ENCYCLOPEDIA OF
WORLD
HISTORY

This is a Dempsey Parr Book
This edition published in 2000

Dempsey Parr is an imprint of Parragon
Parragon
Queen Street House
4 Queen Street
Bath BA1 1HE, UK

ISBN 0 75500 012 9

Produced for Parragon by
Foundry Design & Production, a part of
The Foundry Creative Media Company Ltd
Crabtree Hall, Crabtree Lane
Fulham, London, SW6 6TY

Thanks to: Sonya Newland, Claire Dashwood and Ian Powling.

A copy of the CIP data for this book is available from the British Library.

Printed in Singapore.

ENCYCLOPEDIA OF
WORLD HISTORY

Paul Brewer, Malcolm Chandler, Gerard Cheshire, Ingrid Cranfield,
Brenda Ralph Lewis, Anthony Shaw, Jon Sutherland and Robert Vint

GENERAL EDITOR

Professor Jeremy Black

Contents

HOW TO USE THIS BOOK

The entries in this encyclopedia are organised into seven thematic chapters, each with an introductory synopsis, including a timeline and details of some of the key events covered.

- To find information on a particular era or year, use the Chronological List of Entries on pages 6–13.
- To follow a particular sub-theme within a chapter, use the key and the cross-references indicated next to the entry heading.
- To find information on a specific event, person or subject, use the Index on pages 314–20.
- Events that have had a particularly significant impact on history can be traced through the 'Triumphs & Tragedies' theme recurring throughout the book.
- Each spread contains a 'Distant Voices' quotation, offering a contemporary insight into subjects and events.

Chronological List of Entries

Introduction

THIS IS AN ACCESSIBLE HISTORY for the close of one millennium and the start of another. In looking back we understand better not only the fascination of the past, but also ourselves, our world and our possibilities for the future. This, then, is an exciting tale of bold coverage. The key thematic perspectives through which each century is seen offer both a comprehensive account of world history and provide coherent coverage of crucial dynamics of the human past. Individually they offer important perspectives and collectively they build towards a compelling whole, in which aspects of all cultures, regions and periods are covered.

Each chapter is a broadly chronological sequence of self-contained spreads, beginning with a general spread that introduces the theme of the chapter; but this approach is not simply a matter of 'as time goes by'. Instead, the entries are organised so as to explore and develop a set of sub-themes within each chapter. This enables an identification of many of the key developments throughout history. The entries can be meaningfully read in isolation from the spread, but it is best to see them as part of the whole, providing both a narrative sequence and analytical coherence.

Each chapter has its own strong thematic voice and chronological spans are adapted to suit the dynamic of the theme. The chapters do not have a matching sequence of periods, but there is a strong correlation. The text is enlivened and enriched by 'Distant Voices' quotations – either spoken or written – illustrations and maps. The themes have all been constructed on a global perspective, providing balanced coverage of all cultures, regions and periods.

It is important to remember this organisation when reading and using this book. Yes, it may seem strange to read about the Protestant Reformation of the sixteenth century after the construction of the railways in the nineteenth, but this is the most helpful way to approach the past if you want to give it shape and meaning. Our societies are the products of broad developments that can only be understood if seen not as a series of disconnected facts, but as long-term developments with their own chronologies. This is true, for example, of industrialisation, or the creation of a culture of mass literacy or of the modern states system.

Overarching issues in human history covered here – all as important for our future as for our past – include human relations with the environment; the demographic history of the species; relations between the generations and the sexes – the crucial issues in social structure; the structures of productive society, such as class; the world belief, particularly religion; the ways in which people identify themselves, their families and their worlds: place, ethnic group, language, religion, each of which is often in a dynamic but also unsteady relation with the others; the organisation of political society: units of authority and their objectives; relations within and between states; and the march of scientific knowledge, technological capability and economic development.

These issues are all approached through the themes and entries of this book. The issues link. Greater technological strength requires more resources and thus puts more pressure on the environment. Indeed, in this century, man has altered his environment more than in any other. Yet, this process of change is not new and an understanding of the ongoing nature of change is important when looking at our own age. Thus, deforestation – the clearing of natural woodland to provide agriculture and settlement – has been going on for centuries.

Change is the issue in history. The past is not a series of static shots, frozen in time – for example, Paris in 1650 or the life of the factory worker in 1850. Such an approach can yield interesting images, but it is essentially rigid. Instead it is necessary to understand how the past is part of a living process of change, and was and is given energy and meaning, importance and explanation by this change. Without an understanding of change, we cannot appreciate the 'whys' of the past and thus of the present: why did they do this in 1700, 1900, 2000? Change also provides the dynamic of history. The effects of, for example, rising or falling populations, economies, govern-ments and religions were the fabric of the past and the cause of altering experiences for its people.

The reality is with us today. Take anyone of 80. In their life they have seen what would have been regarded as inconceivable or unlikely when they were born: space rockets and microchips, anti-biotics and artificial hips. We take all this for granted but also know how important it is to understand these changes. History is not just a record of change; it also helps us understand it.

At the cusp of the millennium there is both hope and uncertainty; a sense of particular balance

between past and future. That is a useful image, but much of the thrust of this book rests on the notion that past and future are not rival worlds. Instead we see them as part of a

continuous process, bound together by the energy of change. The people of the past knew there would be a future and were affected by this knowledge. If in the sixteenth century Europeans explored the – to them – New World, they did so knowing there were other worlds to explore.

This is part of the excitement of history: purposeful exploration and understanding of others and ourselves. Take, for example, an obvious feature of life, the darkness of night. The modern world can overcome this with electric lighting, but earlier the dark was a world of danger and menace. This was especially true for the traveller literally unable to see his route, as in Shakespeare's *Macbeth*:

> *The west yet glimmers with some streaks of day;*
> *Now spurs the lated traveller apace,*
> *To gain the timely inn.*

To see how we have overcome the abrupt shift from light to darkness, one has to see the fearful world of dark in the past. Look at the pictures from the period. In twilight and at night, space shrank to the shadowy spots lit by flickering lights.

Different readers will draw varied conclusions from history. Some see it as a cause for celebration or optimism; others are more pessimistic. Both interpretations can find support. What is clear, however, is that in assessing how far and why we have done better or worse, it is necessary to look back and around us, to consider history as a source of our world, not as something that is past and gone. History is interesting and fun, stimulating and thought-provoking. It is also valuable, an important source of knowledge, reflection and understanding.

PROFESSOR JEREMY BLACK

Power and Politics

KEY THEMES

- ✤ UNIFICATION
- ♣ CIVIL WAR
- ✳ CRISES
- ✴ EMPIRES
- ✪ DEMOCRACY
- ✈ CONQUEST
- ✠ DICTATORSHIP
- ✕ DECLINE
- ✍ AGREEMENTS
- ☭ REVOLUTION

T HERE HAVE BEEN VERY FEW societies and civilisations in which power has not been of vital importance. In the ancient world, power was usually in the hands of a king, who frequently assumed a religious, or even divine status; Roman emperors were believed to be gods. The spread of Christianity and the rise of Islam ended such beliefs in Europe, but they continued in Japan and China and were common in the civilisations of Central and South America. Instead kings began to control their subjects by feudalism, where power was passed on to local barons in return for oaths of allegiance. Different forms of this existed in Europe, China and Japan. Its greatest weakness was that it encouraged powerful barons to challenge the monarch in times of trouble. Autocratic royal power lasted until the twentieth century in some areas: Russia, the Austrian Empire, China and Japan. It was eventually undermined by the growth of democratic institutions, which led to the growth of politics. Democracy could fail, however, especially in countries humiliated by war, or where groups refused to accept the verdict of the people. In the twentieth century, as in every century, the temptation has existed for power to be seized by dictators, with disastrous consequence.

KEY EVENTS

① 27 BC
THE CREATION OF THE ROMAN EMPIRE

Octavian, the great-nephew of Julius Caesar, became emperor of Rome in 27 BC. As he was unwilling to upset the Roman people by taking the title of king, he took the title of Princeps and referred to himself as the 'First Citizen'. However, when the Roman Senate decided to offer Octavian the title of 'Augustus' (the 'respected one'), he was quite prepared to accept.

② AD 622
THE HEGIRA

In AD 612 the Prophet Muhammad began to preach in Mecca. He gained few followers and in 622 was forced to flee from Mecca to Medina. Here the impact of the teachings of the Prophet Muhammad was immediate. After the Hegira, he organised an alliance of the tribes in Medina and attacked and captured Mecca in 630.

③ 1776
DECLARATION OF INDEPENDENCE

The American Declaration of Independence was drawn up by Thomas Jefferson on 4 July 1776. The actions of the Americans set a new precedent in power and politics. They asserted the right of a people to throw off their allegiance to their king and establish for themselves a new and different form of government.

④ 1789
THE FRENCH REVOLUTION

On 14 July 1789 a crowd of Parisians attacked the Bastille, a royal fortress in Paris that was used as a prison and an arsenal. The fall of the Bastille was a symbol that the power of the king could be challenged. It was an ominous step.

⑤ 1914
THE ASSASSINATION OF ARCHDUKE FRANZ FERDINAND

On 28 June 1914, the Archduke Franz Ferdinand, heir to the Austrian throne, and his wife were shot dead by a Serbian terrorist. When Russia mobilised in support of the Serbs, Germany automatically became involved and this drew in France. By 12 August, all the major European powers were involved.

⑥ 1917
THE OCTOBER REVOLUTION

On 24–25 October 1917 the Bolsheviks overthrew the Russian Provisional Government in a coup planned and led by Leon Trotsky, Lenin's second-in-command. The general election was won by the Socialist-Revolutionary Party, but when the Assembly met in January, Lenin dissolved it by force and began to rule as a dictator.

⑦ 1933
HITLER COMES TO POWER

Hitler became chancellor of Germany in January 1933 and was given total power when the Enabling Act was passed in March. This allowed him to govern without the Reichstag, the German Parliament, for the next four years. By then a total dictatorship had been set up in Germany.

1945
⑧ HIROSHIMA

In 1945 an atomic bomb was dropped on the city of Hiroshima and some 70,000 people were killed. The bomb not only marked the beginning of a new period in the history of mankind, but also increased the hostility between US president Truman and the Soviet leader Stalin. It became a major factor in the development of the Cold War.

TIMELINE

2850 BC	Unification of Upper and Lower Egypt
1532 BC	Founding of the Egyptian New Kingdom
753 BC	Founding of Rome
492 BC	Persians invade Greece
480 BC	Battle of Thermopylae
403 BC	Spartans defeat Athens
323 BC	Death of Alexander the Great
214 BC	Great Wall of China begun
❶ 27 BC	Octavius becomes emperor of Rome
AD 98	Trajan becomes emperor of Rome
AD 306	Constantine becomes emperor of Rome
❷ AD 630	Muhammad captures Mecca
1066	Battle of Hastings
1096	First Crusade
1215	Signing of the Magna Carta
1453	Muhammad II captures Constantinople
1492	Christopher Columbus sails for the New World
1517	Martin Luther posts his 95 Theses
1519	Cortés attacks the Aztec Empire
1558	Elizabeth I becomes Queen of England
1618	Thirty Years' War begins
1642	English Civil War begins
1763	Treaty of Paris
❸ 1776	American Declaration of Independence
1787	Constitution of the USA
❹ 1789	Storming of the Bastille
1792	National Assembly set up in France
1804	Napoleon appoints himself emperor of France
1815	Battle of Waterloo
1815	Treaty of Vienna
1842	Britain forces China to sign the Treaty of Nanking
1857	Indian Mutiny
1862	Bismarck becomes chancellor of Germany
1878	Congress of Berlin
1904	Russo-Japanese War
1911	Chinese Revolution
❺ 1914	First World War begins
❻ 1917	Revolution in Russia
1928	Stalin announces the Five Year Plan
1929	Wall Street Crash
❼ 1933	Hitler becomes chancellor of Germany
1936	Spanish Civil War
1939	Second World War begins
1941	Japanese attack Pearl Harbor
❽ 1945	Atomic bomb dropped on Hiroshima
1949	Chinese Communist Party seizes power
1950	North Korea invades South Korea
1965	Chairman Mao's Cultural Revolution in China
1989	Destruction of the Berlin Wall
1998	Launch of the Euro

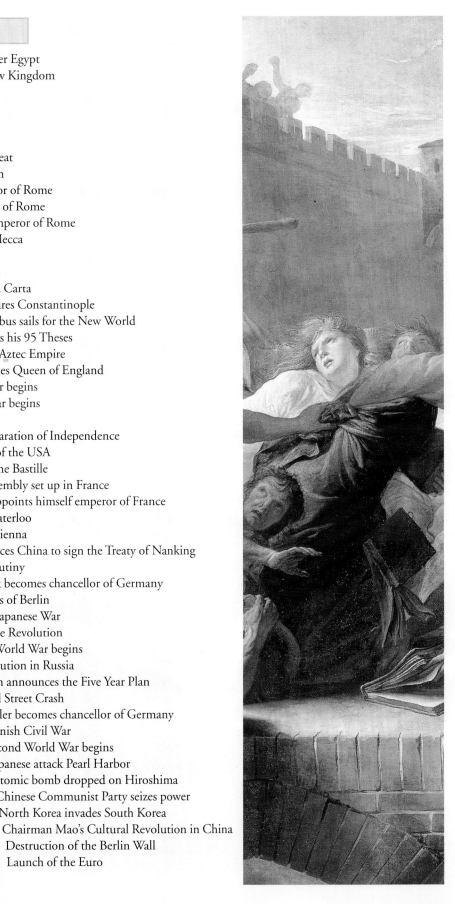

The 3,000-Year Empire
2850–30 BC

MOST PEOPLE'S ideas of Ancient Egypt are based on the Pyramids at Giza and the Sphinx. The Great Pyramid is the only remaining one of the Seven Wonders of the Ancient World, and it gives the impression of immense strength and power, of a strong centralised state, which was capable of building such vast structures. In fact the pyramids were built almost at the beginning of the Egyptian Empire and they had been completed by 2300 BC. The strength that they represent did not last. For more than two thousand years the kings of Egypt fought to defend and to extend their empire and to control powerful nobles who ruled local areas.

◆ ▶ p. 32

2850 BC
THE NARMER PALETTE

Until the beginning of the third millennium BC, Egypt was divided into two parts. The kingdom of Lower Egypt was in the north and centred on the Nile Delta. The kingdom of Upper Egypt was in the south below the Fayum. In about 2850 BC the king of Upper Egypt, Narmer, defeated the king of Lower Egypt in battle and united the two kingdoms. The union was symbolised by the creation of a new crown, an amalgamation of the crowns of the two kingdoms. Narmer became the first king of the new state and founded the first dynasty. He then became known as Menes and built a new capital at Memphis. The victory of Narmer may have come about because Upper Egypt was more rugged and the people hardier.

2615 BC
THE OLD KINGDOM

The Old Kingdom was founded by King Zoser at the beginning of the Third Dynasty, in about 2615 BC. It lasted until about 2175 BC, when royal authority broke down. During the Old Kingdom Egypt was divided into 42 districts, or *nomes*, each one ruled by a representative of the king. The kings ruled Egypt as if it was their own personal property, so kingship was personal. Kings were required to establish their authority by the force of their own character. Strong kings were successful, weak kings were not. There was no permanent capital, no seat of government. The capital was where the king chose to build his palace. This fundamental weakness of hereditary monarchy was to last, in some European countries, until the twentieth century.

▼ *The Great Pyramid at Giza, the last remaining Wonder of the Ancient World.*

2600 BC
PYRAMIDS AND POWER

King Zoser built the first pyramid in about the year 2600 BC; it was a step pyramid at Saqqarah. The biggest of the pyramids were built in the next two centuries and would have involved colossal effort. In the great Pyramid there are two million limestone blocks covering an area of thirteen acres and rising originally to over 150 m (492 ft). Building must have commenced soon after a king succeeded to the throne and continued throughout the reign. Some pyramids were never completed. It used to be believed that the pyramids were built by slave labour, but modern research suggests that the workers were paid. Either way, the effort involved in bringing limestone and the marble cladding to Giza was immense. It suggests a strongly centralised and well-organised state and a strong economy.

▼ *Statue of the god Horus in the temple complex at Luxor.*

2400 BC
PHARAOHS AND GODS

Egyptians believed that life was only a preparation for death and the afterlife. Consequently they took enormous trouble over their preparations for death. The pyramids were only one example of this. The body also had to be preserved so that the soul could recognise it when it returned to find the body in the tomb, hence the long and complicated process of mummification. These beliefs meant that priests had great power and authority in Egypt. The king himself was believed to be a god and the previous kings were the god Osiris, the lord of the Underworld. From about 2400 BC, the king was identified with the sun god Re and was addressed as 'Son of Re'.

❖ ▶ p. 23   **1991 BC**
THE MIDDLE KINGDOM

In about 2175 BC the authority of the kings of Egypt collapsed and the rulers of the *nomes* began to acquire independence. For almost two centuries there was a series of civil wars and unrest between groups of families. This came to an end with the reign of Ammenemes (1991–62 BC). He founded the Middle Kingdom by destroying the power of the nobles and securing the borders of Egypt on all sides. This led to a period of prosperity and artistic and literary development. After 200 years, however, the power of the king collapsed again in about 1785 BC and Egypt was then invaded and conquered by the Hyksos peoples from the north.

1570 BC
THE NEW KINGDOM

The New Kingdom was founded by Amosis in 1570 BC. He drove out the Hyksos and began a period of expansion. Egypt was reorganised as a military state and a series of kings conquered Syria, Palestine, Nubia and eventually extended the empire as far as the Euphrates. Under Amenophis III (c. 1417–1379 BC) Egypt reached the height of its power and wealth. He began building the great complex of temples at Luxor in honour of the god Amun. The kings of Egypt now ruled an enormous empire

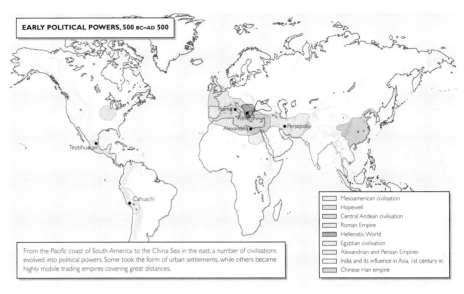

EARLY POLITICAL POWERS, 500 BC–AD 500

From the Pacific coast of South America to the China Sea in the east, a number of civilisations evolved into political powers. Some took the form of urban settlements, while others became highly mobile trading empires covering great distances.

- Mesoamerican civilisation
- Hopewell
- Central Andean civilisation
- Roman Empire
- Hellenistic World
- Egyptian civilisation
- Alexandrian and Persian Empires
- India and its influence in Asia, 1st century BC
- Chinese Han empire

stretching from Libya in the west to Mesopotamia in the east, and from Syria in the north to Nubia in the south. However, the empire lacked natural borders and was constantly under attack, thus obliging each king to undertake campaigns to prevent the empire being undermined.

✸ ▶ p. 25   **1350 BC**
AKHENATEN'S REVOLUTION

Akhenaten was king of Egypt in the middle of the fourteenth century BC. He was entirely absorbed in religion and changed his court from the worship of the god Amun to that of Aten. He even changed his own name from Amenhotep. The changes were opposed by the entire priesthood of Amun. Akhenaten was so preoccupied with his religious changes that he took no action to defend the empire. As a result, all the provinces conquered in Asia over the previous 200 years were lost and had to be regained by his successors, notably Seti I and Rameses II. This was to be the last period of Egyptian greatness. There were kings for another 900 years, until Egypt was conquered by Persia in 334 BC and then by Alexander the Great in 332 BC.

30 BC
A PROVINCE OF ROME

From 305 to 30 BC, Egypt was ruled by Greek kings, the Ptolemys, who were descended from one of Alexander the Great's generals. They fought a long series of wars with Syria and also occasionally held islands and ports in the Aegean, but apart from that the empire had all but disappeared. In the first century BC corruption and intrigue became widespread in Ptolemaic Egypt and a number of kings were murdered; Cleopatra murdered her own brother in 44 BC. When Cleopatra herself committed suicide in 30 BC, Egypt became a province of the Roman Empire and one of its main sources of wheat. It remained under Roman and later Byzantine control for almost seven centuries.

Distant Voices ▶ p. 21

Thy dawning is beautiful in the horizon of heaven
O living Aten, beginning of life!
When thou risest in the eastern horizon of heaven
Thou fillest every land with thy beauty,
For thou art beautiful, great, glittering, high over the earth
Thy rays, they encompass the lands, even all thou hast made.

A poem written by Akhenaten in honour of the god Aten (c. 1350 BC)

The Birth of Democracy
800–322 BC

ANCIENT GREECE was a strange mixture of intellectual brilliance and violent warfare. Many of the cities had detailed constitutions and the development of the Greek language and script meant that the study of philosophy and politics became highly developed by the fourth century BC. Indeed the Greeks were the first people to develop theories about power and politics. However this did not enable the city-states to get on with one another, and consequently Greek history is made up of a long series of wars between state and leagues of cities. Just occasionally the city-states united in the face of a foreign invader, but once the danger passed they returned to fighting amongst themselves. In the end they fell easy prey to Alexander the Great and, later, the Romans.

✳ ▶ p. 22
800 BC
MAGNA GRAECIA

'Magna Graecia' was the name given to the colonies founded by the Greek city states. Although they never recovered from the invasions of Philip of Macedon and his son Alexander the Great, Greek ideas came to dominate the ancient world. One reason for this was the planting of colonies by the states throughout the Mediterranean. Southern Italy and Sicily were colonised from the seventh century BC onwards. Some of the finest Greek temples can be found around the Gulf of Salerno. These colonies were later to be absorbed into the Roman Republic and Empire. Another reason for the spread of Greek ideas was the conquests of Alexander the Great. When his empire was broken up after his death, Greek influence became particularly strong in Egypt, where the descendants of Alexander's general, Ptolemy, ruled for three centuries.

✪ ▶ p. 21
594 BC
DEMOCRACY IN ANCIENT GREECE

Democracy was first developed in Athens, where there was an Assembly which citizens were invited to attend and address. After the Reforms of Solon in 594 BC, the Assembly had the right to reject or approve legislation. Laws were introduced by the council which, after 508 BC, was chosen by lot. Real power, however, was exercised by the nobles through their council, the 'Areopagus'. They elected the Archons, who ran the city, but from 488 BC, the Archons were also chosen by lot. This meant that the nobles lost much of their power. Magistrates were elected by all freemen; jurors in trials were paid fees, which meant that any citizen was able to sit. Athenian democracy did not involve equality, but it did accept the right of all citizens to be involved in the government of their city.

▼ *Alexander the Great in battle against the Persians.*

✦ ▶ p. 32
492 BC
THE PERSIAN WARS

In 492 BC the Persian army invaded Greece. It conquered the north but then returned to Persia when its fleet was destroyed in a storm. The Persians returned in 490 BC and this time were completely defeated by the Athenian army at the Battle of Marathon. A further invasion by a Persian army of 180,000 men took place in 480 BC. The army was held up at the pass of Thermopylae by the Greek army. Leonidas, king of Sparta, and 300 of his army fought to the last man to allow the rest of the Greeks to escape. The Greeks then destroyed the Persian fleet at Salamis and the following year defeated the Persian army at Plataea. Once again it was the heavily armed Spartan infantry that was responsible for the victory.

460 BC
THE PELOPONNESIAN WARS

During the fifth century BC Sparta and Athens competed for the leadership of Greece. Fighting broke out in 460 BC and lasted until 445 BC; it began again in 431 BC. The Athenians tried to avoid battles on land, because they believed the Spartan army was too strong. They used their navy to attack the coast of the Peloponnese and disrupt Spartan trade, while they remained inside their city walls. The Spartans used

✛ UNIFICATION ♣ CIVIL WAR ✳ CRISES ✲ EMPIRES ✪ DEMOCRACY

their army to destroy the countryside around Athens, hoping to lure the Athenians out. The result was a destructive war, ending with the defeat of Athens in 403 BC. For 30 years afterwards Sparta was the most powerful city in Greece, but by the middle of the third century BC a far more dangerous enemy was threatening Greece – Philip of Macedon.

▲ *The Greek philosopher Plato, who continued the beliefs of his teacher Socrates.*

457 BC
TRADE IN ATHENS

The Greek city-states emerged in the seventh century BC, when the kings and tyrants were driven out. Over the next 200 years the states fought for territory, forming themselves into leagues to try to gain advantage over their rivals. By the middle of the fifth century there were two main leagues, to which most of the city-states belonged, the Athenian League and the Peloponnesian League. Athens was the main city of Attica in eastern Greece. Athens had developed trading links with many parts of the eastern Mediterranean, including Egypt, and had a strong navy. To ensure access to the sea, the Athenians had built a port in Piraeus, which in 457 BC was linked to Athens by two long walls to enable the Athenians to reach it when they were attacked.

Triumphs & Tragedies ▶ p. 29
336 BC
ALEXANDER THE GREAT

Alexander the Great was the son of Philip of Macedon and succeeded his father in 336 BC, at the age of 20. Philip had crushed the army of the Greek city states at the Battle of Chaeronea in 338 BC and had forced the states to join the Hellenic League – only Sparta refused. He then planned to invade Asia, but was murdered before he was able to put his plans into action. After this, the Greek states revolted, but Alexander crushed the rebellion and appointed a governor in Greece before he left for his invasion of Persia. When Alexander died in 322 BC Athens rebelled again and formed a new Hellenic League. The revolt was once again crushed and the Athenian navy completely destroyed. The Macedonians had changed the face of Greece for good.

450 BC
SPARTA

At its height around 450 BC, Sparta was the most important city-state in the Peloponnese in southern Greece. The Spartans came from the area of Laconia, which is the origin of the word 'laconic', meaning a person of very few words. Spartans were famous for their ability to endure very harsh conditions and had, therefore, a very strong army. All citizens had to serve in the army and legend has it that their city had no walls in order to make the citizens fight more desperately. Spartans were also famous for being slow to make up their minds. They followed strict religious rules and on a number of occasions delayed action until it was too late. However, the Spartan army was renowned for its bravery.

✪ ▶ p. 22
399 BC
PHILOSOPHERS AND KINGS

The Greeks were the first people in Europe to develop a cursive script. Although Egyptian hieroglyphics and Babylonic cuneiform were efficient for making lists, writing records and publishing laws, they

▲ *Plato, one of the earliest exponents of political ideals.*

did not allow sophisticated analysis or discussion. Socrates founded a school of philosophy, which was continued by his pupil Plato after Socrates's death in 399 BC. Plato's *Republic* was the first treatise on political ideals written in Europe. The Greeks were, therefore, the first Europeans who were capable of analysing and explaining political institutions and considering alternatives. Socrates, Plato and Aristotle provided an analysis of human behaviour which was not to be equalled until the seventeenth century.

p. 19◀ **Distant Voices** ▶p. 23

Now they drew up for battle beyond the pass and attacked the enemy, who fell in heaps. By this time the spears of the Spartans were broken. With their swords they hacked down the ranks of the Persians. As they struggled, Leonidas fell fighting bravely, together with many other famous Spartans. They drew back into the narrowest part of the pass. Here they defended themselves to the last.

A description of the battle of Thermopylae, written by the Greek historian Herodotus (484–425 BC)

From Republic to Empire
752 BC–AD 337

O N THE BANKS OF THE TIBER, in about 752 BC, twin brothers founded the city of Rome. At least, that was the version of the legend the Romans came to believe. This city became the centre of one of the most powerful empires the world has ever known. The Romans' greatest advantages were their determination and their organisation. Because of these abilities they were able to take on more numerous and far better equipped opponents and defeat them comprehensively. With an army of only 160,000 legionaries, in the time of Augustus, they were able to rule most of Europe, the Middle East and North Africa. For hundreds of years the Pax Romana guaranteed stability and order for millions of people.

752 BC
THE KINGDOM

From 752 until 509 BC, Rome was ruled by seven kings. The first was Romulus, one of the twin brothers who founded the city. According to legend, Romulus and his brother Remus were brought up by a she-wolf on the banks of the Tiber. The last kings of Rome were Etruscans, members of a mysterious people who lived to the north of Rome. Even today, little is known about their way of life and their script has still not been deciphered. The rule of the kings

▼ *Marble busts depicting a Roman consul and his wife.*

became dictatorial and, in 509 BC, the Romans turned against their king Tarquinius and drove him out of the city. Despite the efforts of the Etruscan king, Lars Porsenna, the Romans were able to prevent him restoring the monarchy and set up a republic in its place.

✪ ▶ p. 29

509 BC
THE REPUBLIC

The Roman Republic was set up in 509 BC. Because their kings had been dictators, the Romans were determined that no one should gain complete power in the city, so they created a complex system of controls on all officers of state. Power was exercised by two officials, called consuls, who were elected every year. One stayed in Rome and one took command of the army. There were also elected officials in charge of the treasury, the police and the city itself. The Romans hoped that the rapid change of personnel would stop anyone seizing total power, but they also realised that in an emer-gency it might be necessary to allow one man to take charge; so the Republic allowed the appointment of a 'dictator' for a period of up to six months.

✠ ▶ p. 39

107–79 BC
MARIUS AND SULLA

The Roman Republic lasted for almost 500 years, but as Rome became more powerful and much richer, it also became an increasingly attractive prospect for ambitious and unscrupulous politicians. At the end of the second century BC, power was seized by a general, Marius, who was elected consul in 107 BC. In 82 BC, Sulla, one of Marius's protégés, had himself elected dictator and held power for three years. While in power, Sulla carried out extensive reforms of the Roman legal system and the courts of law, but when he resigned and returned to private life in 79 BC, the way was open for others – who did not have his scruples – to try to seize control of the republic. Three figures emerged: Crassus, Pompey and Julius Caesar. In 60 BC they formed the First Triumvirate.

60 BC
THE TRIUMVIRATES

Between 60 and 48 BC, Caesar and Pompey fought a civil war, which became even more violent after the death of Crassus, the third member of the First Triumvirate, in 53 BC. After the Battle of Pharsalus in 48 BC and Pompey's murder in Egypt in the same year, Julius Caesar was the undisputed master of Rome. Increasingly he acted like a king, and it was this behaviour that brought about his murder at the hands of a group of Republicans in 44 BC. This act led to the formation of the Second Triumvirate in 43 BC; the members, Mark Antony, Lepidus and Octavian, hunted down Caesar's murderers, but then fell out amongst themselves. Finally, Octavian defeated Mark Antony at Actium in 31 BC, after which Mark Antony and his wife Cleopatra committed suicide.

✳ ▶ p. 25

27 BC
AUGUSTUS

Octavian, the great-nephew of Julius Caesar, became emperor of Rome in 27 BC. As he was unwilling to upset the Roman people by taking the title of king, he took the title of Princeps and referred to himself as the 'First

▲ *The great Roman emperor Julius Caesar, holding a globe, symbolic of his empirical success.*

X ▶ p. 25

AD 324
CONSTANTINE

By the early fourth century, it was becoming increasingly obvious that the Empire could not be governed by one man. In AD 324 Constantine (r. AD 306–337) took divided the empire in half and built a new capital for the eastern half at Constantinople. For all the strength of its army, the Roman Empire never developed real political stability; success depended upon the character of the emperor and on the support of the army. When the empire came increasingly under attack from outside forces, the chaos that ensued only encouraged attempts to seize control. These attempts were a major factor in the collapse of the Roman Empire in the West by the end of the fifth century. But Constantine's creation, the Empire in the East, survived, in one form or another, for more than a thousand years.

▼ *The Roman emperor Constantine, who built the great city of Constantinople.*

Citizen'; this was to be copied by Adolf Hitler nearly 2,000 years later. However, when the Roman Senate decided to offer Octavian the title of 'Augustus', the 'respected one', he was quite prepared to accept. Augustus then set about reforming the empire, which had grown up haphazardly over the last two centuries. He took charge of the appointment of governors of the 30 or so provinces of the empire. He reorganised the army, reducing the number of legions from 62 to 28, and appointing all senior commanders.

❖ ▶ p. 35

AD 41
EMPIRICAL RIVALRY

There was no line of succession to the throne of the Roman Empire; each emperor had, in theory at least, to be elected to the office. Augustus was elected consul every year, along with another nominal colleague. From the early first century AD it was obvious that emperors depended on the army to support their claims to the throne. But if the army could make an emperor, it could also break him. In AD 41 Gaius Caligula was murdered by guards, who then pronounced his uncle, Claudius, as successor. In AD 68–69, after

the suicide of Nero, there were four rival emperors, all trying to seize power. In the third century, however, violent death was a common end for emperors – there were 27 in 73 years, and in the year AD 238, five emperors were killed.

AD 98
EMPEROR TRAJAN

The Roman Empire was at its most successful during the second century AD. From AD 98 onwards there was a long succession of able and conscientious emperors, of whom the first was Trajan (AD 98–117). Much is known about the methods used by Trajan to govern the empire because he wrote many letters to his friend and former tutor, Pliny the Younger, who he appointed as Governor of the province of Bithynia-Pontus. The letters reveal Trajan as an intelligent politician and statesman. He rejected widespread persecution of Christians and showed interest in all aspects of the life of the province. Under him the empire reached its greatest size, with the occupation of Armenia, Assyria and Mesopotamia. The River Tigris became the eastern boundary of the empire.

p. 21 ◀ **Distant Voices** ▶ p. 25

You have my permission to set up my statue in the place you have chosen for it. I have no wish to accept honours of this kind. But I do not wish it to seem that I have put a check on your loyal feelings to me.

From letters written by Emperor Trajan to his friend Pliny, the Governor of Bithynia-Pontus (AD 112–113)

The Rise and Decline of Islam
AD 612–1900

I N THE EARLY SEVENTH CENTURY a new and dynamic political power emerged in the Middle East. It sprang from the teachings of the Prophet Muhammad, who fled from Mecca to Medina in 622 AD, but returned in 630 to drive out his opponents. Within 100 years, his followers had conquered most of the Middle East, much of Asia, North Africa, Spain and had advanced as far as Tours in central France. There they were defeated by Charles Martel, king of the Franks. The success of the Muslim forces was partly brought about by the weakness of their opponents. The Byzantine Empire, which had succeeded the Roman Empire in the East, often used violence and cruelty and its provinces in Egypt fell easily. But Muslim success also resulted from the teachings of the Prophet Muhammad, tolerance of other faiths and equality.

▲ *The Dome of the Rock mosque in Jerusalem, built on the site of the Prophet Muhammad's ascension.*

AD 622
THE HEGIRA

Arabia at the beginning of the seventh century was wild, pagan and unsafe when, in AD 612, the Prophet Muhammad began to preach in Mecca. He gained few followers and in 622 was forced to flee from Mecca to Medina; this became known as the Hegira ('flight'). In Medina the impact of the teachings of the Prophet Muhammad was immediate. After the Hegira, he organised an alliance of the tribes in Medina and attacked and captured Mecca in 630. By the time of the Prophet Muhammad's death in 632, most of Arabia was Muslim. Muhammad's teachings were based on the Five Pillars of Islam and it was the belief and hope which they offered that attracted so many followers and made Islam such a powerful force.

AD 632
THE CALIPHS

When the Prophet Muhammad died in AD 632, he was succeeded by the caliph Abu Bakr, who was chosen by popular acclaim. When he died in 634, he was succeeded by Omar. The first two caliphs began the conquest of the Middle East. Egypt, Palestine, Syria, Iraq, Persia and Mesopotamia were all occupied. In 644 Omar was assassinated and was succeeded by Othman, who was responsible for producing the first version of the Qur'an. He also captured Cyprus and attacked Constantinople for the first time, destroying a Byzantine fleet. When Othman was murdered in 656 he was succeeded by Ali, but civil war broke out and in 661 power was seized by the Umayyads. They moved the capital of the empire from Mecca to Damascus.

AD 661
DAMASCUS

Damascus was the centre of the Islamic Empire from AD 661 to 750. It became a great trading centre and famous for elaborate embroidered cloth, known as damask, and for fine steel Damascening. The Umayyads ruled in Damascus and extended the Empire as far as Afghanistan in the east and then conquered all of North Africa and Spain in the west. One important reason for these conquests was that subject peoples were treated fairly. Many Jews and Christians preferred life under Muslim rulers, because they were allowed to practise their religion and simply had to pay an extra tax. Another reason was that Muslims also believed that death on the battlefield fighting for Islam would mean passage straight to heaven.

AD 750
CITIES OF ISLAM

Baghdad became the centre of the Islamic Empire in the years after AD 750. The Ummayads were replaced after the civil wars by the Abbasids who built Baghdad. It was a round city surrounded by a wall with four gates. Each gate was defended by 1,000 men. This shows the power and importance of the caliph, who lived in the centre of the city in

❖ UNIFICATION   ♣ CIVIL WAR   ✳ CRISES   ✳ EMPIRES   ✪ DEMOCRACY an enormous palace. The most famous of the Abbasid caliphs was Haroun al-Rashid. He had an inventory drawn up of all the objects in the palace, and it included 4,000 different sets of clothing. The Abbasids also encouraged learning and medicine. Libraries were set up throughout the empire and there were hospitals in every city.

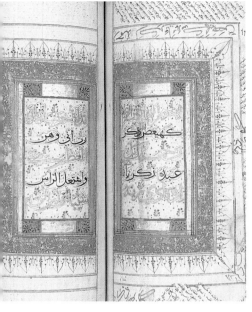

▲ *The Qur'an, the Holy Book of the Islamic faith.*

✳ ▶ p. 30   **1096**
THE FRANKISH INVASIONS

Muslims believed that the Prophet Muhammad rose to heaven from Jerusalem. On the spot they built a mosque, the Dome of the Rock. Jerusalem was, therefore, a very important city in the Islamic religion. To Christians, it was the very centre of their religion. Despite repeated wars between the Islamic and Byzantine Empires, Christian pilgrims were allowed to visit Jerusalem on pilgrimage. In the eleventh century, a few groups of pilgrims were attacked and in 1095 Pope Urban appealed for help to defend pilgrims and recapture Jerusalem. In 1096 a force of 30,000 men set out from western Europe. To Christians this was the start of the crusades. To Muslims it was the beginning of the Frankish Invasions. They were to last for nearly 200 years.

1187
SALADIN'S WAR FOR JERUSALEM

Saladin was the sultan of Egypt at the end of the twelfth century; he was a humane and intelligent ruler. In 1187 he declared war on the Christian kingdom of Jerusalem and captured the city. He did not, however, allow his army to sack the city, so there were no unnecessary casualties. The war began because Christians attacked a caravan, which was said to be escorting Saladin's sister. This led to the Third Crusade; Richard I of England, Philip II of France and Frederick Barbarossa, the Holy Roman Emperor, all took part. The Christians failed to capture Jerusalem, but did take Acre, which was sacked and many people killed. Richard I also had 3,000 Muslim prisoners killed. A truce was agreed in 1192 and the crusade came to an end. Saladin died in 1193.

✳ ▶ p. 34   **1453**
THE OTTOMANS INVADE ISLAM

In the fourteenth century, the Ottoman Turks conquered the Islamic Empire and began to advance into Europe. Mehmet II (1451–81) captured Constantinople in 1453 and then invaded the Balkans. For the next 200 years the Turks launched various invasions on eastern Europe. Belgrade was captured in 1521 and Vienna was besieged in 1526 and again in 1683, when it was only saved by the arrival of the Polish army, commanded by John Sobieski. The Ottoman sultans ruled a huge empire in the Middle East, North Africa and the Balkans. Their capital was Constantinople, but the empire was divided into provinces, each ruled by a governor. The extreme wealth of the empire led to increasing corruption and, in the nineteenth century, governors like Mehmet Ali in Egypt began to try to break away from central control.

✗ ▶ p. 27   **1850s**
A POWER VACUUM

Turkish power in the Balkans began to collapse in the middle of the nineteenth century. Greece became independent in the 1820s, and Romania, Bulgaria and Serbia emerged at the end of the nineteenth

▲ *A plan of early Jerusalem, a holy city for Muslims and Christians.*

century. This created an area in south-east Europe in which there were many small states, but no dominant great power. Both Russia and the Austrian Empire tried to advance into the Balkans. Austria was given control of Bosnia and Herzegovina in 1878 and annexed the territories in 1908. Russia formed an alliance with Serbia. They had a common script and the same religion. It was to be the clash between these two powers, which was to lead to the outbreak of the First World War in 1914.

p. 23 ◀ **Distant Voices** ▶ p. 27

A scout came to us with a sobbing Frankish woman. 'Yesterday some Muslim thieves entered my tent and stole my little girl. I cried all night and our commanders told me: "the King of the Muslims is merciful."' Saladin was touched, and tears came to his eyes. He sent someone to look for the girl. Less than an hour later a horseman arrived bearing the child on his shoulders. Thus was her daughter returned to her.

A description of Saladin by the Muslim writer Baha al-Din (c. 1191)

The Feudal System in England
1066–1471

DURING THE TENTH and eleventh centuries, the first nation states began to appear in Europe, as kings tried to establish their authority by forcing their barons to swear allegiance to them in return for land. Barons had to perform military service for 40 days a year. At first this solved the problem of loyalty and also meant that kings did not have to pay for an army, but in the long run the feudal system, as it became known, led to barons challenging, and even deposing, their overlords. It encouraged barons to believe that they were the equals of the king in all but name. The feudal system also gave them the right to maintain private armies, which were loyal to them personally. By the fifteenth century feudalism was a major hindrance to the development of a centralised state.

1066
THE BEGINNINGS OF FEUDALISM

When William, Duke of Normandy, became king of England in 1066, he took control of all land. Faced with the problem of ruling and controlling a large country, William imposed feudalism upon England. His main aim was to ensure that he had military forces at his disposal and that the dangerous areas of the country were under control. His most important barons were given estates throughout the country. His own half-brother Odo, Bishop of Bayeux, held many areas of Kent, the site of a likely invasion. When the kingdom of France emerged, a similar process was followed. In origin, kings were only the most powerful and successful barons. Their position depended upon their ability to handle and control their own subjects.

1100s
HOMAGE

Homage was one method used by kings to try to compel barons to obey them. The origin of the term was the French word *homme*, meaning man. When a baron became the king's man he swore to obey him. It was religious ceremony, usually held in a church, with a bishop present. The baron knelt before the king and swore an oath to obey him. By making the ceremony as religious as possible, kings hoped that they would be able to force their barons to take the oath seriously, however, this was

▼ *An early manuscript depicting baron knights.*

often not the case. Even Odo of Bayeux, the brother of William the Conqueror, broke his oath and was forced to go into exile.

1100s
TENANTS-IN-CHIEF

Tenants-in-chief were the king's most senior and most trusted barons. They held estates throughout the country and were responsible for bringing a fixed number of knights with them to do military service. The number of knights was based on the amount of land held by the baron. In England, five hides (600 acres) represented one knight. However, although tenants-in-chief were the king's most trusted barons, they could rarely be totally relied upon. William the Conqueror made sure that none of his barons held all their land in one place. Instead, they were each given estates all over the country; this would make the organising of an army and therefore military opposition much more difficult.

▲ *Peasants tilling the land in the Middle Ages.*

1100s
LAND

In most European countries until the middle of the nineteenth century, land was the most important factor in deciding how wealthy and powerful a person was. The king's most important barons held the most land. They also tried to extend their estates by marriage and tried to prevent their break-up by passing land on to the eldest son. This system became known as 'primogeniture'. In addition, they frequently imposed legal restrictions on the sale or disposal of land. These processes meant that larger and larger holdings of land came into the hands of fewer and fewer barons. In England in the fifteenth century this led to a civil war, known as the Wars of the Roses, where rival barons fought over the crown.

1100s
MILITARY SERVICE

In return for land, barons had to perform military service for their lord. This was normally in the form of 40 days' military action every year. Barons were expected to attend the king's summons, with the correct number of knights, and follow their lord into battle. At first this seemed a good solution to the problem of raising an army, but by the twelfth century there were already obvious weaknesses. Forty days was not a long time for a campaign and the timing might be difficult; the army could be slow in assembling. In England during the reign of Henry II (1154–89), the king began to accept the payment of tax instead of military service. The tax became known as 'scutage', from the Latin word *scuta*, meaning a shield.

1100s
KNIGHTS

When barons came to perform military service, they had to be accompanied by the correct number of knights, and each knight had to be properly equipped. Different kings set different standards of equipment, but horse, spear, sword, helmet, hauberk (armour) were common. Barons solved the problem of providing knights by passing on their land to tenants, who had to perform knight service when required. Knights were professional soldiers, they did little else but prepare and practise for war. The vast number of knights, with little to do, was one factor in the development of the crusades from the late eleventh century onwards. To try to ensure that knights performed military service when needed, barons forced them to go through the same ritual of homage and swearing allegiance.

1100s
PEASANTS

Peasants were the lowest level in English medieval society. There were villeins, who owned some land; cottars, who owned a cottage; and bordars, who owned virtually nothing. What they all had in common was the obligation to work for, and pay taxes to, their lord, whether he was a knight, a baron, or even the king. Work meant tilling their lord's fields for several days every week. Taxes meant handing over a proportion of their produce to their lord or to the church and also paying to use their lord's mill to grind their wheat. In addition they could neither leave the village nor marry without his permission.

✕ ▶ p. 39 1471
THE END OF FEUDALISM

One of the consequences of feudalism was that barons came to see the king as little better than themselves. If the king was weak or unsuccessful, it was very tempting to try to overthrow him. When Henry V of England died in 1422, his nine-month-old son, Henry VI, was unable to rule. When he took power, he was a poor ruler and failed to hold on to the English empire in France.

His failures encouraged his enemies, the Yorkists, to try to seize power, and eventually Henry was captured in 1461 and held prisoner in the Tower of London. He was murdered in 1471. This was the final chapter of feudalism. Kings realised that they needed some greater degree of certainty in their control of the country and could not afford to allow powerful barons to challenge them.

p. 25 ◀ **Distant Voices** ▶ p. 29

Baron: I promise to become your man, to hold these lands faithfully and perform due service, preserving your earthly honour in all things.

King: I take you to be my man.

The oaths used at the homage ceremony by William I (*c.* 1027–87)

▼ *The marriage of King Henry VI of England, whose death marked the final chapter of feudalism.*

Kings, Lords and Commons
1066–1688

I N ENGLAND, UNLIKE almost any other country in Europe during the Middle Ages, a Parliament began to develop. The Anglo-Saxon kings had had a council of their earls called the Witan. William I and his successors continued the practice. Representatives of the Commons began to attend in the thirteenth century and by the following century were approving the raising of finance. In the long run this was to be the key to the increasing power of Parliament. So long as the king could survive without taxation, he did not need to summon Parliament. But if he became involved in a war, or fell into debt, Parliament would be summoned and the king might have to face grievances from his subjects.

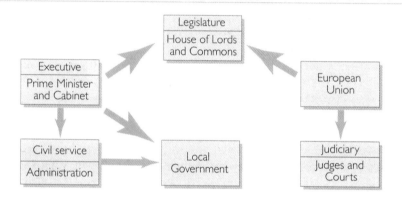

THE BRITISH PARLIAMENTARY SYSTEM
The British system became the model upon which many Parliaments around the world were based. The British parliamentary system continues to evolve due to the developing powers of the European Union and devolved assemblies in Belfast, Cardiff and Edinburgh.

1066
THE WITAN
The Witan was the council of the Anglo-Saxon kings of England. It contained the most important earls and bishops of the kingdom. It met, whenever the king summoned it, to offer advice and probably to approve his actions. William the Conqueror continued this practice. Feudal kings depended upon the support of their barons and needed to make them feel that they were being consulted, because the essence of feudalism was a bargain between king and barons. If the king was successful, barons were usually ready to accept his decisions. William the Conqueror

(r. 1066–87) and his youngest son Henry I (r. 1100–35) met little opposition, but Stephen (r. 1135–54) was forced to fight long civil wars, and John (r. 1199–1216) found himself involved in long-running disputes with his barons. Eventually he was forced to accept the Magna Carta.

✍ ▶ p. 31

1215
MAGNA CARTA
King John was faced by enormous debts as a result of his brother's continual campaigns on the Third Crusade and in France. This forced him to raise higher taxes. John's attempts to recapture the English possessions in France failed when he was

defeated at the Battle of Bouvines by Philip II of France. Finally, John's barons forced him to accept the Magna Carta at Runnymede in 1215. In theory, this guaranteed the rights of freemen, but in fact the most important clauses were attempts to limit the king's power and protect the rights of the barons. John probably intended to disregard the Magna Carta as soon as he felt strong enough, but he died the following year and left the throne to his young son, who became Henry III.

▲ *King John was forced by his barons to sign the Magna Carta, a document limiting the power of the monarch.*

➰ ▶ p. 29

1264
SIMON DE MONTFORT
Medieval kings were expected to lead their barons into battle and win victories. Henry III, the son of John, was only nine when he became king in 1216. When he took control of the kingdom he proved to be a poor military leader. In 1264 there was a revolt against him led by Simon de Montfort (1208–65), who captured the king. Simon de Montfort then summoned a 'Parliament' to which he invited both the barons, or 'lords' as they came to be called,

p. 21 ◀ **Triumphs & Tragedies** ▶ p. 30

1649
THE DEATH OF A KING

Both the Stuart kings, James I (r. 1603–25) and his son Charles I (r. 1625–49), tried to avoid Parliament as much as possible. By being frugal, James was able to avoid summoning Parliament for many years. Charles I did not summon Parliament from 1629 until 1640, but he did not realise that in order to do without, he also needed to reduce expenditure. When he did call them to pay for a war with the Scots, he was faced with a barrage of complaints. For two years arguments raged, then, in August 1642, Charles lost his patience and declared war on Parliament – a war he was to lose. In 1646 the king surrendered to Parliament and after three more years of arguing – in January 1649 – the parliamentary leaders reluctantly put Charles to death.

and also, for the first time, representatives of the Commons. Two knights were summoned from every shire, or county, and two burgesses from every town. This is regarded as the first real evidence of the existence of Parliament, although the name had been used since the 1240s.

1327
EDWARD III AND PARLIAMENT

Parliament became firmly established during the reign of Edward III (1327–77). In the 1340s Parliament began to grant money to the king. This became increasingly important as Edward embarked on his campaigns against France, which became known as the Hundred Years' War. In the 1350s the Commons and Lords began to meet as distinct bodies at the same time and the post of Speaker – someone who would put forward the views of the Commons after their debates – was created. Royal officials also stopped attending meetings of the Lords, which meant that the house was now made up exclusively of bishops and barons. By the end of Edward's reign, the two houses had developed into something like their modern form.

✪ ▶ p. 37

1534
THE TUDOR PARLIAMENT

When the Tudor monarchs tried to bring an end to the chaos of the Wars of the Roses and establish an omnipotent monarchy in England, they used Parliament as a means of helping them. In 1534, Henry VIII passed the Act of Supremacy, which cut the Church of England off from Rome. This set a dangerous precedent for the future. If the king needed to ask for Parliament's help, Parliament might have more power than the monarch himself; however, in the sixteenth century little came of this. Parliament met only when the monarch summoned it and Elizabeth I actually forbade Parliament to discuss some topics – religion for example. But it did mean that weaker, or more careless, monarchs might find Parliament troublesome in the future.

1660
WHIGS AND TORIES

Charles II (1630–85) was restored to the throne in 1660, after 11 years of a republic. He was a very popular king, but as he grew older it became clear that he would have no legitimate children. Charles's successor would be his brother James, the Duke of York. But James was a Catholic and many people were afraid that this would lead to a Catholic revival in England. Some members of Parliament tried to prevent James becoming king, others supported him. His supporters became known as Tories, his opponents as Whigs. Both names were terms of abuse. These were the first political groups in Parliament; they were not really political parties, but they became the basis of the Liberal and Conservative Parties of the nineteenth century.

⚷ ▶ p. 31

1688
THE GLORIOUS REVOLUTION

James II (1633–1701) was forced to flee from England in 1688, and was replaced by his daughter Mary. Her husband, William of Orange, became king. After 1689, a series of Acts of Parliament were passed to limit the power of the Crown. Parliament had to meet every year; taxes could only be

▲ *The execution of Charles I in January 1649.*

collected for one year at a time; the monarch had to be a Protestant and could not leave the country without Parliament's knowledge. Despite these laws, the king could still appoint and dismiss ministers and decide all policy. But William III, and his successors Queen Anne and George I, became less involved in the government of England (and Scotland after 1707) and the post of prime minister developed, as well as the beginnings of the Cabinet. Britain was becoming a constitutional monarchy.

p. 27 ◀ **Distant Voices** ▶ p. 31

No constable or other royal official shall take corn or other moveable goods from any man without immediate payment.

In future no official shall place a man on trial unless he can produce believable witnesses to support his accusation.

No free man shall be seized or imprisoned, except by lawful judgement of his equals or by the law of the land.

From the Magna Carta (1215)

Reformation and Counter-Reformation
1482–1648

DURING THE FOURTEENTH and fifteenth centuries there was increasing protest at the power and authority of the pope in Rome. This was largely brought on by the luxurious lifestyle of the popes. The protesters became known as 'Protestants' and in the sixteenth century, Protestant churches appeared in many parts of Europe, especially in the north. England, Holland, Sweden and northern Germany all became Protestant. This produced a deep division, which led to prolonged warfare in Europe, as the Catholic south attempted to reconvert the Protestant north. Philip II of Spain sent the Armada against England in 1588 and in France there was a series of civil wars brought about by religion. Finally, the Thirty Years' War (1618–48) laid waste to many areas of Germany.

✴ ▶ p. 47

1482
CORRUPTION IN THE PAPACY

The pope was the leader of the Catholic Church; he was also the ruler of a large part of central Italy and was involved in wars with the other Italian states. Usually the pope was an Italian and, in the late fifteenth century, most popes came from wealthy noble families. The pope controlled the wealth of the Catholic Church and had the power to promote his supporters and the members of his own family. Innocent VIII (1482–92) and Alexander VI (1492–1503) were both corrupt and immoral. Alexander was a member of the notorious Borgia family and appointed his own son as commander of the papal armies. These two popes attracted a great deal of criticism and brought the papacy into great disrepute.

1500s
REFORMATION

The Reformation is the name given to the protests against corruption in the Catholic Church at the beginning of the sixteenth century, which led to a split in the Christian Chuch and the establishment of Protestant-ism. Protestants believed that it was what an individual did during his life that was important, rather than the organisation of the Church. They rejected the authority of the Catholic Church and turned to the Bible instead. Protestantism, therefore, was a very serious threat to the Catholic Church, and it divided Europe. Northern Germany, Scandinavia, Holland and England became Protestant; Spain, France, the Italian States, Austria and southern Germany remained Catholic.

▼ *Martin Luther (far left) with other leaders of the Reformation in Europe.*

1517
MARTIN LUTHER

In 1517, Johann Tetzel, an agent of the pope, arrived in Wittenberg selling indulgences. These were certificates that absolved the buyer of sin and they were used by popes and corrupt clergy members as a way of raising money. Martin Luther, a professor at Wittenberg University, nailed a list of objections to the sale of indulgences on a church door. He stated that sins could not be absolved by buying an indulgence, but only by true repentance by the individual. This was the start of the Reformation and the beginning of the Lutheran Church, which believed that the papacy was unnecessary. Luther defended his views at the Diet of Worms in 1521, but was banned from the Catholic Church.

p. 29 ◀ **Triumphs & Tragedies** ▶ p. 37

1542
THE HOLY OFFICE

The Holy Office was the Inquisition, which had originally been set up in Spain in 1478, to find converted Jews who continued practising Judaism. It was originally under the personal control of the king of Spain. In 1542, the Universal Inquisition was set up by Pope Paul III. This operated in Catholic countries to seek out Protestants and try to force them to recant. In particular, the Inquisition was used to find Protestants who claimed to have reverted to Catholicism, but practised their new beliefs in secret. Any form of pressure was used, including torture. If Protestants refused to recant they were brought before a Tribunal and tried; they would usually be sentenced to death by burning. It was believed that fire purified the body.

1534
THE JESUITS

The Counter-Reformation was the Catholic Church's reply to the Reformation. At first the papacy took little notice of the Protestants, but in 1534 Ignatius Loyola set up the Society of Jesus, which became known as the Jesuits. The Jesuits were

▲ *The Diet of Worms at which Martin Luther was exiled from the Catholic Church.*

organised along military lines and came under the direct control of the pope; they led the reply to the Reformation. In European countries they were used to reconvert Protestants, and overseas they were used as missionaries, travelling to South America and the Far East. Their actions made them unpopular, however, as they often interfered in the internal affairs of European states. Eventually they were banned from most countries.

⚒ ▶ p. 35
1568
THE DUTCH REVOLT

In the sixteenth century the Netherlands were part of the Holy Roman Empire. Philip II of Spain planned to introduce the Inquisition into the Netherlands, where many people were Protestant, and this led to a revolt in 1568 by the Dutch. It was the first of a series of wars between Catholics and Protestants, which was to continue for almost a century. Philip tried to crush the revolt by force. He sent 20,000 troops and executed the leaders of the revolt. He managed to regain control of the southern provinces, but the north held out and eventually became independent in 1648 as the United Provinces, often known as the Netherlands, or Holland, after the name of the largest province.

✍ ▶ p. 36
1598
THE EDICT OF NANTES

From 1562 to 1598 there was a series of eight wars between Catholics and Protestants (called Huguenots) in France. The Huguenots were concentrated in the south-west of France, but Paris and the north-east remained Catholic. The wars came to an end when Henry of Navarre became King Henry IV in 1589. He was a Huguenot, but converted to Catholicism to ensure that the Catholics would accept him. In 1598 he issued the Edict of Nantes, which gave Huguenots equal political rights with Catholics and allowed the Protestant religion to be practised in some parts of France, but not in Paris and some other cities. It was the first example, however, of acceptance of Protestantism in a major Catholic country.

1618
THE THIRTY YEARS' WAR

The Thirty Years' War broke out in 1618. The war began as a revolt in Bohemia against Habsburg rule. The conflict spread in 1625, when Denmark became involved. In 1630 the

▼ *The expulsion of the Huguenots (French Protestants).*

Swedish army landed in Germany and finally France entered the war in 1635. The war caused appalling destruction and loss of life in Germany, where most of the fighting took place. It came to an end in 1648 at the Treaty of Westphalia. In religious terms this said that states could revert to the religion that they had had in 1618, or the ruler could decide the religion of his people. Absolutist monarchy was the main political institution of the day.

p. 29 ◀ **Distant Voices** ▶ p. 33

If he refuses to be converted, he is sent to a large town to be burned on the pyre, perhaps alone, perhaps with others like him. Wearing a gown on which are pictures of devils pulling him to hell and tormenting him in a thousand ways, he is put to death in the most atrocious manner. But for the martyrs this death is glory.

A description of the working of the Inquisition, written by a Swiss traveller (1599)

Majesty
1469–1715

IN THE SECOND HALF of the fifteenth century an important change took place in the government of many countries in western Europe. In England, France and Spain, strong centralised monarchies appeared that tried to reduce the power of the barons and landed aristocracy. In France the monarchy finally won the battle with the Dukes of Burgundy and forced the English out of all their French territories. Spain was united as a country for the first time, and then began a period of expansion which made Spain the most powerful, as well as the richest country in Europe. The result of this development of royal power and prestige was a series of wars, which lasted for almost three centuries, as the royal families of Europe struggled for ascendancy.

▲ *Holy Roman Emperor Charles V, founder of the Habsburg dynasty.*

✜ ▶ p. 37

1469
FERDINAND AND ISABELLA

Ferdinand of Aragon (r. 1479–1516) and Isabella of Castile (r. 1474–1504) were the king and queen who united Spain at the end of the fifteenth century. Spain became the most powerful force in Europe for the next hundred years. The power of the nobles, especially in Castile, was reduced and a centralised government was set up. The Moors were driven from Granada, their last stronghold, in 1492. Ferdinand and Isabella also opened up a new field of power struggle when they sent Christopher Columbus to the New World in the same year. Their grandson, Charles I, who became the Holy Roman Emperor Charles V, played a key role in developing a new order in Europe. He set up a centralised administration for the whole empire and founded the Habsburg family, which was to rule the Holy Roman Empire, and later Austria, until the end of the First World War.

1485
HENRY VII

Henry VII became king of England in 1485. His immediate aim was to solve the remaining problems from the wars that had lasted on and off for 30 years. His methods were simple and, at times, brutal. Any possible rivals to the throne were imprisoned and executed; the noble families who had fought for the throne were forced to give up their private armies. Henry also built up a strong treasury, which gave him a high degree of independence. On the one occasion that he went to war – with France in 1492 – he signed an armistice almost immediately. The French agreed to pay him £50,000, which more than covered his costs. Henry VII set a pattern that later monarchs followed; but few had his ability to manage their resources as effectively.

♣ ▶ p. 39

1519
THE SPANISH EMPIRE

The desire for wealth and power brought the Spanish Empire into conflict with the civilisations of Central America. The Aztec civilisation had evolved over a period of a thousand years, and in 1519 had a capital city of perhaps 200,000 people. The Aztecs were ruled by a king who was elected and who appointed provincial governors. There was an effective system of law courts and a large army. Altogether the empire had about five million inhabitants. The Aztecs had developed the principles of architecture and engineering, and by the sixteenth century were on the verge of developing a cursive script. In 1519, the Aztec Empire was attacked by the Spanish under Hernán Cortés and was destroyed within two years. The capital Tenochtitlán was obliterated.

1556
PHILIP II

Philip II became king of Spain in 1556. He was a hard-working bureaucratic administrator who continued his father's policy of centralisation. He worked long hours in his office, reading and signing documents. Under Philip II, Spain became the most powerful country in Europe and the western world. The Spanish infantry, armed with long pikes, became a feared military force, and twice a year the Flota returned from the Americas with vast amounts of gold and silver. But Philip set an example that few monarchs could follow. His son, Philip III, showed little interest in politics and almost immediately the power of Spain began to subside. Philip II had also bankrupted Spain; despite the immense wealth brought by the Flotas, Philip's attempts to destroy Protestantism led to vast expense and constant interference in wars throughout Europe.

1558
THE VIRGIN QUEEN

In 1558, Elizabeth I became queen of England. She was 25 years old. During her lifetime she had seen her father, Henry VIII, grow old and increasingly unhappy, her

▲ *Elizabeth I began to re-establish the authority of the monarchy in England.*

brother Edward VI die at the age of 15, and her elder sister Mary become very unpopular after she married Philip II of Spain and then tried to reimpose Catholicism on England. Elizabeth was determined to re-establish the authority of the Crown. Traditionally the monarch in England was referred to as 'Your Grace'; this was the same title as was used for a duke and an archbishop. Elizabeth forced her courtiers – as they now became called – to address her as 'Your Majesty', implying that there was something different and remote about royalty. This set a pattern that other monarchs were to follow.

1560s
COURTLY LIFE
Until the sixteenth century, most nobles lived on their estates, holding sway over their land and their subjects. In some countries, such as France and Spain, they were the source of justice and even had the right to perform executions. Elizabeth I realised the potential dangers of this situation and developed the idea of the

court. She persuaded her nobles that the proper place for them was with her, where she could keep an eye on them. Their main function was to pay court to the queen. They wrote poems, songs and music about her and gave her expensive gifts. She gave them the privilege of being near her. To be banished from court was a sign of extreme disfavour. In countries where the monarch remained the centre of political power, the court remained crucial until the early twentieth century.

1642
THE DIVINE RIGHT OF KINGS
The Divine Right of Kings was a concept that developed throughout the sixteenth and early seventeenth centuries. It simply stated that kings were appointed by God and could only be punished by God. Opposition to the monarch was, therefore, impossible. In France, Spain and the Holy Roman Empire, all Catholic countries, Divine Right was accepted almost as a matter of course; it was a further source of royal authority and power. It also gave the church a privileged position. In Protestant countries Divine Right was not popular. Charles I's belief in it was one factor in the outbreak of civil war in England in 1642, and also in his execution in 1649. Overall, Divine Right stabilised but also ossified politics. Opposition became more difficult and the development of democracy was virtually impossible.

1661
THE SUN KING
The Sun King was Louis XIV, king of France (1643–1715). He made France the most powerful country in Europe. Louis was only five when he became king and did not rule in person until 1661. He followed the practice of centralising power into his own hands. Louis also established a dazzling court at his new Palace of Versailles, just outside Paris. The bishops and nobles of France flocked there to pay court to the king. Their days were often spent watching the king get up, the *levée*, or go to bed, the *couchée*. They were also expected to watch

him have breakfast, lunch and dinner. Extra privileges included carrying the king's bedrobe or walking before him with a candle as he went to his bedroom.

p. 31 ◄ **Distant Voices** ► p. 35

I am come amongst you as you can see ... being resolved in the midst and heat of the battle to live and die amongst you all.

I know I have the body of a weak and feeble woman, but I have the heart and stomach of a king, and a king of England too, and I think foul scorn that ... any prince of Europe should dare to invade the borders of my realm.

From a speech made by Queen Elizabeth I to her army, while they were awaiting the Spanish Armada (1588)

▼ *Louis XIV of France, known as the 'Sun King'.*

India
1526–1947

UNTIL THE SIXTEENTH CENTURY, the vast area of India was divided into different states. In the west were Muslim states, in the north Buddhist and in the south Tamil, Jainist and Sivaist. There was continual conflict in each area as noble families attempted to extend their territories. In the sixteenth century, much of central and northern India fell under the control of the Muslim Mogul emperors. When this empire declined in the eighteenth century, they were replaced by the Hindu Marathas. During the nineteenth century, the Marathas gradually came under increasing British control. In the twentieth century, both Hindus and Muslims tried to force the British to leave India and in so doing created the two states of India and Pakistan.

✴ ▶ p. 52

1526
THE FOUNDING OF THE MOGUL EMPIRE

The Mogul Empire was founded by Babar (r. 1526–30), but the organisation of the empire was the work of Akbar (1556–1605). He took control of all land and arranged for it to be administered directly by the Crown. He also set up a state civil service to carry out his orders. Non-Muslims within the empire were treated as equals and were not subject to any special laws or taxes. In 1578 Akbar allowed public debates on religion involving all faiths, including Christians. Akbar strengthened the empire by conquering Gujarat and Bengal to the west and beginning the conquest of the Deccan to the south. This was the first time that a large part of India had been unified.

▼ *Babar, the founder of the Mogul Empire, invading Persia.*

1658
AURANGZEB

Aurangzeb was the last of the Mogul emperors. He seized power in 1658, when he rebelled against the emperor Shah Jahan, the builder of the Taj Mahal. Under Aurangzeb the Mogul Empire began to break up. This was partly the result of his attacks on Hinduism, which led to rebellions by Hindus and Sikhs. It was also brought on by Aurangzeb's failure to control his own regional governors, who increasingly began to ignore his authority and raise taxes for themselves. Aurangzeb faced opposition from the Hindu Maratha princes from southern India and from the British, who had arrived in India in the early seventeenth century. When he died in 1707, the Mogul Empire began to disintegrate.

1775
THE MARATHA WARS

The Marathas were Hindu princes from southern India, who attacked the remnants of the Mogul Empire in the mid-eighteenth century. They were organised into a loose confederacy and competed amongst themselves for leadership. Their success against the Mogul Empire brought them into conflict with the British, leading to the first Maratha War from 1775–82. A second war broke out in 1802, which resulted in the Marathas being defeated at the battles of Assaye and Argaum by Sir Arthur Wellesley (later the Duke of Wellington). This led to the collapse of Maratha power. They retained control of their lands, but were under the indirect control of the British.

1784
THE INDIA ACT

The British landed in India for the first time in 1603. They were representatives of the East India Company for which a charter had been granted by Elizabeth I in 1600. For more than a century they occupied coastal trading posts, such as Madras, but in the mid-eighteenth century they were able to defeat both the Dutch and the French and take control of the trade on the subcontinent. In 1784, Pitt's India Act prevented the East

✜ UNIFICATION   ♣ CIVIL WAR   ✱ CRISES   ✳ EMPIRES   ✪ DEMOCRACY

India company from interfering in the affairs of Indian states, but in the early nineteenth century, after the Maratha Wars, the Company acquired more and more influence across India. By the 1820s, almost all of India was governed, directly or indirectly, by the East India Company.

▲ *The British first settled in India in 1603; it was only in the twentieth century that Indians once again began to govern their own country.*

⚒ ▶ p. 38   **1857**
THE 'INDIAN MUTINY'
In 1857 there was a revolt against the East India Company by members of its army. To the British it was a mutiny; to Indians it marked the beginnings of Indian Nationalism. The revolt began when a new cartridge was introduced which Muslims came to believe was smeared with pig fat. Hindus came to believe that it was smeared with cow fat. East India Company control broke down in many parts of northern India and in 1858 the British Government took over the government of India. In the 1860s and 1870s a number of nationalist movements were set up, culminating in the Indian National Congress in 1885. It was this organisation that led the fight for independence in the twentieth century.

1915
MOHANDAS GANDHI
Mohandas Gandhi became the leader of the Congress Party when he returned to India in 1915. He began a campaign of Satyagraha, or peaceful civil disobedience, to force the British to leave India. Gandhi began to spin

cotton, in defiance of British laws which said that raw cotton had to be sent to Britain, and in 1930 he organised a 'March to the Sea' to make salt, again in defiance of the British. His self-restraint won him a place at the Round Table Conferences in London in 1930–32. These conferences were intended to find a compromise between the British and the Indians. The result was the Government of India Act in 1935. For the first time Indians played a significant part in the government of their country.

1945
THE IMPACT OF THE SECOND WORLD WAR
During the Second World War, Gandhi organised the 'Quit India' campaign. This was a response to the British government's decision to announce that India had declared war on Germany without consulting Indians. Gandhi's campaign increased the influence of the Muslim League, which was led by M. A. Jinnah. When the war ended in 1945, Jinnah demanded a separate Muslim state, Pakistan. For the first time, there was widespread violence between Hindus and Muslims, especially in Calcutta in August 1946, when Jinnah attempted to put pressure on the British to allow 'partition'. It became increasingly obvious that the two religions could not coexist.

▼ *The 'Indian Mutiny' marked the beginning of the campaign for Indian Nationalism.*

❖ ▶ p. 48   **1947**
INDEPENDENCE AND PARTITION
On 15 August 1947, India and Pakistan became independent. To the last, Gandhi wanted Hindus and Muslims to live together in a united India, but rivalries and jealousies between Congress and the Muslim League made that impossible. A dividing line was drawn up which left many Muslims in India and many Hindus in Pakistan. As hundreds of thousands tried to cross the border in both directions there was widespread violence. Partition did not solve the disputes between Hindus and Muslims. Kashmir in the north has been argued and fought over since 1947 and periods of normal relations between the two governments have been rare.

p. 33 ◀ **Distant Voices** ▶ p. 37

Passive resistance … is superior to the force of arms … even a man weak in body is capable of offering this resistance. One man can offer it as well as millions. Both men and women can indulge in it. Control over the mind alone is necessary, and when that is attained man is free like the king of the forest and his very glance withers the enemy.

From an article written by Mohandas Gandhi, describing his idea of passive resistance (1909)

Government of the People
1755–1890

O F ALL THE COLONIES created by the European powers in the seventeenth and eighteenth centuries, America was by far the most developed. In fact there were 13 colonies, all very different in make-up, economy and size. Until 1763 they all had one thing in common: they needed British protection from the French and the Indians. After 1763, when the French had been defeated, there appeared to be less need for such British protection and for government from London, and resentment began to brew. Americans, many of whom did not originate in Britain, came to see themselves as owing allegiance to no one other than themselves. A new experiment in democracy followed.

1755
THE SEVEN YEARS' WAR
In 1755, war broke out between the American colonists and the French, who were allied to the native American Indians. At first the war went badly for the colonists and the French captured Forts Oswego, George and Ticerondoga, but in 1758, the tide began to turn. Louisburg, Fort Frontenac and Fort Duquesne were all captured by the British and in 1759 General Wolfe attacked Quebec, the centre of French Canada. At the Battle of the Heights of Abraham in September 1759, the British forces destroyed the army of General Montcalm. They moved towards Quebec and captured it five days later. French power in North America was ended.

✏ ▶ p. 44   ### 1763
THE TREATY OF PARIS
The Treaty of Paris in 1763 brought to an end the Seven Years' War (called in the USA the French and Indian War). The war had resulted in a comprehensive victory for Britain over France. The French forces had been driven out of America and India and the French navy had been crushed at Quiberon Bay in 1759. The British army had even won a victory on the continent at Minden in the same year. The end of the war had two principal effects. Firstly it built up resentment in France against Britain, which led to the search for an opportunity

to gain revenge, and secondly – and much more importantly – it led to increasing opposition from the colonists to British rule, especially when this involved increased taxes to help pay for the cost of the war.

1764–67
ACTS AND DUTIES
After the Treaty of Paris in 1763, the British had acquired vast new territories in North America and large debts as a result of seven years of fighting. The British government expected the American colonists to share the cost of the war and introduced a number of taxes to raise money: the Sugar Act in 1764; the Stamp Act in 1765; and the Townshend Duties on glass, lead, tea and paper (amongst other commodities) in 1767. Each of these measures was met with increased opposition and helped to create a sense of unity between the colonies. In 1765 there

was a Stamp Act Congress, with delegates from nine of the colonies, which led to a Declaration of Rights and Liberties. This was the first occasion on which the colonies had actually worked together.

1773
THE BOSTON TEA PARTY
The centre of resistance to British rule in the 1760s and 1770s was the port of Boston in Massachusetts. Because they relied on trade, Bostonians were far more affected by restrictions imposed by the British government than other colonies to the south. In 1770 this led to an attack on a group of soldiers which resulted in the deaths of five Bostonians. In December 1773, when tea from India arrived in Boston, it was dumped into the sea by Bostonians disguised as Indians. This action became known afterwards as the 'Boston Tea Party'. In June 1774 the port of Boston was closed and the colony of Massachusetts lost many of its rights of self-government and justice. Representatives of all of the colonies, except Georgia, met at Philadelphia in September 1774 in the First Continental Congress. They agreed to refuse to import British goods from December 1774.

1776
THE DECLARATION OF INDEPENDENCE
War broke out between the colonists and the British in April 1775. Much of the early

▼ *Bostonians disguised as Indians throw tea into Boston Port in defiance of British trade restrictions.*

     ✣ UNIFICATION   ♣ CIVIL WAR   ✳ CRISES   ✳ EMPIRES   ✪ DEMOCRACY

fighting centred on Boston, which the British were forced to evacuate in March 1776. Congress then announced that the authority of the British Crown was at an end. The Declaration of Independence was drawn up by Thomas Jefferson on 4 July. The actions of the Americans set a new precedent in power and politics. They asserted the right of a people to throw off their allegiance to their king and establish for themselves a new and different form of government. The next step was the Articles of Confederation and Perpetual Union, which were signed in November 1777. This set out the basis for a United States of America, which came into being in 1781, when the British forces in America surrendered.

p. 30 ◀ **Triumphs & Tragedies** ▶ p. 41

1830s
THE TRAIL OF TEARS

The States of the Union began to expand as soon as the Constitution was ratified. This began the long period of conflict between the colonists and the Native American Indians, who found themselves being forced further and further west. In Georgia, the Cherokee Indians, who had developed an advanced culture with newspapers, schools and libraries, were evicted from their homelands. President Jackson forced them to move west of the Mississippi. The journey west became known as the Trail of Tears, as so many died en route. This was only the first of a series of evictions, culminating in the obliteration of the Sioux tribe at the Battle of Wounded Knee in 1890.

✤ ▶ p. 40   **1787**
THE CONSTITUTION

The Constitution of the United States of America was signed on 17 September 1787. The Constitution came into effect in June 1788 when the ninth state, New Hampshire, ratified it. The drafting of the Constitution had proved difficult. Until the 1770s the states had all had their own governments and it had been opposition to British rule that had united them. Once the British left, some

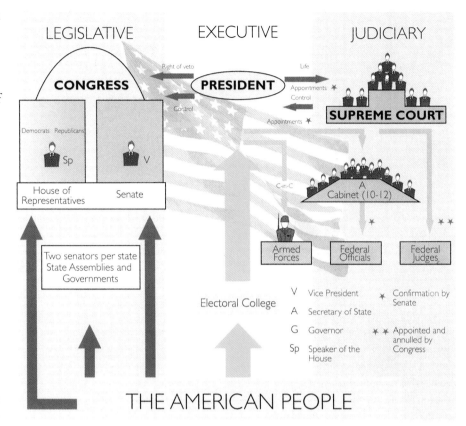

LEGISLATIVE   EXECUTIVE   JUDICIARY

THE AMERICAN PEOPLE

of the old rivalries reappeared. States were reluctant to raise taxes for the federal government, there were disagreements over trade and between the agricultural states of the South and the more industrialised in the North. In addition, the smaller states, such as Connecticut and Rhode Island, feared that they would be swamped by the larger states such as Massachusetts and New York. What resulted was a compromise.

✪ ▶ p. 38   **1789**
THE PRESIDENT

The office of president of the United States was created by the Constitution, and the first president, George Washington, was inaugurated on 5 March 1789. Americans had wanted to avoid giving their president prerogative power, so he was subject to the control of the legislature, or Congress. Presidential actions, such as the budget or declarations of war, had to be approved by both houses of Congress. The president was also subject to the Supreme Court, which had the power to declare his actions

unconstitutional. It was a complicated system of checks and balances, which was intended to prevent presidents acting dictatorially. Many presidents, however, have found ways of extending their executive power.

p. 35 ◀ **Distant Voices** ▶ p. 39

We hold these truths to be self-evident, that all men are created equal, that they are endowed by their Creator with certain unalienable rights, that among these are life, liberty and the pursuit of happiness. That to secure these rights, Governments are instituted among men, deriving their just powers from the consent of the governed. That whenever any form of Government becomes destructive to these ends, it is the right of the people to alter or abolish it....

From the Declaration of Independence (1776)

The French Revolution … and Beyond
1774–1818

IN 1780 LOUIS XVI sent French troops to help the American Colonies win independence from Britain. In 1781, after the surrender of the British forces at Yorktown, the French soldiers returned home. They brought with them the idea that a king could be overthrown by his own people and that a republic could be set up instead. Whether this was an important factor in the events of the next 15 years is uncertain. What is certain is that the cost of helping the Americans was very high and was financed by loans. As a result, the French monarchy became increasingly hard up. By 1788, half of the government's annual expenditure went on interest on debts.

1774
LOUIS XVI

Louis XVI became king of France in 1774. He was a pleasant, unintelligent family man who was totally unsuited for the role that he had to play as an autocratic monarch. In the 1780s, Louis relied on a series of ministers, each of whom tried to solve the financial problems of France. The central issue was that the First and Second Estates (the clergy and the nobility) were exempt from all taxes. This meant that the Third Estate had to pay for everything. This not only reduced the potential income of the state, but it also became an increasing source of grievance with the rich bourgeoisie, the lawyers and merchants, who emerged as the leaders of the Third Estate. Louis XVI was not prepared to break this system; if a minister suggested radical change, he was replaced.

✪ ▶ p. 57

1789
THE ESTATES-GENERAL

The Estates-General was the nearest that France had to a Parliament. It was a body that represented the three Estates of France, the Clergy, the Nobility and the rest, the Third Estate. It had met in 1614, but had never been summoned since. The financial state of the French monarchy was so bad that Louis was forced to summon the Estates-General in May 1789. However, the meeting did not go as Louis and his ministers had anticipated. The Third Estate refused to co-operate with the other two and left the meeting in June. They swore that they would not return unless their grievances were met. The situation soon became much worse as rumours began to spread that Louis was about to use force to solve the problem.

⚒ ▶ p. 43

1789
THE BASTILLE

In May and June of 1789, while the Estates-General was arguing at Versailles, bread prices in Paris reached record levels. On 14 July 1789 a crowd of Parisians attacked the Bastille, a royal fortress in Paris, that was used as both a prison and an arsenal. They were looking for weapons to defend Paris against a possible attack by Louis XVI's forces. The attack was a complete success and the governor of the prison surrendered, but the mob killed him immediately. The fall of the Bastille was a symbol that the power of the king could be challenged, and it had been the working people of Paris who had played the most important role in the events. It was an ominous step for the aristocracy.

1792
MASSACRE IN PARIS

From 1789 to 1792 France was a constitutional monarchy. The National Assembly (1789–91) and the Constituent Assembly which succeeded it, were elected by virtually universal manhood suffrage and different political parties began to appear. However, it was the Paris mob that became

▼ *The Storming of the Bastille: the first step on the road to revolution in France.*

✜ UNIFICATION   ♣ CIVIL   ✳ CRISES   ✳ EMPIRES   ✪ DEMOCRACY

▲ *The Jacobin Maximilien Robespierre, leader of the Reign of Terror in France.*

the most important force in the capital. They were known as the 'Sans-Culottes' because they they wore sriped trousers instead of breeches. In October 1789 the mob marched to Versailles and forced the king to return to Paris. In June 1792 they attacked the royal palace, and then stormed it in August, killing the guards. In September 1792 there were massacres in Paris, which spread to many other cities. The leaders of the Sans-Culottes were members of political clubs, which had been meeting in Paris since 1789.

✠ ▶ p. 43
1792
THE JACOBINS

In September 1792 the National Assembly was set up in France. This soon fell under the control of the Jacobins, who were members of a club, which met in a monastery in the rue St Jacques. Their leader was Maximilien Robespierre. The monarchy was abolished and Louis XVI was put on trial and executed in January 1793. Robespierre then began the Reign of Terror, in which all his political opponents, including members of his own party, were brought before Revolutionary Tribunals and

then executed, usually by the guillotine. Robespierre became virtual dictator of France, even introducing a Law of Suspects, which allowed people suspected of planning crimes to be tried.

✗ ▶ p. 57
1792
EUROPE DIVIDED

The effects of the Revolution were not confined to France; all over Europe opinion divided on the rights and wrongs of such dramatic social upheaval. The vigour and ruthlessness with which the French Revolution and the subsequent Reign of Terror were conducted put fear into the hearts of political establishments across the continent, particularly in Britain, which had become a haven for escaped 'aristos'. Such fear led to persecution of those radicals who voiced support for the revolutionary cause, such as Thomas Paine, whose *The Rights of Man* (1792) expressed a need for united moves towards reform in the case of corrupt or evil government.

1799
NAPOLEON

In July 1794 the Reign of Terror came to an end and its leader, Maximilien Robespierre, was executed. From 1795, France was governed by five 'Directors'. The Directory, however, was accused of dishonesty and corruption and in November 1799, Napoleon Bonaparte and his brother Lucien carried out the *coup d'état* of 'Brumaire' and

▼ *Napoleon Bonaparte declared himself emperor of France in 1804 and began to rule with a military dictatorship.*

set up the Consulate. This was to be the beginning of an illustrious career. Although in theory Napoleon was only one of three consuls, he was the most important, and in 1801 he became consul for life. In 1804 he declared himself emperor. Not for the first time, or the last, a general took advantage of political instability to set up a dictatorship.

♣ ▶ p. 46
1804
THE EMPIRE OF FRANCE

When he appointed himself emperor in 1804, Napoleon wanted the other crowned heads of Europe to regard him as a legitimate monarch. He established a court and a new nobility, which was much grander than that of Louis XVI. There were 18 Marshals of France and many other titles, privileges and honours. The main difference was that Napoleon's empire valued achievement and merit, rather than birth. He married Marie Louise, the daughter of the Austrian emperor, in 1810, and their son was to succeed him. In acting like this, Napoleon was hoping that his seizure of power and his wars of conquest would be accepted both at home and abroad. He was wrong – although many French people regarded him as a hero, throughout Europe he was regarded as a tyrant.

p. 37 ◀ **Distant Voices** ▶ p. 41

As I left the Hotel de Ville I heard someone say that the Bastille was being attacked. I prepared and greased my gun and set off for the Bastille, loading my gun as I went. It was about half past three. The first bridge had been lowered, and the chains cut, but the portcullis barred the way; people were trying to bring in some cannon, which had previously been dismantled. I crossed over by the small bridge and helped to bring in the two guns.

A description of the storming of the Bastille, written by one of the attackers (1789)

The Nation State
1815–71

WHEN HE CONQUERED his empire from 1799 to 1811, Napoleon destroyed the political system of Europe. Every country in Europe was defeated or became allied to France, with the exception of Britain. In place of the old order, Napoleon created new countries, which were given to members of his family or to his marshals. These changes were redressed in the Treaty of Vienna in 1815, after the final defeat of Napoleon at Waterloo. Napoleon's creations were swept away and the principle of legitimacy was enforced. The rulers of 1799 were restored. But Napoleon's work was not completely swept away. In Germany, Austria and Italy, he had aroused ideas of nationalism that were to reappear later in the century.

▲ *Napoleon's last stand: the Battle of Waterloo in 1815.*

1815
THE HABSBURGS

The Habsburgs, the Austrian royal family, ruled a large empire, that covered much of central Europe. At the end of the Napoleonic War they had been given, in addition, most of northern and central Italy. Their empire was governed from Vienna by the emperor, but was multinational and multilingual in character. To the east were Hungarians, Czechs, Slovaks and Ruthenians; to the south there were Italians, Croats and Slovenes; and to the north there were Poles. The Habsburgs knew that, of all the empires of Europe, theirs was the most vulnerable to nationalism. And for 33 years, from 1815 to 1848, any sign of nationalism was eradicated without mercy.

✥ ▶ p. 41

1819
THE ZOLLVEREIN

The Zollverein was an economic union set up by Prussia in 1819. The Rhineland had been given to Prussia at the Treaty of Vienna in 1815 and the Prussians decided to set common tariffs for all their territories, creating a customs union, or Zollverein. Other German states joined and by 1844 almost all of Germany was included. Although the Zollverein was not a political force, it led to Prussia being seen as the leader of Germany, with the result that many German states were drawn into a Prussian sphere of influence and away from Austria. It laid the basis for the nation state of Germany and challenged the German Confederation, set up in 1815, and dominated by Austria.

1820s
THE RISE OF NATIONALISM

Nationalism, the concept of the nation state, was uncommon in the eighteenth century. At that time, autocratic power was exercised by hereditary royal families, rather

▼ *Maximilian de Habsburg; the Habsburg dynasty was founded by Holy Roman Emperor Charles V in the sixteenth century.*

than by the people whom they ruled. The French Revolution and Napoleon's empire created a new sense of national identity in France and abroad, and as early as the 1790s there were demands for reform in both Britain and Austria. In the 1820s, radical movements throughout Europe were crushed by the armies of Russia, Austria and Prussia. The demands in Britain succeeded in the 1830s, but elsewhere, autocracy struck back using repression.

1832
MAZZINI AND YOUNG ITALY

The most troublesome part of the Austrian Empire from the 1820s onwards turned out to be the Italian provinces. Much of the trouble was caused by Giuseppe Mazzini, who set up the Young Italy movement in 1832. He wanted to overthrow the rulers of the different states in Italy and set up a republic with its capital at Rome. From 1832 onwards there was a series of uprisings in almost every Italian state, which all failed disastrously. Mazzini fled abroad, eventually to London, from where he published a stream of pamphlets and journals. In terms of the 1830s and 1840s his ideas were too radical, but he kept the flame of Italian nationalism alive and spread it to other countries throughout Europe.

✤ ▶ p. 55
1860
GARIBALDI

Giuseppe Garibaldi was a republican guerrilla leader. He first became famous when he defended Rome against the French army after it had been seized by Italians in 1848. He surrendered after a siege lasting a month. In 1860, after the Piedmontese army had occupied Lombardy, Garibaldi sailed from Genoa and landed with 1,000 men on Sicily, which was part of the kingdom of Naples. In less than three months he had driven the Neapolitan army out of Sicily and in August he invaded the mainland. The city of Naples was occupied within a fortnight and the king of Naples fled. Garibaldi planned to invade the Papal States and then to attack Venetia, but before he could, the Piedmontese army invaded the

▲ *Prussian politician Otto von Bismarck became chancellor of Germany in 1862.*

p. 37 ◀ **Triumphs & Tragedies** ▶ p. 43
1852–61
CAVOUR

Count Camillo di Cavour was prime minister of Piedmont from 1852–59 and again in 1860–61. His aim was to unify Italy under the king of Piedmont, but he realised that he would need powerful allies if he were to be successful. In 1855 he sent the Piedmontese army to fight in the Crimea alongside the Franco-British force, hoping this would win him support. Emperor Napoleon III did indeed send forces against the Austrians in 1859, winning the battles of Magenta and Solferino. However, he was so shocked by the losses his army suffered that he withdrew from the campaign. In 1860 Cavour cleverly took advantage of the campaign of Garibaldi to take over most of southern and central Italy. Cavour was prepared to use any means at his disposal to gain his objective. This policy became known as *realpolitik* – 'realistic politics'.

Papal States from the north and Garibaldi handed over all his conquests to Victor Emmanuel, the king of Piedmont.

1862
BISMARCK

Otto von Bismarck became chancellor of Germany in 1862. He was a conservative Prussian politician, who wanted to extend

Prussia's dominance in Germany by uniting the country under the king of Prussia. He followed the policy of *realpolitik*. In 1864 Bismarck, in alliance with Austria, declared war on Denmark and took Schleswig. In 1866 he first signed a treaty with France and then picked a quarrel with Austria. The French remained neutral, but the Austrian army was crushed in seven weeks. When the peace terms were discussed. Bismarck insisted on being lenient to Austria; he knew that he would want its support in the future.

1870
THE FRANCO-PRUSSIAN WAR

In July 1870 Bismarck, the chancellor of Germany, managed to bring about a French declaration of war on Prussia. He altered a telegram sent to the king of Prussia, which made it appear to be offensive. The war was a disaster for the French; all their armies were defeated and the emperor Napoleon III was captured at Sedan. On 18 January 1871, the German Empire was proclaimed in the Hall of Mirrors in the Palace of Versailles. All the German states were now members of the empire. Many of them retained their own heads of state and their government, but in reality it was Prussia that mattered. In May the peace treaty with France was signed and the two provinces of Alsace and Lorraine were ceded to Germany.

p. 39 ◀ **Distant Voices** ▶ p. 43

During the defence of Rome I had often had occasion to admire Garibaldi's sure hand in directing a battle and his quick and sure eye for detail…. His energy is boundless. He had acquired his ability in long years of warfare with lightly armed troops. Whenever we left camp he first found guides and then gave instructions to those officers whose job it was to procure information about the enemy movements.

A Swiss officer who served with Garibaldi describes his military qualities (1849)

China
214 BC–AD 1967

ACCORDING TO LEGEND, Chinese civilisation began during the second millennium BC, but detailed records exist from the ninth century. The first emperor was Shih Luang Ti, from 247–210 BC, who founded the Ch'in dynasty. He established the pattern of Imperial rule which continued until the founding of the T'ang dynasty in AD 618. Their system of government remained virtually unchanged until 1912. China was a centralised autocracy, which put enormous power in the hands of the emperor. This encouraged almost continuous rebellions and attempted breakaways by border states. Many of these were prompted by religious ideas, as in the case of the Taiping Rebellion in 1850. Emperors had constantly to re-establish their authority.

▲ *The immense Great Wall of China, built to defend the empire against invaders.*

214 BC
THE CH'IN DYNASTY

The first emperor, Shih Luang Ti, organised China as a centralised and orderly state. Many of his reforms were surprisingly modern. He set up 36 regions, or *chun*, each with civil, military and governing civil servants. Laws and weights and measures were standardised, as were the characters in the written script. Older, more complicated characters were abolished. Axle lengths in carts were also controlled to make commerce easier. These changes show that Shih was aware that there was more to centralisation than merely giving orders. To defend the empire he carried out conquests in the south and linked earlier fortifications to build the Great Wall in 214 BC.

AD 618
THE T'ANG DYNASTY

In the seventh century AD, the T'ang dynasty, founded in AD 618, reorganised the empire into 10, later 15, districts which were subdivided into prefectures. Each prefect was responsible for the administration of his area directly to the court. At the centre, the emperor met his Grand Council every day. There were six ministries and 10 other offices, including a flood-prevention bureau and a national college to train officials. There were two state universities that trained civil servants, who were promoted at first on the basis of written examinations. Higher promotion depended upon performance. The T'ang administration depended upon able emperors; a minority or weakness could lead to chaos.

1841
CHINA VS BRITAIN

In the nineteenth century, China came increasingly into contact with the west. The initial reaction of the Chinese was to resist foreign interference, but Britain and France used military force to compel China to open its ports to Western trade. In 1841–42, Britain seized several coastal ports and forced China to sign the Treaty of Nanking, which ceded Hong Kong to Britain. China was also forced to accept the trade in opium, which had been banned hitherto. In 1857–58 Britain and France seized Canton and then signed the Treaties of Tientsin with China. Eleven more ports were opened to the West and foreign missions were allowed in Peking.

1890s
UNEQUAL TREATIES

In 1895–96 China fought a disastrous war with Japan over Korea. This was followed by a series of treaties with the European powers and the USA to obtain concessions from the Chinese government. In 1897 Russia was allowed to build and operate railways in China and in 1898 Britain was allowed to operate steamships on Chinese inland waters. Germany seized Kiaochow and was granted a 99-year lease. It was allowed to build railways and to develop mines. On 9 June 1898 Britain secured a 99-year lease on Kowloon and Hong Kong. France acquired Kuang-chou and the right to build railways. The Unequal Treaties showed the weakness of the Chinese Empire. In 1908 the throne passed to the boy emperor P'u-i.

1912
SUN YAT-SEN AND THE CHINESE REPUBLIC

Sun Yat-Sen was a western-educated politician who led the Chinese Revolution of 1911. The emperor, P'u-i, abdicated in February 1912 and a republic was set up with Sun as president. An Assembly was established with two houses. Sun, however, resigned almost immediately to allow Yuan Shih-k'ai to unite the country. Sun set up the Kuomintang, or Nationalist Party. In 1913 Yuan forced the Kuomintang

❖ UNIFICATION   ♣ CIVIL WAR   ✳ CRISES   ✳ EMPIRES   ◉ DEMOCRACY

p. 41 ◀ **Triumphs & Tragedies** ▶ p. 45

1963
THE CULTURAL REVOLUTION

In 1965, Mao announced the beginning of the Cultural Revolution. This was an attempt by Mao to regain his dominant position in the party. He set up soldiers called 'Red Guards', who put up posters throughout the country praising the 'thoughts of Chairman Mao', which were published in a 'Red Book'. They attacked teachers, intellectuals, scientists and civil servants, who were often humiliated by being and forced to recite from Mao's book. All forms of traditional Chinese culture were ridiculed. Within two years the country was in complete chaos and even Mao was forced to order the Red Guards to stop their attacks in 1967.

▲ *Chinese citizens show their support for Chairman Mao during the Cultural Revolution.*

members of the Assembly to leave and in 1914 dissolved the Assembly. In 1915 he declared himself emperor. Yuan's behaviour had important consequences in the long run. When the Kuomintang held its first national congress in 1924, Communists were admitted and there were Russian and German military advisers headed by Jiang-Jieshi, who had been trained in Japan. They set up a military academy and when Sun died in 1925, Jiang-Jieshi became the leader of the Kuomintang.

▼ *Prince Yuan Shi-k'ai of China.*

✠ ▶ p. 49   ### 1920s
THE WARLORDS

In the 1920s, central government in China broke down and power fell into the hands of local rulers who became known as the 'Warlords'. Although some, such as Yen Hsi-shan of Shansi, ruled efficiently, most were simply local dictators taking advantage of the situation. The Warlords were crushed by military campaigns by Jiang-Jieshi, which gave him even more power within the Kuomintang and led to a split in 1927 between the Nationalist members of the party and the Radicals on one side, and Communists on the other. The Communists, led by Mao Zedong, set up a commune in Kiangsi, where they lived until 1934. They were then forced to leave by attacks from the Kuomintang and set out on the Long March to the province of Shensi. This became part of Chinese Communist mythology.

⚒ ▶ p. 48   ### 1949
THE COMMUNIST REVOLUTION

In 1949, after years of fighting, the Chinese Communist Party seized power and the Kuomintang, led by Jiang-Jieshi, fled to the island of Formosa, where they eventually established the state of Taiwan. Mao Zedong set up a programme of industrial

development based on Five-Year Plans; however, his distrust of intellectuals and technical experts held back progress. Much of the work in building dams and other large-scale enterprises was done by manual labour. In 1957 the 'Great Leap Forward', in which people throughout China were asked to set up blast furnaces in their back gardens was a disaster. All over China the harvest was left to rot and there was widespread famine.

p. 41 ◀ **Distant Voices** ▶ p. 45

On the athletic field, I saw rows of teachers, about forty or fifty in all, with black ink poured over their heads and faces. Hanging around their necks were placards with such words as 'class enemy so and so'…. They all wore dunce caps. Hanging from their necks were pails filled with rocks. I saw the principal, the pail round his neck was so heavy that the wire had cut into his neck.

An eyewitness describes an incident during the Cultural Revolution, from *The Red Guard*, by Ken Ling (1972)

The Balance of Power in Europe
1871–1914

THE FRANCO-PRUSSIAN WAR of 1870–71 changed the face of Europe and led eventually to fundamental alterations in the workings of European politics; it also gave rise to increasing friction between European nations. After the war, the most powerful state in Europe was the new united Germany. The war also created intense hostility between France and Germany. Bismarck, the German chancellor, believed that he could counteract France by creating a series of alliances with the other great powers, so that France was isolated. At all costs he wanted to avoid a war on two fronts, a simultaneous attack by both France and Russia. For 20 years he tried successfully to hold the balance of power in Europe.

1871
ALSACE-LORRAINE

The provinces of Alsace and Lorraine were taken by Germany at the end of the Franco-Prussian War. They became part of the new German Empire. This was bitterly resented

▼ *German chancellor Bismarck with French emperor Napoleon.*

in France. For more than 40 years the statue in Paris that represented the city of Strasbourg, the capital of Alsace, was draped in black cloth. *Revanchisme*, 'revenge', became important in French politics. The French actress, Sarah Bernhardt, refused to appear in Germany. When she was asked to name her fee by a theatre manager, she sent a telegram with the words 'Alsace-Lorraine'. It was obvious that sooner or later France would attempt to regain the lost provinces and the main battle plan of the French Army, 'Plan 17', involved a direct assault from Champagne into Germany.

1873
THE DREIKAISERBUND

In 1873 the DreiKaiserBund, the Three Emperors' League, was signed by the emperors of Germany and Austria and the tsar of Russia. Agreements already existed between each of the three powers and the League was the last in this sequence of alliances. The League was the first of Otto von Bismarck's attempts to guarantee the security of Germany and protect it from an attack by France. The League did not have exact, binding clauses, but the powers agreed to crush any subversive movements and to defend the monarchy. The three great powers of central and eastern Europe were now linked in a loose agreement, which was intended to maintain the status quo.

1878
THE CONGRESS OF BERLIN

In 1877 war broke out between Russia and Turkey. The two countries had been at war intermittently for centuries, but during the nineteenth century Turkey declined as a military power and Russia advanced into the Balkans. In March 1878 the Treaty of San Stefano was signed between Turkey and Russia, which gave the Russians territory in the Balkans and also set up a new country, Bulgaria, which was to be occupied by the Russians for two years. Both Britain and Austria protested that this gave Russia too much influence in the Balkans and Britain threatened to go to war. The crisis was solved by Bismarck at the Congress of Berlin. Bulgaria was divided into three parts, Austria was allowed to occupy Bosnia-Herzegovina and Britain was allowed to occupy Cyprus.

✐ ▶ p. 52 **1879 AND 1882**
THE DUAL AND TRIPLE ALLIANCES

The Dual Alliance was signed between Germany and Austria in 1879. It became the most important part of Bismarck's attempts to give Germany security. It was aimed at Russia. If either power was attacked by Russia, the other would declare war immediately. In 1882 the Dual Alliance was extended to become the Triple Alliance, with the inclusion of Italy. While these agreements gave Bismarck some security, they isolated Russia, so in 1881 he had arranged the Alliance of Three Emperors, between Germany, Austria and Russia. This was based on the DreiKaiserBund, but this time contained a series of terms. This agreement was renewed in 1884, but in 1887 Russia refused to sign. Bismarck quickly concluded a secret treaty with Russia, the Reinsurance Treaty, which was designed to prevent Russia forming an alliance with France.

1894
THE DUAL ENTENTE

In 1887 Wilhelm II became emperor of Germany. He soon disagreed with Bismarck and demanded his resignation in 1890. As a result, Russia refused to renew the Reinsurance Treaty in 1890. Instead, relations between Russia and France grew much closer. In January 1894 they signed the Dual Entente, which was intended to be a counterweight to the Triple Alliance. Both powers agreed to defend the other if attacked by Germany and to mobilise their forces immediately if the powers of the Triple Alliance mobilised. The Dual Entente created the situation which Bismarck had tried for so long to avoid, the possibility of a war on two fronts, with Germany caught between the armies of France and Russia.

1904
THE ENTENTE CORDIALE

Throughout the second half of the nineteenth century, Britain had avoided any long-term European commitments. British politicians took part in conferences and agreements, but undertook no treaty obligations. In 1902, however, Britain signed a treaty with Japan and in 1904 signed the much more important Entente Cordiale with France. These treaties brought to an end the period of 'Splendid Isolation' in British foreign policy. Three years later, Britain signed an entente with

▼ *Kaiser Wilhelm II of Germany.*

Russia, so creating the Triple Entente. This effectively meant that Europe was now divided into two armed camps, each made up of three powers and each with a series of built-in clauses, which involved automatic and immediate military action. The stage was now set for a showdown.

p. 43 ◀ **Triumphs & Tragedies** ▶ p. 47
1914
SARAJEVO

On 28 June 1914, Archduke Franz Ferdinand – the heir to the Austrian throne – and his wife were shot dead by Serbian terrorist Gavrilo Princip. Under normal circumstances this incident would have passed without major repercussions, but the build-up of alliances and the consequent heightening of tensions turned what was a political matter into an international tragedy. The Austrian government had been looking for an excuse to crush Serbia, which stood in their way in the Balkans. When Russia mobilised in support of the Serbs, Germany automatically became involved and this brought in France. By 12 August all the major European powers were involved in a catastrophic slogging match, which would last for more than four years.

1905
THE SCHLIEFFEN PLAN

Count Alfred von Schlieffen was the chief of the German general staff and in 1905 he drew a military strategy to counter a possible attack on two fronts by France and Russia. He believed that the immediate threat would come from France, but the more serious threat would come from Russia. The Schlieffen Plan involved a sudden attack through Belgium, a neutral country, which would outflank the French Army and surround Paris. This would force the French to surrender. German forces could then be moved east by train to face the Russian armies. Schlieffen believed that the Russians would take six weeks to mobilise. The plan became fundamental to German strategy.

▲ *The assassination of Archduke Franz Ferdinand, the spark that ignited the Great War.*

p. 43 ◀ **Distant Voices** ▶ p. 47

If France is attacked by Germany, or by Italy supported by Germany, Russia shall use all her available forces to attack Germany.

If Russia is attacked by Germany, or by Austria supported by Germany, France shall use all of her available forces to attack Germany.

If the forces of the Triple Alliance, or of one of the Powers of the Triple Alliance, shall be mobilised, France and Russia shall immediately mobilise their forces and shall move them as close as possible to their frontiers.

From the Franco-Russian military agreement which became part of the Dual Entente (1892)

Japan
1853–1945

UNTIL THE LATE NINETEENTH CENTURY, Japan was a feudal society ruled by a military dictator called the 'shogun'. This was short for *Seiidaishshogun*, or 'Barbarian-subduing great general'. Families competed for the post, which was more important than that of emperor. There were long periods of prosperity under some families, for example the Fujiwaras from 866 to 1160, but there were also periods of intense rivalry and civil war. From 1600 to 1868, Japan was dominated by the Tokugawa family. The law code was based upon the concept of loyalty and society was strictly classified. The country was ruled by feudal lords, who had to provide hostages to the central government. The lords were left to govern their regions, but were expected to follow the law and organisation of the state.

1853
THE ARRIVAL OF THE WEST

Until the 1850s Japan resisted almost all contact with the West. There were many missions, but only a few amounted to anything. But in 1853 Commodore Matthew Perry arrived in Tokyo with a letter for the emperor from the US president. The letter was taken to the local feudal lord and was then sent to the emperor. A treaty was signed with the USA in 1854 and others followed with Britain, Russia, and the Netherlands. Opinion in Japan was divided over the issue of foreign influence. This lasted until 1868 when the new emperor Mutsuhito took control of the government himself and dismissed the shogun. This brought to an end feudal rule in Japan. The new royal family the Meiji began a policy of Westernisation.

1868
COPYING THE WEST

From 1868 onwards Japan began to learn as much as possible from the West. Naval cadets were sent to study in Britain and military cadets were sent to Germany. Industrialisation was introduced and advanced rapidly. A strong centralised bureaucratic government was introduced. The feudal lords were dismissed and local government was put in the hands of

prefects. In 1880 a new law code was published, based on the French system. In 1881 two political parties appeared, the Liberals and the Progressives. By 1889 a new constitution was in place which safeguarded the position of emperor; only he could declare war, for example, and which set up two houses in a Parliament. The government was carried on by a prime minister and a cabinet of nine ministers.

▼ *The Japanese cavalry fighting Russian sentries during the Russo-Japanese War of 1904.*

1904
THE RUSSO-JAPANESE WAR

War broke out between Japan and Russia over Korea in February 1904. The Russians had advanced into Korea and refused to withdraw. The war was a complete victory for Japan. Port Arthur was besieged and the Russian army was defeated at Mukden. The Russian Baltic Fleet was sent on a 35,400-km (22,000-mile) journey around the world to break the siege of Port Arthur, but was destroyed in 45 minutes at the battle of Tsu Tshima. This was the first time that a major European power had been defeated by an Asian country. It revealed the extent to which Japan had developed since the coming to power of the Meiji.

✦ 1931
THE OCCUPATION OF MANCHURIA

The links between Japan and the West developed further with an alliance with Britain in 1904 and a declaration of war on Germany in 1914. In the 1920s, however, there was a revival of traditional Japanese ideas. The first reason for this was the failure of Japan to gain what it was expecting at the Treaty of Versailles. A second factor was the international reaction to the occupation of Manchuria in 1931. The Japanese army invaded Manchuria – which was part of China – and set up a puppet government.

There was international condemnation, but little else was done. In Japan, the government fell under the control of the army and the country began a period of territorial expansion on the mainland.

1937
JAPAN VS CHINA

In July 1937 the Japanese army invaded northern China. The following month two Japanese sailors were killed at a Chinese aerodrome in Shanghai. This led to the landing of an army, which then forced its way inland. The Japanese airforce was used to bomb Chinese cities into submission. Within a year Nanking, the capital, Tsingtao, Canton and Hankow had all been taken. Britain and the USA gave large loans to the Kuomintang government of China, but the Japanese government began to demand that Britain and the other Western countries should give up supporting China and co-operate with Japan in establishing a 'new order' in the Far East.

✳ ▶ p. 54　1941
PEARL HARBOR

In the 1930s the Japanese government intended to set up a 'Greater South-east Asia Co-prosperity Sphere'. In fact, this was to be nothing more than a Japanese Empire, intended to provide living space for Japan's growing population and to enable Japan to acquire the raw materials which it desperately needed, the most crucial of which was oil. When the USA cut off supplies of oil to Japan in July 1941 in protest against Japan's expansion in China and Indochina, the Japanese government decided to attack the USA before it was ready. On 7 December

▼ *US president Harry S. Truman, who authorised the dropping of the atomic bomb on Hiroshima.*

▲ *Japanese forces fighting in Manchuria.*

1941, the Japanese navy attacked the US base of Pearl Harbor on Hawaii without warning. Eight battleships were destroyed, but the crucial aircraft carriers were at sea on manoeuvres. The USA declared war on Japan the following day.

p. 45 ◀ **Triumphs & Tragedies** ▶ p. 50
1941
HIROSHIMA

On 12 April 1945, Harry S. Truman became president of the USA after the death of Franklin Roosevelt. While at the Potsdam Conference he was told that the Atomic Bomb was ready to be used on Japan. After lengthy discussion, Truman decided to use the bomb. He was told by his chiefs of staff that one million casualties would be caused if Japan were to be invaded. The bomb was dropped on 6 August 1945 on the city of Hiroshima, where some 70,000 people were killed. The bomb not only marked the beginning of a new period in the history of mankind, but also increased the hostility between Truman and the Soviet leader Stalin, who had not been told about the bomb in advance. It became a major factor in the development of the Cold War.

1945
RECOVERY

After 1945, Japan developed a new form of power. The new Japanese constitution severely restricted the power of the military and stated that the Japanese army would not be allowed to serve overseas. All executive power was transferred from the emperor and sovereignty was given to the people through elections to both houses of parliament. The emperor was specifically prohibited from interfering in politics and all his speeches had to be approved by the government in advance. Almost overnight Japan changed from a military dictatorship to a constitutional monarchy. Instead, the Japanese turned the devotion to duty, which was shown in their armed forces, to industrial and economic revival.

p. 45 ◀ **Distant Voices** ▶ p. 49

I see those faces, hear those voices.
My son and wife are waving,
Waving flags until they break.
Their message to me is to fight well.
I look at the sky, and in the spaces
Between the clouds I see them waving
*　still.*
From the deck of the great fleet of
*　battleships*
I say goodbye to the land of my birth,
Goodbye to my wife and my son.
I look to the place where the sky arches
Above the Imperial Palace
And I swear that I will fight well.

A song taught in Japanese schools in the 1930s

All Power to the Soviets
1914–34

RUSSIA WAS THE LARGEST of the European empires, and in 1900 it was still ruled by an autocratic tsar. Although a Duma, or Parliament, was set up in 1906, it had little influence and the tsar continued to appoint and dismiss ministers at will. Russia was a country where the rich were very rich, and the poor very poor, and many Russians lived in appalling poverty. But despite an attempted revolution in 1905 and many assassinations of ministers and members of the royal family, Tsar Nicholas II showed no inclination to carry out reforms. This led to increasing support for opposition groups, some of which used violence. The most important of these became the Bolsheviks led by Vladimir Lenin.

▲ *Tsar Nicholas II abdicated after the February Revolution in 1917.*

1914
NICHOLAS II

Tsar Nicholas II was an unintelligent family man who was completely unsuited to being the autocratic ruler of 140 million people. He was easily influenced by others and lacked the determination to carry out serious changes in Russia. He believed that it was his duty to pass on the power that he had inherited to his son, so he tended always to side with his most conservative, even reactionary ministers. Nicholas allowed Russia to be rushed headlong into war in 1914, and when the Russian army was badly beaten by the Germans in the early battles, appointed himself commander-in-chief in August 1915. This was typical of his complete lack of political judgement. As a result, and for the first time, Russians began to blame the tsar personally for Russian failures.

1917
THE FEBRUARY REVOLUTION

In February 1917 revolution broke out in Petrograd, the capital of Russia. It was not a planned uprising, but a series of protests against food shortages, inflation and rumours about the tsarina, Alexandra, who was believed to be a German spy. She was also believed to have had an affair with Gregory Rasputin, a mysterious monk who had been murdered in December 1916. The protests were joined by strikers from factories in Petrograd and by soldiers sent to deal with the demonstrators. Even some of the tsar's most loyal troops, the Cossacks, joined in. When Nicholas heard of the events, he tried to return to Petrograd from his headquarters, but his train was not allowed through. On 2 March 1917 the tsar of Russia abdicated.

1917
THE OCTOBER REVOLUTION

From March to October 1917, Russia was ruled by the Provisional Government. This had no legal standing, but was intended to govern until a general election could be held; this was planned for November. The Provisional Government gradually became more and more unpopular, partly because it decided to continue the war against Germany, but also because food shortages and inflation grew even worse. On 24–25 October the Bolsheviks overthrew the Provisional Government in a coup planned and led by Leon Trotsky, Lenin's second-in-command. A month later the general election was held. This was won by the Socialist-Revolutionary Party, but when the Assembly met in January, Lenin dissolved it by force and began to rule as a dictator.

1918
BOLSHEVISM IN ACTION

The Bolsheviks were Marxists; Lenin and his followers believed that private property was wrong, that all businesses, farms and public services should be owned by the state. Workers should be paid according to the value of the work that they did, and not according to who they were or what they could demand. Not surprisingly, therefore, in the months after the Bolsheviks seized power, all businesses, banks and so on were taken over by the state; land, houses and money were all confiscated. To enforce his actions, Lenin set up a secret police force, the Cheka, led by Felix Dzerzhinsky, which ruthlessly murdered Lenin's opponents. Russia became a dictatorship far more violent and far more extreme than it had been under the tsars.

♣ ▶ p. 51 ## 1918
CIVIL WAR

In the summer of 1918, civil war broke out between the Bolsheviks and their opponents. At first it seemed inevitable that the Bolsheviks would be defeated as they were completely surrounded and had few effective forces. However, by the end of 1920 all the White armies, as the Bolshevik's

✢ UNIFICATION   ♣ CIVIL WAR   ✳ CRISES   ✳ EMPIRES   ✪ DEMOCRACY

▲ *Bolshevik leader Leon Trotsky, who planned and led the overthrow of the Russian Provisional Government.*

opponents were known, had been defeated. The Bolsheviks controlled the main centres of industry and the railway network. They were supported by many of the officers of the tsar's army and by some of the people of Russia. The Whites were disorganised and had few reserves or supplies, despite being supported by Britain and the USA. One by one, their armies were defeated and their commanders captured.

▲ *Armed Bolsheviks taking a suspect to a revolutionary tribunal.*

1928
SOCIALISM IN ONE COUNTRY

Lenin had intended that his successor should be Leon Trotsky, but, after a power struggle lasting over two years, Joseph Stalin emerged as the new leader of the Soviet Union, as Russia and the 14 surrounding countries, was now known. A ruthless dictator, Stalin believed that his first priority must be to make Communism safe in the Soviet Union. He was afraid that the countries of western Europe might try to interfere, as they had done during the civil war in 1918. He called his policy 'Socialism in one Country'. From 1928 Stalin set about modernising and strengthening Soviet industry and agriculture as quickly as possible. This meant that the standard of living generally in the Soviet Union fell and the NKVD, Stalin's secret police, were used even more frequently.

✠ ▶ p. 50

1928
THE FIVE-YEAR PLANS

In 1928 Stalin announced the First Five-Year Plan. This was an attempt to develop Soviet industry, which Stalin believed was one hundred years behind the West. Every factory, coal-mine and industrial plant in the Soviet Union was set a series of targets for the next five years, which it had to meet.

The targets were worked out in Moscow by the state-planning agency, Gosplan. The First Five-Year Plan also included the Collectivisation of all the farms in the Soviet Union. Farmers and peasants were forced to amalgamate their farms into large state farms. Second and Third Five-Year Plans followed in the 1930s. Overall, industrial production increased by about 400 per cent, but the plans encouraged quantity not quality. Fifty per cent of tractors broke down and could not be repaired.

1934
THE PURGES

In 1934 Stalin began his most sinister use of power. He began to systematically eliminate anyone whom he suspected of opposing him throughout the Soviet Union. Other leaders of the Communist Party were put on trial and forced to confess to crimes that they could not possibly have committed. Generals and admirals were executed on suspicion of treason. Managers of state farms and factories were shot. Poets, musicians, scientists who did not agree with Stalin, were rounded up and sent to slave-labour camps, along with millions of others. The final total is unknown, but may have been as high as 20 million. Soviet citizens learnt to dread the arrival of the secret police in the early hours and the disappearance, without warning or explanation, of a member of the family, usually the husband or father.

p. 47 ◀ **Distant Voices** ▶ p. 51

Thank you, Stalin. Thank you because I am joyful. Thank you because I am well ... centuries will pass, and the generations still to come will regard us as the happiest of mortals, as the most fortunate of men ... because we were privileged to see Stalin.... We regard ourselves as the happiest of mortals because we live at the same time as a man who never had an equal in world history.

From a speech given in Stalin's honour (1935)

Dictatorship
1919–45

THE DEFEAT OF GERMANY in 1918, at the end of the First World War, led to the growth of a number of extremist parties. When the terms of the Treaty of Versailles were announced in 1919 the situation became even more dangerous. In some parts of Germany law and order almost broke down altogether. A similar situation developed in Italy. In fact Italy had been one of the victors in the First World War, but at the Peace Conference at Versailles had not been given the territory that it had expected. Instead Italy received only two small areas, the South Tyrol and Istria. Italy's debts, however, were enormous and 460,000 Italians had been killed in the fighting. Many Italians felt that they had actually lost the war.

1919
FASCISM

Fascism developed in Italy after the First World War. The term came from the Roman word *fasces*, a bundle of rods and an axe, which was carried before a Roman magistrate. They represented the power of

▼ *Italian fascist dictator Benito Mussolini.*

a magistrate to order corporal punishment and capital punishment. The *fasces* became the symbol of the Fascist Party. Fascists believed in a strong central government headed by a dictator. They thought that ordinary people should be prepared to sacrifice their own personal liberty for the good of the state. For example they believed that men and women had different roles in society. They opposed foreign influences and instead wanted Italy to be self-sufficient. They described this economic system as 'Autarky'.

✠ ▶ p. 54
1919
MUSSOLINI

Benito Mussolini was the leader of the Fascist Party in Italy. He had fought in the First World War and was very angry at the treatment Italy had received at the Treaty of Versailles. From 1919 he organised a propaganda campaign through his paper *Il Popolo d'Italia*. He made himself out to be a strong man who could solve Italy's problems. His supporters, known as the Blackshirts, were organised into *Fascio di Combattimento*. In some parts of Italy, Bologna for example, they were the main source of law and order. They punished criminals, broke up strikes and attacked Mussolini's opponents. In October 1922 Mussolini organised a 'March on Rome' by

his Blackshirts. This was intended to put pressure on the government; in fact it led to Mussolini being appointed prime minister of Italy. He became the first dictator in western Europe.

1920s
NATIONAL SOCIALISM

National Socialism was the name that Hitler gave to the ideas that he developed in the 1920s. He hoped that the word 'Nationalist' would attract right wing conservatives and that the word 'Socialist' would attract left wing workers. At first Hitler was only well-known in Bavaria in southern Germany but, after the Wall Street Crash in 1929 and the beginning of the Depression, he began to attract much wider support. National Socialists, or Nazis as their enemies called them, believed that Germany was the most important country in the world. They called Germans the 'Master Race'. All foreign influences should be eradicated, especially that of the Jews, who the racist Nazis unfairly blamed for the defeat of Germany in the First World War.

p. 47 ◀ **Triumphs & Tragedies** ▶ p. 62
1939
THE PERSECUTION OF THE JEWS

Hitler blamed the Jews for causing the defeat of Germany during the First World War and believed that he could 'purify' the German race by ridding it of certain groups of people. This included gypsies, Slavs, cripples and the mentally ill as well as Jews. At first the Nazis tried to force the Jews to leave Germany by banning them from the professions, preventing them from voting and making it more and more difficult for them to earn a living. Jews were attacked on the street and their property was smashed. But after the outbreak of war Hitler began to force Jews to live in ghettos, and then, from January 1942, began systematic mass murder in extermination camps using poison gas. By the end of the war in 1945 about six million people had been killed.

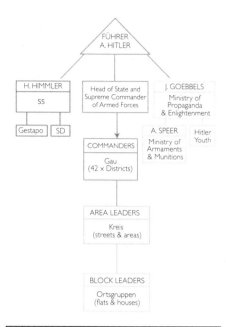

THE POLITICAL STRUCTURE OF NAZI GERMANY, 1933–45
The Nazi party had a structure separate to that of the German government. Competition between the two helped to lessen the efficiency of the German state. In a climate in which the SS competed with the army, Hitler valued loyalty above competence. The party failed to survive its leader in part because it became an extension of his own personality.

1922
THE CORPORATE STATE
Italy under Mussolini set the tone for the dictators who were to follow him in Europe. He banned all other political parties; he controlled newspapers and radio programmes, and had school textbooks rewritten. Women were banned from working and were encouraged to have as many children as possible. He set up a secret police force, the OVRA. Industry was reorganised into corporations; trade unions were banned and instead workers and employers were made to work together on committees, with fascist representatives as chairmen. But Mussolini's great weakness was that his plans were rarely carried through. If he encountered difficulties he usually gave up, as he did when he tried to found a new city in southern Italy, 'Mussolinia'. It was never built.

1933
HITLER IN POWER
Hitler became chancellor of Germany in January 1933 and was given total power when the Enabling Act was passed in March. This allowed him to govern without the Reichstag, the German Parliament for the next four years. By then, the very infrastructure of the country had been changed completely. All political parties and trade unions had been banned. Children were indoctrinated in Nazi ideas by schools and youth organisations, such as the Hitler Youth. Almost all married women had been forced to give up work and were encouraged to have at least four babies. Newspapers, the cinema, books, the arts, music and radio were all controlled by the Nazis and their laws were enforced by the secret state police known as the Gestapo. A total dictatorship had been set up in Germany.

1935
REARMAMENT
One of Hitler's main aims was to re-establish Germany as a major power and overturn the Treaty of Versailles. To do this he needed military strength. From 1935 he began to build up the German armed forces, by first introducing conscription and then producing warships and military aircraft. In 1936 he reoccupied the Rhineland, and in 1938 he occupied Austria and then demanded – and was given – the Sudetenland, the German-speaking part of Czechoslovakia. All these acts had been banned by the Treaty of Versailles, but apart from a few protests by the British and French governments, nothing was done to stop him. It was only when the remainder of Czechoslovakia was occupied in March 1939 that Britain agreed to defend Poland if it was attacked.

♣ 1936
THE SPANISH CIVIL WAR
The Spanish Civil War broke out in the summer of 1936. It was fought between the forces of the Popular Front, the elected government of Spain, and the rebel Falangists, led by General Francisco Franco. The Falangists wanted to overthrow the Popular Front Republicans, who had begun to undermine the power of the Church and the position of the landowners. Because Franco was a Fascist, he received aid from both Mussolini, who sent 70,000 men, and Hitler, who sent the Condor Legion of 10,000 men. Hitler used the war as an opportunity to try out the strength of his new armed forces and to practise 'Blitzkrieg', the strategy of mobile warfare that he was to use at the beginning of the Second World War.

p. 49 ◀ **Distant Voices** ▶ p. 53

In the course of the Final Solution, the Jews will be brought to the East for labour. Large labour camps will be formed, with the sexes separated, which will be used for road construction. No doubt a lot will drop out through natural wastage. The remainder who survive will have to be dealt with accordingly.

From the minutes of the Nazi meeting at the Wannsee Hotel, in which they planned the Final Solution (1942)

▼ *General Francisco Franco, leader of the rebel group the Falangists during the Spanish Civil War.*

Cold War
1945–55

WITH THE END OF THE SECOND WORLD WAR in 1945, a whole new era of power and politics opened up. The atomic bomb gave mankind the power to destroy on a hitherto unimaginable scale. The war had also brought into existence two superpowers, which were to compete for supremacy for almost half a century, by the formation of power blocs and military alliances, which encircled the world. The leaders of East and West no longer represented countries, but ideologies and political systems and it began to appear that one of the two must prevail and one must collapse. But how would that *denouement* come about? Would the new rivalry lead to warfare that might destroy the planet itself?

✍ ▶ p. 52 **1945**
YALTA AND POTSDAM
The conferences at Yalta and Potsdam were both held in 1945. At Yalta in February the mood was friendly, when the leaders of Britain, the USA and the USSR met to decide the fate of Germany. It was decided to divide it into four zones, to be occupied by each of the powers present plus France. Stalin promised to allow free elections in the countries of eastern Europe that he had occupied. He also agreed to allow exiled Poles to join the government that he had set up in Poland. Five months later at Potsdam the mood was very different. US president Truman took a much stronger line with Stalin, who had not allowed the free elections he had promised. Stalin was angry that Truman had not informed him before about the development of the atomic bomb. The Cold War had begun.

✳ ▶ p. 55 **1945**
THE IRON CURTAIN
In 1945 and 1946 Stalin built the Iron Curtain across Europe. It was a barrier that ran for 1,000 miles from the Baltic to the Adriatic, cutting Europe in two. Its purpose was to prevent any western influence from reaching the eastern European countries controlled by Stalin. In particular, it cut Germany into sections, the Soviet zone and the three western zones. The Iron Curtain

received a very hostile reception in the West, which surprised Stalin. At Yalta and Potsdam he had agreed that the West could do as it liked in western Europe and he assumed, therefore, that he could do as he liked in the East. As always, Stalin's main preoccupation was security, and the Iron Curtain seemed to him a natural step. To the West it correctly suggested the beginning of another form of dictatorship.

1946
GERMANY
After 1945, the fundamental difference between East and West was over Germany. To Stalin, Germany remained a serious threat that had to be kept under control. Russia and the Soviet Union had been invaded twice by Germany during the twentieth century, at tremendous cost to the land and the people. Stalin did not want this to happen again. He envisaged a Germany occupied by the Allies, paying reparations and subject to the tightest control. The West believed that if Germany was treated too harshly there could be a reaction, as there had been after the First World War. The Allies wanted a Germany which was occupied, but which was helped to recover from the damage inflicted upon it by the war.

▶ *World leaders at the Yalta Conference in February 1945.*

1948
THE BERLIN BLOCKADE
Berlin, the capital of Germany was divided into four sectors after the war. Each sector was governed by one of the Allies. In the British, US and French sectors, people began to benefit from Allied rebuilding and Marshall Aid. As East Berliners from the Soviet sector were free to travel into the three western sectors, they were able to see the many advantages of life in the West. In June 1948 Stalin tried to cut off West Berlin from the Allied zones in Germany. He stopped all traffic by road, rail and canal. The Allies refused to be beaten and continued to supply Berlin by air. The Berlin Airlift lasted for 10-and-a-half months and at its peak the Allies were carrying in 8,000 tonnes of supplies a day – twice what was required. In May 1949 Stalin gave up. The West had won the first real trial of strength in the Cold War.

✍ **1949**
NATO
NATO was set up in 1949 after the Berlin Blockade. It was a military alliance involving countries on either side of the North Atlantic. It changed relations between East and West by uniting the countries of the West leading to the stationing of US forces in western Europe for the first time. The most important clause in the NATO treaty was that an attack on one country would be considered an attack on all of them. In other words, the East could not pick off democratic countries without the risk of a war with NATO. The

❖ UNIFICATION   ♣ CIVIL WAR   ✳ CRISES   ✳ EMPIRES   ✪ DEMOCRACY

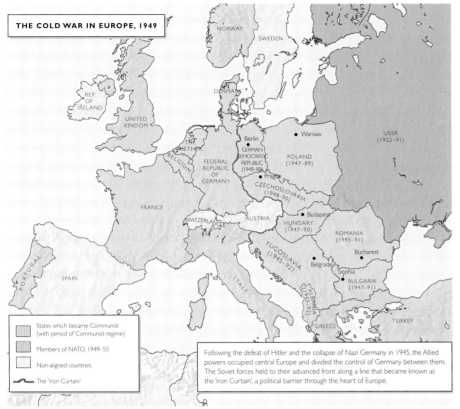

Following the defeat of Hitler and the collapse of Nazi Germany in 1945, the Allied powers occupied central Europe and divided the control of Germany between them. The Soviet forces held to their advanced front along a line that became known as the 'Iron Curtain', a political barrier through the heart of Europe.

States which became Communist (with period of Communist regime)

Members of NATO, 1949–55

Non-aligned countries

The 'Iron Curtain'

existed and had to try to compete with it and prove that the Soviet system was better than any other. One form of this competition was the 'Space Race', which the Soviet Union eventually won with the first satellite in 1957, and the first man in space in 1961. Soviet athletes also began to dominate the Olympic Games from 1956. Khrushchev was a lively character who enjoyed travel and meeting people. He set out to hit the headlines and produce a popular image for Communism.

1955
SUMMITS

From 1955 the leaders of the USA, the USSR, Britain and France began to meet regularly. The meetings were called Summits. Very little ever came of these meetings in terms of actual agreements, but they were a sign that relations between East and West were improving. In fact, the Soviet prime minister, Nikita Khrushchev, used the meetings as a means of winning popular support throughout the world. When he visited Britain in 1957 he broke with protocol and shook hands with workers at a factory. He also decided, after a meeting with the US president Kennedy at Vienna in 1961, that he could take advantage of the young president's political inexperience.

Soviet Union did not react to NATO until West Germany was admitted as a member in 1955. After this, it set up the Warsaw Pact, a military alliance between the Communist countries of eastern Europe.

1950
KOREA

At the end of the Second World War, Korea had been divided into a Communist North and a non-Communist South. In 1950 North Korea invaded the South and quickly overran all but the very southern-most tip of the peninsula. The USA took the matter to the United Nations Security Council, which agreed to send a UN force to support South Korea. UN forces landed in the south and also behind North Korean lines at Inchon. The North Koreans were forced back and retreated almost to the Chinese border. However, the Chinese army invaded to support them and the UN forces were forced to retreat. A cease-fire was finally agreed in 1953. The border between the North and the South was then fixed at exactly the same point as it had been when the war began.

1953
COEXISTENCE

In March 1953 Stalin died; after a period of rivalry he was replaced by Nikita Khrushchev, who immediately brought about a change in East-West relations, by introducing the policy of Coexistence. Khrushchev believed that there was nothing to be gained by trying to destroy the West; the Soviet Union had to accept that it

▲ *Memorial to those who died in the Korean War.*

p. 51 ◀ **Distant Voices** ▶ p. 55

From Stettin, in the Baltic, to Trieste, in the Adriatic, an iron curtain has descended across the continent. Behind that line lie all the capitals of the ancient states of Central and Eastern Europe – Warsaw, Berlin, Prague, Vienna, Budapest, Belgrade, Bucharest and Sofia. All these famous cities ... are subject ... to a very high and increasing measure of control from Moscow.

From a speech made by Winston Churchill, warning Americans about the dangers of Soviet advances in Europe (1946).

Détente
1959–89

AFTER STEADY IMPROVEMENT in the late 1950s, relations between the superpowers deteriorated very quickly from 1959 onwards and reached an all-time low in 1962 with the Cuban Missile Crisis. The effect of the crisis was so dramatic that both superpowers realised that this could not be allowed to happen again. The result was a period known as *détente*, in which the superpowers tried to find ways of reducing the threat of nuclear war. Despite some difficulties, especially after the Soviet invasion of Afghanistan in 1979, the enormous cost of maintaining nuclear arsenals and the emergence of Mikhail Gorbachev in the Soviet Union eventually led to the end of the Cold War in 1989.

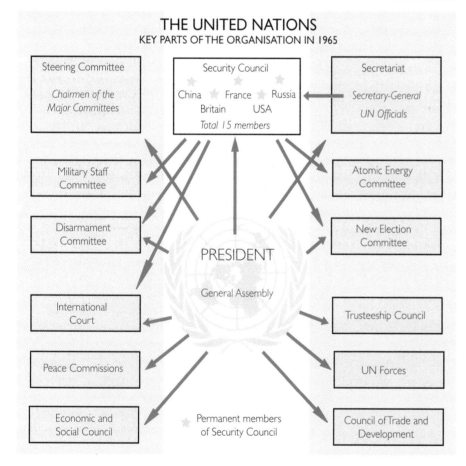

THE UNITED NATIONS
KEY PARTS OF THE ORGANISATION IN 1965

Steering Committee
Chairmen of the Major Committees

Security Council
China   France   Russia
Britain   USA
Total 15 members

Secretariat
Secretary-General
UN Officials

Military Staff Committee

Atomic Energy Committee

Disarmament Committee

New Election Committee

PRESIDENT
General Assembly

International Court

Trusteeship Council

Peace Commissions

UN Forces

Economic and Social Council

Permanent members of Security Council

Council of Trade and Development

1959
CUBA

Until 1959 Cuba was governed by a pro-American dictator Batista, but in 1959 he was overthrown by a group of rebels led by Fidel Castro. The USA cut off all aid to Cuba, and Castro in turn nationalised all US assets and property in Cuba. Soviet leader Khrushchev took advantage of the situation by agreeing to buy one million tonnes of Cuban sugar every year at inflated prices. This brought Cuba Soviet influence and

Castro set up a Communist regime. Many US citizens were horrified. Communism now existed only 70 miles off the coast of Florida. Eisenhower, the US president, authorised an attempt to overthrow Castro by landing a force of Cuban exiles at the Bay of Pigs. The landing actually took place in April 1961, after Eisenhower had left office and was a disaster. The 1,500 Cubans were all killed or captured.

1961
THE BERLIN WALL

The construction of the Berlin Wall was started in August 1961. It separated families and trapped people who had crossed to the other side of Berlin. For 12 years people had been escaping from East Berlin to West Berlin, and by 1961 their numbers were reaching thousands every week. Most of the people who escaped were skilled workers, doctors or engineers. The Wall was an attempt to stop the drain of people from East to West. It was very effective, but it did not stop people trying to escape. The Wall also increased tension between the superpowers. The US president Kennedy visited West Berlin to show his support for its citizens.

1962
EYEBALL TO EYEBALL

On 17 October 1962 John F. Kennedy, the president of the USA, was shown photographs of Soviet missile bases in Cuba. This meant that Soviet missiles could be launched at most US cities and there would be no defence against these attacks. After a week of discussions, Kennedy decided to blockade Cuba and stop any more Soviet ships going there. For a week US forces were on full alert and many people around the world expected that nuclear war would break out. In fact Nikita Khrushchev, the Soviet prime minister, realised that he had made a mistake and sent two messages to Kennedy – one was threatening, the other conciliatory. Kennedy replied to the conciliatory message and the crisis was settled peacefully. The Soviet bases in Cuba were destroyed and the USA agreed not to interfere in Cuban affairs.

▲ *Soldiers returning from the failed US invasion at the Bay of Pigs.*

1963
THE HOTLINE

The Cuban Missile Crisis was a turning point in relations between the superpowers. The leaders of the USA and the USSR realised that such a situation could not be allowed to happen again and both used the word *détente*, a lessening of tension, for the first time towards the end of the crisis. The first real sign of *détente* was the setting up of the Hotline in 1963. This was a direct teleprinter link between the Kremlin and the White House. It enabled the two leaders to get in touch immediately. It was hardly ever used, but it was a sign to the rest of the world that the two sides were talking to each other.

1972
SALT

In 1969 the superpowers began Strategic Arms Limitation Talks. These were aimed at limiting the numbers of the very biggest nuclear weapons. The first treaty, known as SALT 1, was signed in 1972. Its most important clause was a five-year moratorium on the building of strategic weapons. This agreement did not lessen the risk of nuclear war, the superpowers had more than enough weapons already, and it did not affect intermediate or tactical weapons, but it was the first agreement of its kind. SALT 2 was agreed in 1979. This was a much more important treaty as it limited the number of strategic weapons that the two superpowers could build. Each would have no more than 2,500. However, the treaty was never ratified by the US Congress, because of the Soviet invasion of Afghanistan in December 1979.

✳
1980
THE EVIL EMPIRE

In 1981 Ronald Reagan became president of the USA. He was a fierce opponent of Communism and relations between the superpowers deteriorated once again. In 1980 the USA had boycotted the Olympic Games in Moscow and in 1984 the USSR boycotted the Games in Los Angeles. Disarmament talks made no progress for years. The situation was made worse by internal politics in the Soviet Union. Leonid Brezhnev, who had been president since 1964, was very ill, and corruption was widespread. When Brezhnev died in 1982, Yuri Andropov replaced him, but he also soon fell ill and died in 1984. His successor, Konstantin Chernenko died in 1985. For five years there had been little prospect of real change, either internally or externally.

1985
GORBACHEV

In 1985 Mikhail Gorbachev became the president of the Soviet Union and announced his policies of Perestroika and Glasnost. Perestroika involved the restructuring of the Soviet economy and Glasnost meant openness. This applied both internally and externally. Gorbachev was aware that the Soviet Union was bankrupt and that he had to find ways of saving money as quickly as possible, so he immediately restarted disarmament talks with the USA and became very well known and very popular in the West. He was able to develop a close friendship with the Western leaders, which enabled a number of treaties to be signed in the years from 1986 to 1991. In 1989 Gorbachev and President

Bush of the USA were able to announce that the Cold War was over.

✢ ▶ p. 56
1989
THE WALL COMES DOWN

Since 1945 the Soviet Union had kept military forces in the countries of eastern Europe. Those countries had been cut off from the West by the Iron Curtain that Stalin had built in 1945–46. The most famous example of the Iron Curtain was the Berlin Wall, which had been built on Khrushchev's orders in 1961. These actions had been very expensive. In 1989 Mikhail Gorbachev, the Soviet president, began to withdraw forces from eastern Europe in an effort to save money. The West German government paid the expenses of the forces which left East Germany. As Soviet troops withdrew, country after country left the Warsaw Pact and threw off Communism. Finally, in November 1989, crowds in Berlin began to dismantle the Berlin Wall. By the end of the year pieces were being sold as souvenirs.

p. 53 ◀ **Distant Voices** ▶ p. 57

For most west Europeans now alive, the world has always ended at the East German border and the wall; beyond lay darkness. The opening of the frontier declares that the world has no edge any more. Europe is becoming whole.

From an article in the *Independent*, 10 November 1989.

▼ *Crowds in the Postdamer Platz in Berlin celebrate the destruction of the Wall in 1989.*

European Unity
1947–99

AT THE END of the Second World War many European countries were in a desperate state. To help recovery there were discussions about possible co-operation between European countries on economic, military and even political issues. The development of the Cold War and rivalry between the superpowers increased interest in co-operation and some politicians saw the possibility of developing Europe as a third force in the world, a counterweight to the military and economic might of the USA and the USSR. Consequently a new form of political institution was created, one in which nation states surrendered some of their sovereignty to an international organisation.

1947
THE MARSHALL PLAN

The Marshall Plan was proposed in July 1947 by the US secretary of state George Marshall. It set up a European Recovery Programme, that offered money to countries in Europe to help them rebuild after the war. All countries in Europe were invited to apply for aid and, at first, the Soviet Union and the countries of eastern Europe were involved. However, when they discovered that Marshall Aid would involve membership of the Organisation for European Economic Co-operation, Stalin the Soviet leader, withdrew. Even so, Poland and Czechoslovakia still tried to obtain aid until Stalin banned their applications. Altogether about $13.5 billion was given out in aid from 1948 to 1951.

1948
THE BEGINNINGS OF UNION

The first moves towards European Union took place in the years after the Second World War. In March 1948 the Brussels Treaty was signed by Britain, France, Belgium, the Netherlands and Luxembourg. This included plans for economic, social and military co-operation. In May 1948 a Congress of Europe was held to discuss plans for European union, and in May 1949 the Council of Europe was set up, with headquarters at Strasbourg. In May 1952, a European Defence Community was set up by Italy, France, the Netherlands, West Germany, Belgium and Luxembourg. This could have led to an integrated European army, but it collapsed when the French Parliament rejected the treaty in 1954. This was the first sign that national politics could make integration increasingly difficult.

1950
THE SCHUMAN PLAN

The Schuman Plan was proposed by the French foreign minister, Robert Schuman, in May 1950. It was a plan to integrate the coal and steel industries of western Europe. In April 1951 the plan was put into effect when France, West Germany, Italy, Belgium, the Netherlands and Luxembourg signed a treaty setting up a single market for coal and steel. This became known as the European Coal and Steel Community, which met for the first time in August 1952. The Community was the prototype for the European Economic Community, which the members began to discuss almost immediately in 1953. These discussions continued for three years and resulted in the drawing up of the terms of the Treaty of Rome in 1957.

✢ 1957
THE TREATY OF ROME

The Treaty of Rome established the European Economic Community and it was signed in March 1957. There were six member countries at first: France, West Germany, Italy, Belgium, the Netherlands and Luxembourg, all members of the European Coal and Steel Community. The EEC came into effect on 1 January 1958; at the same time the European Atomic Community was set up. Delegates from the six countries met in the European Economic Assembly in March 1958, under the presidency of Robert Schuman. At first the EEC, or the Common Market, was a strictly economic body. It encouraged trade between the members and set tariffs on imports from outside. The Treaty of Rome, however, contained clauses, which allowed for political union at some future date.

▼ *Western powers signing the Brussels Pact, one of the first steps towards European Union.*

✪ 1960s
THE EEC

The EEC developed three main organisations. The Commission, in Brussels, was made up of representatives from all of the member countries, who were appointed by their governments. Each 'Commissioner' was responsible for an area of policy. The role of the Commission was to carry out the policies of the EEC. Policies were decided by the Council of Ministers, which was made up of politicians from each of the member countries. This could meet anywhere. At important meetings, the prime ministers would attend, on other occasions, it would be the minister responsible for the area of policy to be discussed, such as farming for example. Finally there was a European Parliament in Strasbourg, which contained elected representatives from each member country. The Parliament could discuss, argue and even question Commissioners, but it had no legislative power.

✗ 1960s
DECOLONISATION

Just as European countries were drawing closer together in the EEC, their colonies in Africa and Asia were gaining independence. The French were forced out of Vietnam in 1954 and left Algeria in 1962. Belgium gave up the Congo in 1960. Britain allowed all its African colonies to become independent at the same time. Although many British colonies became members of the Commonwealth and so retained close ties with Britain, decolonisation created a large block of countries that was linked neither with East or West. In the 1950s and 1960s both superpowers tried to draw these countries into their spheres of influence, adding an extra dimension to their rivalry.

1973
EXPANSION

The EEC proved very successful economically. Trade between the members increased and in 1961 Britain applied to join. Britain had not taken part in the earlier developments towards economic unity because of her links with the

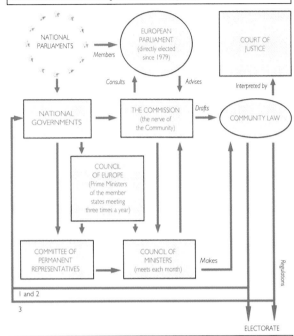

THE EUROPEAN ECONOMIC COMMUNITY, 1957
The EEC was formed with the signing of the Treaty of Rome on 25 March 1957. The original members were Belgium, France, Italy, Luxembourg, West Germany and the Netherlands, with Britain, Ireland and Denmark joining on 1 January 1973. The body has continued to expand and uneasy relations between all the constituent bodies reveal the tensions inherent in reconciling national and communal aspirations.

1 **Directives** binding on member states but each country decides how to carry them out
2 **Decisions** binding on those to whom they are addressed
3 **Regulations** have the force of national law and need not be passed by individual parliaments

▲ *The opening of the European Parliament in Strasbourg, 7 July 1979.*

Commonwealth, but it soon became clear that membership of the EEC was very advantageous. However, in both 1963 and 1967, Britain's applications for membership were vetoed by France. The French president, Charles de Gaulle, believed that Britain was too closely linked to the USA to be a real member of the EEC. Britain eventually joined in 1973, along with

Denmark and Ireland. In the 1980s Spain, Portugal and Greece were admitted and in the 1990s Sweden, Austria and Finland.

1992
A SINGLE MARKET

The EEC became the European Community in the 1970s and then became known as the European Union in the 1990s. This was a sign that the Community was changing significantly. In particular a much higher level of integration was taking place. Taxes and laws were being brought into line. In 1992 the Single Market was set up, all goods and people could now travel freely throughout the member countries. Work permits were not required. Terms for a single currency were agreed in 1997, and came into effect in 1999. Co-operation between police and armed forces increased and the Community, in addition, began to be seen as a political force. It attempted to intervene in the Balkans and made common representations on worldwide issues.

p. 55 ◀ **Distant Voices** ▶ p. 61

If Europe is to be saved from infinite misery, and indeed from final doom, there must be an act of faith in the European family. What is the sovereign remedy? It is to recreate the European family, or as much of it as we can and provide it with a structure under which it can dwell in peace, safety and freedom. We must build a United States of Europe.

From a speech made by Winston Churchill, at a conference on European Unity (1946)

War and Peace

KEY THEMES

- ▤ TECHNOLOGY
- ☆ GENERALS
- ⌐ STRATEGY
- ◉ WEAPONS
- ◎ ARMIES
- ✈ CONQUEST
- ✠ SIEGES
- ✋ DECLARATIONS
- ⊕ CAUSES
- ⊂ SEA WARFARE

WAR STIRS IN HUMANKIND great passion, moral force and consuming capacity. To most it is a curse. War can annihilate, in a few brief moments in time, the work of centuries or a whole civilisation. Throughout the evolution of society, tribes, cities, nations and empires have each been preoccupied in protecting or extending their boundaries. The stakes are high, the cost of defeat has led to the loss of territory, migration, slavery or extermination. As humans have harnessed nature, developing weapons of ever-increasing destruction, the nature of war has been revolutionised. Tactics, with all of their infinite variety, have quickly become outdated. Temporary advantage, dependent upon terrain, climate or the courage of an army, has been countered with new developments or the emergence of a great leader. A general's judgement and versatility has often meant the difference between victory and defeat. In this chapter, we investigate the nature of war and its place in history. From the earliest times to the last shots of the twentieth century, we encounter places, armies and characters fighting for causes, beliefs, religions and for other less noble reasons. The only constant is the fighter on foot, on horseback, at sea, or in man-made machines – the very core of a war and the tools upon which empires rise and fall.

KEY EVENTS

❶ 752 BC
THE RISE OF ROME

From the founding of the city in 752 BC to becoming the centre of one of the most powerful empires the world has ever seen, Rome dominated the world for over a thousand years. Although it brought civilisation to millions, Rome finally fell, its armies scattered and its cities afire.

❷ 400s BC
THE ANCIENT GREEKS AND PERSIANS

Through centuries of conflict, the Greeks and Persians waged war in the Eastern Mediterranean and Asia Minor. With radically different approaches to war and changing fortunes in battles including Marathon and Salamis, Gaugamela and Arbela, these implacable foes finally exhausted one another, leading to Roman domination.

❸ 1096
THE CRUSADES

When European monarchs sent the cream of their armies to the east to forge a Christian empire in the Holy Land, they found that they would face the rising armies of Islam. A series of battles ensued that would last for many centuries.

❹ 1815
THE ERA OF NELSON, NAPOLEON AND WELLINGTON

After the French Revolution, Europe was again plunged into war with the rise of Napoleon. Conflict raged from the steppes of Russia to the coast of Spain. Great battles at Waterloo, Austerlitz and Trafalgar forged Europe's borders and alliances that would endure throughout the century. It was an era of great generals and sweeping tactics.

❺ 1879
THE ZULU WAR

Convinced that the independent Zulu kingdom adjoining the new British possessions in South Africa was a serious threat, an ultimatum was delivered ordering the Zulus to disband their army. When the Zulus refused the British army attacked but, hopelessly underestimating the tactical ability of the Zulus, suffered massive casualties.

❻ 1914–18
THE GREAT WAR

Stalemate on the western front led to enormous casualties in the First World War. The conflict, dominated by weapons rather than tactics, saw hundreds of thousands die for inches of land. The courage of the soldiers meant little against massed guns. Despite the heavy losses, there was still unfinished business between the belligerents.

❼ 1942
THE WORLD AT WAR

1942 saw the high point of the Axis powers in the Second World War. After Stalingrad and El Alamein, the Germans and their allies desperately fought to survive on two fronts. Meanwhile, the Japanese had been defeated at the Battle of Midway. War for them would end after two atomic bombs had been dropped on them.

❽ 1961
VIETNAM

The Vietnam War was fought between communist North Vietnam and US-backed South Vietnam. Some 2000,000 South Vietnamese soldiers, one million North Vietnamese soldiers, and 500,000 civilians were killed. From 1961 to 1975, exactly 56,555 US soldiers were killed.

TIMELINE

3000 BC Chariots first used
1288 BC Rameses II and the Battle of Kadesh
① • • 752 BC Rome founded
② • • 480 BC Battle of Thermopylae
331 BC Alexander the Great and Gaugamela
265 BC First Punic War
57 BC Caesar defeats the Belgae at Aisne
AD 717 Siege of Constantinople
1066 Battle of Hastings
③ • • • • 1096 Launch of the First Crusade
1211 Ghengis Khan breaches the Great Wall of China
1327 Hundred Years' War begins
1415 Battle of Agincourt
1494 Italian Wars begin
1521 Hernan Cortés conquers Mexico
1526 Suleiman the Magnificent's campaign on the Danube
1568 Dutch Wars of Independence
1588 Spanish Armada
1618 Thirty Years' War begins
1700 The Great Northern War begins
1704 Battle of Blenheim
1756 Seven Years' War begins
1775 American War of Independence
1805 Battles of Austerlitz and Trafalgar
1806 Battles of Jena and Auerstadt
1812 French invasion of Russia
④ • • • • • • • • • 1815 Battle of Waterloo
1835 Texan War of Independence
1853 Crimean War begins
1861 American Civil War begins
1870 Franco-Prussian War
⑤ • • • • • • • • • • 1879 Zulu War
1898 Spanish-American war
1899 First Boer War begins
1904 Russo-Japanese War
⑥ • • • • • • • • • • • 1916 Somme and Verdun offensives
1936 Spanish Civil War
1939 Blitzkrieg
1940 Battle of Britain
1941 Japanese bomb Pearl Harbor
⑦ • • • • • • • • • • • • 1942 Battle of Midway; Siege of Stalingrad
1944 D-Day landings
1945 Hiroshima
1950 Korean War begins
⑧ • • • • • • • • • • • • • 1961 Vietnam War starts
1967 Six-Day War
1968 The Tet Offensive
1973 Yom Kippur War
1982 Falklands War
1991 Gulf War
1999 Crisis in Kosovo

War in the Earliest Times
4000–612 BC

THE SIMPLEST FORM of warfare began in the Stone Age. Rival tribes fought running skirmishes over territory, shelter and women. Armed with wooden clubs and stone axes, war was hard and brutal. At some point between 7000–5000 BC, the roving hunters developed into primitive farmers, settling for the first time. A new motive had emerged for war – to protect what was yours and to take what you could by force of arms. The earliest known example of a military fortification is at Jericho, near the Dead Sea. A stone wall and a moat surround the 10-acre town. At its peak, it would have protected around 2,500 people, up to a quarter of whom would have been armed soldiers.

4000 BC
SUMER AND THE SEMITES

Historians' first real understanding of warfare begins somewhere between 4000 and 3500 BC, in Mesopotamia and Egypt. These relatively small areas of fertile river territories were constantly being fought over. By this time, the Sumerians in Mesopotamia, were fighting as close order foot soldiers with spears and shields. Between 3500–2000 BC, the main

▼ *Early relief carving showing a horse-drawn chariot.*

principles of warfare and weapons developed that would remain until the introduction of gunpowder in the fourteenth century. Sargon, the leader of the Semites, conquered all of Sumer, Syria, Palestine and the rest of the fertile Mesopotamian area, uniting them with Babylonia to form the powerful Akkadian dynasty. By this time, around 2340 BC, his soldiers were mainly armed with javelins and spears, but he had also introduced the chariot as a new development in war.

▶ p. 68

3000 BC
THE CHARIOT

The chariot first appeared in Mesopotamia around 3000 BC. Drawn by four asses, this revolutionised warfare, giving it a flexibility and mobility never known before. Some had two wheels, others four, with a charioteer and soldier armed with a spear and javelin. A line of charging chariots would throw the enemy into panic and disorder; attack would then follow from foot soldiers armed with spears and shields. Chariots improved over the next few centuries with lighter bodies, spoked wheels and axles placed further back to give better balance and manoeuvrability. By 2000 BC, the asses had been replaced by horses. During the New Kingdom period in Egypt (1570–1100 BC), highly trained crews, in light chariots, were armed with bows and javelins for long- and close-range attacks.

2700–1800 BC
THE OLD AND MIDDLE KINGDOMS OF EGYPT

Although the Egyptians lagged behind the Mesopotamian civilisations in their weapons and warfare, they managed to create one of the longest and greatest civilisations, which endured for 3,000 years. During the Old Kingdom (2700–2200 BC) and the Middle Kingdom (2100–1800 BC) periods, they fought a series of wars against the Nubians and the Semites. Unfortunately, despite the Egyptians' ability to protect themselves, towards the end of the Middle Kingdom, a century of rivalry for the throne left them open to attack from outside. The Hyksos, or 'Shepherd Kings', from Syria swiftly overran Egypt and dominated the region for two centuries. Their garrisons in huge fortresses assured control of the country until around 1570 BC, when King Ahmose I, the first pharaoh of the New Kingdom, drove them out.

▼ *Statue of a warrior guard discovered in the tomb of the pharaoh Tutankhamen.*

 TECHNOLOGY ☆ GENERALS ⇨ STRATEGY ● WEAPONS ◎ ARMIES

● ▶ p. 70

2500 BC
EARLY METALWORKING

The mace was the preferred weapon of the Egyptians until around 2500 BC. But as copper came into wider use, early civilisations realised that they could produce effective cutting edges; thus the axe was born. Soldiers began to be provided with metal helmets and caps studded with metal discs, making the mace ineffectual against these troops. The sword did not become widely used until after 2000 BC. By this time bronze had replaced copper and sturdier blades could be made, some being sickle-shaped. The spear and the javelin remained the primary weapons until the sword was introduced; the former had a vicious leaf-shaped tip and the latter was mainly used as a hand-hurled missile, often five or six being carried in a quiver into battle.

✰ ▶ p. 63

1570 BC
WARFARE IN THE NEW KINGDOM

When King Ahmose I established the New Kingdom in Egypt (1570–1100 BC), he realised that he needed a large standing army to ensure that the country would be adequately protected at all times. He created two vast armies, one to protect the Nile Delta and one to garrison the south of the country. For the first time, strategy and tactics became an established part of warfare. New-style Egyptian troops were raised, spear-armed troops were issued with a battleaxe and bowmen were trained to fire in volleys. New divisions of chariots and infantry were created to work in close support of one another. King Amenhotep added Nubia, Libya and Syria to the Euphrates. His son, Thutmosis I, seized Mittani, which was north-west of Nineveh.

⌔ ▶ p. 62

1288 BC
THE HITTITES

The pharaoh Rameses II was determined to eliminate a new threat emanating from the Hittites, who were based in Syria. Dividing his army of 20,000 into four divisions, Rameses advanced towards the city of Kadesh with one division. The Hittite general, Mutallu, slipped his force behind

▲ *One of many massive statues of the warrior-king Rameses II of Egypt.*

Rameses and attacked the supporting division. As the Egyptians fled towards Rameses, the Hittites pursued them and shattered the Egyptian army. With the Hittites more interested in looting the Egyptian camp, Rameses threw his crack Canaanite mercenaries at the Hittites and wiped out the centre of their army. As a fresh Egyptian division threatened, the Hittites fell back into Kadesh. The battle was indecisive and the two civilisations eventually signed a peace pact.

911 BC
THE RISE OF THE ASSYRIANS

The Egyptians managed to save themselves from invasion during the reign of Rameses III by making successful attacks on the dangerous tribes of the Aegean. A new and more sinister threat was arising in the arid lands of the upper Tigris; perhaps the most warlike nation of the ancient times. The Assyrians began their conquests in 911 BC, gradually absorbing civilisation after civilisation. Eventually, their empire was to stretch from the Mediterranean to the Persian Gulf and from the former Hittite lands to Egypt itself. Their principal reasons for conquest and war was the sheer love of fighting, and their warrior kings aimed to instil fear in the ancient world. Their art of siege warfare became a trademark and their well-armed troops swept all before them.

612 BC
THE FALL OF ASSYRIA

By 639 BC, the Assyrian king, Ashurbanipal, had managed to secure the borders of the Empire, allying with the Lydians and maintaining good relations with the Babylonians and the Scythians. When he died, the inevitable struggle for the throne sparked off a civil war that would lead to the downfall of the empire. The king of Babylon, Nabopolassar, allied with Cyaxares the Mede and hemmed the Assyrians into their homeland. In 616 BC, Nabopolassar defeated the Assyrians at Kablinu and then sacked the Assyrian city of Ashur in 614 BC. The Assyrians hung on by a thread until the Scythians joined the alliance in 612 BC and besieged the capital Nineveh. For three months, the city held out, but with the capital in flames, the last Assyrian king, Sin-Shar-Ishkun, killed himself.

p. 57 ◀ **Distant Voices** ▶ p. 63

And it came to pass, when the Philistine came to meet David, that David put his hand in his bag and took out a stone. David slung it and hit the Philistine's forehead and he fell upon his face to the earth. David ran and stood upon the Philistine and took his sword and drew it out of the sheath, slew him and cut off his head. When the Philistines saw their champion was dead, they fled. And the men of Israel and of Judah arose, and shouted, and pursued the Philistines, until they reached the valley and the gates of Ekron.

Old Testament, *1 Samuel* 17: 48

The Ancient Greeks and Persians
740–275 BC

LESS THAN 80 YEARS after the end of the Assyrian Empire, the victors were in turn overrun by the Persians. Cyrus the Great (600–529 BC) had forged a vast empire in the east with a formidable army of light and heavy infantry, chariots, archers and specialist troops including elephants and camelry. At its height, the Persian Empire stretched from Asia Minor to India. Early in the fifth century BC, the Persian king, Darius I, sent a powerful force to conquer the Greeks. Only one major state stood in his way: the Athenians. This was the first era of large-scale organised warfare, with a new sense of importance placed on the logistics of a campaign. By 490 BC, the vast Persian Empire was ready to deliver the attack.

740 BC
THE SPARTANS

Greek warriors of the heroic age would ride into battle on chariots, dismount and fight in single combat with their foes. The bow was considered a coward's weapon and the warriors would be armed with two spears, a shield and a short sword. After the Trojan War, Greece was dominated by the Dorian city of Argos, but sometime between 740 and 710 BC, Sparta rose to prominence. This southern city state, under the rule of King Theopompus, annexed Messenia and Laconia, securing the all-important iron supplies. They were defeated by King Pheidon of Argos in 699 BC, but survived to dominate Greek military thinking for 250 years. Spartan males aged from seven to 30 years were trained as soldiers; they would be needed when the Persians arrived.

◎ ▶ p. 66   669 BC
THE HOPLITES

The first true Hoplite force was created by the Argives and used at the Battle of Hysiae in 669 BC. These close-order formations of heavy infantry consisted of men armed with a long thrusting spear, sword, helmet, breast-plate, greaves and a 1-m (3-ft) round shield. They confronted the enemy with a solid line of alternating shields and spears; the continuity of the line was all-important and each man depended on his neighbour. At Plataea (479 BC), the Spartans fought eight deep, the rear ranks filling in at the front as men fell. Steadiness and weight of numbers in the right place were the key to victories on the field. Tactics were still rather limited and sieges rare.

⤳ ▶ p. 80   490 BC
THE BATTLE OF MARATHON

When the Persians landed at Marathon, 20 miles to the north-west of Athens, this was just part of the overall strategy of the campaign. The strategy worked: the Greeks were lured towards the landing site as a second Persian amphibious force was poised to land at Phalerum and take Athens. The Greeks, about 11,000-strong under the leadership of Miltiades, were hopelessly outnumbered. Frightened of being outflanked and overwhelmed, the Greeks extended their lines across the whole valley. The Greek centre collapsed, but the wings drove the Persians back in confusion. The Persian force escaped by ship, leaving 6,400 dead. The Greeks then turned back and countered the second invasion force; they had lost just 192 men.

p. 50 ◀ Triumphs & Tragedies ▶ p. 69
480 BC
THE BATTLE OF THERMOPYLAE

Xerxes had succeeded Darius and, by 484 BC, he was ready for another attempt at invasion. Harpalus, a Greek engineer working for the Persians, bridged the Hellespont and in the spring of 480 BC a massive force of 160,000 troops supported by over 1,200 warships advanced into northern Greece. The Greeks met the invaders at the narrow pass of Thermopylae (80 miles north of Athens) with just 7,000 Hoplites. All was staked on the Persians sending their fleet south to outflank Thermopylae. The Persians landed near Athens, the Greeks sprung the trap and, after a hard struggle, scattered the Persians who lost over half their ships. In the following year, at Plataea, the Greeks defeated the Persians once more and Greece was freed from the threat.

▼ *Chariots changed the way in which warfare could be conducted in the Ancient World.*

🔲 TECHNOLOGY   ☆ GENERALS   ⤳ STRATEGY   ● WEAPONS   ◎ ARMIES

431 BC
THE PELOPONNESIAN WAR

The Delian League was formed by the Greeks in 478 BC with the aim of driving the Persians out of the Aegean Sea. The Athenians took control and absorbed 150 states into their empire. The Spartans reacted violently and, in 431 BC, the Peloponnesian War broke out. For the next 27 years, the Greek states would be at war. The Athenians ruled the seas, whilst the Spartans were dominant on land. The Spartans won the Battle of Mantinea (418 BC), forcing the Athenians to risk all. They invaded Sicily in 415 BC in the hope of cutting off Spartan trade and supplies, but in 413 BC the fleet was lost at Syracuse. The Athenian army hung on until 405 BC, losing another fleet at Aegospotami; they surrendered the following year.

▼ *Classical vase from Ancient Greece; although a warlike nation, the Greeks produced many beautiful works of art.*

359 BC
THE RISE OF MACEDONIA

In 359 BC, Philip II became the king of Macedonia. He was ambitious, clear-sighted and a great organiser. He reasoned that the Greek states, having been constantly at war with one another for the past 70 years, would be in no position to ally against him. He first conquered Illyria, then turned on Thebes and Athens, beating them at the Battle of Chaeronea in 338 BC. After installing friendly governments in most cities and garrisons in some, Philip forced the Greeks to join a Hellenic league. In 336 BC, he successfully launched an invasion of Asia, but dynastic troubles supervened. He divorced his wife Olympias, exiled his son Alexander, and remarried. However, Philip was assassinated at his daughter's wedding, and Alexander was at once presented to the army as king.

☆ ▶ p. 64

336 BC
WAR WITH PERSIA

Alexander took up Philip's war of aggression against Persia on his accession in 336 BC. He defeated the small force defending Anatolia and met and defeated the Persian army under Darius III at Issus. Alexander occupied Syria and Phoenicia, then entered Egypt. In the autumn of 331 BC he defeated Darius's grand army at Gaugamela and occupied Babylon, the imperial capital Susa and Persepolis. He then pursued Darius, who had turned eastward. Darius was at once assassinated by Bessus, and Alexander proclaimed himself king. Alexander invaded the Punjab (327 BC), but after conquering most of it, he was stopped from pressing on to the distant Ganges by a mutiny of his soldiers. He returned to Babylon, where he prepared an expedition for the conquest of Arabia.

323 BC
THE RISE OF HELLENISTIC WARFARE

Alexander died without naming a successor and, once deprived of his personality and stature, his empire began to disintegrate. Despite his warlike life, Alexander had hoped that the lands could be melded together, but instead all his governors claimed territories. Chief among them were Antigonus I, Antipater, Demetrius I, Poliorcetes, Lysimachus, Perdiccas, Ptolemy I and Seleucus I. This period is known as *diadochi* ('successors') and was marked by the extensive use of the phalanx (pike blocks of infantry), Persian cavalry, siege equipment, elephants and camels. This generation is taken to the end with Seleucus's death in 281 BC. Pyrrhus, the king of Epirus, continued the Hellenistic style of warfare, beating the Romans in 280 BC using elephants, but he was decisively defeated by their infantry at Beneventum in 275 BC.

▲ *Mosaic depicting Alexander the Great in battle against the Persians.*

p. 61 ◀ **Distant Voices** ▶ p. 65

Hear your fate, O dwellers in Sparta of the wide spaces;
Either your famed, great town must be sacked by Perseus' sons,
Or, if that be not, the whole land of Lacedaemon
Shall mourn the death of a king of the house of Heracles,
For not the strength of lions or bulls shall hold him,
Strength against strength; for he has the power of Zeus,
And will not be checked till one of these two he has consumed.

The words of the Oracle before the Battle of Thermopylae, from Heredotus (480 BC)

Rome at War
391 BC–AD 540

WHEN ROME WAS founded in 745 BC, it was just one of the many city states on the Italian peninsula. Within 500 years, Rome would come to dominate the whole of the peninsula and within 750 years, it would rule the whole of western Europe and the Mediterranean. The constant demands for self-defence in the early days had prepared its people well; they were militaristic and aggressive. Over the centuries the Etruscans, the Samnites and Volsci were all conquered and the attempted Gallic invasion was averted, but little is known about the early Roman armies, except that all males aged between 17 and 46 were liable for military service, and those up to 60 could be called up as reservists. In the fourth century BC, they were still Hoplites.

391 BC
THE MANIPULAR SYSTEM

Following a disastrous defeat at the hands of the Gauls at Allia in 391 BC, the Romans realised that they would have to reorganise their army. The legion, heavy infantry supported by light velites and cavalry, replaced the Hoplite phalanx. The infantry were organised into three lines, each four deep. The first two lines were armed with javelins and swords and protected by a bronze helmet and breastplate and a rectangular shield. The third line was similarly armed, but had long spears. The velites formed a screen in front of the main force and the cavalry protected their flanks. At the end of every day, the Romans would build a fortified camp, so that they would have both protection and somewhere to retreat if there was a disaster.

265–146 BC
THE PUNIC WARS

As a result of Rome's increasing political and commercial influence, it came into conflict with Carthage over Sicily. Carthage had a considerable empire in North Africa, Spain and on the Mediterranean islands. The First Punic War (265–241 BC) ended after a series of Roman naval victories. In 218 BC, the Carthaginian general, Hannibal crossed the Pyrenees and invaded Italy; this marked the beginning of the Second Punic War

(218–201 BC). Hannibal won three quick victories, defeating each Roman army that faced him. At Cannae (216 BC), he defeated 70,000 Romans and most of southern Italy went over to Carthage. Scipio, a new Roman general, took command in 210 BC and pushed the Carthaginians out of Spain, Sicily and finally Italy. Carthage fell in 146 BC.

♣ ▶ p. 65 **197–67 BC**
ROMAN EXPANSION

At the battles of Cynoscephalae (197 BC) and Pydna (168 BC), the more flexible Roman legions overcame the Hellenistic phalanx. Further territories were added to the empire, including North Africa, Macedonia, Greece and Asia Minor. The Marian Reforms (104–101 BC) established

the organisation of the army for years to come; the cohort was created (600 men) and 10 cohorts made a legion. Long spears disappeared, along with the velites and allies provided all light infantry and cavalry. When Sulla returned to Rome in 82 BC, he became a dictator, sparking off a series of revolts against Rome. Pompey regained control of Spain for the Romans by 72 BC, Crassus crushed the slave revolt led by Spartacus, and the pirates based in Crete and Cilicia were defeated in just three months (67 BC).

☆ ▶ p. 67 **59 BC**
JULIUS CAESAR

In 57 BC, at the age of 41, Julius Caesar was thrust into prominence when he became governor of Illyricum, Cisalpine and Transalpine Gaul. He checked the threat of the Helvetii in 58 BC and advanced north of the old Roman frontier to clear Alsace of the German tribes. In the spring of 57 BC, he defeated a massive 300,000-strong Belgae army on the Aisne and, by 56 BC, had added nearly all of Gaul to the empire. He landed in Britain in 55 BC, but had to turn his attention elsewhere. The Gauls, under Vercingetorix, rebelled in 52 BC, and at the siege of Alesia, they were crushed for many years. Caesar faced Pompey in a civil war that lasted until 45 BC, but was murdered by Brutus and Cassius the following year.

▼ *The emperor Julius Caesar, who increased the power and dominance of the Roman Empire.*

 TECHNOLOGY GENERALS STRATEGY ● WEAPONS ◎ ARMIES

▲ *The barbarian leader Attila, king of the Huns.*

31 BC–AD 125
AUGUSTUS TO HADRIAN

By 31 BC, the Roman army could boast 60 legions, but these were reduced to 28 by Augustus; 168,000 legionaries and 150,000 auxiliaries protected the empire. Augustus also created the Praetorian Guard, some 9,000 men to act as a bodyguard. The Romans no longer ignored sea-power as a major factor; all of the provinces had fleets. Augustus pushed the northern frontier forward to the Danube and the Elbe (17–11 BC). After the death of Augustus (AD 14) Britain and Dacia were added. Between AD 70 and 130, during the reigns of Vespasian, Domitian and Hadrian, the frontier was fortified. Hadrian's Wall in northern Britain is a typical example (AD 122–125). Auxiliaries were used for frontier defence and the legions held back as a mobile reserve.

AD 250
THE BARBARIANS

Emperor Gallienus (AD 260–266) continued to improve the army not a moment too soon. The Sassanid Persians were threatening the Eastern Empire, but Odenathus, the Palmyran governor, repelled this. In the north, by AD 251, the Ostrogoths had overrun the Balkans and killed Emperor Decius in battle. The Alemanni pushed into Italy, but were checked at Metaurus in 258. During the reign of Constantine (AD 306–37), a second imperial capital was established in Byzantium. The empire was suffering from economic weakness and a fall in population; it had also embraced Christianity. Old Rome had long since been swept away. The Goths, at Adrianople, defeated Emperor Valens in 378 and Alaric the Visigoth sacked Rome for the first time in 410.

AD 476
THE FALL OF ROME

After AD 410, there was a lull in warfare. The Vandals had settled in North Africa, the Burgundians and Franks in France and the Visigoths had moved on to Spain and Gaul. A graver danger for all lay ahead. By the middle of the fifth century, under the leadership of Attila, the Huns descended on

▼ *The emperor Hadrian, who ordered a wall to be built from coast to coast across northern Britain, to keep out invaders.*

the western world. The Chinese had repelled them between 207 BC and AD 39, so they had turned west. Attila came to power in 433 and after invading the Balkans in 440–447, he crossed the Rhine and faced the Visigoths and Romans at Champagne. Attila was defeated, but in 451, he invaded northern Italy. The Huns were turned back, but Rome was not saved. Odovacar, commander of the Roman army was a barbarian, and he seized the capital in 476.

✈ ▶ p. 68

AD 520
BELISARIUS

Belisarius, the great Byzantine commander, reorganised the Eastern Empire's troops in the AD 520s. In 532, he was given the task of defeating the Vandals in North Africa with 15,000 men and over 500 ships. He met them outside Carthage, and by repeated charges, finally annihilated them. By 535, the Vandals were conquered. Landing in Italy, he defeated the Ostrogoths with a force of only 7,500 men. His emperor, Justinian, had drained the east of troops, despite the building of 700 fortifications. With Belisarius committed in Italy, defending Rome and attempting to prevent the fall of the country to the Lombards, Antioch fell to the Persians in 540. The Lombards were the last of the northern barbarians, but North Africa would soon fall to the Arabs.

p. 63 ◀ **Distant Voices** ▶ p. 67

As Caesar rode through the Velabrum on the day of his Gallic triumph, the axle of the triumphal chariot broke, and he nearly took a toss; but afterwards he ascended to the Capitol between two lines of elephants, forty in all, which acted as his torch bearers. In the Pontic triumph one of the decorated wagons, instead of a stage-set representing scenes from the war, like the rest, carried a simple three-word inscription: I came, I saw, I conquered!

Suetonius

Early Medieval Warfare
AD 476–866

WHEN THE WESTERN Roman Empire ceased to exist in AD 476, Byzantium continued to struggle for survival, first against the Arabs, then the Turks and the Bulgars. By AD 713, they had beaten the Arabs in North Africa and had conquered Spain. In 720, they entered southern France. This area was dominated by a Germanic civilisation, the Franks. By the eighth century, the Vikings had started raiding western Europe from Scandinavia, but by the ninth century the English and the Franks had managed to counter this threat. Between the seventh and eleventh centuries, the feudal system emerged and the mounted knight became the dominant force on the battlefield. During these years, many able generals were victorious against far more numerous foes, and new tactics and weapons were evolved.

◎ ▶ p. 70 AD 476
THE BYZANTINE MILITARY SYSTEM
Byzantium continually faced vastly superior enemies in terms of numbers, but they made up for this deficiency by the quality of their warfare. The army forged by Belisarius, Maurice and Heraclius at the end of the sixth century remained in place for the rest of Byzantine history. Heavy cavalry were the mainstay of the army, with a mail shirt from neck to thigh, a medium-sized shield, steel cap, gauntlets and shoes. They were armed with a broadsword, dagger, short bow, axe and lance. Infantry tended to be used for defensive work, but were equally well-equipped. A corps of engineers marched with the army and an ambulance corps was also added with stretchers. The army had to be flexible; the fact that Byzantium lasted so long is testimony to this fact.

⊕ ▶ p. 71 AD 622
ISLAM
When the Prophet Muhammad moved with his followers from Medina to Mecca in AD 622, the period of Arabianism and Islam had begun. By 632, his disciples had taken Syria and Egypt from the Byzantines and Persia had been overthrown. Within 900 years, the Islamic Empire extended from the Aral Sea in the north to the Nile Delta and from China in the east to Spain in the west.

In AD 636 Khalid defeated Heraclius. Alexandria fell, the Berbers of Libya were converted and Spain was conquered all between 710–713. In six campaigns after 623, the Arabs had forced the Byzantines back in the north and north-east. In 668 and every year between 672 and 677, the Arabs attacked the Byzantines, only to be frustrated each time.

▼ *The reign of Emperor Charlemagne was a period of relative peace and stability.*

✤ ▶ p. 75 AD 717
THE SIEGE OF CONSTANTINOPLE
In August AD 717, the Arab general Maslama attacked the city of Constantinople. Having been repulsed by the city's catapults, he organised a blockade. The Arab fleet, under Suleiman was ordered to intercept any Byzantine ship, and to block the Bosphorus and entry into the Black Sea. As an Arab fleet passed the harbour, the Byzantines struck with their warships, sinking over 20 of them. In the following spring, the Arabs were reinforced, but again the Byzantines struck and sunk many vessels. By August 718, believing that the Franks were *en route* to raise the siege, the caliph gave up; few of his troops made it home. Leo, the Byzantine emperor, pursued the Arabs, but his victory in 739 at Acroninon in Phrygia finally forced the Arabs out of Asia Minor.

AD 718
THE ARAB INVASIONS
In AD 718, the Arabs flooded over the Pyrenees and ravaged the Visigoth Kingdom of Aquitaine. When Abd-al-Rahman led an Arab army into Tours in 732, the Franks realised that they must react or face a similar fate. Charles the Hammer advanced against the Arabs who were retreating with their plunder in the direction of Poitiers. For seven days, the two armies faced each another then finally, the Arabs attacked. The Arab king was killed in an early attack and his army was scattered. The Islamic threat to Europe had been defeated. However, in 743, the Arabs captured Lyons, but retreated beyond the Pyrenees once more after 759. This left Martel as the most powerful figure in the Frankish Empire.

AD 732
THE FRANKS DOMINATE EUROPE
The Franks had come to prominence in western Europe after their victory at Vougle in AD 507 they then followed the Byzantine pattern in which cavalry became the most important force in their armies. During the sixth and seventh centuries, the Frankish infantry were dominant. They tended to be

🖥 TECHNOLOGY ☆ GENERALS ⤳ STRATEGY ◦ WEAPONS ◎ ARMIES

▲ *Viking raiders first invaded England in* AD *789; they went on to pillage and plunder areas all over Europe.*

lightly armoured, but used a characteristic weapon. The francisa was a throwing axe, its heavy head consisting of a long curved blade. Once this had been thrown, the Franks would charge in with a double-edged sword, protected by an oval shield. Frankish cavalry was probably first used against the Saxons in AD 626, but only rich men could afford this luxury. After the Arabs were beaten back in 732, the Franks would dominate Europe under Charlemagne.

☆ ▶ p. 76
AD 768
CHARLEMAGNE

Charlemagne was Charles the Hammer's grandson and became king in AD 768. Between 768–814, Charlemagne fought against the Saxons, Lombards, Spanish Muslims, Avars, Frisians, Bretons and Byzantines. His empire covered the major part of western Europe and the Pope crowned him emperor in Rome in AD 800. It is for his wars against the Muslims in Spain that he is best remembered, but his introduction of the feudal system allowed him to maintain a strong cavalry force, so vital for defending the enormous borders of his empire and for striking out at his enemies. After his death in 814, the empire fragmented under the pressure of the combined raids from the Arabs, Magyars and Vikings in the ninth and tenth centuries; the latter proved the most dangerous.

AD 789
THE VIKINGS

The initial purpose of Viking raids seemed to be plundering rather than colonisation, but many of them did settle in the lands that they overran. Vikings were first spotted off the Dorset coast in AD 789, and in the following decade, they attacked the English, Irish, and French coasts. In 832, they invaded Ireland; in 834, they sacked Utrecht; and in 851, London and Canterbury were plundered. Northern and eastern England became Viking lands over the next 50 years and, importantly, Normandy was ceded to them in 911. Their sea battles were fought close to land; they would bombard the enemy with missiles, including arrows and lumps of stone, then grapple the enemy ships and board for hand-to-hand fighting.

AD 866
CHARLES THE BALD AND ALFRED THE GREAT

By the end of the ninth century, both the Franks and the English had learned to cope with the Vikings. The Franks could now raise a large force of cavalry, vital in being able to catch and fight the fast-moving Vikings. In AD 866, Charles the Bald completed a series of fortifications along the Seine and the Loire. In England, Alfred the Great had built up a strong force of heavy

infantry and an impressive fleet to counter the Vikings. When Canute became king of England (1016–35) after the death of Aethelred's son, Edmund Ironside, he won acceptance by the English nobility, to whom he promised – and gave – strong government. He forged links with the Viking successors, the Normans, and other Scandinavian civilisations.

▲ *Charles the Bald, Holy Roman Emperor and king of France.*

p. 65 ◀ **Distant Voices** ▶ p. 69

The Danish army then came to Thetford within three weeks after their ravaging of Norwich, and remained inside there one night. Then in the morning, when they wished to go to their ships, Ulfcetel arrived with his troops to offer battle there. And they resolutely joined battle, and many fell slain on both sides. There the flower of the East Anglian people were killed, but if their full strength had been there, the Danes would never have got back to their ships.

From the *Anglo-Saxon Chronicle*

The Norman Conquests and the Crusades
1060–1261

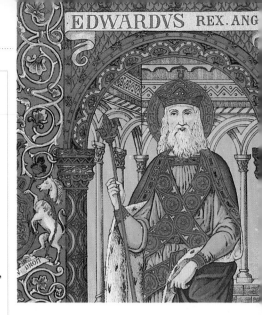

THE NORMANS WERE VIKINGS, or Norsemen, who settled in western France in the ninth and tenth centuries. In AD 911, the weak French monarchy under the Carolingian Charles III granted the lands at the estuary of the River Seine to Rollo, a Norwegian Viking, and his Danish followers, in return for an alliance against other Vikings, thus laying the foundation for the duchy of Normandy. The crusades were Christian military expeditions undertaken between the eleventh and fourteenth centuries to recapture the Holy Land from the Muslims. The word 'crusade', which is derived from the Latin *crux* ('cross'), is a reference to the biblical injunction that Christians carry their cross. Crusaders wore a red cloth cross sewn on their tunics, to indicate that they had assumed the cross and were soldiers of Christ.

▲ *Edward the Confessor, whose death resulted in disputes over the succession and eventually the Norman conquest.*

▶ p. 71 **1000s**
NORMAN FORTIFICATIONS

By the middle of the eleventh century, the Normans had developed and introduced to most of Europe a new type of fortification. The motte and bailey castle was a mound (motte) surrounded by a ditch. On the motte was a wooden stockade, where a keep and several buildings would be constructed. The bailey was another stockade below the motte, used to protect the domestic animals. The outer entrance to the castle

▼ *The arrival of the Normans in England saw developments in defensive fortifications, and castles were changed and adapted over the next few centuries.*

was by way of a drawbridge. By the end of the eleventh century, the castles were being constructed in stone and were considerably larger. By the twelfth century, great curtain walls and multiple baileys were constructed to deal with the increasingly effective siege equipment. Very few sieges were successful, but those that were used mining, starvation and treachery as their weapons.

✦ ▶ p. 72 **1060–91**
CONQUEST OF SICILY

As early as the first half of the eleventh century, some Normans sought adventure far from home in Mediterranean lands. The numerous sons of Tancred of Hauteville entered the service of Lombard rebels against the Byzantine Empire in southern Italy. One of them, Robert Guiscard, established himself as an independent ruler in Calabria and Apulia. Between 1060–91 he and his brother, Roger I, undertook the conquest of Sicily from the Muslims. By 1139, Roger II made good his effort to mould these Norman conquests into the kingdom of Sicily, which served as a base for further Norman expansion in North Africa and Dalmatia in the later twelfth century.

1066
NORMANS AND SAXONS

Harold II was the last Anglo-Saxon king of England. Harold succeeded his father Godwine (d. 1053) to the powerful earldom of Wessex, and was named heir to the English throne by Edward the Confessor when Edward was on his deathbed in January 1066. However, Harold's claim to the throne was immediately challenged by William of Normandy and by the Norwegian king, Harold III. Harold III allied himself with Tostig, the brother of the English Harold, and invaded northern England. Harold II stopped this attack at Stamford Bridge in Yorkshire on 25 September 1066, but had to make a forced march south to confront the Norman invaders who landed in England on 28 September. He was ill prepared for the decisive encounter that would follow at Hastings.

📼 TECHNOLOGY   ☆ GENERALS   ➦ STRATEGY   ◗ WEAPONS   ◎ ARMIES

✂ ▶ p. 76

1096
LAUNCH OF THE FIRST CRUSADE

The First Crusade (1096–99) was launched by Pope Urban II; he appealed for volunteers to help the Christian East and to stop the desecration of the holy places. The Muslims destroyed bands of poorly armed pilgrims – most of them inexperienced and poor – when they crossed into Anatolia. The main army, under Godfrey of Bouillon, Baldwin of Flanders, Raymond of Toulouse, Robert of Normandy and Bohemond of Taranto, assembled at Constantinople. They captured Antioch (3 June 1098) and finally Jerusalem (15 July 1099) in savage battles. The end of the campaign had formed four crusader states along the Syrian and Palestinian coast: the County of Edessa, the Principality of Antioch, the County of Tripoli, and the Kingdom of Jerusalem.

1144
THE SECOND CRUSADE

Almost from the beginning, continuing rivalry among the leaders and the other nobles undermined any chance of

▼ *William the Conqueror defeating Harold's English army at the Battle of Hastings in 1066.*

p. 62 ◀ **Triumphs & Tragedies** ▶ p. 71

1066
THE BATTLE OF HASTINGS

On 28 September William landed his army at Pevensey and moved eastwards along the coast to Hastings. Harold hurried from the north of England with his army of about 7,000 men. On 13 October Harold took a strong position on a hill near Hastings. Norman horsemen pressed up the hill. Standing close together and protected by great shields, the English wielded their long-handled battle-axes. William alternated cavalry charges with flights of arrows from his archers. Pretending retreat, he drew the English from their position and then attacked and destroyed them. Harold was killed when an arrow pierced his eye. After the battle, William and his army moved northward, to isolate London. On Christmas Day William, Duke of Normandy, was crowned king. He became known as William the Conqueror.

consolidating the acquisitions made in the First Crusade. The next crusade had its immediate cause in the loss of Edessa to the Muslims of Mosul and Aleppo (1144). Encouraged by St Bernard of Clairvaux, King Louis VII of France and King Conrad III of Germany tried to lead separate armies through Anatolia. What remained of them joined in an unsuccessful siege of Damascus. The only success of this crusade was the capture in 1147 of Lisbon in Portugal from the Arabs, by English and Frisian crusaders on their way to the East. St Bernard was a trusted advisor of the pope; he helped create the Order of the Knights Templars.

1189
THE THIRD CRUSADE

The Third Crusade was a response to the conquest of almost all of Palestine, including Jerusalem, by Sultan Saladin (1187), who had consolidated Muslim power in Mesopotamia, Syria, and Egypt. The crusade's illustrious leadership included Philip II of France, Holy Roman Emperor Frederick I, and Richard I of England. Frederick, however, drowned *en route* in

Cilicia, and the crusading effort disintegrated through attrition and lack of co-operation. Acre was recaptured (1191), but Philip returned to France soon after. Jaffa was secured, mainly through the initiative of Richard, who also occupied Cyprus. Richard was shipwrecked near Venice on his return in 1192 and imprisoned by Duke Leopold of Austria. Leopold turned Richard over to Holy Roman Emperor Henry VI, who released him in February 1194, but only after a huge ransom had been pledged.

1202
THE FOURTH CRUSADE

Pope Innocent III attempted to reorganise the crusading efforts under papal auspices, but lack of funds to pay for the passage of the 10,000 crusaders in Venice forced a diversion of the army. At the request of the Venetians, the crusaders first attacked the Christian city of Zara, in Dalmatia. They then sailed on to lay siege to Constantinople. The Byzantine capital fell in 1204; it was looted and made the residence of a Latin emperor, Baldwin, count of Flanders. A Greek army easily recaptured the city in 1261. During the crusades, the fabulous riches of the East lured many participants. The major European powers and the rising Italian cities saw the crusades as a means of establishing and extending trade routes.

p. 67 ◀ **Distant Voices** ▶ p. 71

Outside the walls of Acre during the Third Crusade, a Welsh and a Turkish archer agreed to a trial of skills. Each promised to stand still while his adversary took a shot at him. The Turk fired and missed, then suggested they allow two shots each. The Welsh archer agreed, but while the Turk was getting his second arrow ready, the Welshman took careful aim and shot him through the heart.

Ambroise (and Ronald Finucane)

The High Middle Ages
1200–1415

DURING THE HIGH MIDDLE AGES warfare raged across Europe. The Holy Roman Empire was fast reaching a crisis point, helped by the struggle in the thirteenth century between the pope and the imperial family, the Swiss Wars of Independence (from 1291) and the Hussite Wars (1337–1453). England, under Edward I, became a dominant state, conquering Wales (1277–95), but failing to subjugate Scotland (1296–1328). The Hundred Years' War (1337–1453), fought between England and France, would change the map of medieval Europe. The knight and the castle would give way to infantry, firearms and professional soldiers. New missile weapons took over the role of hand-to-hand weapons. The cavalry's 1,000-year mastery of the battlefield was over; the gun would become all-powerful for the next 600 years.

1200s
THE DEVELOPMENT OF ARMOUR

Armour developed rapidly during the twelfth and thirteenth centuries; conical helmets gave way to pot-helms, with visors added, around 1300. Long mail tunics became lighter, more supple and better fitting, with a quilted surcoat adding to the protection of the rider. By 1250, metal caps were being added to elbows and knees for greater protection, soon to be replaced with a cuirass, which covered the whole of the upper body. Light cavalry re-emerged for skirmishing and scouting. The main fighting was still the task of the man-at-arms, flung at the enemy in a series of mass charges. Simon de Montfort used this tactic at Lewes against Henry III in 1264, and Charles of Anjou used the same methods at Benevento against Manfred in 1266.

◉ ▶ p. 74
1214
THE NEW INFANTRY

Cavalry had reigned supreme from Adrianople in AD 378; infantry were despised, reduced to a supporting role at best. Yet some were beginning to realise that using cavalry and infantry together proved more effective than using a single arm alone. Infantry needed to win their place on the battlefield; this began at Bouvines in 1214, when Philip Augustus used them to great effect. New mercenary infantry, mainly Genoese, armed with a crossbow became commonplace. It was the pikemen, such as the North Italian League troops who held off Frederick II's cavalry at Cortenuova in 1266, that proved that slower moving infantry were a match for the finest cavalry in the world. Their defensive capacity was becoming recognised by all commanders.

◉ ▶ p. 83
1252
THE LONGBOW

One of Edward I's great innovations was the longbow. It was during the Welsh Wars (1277–95) that it came to the fore, and the English victory at Orewin Bridge (1282) owes much to this weapon. They were over 2 m (6 ft), requiring a muscular pull of 4.5 kg (10 lb) and usually made of yew or elm. The arrows were 1 m (3 ft) long and could be used to a range of around 350 yds. From 1252, all freeholders in England were required to possess a bow and regular archery practice was obligatory. A trained archer could fire at least four times to every one shot from a seasoned crossbow man. A shower of arrows peppering the enemy as they charged was often decisive in battle.

1260
GUNPOWDER

Roger Bacon, an English monk, was the first to record the process and composition of gunpowder in 1260; it would be 50 years before anyone took the concept seriously. A gun was fired at Metz in 1324 and Edward III probably used cannon against the Scots

▼ *Troops in the Hundred Years' War, showing how armour and weaponry had developed.*

🔲 TECHNOLOGY ☆ GENERALS ⤷ STRATEGY ◦ WEAPONS ◉ ARMIES

at Berwick in 1327. The French also used cannon against the English at Quesnoi in 1340 and Edward repaid the compliment at Calais in 1346. At the same time another new firearm was being developed, the ribauldequin, which consisted of several tubes mounted on a wagon that could be fired at the same time. It was a primitive rocket battery. Edward ordered 100 of these to be made in 1345. By the mid-fourteenth century, firearms were coming into regular use, but they had not yet made a significant impact on warfare.

1300s
▶ p. 86
CASTLE DESIGN

The castle managed to outlive the knight by adapting to the times, and some of the most effective fortifications were built during this period. The main style of fortification involved the building of several concentric curtain walls and by the fourteenth century moats had become lakes. The gatehouses were three or four storeys high with two towers, and one or more drawbridges could defend approaches to the castle. The central bailey often included a town, such as those

▼ *The longbow was the innovation of English king Edward I, and was to prove indispensable during the wars of the Middle Ages.*

built by Edward I in Wales and the Teutonic knights in Eastern Europe. The Bastille in Paris was built (1370–83) with eight towers, thick walls and a continuous parapet in addition to the wide moat. Even churches, cathedrals and houses were fortified in this period.

1315
THE SWISS VICTORY AT MORGARTEN

When the Austrian Duke Leopold failed to send scouts ahead as his army passed through a narrow Alpine pass in 1315, he found his route barricaded by Swiss Confederate infantry. Although the Austrians were more numerous, they were jammed together and slaughtered. Morgarten was just the first of a string of Swiss victories over the next two centuries, which included Laupen (1339), Sempach (1386), Granson (1476) and Morat (1476). By the mid-fourteenth century, the Swiss had dispensed with their halberds and spears and replaced them with pikes and short swords. In battle, they presented an impenetrable, bristling hedge of pikes with at least four ranks of points projecting in front of the first row of men. Their system of war was not unlike the Greeks many centuries before.

1327
⊕ ▶ p. 78
THE HUNDRED YEARS' WAR

The Hundred Years' War began as a result of Edward III's claim to the French throne, and a series of territorial and trade disputes between the two nations. England won a comprehensive naval victory off Sluys in 1340, but it was not until 1346 that Edward felt strong enough to face the French in a decisive battle. Edward landed in France and headed for Calais with 15,000 men. He was immediately pursued by Philip VI with around 40,000 troops, including 29,000 mounted knights. Taking up a position overlooking a valley, Edward turned to face them. The French advanced to within 150 metres and the skies filled with English arrows, slaughtering the French. They lost 10,000 men to England's 200.

p. 69 ◀ **Triumphs & Tragedies** ▶ p. 80

1415
THE BATTLE OF AGINCOURT

The English spent the latter half of the fourteenth century sending out forces around France, in vain attempts to search for the elusive French army. A peace treaty was finally signed in 1396, but it did not last very long. Henry V, keen to press his claim to the French throne, took advantage of French indecision and renewed the war in 1415. He captured Harfleur and marched on Calais. A huge French army was lured out in pursuit against his army of less than 6,000. The armies met at Agincourt, where the French showed that they had ignored the lessons of previous encounters with the English. In a little more than half an hour, Henry's archers slaughtered 6,000 of the 25,000-strong French army.

▲ *Henry V of England, who led his army to victory against a numerically superior French force at Agincourt.*

p. 69 ◀ **Distant Voices** ▶ p. 73

Lord Wenlock, not having advanced to the support of the first line but remaining stationary, contrary to the expectations of Somerset, the latter, in a rage, rode up to him, reviled him, and beat his brains out with an axe.

Richard Brooke, on the Battle of Tewkesbury (1471)

The Greatness of Spain
1474–1588

THE LEADING NATION in the sixteenth century – as far as warfare was concerned – was Spain. By the beginning of the sixteenth century, the foundations had been laid by Ferdinand and Isabella to create a vast and powerful empire. Spain took part in all the major wars in Europe during the sixteenth century, including the Habsburg-Valois Wars (1494–1559), the French Wars of Religion (1562–98) and the Dutch War of Independence (1568–1609). Closely followed by England, Spain's massive fleets ranged around Europe, across the Atlantic and into the newly colonised continent of America. They were at the forefront of developments in naval and military technology. Spain reached the height of its power in 1550, under Charles I, but by 1600, under Philip III (1598–1621), the empire was in serious difficulties.

1474
FERDINAND AND ISABELLA

By a chance of dynastic fortune – the accession of Isabella I to the throne of Castile in 1474 and of her husband Ferdinand II to that of Aragon in 1479 – the two most important kingdoms of Spain were joined. The 'Catholic kings' were exceptionally gifted, Isabella in internal politics and Ferdinand in foreign policy. Ferdinand turned his attention to the conquest of Naples and to disputes with France over the control of Italy. In addition, he added Navarre and territories on the French border to the family's domains. In 1492, Granada was conquered, ending the re-conquest of Spain from the Arabs. Isabella died in 1504 and, upon Ferdinand's death in 1516, both their crowns went to their grandson, Charles I.

1492
GONZALO DE CORDOBA

Gonzalo Fernandez de Cordoba was a Spanish general, known as 'el Gran Capitan'. He fought in the wars to drive the Muslims from Spain and helped negotiate the surrender of the Moorish kingdom of Granada (1492). He was sent to Italy (1495) with an army and soon forced the French to withdraw. His brilliant victories at Cerignola and at Garigliano (1503) brought all of Naples under Spanish rule. He is credited with the introduction of the *arquebusier* – men armed with the latest handguns. Each had a bullet pouch, match, ramrod and powder in tubes hung on a bandolier; they also had a sword and helmet. He realised that these troops were perfectly capable of checking the assault of any enemy facing them.

1494
THE START OF THE ITALIAN WARS

After the Peace of Lodi (1454), a precarious balance of power had been maintained among the chief Italian states: Florence,

▲ *Charles VIII of France descending into Naples in Italy in February 1495.*

Milan, Naples, the papacy, and Venice. This equilibrium was upset when Ludovico Sforza of Milan appealed to France for aid against a secret league of Florence and Naples. The French king, Charles VIII, descended into Italy with his army (1494), expelled the Florentine ruler Piero de Medici and entered Naples in February 1495. Threatened by a coalition of Italian states allied with Emperor Maximilian I and King Ferdinand II of Aragon, Charles soon withdrew. A period of intermittent warfare followed, during which the Spanish general Gonzalo de Cordoba conquered Naples (1503–04), bringing southern Italy under Spanish control, whereas France dominated the northern half of the peninsula.

1508
KEEPING ENEMIES CLOSE

Venice seemed to pose the next threat and in response France, the Habsburg Empire, the papacy and Spain formed the League of Cambrai (1508). Following its victory at Agnadello (1509), the League conquered all of Venice's mainland possessions. In 1512 the Habsburgs restored de Medici to Florence and, in 1515, they were defeated by the French at the Battle of Marignano. By the Treaty of Noyon (1516), France gained Milan but renounced its claim to Naples. During the 1520s, France and the empire continued to fight over Lombardy. The French defeat at Pavia (1525) doomed French influence in Italy. The League of Cognac (1526) allied France, Florence, Milan, Venice and the papacy against the Habsburgs, but Spanish pikemen quickly conquered Milan and, in May 1527, sacked Rome.

✈ ▶ p. 74 ### 1519–33
THE CONQUESTS OF MEXICO AND PERU

Charles I had hardly set foot in his new kingdoms when he was elected Holy Roman Emperor Charles V and had to leave for Germany. For the next two centuries, the fate of Spain was tied to that of the Habsburg dynasty. Charles spent most of his life defending his scattered domains against French, Turkish and Protestant enemies. The

🖿 TECHNOLOGY   ☆ GENERALS   ⮑ STRATEGY   ◉ WEAPONS   ◎ ARMIES

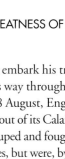

▲ *Contemporary illustration showing the fall of the Aztec capital Tenochtitlán at the hands of Hernán Cortés.*

conquest of Mexico (1519–21) by Hernán Cortés, and the conquest of Peru (1531–33) by Francisco Pizarro, resulted in an influx of gold and silver from America making Spain the greatest European power of the age. Charles abdicated in 1555–56, leaving Spain to his son, Philip II, and his German dominions to his brother, later Holy Roman Emperor Ferdinand I.

1562
THE FRENCH WARS OF RELIGION
The rise in the number of French Protestants excited the alarm of the French Roman Catholics. Religious intolerance was intensified by political rivalry between the house of Valois – then in possession of the French throne – and the house of Guise. Catherine de Medici, widow of Henry II, who governed in the name of her son, Charles IX, at times allied herself with the Huguenots for political reasons, but generally sided against them. The Huguenots were persecuted throughout Charles's reign, and they in turn made reprisals upon the Roman Catholics. Finally, in 1562, open civil war broke out and eight bitter wars were fought. In 1598, Henry IV issued the Edict of Nantes, by which the Huguenots received almost complete religious freedom.

1578
THE DUTCH WAR OF INDEPENDENCE
Religious and political factors fuelled a revolt in the Netherlands in 1578. The revolt actually began in the southern provinces in 1566. In 1567 the duque de Alba was sent to quell the uprising, but the revolt spread under the leadership of William I of Orange (William the Silent). Under the treaty known as the Pacification of Ghent (1576) all the provinces united to drive out the Spanish. Beginning in 1578 the Spanish governor Alessandro Farnese won back the southern provinces by political concessions. The northern provinces of Holland formed the Union of Utrecht (1579) and declared themselves a republic in 1581. The Dutch were aided by the war between Spain and England, which forced the Spanish to fight on two fronts and made England a valuable Dutch ally.

◢ ▶ p. 75

1588
THE SPANISH ARMADA
The Armada was a great Spanish fleet, assembled in 1588 as part of an attempt by Philip II to invade England. The plan was to send a fleet of 130 ships, commanded by the duque de Medina Sidonia, to cover an invasion force from Flanders under Alessandro Farnese. Lacking adequate ships of his own and blockaded by Dutch rebels, Farnese could not embark his troops. The Armada fought its way through the English Channel but, on 8 August, English fireships drove the Armada out of its Calais anchorage. The Spanish regrouped and fought another battle off Gravelines, but were, by this time, out of ammunition. Realising that the situation was lost, Medina Sidonia sailed north around Scotland and Ireland and returned to Spain. He suffered heavy losses along the way because of disease and shipwreck.

p. 71 ◀ **Distant Voices** ▶ p. 75

Sir Philip being thirstie with excess bleeding, he called for a drink, which was presently brought to him; but as he was putting the bottle to his mouth, he saw a poor Souldier carryed along, gastly casting up his eyes at the bottle. Which Sir Philip perceiving took it from his head before he drank, and delivered it to the poor man, with these words, 'Thy necessity is yet greater than mine'.

Sir Fulke Greville, on an incident in the Low Countries (1586)

▼ *The Spanish Armada, which was defeated by the English fleet in 1588.*

 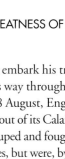

The Ottoman Empire
1071–1571

BY 1000, THE NORTHERN INVADERS had been assimilated into Europe and by 1500 technological progress had allowed the European powers to begin extending their influence around the world. Europe's failure to deal with the Turkish threat to Asia and the Mediterranean can be explained by a number of factors. Europe population growth was, at best, stagnant during this period, whilst the Turkish groups seemed to have infinite numbers. The Turks were not a primitive race, indeed their war technology was far superior to that of the Europeans. The Turks had elements of two important cultures, Islam and the Steppe Nomads, that filled the vacuum left by the Arabs and encountered the dying civilisation of Byzantium.

✦ ▶ p. 82 **1071**
THE RISE OF THE OTTOMANS
The Seljuk Turk victory over the Byzantines at Manzikert in 1071 opened the way for a Turkish invasion of Asia Minor. The Turks had been interested in settling in Arabia, but the attractive land of Anatolia was too good an option to ignore. Inspired by their faith as *ghazis* (warriors of the Muslim faith), they attacked the ruins of the Byzantine Empire. Osman (1281–1326) fearlessly led the Ottomans in the early days, followed by Orkhan (1326–62); Europe was in no condition to repel them. When the crusaders sacked Constantinople in 1204, the Ottomans quickly annexed Anatolia. The Europeans failed to support Byzantium and they knew that a superior military force faced them. The poor performance of the crusaders was confirmed by a string of defeats against the Turks.

◎ ▶ p. 86 **1356**
THE OTTOMAN MILITARY SYSTEM
By 1356, the Turks were ready to cross into Europe. They took Adrianople and surged towards the Danube, beating the Serbs at Maritza (1378) and Kosovo (1389), then destroying a Hungarian army at Nicopolis (1396). Two more victories at Varna (1444) and Kosovo (1448) sealed the fate of Constantinople. The Ottoman army resembled a feudal force, the bulk of the army being militia. These were mainly cavalry, supported by hordes of irregular troops, who were unpaid and fought for plunder. The elite troops of the Turkish army were the Janissaries. These were recruited from Christian families, taken away to monastery-barracks and trained in warfare. Initially armed with bows and hand-weapons, they were eventually re-equipped with firearms; they numbered at least 15,000.

1453
THE FALL OF CONSTANTINOPLE
When Urban, a Hungarian engineer, was turned away by Constantine, the Byzantine emperor, in 1452, he was employed by Mehmet II to construct a cannon, 8.2 m (27 ft) long and with a range of a mile. The Ottomans had already realised the im-portance of cannon and by 1364 had begun mass production; they had used field artillery at Kosovo in 1389. Mehmet arrived with his 100,000 men and a huge siege train, and kept up a ceaseless bombardment of Constantinople for six weeks. Within a week, the outer wall had been breached in several places and when the Ottomans placed more cannon on a pontoon across the Golden Horn, none of the city was safe from their bombardment. On two occasions, Mehmet thought that the bombardment had done enough, but was repulsed each time. On the third attempt, the city fell.

1480
THE OTTOMANS VS THE KNIGHTS OF ST JOHN
When the Ottomans took Constantinople, they also captured one of the greatest shipbuilding centres in the world. The Turkish fleet grew enormously during the late fifteenth century, with notable victories against the Venetians leading to the occupation of Albania in 1478. In 1480, Mehmet failed in his attempt to take Rhodes from the Knights of St John of Jerusalem, but when Suleiman the Magnificent landed on the island in 1522, it was clear that he meant to stay. The town was surrounded by a wall 9.1 m (30 ft) high and 12.2 m (40 ft) thick - a formidable proposition. Four assaults were beaten off in September, but by December the defenders had had enough and they departed to Malta; this too was besieged in 1565.

▼ *One of the Knights of St John of Jerusalem.*

 TECHNOLOGY ☆ GENERALS STRATEGY ● WEAPONS ◎ ARMIES

▲ *The Ottoman ruler Suleiman the Magnificent, who mounted a campaign to capture Vienna.*

1525
SULEIMAN THE MAGNIFICENT
Suleiman led a major campaign on the Danube front in 1525–26, the first in this region for 50 years. There was no united opposition from the barons on the frontier. Despite the warning signs, the Hungarians were unprepared and the Ottomans reached Belgrade in July 1526. When Suleiman met the Hungarian army of King Louis at Mohacs in August, his army had swelled to 70,000, outnumbering the Christians two to one. At first the Hungarian cavalry attacks threw the Ottomans into disorder, but as they broke through the Turkish lines they were destroyed by the Janissaries. The Hungarians left 22,000 dead including the king, seven bishops and over 500 nobles. Budapest fell immediately; the road to Vienna was clear.

✛ ▶ p. 77 　　**1529**
THE SIEGE OF VIENNA
At the head of an Ottoman army of 120,000, Suleiman the Magnificent arrived at the gates of Vienna on 27 September 1529. A series of assaults were made during October, culminating in an attack on a breach in the walls. All were repulsed with

heavy losses. With the winter drawing in and the prospect of defending a long supply route, Suleiman abandoned the siege. The new frontier was set from Zengg on the Adriatic to Gran on the Danube. Meanwhile, on the south-eastern front, Suleiman had extended his empire as far as Basra and with it, a port on the Persian Gulf. He allied with the Gujarati prince, Bahadur, and participated in a fruitless siege of Portuguese Diu.

🚢 ▶ p. 76 　　**1538**
PHILIP II AND BARBAROSSA
By the mid-sixteenth century, Spain had become the dominant European sea power in the Mediterranean, but western expansion plans were a key part of Suleiman's overall policies. His chief allies in this aim were the Barbary Corsairs, led by Khair-ed-din Barbarossa. They quickly built up a fleet and decisively defeated a Christian force off the Albanian coast in 1538. This meant that the Ottomans had sea supremacy east of Italy. Dragut captured Tripoli in 1559 for the Corsairs, but the massive Turkish attempt to capture Malta in 1565 failed. By this time Philip II of Spain had massively increased his fleets and, after Suleiman died in 1566, the tide began to turn in favour of the Christians.

▼ *Barbarossa, leader of the Barbary Corsairs.*

1571
LEPANTO
When the Christian fleet, under Don John of Austria, assembled at Messina in September 1571, it could boast 200 galleys, six galleasses, 24 large transports and 50 other craft. There were 50,000 seamen – most still shackled to their rowing positions – and 30,000 fighting men. Against them, the Ottoman fleet under Ali Pasha mustered 250 galleys, 40 galliots and 20 other craft, together with some 25,000 fighting men. The fleets spotted each another off Lepanto near the Gulf of Corinth on 7 October. The Turkish centre and right were destroyed, with a loss of around 200 ships and 30,000 men. This was the last time that oar-driven ships were used in a naval battle. Lepanto ended Ottoman naval supremacy in the Mediterranean.

p. 73 ◀ **Distant Voices** ▶ p. 77

The Turks surpass our soldiers for three reasons: they obey their commanders promptly; they never show the least concern for their lives in battle; they can live a long time without bread and wine, content with barley and water.

Givio

States in Conflict
1618–1704

ONE STRIKING DEVELOPMENT in seventeenth-century warfare was the sheer scale of armies. Gustavus Adolphus (r. 1611–32) allocated half of Sweden's budget to military expenditure. Smaller states, such as Scotland and Switzerland, sold their manpower to the greater nations. The Thirty Years' War (1618–48) marked the beginning of modern warfare. During that conflict Gustavus Adolphus of Sweden greatly improved army organisation and discipline, introducing more powerful artillery and a lighter infantry musket that permitted soldiers to load and fire faster. During the English Civil War (1642–49), Oliver Cromwell raised an extremely effective fighting force by conscription. Law fixed pay, supplies and discipline, and for the first time the scarlet coat became the badge of English troops.

▲ *Oliver Cromwell, leader in the English Civil Wars and later Lord Protector of England.*

1618
EUROPEAN CONFLICT

The Thirty Years' War was the last major European war of religion and the first all-European struggle for power. Hostilities broke out on 23 May 1618, when a number of Protestant Bohemian noblemen threw two royal governors of their country out of the windows of the Hradcany Palace in Prague. The Bohemians appealed to the Protestant prince of Transylvania, who, with the encouragement of his overlord, the Ottoman sultan of Turkey, was hoping to win the crown of Hungary from the Habsburgs. They also elected Frederick V of the Palatinate as their new king. They hoped that Frederick's father-in-law, James I of England, and his uncle, virtual ruler of the United Provinces of the Netherlands, Maurice of Nassau, would lend him support.

❀ ▶ p. 78 **1630**
THE LION OF THE NORTH

In July 1630 the Swedish king Gustavus Adolphus landed in Pomerania to begin a eries of victorious campaigns against the imperial armies. At Breitenfeld (17 September 1631) and at the Lech River (15 April 1632) he defeated Tilly, and at Lutzen (16 November 1632) the Swedes defeated Wallenstein, although Gustavus Adolfus was killed. The intervention of France (1635) on the 'Protestant' side cut across the religious alignments of the combatants. In 1640 both Catalonia and Portugal rebelled against Spain, although all three were Catholic. In 1643, the Protestant Christian of Denmark, fearing the increasing power of Protestant Sweden, restarted the old Danish-Swedish rivalry for the control of the western entrance to the Baltic. Once more the Danes were heavily defeated and lost their monopoly control over the Sound.

1642
THE START OF THE ENGLISH CIVIL WAR

After a drawn battle at Edgehill in Warwickshire (1642), the royalists threatened London. In 1643, the royalists were victorious in most parts of England except London and the east. Charles was defeated at Newbury (20 September 1643) and the tide turned for the parliamentarians for good in 1644, when the royalists were beaten at Marston Moor in Yorkshire (2 July). In 1645 the royalists were defeated by Thomas Fairfax's New Model Army at Naseby. Oxford fell in 1646, and Charles, who had surrendered himself to the Scots, was turned over to Parliament and became a prisoner. After Charles I's execution (30 January 1649), his son Charles II renewed the war, sustained by royalists in Ireland and Scotland. Cromwell defeated the Irish and then invaded Scotland, where he crushed the Scots at Dunbar (1650).

⛵ ▶ p. 87 **1650**
MARITIME SUPREMACY

The leading maritime nation of the first half of the seventeenth century was Holland. From 1650, at the height of their prosperity, Spain ceased to be a menace to the French and the British. Consequently, the Dutch were thrown into direct competition with the British. Between 1650 and 1652, the British passed three Navigation Acts, excluding the Dutch from their trade. By 1652, the British had over 60 large warships with over 100 guns each in preparation for impending war. Three Anglo-Dutch Wars were fought (1652–54, 1665–67 and 1672–74), after which the British overtook the Dutch as the major maritime power. As a result of the war, the British came to own much of the Atlantic coast of America, including New Amsterdam, which became New York.

☆ ▶ p. 80 **1667**
MARLBOROUGH

John Churchill, 1st Duke of Marlborough, entered the English army in 1667; he first distinguished himself by helping defeat the

rebellion of the Duke of Monmouth (1685). King James raised him to the peerage and promoted him to the rank of lieutenant general. When James was deposed and replaced by William II of Orange, Churchill was quick to shift his allegiance. Churchill campaigned for William during the war against France in Flanders and Ireland. When Anne became queen in 1702, she appointed Marlborough commander-in-chief and first minister. During the long war against France, he won victories at Blenheim (1704), Ramillies (1706), Oudenarde (1708) and Malplaquet (1709). Marlborough is acknowledged as a master military strategist and as one of the great generals in British history.

▼ *John Churchill, the Duke of Marlborough, one of England's greatest military figures.*

▲ *The Battle of Edgehill, the first of the English Civil Wars.*

1670s
SEBASTIEN DE VAUBAN

The effectiveness of citadels for defence was greatly enhanced in the seventeenth century by the work of a French military engineering genius named Sebastien de Vauban (1633–1707). Retaining the basic features of the citadel structure, he devised a means of extending the outer-works so far that no enemy could begin siege operations at close range. Vauban was also a master of offensive siege-craft; he developed the concept of using parallel trenches to connect the zigzag trenches used by besieging troops, and the use of the ricochet shot from cannon plunging over the walls to drop on the defenders beyond. The best examples of Vauban's work can be seen at Neuf Brisach and Lille, which are typical of his 'star fort' designs.

1700
THE GREAT NORTHERN WAR

Sweden, the dominant power in northern Europe when the war began, fought against an alliance intent on seizing its empire. After Charles XII inherited the Swedish throne (1697), Denmark, Saxony and Russia attacked Sweden. Charles defeated the Danes, then turned his attention to Russia, destroying the Russian army that was besieging Narva (1700). Charles toppled Augustus from the throne of Poland (1704) and broke his power in Saxony (1706). In 1707, Charles was decisively

defeated at Poltava by Peter the Great and fled to the Ottoman Empire. Russia seized Livonia, Estonia and the Gulf of Finland. Charles returned to the north in 1714, but was killed during a campaign against Danish-ruled Norway (1718). This signalled the emergence of Russia as the strongest power in the Baltic.

❖ ▶ p. 82 **1704 AND 1709**
BLENHEIM AND MALPLAQUET

The English and imperialist army of 52,000, under the Duke of Marlborough and Prince Eugene, faced a Franco-Bavarian army of 56,000 under Tallard in August 1704. The latter were in strong defensive positions behind a stream, a marsh and fortified in a series of villages. Marlborough made a series of diversionary attacks to draw off the enemy then launched his troops, routing the Franco-Bavarians, who lost 40,000 including 16,000 who were taken prisoner. The allies lost around 12,000. In 1709, Marlborough again faced the French at Malplaquet. The 80,000-strong French army with 60 guns attempted to break the siege of Mons. Marlborough, who had a numerical advantage, attacked them near Tournai. The desperate fighting – the bloodiest of the war – resulted in 12,000 French dead or wounded and 24,000 allied casualties.

p. 75 ◀ **Distant Voices** ▶ p. 79

In Wendover, a pulpit was built in the market place, where we heard two worthy sermons. This evening our ungodly Lieutenant-Colonel, upon an ungrounded whimsy, commanded two of our captains, with their companies, to march out the town, but they went not. I humbly entreat you, as you desire the success of our just and honourable cause, that you would endeavour to root out our Lieutenant-Colonel for if we march further under his command, we fear, upon sufficient grounds, we are all but dead men.

Sergeant Nehemiah Wharton
(August 1642)

War in the Eighteenth Century
1739–81

THE TREATY OF UTRECHT (1713) ended France's attempts to dominate Europe; however, there was still the question of colonies and trade. The Dutch were no longer a problem and the Spanish were content to ally themselves with France when it suited them. The Anglo-Spanish War of Jenkins' Ear (1739–48) proved to be the first flash-point, followed by the Austrian War of Succession (1740–48), in which Britain and France fought from 1743. After a brief pause, France and Britain clashed in the Seven Years' War (1756–63) which continued as the American War of Independence (1775–83), although this was effectively over after Cornwallis surrendered at Yorktown in 1781.

▲ *The signing of the Treaty of Utrecht in 1713, marking the end of French domination in Europe.*

⊕ ▶ p. 79 **1739**
THE WAR OF JENKINS' EAR
When the English brig Rebecca, was boarded by a Spanish ship on its way home from the West Indies, the Spanish commander cut off the ear of the English captain, Robert Jenkins. He complained about this treatment when he returned home, but was largely ignored. Seven years later, when he retold his story in front of the House of Commons, Sir Robert Walpole, the prime minister, gave in to the calls for war. Admiral Vernon captured Porto Bello in 1740, one of the first amphibious operations in warfare. Meanwhile,

Commodore Anson sank Spanish ships and circumnavigated the world, bringing back the richest prize cargo in history. He went on to sink 10 French ships and capture 3,000 prisoners off Cape Finisterre in 1747.

1740
THE WAR OF THE AUSTRIAN SUCCESSION
In 1740, Emperor Charles VI died without a male heir, and his lands passed to a daughter, Maria Theresa. Two months later, Frederick II of Prussia, anticipating a partition of Habsburg domains, invaded Silesia. A Prussian victory at Mollwitz in 1741 hastened the formation of an anti-Habsburg coalition that included Bavaria, Spain, and France as well as Prussia. Illustrious victories by Frederick II in 1745 compelled Maria Theresa to sign the Treaty of Dresden on 25 December 1745, reaffirming Prussian control of Silesia. In 1745, the French had won a tremendous battle over a combined Austrian, English and Dutch force at Fontenoy, but had lost Canada. A general peace was finally concluded at Aix-la-Chapelle on 18 October 1748.

1755
THE BRADDOCK MASSACRE
In 1754, the Ohio Company of Virginia – a group of land speculators – began building a fort at the Forks, only to have the workers

ejected by a strong French expedition, which then proceeded to construct Fort Duquesne on the site. Virginia militia, commanded by a young George Washington proved no match for the French and Indians from Fort Duquesne. Defeated at Fort Necessity (July 1754), they were forced to withdraw east of the mountains. The British government in London, realising that the colonies by themselves were unable to prevent the French advance into the Ohio Valley, sent a force of regulars under Braddock to uphold the British territorial claims. In July 1755, to the consternation of all the English colonies, Braddock's army was disastrously defeated as it approached Fort Duquesne.

✄ ▶ p.85 **1756**
THE SEVEN YEARS' WAR
The Seven Years' War pitted Britain and Prussia against Austria, France, Russia, Saxony, Sweden and (after 1762) Spain. On the European continent hostilities began in 1756, when Frederick II (the Great) of Prussia, anticipating an assault from Maria Theresa of Austria and Elizabeth of Russia, launched a surprise offensive through the electorate of Saxony, a minor Austrian ally. Sweden aligned itself against Prussia, and Frederick's advance into Bohemia led to a Prussian defeat at Kolin in June 1757. A Russian army marched into East Prussia in August, and Austrian troops occupied Berlin for several days in October. Only Frederick's outstanding victories at Rossbach in November and at Leuthen a month later, prevented the allies from overwhelming his kingdom.

1756
WOLFE AND MONTCALM
In 1756, Montcalm forced the surrender of the British fort at Oswego on Lake Ontario, thereby breaking the British hold on the Great Lakes. By 1758, a British expedition, employing increasing numbers of regulars, forced the surrender of Louisbourg, and another expedition advancing west from Philadelphia caused the French to abandon the Forks of the Ohio. For the British, 1759

proved to be a year of stunning successes in America. One British expedition took Niagara; another, led by Amherst himself, seized both Ticonderoga and Crown Point, thereby opening the way to Montreal. A third, commanded by Wolfe, sailed up the Saint Lawrence and, after much difficulty, defeated Montcalm on the Plains of Abraham just outside Quebec. The war-weary nations began negotiations that, in February 1763, produced the decisive Treaty of Paris.

▲ *Frederick II of Prussia, known as Frederick the Great.*

1758
FREDERICK THE GREAT

Costly Prussian successes at Zorndorf in 1758 and again at Leignitz and Torgau in 1760, only drained Frederick's limited resources. He suffered another defeat against the Russians at Kunersdorf in 1759. By the end of 1761 the Austrians had moved into Saxony and Silesia, and Russian troops held Prussian Pomerania. With enemy armies closing in around him, Frederick seemed incapable of further resistance. At this critical moment the Russian empress died and was succeeded by Peter III, one of Frederick's devoted admirers. Peter immediately withdrew from the war and Austria, unable to defeat Prussia alone, was compelled to end the fighting in Germany. A treaty confirming Prussian sovereignty over Silesia was signed at Hubertusberg in 1763.

⊕ ▶ p. 85

1775
AMERICAN REVOLUTION

The American Revolution was caused by colonial opposition to British economic exploitation and anti-monarchist sentiment. The spark, which ignited wholesale revolution, came at Lexington, Massachusetts on 19 April 1775. General Gage despatched a small force to seize illegal military stores at Lexington. The local colonists' militia, known as 'minutemen', exchanged fire with the British troops and the Battle of Lexington and Concord began the Revolution. The second Continental Congress met in Philadelphia in May 1775 and adopted the rebel militias in the field as the Continental Army; George Washington was appointed commander-in-chief. The British were reinforced by the arrival in Boston of William Howe, Sir Henry Clinton and John Burgoyne with additional troops, raising their total force to 10,000.

1775
THE WORLD TURNED UPSIDE DOWN

The first significant engagement of the American Revolution came at Bunker Hill (1775), which the British won only at a great cost. The Americans invaded Canada but were forced to retreat after defeat at Quebec (December). Washington bombarded Boston (March 1776), forcing Howe to evacuate. Washington was defeated at Long Island (August), but the Americans defeated the British at Trenton (December) and Princeton (January 1777). However, Washington suffered major reverses at the Brandywine (September) and Germantown (October) and Howe occupied Philadelphia. The British suffered a major setback when Burgoyne surrendered after Saratoga. In 1781, Washington besieged Lord Cornwallis in Yorktown. Cornwallis's last hope of evacuation by sea was dashed by the French victory over the British fleet at Chesapeake Bay, isolating him and his troops who were forced to surrender.

p. 77 ◀ **Distant Voices** ▶ p. 81

Came a deserter who reports that while our guns were firing at them an officer pulled off his hat, huzzaed and called God to damn us all, when one of our balls with unerring justice took off the miserable man's head and left him a wretched example of the Divine justice. A recruit who refused to work, carry arms, eat or drink was whipped for the fifth time, after which being asked by the officer he said that he was now ready to do his duty.

From the diary of an unknown soldier at the Siege of Gibraltar (1727)

▼ *The Battle of Bunker Hill during the American Revolution.*

The Era of Nelson, Napoleon and Wellington
1792–1815

I N 1789, GROWING DISCONTENT with France's government suddenly exploded into an open revolt which drew the attention of all the nations of Europe. The ensuing violence and international involvement triggered more than two decades of nearly continuous warfare. The former king and queen were cruelly put to death. This act galvanised the other nations of Europe against France. Army general Napoleon Bonaparte seized control of the government. The presence of this charismatic military genius as the head of France meant that confrontation was destined to continue until one of the two sides was defeated. It was not until 1815 that the wars ended with the Battle of Waterloo and a monarch returned to Paris.

1792
VALMY AND JEMAPPES

The nations of Europe began moving against revolutionary France even before the execution of Louis. In August 1792, a joint Prussian-Austrian army invaded north-eastern France. They were met at Valmy, where the day was won by the French. Other French forces pushed back the Austrian army at the Battle of Jemappes. In January 1793, the revolutionary government in Paris issued the infamous

▼ *Napoleon and his* Grande Armée *defeated the Allied forces at the Battle of Austerlitz in the Napoleonic Wars.*

orders to execute King Louis and Marie-Antoinette. Britain was transformed from a concerned observer to an implacable foe. The Austrians were driven from the Netherlands, and the United Provinces (Northern Holland) were annexed. By 1795 Prussia, Spain, Hanover and Saxony had all opted out of the coalition, leaving Britain and Austria to continue the fight against France's revolutionary government.

☆ ▶ p. 84
1799
THE RISE OF BONAPARTE

Austria was now fighting a lone war on the Continent. In Italy, Napoleon Bonaparte expelled the Austrians from northern Italy in a lightning campaign. His army then joined up with Joubert's troops marching out of southern Germany and advanced on Vienna, forcing the Austrians to sue for peace. An Egyptian campaign in 1798 was a strategic failure. Back in Europe, a joint Austrian-Russian army managed to wrest most of northern Italy away from the French. Napoleon seized power in 1799 and a fresh French army defeated the Austrians at Marengo in Italy. By the end of 1800, the French were driving into southern Germany and the Austrian government again sued for peace, bringing the French Revolutionary Wars to a close in early 1801.

➥ ▶ p. 86
1801
THREAT OF INVASION

Britain remained openly hostile to the French and for all but 14 months of that time, the Royal Navy maintained a tight commercial blockade of the Continent. In 1801, Admiral Horatio Nelson took matters into his own hands and attacked a Danish fleet at Copenhagen. The Russian fleet would probably have been next had not the anti-British tsar been killed and replaced by his son, who quickly came to an agreement with England. France, in turn, planned an invasion of England. Numerous newly formed French army corps were stationed along the English Channel in training camps. The invasion plans were finally brought to a close, however, when Austria and Russia again declared war and invaded southern Germany.

p. 71 ◀ **Triumphs & Tragedies** ▶ p. 85
1805
AUSTERLITZ AND TRAFALGAR

In one of history's most famous military manoeuvres, Napoleon marched his main *Grande Armée* into Germany and surrounded the Austrian army. With their strategic centre breached, the Austrians were unable to prevent the French occupation of Vienna, and in December 1805 the remaining Allied army catastrophically lost the Battle of Austerlitz to Napoleon, knocking Austria out of the wars for several years. In the Atlantic, the French and Spanish navies were caught by the British fleet after their attempt to secure the English Channel for Napoleon. The resulting naval battle off Cape Trafalgar ended in the destruction of both the French and Spanish fleets, but at the cost of Nelson's life.

1806–1809
JENA TO WAGRAM

Prussia declared war on France in 1806, but was decisively beaten at the twin battles of Jena and Auerstadt that October. After bloodily halting the French army at Eylau in

1807, the Russians lost at the Battle of Friedland later the same summer. In March 1808, a large French army entered Spain and the Spanish king was deposed. Within weeks a British army landed in Portugal and defeated Junot's main force. Wellington returned to Portugal and in May 1809 defeated Soult, who had been left in overall military command. By this time, only Wellington's army in western Portugal remained to offer organised resistance. In central Europe, the Austrians had decided to declare war on France, but they managed to push back the Austrians at Wagram (1809).

1812
THE RUSSIAN CAMPAIGN

The French invasion of Russia began with the crossing of the Niemen River on 24 June 1812. By the time the invading army fought its first major battle at Smolensk, it was reduced to half its original size due to detachments, death and desertion. The Russians finally fought at the Battle of Borodino in September, the French battering themselves against the Russian defences. The Russians evacuated Moscow. Winter was drawing in; a French retreat was the only choice and severe cold had turned half the army into a mass of fugitives. The Berezina River crossing was a catastrophe, killing half of the remaining 60,000 troops. When the few thousand remaining men abandoned their wagons and artillery at the base of an icy hill west of Vilna, the army effectively disintegrated.

1813
THE BATTLE OF LEIPZIG

The new allied coalition of Britain, Russia, Prussia, Spain, Portugal, Austria and Sweden slowly ground down the remaining French armies. Austria especially had not suffered a significant military defeat in eight years and her relatively intact armies were to form the backbone of the 1813 and 1814 campaigns. Despite victories at the battles of Lutzen, Bautzen and Dresden, the French Army suffered a crushing defeat at the huge three-day Battle of Leipzig in October 1813. By 1814, allied armies were advancing into France from every direction and despite continuing French resistance, Paris surrendered on 31 March 1814. A few days later Napoleon surrendered unconditionally, and was exiled to the island of Elba in the Mediterranean.

1815
THE HUNDRED DAYS

By the spring of 1815, Napoleon had returned to southern France and marched toward Paris, drawing most of the army to his side as he approached. The recently installed king, Louis XVIII, quickly evacuated the capital and Napoleon again took control of the government. Allied countries mobilised for war. Napoleon decided to administer a quick and decisive

▼ *Admiral Nelson on his flagship, the HMS* Victory, *during the naval battle against the French in 1805.*

▲ *A French offensive during the Russian campaign of 1812.*

blow by moving against the Anglo-German armies then in Belgium and Holland under the commands of Generals Wellington and Blucher. The campaign did not go according to plan, however, climaxing at the Battle of Waterloo, during which the French army virtually disintegrated. Napoleon's reign had lasted just 100 days. Napoleon was sent to his final exile on the island of Saint Helena, where he died in 1821.

p. 79 ◀ **Distant Voices** ▶ p. 83

Looting the enemy's dead was a soldier's right, and fortunes were lying on the field for anyone cold-blooded enough to take them. Dead officers had purses, watches, pistols, swords and lockets. Their epaulettes and gold braid were worth money. When all those were gone, there were clothes and equipment. False teeth were either carved out of ivory or made up of human teeth, and dentists would pay well for the raw materials. Such a haul was made from the field of Waterloo that dentures for years afterwards were often called Waterloo teeth.

From *A Near Run Thing*, by David Howarth

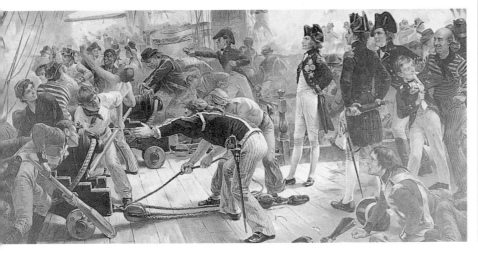

Eastern Warfare
246 BC–AD 1757

ANY STUDY of the history of warfare would be incomplete without considering the Near and Far East. The Mongols were once a totally warrior society, perhaps the most successful the world has ever seen. The Chinese, although not a warlike and aggressive race throughout history, were perfectly able to defend themselves and launch fierce counter-offensives. The Japanese, an intensely militaristic nation, developed the samurai – a distinctive and outstanding warrior. As far as the Indians were concerned, complex mixtures of no less than eight different races, 200 languages and 1.5 million square miles, meant that the opportunities for conflict were immense. The Moguls and the Marathas dominated the history of India, but after the eighteenth century India, like most of Asia, became embroiled in European struggles.

▲ *The Great Wall of China, built during the Chin dynasty – one of the greatest feats of ancient engineering.*

✥ ▶ p. 94 **246 BC**
THE GREAT WALL

The Chin dynasty were great exponents of siege warfare. They developed catapults, scaling ladders and other equipment, thus requiring more sophisticated fortifications to be built. This culminated in the building of the Great Wall of China, which stretched 2,574 km (1,600 miles) along the nomad frontier south of the Gobi Desert. It was constructed to be a standard 7.6 m (25 ft) wide at the base, and 5.2 m (17 ft) wide at the top; it averaged 7.6–9.1 m (25–30 ft) high with crenellated parapets 1.5 m (5 ft) above the walkways, and was punctuated with regular towers. Cities such as Nanking and Sian could boast walls of 15.2–21.3 m (50–70 ft) thick, with large numbers of soldiers to defend the walls and gates.

AD 249
THE WARRING STATES

The earliest reliable period in Chinese history is known as the Chou dynasty. China was a feudal land, and champions and their retinues fighting small pitched battles dealt with many of the conflicts. As the strength of the Chou declined, warfare became a more serious game; chariots remained the important factor, but foot soldiers were fast becoming the dominant force on the battlefield. When the Chou dynasty fell in AD 249, the Chin took control and it became essential to present a united front against incursions from outside the empire. As the Chin had fought for years against the nomads in the north, it was natural that they should adopt the horse as their main method of warfare.

AD 900s
THE WAY OF THE WARRIOR

Two and a half centuries of desperate warfare over the rugged countryside of Japan led to the emergence of a privileged class, the samurai. The chief weapon was the bow but by the tenth century, the art of sword-making had reached a high level and the samurai devoted much of their time to acquiring skills in swordsmanship. They were also highly skilled in unarmed combat. The samurai rode to battle on sturdy ponies, but battle often became a series of single combats as each of the samurai strove to defeat an individual opponent. A samurai would die for his lord; if he chose surrender rather than death, he would be the object of utter contempt.

✥ ▶ p. 95 **1211**
MONGOLS IN CHINA

Son of a minor chieftain, Genghis Khan moulded the warring Mongol clans into an unstoppable force. He organised his armies in multiples of 10, with the touman (10,000) as the largest tactical unit. By the time he unified all the tribes, his empire stretched 1,000 miles from east to west. His army, known as the Horde, even breached the Great Wall of China in 1211, devastating the Chinese country. Genghis was bought off by the Chinese and turned his

▼ *The great Mongol leader Genghis Khan.*

 TECHNOLOGY ☆ GENERALS ⤳ STRATEGY ● WEAPONS   ARMIES

▲ *The Japanese warlord Yorimoto.*

attention to the west. By 1221, he had conquered the Khwarizarmians and had extended his empire from Tibet to the Caspian Sea and the Persian Gulf. He turned again to China, overrunning the Hsia and southern China. He died in 1227.

1274
MONGOLS IN JAPAN

Yorimoto emerged as a great leader of the Japanese in 1185, establishing a strong central government, whilst maintaining the feudalism and fighting character of the nation. Japan was well prepared for the first Mongol invasion in 1274. For a whole day the Japanese held the Mongols at their landing point on Kyushu until a storm forced the Mongols to retire to Korea. The Japanese had underestimated the fighting skills and great numbers of Mongols and it was inevitable the Horde would be back. The Japanese did not waste the seven years' respite, though, they built a stone wall along the shore of Hakozaki Bay, from which

they would defend their country. The Mongols reappeared off the coast in 1281, but were unable to breach the defences. They never returned.

1543
CONTACT WITH EUROPE

Throughout the fourteenth to sixteenth centuries, Japan was torn apart by civil war, but in 1543 contact was made with the Europeans. Using European weapons mixed with traditional Japanese martial skills, Nobunga became shogun of Japan in 1573. He established the Japanese firearms industry and began producing European-style ships. After he was assassinated in 1582, his lieutenant, Hideyoshi, crushed the dissidents and reunited Japan. In 1592 he invaded Korea, taking Seoul in just three weeks. At sea, things did not go so well; the Korean admiral Yi-sun, with his iron-clad ships, defeated the Japanese. Hideyoshi tried again in 1597, but suffered the same fate. Iyeyasu, another of Nobunga's generals, took control and established the Tokugawa dynasty which would last until 1867.

● ▶ p. 87

1700s
MISSILE WEAPONS

Rockets were an old Hindu weapon, but they remained in use in the Mogul and Maratha armies of the eighteenth century. The rocket was fired from an iron tube about 30 cm (1 ft) long and 2.5 cm (1 in) in diameter; this tube was fixed to a bamboo stick. Although it had an effective range of around 91 m (1,000 yards), it was probably as dangerous to the person firing it as to the intended target. If it exploded on contact, it could cause a fire, stampede mounts or scatter raw and inexperienced troops. By the fourteenth century, cannon and guns were being imported from Europe, but the Indians were perfectly capable of producing their own huge artillery pieces. Swivel guns were even attached to elephants and camels, yet as late as 1857, bows were still in common use.

1757
THE BATTLE OF PLASSEY

Indian hill forts were as good as any fortifications built in Europe. Typical of these forts is Mandu in Gujarat, built by Shah Hoshang Ghori (1406–35). Its powerful walls, bastions and gates stand 35 m (1,000 ft) above the plain, with sheer sides to the south. The Indians were forced to accept the arrival of the Portuguese, the French, the Dutch and the British. But it was the last that would expel the others and finally bring India into their own empire. At Plassey in 1757, Clive, with less than 3,000 men, defeated the Indians under Suraj-ud-Dowah, leading to the establishment of the British in the wealthy region of Bengal. Nevertheless, there was still much fighting before the British could dominate all of India.

p. 81 ◀ **Distant Voices** ▶ p. 85

Will your Excellency permit our knights and yours to play a game?

A Chou general challenge to the Chin ruler (623 BC)

The Beginnings of Modern Warfare
1810–65

THE INDUSTRIAL REVOLUTION and the general rise in population around the world caused societies to organise themselves for war in a more complete way. Weapons were also becoming increasing more effective. Despite this, the period after the Napoleonic Wars until about 1848, was one period of relative peace in Europe. This, however, was not the case elsewhere. In every other continent around the world, nations began their struggle for independence or found themselves in direct conflict with the European powers. As the weaker European empires lost their overseas territories, the threat of civil war gathered in North America, pitching brother against brother in a potentially ruinous war that would rage for four years from 1861–65.

▶ p. 96

1810
SIMON BOLIVAR
Simon Bolívar fought against the Spanish in Venezuela in 1810. The rebels were defeated by the Spanish royalists, and Bolívar was forced to flee the country. In 1812 he led another expedition to Venezuela; he captured Caracas in 1813 and assumed dictatorship. In 1819 Bolívar's army crossed the Andes mountains into New Granada (now Colombia), defeating the Spanish at Boyacá. The republic of Colombia was proclaimed, consisting of Venezuela and New Granada, with Bolívar as president. Bolivar, with a vision of a united Spanish America, secured independence for Quito (now Ecuador) in 1822, which then became part of Colombia. In 1824 he led the revolutionary forces of Peru in their fight for independence. Victorious, he was elected president of Peru in February 1825.

1835
THE TEXAN WAR OF INDEPENDENCE
In November 1835, a convention of Anglo-American settlers set up a provisional state government and declared that Texans were fighting for the rights due them under the Mexican Constitution. A Texan army was quickly gathered and marched to attack the Mexican garrison at San Antonio. For 13 days the small force defended the Alamo there against more than 5,000 Mexican troops. On 6 March, the Alamo fell. The Texans had almost 800 men when they faced Santa Anna's force of about 1,600 soldiers at San Jacinto. The Mexican army was taken by surprise and most of Santa Anna's troops were killed or wounded. Santa Anna was captured the next day, and in Velasco on 14 May, he was forced to recognise Texas's independence and to withdraw south of the Rio Grande.

1839
THE START OF THE OPIUM WARS
The first Opium War started in 1839 when the Chinese government confiscated opium warehouses in Canton. The British won a quick victory and the conflict was ended; China was forced to pay a large indemnity, open five ports to British trade and residence, and cede Hong Kong to Great Britain. In October 1856, Chinese police boarded the British ship *Arrow* and charged its crew with smuggling. The British used the incident to launch another offensive, precipitating the second Opium War. British forces, aided by the French, won another quick military victory in 1857. When the Chinese government refused to ratify the Treaty of Tientsin, which had been signed in 1858, the hostilities resumed. In 1860, after British and French troops had occupied Beijing and burned the Summer Palace, the Chinese eventually agreed to ratify the treaty.

1839–43
WARS IN AFGHANISTAN
During the nineteenth and early twentieth centuries there were three wars between Afghanistani fighters and British forces in India. The origin of the wars lay in the weakness of the Afghan state. The nation had become independent in the mid-eighteenth century, but local chieftains attempted to establish their own power against the government. The British, who were consolidating their hold on India, wanted a strong Afghanistan between Persia and Russia. The first Afghan War (1839–42) started when the ruler of Afghanistan, Dost Mohammad Khan, refused to make an alliance with the British. The British invaded the country and restored a former king, Shah Shoja, to the throne. Local uprisings throughout the country eventually drove the British out, and Dost Muhammad returned as ruler in 1843.

▲ *The Mexicans taking the Alamo in the Texan War of Independence.*

 TECHNOLOGY ☆ GENERALS STRATEGY ● WEAPONS ◎ ARMIES

p. 80 ◀ **Triumphs & Tragedies** ▶ p. 91

1853
THE CRIMEAN WAR

In 1853 Tsar Nicholas I of Russia demanded the right to protect Christian shrines in Jerusalem, then part of the Turkish Empire. As a first step, his troops moved into the Turkish Balkans. By August 1854, Turkey, with the help of Britain, France and Sardinia, had driven the Russian forces out of the Balkans. There their troops landed in the Crimean Peninsula on 16 September 1854 and laid siege to the Russian fortress of Sevastopol. Battles were fought at the Alma River, at Balaklava and Inkerman. During the siege of Sevastopol disease took a dreadful toll on French and British troops. Florence Nightingale's heroic work as head of the hospital service did much to improve conditions. By September 1855, Sevastopol was in allied hands.

⊕ ▶ p. 89   ## 1845
BEGINNINGS OF MAORI WARS

In 1841 New Zealand became a separate colony of Great Britain, and British government and settlements were established there. The resultant loss of Maori tribal lands triggered Maori revolts against British rule from 1845 to 1848 and again from 1860 to 1870. At Gate Pah, in 1864, the British attacked the Maori stockade with an overwhelming force. After a bombardment and several assaults the stockade fell with the loss of more than 100 men. The Maoris had lost just 30, having abandoned their defences just before the final assault. Peace was permanently established in 1871, after which the Maori gained representation in the New Zealand Parliament that had been established in 1852

⚘ ▶ p. 96   ## 1861
THE WAR BETWEEN THE STATES

The American Civil War was the climax of a long series of quarrels between the North and South over the interpretation of the United States Constitution. The North

▲ *Florence Nightingale's work in the Crimea did much to improve hospital conditions.*

favoured a loose interpretation that would grant the federal government expanded powers. The South wanted to reserve all undefined powers to the individual states. Confederate land batteries opened fire on Fort Sumter on 12 April 1861. The small federal garrison surrendered the next day and this attack ended all hope of peace. Abraham Lincoln at once called upon the loyal states to furnish 75,000 state militia, and Confederate president Jefferson Davis asked for 100,000 volunteers from the Southern states. Both sections were eager for battle. Virginia, North Carolina, Tennessee and Arkansas now joined the Confederacy. The four border states – Maryland, Delaware, Kentucky and Missouri – stayed with the North.

1865
UNION

Throughout the American Civil War, the South were disadvantaged in terms of manpower and materials. The more populous and industrialised North could always deploy larger and better-equipped armies in the field. The South, however, boasted some of the most talented commanders of the century: Stonewall Jackson, J. E. B. Stuart, Jubal Early and

their senior commander, Robert E. Lee. Lee sustained the South far beyond their true capacity, defeating numerous Union generals in decisive and well-managed battles. He failed to defeat the Union army at Gettysburg and, in 1864, faced U. S. Grant, the new northern commander. Forced onto the defensive, he nevertheless inflicted heavy losses on Grant at the battles of the Wilderness, Spotsylvania and Cold Harbor. Early in April 1865 he met Grant at Appomattox and surrendered the army of Northern Virginia.

p. 83 ◀ **Distant Voices** ▶ p. 87

During the morning, after a conference with Grant, Sedgewick rode forward to an elevation near the centre of his position, found that his men were a little nervous because of the fire of Confederate sharpshooters, assured them that there was nothing to worry about because 'they couldn't hit an elephant at this distance' and then himself fell dead with a sharpshooter's bullet in his brain.

Bruce Catton, on the death of General Sedgewick at Spotsylvania Court House (1864)

Towards World War
1870–1914

THE YEARS BETWEEN 1870 and the outbreak of the First World War began with a series of sharp and significant indicators as to the nature of war. Lessons were not learnt, however, as war again raged across central Europe, the Russians attempted to wrestle territory from the Ottoman Empire and as Japan took advantage of the out-dated and poorly led Russian army. In the last 30 years of the nineteenth century, the European population rose by 10 per cent each decade, during a period in which industrialisation revolutionised the armaments industry. By the turn of the century, the Germans and French could put three million men into the field, the Russians four million and the Austrians two million. In total, the European armies amounted to well over 10 million men.

▲ *The Prussian leader Otto von Bismarck.*

1870s
STAFF COLLEGES

As an integral part of the sweeping changes to the armies, it was recognised that efficient general staff were needed. The German model proved to be the system most copied by other nations, with a tight control over the training of senior officers and a powerful leading commander. The Russian Nicholas Staff Academy in St Petersburg and the Staff College at Camberley were both heavily influenced by the German system. Not only were the armies becoming more professional, but the general staff faced tougher and more testing training at the Staff Colleges, and it was becoming more difficult to gain entry unless an individual was well educated. In Britain, Edward Cardwell introduced sweeping reforms to the army, followed by further changes from Wolseley and Lord Roberts.

1870s
ARMAMENTS

During this period, the corps became the key unit of the majority of armies. With 30,000 men, this well-organised and self-contained unit was usually linked to a particular territorial area, with the commander responsible for training, recruitment, supply and mobilisation. Typical corps consisted of two divisions, each with two brigades of infantry, one of cavalry and an artillery regiment. The corps would also have a heavy artillery regiment, engineers, supply troops, medical units, telegraph units, railway and balloon attachments, bridge trains, cyclists and administrative services. By the turn of the century, the majority of the infantry were armed with 8–9 mm magazine rifles, the artillery with 8 cm steel guns and heavy pieces (15–21 cm) for sieges.

▶ p. 89

1870
FRANCE VS RUSSIA

Bismarck put forward a German candidate for the vacant Spanish throne with the deliberate, and successful, intention of provoking the French emperor, Napoleon III. The Prussians defeated the French at Sedan, then moved on and besieged Paris. At Sedan, the French were commanded by Comte Marie Edme Patrice Maurice de MacMahon until he was wounded, and then by General Emmanuel Felix de Wimpffen; the Germans were under Count Helmuth von Moltke. The conflict resulted in a German victory. Napoleon, who had joined the French forces in the afternoon, was also captured. The French casualties were approximately 17,000; German casualties about 9,000. The Treaty of Frankfurt in May 1871 gave Alsace, Lorraine, and a large French indemnity to Prussia.

1899
MILITARY EXPENDITURE

Between 1874 and 1896, European military expenditure increased by 50 per cent. Concerned by the rise in spending and the expansion of the armies, as well as fearing the horrors of modern warfare, the tsar called a disarmament conference at the Hague in 1899. Even the Americans, who had only just recovered from a devastating civil war, took the position that any reduction in arms and troops should be considered potentially dangerous to peace. In the event, the conference was doomed to failure and no meaningful agreements were reached. As the size of armies increased, so too did the organisation of the forces with each country matching and borrowing from one another whilst still maintaining some degree of individuality.

▶ p. 87

1899
THE FIRST SUBMARINE

The Russians had used the torpedo against the Turks in 1877, signalling the introduction of torpedo boats into most naval forces. In the same year the horizontal rudder was designed, making a controlled dive possible. With the development of the petrol engine and the accumulator battery, the submarine was now a viable option. The

▉ ▶ TECHNOLOGY   ☆ GENERALS   ⤳ STRATEGY   ● WEAPONS   ◎ ARMIES

Gustave Zede was a French invention and was designed and tested in 1899, capable of travelling at 8 knots at 18.3 m (60 ft) below the surface. By 1901, the French had 23 submarines in production, Britain had commissioned five. By 1912, submarines had been extensively tested in manoeuvres and finally the naval authorities in the majority of countries had been convinced to include them in their plans.

❄ ▶ p. 90
1900
WAR TECHNOLOGY

By 1900, most armies were equipped with the rifles, pistols, carbines and machine guns that they would use in the First World War. James Lee's magazine system for rifles allowed smaller calibre bullets to travel faster and with a flatter trajectory. The French had introduced smokeless powder in 1884, with the new ingredient of granular nitrocellulose. Nobel had introduced dynamite in 1860 and cordite was being mass-produced by 1890. Bordchardt had designed the first automatic pistol in 1893, using the gas from the explosion to operate the mechanism. By 1898, the Mauser had become the more popular and reliable automatic; a 10-shot version was used extensively by the Boers in South Africa.

▼ *The steel battleship Dreadnought, first unveiled in 1904, was to change the face of naval warfare.*

These developments in small arms greatly improved the overall firepower of the infantry.

🚢 ▶ p. 93
1904
DREADNOUGHT

The development of steel manufacturing allowed enormous steps to be made in the production of ships from 1870 onwards. By 1900, however, the thin steel battleships, with a displacement of 15,000 tons and a speed of 18 knots were fast becoming the norm. Britain had intensified the fleet build-up in 1899, concerned that the joint fleets of France and Russia rivalled its own. The first Dreadnought was laid down in 1904; it was a significant improvement on anything produced elsewhere in the world. This British vessel, with a speed of between 18–25 knots, boasted ten 12-in guns and would become the model for capital ships until the Second World War. Britain and Germany now dominated the seas around Europe.

🗃 ▶ p. 92
1909
WAR IN THE AIR

The first army Balloon School was established in Woolwich in 1874, and most countries soon realised the potential of observation from the air. The Germans developed the Zeppelin and by 1909, the race to produce reliable and effective air corps was reaching its height. France had been the first country to recognise the value

▲ *Zeppelins were developed by the Germans and used as the first method of air attack in the First World War.*

of the aeroplane for military purposes, and by 1914, aircraft could reach a speed of 121 kph (75 mph) and remain airborne for up to three hours. By the outbreak of the First World War, it was still believed that the aircraft would be a reconnaissance weapon and not a frontline fighting machine. Most countries chose to attach small groups of aircraft to corps rather than concentrating them in bigger units.

p. 85 ◀ **Distant Voices** ▶ p. 89

Queen Victoria, listening to a military band at Windsor, was captivated by a certain tune and sent a messenger to ascertain the title of it. He returned in some embarrassment and said that it was called 'Come Where the Booze is Cheaper'.

They Were Singing, by Christopher Pulling.

Learning the Hard Way
1877–1905

DURING THE LAST QUARTER of the nineteenth century, the majority of the more powerful nations of the world were involved in a desperate scramble to enlarge their empires. To this end, there were a series of limited wars in Africa and Asia. Important though these diversions were at the time, the major powers failed to pick up on a number of lessons that should have been learnt from the American Civil War, the Crimean War and the Franco-Prussian War. It was inevitable that any future, major conflict between the leading states of the world would descend into a blood-bath. With the massive leaps in weapons technology, added to the increased size of standing armies, the signals were there, but for the moment the world's attention was elsewhere.

1877
THE RUSSO-TURKISH WAR

Turkish efforts to suppress nationalist agitation in the Balkans, particularly in Bulgaria, Serbia and Bosnia-Herzegovina, led to the Russo-Turkish War of 1877–78. After a difficult military campaign, Russia compelled the Ottoman Empire to sign the Treaty of San Stefano (1878). Because the

extensive rights and territories surrendered by Constantinople augmented St Petersburg's strength and thus threatened the European balance of power, the other great powers pressured Russia to attend the Congress of Berlin. The resulting Treaty of Berlin (1878) reversed some Russian gains but also brought changes to the Balkan peninsula and recognised Russia's acquisition of Batum, Kars and Ardahan in the Caucasus region and southern Bessarabia.

▼ *British troops defending the hospital at Rorke's Drift against the Zulus.*

1879
THE ZULU WAR

Convinced that the independent Zulu kingdom adjoining the new British possessions in South Africa was a serious threat, an ultimatum was delivered ordering the Zulus to disband their army. Knowing that the Zulus would refuse, a British and colonial army under Lord Chelmsford crossed the Buffalo River in January 1879. Hopelessly under-estimating the tactical ability of the Zulus, Chelmsford split his forces and left the way clear for the enemy to attack the British camp. A full six British companies were slaughtered, in addition to several hundred colonial troops. A wing of the huge Zulu army crossed the Buffalo, but were driven off at high cost by a small force at the hospital station at Rorke's Drift.

1881
THE MAHDI

In 1881 Muhammad Ahmed declared himself the Mahdi – the prophesied Muslim messiah who would rid the world of evil – and launched a holy war on the infidel occupiers of Sudan. The Mahdi led a victorious attack on Al Ubayyid in 1883, and went on to capture all of the Darfur region of western Sudan, defeating an Egyptian army led by British colonel William Hicks. In 1884 General Charles George Gordon was dispatched to Khartoum to evacuate Egyptian troops. The Mahdi's forces surrounded Khartoum and besieged the city for 10 months, while Gordon begged the British government for reinforcements. On 26 January 1885, two days before British reinforcements arrived, Khartoum fell and Gordon and his entire garrison were massacred. The British reconquered Sudan in 1898.

1898
ROUGH RIDERS

The Spanish-American War lasted less than four months, from 25 April to 12 August 1898. The sinking of the US battleship *Maine* in Havana harbour sparked off hostilities. Most of the fighting occurred in or near the Spanish colonial possessions of

 TECHNOLOGY   GENERALS   STRATEGY ● WEAPONS ◎ ARMIES

▲ *Muhammad Ahmed – the Mahdi – who instigated a holy war against the 'infidels' in Sudan.*

Cuba and the Philippines, nearly halfway around the world from each other. In both theatres, the decisive military event was the complete destruction of a Spanish naval squadron by a vastly superior US fleet. These victories left the Spanish land forces isolated from their homeland and, after brief resistance, brought about their surrender to US military forces. The defeat marked the end of Spain's colonial empire and the rise of the United States as a global military power.

⊕ ▶ p. 96

1900
THE BOXER REBELLION

In the late nineteenth century, Chinese resentment grew toward Japan and western countries because of their economic and political exploitation, and humiliating military defeats of China. A secret society of Chinese called the Boxers began terrorising Christian missionaries in 1899. In 1900 these attacks culminated in the violent Boxer uprising in Beijing, which claimed the lives of many Chinese and foreigners. A large relief expedition consisting of British, French, Japanese, Russian, German and American troops relieved the besieged quarter and occupied Beijing on 14 August 1900. The relief forces retained possession of the city, looking for and punishing anti-foreign actions, until a peace treaty was signed on 7 September 1901.

▷ ▶ p. 90

1900
THE FIRST BOER WAR

On 10 January 1900, General Lord Roberts was sent to replace Sir Redvers Buller as commander-in-chief of British forces in South Africa. Early in February, Roberts ordered General French north to relieve the city of Kimberley, and this was attained four days later. Simultaneously, Roberts marched from Cape Colony into the Orange Free State. Attacked by the Afrikaaner general Piet Cronje on 27 February, Roberts forced the surrender of Cronje and his troops (4,000 men). On 13 March, Roberts entered Bloemfontein, capital of the Orange Free State. Two months later, the besieged town of Mafeking, defended by troops under the command of Robert Baden-Powell, was relieved. Roberts captured Johannesburg on 31 May, and Pretoria, the capital of the South African Republic, on 5 June.

1901
AFTER PRETORIA

No sooner had the British begun to reduce the number of troops in South Africa than Boer leaders – among them such soldiers and future statesmen as Louis Botha and Jan Christian Smuts – launched extensive and well-planned guerrilla warfare against the occupying British troops. The fighting continued for the next year and was only finally quelled through the severe tactics of the new British commander-in-chief, Lord

▼ *Lord Kitchener, commander-in-chief of British forces in South Africa during the Boer War.*

Kitchener. He exhausted the Boers by devastating the Afrikaaner farms that sustained and sheltered the guerrillas, placing black African and Afrikaaner women and children in concentration camps and building a strategic chain of formidable iron blockhouses for his troops. British losses totalled about 28,000 men. Afrikaaner losses were about 4,000 men, plus more than 20,000 civilians, who died from disease in concentration camps.

1904
RUSSIA VS JAPAN

This war was the first conflict in modern times in which an Asian power defeated a European country. The war resulted from the conflicting ambitions of Russia and Japan to control Manchuria and Korea. Fighting began when the Japanese attacked and bottled up the Russian fleet at Port Arthur after Russia – which had occupied Manchuria during the Boxer Rebellion in China – refused to withdraw its troops. Despite the recent construction of the Trans-Siberian Railroad, the Russians were unable to transport adequate troops and supplies to the east and suffered a series of defeats, including the loss of Port Arthur (January 1905) and the Battle of Mukden (February–March). Russia acknowledged Japanese predominance in Korea and ceded the southern half of Sakhalin.

p. 87 ◀ **Distant Voices** ▶ p. 91

He was a plucky young man, and he died a soldier's death. What on earth could have been better? Many other brave men have also fallen during this war, and with the Prince's fate England has no concern. Perhaps I have insufficient sympathy with foreign nations; I reserve all my deep feeling for Her Majesty's subjects.

Wolseley to his wife, on the death of the French Prince Imperial in a skirmish against the Zulus (1 June 1879)

The Great War

1914–18

T HE FIRST GREAT WAR of the twentieth century began on 4 August 1914. It eventually grew into a worldwide conflict that has since become a symbol of senseless slaughter. Two of the greatest bloodlettings in world history – the battles of the Somme and Verdun – occurred within months of each other at the height of the war. The western section of the conflict, which took place in Belgium and France, started off as a war of 'grand manoeuvres'. As more troops were poured into an increasingly cramped area,

there eventually came a time when the antagonists could no longer manoeuvre against their enemies in any operational sense. When this occurred, the forces involved began entrenching in the face of increasingly lethal concentrations of firepower.

THE FIRST WORLD WAR: EASTERN & WESTERN FRONTS, 1914–18

Central Powers	Neutral Countries	Western Front trench line November 1914
Allied Nations	Maximum advances of Central Powers	Russian advances by end of 1914
Areas occupied by Central Powers		Eastern Front December 1917
		Armistice Line November 1918

In 1914, the wealthy and competitive European empires embarked on a costly war. It was marked by the attrition of trench warfare, slow-moving infantry and the advent of tanks and gas. The map shows how the Central Powers were eventually driven back from their front lines of maximum advance to the Brest-Litovsk Armistice Line on the Eastern Front in December 1917, and the Armistice Line on the Western Front on 11 November 1918.

⤳ ▶ p. 98

1914
THE SCHLIEFFEN PLAN

On 4 August 1914, German troops from seven armies swept into Luxembourg and Belgium as part of their 'Schlieffen plan', which proposed a sweeping move into Belgium and down to Paris from the north. The German armies were finally stopped at the River Marne when General von Kluck, moving to pursue the French, tried to sweep behind the French corps, exposing his own right flank in the process. French general Gallieni quickly assembled an ad-hoc force and, co-ordinating with General Joffre, assaulted Kluck's exposed flank. In the process of defending himself, Kluck redirected his corps westwards, allowing yet another dangerous gap to open between him and Bulow. The Germans withdrew back across the Marne, where they resisted attempts by the French to dislodge them.

1914
THE WAR IN THE EAST

The eastern war began on 17 August 1914, when the Russians invaded eastern Prussia in a full-scale offensive. Two days later, General Alexander Samsonov's Second Army attacked around the right flank of the German Eighth Army commanded by General Friedrich von Prittwitz. Prittwitz proposed abandoning most of East Prussia, including Königsberg. He was immediately replaced by Field Marshall Paul von Hindenburg and his new chief-of-staff, Erich von Ludendorff. By 27 August they had fallen on Samsonov's army, taking it in both flanks in a near-perfect double envelopment. The Battle of Tannenberg was over by 30 August when Samsonov's command disintegrated at a cost of 92,000 captives. By 5 September, German forces under General August Mackensen had defeated General Rennenkampf at the Battle of Masurian Lakes, where the Russians suffered over 100,000 casualties.

● ▶ p. 95

1914
GAS

In November 1914, the Germans attacked at Ypres and conducted a close-order frontal

🔲 TECHNOLOGY   ☆ GENERALS   ⇨ STRATEGY   ● WEAPONS   ◎ ARMIES

▲ *The Battle of the Somme, one of the greatest Allied offensives in the First World War.*

assault on prepared British trenches, losing hundreds of men and officers without having secured an inch of ground. In February 1915, they began another series of offensives in the Soissons. The British then attacked in the Artois region and broke through at Neuve Chapelle, but were unable to exploit the advantage. The Germans quickly closed the gap and, in April, successfully used gas for the first time on the western front at Ypres. These assaults also failed at a cost of 300,000 Allied casualties. The French then attempted another campaign against the German lines in the Champagne region, preceded by a lengthy artillery bombardment. After 250,000 casualties, the French commander Joffre called off the assaults.

1916
THE VERDUN BULGE
In 1916, the German commander-in-chief, Erich von Falkenhayn, put into action his idea for 'bleeding white' the French army. His plan was to attack a point which the French would not allow to fall and ensure that the point was well covered by artillery. His target was the 'Verdun Bulge', which his troops first assaulted on 21 February, after the most concentrated bombardment of the war. The campaign carried on for four terrible months, during which 300,000 Germans and 460,000 French were killed or wounded. This series of battles, one of the most horrific slaughters in history until this time, only marginally achieved the original German goals. The French were indeed 'bled white', but not as severely as hoped.

1916
THE BRUSILOV OFFENSIVE
The next major offensive in the east was undertaken by the Russian general Alexei Brusilov. His four armies, the seventh, eighth, ninth and eleventh, were poised along the Galician border facing the Austrian army. In June 1916, the Russians attacked, penetrating deep into Austrian positions and taking 13,000 prisoners on the first day. The entire Austro-Hungarian empire was in danger of falling, but the

p. 85 ◀ **Triumphs & Tragedies** ▶ p. 95

1916
THE SOMME OFFENSIVE
On 1 July 1916, the British and French launched the Somme offensive. This brought them face to face with some of the heaviest German fortifications on the entire western front. The British general Douglas Haig resisted the idea, but French commander Joffre won the argument and the campaign began. The Somme saw the first use of tanks in warfare, and was preceded by the war's greatest artillery barrage. Despite these advantages, the general slaughter of Allied troops that occurred is infamous, with the British suffering 65,000 casualties on the first day alone. When the October rains finally put an end to the prolonged carnage, 400,000 British, 200,000 French and 450,000 Germans had become casualties. The Allies captured only a few miles of ground, but the Germans responded by withdrawing to their new Hindenburg Line in early 1917.

Germans counter-attacked, knocking Romania out of the war. Germany and Austria gained control of vast coal and wheat fields, although they also added over 200 miles of front to their lines. In September, the offensive was continued, completing the conquest of Galicia. However, Russia's army had suffered almost one million casualties and discipline was breaking down. The country was moving toward revolution.

1918
THE YANKS ARE COMING
The British attacked at Arras on 9 April, suffering 84,000 casualties, but achieved no breakthrough. Before this battle had ended, the new French commander, Nivelle, launched his own offensive from Soissons to Rheims. This offensive ground to a halt on its first day, and by the time the assault was over the French had suffered 220,000 casualties. Many French soldiers mutinied. In November, the British launched an attack toward Cambrai using hundreds of tanks. All three German lines were broken, but

within days, German counter-attacks drove the British back to their starting positions. The last great German offensive was launched on 21 March 1918, with a 6,000-gun barrage and a heavy gas attack. The Allies suffered 350,000 casualties, but more troops were rushed in from across the Channel, and American troops began arriving for the first time.

1918
THE FINAL OFFENSIVES
By late June 1918, German strength on the western front fell below that of the Allies, and the final Allied assault was not long in coming. The first attacks were made in July by the French, west of Rheims, followed by a British offensive at Amiens and a general offensive toward the Hindenburg line. The Americans attacked the St Mihiel salient south of Verdun. The Germans were now steadily pulling back and even though the Allies continued to suffer tremendous losses, they were inspired by the continued German retreat. The only German to keep fighting after the armistice was Field Marshal Paul von Lettow-Vorbeck in East Africa, who was beginning his tiny invasion of Rhodesia. He surrendered on 23 November, upon hearing of the armistice.

p. 89 ◀ **Distant Voices** ▶ p. 93

At this hour of England's grave peril and desperate need I do hereby pledge myself most solemnly in the name of my King and Country to persuade every man I know to offer his services to the country, and I also pledge myself never to be seen in public with any man who, being in every way fit and free for service, has refused to respond to his country's call.

The Active Service League (1915)

The Beginnings of the Next War
1930–41

THE PRINCIPLE OF TOTAL WAR was the dominating feature of conflict in the middle of the twentieth century. The half-hearted peace and resolution of the First World War had done little to diffuse the smouldering discontent and rivalry in Europe. Elsewhere, the Japanese had succeeded in catching up with the West in military and technological terms, but were still preoccupied with their feudal past. This would be a dangerous mixture for both the Japanese and their foes during the Second World War. As Germany transformed into the Nazi state during the 1930s, Hitler galvanised his nation into a war machine. All the signals were there, and the Spanish Civil War was just the prelude to global blood-letting.

▲ *Spanish troops during the Civil War of 1936.*

1936
UNREST IN SPAIN
During its first months, the Spanish Civil War acquired international political and ideological significance. Less than a year from the conflict's onset, fascist Italy sent about 70,000 ground troops to aid the nationalists, and Nazi Germany provided planes, pilots, arms and technicians. The

USSR sent weapons and advisors to the republicans; the Comintern organised thousands of liberals and leftists from 53 foreign countries into Volunteer International Brigades formed to fight fascism. Both sides engaged in mass arrests and executions in the name of anti-communism or anti-fascism. Serving as a battle-ground for conflicting nations and as a proving-ground for new weapons, the civil war later became known as a dress rehearsal for the Second World War.

1939
BLITZKRIEG
On the morning of 1 September 1939, waves of German bombers attacked Poland, hit the railways and hopelessly snarled Polish mobilisation. In four more days, two army groups, one on the north out of East Prussia, the other on the south out of Silesia, had broken through on relatively narrow fronts and were sending armoured spearheads on fast drives toward Warsaw and Brêst. This was *blitzkrieg* ('lightning war'); the use of armour, air power and mobile infantry in a pincer movement to encircle the enemy. On 17 September, a second, deeper encirclement closed 160 km (100 miles) east, near Brêst Litovsk. By 20 September, practically the whole country was in German or Soviet hands and only isolated pockets continued to resist until 6 October.

1940
THE FALL OF FRANCE
On 20 May a panzer group took Abbeville at the mouth of the Somme River and began to push north along the coast; it covered 400 km (250 miles) in 11 days. By 26 May, the British and French were pushed into a narrow beachhead around Dunkirk. Destroyers and smaller craft rescued 338,226 men from Dunkirk. On 5 June the Germans launched a new assault against France. Italy declared war on France and Britain on 10 June. The Maginot line, which only extended to the Belgian border, was intact, but the French commander, General Maxime Weygand, had no troops to screen it, or Paris on the north and west. France capitulated and the armistice was signed on 25 June.

▶ p. 95 ### 1940
THE BATTLE OF BRITAIN
Following the fall of France, Hitler hoped that Britain would accept German control of the Continent and seek peace. But Britain shunned the chancellor's overtures of July 1940, and, in August, Hermann Goering's Luftwaffe began an all-out attack on British ports, airfields, and industrial centres and, finally, on London. The goal was to crush British morale and wipe out the RAF in preparation for Operation Sea Lion, an invasion of England. The Battle of Britain was the first great air battle in history. For 57 nights, an average force of 160 bombers attacked London. The outnumbered RAF, employing the effective Spitfire fighter and aided by radar, destroyed 1,733 aircraft while losing 915 fighters.

1940
THE DESERT FOX
Italy managed to overrun British Somaliland, defended only by a small garrison, in August 1940. Mussolini's triumph was short-lived, though, for by the next summer the British had not only recaptured that territory but had driven the Italians from their East African possessions. In September 1940, Mussolini moved a second army of Italians and North African

▲ *German fighter planes during the Second World War.*

wave followed. Eighteen US ships were hit and more than 200 aircraft destroyed or damaged. The attack was, however, a colossal political and psychological blunder, for it mobilised US public opinion against the Japanese and served as the catalyst that brought the United States into the war.

p. 91 ◄ **Distant Voices** ► p. 95

Prime minister: Is that M.O.5?
Voice: Yes.
Prime minister: How do you think the operations are going in Syria?
Voice: Oh, I think everything is going all right.
Prime minister: What about that turning movement the French are trying to make?
Voice: Oh, that seems to be all right.
Prime minister: Who are you?
Voice: Corporal Jones, Duty Clerk, M.O.5.

Winston Churchill had the habit of calling junior officers in the War Office, as recalled by Sir John Kennedy, Director of Military Operations.

troops across the Libyan border to establish themselves about 100 km (60 miles) inside Egypt. The British struck back in December in a surprise attack that had carried them halfway across Libya by early February 1941. In March 1941, Germany's Afrika Korps, commanded by General Erwin Rommel, arrived at Tripoli. By mid-April, Rommel had reconquered all of Libya except Tobruk; his exploits earned him the nickname 'the Desert Fox'.

1941
BATTLE OF THE ATLANTIC

► p. 94

By the spring of 1941 the number of supply ships sunk by German U-boats reached such a critical level that Churchill called the attacks the Battle of the Atlantic. Still the British managed to keep the sea-lanes open for desperately needed supplies from the United States. In the midst of the havoc wrought upon Britain's trade, the country won an important morale-boosting victory. On 24 May 1941, the German battleship Bismarck, the pride of Hitler's navy, sank the British battle cruiser Hood off Greenland. On 27 May, however, the Bismarck was intercepted by a British task force while returning home, and was sent to the bottom of the sea. To a large extent, this ended the threat of the German surface fleet, although the U-boats remained.

1941
OPERATION BARBAROSSA

Originally scheduled for mid-May 1941, the invasion of the USSR, called Operation Barbarossa, was delayed until 22 June by Hitler's campaign in the Balkans. Launching a blitzkrieg, with 121 divisions on a 3,200-km (2,000-mile) front from the Baltic to the Black Sea, the Germans employed a three-pronged assault. In the north they moved on Leningrad via the Baltic states. Forces moving east to Smolensk approached Moscow, the target of the German centre. In the south the invaders marched towards the Ukraine and Kiev, where they planned to turn south to the Crimea and cross the Don to the Caucasus and to Stalingrad on the Volga. A smaller force of Romanians and Germans attacked in the extreme south.

1941
PEARL HARBOR

In late 1941 more than 75 US warships were based at this 'Gibraltar of the Pacific'. All US aircraft carriers were elsewhere. On 26 November a Japanese task force departed in secret from the Kuril Islands. Observing radio silence, it reached a launching point on 7 December. At 7.50 a.m., the first wave of Japanese planes struck Pearl Harbor, bombarding airfields and battleships moored at the concrete quays. A second

▲ *The Japanese bombing of the US naval base at Pearl Harbor.*

The World at War
1942–45

TO ARRANGE THE UNION of the two Allied operations in North Africa and to plan subsequent strategy, Roosevelt and Churchill met at the Casablanca Conference (January 1943) on the Moroccan coast. Stalin, who claimed that he had been promised a European second front by the spring of 1942, refused to attend. The conferees agreed that a cross-Channel invasion of Europe was still out of the question. Instead, they decided to follow the North African union operation with an invasion of Sicily. They concurred that, pending a second front, strategic bombing of German industry would be intensified. At the conclusion of the conference, Roosevelt announced that Allied policy was to impose 'unconditional surrender' on Germany.

1942
1,000-BOMBER RAID

Aided by rapid production of aircraft in the US, the Allied forces began making major air raids on Germany in 1942. The RAF attacked the cities of the Ruhr Valley – a major centre of German heavy industry – in crippling raids. In May 1942 the first RAF 1,000-bomber raid was directed against the Rhineland city of Cologne, destroying much of the city. In the summer of 1942 the US joined in the operations against Germany. American B-17 Flying Fortresses and B-24 Liberators concentrated on daylight precision bombing of industrial targets, whereas the British struck at night. In the summer of 1943, three-quarters of Hamburg was destroyed in combined raids. Round-the-clock bombing mounted steadily until all Germany was subjected to massive air raids.

1942
BATTLE OF MIDWAY

On the afternoon of 3 June 1942, a patrol plane sighted a Japanese force approaching Midway. The next day 100 Japanese bombers took off from their carriers and headed for Midway. In wait for the invaders was a strong force of American torpedo planes and fighters. The US aircraft launched off the carriers Hornet, Yorktown and Enterprise and sank four Japanese carriers. Within four days Japanese losses, in addition to the four aircraft carriers, included two heavy cruisers and three destroyers badly damaged, and 322 aircraft. The Americans lost the carrier Yorktown, a destroyer and 147 aircraft. Midway remained in American hands, and the Japanese fleet was so severely damaged that Japan's war effort changed from an offensive thrust to a holding operation.

1942
STALINGRAD

Stalingrad was the site of a critical Soviet victory that reversed Germany's advance to the east. The first phase of the battle lasted from 17 July to 18 November 1942, when the German 6th Army under Friedrich von Paulus closed in on the heart of the city, which was being tenaciously defended by General Vasily Chuikov's 62nd Army. On 19 November, Soviet forces under General Georgy Zhukov attacked north and south of the city, encircling the Germans, who finally surrendered on 2 February 1943. Soviet losses numbered 750,000, whereas Germany and its allies lost 850,000. Coupled with the defeat of Rommel at El Alamein in Egypt at the hands of a British army under General Montgomery the month previously, the end of 1942 saw the turning point of the war.

Neutral nations
Allied & Allied-controlled areas Nov. 1942
Axis powers
Axis-controlled areas Nov. 1942
⊗ Major battles

1 D-Day, 6 June 1944
2 Battle of the Bulge, Dec. 1944–Jan. 1945
3 Berlin, May 1945
4 Anzio, Jan.–May 1944
5 Monte Cassino, Jan.–May 1944
6 Warsaw, Aug.–Oct. 1944
7 Kursk, July 1943
8 Minsk, July 1944
9 Moscow, Sept. 1941–Spring 1942
10 Siege of Leningrad, Sept. 1941–Jan. 1944
11 Kasserine Pass, Feb. 1943
12 El Alamein, Oct.–Nov. 1942

THE SECOND WORLD WAR: EUROPEAN THEATRE, 1941–45
Hitler's invasion of Poland in 1939 prompted a British declaration of war. In the spring of 1940, the Nazi military expansion drove north into Scandinavia and west into the Netherlands, Belgium and France. By 1942 the Axis Powers had taken control of a vast area. The map shows the battles that played a decisive role in the reversal of this expansionism.

 TECHNOLOGY   GENERALS ⬑ STRATEGY ● WEAPONS   ARMIES

1943

TANK WARFARE

On the eastern front, the situation had changed slightly in Germany's favour since Stalingrad. They had shortened their lines, while the Soviet troops were stretched over a massive front with a bulge westward around Kursk. On 5 July 1943 the Germans, using their new Tiger and Panther tanks, struck at this Soviet salient. Hitler committed more than 1,000 planes against the Red Army's enormous concentration of troops, artillery pieces and tanks. The encounter developed into one of the largest and most vicious armour battles ever fought. More than 3,000 tanks were engaged on the grasslands. On 12 July 1943, the Soviets moved in fresh tank divisions and the advantage finally swung to the Russians. Manstein, having lost 70,000 men, half his tanks and more than 1,000 planes, was forced to withdraw.

1944

THE BATTLE OF THE BULGE

German resistance stiffened in the last months of 1944. In late September a British airborne division was dropped behind German lines across the Rhine near Arnhem in the Netherlands. Of the 10,000 troops landed, more than 1,000 were killed and 6,400 were taken prisoner. On 16 December 1944, von Rundstedt launched a counter-offensive, known as the Battle of the Bulge, which took the Allies by surprise. In eight days the Germans cut deep into Allied-held territory. US president Eisenhower ordered Patton and his 3rd Army to turn north towards the fighting. Allied air

▲ *The last great push of the Second World War: Allied troops land on the beaches of Normandy on D-Day.*

p. 91 ◀ **Triumphs & Tragedies** ▶ p. 99

1944

D-DAY

On 6 June 1944, waves of Allied troops moved ashore between Cherbourg and Le Havre in history's largest amphibious operation, involving approximately 5,000 ships of all kinds. About 11,000 Allied aircraft operated over the invasion area. More than 150,000 troops disembarked at Normandy on D-Day. The Germans struck back vigorously; for more than a month they resisted while Allied forces built up on the crowded beaches. On 15 August 1944, a fleet of Allied warships appeared off the French Mediterranean coast between Toulon and Cannes. Following a heavy bombardment, they unloaded an army of US and French troops. Speedily taking Marseilles and Nice, the Allies headed northwards along the Rhone River. German troops in western France were now threatened with isolation.

power hit hard at the Germans. In early January 1945 the German thrust was contained. The last great German offensive in the West had failed to terminate the Allied drive to the heartland of Germany.

1945

GERMAN SURRENDER

On 16 April 1945, Zhukov launched his final attack on Berlin. By the end of the

month the Soviets had penetrated to the centre of the city. German soldiers and civilians, fearful of the revenge expected from the Soviets, hastened to surrender to the Americans and the British in the belief that they would receive better treatment from the western Allies. On 25 April 1945, Soviet troops, who had now encircled Berlin, met the Americans at Torgau on the Elbe. While the Soviets were making their final drive on Berlin, Allied troops liberated one concentration camp after another. In April they reached Buchenwald as well as Belsen and Dachau. Hitler committed suicide in his Berlin bunker on 30 April.

1945

THE FALL OF THE RISING SUN

On 6 August 1945, an atomic bomb was dropped on Hiroshima, a Japanese city with a population of about 300,000. At least 78,000 people were killed outright, 10,000 were never found, and more than 70,000 were injured. Almost two-thirds of the city was destroyed. On 9 August, the day after the USSR declared war on Japan, an atomic bomb was dropped on Nagasaki, a city whose population numbered 250,000. About 40,000 people were killed, and about the same number were injured. On 10 August, Japan sued for peace on the condition that the emperor's position as sovereign ruler be maintained. At the behest of the emperor, an imperial conference on 14 August accepted the Allied terms.

p. 93 ◀ **Distant Voices** ▶ p. 97

If you don't understand what 'nuts' means, in plain English it is the same as 'go to hell'. I will tell you something else – if you continue to attack, we will kill every goddamn German that tries to break into this city.

Colonel Joseph H. Harper (327th US Infantry Division), to the German commander outside Bastogne (December 1944).

Korea and Vietnam
1945–76

DURING THE KOREAN WAR (1950–53), a US-dominated coalition came to the aid of South Korea after an invasion by North Korea, which was aided by the USSR and China; the war ended in a military stalemate and the restoration of the political status quo. As the Cold War heated up, it brought the United States into a military confrontation with Communist forces in Korea. In the Vietnam War, which lasted from the mid-1950s until 1975, the United States and the southern-based Republic of Vietnam (RVN) opposed the southern-based revolutionary movement known as the Viet Cong and its sponsor, the Communist Democratic Republic of Vietnam. The war was the second of two major conflicts that spread throughout Indochina, with Vietnam as its focal point.

1945
THE ORIGINS OF THE VIETNAM WAR

French Indochina, which included Vietnam, Cambodia (Kampuchea) and Laos, was occupied by Japanese forces during the Second World War. Communist leader Ho Chi Minh and his Viet declared Vietnam an independent republic in 1945. The United States supported the restoration of French rule. When fighting erupted between France and the Viet Minh in 1947, the Americans aided the French and backed Emperor Bao Dai. By 1953 they were providing 80 per cent of the cost of France's war effort. In 1954 the French, hoping to win a decisive victory, lured the Viet Minh into a set-piece battle at Dien Bien Phu, but were in turn besieged there. Defeat at Dien Bien Phu caused France to decide to withdraw from Indochina.

1950
INVASION

The Korean War began between North Korea (supported by China) and South Korea, aided by the United Nations (although the bulk of the troops were provided by the US). North Korean forces invaded the South on 25 June 1950. The Security Council of the United Nations – owing to a walk-out by the USSR – voted to oppose them. By September 1950 the

▲ *A memorial to those who died during the Korean War.*

North Koreans had overrun most of the South, with the UN forces holding a small area, the Pusan perimeter, in the south-east. The course of the war changed after the surprise landing of US troops later the same month at Inchon, on South Korea's north-west coast. This dramatic counter-attack caught the North Koreans off-guard and it was their turn to retreat in confusion.

1950
DOUGLAS MACARTHUR

After the Inchon landings, the United Nations forces, led by General Douglas MacArthur, fought their way through North Korea to the Chinese border in little over a month. On 25 October 1950, Chinese troops attacked across the Yalu river, driving the UN forces below the 38th Parallel. Truce talks began in July 1951 and the war ended two years later, with the restoration of the original boundary on the 38th Parallel. The armistice was signed with North Korea; South Korea did not participate. MacArthur had made his reputation in the Second World War as a commander in the Pacific Theatre. After his evacuation of the Philippines, he had vowed that he would return to liberate the country. True to his word, he achieved this and was present at the formal capitulation of the Japanese armed forces in 1945.

1954
GENEVA AND BEYOND

Following the Geneva agreement of 1954, there were five years of relative calm until, in 1959 relations between North and South Vietnam again became critical. The Ngo Dinh Diem regime in Saigon tried to eliminate the remaining Communists in the South, and the Communist government of Ho Chi Minh in Hanoi decided to assist a new rebellion south of the 17th Parallel. By the end of 1960, the anti-Diem forces in the South had formed a national liberation front under the leadership of the southern Communists and during 1961 Diem, who had depended on US aid since 1954, sought additional protection. When Kennedy died in 1963, there were about 16,700 US troops in South Vietnam, but the situation was still far from under control.

1964
TONKIN GULF INCIDENT

After the Tonkin Gulf Incident in August 1964, in which the US navy claimed that two of its ships were attacked by North Vietnamese patrol boats, US Congress passed a resolution to take unlimited action

to resolve the crisis in South-east Asia. An attack on a US base at Pleiku in February 1965 was used as the justification for starting air attacks on the North; these were to be a daily feature of the war until 1968. The US began sending in combat troops to Vietnam in April 1965, increasing steadily until March 1968. The political crisis in Saigon was eased with the emergence of Nguyen Cao Ky as prime minister (1965–67), the establishment of a new constitution 1966 and the election of Nguyen Van Thieu as president in 1967.

1968
THE TET OFFENSIVE

US resolve was seriously shaken in February 1968 by the Tet Offensive, in which the communist Viet Cong guerrillas initiated major battles in Hue, Saigon and other towns. A crisis was reached in March 1968 when the US commander General Westmoreland asked for another 200,000 troops to go to Vietnam in addition to the 550,000 already there. By this time, there were also Koreans and Australians in Vietnam plus the 400,000 South Vietnamese under arms. Faced with a serious monetary crisis at precisely the same time, President Johnson decided against

sending any more troops to Vietnam, and announced a limitation of bombing raids on the North. Before the end of 1968 the bombing had been halted completely and peace talks had opened in Paris.

1969
CAMBODIA

The war continued throughout 1969–71 and spread across the region. The US brought Cambodia into the war, securing the removal of Sihanouk's neutral regime in Phnom Penh. Heavy bombing of Cambodia drew that country into the conflict and ultimately resulted in the Khmer Rouge government. Anxious to break the stalemate, North Vietnam launched a new and much heavier offensive against the South Vietnamese army in the Quang Tri province and in the region of An Loc (north of Saigon) in spring 1972. There were now fewer than 100,000 US troops in Vietnam, so the Americans responded with intense bombing of the north, the mining of Haiphong harbour and unlimited air support for South Vietnamese ground troops.

▼ *A US soldier in Saigon in 1972.*

▲ *Soldiers in Pleiku, South Vietnam, where an attack on the US base initiated retaliatory action in the North.*

1975
THE FALL OF SAIGON

Contacts between Hanoi and Washington during 1972 led eventually to the signing of the Paris Treaty in January 1973. US forces finally left South Vietnam in March 1973, and for two years the South Vietnamese government of Nguyen Van Thieu sought to continue the US policy of pacification. But the Viet Cong provisional revolutionary government of South Vietnam was making substantial political gains in the countryside and in late 1974 North Vietnam breached the cease-fire with a final offensive against the South. By March 1975 South Vietnamese morale had collapsed and in April the communist forces took Saigon with only a limited amount of fighting. The war was over and Vietnam was reunited as the Socialist Republic of Vietnam in July 1976.

p. 95 ◀ **Distant Voices** ▶ p. 99

Help us! Parachute us at least some ammunition so that we can die fighting instead of being slaughtered like animals.

Radio message from French soldiers trapped in North Vietnam (1954)

War in Peace
1965–99

THE TWO WORLD WARS in the twentieth century left behind them a trail of unresolved local and civil wars that took time to settle. Equally, the collapse or retreat of old empires such as France, Britain and the Soviet Union triggered off a series of wars and disputes that destabilised regions for many years. Economic wars were increasingly fought, notably over oil, and various would-be dictators attempted to seize territories and bring neighbours under their control. Despite the threat of a Third World War being averted, the later years of the twentieth century saw just as many conflicts and wars as previous centuries. Despite immense leaps in war technology, brutal and violent conflicts still raged around the world, from the Gulf to Africa and from the former Yugoslavia to South America.

1965
THE INDO-PAKISTAN (BANGLADESH) WAR

As a result of border violations, the Pakistanis crossed into Indian territory on 14 August 1965. The Indians rushed troops to seal the Haji Pir pass, leading to a large tank battle on 1 September. Under air cover, the Indians counter-attacked and crossed the border in the Lahore sector of western Pakistan, making thrusts towards Sialkot and the Sind. The ensuing tank battles were the biggest seen since the Second World War. On 22 September, after seven weeks of fighting, more than 20,000 were killed or wounded, nearly 600 tanks destroyed and more than 100 aircraft shot down. Under the terms of the Tashkent Agreement (1966), the two sides agreed to settle their disputes by peaceful means.

1967
THE SIX-DAY WAR

The war grew out of the general Arab-Israeli struggle; Egypt subsequently blockaded the Gulf of Aqaba, a vital transportation route to Israeli shipping – a move that Israel regarded as an act of aggression. Hostilities began on 5 June 1967 with a massive pre-emptive strike by Israel that crippled the Arabs' air capacity. Israeli forces then quickly moved to occupy the Gaza Strip and pushed into the Sinai. At the same time Israelis fought Jordanians in Old Jerusalem and advanced into Syria. By 10 June, when the fighting was halted, Israel controlled the entire Sinai Peninsula and all Jordanian territory west of the River Jordan, as well as the strategic Golan Heights of Syria. The Suez Canal was almost impassable until 1975.

1973
THE YOM KIPPUR WAR

On 6 October 1973, Egypt and Syria, frustrated by Israel's refusal to give up Arab territory, joined to launch a surprise attack on Israeli occupation forces. The Syrians, aided by troops from Jordan and Iraq, initially made some gains in the north, but by 11 October they had been turned back, and the Israelis advanced into Syria. In the south, the Egyptians crossed the Suez Canal and penetrated about 10 km (6.2 miles) into the Israeli-occupied Sinai before they were stalled. On 16 October the Israelis counter-attacked and invaded Egypt itself. A cease-fire took effect on the Syrian front on 22 October and in Egypt two days later. Although militarily won by Israel, Egypt, by the initial performance of its army, managed to turn the war into a psychological victory.

1980
SADDAM HUSSEIN

In 1980 Iraqi president Saddam Hussein invaded Iran, hoping to reverse the 1975 border settlement and perhaps to gain control of the rich, oil-producing Iranian province of Khuzestan. Although Iraqi forces won early successes, Iran rallied, held the invaders, formed new armies and eventually took the offensive. Iran mounted offensives all along the border between the two countries, but especially in the south, where Iran tried to capture Al Basrah, Iraq's main port. Iraq resisted stubbornly; it held back Iranian troops with superior firepower and gas warfare, while the Iraqi air force

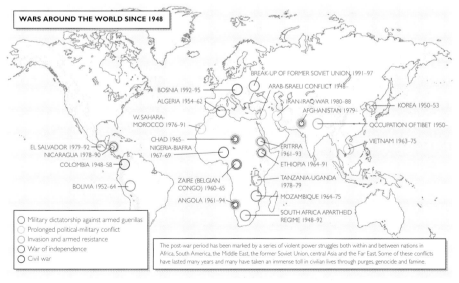

WARS AROUND THE WORLD SINCE 1948

BREAK-UP OF FORMER SOVIET UNION 1991–97
BOSNIA 1992–95
ALGERIA 1954–62
ARAB-ISRAELI CONFLICT 1948–
IRAN-IRAQ WAR 1980–88
AFGHANISTAN 1979–
KOREA 1950–53
W. SAHARA-MOROCCO 1976–91
OCCUPATION OF TIBET 1950–
CHAD 1965–
NIGERIA-BIAFRA 1967–69
ERITRRA 1961–93
VIETNAM 1963–75
EL SALVADOR 1979–92
NICARAGUA 1978–90
ETHIOPIA 1964–91
COLOMBIA 1948–58
ZAIRE (BELGIAN CONGO) 1960–65
TANZANIA-UGANDA 1978–79
BOLIVIA 1952–64
MOZAMBIQUE 1964–75
ANGOLA 1961–94
SOUTH AFRICA APARTHEID REGIME 1948–92

○ Military dictatorship against armed guerillas
○ Prolonged political-military conflict
○ Invasion and armed resistance
○ War of independence
○ Civil war

The post-war period has been marked by a series of violent power struggles both within and between nations in Africa, South America, the Middle East, the former Soviet Union, central Asia and the Far East. Some of these conflicts have lasted many years and many have taken an immense toll in civilian lives through purges, genocide and famine.

 TECHNOLOGY ☆ GENERALS ⌒ STRATEGY ● WEAPONS ◎ ARMIES

attacked Iranian cities and oil installations, as well as tankers approaching or leaving Iranian ports in the nearby Persian Gulf. An agreement for a cease-fire was reached in August 1988 with the help of the United Nations.

1979
THE RUSSIAN INVASION OF AFGHANISTAN

On 25 December 1979, Soviet forces invaded Afghanistan and quickly won control of Kabul. But the government, dependent on Soviet military forces, was unpopular, and the rebellion intensified. During the next few years about three million war refugees fled to Pakistan and 1.5 million fled to Iran. The anti-government guerrilla forces included dozens of factions. They operated from bases around Peshawar, Pakistan and Iran. Weapons and money from the United States, Saudi Arabia, Iran and China sustained them. During the 1980s Soviet forces increasingly bore the brunt of the fighting. By 1986 about 118,000 Soviet troops and 50,000 Afghan

p. 95 ◀ **Triumphs & Tragedies** ▶ p. 109

1990
THE GULF WAR

The Gulf crisis began in August 1990, when Iraq, led by President Saddam Hussein, invaded and annexed Kuwait. Between August and November the United Nations Security Council passed a series of resolutions that culminated in the demand that Iraq withdraw unconditionally from Kuwait by 15 January 1991. By that time, some 500,000 allied ground, air and naval forces – chiefly from the United States, Saudi Arabia, Great Britain, Egypt, Syria and France – were arrayed against an Iraqi army estimated at that time to number 540,000. The land offensive, Desert Storm, was launched and within 100 hours the city of Kuwait had been liberated, and tens of thousands of Iraqi troops had deserted, surrendered or been captured or killed.

government troops were facing roughly 130,000 guerrillas. Estimates of combat fatalities range between 700,000 and 1.3 million people. The Soviets completed their withdrawal in 1989.

1982
THE FALKLANDS WAR

Negotiations to settle the sovereignty dispute between Argentina and Great Britain over the Falkland Islands, began in the mid-1960s at the United Nations. The talks were still in progress in April 1982, when Argentine forces invaded and occupied the islands for 10 weeks in an attempt to settle the issue by force. They were defeated by a British task force and formally surrendered on 14 June. Although numerically superior, the Argentines were out-fought and out-commanded by the British. Casualties were comparatively light, despite the use of modern weaponry. Argentina continued to claim the islands; the British government refused to participate in further negotiations, but the two nations resumed diplomatic relations in 1990.

1991
THE BREAK-UP OF YUGOSLAVIA

The wars in Yugoslavia began in the summer of 1991, after Slovenia and Croatia declared their independence. In July of that year, the Yugoslav People's Army (JNA), which consisted mainly of Serbs, intervened

▲ *Marines training on board ship during the war in the Falklands.*

in Slovenia with the intention of removing the Slovenian government and disarming its defence forces; Slovenian troops repelled the Yugoslav forces after 10 days. The war in Bosnia began in the spring of 1992, when the new government declared independence from Yugoslavia. Serbian nationalists within Bosnia violently occupied more than 60 per cent of Bosnian territory; thousands of Muslims and Croats were murdered or expelled from their homes. The tribunal for massacring civilians during the war indicted more than 50 Bosnians, the majority of whom were Serbs. They included Bosnian Serb leader Radovan Karadzic and military commander Ratko Mladiç.

p. 97 ◀ **Distant Voices** ▶ p. 103

Avigdor stood in a daze looking down on the Valley of Tears. Some 260 Syrian tanks and hundreds of armoured personnel carriers and vehicles lay scattered and abandoned across this narrow battlefield. In the distance he could see the Syrians withdrawing in a haze of smoke and dust, the Israeli artillery following them.

Chaim Hertzog, on the Golan Heights (6 October 1973)

Society and Culture

☞ CUSTOMS

⬛ DOMESTIC LIFE

▣ TECHNOLOGY

✦ CONFLICT

✿ TRADE

⚒ LEISURE

⊕ CAUSES

⛑ HEALTH

⚖ LAW

✳ EMPIRES

EVOLUTION – FROM APE-LIKE CREATURES to humans capable of organisation, complex social relationships and the use of tools and speech – set up the peoples of the world as its dominant species. In time, they left their original location, believed to be in east Africa, and migrated to settle new lands, seeking better conditions and opportunities. By this means, different races and cultures developed, evincing first of all a degree of control over nature not given to other creatures, as well as a variety of customs and traditions, rules of government and social concepts. Some cultures were more favoured than others, by climate, location and eventually the development of modern technology. Some remained devoted to age-old traditions and one, Japan, modern-ised with amazing rapidity in the second half of the nineteenth century, yet retained its ancient cultural identity beneath its advances. The achievements of human society and culture have been considerable, but at times the price paid has been punishing. Wars, rivalries, ideological disputes, conquest, persecution and what was once called 'man's inhumanity to man' have also marked world progress over the centuries. On the brink of the third millennium, this unfortunate process shows little sign of slackening, but peace on Earth remains the ideal.

KEY EVENTS

① 10,000 BC
FARMING AND THE EARLY CIVILISATIONS

The discovery of farming in about 10000 BC was the greatest single breakthrough of prehistoric times. Now, humans could settle permanently in one fertile place and the first civilisations could evolve, giving humans the chance to explore their many talents, for art, architecture and building, and for systems of government and law.

② 2000 BC
ANCIENT GREECE

Ancient Greece was the fount of Western civilisation. The idea of democracy originated there; so did styles of building that are still seen in today's cities, as well as the beginnings of Western philosophies, medicine, theatre, astronomy – and the concept of the Olympic Games as a unifying factor in the world.

③ 753 BC
THE ANCIENT WORLD OF ROME

From humble beginnings, Ancient Rome became an influential republic and afterwards a huge empire. With its near-invincible army, extensive network of roads, its cities and the Pax Romana (Roman peace), Rome was the ancestor of modern Europe.

④ 1750
THE INDUSTRIAL REVOLUTION

The use of machines during the Industrial Revolution (1750–1840) made a quantum leap in the production of textiles and other goods, and prompted the creation of Britain's canals and railways. The human price paid was, however, a grim one: factory and mine workers were the hapless victims of progress.

⑤ 1789
THE FRENCH REVOLUTION

The French Revolution of 1789 was no ordinary uprising against tyranny by the oppressed and dispossessed. Long after it was over, its influence echoed across Europe, introducing new concepts of equality and human rights which liberalised European thought and spelled the end for autocratic rulers and their despotic ways.

⑥ 1885
THE MOTOR CAR

The motor car was pioneered by Gottlieb Daimler in germany in around 1885. At first a plaything for the rich, the car enabled many townsfolk to venture out into the countryside for the first time, giving thousands the mobility that the horse had never been able to offer.

⑦ 1960s
THE 'SWINGING SIXTIES'

Youth and youthfulness became prominent for the first time during the 1960s, with protests against war, traditional morals, and with new styles of music, dress and ways of thought. During this decade, the 'Establishment' and all its works came under heavy fire and afterwards, it was never quite the same again.

⑧ 1999
THE GLOBAL VILLAGE

Today's world is a 'smaller' place due to the rapid communications and technological possibilities that have enabled it to grow into a 'global village'. Through computers, faxes and e-mail, contact can be made more rapidly than ever before, and fast travel has enabled people to explore further than was previously possible.

TIMELINE

100,000 BC		First hunter-gatherers
❶•• **10,000 BC**		Fire made with flint and stone, first farming methods
7000 BC		Rise of the Sumerian civilisation
❷••• **2000 BC**		Flourishing of Ancient Greece
1200 BC		Rise of the Olmec civilisation
1000 BC		Rise of the Mayan civilisation
900 BC		Formation of Assyrian military state
❸••••• **753 BC**		Foundation of Rome
AD 200		Rise of the Zapotec civilisation
AD 350		Rise of the Byzantine Empire
AD 635		Muslims capture Damascus
AD 762		Caliph Al-Mansur founds Baghdad
AD 800		Charlemagne crowned Holy Roman Emperor
1326		Aztecs found city of Tenochtitlán
1348		The Black Death arrives in Europe
1450		Beginning of the Renaissance
1500		Beginnings of the African Slave Trade
1601		Introduction of the Poor Law in Britain
❹•••••••••• **1750**		Industrial Revolution begins
1787		Abolition Society founded
❺••••••••••• **1789**		Storming of the Bastille
1793		Beginning of the French Reign of Terror
1842		Parliament votes against women and children miners
1847		Introduction of the 10-hour working day in Britain
1864		Henry Dunant founds the Red Cross Society
1866		Ku Klux Klan formed
❻•••••••••••••• **1885**		Daimler pioneers the motor car
1890		Decline of the Native American Indian culture
1895		Lumière brothers give first film performance
1903		Pankhurst founds the Women's Social and Political Union
1926		Television is invented
1928		Women win the vote in Britain
1929		Wall Street Crash
1932		President Roosevelt introduces the New Deal
1940		Rationing introduced in Britain
1948		South Africa imposes apartheid laws
1954		Television comes into common usage
❼•••••••••••••• **1960s**		Ban the Bomb! protests
1966		National Organisation for Women formed
1969		First moon landing
❽••••••••••••• **1999**		The Global Village

Human Beginnings
20 million–10,000 BC

ABOUT 20 MILLION YEARS AGO, somewhere in Africa, ape-like creatures – whom anthropologists call Proconsul – came down out of the trees and began to live on the ground, searching for their food on the broad savannahs. In time, they adapted to this new life, began to walk upright, used tools, made fire and eventually began to talk. Now markedly different from their ape-like ancestors, they had become Hominids, the first creatures to be noticeably human-like. There was a long way to go before the Hominids evolved into Homo sapiens sapiens, our own species. However, the way was now open for gradual development towards organised bands of hunter-gatherers, and cave-dwelling families no different in basic essentials from families today.

▲ *A reconstruction of the human ancestor known as Proconsul, who lived around two million years ago.*

20 MILLION BC
EARLY HUMAN SOCIETY

Fifty years ago, the British anthropologist Mary Leakey, working in Kenya, unearthed the two-million-year-old skull of Proconsul. She also found human footprints about 3.75 million years old. As later investigations confirmed, these were the earliest prehistoric remnants of human-like creatures and the beginnings of a trail of evolution which led to Homo erectus ('upright man'), the first true human through Homo sapiens ('intelligent man') and on to Cro-magnon man or Homo sapiens sapiens ('very intelligent man'). Cro-magnon, who lived around 10,000 BC, was clearly a superior creature, with a larger brain, and the ability to live in mutually supportive societies, delegate tasks, use tools and, unlike animals, co-operate with and use nature to his own advantage.

2 MILLION BC
MIGRATIONS

The quest for food and, with that, survival was a human imperative two million years ago and more. Following herds of animals which provided their food and seeking better environments for gathering more so that they could live, led, eventually, to the circumlocution of humans. Remains of Homo sapiens unearthed in Iraq, China, Russia and Germany proved that migrations were already under way around 98,000 BC. Remains of Cro-magnon man have been discovered in south-eastern Europe, the Middle East and France. Thousands of years later, from about 10,000 BC, when humans had turned from hunting and gathering to farming, they had to migrate in order to find richer land and better water supplies.

1.64 MILLION BC
THE COMING OF THE ICE AGE

Human life has always been vulnerable to climate and climatic change, and after about 1.64 million years BC, the coming of an Ice Age severely affected opportunities for hunter-gatherers. The animals began to migrate to escape the cold and the huge glaciers that spread like great freezing tongues across the inhabited Earth. Plants which could not survive at the new lower temperatures died out. Now, if possible, humans had to find places to settle where the hunting, fishing and vegetation were plentiful. With this, humans began to live permanently in caves. Latecomers, finding the best locations occupied, had to move on, and either remain hunter-gatherers, even in these harsher times, or go further afield to seek caves elsewhere.

10,000 BC
THE RACES OF MANKIND

Eventually, the environments that humans encountered far from Africa created a variety of physical features. Those who remained in the hotter parts of Africa, with its strong sunshine, developed black or brown skins and thick, wiry black hair for protection. Further north, where the sun was less strong, human skin was pale or pinky-white, and hair was fair. Humans venturing into Central Asia developed what appeared to be slanted eyes because of the extra fold of skin on the eyelid, which shielded the eyes from the cold, as well as extra body fat and a high body temperature. Racial differences, the cause of so much conflict and hatred in human history, were, therefore, no more than a matter of geography, environment and climate.

10,000 BC
SEEKING FOOD

Human hunter-gatherers were perpetual nomads, always following where their prey led them or digging for roots, shoots and grubs in the earth. What shelters they enjoyed consisted of temporary 'tents' made from brushwood and leaves or, if their surroundings afforded, caves where they

☞ CUSTOMS ⬠ DOMESTIC LIFE ▮ TECHNOLOGY ✦ CONFLICT

could find protection from the wind, rain or cold. The crucial difference between humans and animals, however, showed in the way humans organised ambushes and laid traps for the bison, rhinoceros, antelopes, reindeer, woolly mammoth and other animals they hunted. If they were lucky enough to find a place where hunting and fishing were plentiful, they might stay there for a while, but sooner or later they had to move on, seeking new sources of sustenance.

☞ ▶ p. 106 **10,000 BC**
GETTING TOGETHER FOR THE HUNT
The co-operation and cunning required for successful hunting was well within the scope of intelligent early humans. Deploying these qualities was vital, since animals were larger, stronger and much more dangerous than humans, and humans lacked the physical defences of their prey, such as thick, furry hides, horns or hooves. Distance gave humans some safety, so spears that could be thrown became important. Driving animals into places from which they could not

escape, often by using fire, was another successful method, and one which was also used to tempt large quantities of fish or whales into creeks. The vital factor here was the human ability to work together, even in those far-off days an essential component of human society.

⌂ ▶ p. 110 **10,000 BC**
LIVING IN CAVES
Pulling together for a common cause – the building-block of human society – was a characteristic of the cave-dwelling life from the first. Everyone had to join in if the family was to survive. The men hunted, or spent long hours chipping sharp edges onto flint weapons and tools, or turning animal bones into needles and other implements. The women and children scraped animal hides to make clothes, or tended the fires. The women prepared food, and in some places preserved it in primitive 'refrigerators' made from holes in the ground covered with snow. Children too young to work were put for safety and visibility in shallow holes dug in the ground.

▲ *Humankind's early ancestors eventually came down from the trees and began to forge a hunter-gather lifestyle on the plains.*

▣ ▶ p. 112 **10,000 BC**
PREHISTORIC TECHNOLOGY
The practical demands of prehistoric life led to a range of technological discoveries. Chipping or flaking flints to produce sharp edges was succeeded by a cleverer method – using stones to grind them. Levers and wedges were developed for lifting heavy objects. So was rope, made from the plaited fur or hair of animals. Making fire by striking flint on stone was a much more convenient method than waiting for lightning to set the forests ablaze, and the supply of long-distance weapons for hunting was extended to bows and arrows, boomerangs and slings for throwing large stones. The greatest prehistoric discovery of all was made when the rolling qualities of large round stones inspired the making of the first wheel.

▼ *Classical depiction of a prehistoric cave-dwelling family.*

p. 99 ◀ **Distant Voices** ▶ p. 105

Deep inside prehistoric cave dwellings at Lascaux in France and Altamira in Spain beautiful paintings have been found depicting animals and armed humans. These pictures do not seem to have been intended for decoration. Rather, it is believed, they represented the hopes of hunters for good luck, as if painting images of a hunt would encourage the spirits in which they believed, to bless their endeavours. The painters worked in dank surroundings surrounded by murky semi-darkness illuminated only by the small glow of oil lamps, using coloured earths or vegetable dyes to record their hopes and aspirations. (See page 229.)

Farming and Early Civilisation
10,000–100 BC

FARMING, WHICH PROBABLY developed between 10,000 and 7000 BC, was the advance that changed forever the human way of life. Once they became farmers, humans were able to put behind them their dependence on the vagaries of hunting and gathering or the need to keeping moving on. They were also able to consign to the primitive past the need to live in caves. Growing crops for food meant permanent settlement in one place, usually close to the rivers which provided continuous water supplies. Being settled, they could develop skills other than those required for survival. Farming, in fact, gave the signal for humans to establish cities and develop a totally new lifestyle.

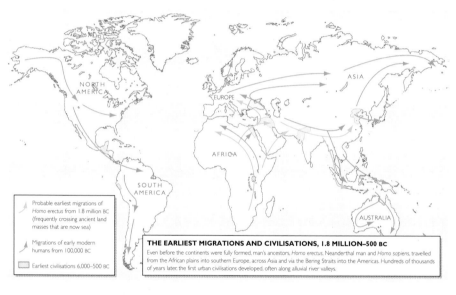

Probable earliest migrations of *Homo erectus* from 1.8 million BC (frequently crossing ancient land masses that are now sea)

Migrations of early modern humans from 100,000 BC

Earliest civilisations 6,000–500 BC

THE EARLIEST MIGRATIONS AND CIVILISATIONS, 1.8 MILLION–500 BC
Even before the continents were fully formed, man's ancestors, *Homo erectus*, Neanderthal man and *Homo sapiens*, travelled from the African plains into southern Europe, across Asia and via the Bering Straits into the Americas. Hundreds of thousands of years later, the first urban civilisations developed, often along alluvial river valleys.

10,000 BC
A NEW WAY OF LIFE

Farming was the first major step that humans took towards loosening the grip nature had over their lives, and using it instead, for their own purposes. Now, nature could be put to work providing for human needs. The hunter-gatherer life did not fade away, of course. Where the hunting was good and the gathering fruitful, there was little point in changing; but it was no longer the only way humans were able to proceed. Not everyone in a society had to be concerned with producing food. Work could now be specialised. While some farmed, hunted and gathered, others were able to

develop technical or artistic skills, create buildings, or concentrate on the work of administration and government. Farming, in other words, freed humans to develop and demonstrate their many talents.

▶ *The pyramids of Egypt are one of the Seven Wonders of the Ancient World.*

7000 BC
SUMERIA, THE FIRST CIVILISATION

Life cannot exist without water, so it is no coincidence that all early civilisations were established close to rivers. The Tigris and Euphrates in Mesopotamia provided particularly fertile ground, and it was here that Sumeria arose – the earliest known civilisation. The land supported sheep, goats and cattle and it grew barley, wheat, vegetables and fruit. This fertility owed much, however, to Sumerian ingenuity. They learned how to control the river, built canals and dykes, devised the plough and constructed terraced ziggurats or temple towers. Sumerians also developed the cuneiform or wedge-shaped writing system, using hard reeds to inscribe letters onto clay tablets. Thousands of years later, these tablets gave archeologists details of Sumerian society, trade, law, monarchy, government and war.

4500 BC
THE INDUS VALLEY

The civilisation in the Indus Valley in north-western India was established in about 4500 BC. Its two chief cities, Mohenjo-Daro and Harappa, possessed streets planned on the grid-system and were provided with drainage systems, baths, temples and splendid private homes and public buildings. A standardised system of weights and measures was used, and it is known to have had trade links with Sumeria. Then, suddenly it seems, the civilisation ceased to exist. Flooding from the River Indus has been blamed; so has an environmental disaster caused by over-use of the local forests. Other suggestions include invasion by the Aryans from central Asia who possibly arrived in about 1500 BC and left behind evidence of fire and slaughter, discovered by archeologists centuries later.

☞ CUSTOMS   🏠 DOMESTIC LIFE   ▣ TECHNOLOGY   ✦ CONFLICT

3000 BC
THE GIFT OF THE NILE

Ancient Egypt has been called 'the gift of the Nile' and without this river, which is surrounded by barren desert, the civilisation might never have existed. Ancient Egypt was characterised by immense luxury and comfort for the rich, but also a well-provided existence for the poor, since the fertile Nile saw to it that there was plenty of food for everyone. The Egyptian pharaohs, regarded as gods, were mummified after death and buried with all their possessions, providing a veritable treasure trove of gold, jewels and ornaments for archeologists to discover. Slaves or prisoners, however, toiled to build pyramids, canals, palaces, temples and other public works, some of which, like the Pyramids of Giza or the Sphinx, survive to this day.

1900 BC
BABYLON

Babylon was one of the most famous and most powerful cities of ancient times. In about 1900 BC, the rule of its warrior king, Hammurabi (c. 1792–1750 BC), extended over almost all of Mesopotamia. Lying on the eastern Bank of the Euphrates, the city was connected to the western bank by bridges made of burnt brick. It contained magnificent palaces and temples and a stone- and brick-paved 'procession' street about 0.8 km (0.5 miles) long. The street, possibly intended for military displays, ran beneath the Ishtar gate, which was decorated with 575 dragons and bulls. Brick lions lined the procession street to add to the daunting display of royal power that Babylon seemed to typify. Inevitably, Babylon became a popular tourist site in the ancient world.

1600 BC
CIVILISATION IN CHINA

The river that permitted early Chinese civilisation was the Hwang-Ho where, from about 1600 BC, farmers grew millet, barley and rice. The early Chinese, had a particular secret – the secret of making silk; this was later considered so important that the death penalty was imposed for anyone who

revealed it. Fine artistic skills were developed, producing beautiful carved jade and bone, bronzework and pottery. This, though, was a militant civilisation. Chinese soldiers were equipped with bronze weapons and chariots, and the dangerous nature of the Chinese environment was evidenced by the building of walled cities. A vibrant intellectual and spiritual life developed over time, characterised by a pictographic writing system, the invention of a calendar and, even at this early stage, a money economy.

► p. 109 ### 900 BC
THE FIRST MILITARY STATE

The Assyrians, who came on the scene after about 900 BC, were the first people to form a military state. In conquering their extensive empire, the Assyrian armies used mighty siege machines, some made of iron, to batter down walls, and shower opponents with missiles. The Assyrians were not all warlike, though. They took care to preserve the libraries they found in captured cities. Assyrian astronomers made observations of the Moon and recorded them on circular clay discs. The knowledge that the Assyrians amassed was considerable. In 1929, the library of Ashurbanipal, who became king in about 626 BC, was discovered at his capital of Nineveh; it contained over 20,000 clay tablets, inscribed with information on mathematics, botany, chemistry, medicine and history.

► p. 113 ### 100 BC
THE SEVEN WONDERS OF THE ANCIENT WORLD

Tourism is not a modern phenomenon. Tourists travelled the ancient world to visit great cities and impressive monuments, buy souvenirs and return home to enthuse about the wonders they had seen. The most comprehensive 'package' tour took in the Seven Wonders of the Ancient World: the pyramids of Egypt; the 'hanging' gardens of Semiramis at Babylon; the statue of Zeus at Olympia; the temple of Artemis; the Mausoleum at Halicarnassus; the Colossus of Rhodes; and the Pharos, or lighthouse at Alexandria in Egypt. It is doubtful if large

numbers of people could afford the time and expense of visiting all seven, but it seems that tourist guides did a lively trade nevertheless.

▲ *The Chinese produced many artefacts in jade, bronze and ceramics.*

p. 103 ◄ **Distant Voices** ► p. 107

Heaven and Earth are the parents of all creatures, and of all creatures, man is the most highly endowed.... Heaven had to help the inferior people, through the provision of rulers and the provision of teachers.... [Furthermore] the One Man, having offered special sacrifice to Heaven and performed the due services to Earth, leads the multitude to execute the will of Shang Di [the ruling house]. Heaven has regard of the inferior people. What they desire, Heaven will effect. So the Son of Heaven [the king] needs their assistance in cleansing all within the four seas.

From the Proclamation of Wu, Lord of Zhou (1000 BC)

Ancient American Civilisations
1200 BC–AD 1513

IN ABOUT 22000 BC, a land bridge existed between the furthest point of eastern Asia and present-day Alaska. Before the ocean covered it, forming the Bering Strait, Asians came across in small groups over a period of several thousand years, to become possibly the first humans to inhabit America. They spread gradually southward until they had peopled both the northern and southern areas of the continent. In the north they became, and until modern times remained, hunter-gatherers blessed with the paradise of plenty that that part of America afforded. However, south of the Rio Grande, in central and south America, civilisations developed which, although they knew nothing of the wheel, evolved into highly complex, artistic and intellectual societies.

▲ *Huge stone head depicting an Olmec god.*

1200 BC
THE FIRST AMERICAN CIVILISATION

The earliest of the ancient American civilisations – that of the Olmecs – grew up around the Gulf of Mexico in about 1200 BC. The most impressive, even daunting, traces the Olmecs left behind were giant heads carved from the basalt that was common in this actively volcanic region. These heads were probably representations of Olmec rulers, and some of them were as

much as 3 m (10 ft) high and up to 14 tonnes (13.8 tons) in weight. Archeological evidence has also been found of some remarkable Olmec talents; they used a form of picture writing and were skilled mathematicians, devising a 'dot and bar' system of arithmetic. The dot represented the figure one, the bar represented five, and a shell represented zero. It was possible for the Olmecs to handle quite complicated calculations using only these three symbols.

1000 BC
THE MAYAS

The Mayas of Yucatán in southern Mexico and neighbouring Guatemala, whose civilisation probably dates back to 1000 BC, were remarkably clever people. Mayan astronomers knew how to predict eclipses of the Sun and to chart the orbit of Venus. Mayan sculptors created beautiful statues and carvings, and their architects built cities such as Tikal, Chichen Itza and Uxmal. These contained pyramid-shaped buildings with steep staircases leading up the sides to the temples at the top, and here there were elaborate carvings and ornamentation. The fate of this brilliant civilisation was a tragic one, however. By about AD 850, most of their cities were deserted and some 50 years later, their civilisation collapsed, maybe through epidemic disease but more possibly through invasion and war.

700 BC
CIVILISATIONS OF THE ANDES

Despite the rigours of high altitude and rugged terrain, the first Americans found ways to live and thrive in the Andes Mountains, establishing first the empire of Chavin (700–200 BC). Chavin left behind the oldest of all Andean buildings – castles, fortresses and temples – as well as ceramics, textiles and objects made of gold. Tihuanaco (AD 400–1000) stood on the southern shore of Lake Titicaca, 3,658 m (12,000 ft) up in the Andes. Here, archaeologists have found a huge 'Gate of the Sun', cut from a single stone, as well as large warlike statues. The empire of Chimu (AD 1000–1466), also centred on Lake Titicaca, contained 10 large walled palaces, tombs containing gold and silver objects and many walls covered in bird and snake designs.

☞ ▶ p. 114

AD 200
THE ZAPOTECS OF MEXICO

The Zapotecs, who settled in the Oaxaca Valley of Mexico, close to the Pacific Ocean around AD 200, believed that rocks, trees and jaguars were the incarnation of their ancestors. The Zapotecs also worshipped the rain god Cosijo, and built a great religious centre for him at Mitla. Such centres were a feature of ancient Mexico and one of the most impressive was the Zapotecs' Monte Alban in Oaxaca. Here, archeologists have uncovered burial chambers with beautiful mural paintings. The Zapotecs adopted the Olmec numerical system and used hieroglyphic writing. The Oaxaca region, however, does not seem to have been a very peaceful place, for traces have also been unearthed of extensive fortifications built by the Zapotecs, probably to fend off rival tribes.

AD 600
THE FALL OF TEOTIHUACAN

Teotihuacan, once called 'the metropolis of the gods', was a very old, very venerable Mayan religious centre – the most important in Mesoamerica. Dedicated to Tlaloc, the water god, it contained the huge Pyramids of the Sun and Moon and the temple of Quetzalcoatl, the feathered serpent, decorated with fierce serpent heads jutting out from the walls. In its heyday, in the first six centuries AD, Teotihuacan may have contained almost a million inhabitants – traders, farmers, potters, fresco-painters, scribes and priests. Then, in about AD 600, it was attacked, probably by the savage, warlike Toltecs. Everything that would burn was set ablaze and what would not was destroyed. Another Teotihuacan rose from the rubble, however, and today it is situated 20 miles north of modern Mexico City.

they founded their own capital city of Tollan (Tula). At Tollan, known as the 'city of reeds', the Toltecs built temples with roofs supported by giant statues. They created massive sculptures of warriors and decorated their pyramids with carvings of Quetzalcoatl. Quetzalcoatl, it appears, was the real-life Ce Acatl Topiltzin, the founder of Tollan. In AD 999, however, Topiltzin was forced into exile and fled east across the Atlantic. A legend arose that one day Quetzalcoatl would return, punish his enemies and reclaim his kingdom.

▲ *Native slaves building Mexico City on the ruins of the Aztec city of Tenochtitlán*

1325
THE AZTECS

The early Aztecs, who eventually settled in Mexico, hired themselves out as mercenaries, but often provoked disgust with their savage habits. These included cutting off the ears of their enemies as proof of their success in battle, and human sacrifice. Spurned by other native Americans, they wandered the Valley of Mexico until, in 1325, they reached Lake Texcoco. Here, they built the magnificent city of Tenochtitlán, with causeways connecting it to the shore, dykes to prevent flooding and *chinampas*, or floating garden islands. After 1440, these one-time pariahs conquered a vast empire in Mexico and from their 12 million subjects exacted heavy tribute – gold, silver, feathers – and human sacrifices.

1513
THE INCA EMPIRE OF TAHUANTINSUYU

The Sapa Inca ('Supreme Lord') of Tahuantinsuyu, stretching 4,828 km (3,000 miles) from Ecuador through Peru to northern Chile, was the most revered ruler in ancient America. As a descendant of Inti, the sun god, the Incas believed he owned everything and everyone on Earth. Whatever they did – cultivating the high mountain terraces, building stepped roads through the Andes, spanning steep ravines with plaited rope bridges – was possible only because the Sapa Inca allowed it. However, this society of

total unquestioning obedience was not without its enterprise. The Incas were able to construct walls made of stones perfectly fitted together, without mortar; and complex records were kept, using nothing more than *quipus* (knotted strings) made of coloured wools. The Inca empire, like so many others, was destroyed in 1513.

▲ *The Toltec god Quetzacoatl.*

✳ ▶ p. 110 **AD 930**
THE TOLTECS – WARRIORS AND CONQUERORS

The Toltecs seem to have lived for war and conquest. They seized power in Yucatán in about AD 930 and occupied Chichen Itza, doubtless with all the ferocity for which they were notorious. Not long afterwards,

p. 105 ◀ **Distant Voices** ▶ p. 109

The Great Montezuma descended from his litter, and ... great caciques [nobles] supported him beneath a marvellously rich canopy of green feathers, decorated with gold work, silver, [and] pearls.... The Great Montezuma was magnificently clad ... and wore sandals ... the soles of which were of gold and upper parts ornamented with precious stones.... Many more lords...walked before the Great Montezuma, sweeping the ground on which he was to tread and laying down cloaks so that his feet should not touch the earth. No one of these lords dared to look him in the face. All kept their eyes lowered most reverently....

The Spanish conquistador Bernal Diaz del Castillo on Montezuma, Great Speaker of the Aztecs of Mexico (1519)

Ancient Greece
3000 BC–AD 200

ANCIENT GREECE was in many ways the crucible of modern Western civilisation. The Greeks were leaders in mathematics, philosophy, medicine and architecture, and were the first to conceive democratic ideas about society and government. Despite its isolated and quarrelsome city states and damaging invasions, from Persia and later, the Romans, ancient Greek ideas survived, spread and remain potent today. Greek architecture can still be seen in today's modern cities. Today's doctors still swear the oath devised by Hippocrates (460–377 BC), the 'founder of medicine'. Every four years, modern athletes contest the Olympic Games, first formulated in Ancient Greece as a means of bringing rivals together; and democratic principles still shape the lives of millions the world over.

3000 BC
THE WONDERS OF KNOSSOS
In 1895, the British archeologist Arthur John Evans (1851–1941) began 40 years of excavation and discovery on the island of Crete. He uncovered what he termed the Minoan civilisation, named after its king, Minos. Dating from about 3000 BC, during the Bronze Age, this civilisation, separate from those of mainland Greece, had previously been unknown. King Minos was considered to be a mythical figure, but Evans' work on the palace complex at Knossos proved otherwise. Here, on a hilltop site, specially chosen for the protection it offered against earthquakes, he discovered buildings up to five storeys high, an elaborate throne room, beautiful friezes, gilded stone roofs, stone conduits and clay water pipes for drainage, staircases constructed on wooden columns and light wells designed to illuminate the interior.

2000 BC
THE HELLENES
Great civilisations always begin humbly and the civilisation of ancient Greece was no exception. Around 2000 BC, the Hellenes – wandering tribes from central Europe – began settling in the mountains and valleys of Greece, living by farming and goat and cattle herding. The terrain was rough, the lifestyle arduous; farmers had a hard time wresting a

living from the unyielding earth. Yet the Hellenes were well suited to these challenges. They were independent-minded, adventurous and not afraid of risk and danger. Physical hardship was something they were prepared to endure and later, they did not shrink from venturing across the sea to trade with other peoples and set up colonies in places as far away as Spain and Byzantium.

 ▶ p. 114 **776 BC**
THE FIRST OLYMPIC GAMES
Every four years the Greek city states, so often at loggerheads, set aside their differences to take part in the Olympic Games. Held on Mount Olympus in east-central Greece, the Games attracted athletes from all over the country, and wars were suspended while they continued. Contestants competed naked in javelin-throwing, boxing, wrestling or chariot-racing. The winners received branches of wild olive. Inaugurated some time before 776 BC, when records began, the Games were held until AD 394, when they were abolished by the Romans – by then the masters of Greece. It was not surprising that these foreign conquerors should take this step, since the basic idea behind the Games was to unify the Greeks, even if only for a short time.

▼ *The great Mount Olympus in Greece, where the original Olympic Games were held.*

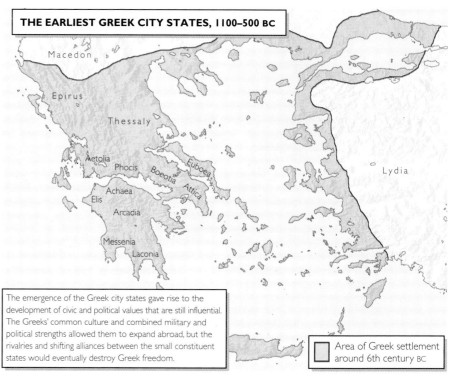

THE EARLIEST GREEK CITY STATES, 1100–500 BC

The emergence of the Greek city states gave rise to the development of civic and political values that are still influential. The Greeks' common culture and combined military and political strengths allowed them to expand abroad, but the rivalries and shifting alliances between the small constituent states would eventually destroy Greek freedom.

Area of Greek settlement around 6th century BC

☞ CUSTOMS ⬢ DOMESTIC LIFE ▣ TECHNOLOGY ✦ CONFLICT

▶ p. 127 **650 BC**

THE CITY STATES
OF ANCIENT GREECE

By around 650 BC, the Hellenic settlements had grown into city states, a natural development when the mountainous terrain isolated communities in their valleys. Just as naturally, these city-states, became tight-knit, individualistic societies which were markedly different from one another. For instance, the city-state of Athens, with its vibrant intellectual life, was a complete contrast to militaristic Sparta. Quarrels and conflict became common, but the Greeks nevertheless had a 'national' sense which was roused when their country was attacked from outside. The states often combined to eject the intruders, as they did in 480 BC when King Xerxes of Persia became their common enemy. The result was a resounding Greek victory, even though at the time, Persia was a great military power.

550 BC
GLITTERING ATHENS

Of all the city states of ancient Greece, which numbered around 30 in all, Athens stood out as the most sophisticated. By the mid-sixth century BC, Athens was a flourishing society, with its lively culture and the fondness the Athenians showed for the comforts of life, including good food. Art, music, poetry, literature and philosophy flourished; craftsmen and artists created beautiful vases, statues and jewellery; Athenian architects designed elegant buildings with fine pillars and decorated walls and roofs. It was here, too, that democracy, taken from *demos*, the Greek word for 'people', first began to show itself, when the Athenian ruler Solon (638–559 BC) gave Athenians the right to make decisions on matters concerning govern-ment and live under a system of law which applied to rich and poor alike.

500s BC
STERN SPARTA

Ancient Sparta rose to its peak as a military state – ruled by warrior kings – during the sixth century BC and the word 'spartan' does

▲ *The Greek physician Hippocrates.*

not mean stern or austere for nothing. Spartans were not without their arts or crafts, but leisure was more often used for hunting or military training, which started at the age of 14. Spartans lived under rigid state control which had no room for the sick or crippled. Weakling infants, in fact, were left on mountain-sides to die, while healthy boys and girls were sent to special schools to toughen them up with training in discipline and physical and mental endurance. The men became full citizens only when they had proved themselves sufficiently hardy and were admitted to the phiditia (army messes) where they spent most of their adult lives.

400s BC
THE ANCIENT GREEKS AT
THE THEATRE

Modern theatre is yet another legacy of ancient Greece and plays written by dramatists such as Aristophanes (448–380 BC) are still performed today. The circular Greek theatres were built in the open air, with the stage, supported by columns known as proskenion, surrounded on three sides by tiers of stone benches for the audience. The proskenion was the predecessor of the proscenium arch on modern theatre stages. Behind it was a building where the actors – all men – changed their costumes or awaited their cues. In order that they could be easily heard, actors wore huge masks which helped 'throw' their voices. These masks were

'comic' or 'tragic' depending on the parts they were playing. Women's parts were played by young boys.

p. 99 ◀ **Triumphs & Tragedies** ▶ p. 117

400 BC–AD 200
THE LEGACY OF ANCIENT GREECE

In about 1450, at the start of the Renaissance in Europe, the ancient Greeks (and ancient Romans who had long ago emulated them) provided the models for a revival of art, archi-tecture and learning. Doctors looked back to the Greek physicians Hippocrates and Galen (c. AD 129–200) and philosophers to Aristotle (384–322 BC). Aristotle's theories on the motion of heavenly bodies were adopted by astronomers; the colonnaded buildings of ancient Greece influenced architects; mathe-maticians consulted the works of Euclid (330–260 BC). Artists and sculptors portrayed Greek mythical characters and other classical subjects. Though the ideas of Galen and Aristotle's theories of astronomy have been superseded, the Renaissance began a long period during which Greek ideas, including their democracy, retained an enduring in-fluence.the hands of just such a state.

p. 107 ◀ **Distant Voices** ▶ p. 111

The regimen I adopt shall be for the benefit of my patients…I will give no deadly drug to any, though it be asked of me, nor will I counsel such, and especially I will not aid a woman to procure abortion. Whatsoever house I enter, there will I go for the benefit of the sick…. Whatsoever things I see or hear concerning the life of men in my attendance on the sick or even apart therefrom, which ought not to be noised abroad, I will keep silence thereon, counting such things to be as sacred secrets.

Extract from the Hippocratic oath, devised by Hippocrates (460–337 BC) and still sworn by doctors today

Ancient Rome
750 BC–AD 476

STARTING OUT IN ABOUT 750 BC as two small farming villages on the hills above the River Tiber in central Italy, Rome grew to become the first great European empire and superpower. The Roman army, on which the empire depended for its security, was the mightiest and most organised force of its time. This not only related to military matters, though. Roman soldiers were also engineers and aqueduct- and road-builders. The Roman way of life, as it developed, offered a good standard of comfort, including central heating, splendid villas and public baths – a standard not known again in Europe until the nineteenth century. Rome fell, as all empires do, but its presence and power lasted longer than any other.

▶ p. 113 **753 BC**
THE BEGINNINGS OF ROME
Traditionally, Rome was founded in 753 BC by the twins Romulus and Remus, or rather by Romulus, who killed his brother in a quarrel. In fact, Rome began much less dramatically. Life was hard and demanding in its original farming villages. The first Romans lived in wood-and-wickerwork huts, plastered with clay and thatched with straw. Like the Spartans, they left sickly infants on the hillsides to die. Later Romans disapproved of this practice. However, their hardy, disciplined, courageous forebears founded a successful society that later grew into the Roman Republic, with its elected consuls and senate, and its plebeians, or ordinary people, who gained the right to take part in government long before their counterparts elsewhere could dream of such things.

▶ p. 116 **600s BC**
FATHER OF THE ROMAN FAMILY
As might be expected of a military power, the social structure of Ancient Rome was hierarchical, with the *paterfamilias* (father) exerting complete power over his family. The *paterfamilias* could demand total obedience from his children; he could sell them into slavery, flog or even kill them. This power extended, too, over the younger siblings of the *paterfamilias*, so that even when adults, with children of their own, they lived their entire lives under his domination. The idea of the *paterfamilias* emerged quite early on in the history of Rome, but this was not power without responsibility. The *paterfamilias* had a duty to educate his family and bring them up as good citizens, worthy of Roman traditions and virtues.

200 BC
THE ROMAN ROADS
From about 200 BC, the cambered Roman roads spanned out from Rome to all parts of the empire. The soldiers chose the best routes, then dug down until they struck the rock or gravel which would form the roadbed. After filling in with rubble, stones and flints, a layer of smaller stones and pebbles was laid on top and covered with a layer of sand and crushed stone. Next, pentagonal stone paving blocks were laid, each cut so precisely that they interlocked. Finally, the blocks were packed with finely-ground gravel for a smooth surface. Apart from the benefit to civilian travellers, the Roman roads enabled the army to move quickly from place to place, a factor vital for a force with an empire to patrol.

✳ ▶ p. 119 **149 BC**
THE ROMAN EMPIRE
The early Romans hated kings and ejected their last tyrannical monarch, Tarquinius Superbus, in 509 BC. Some five centuries later, however, Romans accepted their first emperor, Augustus (63 BC–AD 14), because a strong single individual was needed to cure the anarchy then blighting the Roman Republic. The Roman Empire itself began much earlier, after 149 BC, when the Romans smashed the Carthaginians of northern Africa and took over their territories. In time, the empire stretched from Britannia in the north to the deserts of Saudi Arabia in the south. Within its strongly guarded borders, Pax Romana (the Roman Peace) prevailed, allowing Roman subjects the security to travel and trade – a life of comparative luxury for the rich, and comforts unique in the ancient world.

149 BC
THE ROMAN ARMY
The Roman army lost battles, but it never lost a war. Highly trained, strictly disciplined and innovative, Roman soldiers fought mainly with the *gladius*, or short sword, although they later learned cavalry tactics from some of their defeated enemies. Soldiers lived in stone or wooden barracks in a camp surrounded by strong walls and defensive ditches, all of which they constructed themselves. The soldiers also acted

▼ *Classical frieze depicting a typical Roman family.*

☞ CUSTOMS   ⬠ DOMESTIC LIFE   ▣ TECHNOLOGY   ✦ CONFLICT

▲ *Classical relief carving showing Roman soldiers in battle.*

as smiths, toolmakers, carpenters, stonemasons, engineers and architects. They were even capable of building ships cannibalised from the wreckage of other vessels. Those who survived the 20 years' service of this rough, dangerous life were given about £600 as retirement pay and sometimes a plot of land on which to live.

▶ p. 115

149 BC
LIFE AT RISK IN ANCIENT ROME

Despite public baths, clean water and drainage systems, life in Rome was not all that healthy. The average life expectancy was only about 40, and many never even got that far. Infant mortality was so high that the Romans used to wait a week before naming a child, in case it died. Malaria, influenza, diphtheria, cholera and smallpox were rife and leprosy, the most feared disease of all, a constant danger. Doctors in Rome, who were mainly Greeks, might have been skilled at treating sores or inflammations with poultices, indigestion with peppermint solutions, setting broken bones or performing trepanning to relieve pressure on the brain, but there was little they could do when epidemics struck, killing thousands.

149 BC
EVERYDAY LIFE IN ANCIENT ROME

Not everyone in ancient Rome lived in luxurious villas with private baths, mosaic floors, fountains, beautiful gardens, luxury food and slaves to provide every need. Plebeians lived in overcrowded *insulae* (islands), sprawling multi-storey blocks where apartments were often home to two or more families. The *insulae* were unhealthy and vulnerable to fire or collapse. Rome itself was a very crowded city; many schools, which opened at dawn, were just areas partitioned off from the forum, close to the din that emerged from cobblers, bakeries or wine shops. During leisure hours, gory entertainments were provided in the arena, where gladiators fought to the death to the delight of excited audiences, or chariots, often driven by slaves, sped round the 'circus' at breakneck speeds.

AD 476
THE END OF THE ROMAN EMPIRE

By about AD 400, the Roman army, riddled with corruption and intrigue, could no longer keep invaders at bay. Goths, Visigoths and Vandals eventually swarmed in, Rome was sacked and by about AD 476, its authority had gone. It survived, however, in the eastern Roman – or Byzantine – Empire founded after the overlarge, difficult-to-govern territories were divided in AD 293. Byzantium, a Christian empire, earned a name for military prowess, but was also famed for its skilled sculptors, jewellers, goldsmiths and silversmiths. The Byzantine Empire lasted nearly 1,200 years, but ultimately, in 1453, its beautiful capital, Constantinople, fell to the marauding Ottoman Turks and the civilisation which had begun long ago among the hills of Rome finally ceased to exist.

p. 109 ◀ **Distant Voices** ▶ p. 113

Gentlemen should not soil themselves with means of livelihood which provoke ill will, such as collecting customs dues and money lending. Degrading and vulgar also are the gains of all hired workmen whom we pay for manual labour, and not for their artistic skill, because their wages are the very badge of servitude. All mechanics are occupied in a degrading way, for no workshop can have anything about it worthy of a free man. Least respectable of all are the trades catering for sensual pleasures ... fishmongers, butchers, cooks, poulterers ... fishermen ... perfumers, dancers and variety performers.

Marcus Tullius Cicero (104–34 BC), to his son

The Empire of China
479 BC–AD 1949

CHINESE CIVILISATION is the most ancient of those that survive today; it also has the longest history of violent disruption – rival dynasties continually contested the throne. China was repeatedly unified, then split into separate warring states then unified again. Yet, despite these upheavals, the Chinese developed a sophisticated culture which, at a very early stage, attained high social, intellectual, artistic, philosophical and technological standards. However, although geographically isolated and protected after 214 BC by the Great Wall, China was subject to invasion from aggressive nomads, most notably the Mongols. In the nineteenth century, Western nations humbled and exploited China and in the twentieth century, the country experienced much civil war until a communist dictatorship was imposed in 1949.

▶ p. 116 **479 BC**
PEASANT LIFE IN CHINA

The Chinese peasantry were in a paradoxical position, partly exploited yet partly respected. Though their feudal overlords worked them mercilessly at times, the peasants were regarded as one of the indispensable pillars of Chinese society. The other was the ethical philosophy of Confucius (551–479 BC). Though they received state aid, including technical aid, to produce food, peasant rebellions punctuated several centuries of Chinese history. Peasant life was hard and could be gruelling. Poverty, despite state help, was common and it was said that a Chinese peasant could work all year round and still not earn enough to feed himself and his family. Quite apart from farming, the peasants were duty bound to work on public building projects and do military service as well.

▶ p. 116 **400s BC**
THE INVENTIVE CHINESE

The Chinese were extremely inventive people, displaying an originality which took little or nothing from outside influences. One Chinese invention was the crossbow, a deadly weapon not yet out of date today. Another was paper, an essential for a highly literate society which left minutely detailed records. Printing, also a Chinese invention, was the first mechanised industry in the world. The Chinese learned early on how to irrigate the soil and make silk and had highly developed smelting and metal-working industries. They used paper money, devised a system of weights and measures, established a calendar and discovered the secret of making gunpowder, the oldest known explosive. A further invention was a 'weathercock', an early warning system which detected subterranean seismic disturbances.

214 BC
THE GREAT WALL OF CHINA

In 214 BC, after the Chin dynasty ended nearly two centuries of violent conflict to create the first strong, centralised empire in China in 221 BC, Emperor Shi Luang Ti ordered that great wall, eventually some 2,333 km (1,450 miles) long, be built in the north to keep out aggressive Mongol and Turkish nomads. The 7.6 m (25 ft) high wall, later extended by the Han dynasty (202 BC–AD 220), was made of earth and stone faced with brick, and featured a series of watchtowers. Today, it is Earth's only artificial construction visible from outer space. Though internal Chinese politics remained in flux, this mighty defence line stood for over 1,400 years before the nomads – the much more powerful Mongols – managed to break through.

▼ *The Great Wall of China, ordered by the Chin emperor Shi Luang Ti.*

126 BC
ISOLATIONIST ATTITUDES

The Chinese did not discover other civilisations on Earth until about 126 BC; when they did, their reaction was not one of interest, but of suspicion and dislike. They soon developed a strong dislike of foreigners, or 'foreign devils' together with a stubborn self-sufficiency which even today makes the Chinese spurn outside aid in times of trouble. Despite their many wars, the Chinese were wary of regular standing armies, and had contempt for merchants. In fact, a young man aiming for high office would carefully avoid working in trade in case it ruined his prospects. As Chinese society developed in these inward-looking ways, it became both feudal and hierarchical, with great importance laid on the family and on respect for age.

❀ ▶ p. 122 **AD 618**
TRAVELLERS AND TRADERS IN CHINA

Uncharacteristically for Chinese rulers, the T'ang emperors (AD 618–907) were very receptive to foreign ideas and imports. Subsequently, Arabian, Persian, Korean and Japanese merchants brought spices, which soon found their way into Chinese food, and, as a special delicacy, Persian cakes and sweetmeats. Before long, tales of the gold, jewels and other luxuries in China whetted the appetites of European merchants, for whom spices, vital for preserving meat, were of as much interest as the luxuries. This trade became rich, although Islamic powers blocked the route at times. After the Europeans entered the Indian Ocean in the sixteenth century, sea links from Europe to China developed.

1211
THE MONGOLS

The nomadic Mongols first came to Chinese attention as hit-and-run raiders swooping down to create mayhem, then departing just as suddenly. There was, however, a great deal more to the Mongols, who began as nomads wandering the grassy plains of Mongolia with their sheep, camels, goats and cattle. In time, the Mongols

developed into fierce and skilful warriors, fighting on horseback with a speed and agility that startled their enemies. The Mongols proved so invincible that they created the largest land empire ever known, conquering territory from eastern Europe to the Pacific Ocean. After 1211, when the Mongols broke through the Great Wall, China became part of this empire and the legendary Kublai Khan (1216–94) became the first Yuan emperor of China.

▲ *The legendary Mongol leader Kublai Khan welcoming Marco Polo to his court.*

⊕ ▶ p. 121 **1839–49.**
CHINA HUMBLED AND REVIVED

In 1839–42, the British went to war with China over Chinese reluctance to open its ports to the valuable trade in Indian opium, which the British sought to use as currency for imports such as Chinese porcelain, silk and tea. China, hopelessly outclassed by modern weapons, had to yield Hong Kong and open five 'treaty' ports. Another Opium War, in 1860, wrested more concessions from the Chinese emperor who had to allow the British, French and other foreigners to create enclaves on Chinese territory, where they were immune from Chinese law. Later, wiping out this humiliation became a strong motive for the Communist Mao Zedong (1903–76), who became ruler of China in 1949 and made it a power in the world once again.

1899
REDISCOVERING THE SILK ROAD

The ancient Silk Road, the route cross the Gobi Desert travelled by caravans carrying silk from China to Europe, fell into disuse and decay once the sea route to Asia was found. In 1899 Aurel Stein (1862–1943), a Hungarian-born British archeologist, set out to rediscover the Road and with it an ancient, but lost, Indian Buddhist civilisation, dating from around the second century AD, whose cities once spanned its immense length. Aurel Stein's quest proved to be his life's work. He travelled some 40,225 km (25,000 miles) across central Asia, usually on foot and accompanied by his pet fox-terrier, and uncovered several tombs, temples and their treasures beneath the sand covering the Silk Road. Aurel Stein was still exploring at the age of 80, when he died in Afghanistan.

p. 111 ◀ **Distant Voices** ▶ p. 115

When the people are well off, they will be content with their villages and value their homes ... respect their superiors and be fearful of committing crimes. When they are respectful towards superiors and fearful of committing crimes, they are easy to govern. When people are poor, they cause trouble in the countryside.... They will dare to show disrespect to superiors and break laws. When they show disrespect to superiors and break laws, they are difficult to govern. Therefore those skilled in ruling will first enrich the people.

Guan Zhong (d. 645 BC), chief minister to Huan, Duke of Qi, on government

▼ *The Chinese and the British meet after the Opium Wars between the two nations.*

The World of Islam
AD 622–1653

HISTORIANS OFTEN TALK of the Muslims 'bursting' out of Arabia, on spreading their Islamic faith, which the Prophet Muhammad founded in AD 622. It is certainly true that Islam spread with amazing rapidity, gaining an empire which, by AD 750, stretched from the borders of Afghanistan in the east, to Spain in the west. Islam, however, was not only a religion, but a distinctive culture with a way of life and social rules of its own. Beautiful works of art, decoration and architecture were created as Islam required – without the use of images. In mathematics, medicine, navigation and map-making, Muslim civilisation was far in advance of contemporary Europe.

☞ ▶ p. 125 **AD 622**
WOMEN IN ISLAM

The position of women in Islam has long been misunderstood, especially in the West. Muhammad himself told his followers that women were the equals of men, and that they should profit just as much from advantages such as education. At the same time, the conditions of Muslim life, especially in the desert, required that women be protected. Protection, in fact, was the idea behind the wearing of veils by women and, eventually, their seclusion in harems where eunuchs were set to guard them. The idea was to keep women away from undesirable men. Husbands were fiercely jealous of their wives' honour and wished to reserve them strictly for themselves, which included being the only ones allowed to see their faces.

▼ *Muslim women are still required today to cover their faces; this was originally intended to protect them from the harsh climate.*

AD 622
THE BEDOUINS OF ISLAM

The fierce, warlike, energetic desert Bedouins were among the earliest converts and missionaries of Islam. The rigours of long and punishing campaigns and many battles against the 'infidels', or unbelievers, were well within their scope. They were already toughened by the demanding nomadic life of the desert and lived by strict rules of behaviour and honour. Bedouins had an extraordinary talent for 'navigating' the outwardly featureless desert sands, seeking out oases and precious water for themselves and their camels, sheep and goats. 'Bedouin' came from *badawi*, the Arabic word meaning 'desert dweller', and even after Islam gave rise to great cities and sophisticated cultures, they refused to give up the independence that went with nomadic life.

☞ ▶ p. 132 **AD 635–809**
CITIES OF ISLAM

Early on in the Muslims' campaigns of conversion, they attacked and captured towns such as Damascus (AD 635) or Aleppo (AD 638) and in time turned them into magnificent cities, with elegant mosques, minarets, gardens, fountains, and houses decorated with elaborate mosaics. Such beauties became, and still remain, features of many Muslim cities and the lives of culture and luxury enjoyed by their rulers became legendary. One of the most prominent centres was Baghdad, now the capital of Iraq, which was founded in AD 762 by the Muslim caliph (civil and religious leader) Al-Mansur. Baghdad later became a centre of culture and learning. The most famous Baghdadi caliph of all, Harun al-Raschid (AD 766–809) was himself a great scholar and possessed a library containing some 600,000 books.

1000s
THE MUSLIMS AS SCIENTISTS

Islam did not rule out worldly preoccupations or intellectual pursuits. The Muslim scientist who studied botany and wrote books dealing with plants, how they grew and how the weather affected them, was thought to be glorifying – not running counter to – his faith. The same went for Muslim zoologists who studied animals and passed their knowledge on to veterinary surgeons, and to astronomers who studied the heavens, using astrolabes to measure altitude and the movements of heavenly bodies. Muslim astronomers, in fact, were able to calculate almost exactly, to within one degree, the Earth's circumference. Their discoveries were of great help to navigators, who also benefited from the skill and accuracy of Muslim map-makers.

1096–1303
MUSLIMS AND CRUSADERS: A CLASH OF CULTURES

In 1095, Pope Urban II appealed for an army to 'take the Cross' and rescue the Holy Land from the Muslims, who had been looting and destroying churches and killing Christians. However, the crusades, which lasted from 1096 until the last crusader presence was expunged in 1303, gave Christians a rather different picture from the one many had expected. Instead of the brutish killers they thought to find, they were impressed by Muslim culture, the dedication and sense of honour of the Muslim knights whom they fought, and the practicality of many Muslim ideas, in castle-building, clothing for the desert heat and hygiene. They took much of what they had learned back with them when they returned home.

 CUSTOMS    DOMESTIC LIFE    TECHNOLOGY   CONFLICT

▲ *Muslim knights out hunting.*

 ▶ p. 120
1096–1303
MUSLIM MEDICINE

In crusader times, there was a great contrast between the Muslim and the European practice of medicine. The crusaders went to the Holy Land accustomed to brutal standards of medical care – the amputation of gangrenous legs, cauterising wounds with boiling oil or cutting crosses in patients' foreheads to drive out 'devils'. The Muslims, however, used acupuncture or drugs and ointments to cure diseases or heal wounds. They prescribed poultices to treat inflammations and curative diets for stomach troubles. Muslim physicians naturally had an understanding of diseases and infections prevalent in the Holy Land, but they took no sides. They saved the lives of many children of crusading families, another unexpected feature of Muslim culture which surprised, but gratified, the Christians.

1500s
SAILORS AND GEOGRAPHERS

Muslim seamen and navigators had a great deal to teach Europeans, even long after the crusades were over. European vessels, for instance, routinely used square sails until they discovered how the Muslim triangular lateen sails made better and faster use of the wind at sea. Muslim maps were preferable by far for those venturing out to sea out of the sight of land, since Muslim geographers had a more accurate and comprehensive view of the layout of Earth. In the early sixteenth century, the Muslim map-maker Pir Muhyi al Din Ra'is drew a chart of the South Atlantic Ocean, showing West Africa and South America.

1631
THE TAJ MAHAL

'A dream in marble' and 'a poem in stone' are two of the many attempts to express the phenomenal beauty of the Taj Mahal, built by the Mogul emperor Shah Jahan (1592–1666) for his favourite wife, Mumtaz, who died in 1631. The Taj, a marvel of intricate sculpture and mosaics with walls, floors and screens studded with precious stones, stands on the bank of the River Jumna near Agra and took 22 years – 1631 to 1653 – to construct. More than 20,00 workmen were employed to build it, together with the surrounding gardens and fountains. Nearby stands a mosque where Shah Jahan was able to see the Taj reflected in a stone set in the wall before him as he prayed.

p. 113 ◀ **Distant Voices** ▶ p. 117

The Arabs are the least adapted of all people for empire-building. Their wild disposition makes them intolerant of subordination, while their pride, touchiness and intense jealousy of power render it impossible for them to agree. Only when their nature has been permeated by a religious impulse are they transformed, so that the tendency to anarchy is replaced by a spirit of mutual defence. Consider the moment when religion dominated their policy and led them to observe a religious law deigned to promote the moral and material interests of civilisation.... How vast their empire became and how strongly it was established.

Ibn Khaldoun, writing in the fourteenth century

▼ *The magnificent mausoleum the Taj Mahal, built by the Mogul emperor Shah Jahan.*

The Feudal System
AD 800–1881

FEUDALISM, TAKEN FROM the Latin word *feudum*, meaning land given as a reward or exchange for services, was a system of mutual self-defence which arose at a time when Europe was in fearful danger of assaults by savage raiders who pillaged, burned, raped and killed at will. Faced with the anarchy this implied, feudalism was adopted to provide this mutual self-defence with an interlinked chain of duties and obligations. Though open to abuse from recalcitrant lords, feudalism served to give Europe reasonable law and order for some five centuries. Only when an outbreak of bubonic plague, later called the Black Death (1348–50), killed one quarter of Europe's population, leaving behind deserted villages and a decimated work force, did the feudal system begin to break down.

AD 800
AN INTERVAL OF PEACE

When Charlemagne was crowned Holy Roman Emperor on Christmas Day, AD 800, Europe was able to contemplate a return of law and order and protection from attack that it had not known since the end

▼ *The emperor Charlemagne, who was crowned on Christmas Day AD 800.*

of the western Roman Empire. The respite, however, was brief. Charlemagne died in AD 814 and with that, Europe was once more vulnerable to assaults by Vikings from Scandinavia, Magyars from Hungary and those fiercest of Christendom's foes, the Arabs. The areas most at risk were in France, Germany, Italy and northern Spain, where feudalism was imposed to counter this threat. Tsarist Russia, too, adopted the system and it persisted there for 1,000 years, until the feudal serfs were freed in 1861.

■ ▶ p. 122   AD 800s
HOW THE FEUDAL SYSTEM WORKED

The feudal system was a pyramid. At its apex was the king, whose vassals – the nobility – owed him fealty and the duty of providing forces for his wars. These were recruited from the mass of ordinary people who, in their turn, were the nobles' vassals. Oaths of fealty were solemn, binding contracts, sworn before God. Breaking them was therefore blasphemy, an awesome crime in an age of superstition. However, in return for fealty, and the labour of their humble vassals, the nobles owed them protection, if necessary physical protection within the walls of their castles. Most feudal estates consisted of these castles, together with a church and tracts of land. Outside, any land was common land, there for the use of all.

AD 800s
THE LIFE OF A FEUDAL VILLEIN

Although the feudal system was abused by cruel lords or recalcitrant villeins (their feudal tenants) it served as a practical means of getting work done on the estates. Villeins spent two days a week labouring on their lords' *demesne*, or feudal estate, and did 'boon' work in late summer, when there was the harvest to bring in. Villeins, too, were landowners, though the extent of their land varied widely. Better-off villeins might have up to 30 strips of land of their own, poorer ones only three or four. There was, however, one place totally forbidden to villeins – forests, which were reserved as hunting grounds for the king and lords. Venturing there, to poach game or gather firewood, incurred draconian punishments.

⚖ ▶ p. 121   AD 800s
LORDS OF THE MANOR

A feudal lord might, by the rules of the system, be a vassal doing homage to his king, but his position was extremely powerful. A demanding lord could treat his villeins like slaves, so that runaways were not uncommon. Justice, as dispensed by the lords, could be harsh, and it was incontrovertible. In the manorial courts, the lord's word was law and a villein, or anyone else who dared to challenge it, risked severe punishment. By bending the rules of the feudal system, the armies that lords were supposed to raise for the king could become private armies for use against rivals and many private wars were fought, the lords attacking each other's castles and laying waste their lands.

🔒 ▶ p. 120   AD 800s
THE MEDIEVAL CASTLE

An effective medieval castle was a strong, virtually unassailable fortress. Surrounded by moats with a drawbridge that could be closed in case of attack, castles consisted of mighty stone walls topped by crenellations from which defenders inside could pour down fire on an enemy. These castles occupied dominant geographical

▲ *English peasants, who endured centuries of poverty and suffering under the feudal system.*

positions, so that enemies could be seen coming long before they reached the vicinity. If they managed to penetrate the defences, they were still at risk from defenders who were well protected behind narrow slit windows. There was more risk, too, for enemies trying to fight their way up the narrow winding staircases inside a castle, where it was difficult to maintain a foothold, with parrying sword or spear thrusts from above.

1000s
TOWN LIFE

Until the beginning of the eleventh century, rural life, encased within the feudal system, was the dominant lifestyle across Europe. Rising populations, however, began to result in the growth and spread of towns. Town dwellers were mainly tradesmen and craftsmen, whose livelihood centred on the markets which were the dominant characteristic of these towns. Many of these tradesmen belonged to guilds of societies, established mainly to control the trades, but then becoming social circles. Townspeople campaigned in many areas to work as self-governing bodies, able to elect their own magistrates and be responsible for law and order in their own borough, and eventually, the first charters were awarded.

p. 109 ◀ **Triumphs & Tragedies** ▶ p. 118
1348
THE BLACK DEATH

In 1348, three ships arrived at Genoa in Italy, infected with a deadly disease that became known as bubonic plague. The Genoese drove the ships away, but it was already too late. The Black Death, as the plague was later called, spread throughout Europe and by 1350 had killed one quarter of its population. Another of its casualties was the feudal system. With the workforce drastically reduced, those villeins who survived were able to demand higher wages and greater independence, thus undercutting the power that the lords had once had over them. The Black Death was not the only cause, though. Wealthy merchants in the towns, who had never been included in the feudal system, also contributed to its break-up, as did the development of guns and gunpowder which made the nobles' castles less impregnable.

1881
WHERE FEUDALISM SURVIVED

Though feudalism died in England after 1350, it persisted in France and Russia. In France, the Revolution of 1789 brought it to an abrupt and bloody end. Russia was

more isolated from European trends and it was not until 1861 that Tsar Alexander II (1818–81) abolished feudalism and freed the serfs. Russian feudalism had taken a particularly harsh form, and the serfs had been 'property', sold along with the feudal estates they worked. The tsar was assassinated by anarchists in 1881, but even 20 years of freedom had not released the serfs from their servile mind-set. When anarchists called for rebellion against the tsar, they refused, clinging to their traditional belief that he was the 'Little Father', their protector and friend.

p. 115 ◀ **Distant Voices** ▶ p. 119

The Count [of Mortain] holds Aldbury, it is assessed at ten hides. There is land for seven plough teams. In demesne [feudal esate], six hides and there are there three plough teams ... eight villeins with one sokeman [tenant] and one 'francigena' [Frenchman] have four plough teams. There, one bordar [lowest-ranked villein] and four serfs. Meadow of half a hide. Wood for 500 swine. In all, it is worth 110 shillings. When [the Count] received it, £8 and likewise in the time of King Edward [the Confessor].

Extract from the *Domesday Book* (1087)

▼ *It is believed that rats carried the plague known as the Black Death to Europe.*

THE BLACK RAT

The Conquistadors
1517–1810

WHEN THE SPANISH conquistadors came to the Americas in the wake of Columbus's discovery of 1492, they were looking for gold, converts to Christianity and adventure. Many conquistadors came from Extramadura, a harsh and poor region of Spain which could never have offered them the riches and eminence that America could. What followed was much worse than a culture clash: the Spaniards' arrival signalled a brutal end to the ancient civilisations they encountered. The native Americans were outclassed in every department that mattered – militarily, and also in their deferential mind-set and automatic obedience to authority. As such, they were no match for the Spaniards' rampant individualism and they quickly succumbed to conquest and the dismantling of their societies across much of the continent.

▲ *The building of the great Aztec capital of Tenochtitlán*

1511
TALES OF GOLD

In 1511, Spaniards were already settled in Cuba and Hispaniola in the Caribbean and there, mouthwatering tales reached them of colossal riches on the mainland. There was the legend of El Dorado, a land covered in gold, and a great empire deep in the mountains of Mexico. Determined to see for themselves, the Spaniards ventured into

Yucatán in south-east Mexico in 1517. They came back mauled and bloodied after a savage encounter with the Mayas. This, though, only hardened the Spaniards' resolve and in 1519, Hernán Cortés (1485–1547) set out from Cuba with a force of only 508 men; he landed at Tabasco and set out to cross the mountains and reach the legendary empire of so much wealth and promise.

1519
THE CITY OF THE AZTECS

The thin air and freezing cold made the Spaniards' journey through the mountains a gruelling one, but on 8 November 1519, Cortés and his conquistadors entered Tenochtitlán, the Aztecs' capital city, to be greeted by a gorgeously garbed Montezuma, the Great Speaker and treated like gods. Tenochtitlán was a revelation, with its massive palace and sacrificial towers, the metals that decorated statues and images of the Aztec gods, and its sheer size and complexity. However, the Aztecs, too, were due for a revelation. They had never before seen soldiers mounted on horseback and thought soldier and horse was a single animal. They had never seen, either, the Spanish arquebuses and muskets, which breathed fire and destruction.

p.117 ◀ **Triumphs & Tragedies** ▶ p. 124

1521
THE DOWNFALL OF THE AZTEC EMPIRE

Once the Aztecs realised the Spaniards' aggressive intent, they drove them out of Tenochtitlán. However, the Spaniards soon returned, this time aided by vast numbers of the Aztec Empire's long-misused subjects. After a ferocious struggle, which reduced Tenochtitlán to ruins, the city fell on 13 August 1521. What followed was the total destruction of Aztec society – the end of human sacrifice, which disgusted the Spaniards, forcible conversion to Christianity, the break up of the Aztec calpulli ('clans') and the enslavement of the people. The allies who had helped the Spaniards to their triumph – Tepanecs, Mixtecs, Totonacs, Zapotecs and Mayas – received the same treatment. Mexico became New Spain, and part of the Spanish-American Empire, which was to last 300 years.

1532
THE CONQUEST OF THE INCAS

History repeated itself, though with extra-ordinary variations, in the South American Andes, where, in 1532, the Spaniards under

Francisco Pizarro (*c.* 1475–1541) reached Tahuantinsuyu and imprisoned the Sapa Inca, Atahualpa. These Spaniards, too, had come for gold and, realising this, Atahualpa made them an amazing offer: whole rooms full of gold and silver in exchange for his freedom. The Spaniards could hardly refuse, but they soon realised, and feared, Atahualpa's near-mesmeric power when, without demur, his subjects filled the rooms as ordered. Atahualpa could just as easily have commanded the Spaniards' slaughter. Afraid of this, they contrived a murder charge and executed him on 29 August 1532. At that, the Incas, supine as always before authority, awaited the orders of their new – Spanish – masters.

▲ *The conquistador Francisco Pizarro, who defeated the Inca civilisation in Peru.*

✱ ▶ p. 131 **1540s**
THE SPANIARDS BUILD THEIR EMPIRE
After the exploits of Cortés in Mexico and Pizarro in Peru, Spanish rule extended over almost all of central and southern America. The Spaniards, however, were adventurous as well as cruel, imaginative as well as greedy for riches. Despite considerable dangers, they explored their new possessions, recording invaluable eyewitness accounts of their discoveries. For instance, Francisco de Orellana (*c.* 1500–49) navigated the mighty Amazon River, from Peru to the Atlantic coast – the first man to do so. However, not all the Incas of Tahuantinsuyu had fallen into Spanish hands; some managed to melt away into the tangled forests, never to be found. Others remained secure in Maccu Picchu, a fortress to the north-west of Cuzco, which the Spaniards sought, but never discovered.

1540s
EXCHANGING DISEASES
Medical knowledge in Europe in the sixteenth century did not yet encompass the causes of disease or, in the case of fatal infections, their proper cure. Yet, within the new Spanish-American Empire, realisation dawned before long of the disaster the conquerors had brought with them. When de Orellana voyaged the Amazon, he noted hundreds of people on its banks. Native America was clearly crowded, but not after thousands of people began to die from smallpox and other European diseases to which they had no resistance. Spanish priests who tended the sick realised what had happened. Disease worked both ways, however, and the Spaniards began to die of strange fevers and infections alien to the Spanish physicians.

1550
PROTECTING THE NATIVES
The attitude of Spanish priests, who so eagerly converted thousands in America to Christianity, was the opposite of those Spaniards whose only thought was exploitation. One priest, Bartolomé de Las Casas (1474–1566) became known as the 'Apostle of the Indies' for his work in encouraging King Philip II of Spain to see the rights of natives as equal subjects of the Spanish Crown. Las Casas' mission was not only philanthropic; he believed that contented, unexploited natives were easier to convert to Christianity. His importunings, however, had their effect in Spain, where like-minded people were concerned to justify the American conquests. Gradually, over the years, Las Casas's ideas were adopted and the brutal treatment of the early days was at least partly contained.

1810
THE END OF SPANISH AMERICA
By 1810, Spaniards, natives and the mixed-blood *mestizos*, the products of intermarriage, were united in one stern purpose: to end tyrannical Spanish rule in America. Led by 'El Liberador', the

Venezuelan Simon Bolívar (1783–1830), Colombia (1819), Venezuela (1821), Ecuador (1822), Peru (1824) and Bolivia (1825) fought savagely against the Spaniards, neither side giving any quarter. Bolívar and his fellow liberators, José San Martin of Argentina and Bernardo O'Higgins of Chile, were defeated several times before the rulers suffered disastrous defeat at Boyacá, Colombia on 7 August 1819. Virtually the whole Spanish army surrendered. Meanwhile, Mexico and other central American states also wrenched their freedom from the Spaniards and by 1825, Spanish rule had come to a close.

p. 117 ◀ **Distant Voices** ▶ p. 121

The wretched and tyrannical Spanish worked the Indians night and day in the mines and in other personal services. They collected unbelievable tributes ... forced the Indians to carry burdens on their backs for 100 and 200 leagues as if they were less than beasts. They persecuted and expelled from the Indian villages the preachers of the [Christian] faith ... and I solemnly affirm, as God is my witness ... all the authority of the kings, even if they were resident in the Indies, will not be enough to prevent all the Indians from perishing.

Bartolomé de Las Casas, on the first 50 years of Spanish rule in America

▼ *The Venezuelan Simon Bolívar, known as 'the Liberator'.*

Social Change
1500–1799

THE RENAISSANCE of the sixteenth and seventeenth centuries had a profound effect, not only on art and architecture, but on views of life that were fundamentally different from medieval thinking. Then, humanity had been viewed as inherently sinful and subject to the incontrovertible will of God, who ruled all and decided all. The Renaissance, by contrast, encouraged individualism, nascent concepts of human rights and, above all, the power of men and women to govern their own future. With such concepts gaining ground, people no longer needed to feel that poverty, destitution and even disease and early death were inevitable burdens to be borne powerlessly. Politicians, physicians, scientists and philosophers set out to prove that human fate was, after all, in human hands.

monopoly of riches and power. The opening up of the New World after Columbus's discovery in 1492 offered escape from harsh conditions in Europe and the chance of a new start in a land of opportunity.

▲ *The German industrial philanthropist Georg Bauer, or 'Agricola'.*

▲ *The traditional method of 'bleeding' patients to release evil humours began to decline in the sixteenth century.*

▶ p. 132

1500s
MEDICINE AND MERCY

In medieval medicine, the cure had often been worse than the disease. For instance, bleeding patients to expel evil 'humours' weakened and often killed them. Although this savage approach to medical care did not disappear, more intelligent methods began to appear in the sixteenth century. There was a determined quest to understand disease and the processes of human anatomy. The Italian Girolamo Fracastoro (1483–1553) did important work on how contagion spread. Another Italian, Andreas Vesalius (1514–64) investigated the workings of the human body. In Britain, in 1628, William Harvey (1578–1657) discovered the circulation of the blood. The French army surgeon Ambroise Paré (c. 1509–90) dressed wounds with soothing balms rather than cauterising, and prevented profuse bleeding in amputations by tying off the blood vessels.

1540s
HUMANISM TAKES HOLD

The 'humanist' concept of life promoted by the Renaissance valued human powers and created a new self-sufficiency. In England, the dissolution of the monasteries by King Henry VIII meant that after 1539, when the task was completed, people could no longer rely on the ministrations of monks and nuns as they had done for centuries. Merchants had grown wealthy and the English Parliament more powerful, giving both a certain ascendancy over the kings and nobles who at one time possessed a

▶ p. 139

1600s
SCIENCE AND INVENTION

Scientists, too, were seeking better methods that would lighten workloads, improve working conditions and promote efficiency. The German Georg Bauer, or 'Agricola' (1494–1555), investigated mining technology and described diseases that affected miners. Such work had added importance because of the increasing use of coal to replace the wood formerly used for fires. Later, in 1712, Thomas Newcomen (1663–1729) invented the 'atmospheric engine', designed to pump water from mines and so reduce the danger of flooding which would otherwise overtake workers underground. He was preceded by Thomas Savery (1650–1715), inventor of the water-driven steam engine in 1696. In manufacturing industry, new techniques in glassmaking were introduced and the first frame knitting machine was invented by William Lee (d. 1610).

☞ CUSTOMS   ⌂ DOMESTIC LIFE   ⊟ TECHNOLOGY   ★ CONFLICT

1600s
MEANWHILE, IN OTTOMAN TURKEY…

While Europe was moving towards a more enlightened, humanitarian concept of life, no such freedom was available in the Ottoman Turkish Empire, which had been established after 1453 when the Muslim Turks captured Constantinople. The Ottoman Sultan had numerous Christian and Jewish subjects, in the Balkans, Cyprus, Poland, the Crimea, and in Russia, and they were treated very much as second-class citizens. Organised into minority communities, and known as *rai'yah*, or 'the shepherded people', their lives, their property and their livelihoods depended entirely on the will of the Sultan. They were not allowed to ride horses or carry weapons and they were barred from the Ottoman army and civil service. None of these rules applied to the majority, Muslim, subjects of the Empire.

1600s
LIFE EXPECTANCY

Despite improvements in medicine and a new understanding of the human body, life expectancy in Europe was a great deal shorter than it is today. Though the stirrings of improvement were already there in the seventeenth and eighteenth centuries, they were to take a very long time before the risks to life lessened. Many infants died either at birth or soon after. Many women died in childbirth. Infectious diseases created epidemics in which thousands died, especially in the unhealthy and overcrowded districts of large cities. Since Roman times, life expectancy had barely moved above 40, less than that for women and even lower for others, for example French peasants, who could rarely hope to live more than 22 years.

⊕ ▶ p. 126 **1601**
A LAW FOR THE POOR

In Britain, vagrants and beggars wandering the roads seeking shelter and sustenance, had long been both a scandal and a security problem for the better-settled population. These miserable outcasts from society created fear and trepidation, since what they were not given, they stole. In 1601, the government of Queen Elizabeth I took official action and created a Poor Law, signalling for the first time that the state had assumed responsibility for the less fortunate. The law imposed a 'poor rate' to fund poor relief, and appointed Overseers of the Poor in every parish to buy materials to provide work for the unemployed. The price of grain was controlled and if famine struck, imported grain from abroad was distributed in the affected areas.

⚖ ▶ p. 123 **1670**
THE TRIAL OF WILLIAM PENN

The jury system, brought to England by the Normans after 1066, was often abused by judges bullying juries for the verdict they wanted. This threatening behaviour finally met its match in 1670, when the Quakers William Penn and William Mead were charged with riot for preaching their faith in public. The judge was intent on a 'guilty' verdict, but the jury disagreed. What was more, they refused to give in despite imprisonment, fines and threats. Ultimately, the Lord Chief Justice, Sir John Vaughan, ruled that judges could not 'lead [juries] … by the nose'. The 'not guilty' verdict stood and the case, known as 'Bushell's Case' from the name of the foreman, Edward Bushell, established the right of British juries to independent verdicts.

1700s
THE AGE OF ENLIGHTENMENT

The humanism of the Renaissance also had its effects on philosophy and politics, and gained its most powerful impetus in the eighteenth century. This was the Age of

▲ *The trial of Quaker William Penn brought an end to corruption in the English judicial system.*

Enlightenment, which sought to remake society and its institutions in the light of pure reason. The ancient Greek concept of democracy came to the fore with revived ideas about representative government. The French political philosopher Jean-Jacques Rousseau (1712–78) set out his own theories of democracy, of the right to elementary education. The Scots economist Adam Smith (1723–90) author of The Wealth of Nations (1776) advocated the untrammelled workings of free enterprise and the importance of free trade. All these ideas were revolutionary, given the traditional social and economic values they sought to replace.

---

p. 119 ◀ **Distant Voices** ▶ p. 123

To the King, our Sovereign Lord: Most lamentably complaineth their woeful misery unto your Highness your poor daily beadmen, the wretched hideous monsters on whom scarcely for horror any eye dare look, the foul unhappy sort that live only by alms: how that their number is daily so sore increased that all the alms of all the well-disposed people of this your realm is not half enough to sustain them, but that for very constraint they die for hunger.... Is it any marvel that your people so complain of poverty?

Simon Fish to King Henry VIII, *A Supplication for the Beggars* (1529)

The Industrial Revolution
1700–1847

THE INDUSTRIAL REVOLUTION, which included a revolution in farming and transport, was not only about the introduction of machines and consequent changes in the world of work. It also had tremendous social implications. Workers exchanged their own homes as workplaces for the grim routine of the factory. There, they laboured long hours under draconian rules. In the mines, pregnant women were put to work hauling loads of coal. Serious injury was a constant danger; homes were filthy slums; wages were barely enough to sustain life. Death, all too often, came prematurely. It was a life of misery and deprivation from which workers were not rescued until philanthropists took up their cause and forced Parliament to confront the scandal and act.

▲ *Sir Richard Arkwright, inventor of the first automated spinning machine.*

1700s
WHY THE INDUSTRIAL REVOLUTION?

For a long time before the Industrial Revolution, home and workplace had been the same for thousands of people. Naturally, for the workers, it had its advantages and personal freedom, even though the work involved long hours and much effort. The trouble was that home production was not particularly efficient. After the invention of machines such as John Kay's Flying Shuttle (1733), James Hargreaves' Spinning Jenny (1764–67), Richard Arkwright's Water Frame for twisting yarn (1769), or Edmund Arkwright's Power Loom (1786), employers were given the means to increase production quite dramatically and so create a larger market for their goods. Once they realised that, the traditional, slower methods were on the way out and for the workers, the factory beckoned.

1733
HOME VERSUS FACTORY

The contrast between home and machine production was enormous. For instance, several spinners were needed to produce enough thread for one weaver. By contrast, the Flying Shuttle (1733) could throw a weaving shuttle from side to side in a loom much more quickly than it could be done by hand, so supplying several weavers in far less time. Even greater output and efficiency was promised by the steam engine of 1776, built by James Watt (1736–1818). The new machines, however, could be used only in specially built textile mills and before long other industries – iron, pottery, corn grinding – were following the lead of the mills. The surviving homeworkers, deprived of their living, had no option but to move to the town and the mill.

❀ ▶ p. 128
1759
THE CANALS

The increase in industrial production created problems. Increased production meant that increased transport was required to carry goods to shops and markets and in the mid-eighteenth century, Britain's roads were not capable of standing the strain. They were dusty, pitted, muddy, icy and dangerous depending on the time of year, and factory owners had no faith in their carrying a regular supply of goods safely. The solution was water transport and after 1759, an artificial waterway, the Bridgewater Canal, was built connecting Manchester to the coal mines on the Duke of Bridgewater's estate at Worsley. A network of canals followed, built by gangs of strong but rough-living 'navvies' (navigators), who lived like nomads, moving from one location to the next.

⬛ ▶ p. 135
1770s
MILLS AND SLUMS

Working conditions in mills and factories were terrible. The working day was 14 hours long, and despite the heat generated by the machines, workers were often not allowed to open windows for air. The machinery itself was unfenced, so that horrific injuries could result from falling against them. If a worker was unable to go to the mill for any reason, he had to pay someone else to work in his place. Harsh overseers were little better than slave-drivers and the wages earned were a pittance. The homes specially built for workers were barely habitable and all too often, there was too little food to eat – or none. This could be the case even if a whole family worked at the mill.

1770s
DOWN THE MINES

The mines were even more unhealthy than the mills and factories, if that were possible. Damp, cold, dark, dangerous, they were nevertheless the workplace for men, women and children who spent long hours under-ground. Children of four or five sat all day opening and shutting doors. Pregnant women hauling trucks loaded with coal risked

 CUSTOMS  DOMESTIC LIFE  TECHNOLOGY CONFLICT

▲ *The Bridgewater Canal, built to allow a more accessible trading route between the Worsley coal mines and the industrial centre of Manchester.*

miscarriages or worse. The railways inside the mines could be death traps if, for instance, workers lost their hold on a truck and were knocked down and run over. Gas escaping from the coal-face could choke them to death. Ceilings could cave in and bury or trap them. Yet there was no protection and if mineworkers could not work, they faced dismissal and consequently starvation.

1770
REVOLUTION ON THE FARM

For centuries, people had lived by 'subsistence faming', growing their own food on their own plots of land. This changed dramatically when, in about 1770, more food was required for the growing population of Britain and Europe. The increase was so great that many feared famine lay ahead. Scientific farming, however, saved the day. A Berkshire farmer, Jethro Tull (1674–41) brought a seed-drill from France that enabled three rows of seeds to be planted at once, and a horse-drawn hoe for destroying weeds. Meanwhile, Viscount Townshend (1674–1738) devised the Norfolk System for rotating crops, and fed turnips and hay to his cattle when grass was scarce. Previously, farm animals had to be killed before the winter for want of food.

⚖ ▶ p. 128

1788
THE CONVICT EXILES

In 1788, a convict fleet of 11 ships sailed for Botany Bay in Australia. The second worst punishment for convicts, after the death penalty, was transportation to an unknown land as far from Britain as possible. Fortunately, when they reached Australia, the convicts were able to use their work skills to build houses and lay out streets. They even built prisons. Others were put to work labouring on the land to produce food. Some, however, resorted to crime and were sent as prisoners to nearby Norfolk Island. The conditions there were so frightful that prisoners about to be hanged told a visiting priest that they welcomed the punishment since it would 'take them out of this terrible place'.

▼ *The industrial community at New Lanark, founded by the philanthropist Robert Owen, based on improved conditions and shorter working hours.*

1800
THE PHILANTHROPISTS INTERVENE

After 1800, Robert Owen (1771–1858), manager of the New Lanark Mill in Scotland, showed that factories could be run humanely, yet still show a profit, by providing good working conditions and housing. Other philanthropists laid the plight of cruelly misused workers before Parliament and, against fierce opposition from factory and mine owners, forced through measures to reduce working hours and ban the employment of children under nine. One of the most dramatic moments came when a commission on the coal mines published a report which was so horrifing that, in 1842, Parliament prohibited the employment of women and children in the mines. The 10-hour day followed in 1847, and the pernicious practice of sending child sweeps up chimneys was abolished.

p. 121 ◀ **Distant Voices** ▶ p. 125

I saw little children, three parts naked, tottering under the weight of wet clay, some of it on their heads and some on their shoulders, and little girls with large masses of wet, cold and dripping clay pressing on their abdomens. Moreover, the unhappy children were exposed the most sudden transitions of heat and cold, for after carrying their burdens of wet clay, they had to endure the heat of the kiln and to enter places where the heat was so intense that I was not myself able to remain more than two or three minutes.

The Earl of Shafestbury, on child workers in the brick fields (1871)

The Native North Americans: a Culture Destroyed
1700–1890

A REPEAT OF HISTORY was inevitable after Europeans settled in North America. Just as the Spaniards destroyed the Aztecs, Incas and others further south, there could be only one ending to the clash between the ambitious, enterprising but intolerant and ruthless newcomers and the semi-nomadic first Americans living their simple, traditional life in the north. When the first English settlers established themselves in Virginia in 1607, the natives helped them survive their first winter, teaching them how to hunt and trap animals and raise crops of corn and tobacco. In time, as the United States – which evolved from the early settlements – set out to claim the country from coast to coast, this was something the native Americans would come to regret.

1700s
THE NATIVE WAY OF LIFE

The native North Americans had a harmonious relationship with nature; they respected it. They even respected the buffalo and other animals they hunted for food. It was, in its way, a form of gratitude, for parts of North America provided everything needed for the simple, hunter-gatherer lifestyle. The plains were full of buffalo, the rivers full of fish, the land was fertile. Naturally, different tribes had their rivalries and their wars. However, within their own communities, the natives' watchword was 'sharing' – sharing whatever they had so that all could thrive. Despite nature's gifts, it was a hard, demanding life; yet there was a lot about it that was idyllic. By 1780, however, the idyll was coming to an end.

1750
'GO WEST, YOUNG MAN!'

'Go west, young man and grow up with the country!' advised US newspaperman Horace Greeley in 1851. A better, richer life in the west of the USA had been a popular quest ever since the way there through the Appalachian Mountains had first been discovered in 1750. A century later, the USA was receiving thousands of new immigrants from Europe. The country needed space, and the space lay westwards. Many immigrants joined the wagon trains within days of arriving in America. But the west was to be much harder and more gruelling than these new Americans imagined. For one thing, the country was already occupied, and the native tribes there were going to fight the intruders with great ferocity.

1784
THE UNITED STATES PUSHES WEST

The British, who ruled the colonies which later won independence in 1783 as the new United States, had long contended that a move west was inadvisable until the native Americans had been pacified. How right they were was soon proved after 1784, when the first appreciable body of European settlers came to Kentucky. The natives were resolved to fight, and fight with great savagery, for the land that had been theirs for thousands of years. As the push west continued, the natives obstructed the settlers in every way they knew. They attacked wagon trains, burned settler camps, towns and farms, stole crops and cattle, captured or killed men, women and children, and created havoc and terror wherever they appeared.

1800s
THE NEW AMERICANS

For those who came to America to escape poverty and oppression in Europe, the promise it held was like a dream about to come true. Here, they believed, they would at last find a successful, gratifying life for themselves and their children. The prior claims of the native peoples meant little to them and the more religiously intolerant looked on the first Americans as godless savages. Nevertheless, it took a great deal of courage and enterprise to venture out into the unknown, facing not only the inimical natives, but disease, accidents and natural disasters. The way west, in fact, was marked by the graves of many whose quest ended in death before they had a chance to attain their goals.

1869
THE CENTRAL PACIFIC RAILROAD

Despite the natives' efforts, the new settlers kept on coming and pushed further and further westwards, heading ultimately for the west coast and California. On 10 May

p. 118 ◀ **Triumphs & Tragedies** ▶ p. 128

1876–90
LITTLE BIGHORN AND WOUNDED KNEE

Two bloody engagements typified the fierce struggle between the natives and the United States army. On 25 June 1876, at the Little Bighorn river in Montana, outnumbered US troops led by Lt-General George Custer (1839–76) were wiped out by Sioux Indians under their chiefs Crazy Horse (1849–77) and Sitting Bull (1834–90). The Sioux victory, however, did not change anything. Fourteen years later, on 29 December 1890, Sitting Bull was killed during a confrontation with the army at Wounded Knee on the Sioux reservation in South Dakota, where the tribe was now confined. Some were involved in the Ghost Dance movement which aimed to restore native control over the land with the aid of their dead ancestors; the army surrounded the natives, opened fire and killed 146 of them.

☞ CUSTOMS   ⬛ DOMESTIC LIFE   ▣ TECHNOLOGY   ✦ CONFLICT

▲ *The Battle of the Little Bighorn, in which Custer and his troops were defeated by Indians of the Sioux tribe.*

1869, a ceremony was performed at Promontory, Utah, which emphasised their determination to occupy the entire United States. Six years earlier, the construction of two railroads had begun. One, the Central Pacific Railroad was built eastwards from Sacramento, California. The other, the Union Pacific Railroad was built westwards from Omaha, 2,848 km (1,770 miles) distant. The natives staged raids on the railroads and the gangs that built them, but despite this, in 1869, the tracks met and a golden spike was hammered into the ground where the last two sets of rails joined.

☞ ▶ p. 130
1880
THE GHOST DANCE
In about 1880, with hope fast fading of victory over the newcomers, some native Americans revived the Ghost Dance movement, which originated in Nevada in

1870. The rituals and ceremonies of the Ghost Dance sought to conjure up aid from long-ago ancestors and in particular from the dead braves of the past who, the natives believed, could be persuaded to come back to life and drive out the hated white man. This was not the only purpose of the Ghost Dance, though. The disappearance of the whites would go hand in hand with the return of the buffalo, which had been so essential to native life, and which the whites had brutally decimated as a means of destroying that way of life.

1890
THE RESERVATIONS
Inevitably, in the end, the technologically superior US army prevailed over the native tribes. This, combined with a gradual, but fatal wearing away of their ancient ways of life ultimately gave the native Americans no choice but to surrender. By 1890, when white settlement had reached the west coast, the 'frontier' was declared closed and the lands over which the natives had so freely roamed were gone. Instead, they were herded into reservations where, unable to support themselves in traditional ways, they became dependent on rations from the US

government. Attempts were made to transform them into farmers and assimilate them into the white American culture, but their time-honoured customs and traditions were all the natives had left and overall the policy failed.

p. 123 ◀**Distant Voices** ▶ p. 127

The danger of the chase arises not so much from the onset of the wounded animal as from the nature of the ground which the hunter must ride over. The prairie does not always present a smooth, level and uniform surface. Yet accidents in buffalo running happen less frequently than one would suppose; in the recklessness of the chase, the hunter enjoys all the impunity of a drunken man, and may ride safely over gullies and declivities where, should he attempt to pass in his sober senses, he would infallibly break his neck.

Francis Parkman, US historian and traveller, on the buffalo hunt (1849)

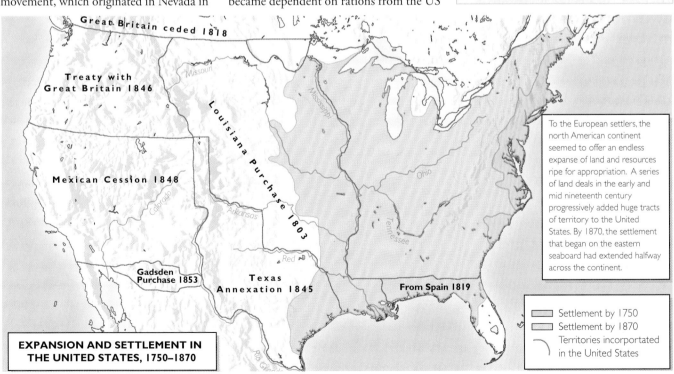

EXPANSION AND SETTLEMENT IN THE UNITED STATES, 1750–1870

Great Britain ceded 1818

Treaty with Great Britain 1846

Mexican Cession 1848

Gadsden Purchase 1853

Texas Annexation 1845

From Spain 1819

Louisiana Purchase 1803

To the European settlers, the north American continent seemed to offer an endless expanse of land and resources ripe for appropriation. A series of land deals in the early and mid nineteenth century progressively added huge tracts of territory to the United States. By 1870, the settlement that began on the eastern seaboard had extended halfway across the continent.

Settlement by 1750
Settlement by 1870
Territories incorporated in the United States

Social and Cultural Effects of the French Revolution
1789–1848

THE FRENCH REVOLUTION of 1789 was not just another uprising of the deprived against authority. It was also a revolution in ideas about society and culture and, in time, exercised an influence that spread worldwide. It gave rise to a new concept of the relationship between ruler and ruled, new appreciation of human rights and, above all, accorded ordinary people a prominence in the scheme of things which had never been known before. Like all revolutions, however, it was bloody and violent and, with the Reign of Terror of 1793–94, reached a peak of horror which appalled the revolutionaries themselves. However, this took nothing from the challenge they mounted against established authority, which was never again the same.

⊕ ▶ p. 132

1789
CAUSES OF THE REVOLUTION

In eighteenth-century France, virtually all power was concentrated in the hands of the king. The nobles and the church enjoyed great privileges and were not required to pay their full share of taxes. Below them were the *bourgeoisie*, the middle-class which enjoyed great riches and influence but lacked the share in government they believed was their due. Finally, there was the great mass of peasants, still living under the feudal system, poverty-stricken, heavily taxed, unenfranchised and frequently hungry. All this invited disaster at a time when traditional concepts of life and government were being widely challenged and the French monarchy, in addition, was too weak and too short of money to put up effective resistance.

1789
THE HATREDS OF THE REVOLUTION

The hatred and resentment that fired the French Revolution ran deep and ferocious. Vengeance was in the air on the very first day, 14 July 1789, when the Bastille prison in Paris was overrun and its governor murdered. Later, government officials were chased through the streets, killed and hung from lamp-posts. Maximilien Robespierre (1758–94), who lorded over the Reign of Terror in 1793–94, harboured a typically vicious hatred towards those he considered the enemies of the Revolution – that is, everyone but the common people. Ghastly scenes took place in Paris when Robespierre's victims were carted to the guillotine and beheaded as the crowds roared their approval, and the women known as *tricoteuses* ('knitters') carried on knitting as the heads fell.

▲ *Philosopher and supporter of the French Revolution, Jean Jacques Rousseau.*

1789
THE IDEAS OF THE REVOLUTION

The Revolution was well primed with liberal ideas through the writings of Voltaire (François-Marie Arouet, 1694–1778) and Jean Jacques Rousseau (1712–78). Its rallying cry 'Liberté, Egalité, Fraternité' – Liberty, Equality, Brotherhood – largely encapsulated their principles. The people became paramount in French revolutionary thinking, which also required a complete break with the repressive past. Now, France was not the king's property, as before, but belonged to all who lived there. A new calendar was introduced, with 1789 as Year One, as well as a new religion and the Cult of the Supreme Being, to replace the old Catholicism. These innovations did not last, but the primacy of the people that the Revolution promoted had come to stay.

▼ *The execution of Louis XVI, the most significant victim of the French Revolution.*

☞ CUSTOMS 　　 🏠 DOMESTIC LIFE 　　 🎞 TECHNOLOGY 　　 ✦ CONFLICT

1791
THE SLAVES RETURN

While the French revolutionaries were fighting to establish their own freedom, an even more disadvantaged society was retrieving theirs through a unique social experiment in Africa. In 1788, Sierra Leone in west Africa was settled as a home for freed slaves. This was a philanthropic enterprise organised by the British abolitionist Granville Sharpe (1735–1813), who called Sierra Leone 'the province of freedom'. A local king, 'Jimmy', drove the settlers away, but they returned in 1791. This second enterprise was sponsored by the Sierra Leone Company which was strongly supported by opponents of the slave trade. They brought over, as settlers, freed negroes from Nova Scotia who had won their liberty fighting for the British in the American War of Independence.

1800s
EUROPE ABSORBS REVOLUTIONARY IDEAS

The egalitarian and other principles of the French Revolution were startling new ideas in Europe. Although, ironically, post-revolutionary France acquired an emperor, Napoleon Bonaparte, the lessons were well learned. Social revolution can be a copycat affair and, in fact, the French learned much from the breakaway United States which won its freedom – with considerable aid from France – six years before the Revolution began. The French revolutionary spirit, in its turn, was passed on to Italy and Hungary which were under Austrian domination, and to the German states where authoritarian kings and dukes imposed draconian rule. What the French Revolution had proved to these people was that seemingly omnipotent power could be challenged and, when challenged, could be overcome.

1800s
BRITAIN STANDS BACK

In Britain, French revolutionary concepts made little headway. The British, in fact, gave sanctuary to French 'aristos' who fled across the English Channel to escape the revolutionaries' slaughter of their class. British kings were not absolute monarchs but rather were constitutional sovereigns, subject in principle to the will of Parliament. Though most ordinary people had no voting rights, they were not brutally oppressed like the French feudal peasants. There was also a degree of religious toleration in Britain, although anti-Catholic and anti-nonconformist laws persisted. Although the system in Britain had its problems, there was no deep-seated popular resentment on which revolution could flourish in Britain.

▶ p. 133 **1848**
EUROPE IN REVOLT

In 1848, the cauldron of libertarian ideas set simmering by the French Revolution boiled over. In France, Prussia, Austria, Italy and Hungary revolutionaries demanded liberal constitutions and popular concessions. The mood was extremely ugly and rulers took fright. Their first instinct was to repress the revolutions by force. The brutality with which they proceeded was such, and the popular reaction so vehement, that in Prussia, for instance, Prince Wilhelm, military commander and heir to the throne, had to flee the country. Nevertheless, many monarchs gave in and granted the constitutions their furious subjects demanded. It was largely a ploy, made to stave off immediate danger and later, with the exception of the kingdom of Sardinia, the constitutions were rescinded after order was restored.

1848
THE FRENCH REVOLUTION – THE LONG TERM

Although most of the revolutions of 1848 failed to achieve their objective, neither Europe nor its despotic rulers were ever the same again. Kings and emperors could never retrieve the total confidence they had once had in the safety of their thrones, or of their persons. Royal families lived smothered in security and, wherever they went, secret services were enlisted to nose out and remove troublemakers before they arrived. This, however, did not prevent the assassination of Empress Elisabeth of Austria in 1898 or, in 1913, the murder of King George I of Greece. Even more fearful for the beleaguered monarchs, revolutionary ideas evolved into communist principles, which at their most extreme advocated the complete destruction and remaking of society.

▲ *The Storming of the Bastille in Paris, the first revolutionary action in France.*

p. 125 ◀ **Distant Voices** ▶ p. 129

All men are born and remain free and have equal rights. Social distinctions are unjustifiable except insofar as they ... serve the common good.... Sovereignty resides ... in the nation as a whole; no group or individual can exercise any authority not expressly delegated to it or him.... Liberty is the right to do anything which does not harm others.... Law is the overt expression of the general will. All citizens have the right to participate in legislation, either in person or through their representatives.... Since all are equal before the law, all are equally eligible, in accordance with their abilities, for all public offices and positions.

Extract from *The Rights of Man and of the Citizen*, proclaimed 26 August 1789

Slavery
1500–1865

SLAVERY HAS BEEN CALLED 'the greatest crime in the world'; it is also a very old one, probably as old as civilisation itself. There were slaves in ancient Judea, where Jewish law decreed that they should be released after a certain time. Ancient Rome teemed with slaves, nearly 21 million throughout Italy by about AD 50. In medieval times and later, Arabs traded in slaves across the Sahara Desert. However, a crime becomes a crime only when people become sufficiently shocked to call it so, and it was not until around 1780 that an increasing level of dismay arose over the transportation of Africans across the Atlantic to work as slaves in the European colonies established there in the previous three centuries.

p. 124 ◀ **Triumphs & Tragedies** ▶ p. 133

1500s
THE MIDDLE PASSAGE
The voyage across the Atlantic to America, known as the 'Middle Passage', meant fearful suffering for slaves. As many as 500 of them were packed into a ship's hold, each crammed into a space no more than about 1.7 m (5.5 ft) long and 40.6 cm (16 in) wide. Half the slaves might die before the voyage was over. They perished from disease, filthy food and drinking water or simply from terror and despair. Others were thrown overboard by the crew if they became troublesome or developed some illness, or the captain thought his 'cargo' too heavy for him to complete his voyage safely and on time. Once in America, the slaves were disembarked and produce and other goods loaded for the return voyage to Europe.

1500s
RAIDING FOR SLAVES
After the Spaniards conquered their empire in America in the sixteenth century and the Portuguese claimed Brazil, they discovered that too many of the natives died when put to hard physical work. This turned their attention to the west coast of Africa. The Portuguese had thoroughly explored the African coasts many years earlier and they knew that Africans were physically strong, accustomed to working long hours in broiling heat and were therefore ideal for labour on farms, estates and down the mines. With that, slave ships began to appear off the west African coasts where African chiefs were willing to sell captured enemies and even members of their own tribes to slave traders who soon included the British and the French.

▶ p. 129 ### 1500s
TRADING IN SLAVES
The sufferings of the slaves began when they were captured by raiding parties sent out by kings or chiefs of rival tribes. Sometimes the raiders ventured far inland for their 'booty', snaring unwary Africans in the forests or kidnapping them from their villages. The raiders took men, women and children and anyone else who looked strong enough to stand the rigours of what lay ahead. Afterwards, a column of slaves might be marched – yoked and chained – for 1,600 km (1,000 miles) before they reached the coast. Many collapsed from exhaustion or died on the way. Those who reached the coast were sold or traded for cloth, ornaments and other manufactured goods which the slave traders had brought specially from Europe.

1500s
HUMANS BOUGHT AND SOLD
By their own lights, the slavers were not evil men; nor did they necessarily feel the need to justify the fact that they were selling other human beings. They did not, in fact, regard black Africans as properly human at all, since they were – in their eyes – uncivilised heathens. These beliefs may lie behind the fact that the British laid down no rules about the humane treatment of slaves. The French and the Spaniards did, and the Spaniards also forbade the breaking up of families. The British, however, had no qualms, and terrible scenes of grief and violence took place at slave markets, for

▼ *Enslaved Africans were often treated brutally by their captors, and many died on the long journeys from their native lands.*

 CUSTOMS   🏠 DOMESTIC LIFE   🖥 TECHNOLOGY   ✦ CONFLICT

▲ *Africans were often captured while out hunting and shipped to Europe and the Americas to be sold as slaves.*

instance in Jamaica, when husbands, wives and children were sold to different owners, never to see each other again.

1500s
SLAVES AT WORK

Not all slaves were sold to brutal masters whose only thought was to get as much work out of them as they could by threats, punishments, deprivation or torture. Decent families, too, purchased slaves and though their lowly position was never in doubt, in these households, they were treated humanely. Even here, though, slaves lived in rough huts, ate plain, cheap food and worked long hours. However, the opposite sort of master was unfortunately far too common. Slaves were flogged, starved and grossly overworked, and could be killed by their masters, even, most sadistically, by being blown up with sticks of gunpowder. Attempted escape was futile and escaped slaves could have their toes amputated on recapture, so that they could not escape again.

1787
THE ABOLITION SOCIETY

Britain had become the major slave trading nation in Europe, yet it was here that positive moves were made to get the trade banned. In 1787 philanthropists, driven by religious belief, formed the Abolition Society. Abolitionists toured ports and interviewed slave-ship captains and crews to build up a picture of the horrors being perpetrated. They faced violent objections – from plantation owners, from those who believed black savages to be 'natural' slaves, and from others who maintained that the slave trade was a training ground for sailors. Twenty years passed before Parliament finally banned the trade in 1807. Another 26 went by before slavery itself was abolished in all British possessions.

1808
BLOCKADING THE SLAVE TRADE

After the Abolition Bill became law on 1 May 1808, the British set out to ensure that no other nation traded in slaves. Royal Navy cruisers blockaded the west African coast to prevent slave ships from leaving port. They patrolled at sea, watching for ships suspected of carrying slaves and fired shots across their bows to make them heave-to. Inspection parties then went aboard to search for slaves. If they were found, the offending ship was seized and impounded. Some of these were British, since there were many slave-ship

▼ *British philanthropist Granville Sharpe, who helped found the Abolition Society and eventually to ban the slave trade.*

captains willing to carry on trading illegally. They disguised their ships as innocent trading vessels and arranged to load their slave cargoes secretly where the watchful Royal Navy could not discover them.

1861
FREEING THE SLAVES OF THE AMERICAN SOUTH

The southern states of America had relied heavily on slaves to work on the cotton and other plantations and by 1860, the South was engaged in disagreements with the non-slave-owning North especially over what southerners felt was undue federal interference from Washington. The matter was settled by the victory of the North in the Civil War (1861–65) after which the slaves were freed. Some southerners refused to accept that slaves were no longer slaves and in 1866, the Ku Klux Klan secret society was founded to reassert white supremacy. The Klan aimed at terrorising the former slaves and anyone who supported them. The Klan disbanded in 1869, but was revived and persists – though to a lesser degree – to this day.

p. 127 ◀ **Distant Voices** ▶ p. 131

As soon as a vessel arrives ... the crew discharge her light cargo, with manacles ... for the slaves, and [also] land the captain.... The vessel ... cruises along the coast to take in ... ivory, gold dust etc. ... and if a British man-of-war be near, the crew have nothing on board to excite suspicion.... They return ... where the cargo had been unloaded and communicate with the captain ... who takes the opportunity of acquainting his crew with the exact time ... he will be in readiness to embark. The vessel cruises up and down the coast a second time ... till the appointed day approaches, when she proceeds to take in her living cargo.

Richard Lander, in a contemporary account of illegal British slave-trading (1830)

Japan Modernises
1636–1941

IN 1636, AN ISOLATION DECREE cut Japan off from the outside world and for three centuries, while Western nations progressed technologically, politically, socially and culturally, the Japanese remained caught in their medieval time-warp. Then, in 1853, the West came to shake them from their slumber, when the American Commodore Matthew Perry arrived to demand that Japan open up her ports to trade. Realising that the only alternative was conquest and subjugation, the Japanese concurred. They proceeded, not only to do as Perry demanded, but to modernise their entire society with quite astounding rapidity. To an extent, though, the changes were superficial and the medieval Japan of the samurai warrior class lived on beneath the surface of modernity.

☞ ▶ p. 138

1636
SAMURAI JAPAN

The Japanese world frozen into stasis by the Decree of 1636 was based on duties and obligations from which there was no escape. Controlled, often brutally, by Shogun warlords and the samurai since the tenth century, the strictly disciplined Japanese lived in an hierarchical society in which failure, or perceived failure, to honour the warrior overlords could mean

▼ *A Japanese warlord.*

instant execution, and the emperor, though a figurehead, was regarded as divine. The strict samurai code of Bushido, in which loss of honour could be assuaged only by *seppuku* (ritual suicide) imbued the civilian mind-set, producing a culture of great formality in which observing proper rituals and expected behaviour and, above all, automatic obedience to all authority, was paramount.

1800s
CAPACITY FOR CHANGE

Japanese leaders had long been aware of the vast strides made in the western world and knew, from Britain's defeat and humiliation of China after 1840, that the same fate awaited Japan if they resisted Perry's demands. There was resistance nevertheless as some Japanese baulked at coming under Western influence with cries of 'Sonno joi! Revere the emperor! Drive out the foreign barbarians!' The modernisation required of the Japanese was not such a hard task, however. They were ingenious, fascinated by foreign innovations, perhaps because of, rather than despite, their isolation, and already had a copyist history: much of their culture had been borrowed from China, including the Buddhist religion, the calendar and even 'bonsai', the practice of dwarfing trees.

1867
FUNDAMENTAL CHANGE

Upending an entire culture rather than gradually changing it was no mean task, but Japan had, as it were, a secret weapon. The Japanese believed that the emperor's decrees must never be questioned and Meiji (Matsuhito, 1852–1912), who became emperor in 1867, was willing to follow modernising advice. After treaties of co-operation were made with the USA in 1854 and with Britain, Russia and the Netherlands in 1856, Meiji commanded in 1871 that all fiefs (feudal lands) be abolished and replaced with prefectures, and that universal education and postal services be established. All these reforms, needless to say, meant fundamental change from the previously existing order, yet the emperor's say-so was incontrovertible and he was obeyed.

1871
MAKING NEW FRIENDS

One of the drawbacks of isolation had been the widespread popular fear of foreigners which prevailed in Japan. A cogent reason why Perry was sent to Japan was the need to put an end to the brutal ill-treatment of foreign sailors whose misfortune it was to be wrecked in or near the Japanese islands. Yet only 18 years later, in 1871, the Japanese signed the Treaty of Tientsin with China and another treaty with Korea in 1876 – and signed them, what was more, as between equals. Even more remarkable for a people whose reaction to foreigners and their doings had long been violent, the Japanese quietly accepted an indemnity from China in 1874 as compensation for the murder of Japanese sailors by the Chinese.

1872
NEW ARMED FORCES

The Japanese had long been a warlike nation and had even turned war into sport, with the martial arts *kung fu*, *jujitsu* and *kendo*. Modern technological warfare, however, was entirely new in their experience as, after 1872, their army was trained by the Germans and their navy by the British. All this meant that modern

▲ *The Japanese emperor Matsuhito, who encouraged the modernising process in Japan.*

battleships and weapons were acquired by a people who, barely 20 years earlier had been so terrified by Perry's steam-assisted sailing ships that they called them kurofune ('smoking dragons'). What was more, before modernisation, so that no one could escape the bonds of isolation, the Japanese had been forbidden to build vessels which could sail more than a certain distance out to sea before they sank.

1877
DEALING WITH THE SAMURAI

Despite the rapid advance of westernisation, the last bastion of the old traditional Japan was bound to be the samurai warrior class. They stood to lose everything – their power, their status, the compliance of the divine but traditionally supine emperor and, after nearly 1,000 years, their paramountcy. In 1877, they staged the Satsuma Rebellion,

which was designed to bring back the ancient ways and preserve their class. The Rebellion was, ironically, suppressed by the new modern Japanese army and the samurai, despite all their efforts, were downgraded. They were forbidden to wear battle cosmetics or carry their characteristic two swords, and the pensions they had previously been awarded were taken from them. Now quite emasculated, the samurai warrior class virtually ceased to exist.

1882
MORE WESTERNISATION

Any other nation but the obedient Japanese might have suffered cultural collapse at the pace and extent of changes which, ultimately, enabled them to leap from medieval to modern practices within a period of 40 years, a tenth of the time it had taken in Europe. By 1882, the Bank of Japan had been established. The Cabinet was reorganised along German lines. Government paper-making and cotton-spinning plants were established, with steam-power introduced into some 200 factories by 1890. Railways, steamships and electric power plants were constructed. The Japanese were soon catching up so fast that they absorbed innovations not long after they appeared in the West, such as telephones, invented in the US in 1869, and the cinema, first introduced in France in 1895.

✳ ▶ p. 136

1891
BENEATH THE MODERNISED SURFACE

It eventually became clear that, beneath the patina of modernisation, warlike samurai Japan persisted, as the Japanese emulated the Western taste for imperialist conquest. They attacked China in 1891, thrashed Russia in 1904–05 and committed later aggressions which ultimately led Japan into the Second World War in 1941. Here, several chilling aspects of traditional Japan surfaced – the Japanese contempt for prisoners-of-war, who, in their eyes, had disgraced themselves by surrender; the willingness of *kamikaze* (suicide) pilots to die by crashing their aircraft onto the decks

of American ships; the equally suicidal *banzai* charges made against American troops and, when defeat or capture was inevitable, the recourse to *seppuku* for which the Japanese sometimes asked permission from their American conquerors.

▼ *Japanese kamikaze pilots.*

p. 129 ◀ **Distant Voices** ▶ p. 133

At about 3 p.m., the guests arrive, frequently attended by servants… Haru receives them at the top of the stone steps and conducts each into the reception room, where they are arranged according to … rules of precedence … (Haru's) neck and throat are much whitened, the paint terminating in three points at the back of the neck… Her lips are slightly touched with red paint. When they are all assembled, Haru and her very graceful mother, squatting before each, present tea and sweetmeats on lacquer trays…. They address each other by their names with the honorific prefix 'O' and the respectful suffix 'San'.

Isabella Bird, visitor to Japan, on a traditional Japanese children's tea party (1878)

The Common Man Advances
1840–1914

BY THE NINETEENTH CENTURY, the human rights first claimed during the French Revolution had evolved into practical concern for humanity as a whole. With this, health, happiness, leisure, work or home environment all acquired a new importance. This helped create a climate of opinion in which it would no longer do for rulers to ignore their subjects' wishes, as had been all too common among Europe's absolute monarchs. Early moves towards a more global concern with humanity were usually pioneered by individuals, but their ideas had influence, and by the turn of the twentieth century, it was no longer good enough for ordinary people to 'know their place'. In this so-called 'Age of the Common Man', the 'place' had significantly altered.

1840s
THE FATALISTIC VIEW

For centuries, humanity had been obliged to accept the pains and perils which, people came to believe, life 'naturally' involved. From the mid-nineteenth century, however, individuals began to challenge this fatalism. In 1847, for instance, anaesthetics – dubbed 'unnatural' by critics – brought an end to the centuries when surgery was both dreaded and often fatal. The Hungarian gynaecologist Ignaz Semmelwiess (1818–65) refused to accept childbed fever and the death of new mothers as just another of life's many cruelties. Instead, he searched for causes and the cures which could save his patients. Likewise, controversial studies into sexual repressions by the Austrian psychiatrist Sigmund Freud (1856–1939) helped many people whose mental distress had long been without sympathy or explanation.

► p. 136 **1854**
'ABANDON HOPE ALL YE WHO ENTER HERE!'

When Florence Nightingale brought a group of nurses to Scutari hospital during the Crimean War (1854–56), she had a double mission: to make nursing a respectable career for women, despite shocked opposition at the idea of ladies doing such work, and to improve medical care for wounded soldiers. Scutari, where the sick and injured lay untended and uncomforted in damp, rat-ridden corridors and food and water was filthy and infected, prompted Nightingale to remark that there should be notice above the hospital entrance reading 'Abandon hope all ye who enter here!' Nevertheless, she and her nurses reduced the death rate at Scutari from 42 to two per cent through better care and hygiene and the psychological balm of personal concern for their patients.

1859
THE RED CROSS

In 1859, Henry Dunant (1828–1910), a Swiss philanthropist, drew the same conclusions about medicine in war as Florence Nightingale, when he witnessed the Battle of Solferino – at which there were 40,000 casualties. Dunant saw soldiers laying ignored on the battlefield, bleeding from wounds and in agony as the fighting raged around them. Dunant, like Nightingle, was shocked and appalled, but refused to shrug off a situation that had been accepted in war for centuries. In 1864, he founded the Red Cross Organisation for the care of battle casualties on both sides in a conflict, and this humanitarian work extended before long to protection for prisoners-of-war and, ultimately, to the relief of suffering throughout the world.

► p. 133 **1885**
THE MOTOR CAR

Machines can liberate; this was certainly true of the bicycle which, after about 1890, enabled women, who took up cycling with especial enthusiasm, to travel further than had ever previously been possible, with or without the bifurcated 'knickerbockers' designed to preserve their modesty. The same could be said of the motor car, pioneered in Germany after 1885 by Gottlieb Daimler (1834–1900). At first a plaything for the rich, the car enabled many townsfolk to venture out into the countryside for the first time. Country folk were not always pleased at the invasion, but when the car gave thousands the sort of mobility that the horse could never offer, it increased knowledge and understanding of rural life and brought people, however reluctantly, closer together.

▲ *The automobile pioneer Gottlieb Daimler.*

1886
POVERTY

Poverty had long been the accepted condition of millions, caused either through their own disinclination and importunity or the fact that this was their 'natural' lot. These ideas did not satisfy Charles Booth (1840–1916), a wealthy Liverpool businessman. In 1886, he set out to discover the extent and nature of poverty in the East End of London and sent investigators to interview the poor and observe their conditions. The approach was strictly factual and Booth's findings, published in

1903, contained no hint of emotion, even though among its conclusions was the damning fact that for nearly 31 per cent of people, poverty derived from inadequate wages and precarious employment. Booth's work later influenced the provision in 1908 of state pensions for the aged.

p. 128 ◄ **Triumphs & Tragedies** ► p. 135

1903
SUFFRAGISM

Women sought the vote as early as 1880, but their polite requests got nowhere. After 1903, when Emmeline Pankhurst (1858–1928) founded the Women's Social and Political Union, suffragism became more militant. Suffragettes chained themselves to railings, smashed windows, set fire to pillarboxes and one, Emily Davison, committed suicide by throwing herself in front of King George V's horse during a race in 1913. Violence was matched by violence, notably the forcible feeding of suffragettes on hunger strike, which so damaged Mrs Pankhurst that it contributed to her death. Her efforts, however, made such a prominent issue of votes for women that after they had taken on men's jobs during the First World War, some were enfranchised in 1918. All adult women in Britain were allowed to vote after 1928.

► p. 134

1895
POPULAR ENTERTAINMENT

The brothers Auguste (1862–1954) and Louis (1864–1948) Lumière gave the first film performance in Paris in 1895. The images were so realistic that the audience, seeing a train coming towards them on screen, panicked and ran out of the theatre. Despite this unfortunate beginning, the cinema became the first mass-entertainment medium, and a rival in Britain to the music hall. The music hall, sentimental, tuneful and rowdy, not only entertained, but expressed working-class aspirations in a particularly touching way. The better life for which they now felt able to hope was

tempered by sadness at their distance from it. 'With a ladder and some glasses,' ran one song 'you could see to Hackney Marshes, if it wasn't for the houses in between'.

1900
REPRESSION RULES

Repression remained the reaction of authority under challenge, even while humanitarians gained ground elsewhere. In 1900, the Boxer Rebellion of Chinese opposed to the powerful influence of foreigners in China was put down with great ferocity. Captured Boxers were beheaded and their executioners posed for photographs with the dismembered bodies. In Russia, protests against tsarist rule in 1901, 1902 and 1905 were put down no less forcefully. However, Russia could no longer afford this kind of response. Millions of peasants lived in extreme poverty and deprivation, and anarchists were willing to murder and terrorise to get what they wanted. Eventually, the Russian tsar,

Nicholas II (1868–1918) and his family faced the ultimate terror – their capture and slaughter by the Bolsheviks in 1918.

p. 131 ◄ **Distant Voices** ► p. 135

On the ground floor lives a hawker with eight children; the eldest, a girl of seventeen…was at home with the two youngest. She makes boot boxes. Wife was out doing half a day's work. A grown-up son lives in Fount Street. The first floor is occupied by Green, a dock labourer, with wife and four children. They suscribe to a clothing club connected with the church. At the top lives Marston, a chair-maker, with wife and four children. They also are in the clothing club. The wife makes match-boxes. She has just been confined, but the baby is dead.

From *The Life and Labour of the Poor in London*, by Charles Booth (1903)

▼ *Emmeline Pankhurst, leader of the Suffragette movement in England, with her daughter Christabel.*

The Social Effects of the First World War

1914–39

THE AGE OF THE COMMON MAN was already under way when the First World War began in 1914. The war accelerated this process, and added to it a new fury against politicians and the militia who, in the popular mind, were responsible for the slaughter of millions. Young people tried to smother the tragedy in the headlong pursuit of pleasure. Others resolved to do absolutely anything to avoid another war. Ordinary Americans, enjoying a new prosperity, invested in stocks and shares, once the monopoly of the rich. However, disillusionment was not far off: the stock market crashed in 1929, impoverishing millions; defeated Germany turned to Nazism; and the 'home fit for heroes' promised to returning British soldiers failed to transpire.

1914
THE WAR TO END ALL WARS

The declaration of war, on 4 August 1914, was greeted in Britain, France and Germany, in the traditional way: by cheering crowds, excitement and patriotic flag-waving. Only three months later, this jubilant mood was replaced by disillusionment as lethal modern weapons forced the combatants in France to retire into trenches and largely remain there, among the mud, sludge, filth, corpses and rats, as long as the fighting lasted. Shock and rage increased, when, in 1915, German zeppelin air raids over Britain made dangerous the one place where people had always presumed themselves to be safe – the home. Even among the victors, the end of the war, on 11 November 1918, was greeted sombrely, with heartfelt relief.

1918
DIVIDE AND RULE

In 1916, the British encouraged the Arabs in Palestine to revolt against their Ottoman Turkish masters – a revolt which succeeded brilliantly – who came to believe that a measure of independence would be their reward. In 1917, in the Balfour Declaration, the British gave a broad hint to the Jews

that Palestine, their ancient ancestral home, would be theirs once again. The result was that Palestine, which became a British mandate from the League of Nations after the war, was the scene of vicious rivalry and hatred, outbreaks of fighting and raiding which the British tried, but ultimately failed, to bring under control. Worse still, both the Jews and the Arabs came to believe that the British were favouring the opposing side in the argument.

1920s
THE ROARING TWENTIES

After the war, many young men and women blanked out their grief for lost friends and relatives with thrills and pleasure. There were wild parties and new, provocative dances such as the 'Black Bottom'. Cars crammed with noisy young people headed for night clubs, from which many did not emerge until dawn. Young women in particular, claimed new freedoms – to cut their hair short, wear 'indecently' short skirts above the knee in 1926, or drink and smoke – things which would never have been permitted them only a short while before. The so-called 'Roaring Twenties' was a crazy time, but not one in which the mass of people could share; their reaction to the war was despair.

1920s
NO HOME FIT FOR HEROES

The 'home fit for heroes' promised by British prime minister David Lloyd George (1863–1945) proved a myth. Many 'heroes' returned home to unemployment. Some sold matches in the streets, displaying their medals to encourage custom. Domestic servants who had hoped to escape the same work, were forced back into service. In defeated Germany, rampant inflation and crippling reparations imposed by the victors led to mass poverty and destitution. The rescue promised by the Nazi leader Adolf Hitler, who came to power in 1933, seemed a tempting way out, with assurances of full employment and socialist benefits. Too late, the Germans realised the price: total submission to Nazi rule and for some – liberals, homosexuals, Jews, gypsies – imprisonment or death.

▼ *The post-war era was characterised by a shaking-off of traditional taboos in attitude, dress and behaviour.*

☞ CUSTOMS   ⬠ DOMESTIC LIFE   ▣ TECHNOLOGY   ✦ CONFLICT

▲ *British prime minister David Lloyd George, with his wife and daughter.*

p. 133◀ **Triumphs & Tragedies** ▶p. 157
1929
THE WALL STREET CRASH

The early post-war period was boom time in the USA. War industries, switching to civilian production, poured out goods for an eager consumer market. Rich dividends were promised to investors, some of whom – the smaller ones – invested their entire savings in stocks and shares. They felt certain of making a profit; instead, they faced ruin. The boom was a bubble which had to burst. Signs that the US economy was not as healthy as investors believed began to appear and stock values began to fall. Then, on 24 October 1929, the pressure became so great that the New York stock exchange crashed. Investors besieged banks clamouring to withdraw their money, but for many it was too late. They had lost everything.

▶ p. 139 ## 1930s
AMERICA ON THE BREADLINE

With the Wall Street Crash, the 'American Dream' – that riches and success were possible for everyone in the land of opportunity – became a nightmare. Jobs disappeared. So did any remaining savings. For millions who now lived on the breadline, queuing for charity food at soup kitchens or living in shanty towns named 'Hoovervilles' after the president of the time, the culture shock was all the greater because their vibrant, success-conscious society, was

psychologically ill-equipped for a national disaster like this. The Americans, however, were lucky. A new president, Franklin D. Roosevelt (1882–1945), elected in 1932, offered Americans a 'New Deal' of socialist-type reforms which enabled them to start digging themselves out of the hole that had opened up when Wall Street crashed.

1935
APPEASEMENT

The ravages of the First World War inspired pacifism in Britain. So much so that appeasement of a now-rampant Nazi Germany became a popular national policy. The urge for peace was so overwhelming that clear signs of Nazi aggressive intent – reviving their forbidden armaments industry, for example – were ignored for the sake of mollifying Adolf Hitler. Meanwhile, the Great Depression had struck Britain hard, throwing millions out of work and onto the 'dole', which barely allowed them to live. In 1936, unemployed men in Jarrow, in north-east England, publicised their plight with a march on London, a token of a new popular idea that society need not be fixed as it was, but could be improved.

1936
PLANNING FOR A BETTER FUTURE

In 1936, British economist John Maynard Keynes (1883–1946) put forward a blueprint for a more stable economy which guaranteed secure employment – a lifeline, in fact, for the millions impoverished by the

Depression. This, Keynes wrote, could be achieved by government spending and control of money to prevent the financial crises which, in the past, had so often destroyed jobs and with them, lives. Keynes' ideas were revolutionary in that they sought to remove the causes of the insecurity that had blighted human life for centuries and to ensure that everyone could earn a decent living. From there, the implications were enormous, for health, proper diet, education, leisure, housing, and, just as important, the hope for the future which the poor had always lacked.

p. 133◀ **Distant Voices** ▶p. 137

Thousands of people gathered in the streets of Jarrow today, and many businesses stopped work as 200 unemployed men began their long march to London. They are carrying with them an oak casket, containing a petition with 11,572 signatures which they hope to present to the government on 4 November. The leaders of the march sported three big banners proclaiming it the 'Jarrow Protest March'. Locals call it the Jarrow Crusade. An appeal raised £800 to support it. The money has been used to buy leather and nails so that the men can mend their boots.

Newspaper report on the Jarrow March (5 October 1936)

▼ *Despair on the streets as the US stock exchange crashes in 1929.*

The Second World War
1939–49

THE DREAD OF ANOTHER WAR, which led to the policy of appeasement, persuaded Adolf Hitler that Britain and France were weak. By 1939, however, the British and French could no longer fool themselves and realised that, as Winston Churchill (1874–1965) had repeatedly warned, Nazi Germany was intent on aggression. The mood on 3 September 1939, when war was finally declared, was sombre but defiant. The British were to prove their backbone in the next six years, and accepted great changes in their daily and family lives. They had to cope with air raids, rationing, dislocation and early on, the threat of Nazi invasion. Socially, these were destructive factors, but in fact the British found a new camaraderie in danger.

▶ p. 141

1940
RATIONING

Because of its island location, rationing became essential in wartime Britain. Luxuries, and certain foodstuffs, especially from distant countries, such as oranges, and for a time, chocolate, virtually disappeared. Essentials – butter, eggs, meat, fish, clothing – were strictly apportioned through ration books containing coupons. It was a well-considered system and in fact provided some Britons with better nutrition than they had had in peacetime, when poor families relied too much on carbohydrates and not enough on vital proteins. The radio and newspapers carried regular hints on how to make the most of the rations, but there were, of course, black marketeers, selling extra goods, and many were willing to buy from them. Others, who told the police about black-marketing activities, could be ostracised.

▲ Rationing was introduced in Britain in 1940.

1940
WARTIME WOMEN

With their menfolk away, women became lone parents, worked in munitions factories, joined the women's sections of the armed services. Countrywomen took evacuees into their homes and were often shocked at the state of them – poor, ignorant, and unfamiliar with toilets, knives and forks and baths. This opened many eyes to the urgent need for social improvement and in 1942, when the Beveridge Report was published outlining the Welfare State, it was widely discussed. Morals, too, were an issue. The dangers of wartime had loosened inhibitions and many children were born outside marriage. Marriage itself became an emergency measure, and couples wed in haste, seeking to seal their relationships before one or the other became casualties of the war.

✳ ▶ p. 138

1940
CONQUERORS AND CONQUERED

Between April and June 1940, Nazi Germany overran Norway, Denmark, France, Belgium and the Netherlands and, in 1941, parts of Russia. Poland had already been conquered n 1939. These countries were now forced to live under foreign and often retributive domination, as the Nazi conquest brought curfews, shortages and savage punishments for disobedience. This produced several reactions: most people simply tried to survive as best they could and keep out of trouble; others risked everything to form resistance movements, and were not always helped by their compatriots who thought it best to keep their heads down. Some collaborated with the Germans, seeking safety by fraternising with the winning side. Their punishment after the war was savage.

1941
THE BLITZ

Air raids were the most feared threat after the Second World War began and there were mass evacuations of children from the big cities, which were most at risk. Those who remained behind in the towns and cities relied on public air raid shelters, or dug up parts of their gardens to install their own. Some, refusing to leave their homes, relied on the space under the staircase for protection. In London, families took over parts of the Underground at night. They operated like a small, isolated community, sharing, cheering each other up, making new friendships, staging sing-songs and dancing, but also behaving somewhat tribally, as they fiercely preserved their own pitches on the cold, uninviting but secure railway platforms.

1941
CONQUERED BY JAPAN

The Japanese, who entered the war in 1941, conquered a large swathe of Pacific Ocean territories, including several belonging to the British, French and Dutch empires. The native peoples suffered their share of Japanese brutality, not least because they had 'offended' their conquerors' Bushido sense of honour which made death preferable to defeat. The Japanese nevertheless presented themselves as liberators from European imperialist aggression. Though many regarded this as exchanging one foreign occupier for another, they still took advantage. The absence of the European rulers encouraged their own resolve for independence, and

☞ CUSTOMS ⬢ DOMESTIC LIFE ▮ TECHNOLOGY ✦ CONFLICT

▲ *Men queue to join the resistance movement in German-occupied countries during the Second World War.*

after Japan's defeat and the war's end, the French in Indochina and the Dutch in Indonesia found determined, well-organised – and successful – resistance to their return.

1941
RESISTING THE NAZIS

In the Nazi-occupied countries, those who chose resistance not only risked their lives every day, but also assumed the tremendous nervous strain of a clandestine existence. Some were simply patriots, determined to eject the hated invader from their land. Others had their own agendas, such as the Communists in Yugoslavia or the supporters of the 'Free French' General Charles de Gaulle (1890–1970), who hoped for political power after the war. Whatever their motives, resistance fighters lived a life of constant suspense, constant watchfulness and always the danger of betrayal. They knew what capture could mean – torture, imprisonment and death – and that all their willpower would be needed not to yield the information the Nazis would try to force out of them.

1941
HITLER'S FINAL SOLUTION

Prejudice, persecution and pogroms had stalked Jews for many centuries, but nothing compared to the Nazis' systematic attempt to exterminate them as a race during the Second World War. All over

occupied Europe, Jews were rounded up, crammed into cattle trucks and transported to the concentration camps the Nazis had set up in Poland and Germany. The Nazis had also constructed gas chambers where the Jews were taken, supposedly to have showers, then shut in and gassed to death en masse. Later, their bodies were burned in ovens. Some six million were wiped out in this horrific fashion. Jews, however, were not the only victims of Nazi 'ethnic cleansing': gypsies, also regarded by the Nazis as a blight on society, received the same sadistic treatment and four million died.

1949
THE STATE OF ISRAEL

In 1944 and 1945, as the Allied forces closed in on Nazi Germany, the ghastly revelations of the liberated camps, with their skeletal, dehumanised survivors, shocked and appalled the world. This gave a powerful impetus to the aspirations of Jews in Palestine who believed that, without a country of their own, this 'Holocaust' could happen again. Once the British, exasperated by the savage Arab-Jewish rivalries and terrorist attacks against them, returned the Palestine mandate to the new United Nations, a vote was taken there in 1947 to create the State of Israel. The new state was immediately challenged by the surrounding Arab countries and a bitter war ensued. By 1949, after nine months, Israel prevailed, but Arab-Israeli hatred survived and has scarred the region ever since.

PALESTINE AND ISRAEL, 1920–49

⌐ Palestine, British
    Mandate 1920–48
⌐ Israel after Declaration
    of Independence
    (1948) & war with
    Arab League 1949
☐ British Mandate
    1920–46
☐ French Mandate
    1920–41
(1946) Date of independence
    of nation

p. 135 ◀ **Distant Voices** ▶ p. 139

At 3 a.m., just as dawn was breaking, hundreds of aeroplanes came over (Amsterdam) and bombs were falling everywhere. I went out onto the balcony and ... the sky seemed filled with planes, and parachute troops were being dropped in large numbers on several parts of the city. Meanwhile the [German] bombers concentrated ... on the important buildings, including barracks. When the smoke and dust had subsided ... several buildings, including the prison, had been destroyed.... The presence of the Fifth Column [traitors] was shown by the way parachute troops approaching main buildings were given directions by residents ... in the houses near.

Eyewitness account of the Nazi invasion of the Netherlands (10 May 1940)

The Years of Freedom
1945–70

THROUGHOUT THE WORLD, the subordination of youth to age has always been a feature of societies and cultures. The 'Swinging Sixties' saw this priority overthrown in many Western democracies, promising anarchy at worst, and at best, giving rise to incomprehension and anger among older generations. The young – that is, those under 30 – set themselves against everything that made society what it was: social rules, moral rules, forms of dress, forms of entertainment and music, and above all, the wars which had been an integral part of life since ancient times. With this, the so-called 'generation gap' opened up and other disgruntled groups – blacks, women, and later, homosexuals – were inspired to make their own bids for freedom.

1945
THE SEEDS OF FREEDOM

The quest for freedom seemed to be in the air once the Second World War was over. As imperial powers, the French and the Dutch had suffered severe loss of face during the War and Britain, though a major victor, had been impoverished by its efforts. The new Labour government elected in Britain in 1945 believed, too, that colonial rule should be decreased and in 1947, with the granting of independence to India and the creation of Pakistan, a long process of decolonisation began. Other lessons had hit home elsewhere. During the war, black Americans had made their own considerable contribution, and suffered their own losses. The segregated regiments in which army GIs had served now seemed iniquitous, and black Americans baulked at returning to their previous, downtrodden status.

1950s
AGAINST WAR

It had always been the fate of young men to fight and die in society's wars. This principle could be maintained as long as war was considered glorious and patriotic, but the young generation, born during or just after the Second World War, sought to break what they saw as a pernicious mould. Pacifism was nothing new at this time, but the scale of it was. The Korean War

(1950–53), and the fighting in French Indochina, Greece and Malaya suggested that nothing had changed. However, vociferous, often violent protests and demonstrations took place as the young challenged the Establishment's presumption that yet another generation would let itself be decimated by war. With this, other Establishment values came under equally heavy fire.

✳ 1957
COLONIAL INDEPENDENCE

The effects of independence in many former colonial territories laid bare the effects of imperialism. Native cultures had necessarily been suppressed during the long decades of colonial rule. When independence revived them, the spectacle was sometimes alarming. For instance, in Africa, where Ghana (the former Gold Coast) was the first imperial possession to be granted independence (1957), the leaders of countries accepted Britain's 'gifts' of a democratic, parliamentary system. Before long, however, their tendency towards rule by one 'strong man', a characteristic of their pre-colonial days, reasserted itself; so did tribalism, now expressed in damaging civil wars. This greatly exacerbated the basic poverty of newly independent countries and sank them in a slough from which many have not yet recovered.

1960s
BAN THE BOMB!

Protest soon became the virtual symbol of the 1960s, with rallies, marches, demonstrations and clashes with the police. The Nuclear Age which followed the atomic bombing of Japan in 1945, produced rowdy, vociferous demonstrations in Britain, France and Germany, demanding that the government eschew atomic weapons. The war in Vietnam, too, roused fury at what young Americans, British and French saw as an immoral conflict. Some Americans went to Canada to avoid being drafted and were dubbed cowards by some, but heroes by others. In America, too, Martin Luther King (1929–68) used peaceful, but determined, methods to promote black equality. Malcolm X (Malcolm Little, 1926–65) preferred more violent ways to achieve the same object. Both were assassinated.

▲ *US Civil Rights leader Martin Luther King, who employed peaceful means to draw attention to black inequality.*

☞ 1960s
GIVE PEACE A CHANCE

The mass social revolt of the young, which left their elders feeling thoroughly beleaguered, seemed to involve everything pugnaciously different from the principles of existing society. Young men grew their hair long. Young women wore revealing miniskirts. They lived together without

☞ CUSTOMS ⬟ DOMESTIC LIFE ▯ TECHNOLOGY ★ CONFLICT

▲ *Malcolm Little, known as Malcolm X, a militant Civil Rights campaigner in America.*

being married, experimented with drugs, embraced mystical religions, such as Zen Buddhism, and gathered at rock festivals to listen to their own brand of popular music. Some, such as the Flower Children, went so far as to create an 'alternative society' with some of the same elements. This included a philosophy which sprang from their idea that if only everyone would 'give peace a chance' – as one of their songs went – then the world would be a wonderful place.

1960s
WOMEN'S LIBERATION

The centuries-old subordination of women could be regarded in two ways: women were either nurturers of children, performing society's most vital single task, or victims of male oppression that denied them their ambitions. The women's liberation movement took the latter view, and the clamour began for equal opportunities as men, abortion 'on demand', access to education and training, and to jobs formerly reserved for men, even access to men's clubs and other 'bastions' of male domination. There was, naturally enough, resistance – and not just from men, either. Concerns were voiced that if women abandoned their traditional role, or even supplemented it with the new roles they demanded, the very fabric of society could suffer.

▶ p. 140

1960s
THE NUCLEAR AGE

In the 1960s and for some time afterwards, the world lived with the awesome knowledge that for the first time in all history, humanity possessed the power to obliterate all life on Earth. For ordinary people, this was a threat almost too terrible to take in. Nevertheless, nuclear power, even in its more peaceful application as energy, provoked atavistic fears. All the more so because the rival superpowers, the US and USSR, possessed nuclear arsenals, and popular anti-nuclear protests had little effect on their leaders, who regarded nuclear weapons as a mutual deterrent. This situation provoked the young, who felt they had the most to lose, to ever more vociferous hatred of the Establishment that had produced this dreadful situation.

1960s
THE DECLINE OF APARTHEID

South Africa imposed apartheid – the separation of the black and white races – in 1948, but this was merely official sanction of a situation that had long existed. The Boers, the white South Africans of Dutch descent, believed blacks to be inferior and had, in fact, found justification for this

belief in the Bible. Their thinking, of course, ran counter to the more liberal ways of thought gaining ground in the West during the 1960s, but South Africa's comparative isolation enabled them to sustain it. The liberalising influences put pressure on South Africa nonetheless. In the West, there began a campaign of sanctions and censure, designed to make apartheid untenable. Over 30 years passed and much suffering took place before it succeeded.

p. 137 ◀ **Distant Voices** ▶ p. 141

The Beatles flew in to Kennedy Airport, New York, today and met their most ecstatic reception yet. Urged on by disc jockeys, who had been broadcasting constant updates on the progress of the Pan Am Flight 101, thousands of American teenagers packed the airport to scream their adulation. They broke through a police cordon, then formed a Beatles motorcade that followed their heroes all the way to the city's Plaza Hotel.

Beatlemania, report from New York
(8 February 1964)

▼ *Mixed bathing on a South African beach after the apartheid regime had been lifted.*

The Global Village
1938–2000

HUMAN SOCIETY, believed to have begun in East Africa some 20 million years ago, became dispersed through migrations, and over aeons of time, separated into different cultures. Today, on the brink of the third millennium, modern technology has enabled it to become reacquainted, through worldwide long-haul travel, computers, faxes, e-mails, as well as the older technologies of radio, television and the telephone. Metaphorically speaking, the world is now a much smaller place – a 'Global Village' as some have come to call it – where contact can be made with far distant places in seconds, news can reach television screens almost as soon as it is made and a multitude of satellites orbit Earth to help make it all happen.

1938
BEFORE THE TECHNOLOGICAL REVOLUTION

In 1938, British prime minister Neville Chamberlain (1869–1940) spoke of Czechoslovakia, about to be devoured by Nazi Germany, as a place 'of which we know nothing'. At the time, most people would have concurred with him. Life in Britain, as elsewhere, was very parochial. Few ordinary people travelled. Even fewer travelled abroad. There was radio, but no television. Localised human existence had been normal for many centuries. In medieval times, for example, many people never left their villages. Until the Spaniards conquered them after 1519, the Aztec and other peoples of Mexico thought they were alone in the world. Even today, remote tribes, for example in the vastnesses of the Brazilian jungle, remain unaware of the outside world.

▼ *Television achieved a huge rise in popularity throughout the 1950s.*

📘 ▶ p. 140 ## 1954
THE WORLD OPENS UP

Television, invented in 1925, was the first to open up a window on the world after it became widely available by about 1954. Through TV, life could be observed going on in distant places, even beneath the sea. 'Jumbo' jets could carry 300 people or more to the other side of the world in a few hours. Today, computer users can make instant links, letters that would take days or weeks to travel by post, appear instantly as faxes. E-mails flash onto computer screens at the touch of a button. These capabilities are so familiar on the brink of the millennium that they have lost much of their wonder, yet barely 40 years ago, they were not yet possible.

1990s
ISLAM VS THE WEST

Islam and Christianity were rivals, often savage rivals, almost from the moment Islam was founded in AD 624. The Western world, which was largely the product of Christianity, has now taken over as Islam's modern challenger, and one that funda-mentalist Muslims in particular regard as an evil to be expunged. Several Muslim countries, such as Iran and Algeria, have sought to close themselves off from 'pernicious' Western influences, though still dealing with the West for political or trade purposes. Their rivalry is, however, a fruitful

ground for Muslim terrorist groups who have used modern weaponry, especially bombs, to make their presence known. This has often resulted in scenes of destruction and carnage, made all the more impactive by graphic television coverage.

1990
SPACE EXPLORATION AND ITS BENEFITS

Space is not simply a playground for scientists or the source of exciting television transmissions. Benefits for humanity can come from space exploration. Medical research could gain much from the germ-free conditions to be found in space. Minerals brought back from the Moon could lead to new drugs. The experiences of astronauts, in particular weightlessness, may lead to new understandings of the human body and its capabilities. The Hubble Space Telescope, launched in 1990, is able to make its observations without the interference from the atmosphere which sometimes complicates the work of Earth-based astronomers. This makes possible closer observations of the stars, including the Sun, and greater understanding of their functions and of the Sun's effects on Earth and its life.

2000
FOOD IS INTERNATIONAL

Food is a great deal more than sustenance. It means social contact, with perhaps traditional or religious meanings, and new gastronomical experiences which bring differing peoples together. Immigration has long been the catalyst here. In the USA, a country of many different communities, a whole world table is laid out in shops, from Italian pasta and pizza and Jewish gefilte fish or lockshen (noodle) soup to Indian, Thai, Malaysian and Indonesian curries. Britain's Indian immigrants, too, have changed the eating habits of the native population, with supermarket shelves full of ready-made curry meals. Anyone almost anywhere can eat Chinese, Greek, Turkish, Creole from the West Indies, traditional French cheeses and German sausage. In the favoured West at least, cuisine is now international.

☞ CUSTOMS   🏠 DOMESTIC LIFE   📘 TECHNOLOGY   ✦ CONFLICT

2000
LONGER, HEALTHIER LIVES

Modern medicine has triumphed over nature at its most destructive in many ways. In recent years, micro- and keyhole surgery has reduced pain and incapacity after operations. Damaged limbs can be saved. Infertility can be helped. Transplants have saved lives that would otherwise have been doomed. Children defective at birth can be treated and survive. AIDS, the great scourge of the twentieth century, is being strongly challenged. But these are not just scientific matters. The fact that solutions have been found for so much that was once incurable has roused new expectations, for longer, healthier and with that, happier, lives.

2000
REMAINING PROBLEMS

The world is not without its serious problems – war, urban crime, economic difficulties, poverty. There is however, a distinct internationalism at work in the search for some solutions. Scientists and governments have come together to tackle AIDS. International aid has many times gone to the rescue of famine sufferers in different parts of the world. Multinational forces have policed trouble spots such as the civil war-torn former Yugoslavia. Among ordinary people, television no sooner shows terrible scenes of suffering and deprivation from anywhere in the world than donations flow in to mitigate them.

2000
SPURNING THE GLOBAL VILLAGE

The materialistic life, with its emphasis on consumerism, is spurned by the unconventional 'hippies' who adhere to their principles even though the Sixties, which gave rise to them, are long past. A great deal about the Swinging Sixties still lives through them: a strong sense of community, the desire for peaceful co-existence and a belief in love as the elixir for a good and happy life. Realising, even so, that most of the world does not seek to run on these lines, hippies tend to live in tight, sometimes remote communities or, in their more recent 'New Age Traveller' persona, they move from place to place like gypsies.

p. 139 ◀ **Distant Voices** ▶ p. 145

Barney Clark, a 61-year old American dentist, stood unaided today, nineteen days after two chambers of his failing heart had been replaced by a mechanised aluminium and polyurethane pump. Two days after the operation, performed by William DeVries in Salt Lake City, Utah, he had a second one to repair his lungs, damaged when air was pumped in during the first. Dr DeVries is the only American surgeon allowed to perform human operations with artificial hearts. It was agreed before the operation that Mr. Clark could end his own life if conditions became unbearable.

Report on the artificial heart
(22 December 1982)

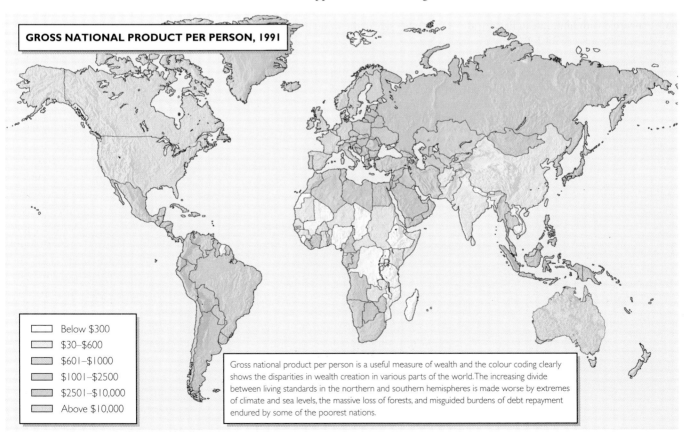

GROSS NATIONAL PRODUCT PER PERSON, 1991

- Below $300
- $30–$600
- $601–$1000
- $1001–$2500
- $2501–$10,000
- Above $10,000

Gross national product per person is a useful measure of wealth and the colour coding clearly shows the disparities in wealth creation in various parts of the world. The increasing divide between living standards in the northern and southern hemispheres is made worse by extremes of climate and sea levels, the massive loss of forests, and misguided burdens of debt repayment endured by some of the poorest nations.

Exploration and Empires

TODAY WE CAN SEE on the daily news images of politicians from many nations assembling to discuss problems that are shared by a region or even by the entire world. Sometimes these reports show areas devastated by famine or other natural disasters, for which the entire international community sends aid. Yet this sense of a planetary society is a remarkably recent achievement. For most of history, the vast distances separating human communities has meant that they have dealt with their problems in isolation. One chapter in the story of humanity must describe just how these far-flung societies have been drawn together into the global village that we live in today. The history of building empires is linked by several recurring themes that recur. It is easy to focus on particular individuals who, through courage and curiosity, have risked dangerous journeys overland or by sea, facing death at the hands of bandits or of nature. But larger movements beyond the direction of single individuals or groups have been equally important. Wars and trade have also made vital contributions and have frequently worked in tandem in bringing the world together. These encounters have enabled societies to adapt their traditional cultures, either making more able to resist the invaders or to transform them into more diverse and dynamic communities.

KEY THEMES

★ CONFLICT

⌐ ENCOUNTERS

❖ FACILITIES

✈ CONQUEST

○ SETTLEMENT

✿ TRADE

✳ CRISES

⊃ PATHFINDER

✳ EMPIRES

⊕ CAUSES

KEY EVENTS

① 2500 BC
CITIES

Urban societies, based on large towns where some residents pursued non-agricultural occupations and exchanged the products of their work for food, are the fundamental building blocks of the modern world. They arose in different places across the planet at different times, but on the Eurasian landmass this development occurred across a 1,000-year period ending in 2500 BC.

② AD 634–698
THE GREAT CONQUESTS

Between AD 634 and 638 Arab armies defeated both the Byzantine heirs of Rome and the Persian Empire. The whole of the Middle East belonged to them when, in AD 639, they invaded Egypt. Arab-led armies marched west across North Africa. Carthage fell to them in AD 698.

③ 1492
SPANISH POWER AND EXPLORATION

Christopher Columbus (1492–1502) discovered the westward passage from Europe to the Americas and found the right winds to achieve this in previously unknown waters without any guide. After securing support from Queen Isabella, his first expedition embarked in September 1492 with three ships carrying 100 men. In October they first landed on present-day Watling Island and proceeded to sail around the Bahamas.

④ 1519
SAILING ROUND THE WORLD

In 1519 Ferdinand Magellan left Spain, explored the east coast of South America and then sailed around the southern tip of the continent. They finally reached the Philippines where Magellan was killed by the indigenous peoples, but the ships continued to India and Africa, thereby making the first circumnavigation of the globe.

⑤ 1549
SLAVERY IN THE NEW WORLD

In 1549, the Portuguese decided to exploit their Brazilian colony by developing a sugar industry there. Brazil was comparatively under-populated and the native Americans who lived there were not farmers, so Africans were brought from Guinea and Angola to work the land.

⑥ 1788
THE PENAL COLONY

Eleven ships carrying 700 convicts, 36 women and guards, plus provisions for two years, arrived in Botany Bay in Australia in 1788; they settled around Sydney Cove. Few people travelled beyond the Great Dividing Range up the east coast. No powerful neighbours threatened the colony, but they faced the problem of economic viability.

⑦ 1947
COLLAPSING EMPIRES

Civil unrest and a naval mutiny (1946) forced Britain to accelerate moves towards independence. In elections Indian Muslims in the north voted overwhelmingly for the Muslim League, which demanded a separate state. In August 1947 the country was partitioned into independent India (mainly Hindu) and Pakistan (mainly Muslim).

⑧ 1969
THE SPACE AGE

Space exploration became entangled with superpower rivalry, particularly between the USA and the Soviet Union and soon became a showpiece to display technical superiority with obvious military implications. One of the greatest missions was the 'race' to the Moon. In July 1969 the United States won when Neil Armstrong, Edwin 'Buzz' Aldrin and Michael Collins landed on lunar soil.

TIMELINE

8000 BC   Neolithic Revolution

2500 BC   Rise of urban societies

814 BC   Carthage is founded

240 BC   Voyage of Pytheas

30 BC   Roman dominance of the Mediterranean

AD 97   Ban Chao reaches Caspian Sea

AD 698   Arabs conquer Carthage

1206   Genghis Khan becomes ruler of the Mongols

1240   Mongols advance into Europe

1368   Establishment of the Ming dynasty

1420   Henry the Navigator makes first expedition to Madeira Islands

1487   Bartholomew Diaz departs for the African coast

1492   Christopher Columbus's first expedition

1497   Vasco da Gama sails around the Cape of Good Hope

1498   Columbus discovers Venezuela

1502   Columbus discovers central America

1511   Albuquerque captures Malacca Port

1516   Ottomans invade Mamluk Empire

1517   Piri Reis draws up first map of the world

1519   Magellan embarks on his circumnavigation of the globe

1519   Vasco Nunez Balboa discovers the Pacific Ocean

1520   Suleiman the Magnificent becomes Ottoman Emperor

1549   Foundations of the slave trade

1577   Drake departs for the Pacific

1733   Great Northern Expedition begins

1788   Penal Colony established in New South Wales

1791   Slave revolt in Haiti

1798   French conquer Egypt

1799   Humboldt explores the Orinoco River

1801   Humboldt explores the Andes

1803   Louisiana Purchase

1830   French invasion of Algiers

1831   Darwin travels to South America

1841   Charles Sturt charts Australia

1849   Livingstone maps central and southern Africa

1860   Burke and Wills cross Australia

1860   Speke visits Uganda

1869   Suez Canal opens

1888   Fridtjof Nansen's first expedition to Greenland icecap

1911   Roald Amundsen reaches the South Pole

1912   Scott's expedition perishes on return from South Pole

1926   Amundsen flies over the North Pole

1929   Byrd flies over South Pole

1947   Separate states of India and Pakistan established

1969   First moon landing

The First Empires
8000–539 BC

THE EXACT ORIGINS of the human species, homo sapiens, remain a matter for debate among anthropologists and archeologists, but it is generally accepted that a genetic heritage can be traced back to an original hominid ancestor in Africa. The spread of humanity across the face of the globe is a testimony to the nomadic lifestyle of man's ancestors in their earliest days. Our ability to adapt to diverse climatic conditions is the consequence of our capacity to manufacture tools from natural resources. Throughout history mankind has been on the move, and our past is as much a story of this perpetual motion as it is of the achievements of a more settled existence.

8000 BC
THE NEOLITHIC REVOLUTION

Around 8000 BC, some nomadic bands in the Middle East realised that cereal grasses could be cultivated, with a consequent increase in the amount of food available. This was such a remarkable discovery that archeologists have called it the 'Neolithic Revolution'. From this moment, humanity started along the path that has brought us to our present way of life. The two main sites uncovered by archeologists demonstrating this are at Jericho in the Jordan Valley and Catal Huyuk in Turkey. Jericho is a smaller settlement, cramped by a defensive rampart of ditch and wall. Catal Huyuk is more sprawling, and also contains evidence of early attempts at working metal. However, they were each constructed by people exclusively using stone tools.

❖ ▶ p. 156 ### 3500 BC
METALS AND TRADE

Some knowledge of metal-working was acquired quite rapidly, using copper ore. This in fact became a kind of luxury good, and there are indications that there was some kind of trade in copper, although whether it was between settlements or simply some kind of exchange made by passing nomads is again a matter of speculation. But it was this exchange between groups that lived in the mountains of the Near East and settlements located on more fertile land along the banks of the rivers Tigris and Euphrates that produced the next stage in the development of human society. Starting around 3500 BC, settlements became larger at the southern end of the Euphrates river valley, and the city became a fact of human life.

3000 BC
CITIES

Urban societies, based on large towns where some residents pursued non-agricultural occupations and exchanged the products of their work for food, are the fundamental building block of the modern world. They arose in different places on the planet at different times, but on the Eurasian landmass this development occurred across 1,000-year period ending in 2500 BC. In Africa, an urban society arose in the Nile Delta around 3000 BC, and at about the same time in the Hwang Ho river valley of East Asia. In India, the first cities were created in the Indus Valley in about 2750 BC. The Americas saw the last urban foundations, in about 1150 BC.

3000 BC
THE URBAN SOCIETY

The leaders of an urban society, almost immediately after its creation, seem to have sought to acquire food, raw materials, or other goods by force. This means that either through exploration or through trade, and probably a combination of the two, they became aware of neighbours. The urban society of Egypt, for example, was a product of the use or threat of force. The first pharaoh, Menes (also known as Narmer), united his lands of Upper Egypt with the settlements in the Nile Delta known as Lower Egypt. That they were aware of other lands beyond Egypt is indicated by an ivory plaque of King Qaa of the 1st dynasty, showing an armed man who apparently fought in defence of a city of Canaan (modern Israel).

▼ *One of the earliest-known civilisations grew up around the River Nile c. 3000 BC.*

 CONFLICT   🖳 ENCOUNTERS   ❖ FACILITIES   ♣ CONQUEST

2600 BC
THE EARLIEST EXPLORATIONS

Once one of these early urban societies became aware of the existence of other lands producing valuable products, it was possible to trade with them. In 2600 BC the Egyptian pharaoh sent a fleet of at least 40 ships north along the Mediterranean coast to the town of Byblos, in modern Lebanon. This expedition brought back shiploads of timber, a commodity in comparatively short supply in the parched lands of the Nile Valley. The Egyptians also explored south, along the Nile and the Red Sea. Somewhere here was a land they called Punt, where a supply of incense was available. During the third millennium BC, two major expeditions are known to have taken place: one during the reign of the pharaoh Sahure and the other led by an Egyptian named Hennu.

▲ *Archeological site in Egypt with the remains of a boat, used for transporting bodies to the pyramid tombs.*

▶ p. 150

2450 BC
BARBARIANS

In Mesopotamia, war also became the means by which individual Sumerian city states expanded at the expense of their neighbours. The Stelae of the Vultures commemorates a war waged by Eannatum, the leader of the city of Lagash, about 2450

BC. They fought over a piece of land; under the terms of the treaty settling the conflict, the land known as the *Gu-Edina* ('the desert's edge') belonged to Lagash, although the defeated city, Umma, was allowed to collect barley from it so long as a heavy tax was paid. The Sumerian city states became victims of an invading people, known as the Akkadians, who spoke a Semitic language. They simply replaced the Sumerian rulers with Akkadian ones.

2371 BC
SARGON THE GREAT

In Mesopotamia, the most dramatic change occurred during the time of Sargon the Great (2371 BC). Where previous victors had allowed the governments of defeated cities to continue to rule, only demanding payment of tribute, Sargon did away with enemy ruling dynasties and placed his conquests under the control of governors appointed by him. This ensured a loyal subordinate who could administer the internal affairs of a city state with a free hand, while still supplying the dominant ruler with the means to support an army capable of enforcing their authority. The effect of the Mesopotamian practice of ruling conquered territories through governors meant that if an empire fell, the bulk of it simply transferred its allegiance to the victor.

650 BC
IMPERIALISM IN THE ANCIENT NEAR EAST

There were three main imperial centres in the Ancient Near East: Egypt, Mesopotamia and Asia Minor. The three fought over the land that lay in between them – modern Syria and Palestine. The eventual winner was Mesopotamia. The Assyrians, who lived in the northern part of the Tigris-Euphrates river system, achieved dominance over both Mesopotamia, Syria, Palestine, and even Egypt by about 650 BC. However, in 609 BC

▼ *Mask depicting the head of Sargon the Great of Mesopotamia.*

this empire collapsed in the face of a Babylonian revolt, supported by the Medes and the Persians. Only Egypt recovered its independence. In 539 BC, the relatively minor region of Persia took advantage of a generation of political instability in the ruling Babylonian house to overthrow the Babylonian Empire and make its own king, Cyrus the Great, king of the Middle East.

p. 141 ◀ **Distant Voices** ▶ p. 147

There is no king who of himself alone is strongest. Ten or fifteen kings follow Hammurabi of Babylon, the same number follow Rim-Sin of Larsa, the same numer follow Ibal-pi-El of Eshnunna, the same number follow Amut-pi-El of Qatanum, and twenty kings follow Yarim-Lim of Yamkhad.

Letter describing early empires of Mesopotamia (*c.* 1814 BC)

Exploration in the Ancient Mediterranean World

700–116 BC

THROUGHOUT THE Ancient World, people began to travel more and more, and as a result, geographical knowledge increased and accumulated correspondingly. This knowledge was largely based on the words and records of anonymous travellers, many of which have not survived to leave a historical record. A few, however, have survived to preserve several stories of the expeditions that revealed the shape and extent of the African and Eurasian land masses. These were some of the greatest early explorations; the beginnings of discovery that were to form the basis of many later adventures that led to the opening up of trade and colonisation in many parts of the Mediterranean world.

▲ *Model of an Egyptian seafaring vessel.*

○ ▶ p. 158 **700 BC**
THE PHOENICIANS

The first people who gained a reputation for skilful navigation and exploration were the Phoenicians, speakers of a Semitic language. They lived in cities along the coast of modern-day Lebanon and Syria around 700 BC, and from there sailed west across the Mediterranean, establishing colonies in Malta, Sicily, North Africa and Spain. The Spanish settlements were, in the long run, the most important. The Iberian Peninsula was a treasure house of metal ores, and Phoenician traders secured a monopoly that lasted two centuries. Phoenician coins have even been found in the Azores. The most important colony was Carthage, which itself became the centre of a major empire encompassing western Sicily, the Spanish coast and North Africa.

⊃ ▶ p. 153 **610 BC**
THE CIRCUMNAVIGATION OF AFRICA

One of the earliest expeditions ever ordered by a government expressly to achieve greater geographical knowledge was made during the reign of Pharaoh Necho (*c.* 610–594 BC). Necho instructed a group of Phoenician sailors to voyage around Libya. The Phoenicians sailed south along the east African coast. During the third year, they sailed through the Strait of Gibraltar and back into the Mediterranean. Herodotus did not believe this account because, when the Phoenicians took a westward heading, the sun was unexpectedly on their right, in the northern quadrant of the sky – which is exactly where it would be if one is sailing west around the Cape of Good Hope!

600 BC
THE GREEKS

Thanks to the survival of a number of historical and literary texts, we know more about Greek explorations than those of any other ancient civilisation. The Greeks travelled west in the wake of the Phoenicians, founding many more colonies. They also ventured into the Black Sea, across Asia to India, north to Britain; and south into Africa. One of the most important Greek cities in this exploratory movement was a

tiny settlement on the coast of Asia Minor, known as Phocaea. One of its citizens may have travelled as far as Britain in the sixth century BC. Many of its inhabitants were sent west to found colonies in Italy, Sicily and, most importantly, at Marseilles in about 600 BC.

450 BC
THE CARTHAGINIANS

The traditional date for the foundation of Carthage is 814 BC. During the sixth century BC it brought under its protection the other Phoenician colonies of the western Mediterranean, and created a network of ports that enabled Carthaginian merchants to control the bulk of trade in the western Mediterranean and the Atlantic. The historical record includes two Carthaginian expeditions that expanded the geographical knowledge of the literate peoples of the Mediterranean basin. Around 450 BC a Carthaginian named Himilco sailed northwards up the Atlantic coast of Europe. The details of his voyage remain sketchy even in our sources, but many historians accept that he reached Britain and possibly Ireland.

▲ *The ancient North African city of Carthage.*

425 BC
HANNO'S WEST AFRICAN VOYAGE

About 25 years later another Carthaginian merchant, named Hanno, sailed through the Strait of Gibraltar and down the west coast of Africa in search of precious metals, especially gold. He left an account of his

 CONFLICT   🖺 ENCOUNTERS   ❖ FACILITIES   ♣ CONQUEST

▲ *The Macedonian king Alexander the Great, who kept a record of the geography of all the lands he conquered.*

geographers of the ancient Greek world. One of them, Eratosthenes of Cyrene, used it to help calculate latitude and longitude, in creating the first scientific map in European history. He reached the south-western coast of England, not an uncommon feat for Carthaginian navigators, but then pressed on. Eventually he made landfall, probably in the Faeroe Islands in the summer, because his account describes nights lasting less than three hours.

116 BC
EUDOXUS OF CYZICUS

India was also the target of at least two expeditions sponsored by the Ptolemaic dynasty in Egypt. A navigator known as Eudoxus of Cyzicus made two voyages into the Indian Ocean, one at an uncertain date between 146 and 116 BC, and another after 116 BC. During the second return voyage, his ship was blown off course and arrived off the coast of Ethiopia (a term that then covered most of East Africa). Here Eudoxus found a ship's figurehead that he believed was without doubt from a vessel that had originated in Gades in Spain (modern Cadiz). Afterwards, he made at least three voyages from Gades in an attempt to find a route to India around Africa.

voyage in a temple at Carthage, which was copied down by a Greek so that a complete text exists. At its end is the description of a gorilla hunt, during which three female gorillas were captured, killed and skinned. However, the description does not exactly match the geography of the coast, and some scholars have speculated that there are intentional inaccuracies to prevent others from following in Hanno's wake. He certainly got as far as Senegal, and possibly all the way to Gabon.

✦ ▶ p. 148 **334 BC**
ALEXANDER THE GREAT
AND HIS LEGACY

When the Greek civilisation expanded outwards from the Aegean basin, interest focused on two important aspects: conquest and trade. Only Alexander the Great, king of Macedon, adopted a scientific method.

When he led an army into the Persian empire in 334 BC, he took with him a number of secretaries who accumulated information about the geography of the lands through which they marched. After Alexander's death, his empire broke up into several individual kingdoms. One of these successor kingdoms sent an emissary named Megasthenes to India. He returned with a highly detailed and accurate account of the empire he found there, albeit a fanciful rather than factual account.

320 BC
THE VOYAGE OF PYTHEAS

One of the most remarkable Greek voyages was made sometime between 320 and 240 BC, by a man named Pytheas, sailing from Marseilles. He wrote a long account of what he had done, which has not survived, but which was used by all the important

p. 145 ◀ **Distant Voices** ▶ p. 149

Loaded with Egyptian and Assyrian goods, [the Phoenicians] called at various places along the coast, including Argos, in those days the most important place in the land, now called Hellas. Here in Argos they displayed their wares, and five or six days later when they were nearly sold out, a number of women came down to the beach to see the fair. These women were standing about near the vessel's stern, buying what they fancied, when suddenly the Phoenician sailors passed the word along and made a rush at them.

Herodotus, describing trade and piracy in the Ancient Near East

Crisis and Recovery
30 BC–AD 1000

D URING THE FIRST CENTURIES of the Christian Era, the temperate regions of the Eurasian landmass were divided between several large empires that managed to maintain a tenuous knowledge of one another. In Europe, the Roman Empire stood alone. The Middle East was divided between the Romans and the Indo-Aryan empires of Parthia and Persia. North-western India was under the sway of the Kushan Empire, founded by nomads from central Asia. In China, the Han dynasty was established in 221 BC, and would last some 500 years. However, none of these regimes was able to impose a stable administration over the lands outside their home geoclimatic regions. They were also vulnerable to attacks by peoples living outside their home regions at moments of internal political crisis.

✦ ▶ p.152
30 BC
THE ROMANS

Carthage and the Greek colonies of Italy fought many wars during the fifth and fourth centuries BC for control of the central Mediterranean, only to lose their independence to another people, the Latin speakers of Rome. But the Romans were even less interested in geographical exploration than the Greeks. Their armies successively defeated the Carthaginians in two wars, the Greek dynasties of south-eastern Europe and Asia, and by 30 BC the city of Rome ruled the entire Mediterranean basin and northern France. This immense empire lasted the longest of any of the ancient ones, enduring until about AD 400. But once it had reached its maximum limits it became a static entity, influencing the people on its borders to adopt those Roman ways that suited them.

▼ *Carved relief showing a Roman battle.*

AD 97
THE FAR EAST

China itself, in the second century AD, was the location of another great empire on Earth. While it had knowledge of south-east Asia and India as well, its information about the lands beyond the central Asian desert were as sketchy as that of the ancient Roman Empire about East Asia. In AD 97, a Chinese general named Ban Chao reached the shores of the Caspian Sea. He sent a subordinate of his, named Gan Ying, further west, and he reached the Black Sea. There he came into contact with the Roman Empire, which he called Da Qin. This was described as a land of great wealth, but the length of the journey further westwards was too daunting for Gan Ying, and both he and Ban Chao returned to China.

✿ ▶ p. 154
AD 100s
VOYAGES TO INDIA

The emperors of Rome occasionally commissioned expeditions, but they were even less interested in exploration than Alexander's successors. During the first century AD, however, a Greek merchant named Hippalus discovered a secret that Arab traders with India had jealously guarded for centuries – that the monsoon winds of the Indian Ocean reverse themselves. Using this information, he became the first European to sail across the Indian Ocean rather than following the coastline, which was a slow and laborious process. Mediterranean merchants and geographers knew of a land beyond India, and a geographer writing in the second century AD described several places in south-east Asia, including Malaya and possibly Hanoi, but the details of distance and location are very vague.

AD 100s
THE INDIAN SUBCONTINENT

India was sufficiently close to the Mediterranean world for it to be almost familiar to readers of the literature of Ancient Greece and Rome. One writer, Pliny the Elder, complained of the amount of gold that was spent on cloth, spices,

✦ CONFLICT   ⑤ ENCOUNTERS   ❖ FACILITIES   ♣ CONQUEST

▲ *The Vikings sailed to many European coasts, where they pillaged, conquered and eventually settled.*

exotic animals and jewels from the Far East. Indian traders travelled east to gather the spices of south-east Asia, and south to get exotic animals from Africa, but their lucrative position in the middle of this commercial system, and the absence of a dominant ruling dynasty, left no incentive for the kind of exploratory expeditions that were mounted from the Mediterranean basin or by China. Arab traders from the south-west of the Arabian peninsula jealously protected their routes south along the east coast of Africa, and competed effectively with the Indian traders for control of the routes to the Middle East.

AD 200–500
THE CLASSICAL CRISIS

Starting in the third century AD, the illiterate tribes of eastern Europe and central Asia began disrupting the emerging Eurasian political and economic system. Some of the Germanic tribes began vigorously attacking the Roman Empire, and during the fourth and fifth centuries the borders finally gave way, leading to the collapse of centralised political authority. At about the same time the Hsiung-Nu nomads crashed through the borders of China and similarly disrupted the Chinese imperial system. The White Huns, another nomadic people, invaded Persia and India during the fifth century. The result of this shifting of peoples was a decline in contact between the civilisations of Eurasia.

AD 700s
RAIDERS AND TRADERS

The collapse of the Roman Empire paradoxically allowed the foundations of the European supremacy of the eighteenth and nineteenth centuries to be laid. The lack of a central bureaucratic authority permitted individual initiatives on the part of different societies that transformed the most backward area of Eurasia into the most dynamic. The Scandinavian region of Denmark, Norway and Sweden, at the end of the eighth century AD, suddenly produced an aggressive seafaring culture that is collectively known as the Vikings. The technological basis for this lay in the excellent ocean-going craft which the Vikings built. The best example that has survived is the Gokstad ship, now in a museum in Oslo.

AD 850s
SCANDINAVIAN RUSSIA

The pattern for European domination was created by probably the least developed region of the continent. Scandinavian traders had been involved in trading amber with the Roman Empire, as is demonstrated by the 7,000 Roman coins that archeologists have found in Scandinavia. After the western half of the Roman Empire collapsed, Swedish traders turned east and found the rivers of Russia a useful highway that brought them to the surviving part of the Roman Empire, the Byzantine Empire based in Constantinople. During the middle of the ninth century, Scandinavian ruling dynasties were established in Kiev and other Russian towns. Thus, like the Europeans in the Great Age of Exploration, the Scandinavians seized control of a society from the top, using trade as the lever to gain entry.

AD 874
VINLAND

From Norway, Vikings voyaged across the Atlantic. Starting in AD 874, they began to establish settlements in Iceland. From here, a voyager named Eric the Red reached Greenland in 982, where he founded a settlement in 986. In 992 his son Leif found land further west, either the island of Newfoundland or the Labrador region of the North American continent. An attempt to create a settlement here, possibly at L'Anse aux Meadows in Newfoundland, in 1005–06, failed, partly on account of the hostility of the Native Americans, whom the Vikings called 'skrfllings'. It would be another 500 years before explorers from Eurasia reached the Americas again.

▲ *Scandinavian voyager Eric the Red, setting sail for Greenland.*

p. 147 ◀ **Distant Voices** ▶ p. 151

The middle three zones are distinguished by the inequalities of their seasons; when the sun holds the first at the summer solstice, the second at the equinox, and the third in winter. The two extreme zones are always without the sun. Wherefore from the island of Thule with one day's sailing to the north the frozen sea is reached.

The Venerable Bede, describing the Earth's climate zones in *De Natura Rerum*

Crescent and Cross
AD 622–1184

IN AD 622, A NEW ERA in world history began with the flight of an Arab prophet and his followers from the city of Mecca to Medina. The Prophet Muhammad had founded a new monotheistic religion, Islam, that considered itself the heir to the Jewish and Christian faiths. The following year Mecca was conquered by the Muslims and a period of military conquest, inspired by devotion to the teachings of Muhammad, began. In 632 Muhammad died. His two successors as spiritual leader, or caliph, of Islam launched the Arabian people on a course of expansion that created a cultural unit that would stretch from the Atlantic to the Indian subcontinent.

AD 634–698
THE GREAT CONQUESTS

Between AD 634 and 638 Arab armies defeated both the Byzantine heirs of Rome and the Persian Empire. They had gained domination over the whole of the Middle

▼ *The North African city of Carthage falls to the Arabs.*

East when, in 639, they invaded Egypt. At the end of 645, all the land in Egypt had become part of the Islamic world. The pace of conquest now slowed, but its movement nevertheless seemed inexorable. In 672 a Muslim fleet began a five-year blockade of the great city of Constantinople, but they lacked sufficiently advanced siege warfare technology to tackle the mighty walls of the Byzantine capital. Arab-led armies marched west across North Africa; Carthage fell to them in 698.

⌐ ▶ p. 168
AD 670
CHRISTIAN PILGRIMAGES

Christians had a long-standing tradition of travelling to the Holy Land. People crossed the Roman Empire to see the places where Christ had preached even as early as the fourth century AD, just years after Christianity had become the empire's official religion. But once the Holy Land had fallen into Muslim hands, this traffic declined. A Frankish bishop named Arculf made one of the first recorded visits after the Muslim conquest in AD 670. He gave a detailed account of the Holy Places, and also his own views about the noisiness of volcanoes. The more peaceful era of the eighth and ninth centuries brought an increase in the number of pilgrims. A regular system of hospices for pilgrims was founded in the Byzantine Empire during the eleventh century.

AD 711
THE MUSLIM ASSAULT ON EUROPE

In AD 711 the Muslims crossed the Strait of Gibraltar and invaded Spain. The Christian kingdoms there were too disorganised to confront the Muslim invaders with any hope of success. The peninsula was conquered rapidly, leaving an independent Christian kingdom only in the far north-west. In 720 an Arab army crossed the Pyrenees and occupied Narbonne. But the Muslim tide had reached its high-water mark in Europe. Three years before, the full might of the Islamic world's military and naval forces had laid siege to Constantinople. The blockade lasted a year, and then the Muslims withdrew. In 732, a raiding force from Spain was defeated at Poitiers in France, marking the end of any attempt on Europe.

AD 751
THE 'NEW ORDER'

In the east, Muslim armies pushed beyond the eastern and northern borders of the Persian Empire, into India and central Asia. In India, the Muslims were as yet unable to make any lasting impact. At the River Talas in AD 751, a Chinese army striking west confronted a Muslim force and was defeated. But internal political turmoil in the Muslim world prevented any further eastward movement for the time being. The Muslim world had grown so large that the authority of the caliph in Baghdad, at its centre, was no longer guaranteed to be effective. By the end of the eighth century, the boundaries of the Muslim world were largely established.

AD 800s
EARLY MUSLIM VISITORS TO CHRISTENDOM

The teaching of the Muslim faith discouraged the faithful from visiting the lands of unbelievers. But some contact was always necessary, whether for diplomatic or commercial reasons. At the beginning of the ninth century, a Muslim emissary named Yahya ibn al-Hakam al Bakri travelled from the emir of Cordova in Spain to a Viking

▲ *Carvings depicting crusader knights, who embarked on the first of their missions in 1096.*

court in either Ireland or Denmark. Another trip was made sometime after AD 953, again on the orders of the emir of Cordova. One member of the embassy was a Jew from Catalonia named Abraham. He wrote a book about his trip, and while the text itself is lost, it was quoted in the work of two eleventh-century geographers.

⊕ ▶ p. 155
1096
THE CRUSADES
In 1095, a council of the Catholic Church met in Clermont. Pope Urban II then called on Christians throughout Europe to fight a holy war to recover Jerusalem. The Christian kings of Spain had begun to use religion as an excuse for waging war against their Muslim neighbours. In northern France, the younger sons of the landed gentry wanted land. The idea of a pilgrimage to the sites of relics in order to gain the remission of sins had become popular. The First Crusade was a great success. In the spring of 1097 a huge army drawn from western Europe had assembled outside Constantinople; it marched across Asia Minor and into Syria. The great city of Antioch was captured in 1098, and Jerusalem in the following year.

1184
ABU HAMID AND IBN JUBAYR
Two Muslim travellers of the twelfth century have left detailed accounts of their journeys into Christendom. Both were originally from Andalus, the Muslim region of Spain. Abu Hamid was a scholar who journeyed into Eastern Europe from the Middle East. His accounts detail his travels through both Russia and Hungary. Ibn Jubayr journeyed to Syria in 1184, visiting some of the Christian cities and recording his views. Their works were, for generations, the main sources of information used by Muslim writers to describe the European world. Ibn Jubayr's account of Acre at this time remains a perfect summary of how the Muslim world viewed the Christian one.

1187
THE KINGDOM OF JERUSALEM
The Christian states of the Middle East became known as *Outre-mer* (French for 'Overseas'). Because the bulk of the crusaders came from France or from parts of Italy and Germany strongly influenced by the kingdom of France, *Outre-mer* was effectively a French colony in the Middle East. It maintained a precarious existence

for some 200 years. Its survival depended on the ability to receive periodic re-inforcements from Europe, in the shape of new crusades, and Muslim disunity, but when the Muslim world was united, the kingdom suffered. In 1187, a combined Syrian-Egyptian army conquered Jerusalem and confined the Christian kingdom to the cities of the coast. The final blow came in 1291, when the stronghold of Acre was captured in a bloody assault.

▼ *An early depiction of the holy kingdom of Jerusalem.*

p. 149 ◀ **Distant Voices** ▶ p. 153

This is the chief city of the Franks in Syria – the assembly point of ships and caravans, the meeting place of Muslim and Christian merchants from all parts. Its streets and roads are thronged with such crowds of people that one can hardly walk. But it is a land of unbelief and impiety, swarming with pigs and crosses, full of filth and ordure, all of it filled with uncleanliness and excrement.

Ibn Jubayr, on the port of Acre (1184)

Hordes from the East
1206–92

THE EURASIAN LANDMASS – since the emergence of literate civilisations – had always been divided into its separate geographical regions. Each one retained its own social, cultural and most importantly, political traditions and practices. However, during the thirteenth century the first attempt to unify these individual areas into a single political unit was made. These attempts originated in a community that had previously been only a marginal element to the literate world – the nomadic cultures of central Asia. This period saw the rise of the Mongol Empire into one of the most feared and powerful in history, setting the stage for some of politics' most infamous figures.

▲ *Kublai Khan receiving Marco Polo and his brothers at his court.*

▲ *The Mongol clans all united under the leadership of the great warrior Genghis Khan.*

1206
THE MONGOLS UNITE

To the north of China, in Mongolia and eastern Siberia, an anarchic world of nomadic and semi-nomadic clans was in a perpetual state of intrigue and warfare. This was partly stimulated by gold that was shipped north by the Chinese emperors. Towards the end of the twelfth century, however, things began to change as a young man named Temujin rose to become 'khan', or 'ruler', of one of these groups – the Mongols. He skilfully manipulated the political situation so that in 1206 all the nomadic groups – the Naiman Turks, the Keraits, and the Tartars – acknowledged his supremacy. He took the name Genghis Khan, and went on to become one of the most infamous warrior leaders in history.

✦ ▶ p. 159
1219
CONQUEST OF CENTRAL ASIA

Genghis Khan directed his Mongol warriors in two directions – south towards China and west towards the Muslim world. The advance west brought the Mongols into contact with the empire of the Shah of Khwarisim, Muhammad. This vast empire extended throughout central Asia and across the Iranian plateau. Its wealth came from the caravan trade between the Muslim and Oriental worlds. Both Muhammad and Genghis were from the same Turkic ethnic background and Genghis angered Muhammad by demanding tribute. War broke out in 1219, and in a rapid campaign lasting two years, the Shah of Khwarisim was crushed. Genghis then moved into Afghanistan and added this land to the Mongol empire.

1223
CONQUEST OF CHINA

China at this time was divided into half, the Chin Empire along the Yellow River and the Sung Empire along the Yangtze. For years the Chinese Empire had demanded tribute from the nomads of the Mongol realm. The Mongols waged a constant war of raiding and plunder against the Chin, but the walled cities were able to hold out until a Chinese engineer named Liu Po-lin joined with Genghis. In 1215, the garrison of Peking opened the gates to the Mongol army after a lengthy siege. Bit by bit, parts of the Chin Empire fell under Mongol control, until the last of the Chin dynasty died in 1223, when the Mongols annexed the remaining provinces.

1231
THE DRIVE WEST

Genghis died in 1227. The division of the empire between his four sons and a revolt in China delayed the return of the Mongols, but in 1231 a huge army arrived in central Asia and founded a permanent camp on the shores of the Caspian Sea. From there it waged a constant war in all directions, bringing Persia, Georgia and Russia under Mongol control. In

 CONFLICT   ENCOUNTERS   ❖ FACILITIES   ♣ CONQUEST

1240 they advanced into Europe, and forced their way into Poland, Hungary and Croatia. It seemed they intended to found a new camp on the Hungarian plain, but in 1242 Genghis' successor Ogodai died and the Mongol commander returned to the capital in east Asia to take part in the discussions about the succession.

1245
PAPAL EMISSARIES

The fact that the Mongols attacked the Muslim world as well was of great interest to European rulers. Pope Innocent IV sent a Franciscan friar, Giovanni de Plano Carpine, offering an alliance. Giovanni's account of his travel has survived; his report warned the pope that the Mongols were only interested in conquest and would prove unreliable allies. A second emissary, the friar William de Rubuquis, travelled to the court of the Great Khan in 1251. He describes how there were embassies from the Byzantine emperor, the caliph of Damascus, the king of Delhi in India, the sultan of the Seljuk Turks and Russian princes. In between these visits from Europe, the Mongols sent their own embassy to King St Louis IX of France, who was on crusade in Cyprus.

✳ ▶ p. 158 **1256**
THE BATTLE FOR THE MIDDLE EAST

For the Mongols, the existence of the Muslim caliphate in Baghdad was a significant political threat. Many of the empire's subjects were Muslims, and they looked to the caliph as the final arbiter and God's representative on earth. In 1254 the Great Khan Mongkë ordered the destruction of Baghdad and in 1256 some 200,000 soldiers crossed the Oxus river in central Asia and began the march on Baghdad. On their way they destroyed the headquarters of a Muslim sect known as the Assassins, who made a religious duty out of political murder and had made orderly government in the Muslim world difficult for a century and a half. On 22 January 1258 the siege of Baghdad began. The caliph surrendered on 10 February. He and 80,000 of the city's residents were massacred.

▲ *Marco Polo and his uncles leaving Venice for the Far East.*

1260
THE MUSLIM RECOVERY

The Mongols continued moving west. In March 1260 they occupied Damascus, then they turned on the last remaining power of the Muslim world – Egypt. A small Mongol army attacked a larger Egyptian one at Ain Jalut in September 1260. The Mongols were defeated. Had they sent another, larger army soon after, Egypt too would probably have become part of the Mongol Empire. But there was civil war in the Far East over the succession to Mongkë, who had died in 1259. The moment to bring Mongol rule to Africa had passed. The Mongol war on the Muslim world ended soon after. The khan of the Golden Horde, based on the Russian steppes, north of the Caspian and Aral seas, embraced Islam openly by 1265.

⊃ ▶ p. 167 **1271**
THE POLO FAMILY

The Mongol Empire had made the caravan routes across central Asia as safe as they had been in the first and second centuries AD. Merchants began moving east, for the products of the Far East – silks and spices – were luxury items in Europe. A pair of Venetian brothers, Niccolo and Maffeo Polo, reached Bokhara in central Asia and then travelled on to Peking before returning briefly to Venice. They then set out once more for the empire of the Great Khan, taking with them their nephew Marco, in 1271. The journey lasted three-and-a-half years, and the Great Khan, Kublai, allowed Marco to remain at his court until 1292, when all three Polos began the three-year journey back to Venice.

p. 151 ◀ **Distant Voices** ▶ p. 155

It is a fact that all over the country of Cathay there is a kind of black stone existing in beds in the mountains, which they dig out and burn like firewood. If you supply the fire with them at night, and see that they are well kindled, you will find them still alight in the morning; and they make such capital fuel that no other is used throughout the country. It is true that they have plenty of wood also, but they do not burn it, because those stones burn better and cost less.

A description of coal, by Marco Polo to Rustichello, a writer of romances, from *The Book of Marco Polo the Venetian*

East Meets West
1294–1499

DURING THE FOURTEENTH CENTURY the connections between the different cultural centres of the Eurasian landmass acquired greater permanence. Western European society gradually took the lead in these developments, although travellers from both the Muslim world and China were active in building links with the other civilisations. However, only the Europeans made a sustained effort at maintaining contacts, in part because they were the poorest region and had the most to gain from trading with the other cultural centres. As the fifteenth century drew to a close, the predominantly commercial causes that had previously propelled these contacts gave way to new motives and the foundations of the modern world were laid.

1325
IBN BATTUTAH

The main Muslim travel narrative from the fourteenth century was written by Ibn Battutah, a Moroccan. He left Tangier in 1325 and crossed the Islamic world to Aden; from there he took a ship down the east coast of Africa. He then went north to visit Russia and the great city of Constantinople, before turning east along the Silk Road. In 1334 he went to Delhi in India, and stayed there for eight years before joining an embassy from the Sultan to the emperor of

▼ *Marco Polo travelled with his uncle to the court of the Mongol leader, the Great Khan, Kublai.*

❀ ▶ p. 155 **1294**
ITALIAN TRADERS IN ASIA

Italian merchants from both Genoa and Venice were slowly spreading along the trade routes between Europe and China. The Genoese were markedly more successful than the Venetians, thanks to their close links with the Byzantine emperors. In 1294 Marco Polo discovered a major Genoese trading centre at Tabriz, capital of the Ilkhanid Empire in Persia. The traffic across the Caspian Sea was sufficiently lucrative at this time to finance the existence of a trading company based in Genoa. The Venetians eventually caught up, signing a trading treaty with the Khan of Persia in 1320, and even establishing a diplomatic legation in Tabriz in 1324. Twenty years later a merchant from Florence, Francesco Balducci Pegolotti, wrote a handbook for his colleague, describing in great detail the itinerary and conditions of trade throughout Asia.

1300s
EARLY MISSIONARIES TO CHINA

While the names of the merchants who ventured east from Italy are largely unknown to history, several missionaries who carried the Christian Gospel to India and China have left more detailed records. One of the best known is Giovanni de Monte Corvino who became the first Christian archbishop of Peking, and

who sent two letters back to Italy in 1305 and 1306. He built a church in Peking and converted some 150 boys to Christianity, teaching them both Greek and Latin. The second letter led to three Franciscan friars being sent to China. One of them, Andrew of Perugia, became bishop in Ts'uenchow on the south-east coast. Giovanni de Monte Corvino died in 1328, and the Khan's own court asked for a successor to be sent to China.

1324
ODERIC OF PORDENONE

Another friar who went east wrote a book about his adventures that has been compared with Marco Polo's own historic work. Oderic of Pordenone travelled by sea from the port of Ormuz in the Persian Gulf in 1324. He visited India, Ceylon, the Indonesian archipelago and entered China through the port of Canton which he declared was 'as big as three Venices'. He described a tremendously fertile land that supported a huge population, and stated that there were two residences of Franciscan friars in Ts'uenchow. He even visited Peking and the court of the Great Khan there. While Oderic, like Giovanni de Monte Corvino, hoped to return home to Italy, he died in China.

★ CONFLICT ⬒ ENCOUNTERS ❖ FACILITIES ♣ CONQUEST

▲ *Timur the Lame established a strict Islamic empire in the Middle East, threatening any Christian travellers.*

China. Ibn Battutah's ship was wrecked on the Malabar coast of southern India, however, and his trip to China was delayed. Instead he went to the Maldives, and then claims to have made a voyage via Sri Lanka and the Malay archipelago to China.

⊕ ▶ p. 162 **1338**
GIOVANNI MARIGNOLLI

To replace Giovanni de Monte Corvino, Pope Benedict XII sent out a Franciscan from the city of Florence, named Giovanni Marignolli. Marignolli spent four years in China and has left an account of his sojourn there, from 1338. He travelled east along the Silk Road and reached Peking, where he found the Christians of China's capital venerating Giovanni de Monte Corvino as a saint. In his works he mentions the presence of European merchants in Ts'uenchow, which he passed through on his way home via southern India. However, Giovanni Marignolli is the last visitor to China to report the presence of the Christian mission there.

1368
BREAKING THE BONDS

The golden age of medieval exploration came to an end in the second half of the fourteenth century. One cause was the great plague in Europe, which significantly reduced the population of many of the richest parts of the continent. The plague itself was a product of the contact between different societies of Eurasia, spread along the Silk Road by flea-infested rats. Another was the rise of a new, militantly Islamic societies in central Asia and Asia Minor. Timur the Lame, a new conqueror worthy

of comparison with Genghis Khan, swept across the Middle East and into India. His savage empire was strictly Islamic, and inhospitable to Christian travellers. Finally, in China itself, the cosmopolitan Yuen dynasty, founded by Genghis Khan, was overthrown by the Ming family, in 1368.

1405
A TURNING POINT

The second Ming emperor, Yung Lo (r.1403–24), for a time considered the possibility of expanding south-eastwards. He had assembled a huge fleet of 62 ships, which he sent into the Indian Ocean under Admiral Cheng-Ho in 1405. Cheng-Ho eventually made seven voyages around the Indian ocean, visiting India, Sri Lanka, and even the coast of East Africa at Mogadishu. He also sailed into the Red Sea and anchored in the Arabian port of Jeddah, the traditional route for pilgrims to the holiest Muslim shrine at Mecca. After Cheng-ho's death in 1434, and given the general preference of the Ming rulers for a self-sufficient economy, the great days of Chinese exploration came to an end. The tentative opening to the world had been shut.

❀ ▶ p. 160 **1493**
THE LURE OF INDIA

At the centre of all this travelling lay the Indian subcontinent. China, the Islamic world and Europe were all drawn towards it. Places such as Calicut, Cambay and the Coromandel coast, were major cosmopolitan commercial centres, with Arab traders, Chinese merchants and spice dealers from the Malay archipelago, all conducting transactions in Indian markets.

In 1493 two Genoese merchants, Hieronimo Santos de Stepahon and Hieronimo Adorno, travelled across Egypt and into the Indian Ocean. They reached Calicut and pressed on further east to Sumatra, but the hardships of the journey killed Adorno. Santos de Stepahon only reached Tripoli in the Lebanon before writing his story in 1499. What happened to him afterwards is unknown.

p. 153 ◀ **Distant Voices** ▶ p. 157

The people of this country are stalwart and fine-looking, and their limbs and faces are of a very dark purple colour. The menfolk bind up their heads; they wear long garments; and on their feet they put leather shoes. The women all wear a covering over their heads, and you cannot see their faces. They speak the A-la-pi [Arabic] language. The law of the country prohibits wine-drinking. The customs of the people are pacific and admirable. There are no poverty-stricken families. They all observe the precepts of their religion, and law-breakers are few. It is in truth a most happy country.

A Chinese account of Arabia in the fifteenth century.

▼ *The Chinese emperor sent Cheng-Ho on seven voyages of discovery in the Indian Ocean.*

By Sea to the East
1420–1580

PORTUGAL'S POSITION on the Atlantic isolated it from the Mediterranean, where Europe's trading routes to Asia lay. Access to Asia's riches was a major motive behind exploration. European trade with Asia was dominated by Venice and Genoa, who traded through Arab commercial centres such as Alexandria. An Islamic resurgence in the 1400s further restricted access to Asia via North Africa, as European Christians met increasing hostility from Muslims. Prince Henry the Navigator led the search for a new route to Asia by funding a series of carefully organised voyages. While in North Africa he had seen Asian cargoes arriving and this encouraged him to find a passage for Portugal. His second motive was to bring Christianity to the pagans.

❖ ▶ p.162

1420
SAILING INTO THE UNKNOWN

It was believed that sailing beyond Morocco led to waters boiled by liquid flames from the Sun; sailing west led to swamps. To prepare crews for these hazards and to overcome fears Henry the Navigator established a maritime centre to equip sailors with knowledge, instruments and vessels. In 1420 storms drove Henry's first expedition to the Madeira islands. These were eventually colonised by Portugal, which introduced new crops and livestock. The islands of the Azores, reached in 1431, became a base for subsequent expeditions. By

the time of Henry's death (1460) his ships had sailed a third of the way down the African coast to present-day Sierra Leone. These ships stopped on coasts and sailed into river mouths to trade with African kingdoms, many of whom had grown rich trading with Arabs.

1482
SPREADING THE FAITH

Portugal marked each 'discovery' with a padrãos – a cross built on a stone pillar. This represented the arrival of the new power and its faith. These Christian symbols were soon followed by missionaries responsible for religious conversion. Diego Cão crossed the Equator in 1482 with four Franciscans and left them in the Congo, in an attempt to convert the natives to the Christian faith. This practice was repeated along the entire route to Asia. The Jesuit Francis Xavier, who arrived in Goa in 1542, moved through south-east Asia to Japan on a 10-year ministry to achieve Portugal's spiritual ambitions in a region of Hindus, Muslims, Buddhists and Annamites.

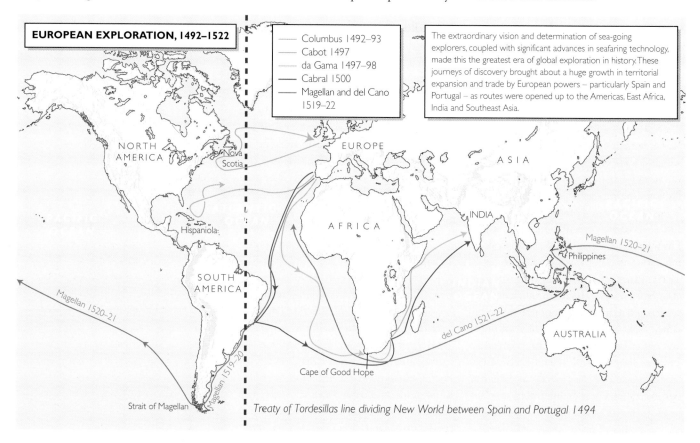

EUROPEAN EXPLORATION, 1492–1522

- Columbus 1492–93
- Cabot 1497
- da Gama 1497–98
- Cabral 1500
- Magellan and del Cano 1519–22

The extraordinary vision and determination of sea-going explorers, coupled with significant advances in seafaring technology, made this the greatest era of global exploration in history. These journeys of discovery brought about a huge growth in territorial expansion and trade by European powers – particularly Spain and Portugal – as routes were opened up to the Americas, East Africa, India and Southeast Asia.

NORTH AMERICA
Nova Scotia
EUROPE
ASIA
INDIA
Magellan 1520–21
Philippines
Hispaniola
AFRICA
SOUTH AMERICA
AUSTRALIA
Magellan 1520–21
del Cano 1521–22
Magellan 1519–20
Cape of Good Hope
Strait of Magellan
Treaty of Tordesillas line dividing New World between Spain and Portugal 1494

★ CONFLICT   ⌐ ENCOUNTERS   ❖ FACILITIES   ♣ CONQUEST

▲ *The Portuguese voyager, Henry the Navigator.*

1487
FINDING A ROUTE TO EAST AFRICA
John II revived interest in exploration, leading to a series of voyages culminating in the first European sailing around the southern tip of Africa. Bartholomew Diaz left Portugal in 1487 with three vessels, sailed along the African coast until blown into open seas by storms. After sailing south for 13 days Diaz, turned east, failed to sight land, so turned north and sighted mountains; and he realised it was east Africa. A mutiny forced him to return home, sailing around Africa's southern tip. John II later called this the Cape of Good Hope. Diaz's critical discovery was not exploited, as disputes over the Portuguese crown and hostility with Spain focused attention on domestic affairs. Despite this delay, Spain had not found a route to Asia, so explorations continued under Manoel I.

1500
BRAZIL
Pedro Alvarez Cabral sailed to Brazil in 1500, supposedly after storms carried him from Africa. This may have been an intentional voyage, however, in response to Spanish imperial ambitions in the Americas. The Italian

p. 135 ◀ **Triumphs & Tragedies** ▶ p. 158
1497
CROSSING THE INDIAN OCEAN
Vasco da Gama finally made the voyage by sea to India with four ships which sailed round the Cape of Good Hope in 1497. Explorations of Mozambique, Malindi and Mombasa revealed abundant trade with Indians and Arabs. Frictions between the Christian explorers and African Muslims led to clashes, but da Gama secured a pilot who guided them to Calicut, an Indian commercial centre, in May 1498. Da Gama had discovered a passage to Asia by finding the best Atlantic winds to make a sailing around the Cape of Good Hope, and had crossed to India in three weeks. Trading fleets emerged to carry cargo between India and Lisbon, which became a major commercial centre.

Amerigo Vespucci made two voyages along the south American coast which convinced him that this was not Asia but a 'New World'. Martin Afonso de Souza established a port (Santos) and mapped the coastline which helped Portugal exploit the colony. Systematic and efficient colonisation developed under Tomé de Souza who united the problematic captains (regional governors), established a capital (Salvador) to co-ordinate key responsibilities such as defence, and attracted farmers to create a permanent settlement.

✳ ▶ p. 158 **1505**
CONSOLIDATING THE EMPIRE
In 1502 the first permanent European naval force in Asian waters appeared, when da Gama led an armed fleet to meet any threats. Francisco d'Almeida, appointed eastern viceroy in 1505, won a major sea battle against an Arab fleet which attempted to seize control of the Indian Ocean in 1509. Portugal did not have the means or manpower to colonise all their 'discoveries'. Instead of settlement, Portugal established fortifications and trading posts to protect harbours and commercial centres. Affonso d'Albuquerque was determined to establish greater control of the sea and land, seizing Goa and transforming it into the eastern empire's capital which controlled administrative and trading affairs. From here, viceroys launched campaigns to expand the empire's frontiers. The crown maintained control through viceroys appointed to safeguard overseas interests and a trade monopoly.

1509
CHINA AND THE SPICE ISLANDS
In 1509, Portugal made its first voyage through the Strait of Malacca (off present-day Malaya), which was used by trading ships from south-east Asia. After d'Albuquerque captured Malacca port in 1511 it became a base for explorations into

the Moluccas (Spice Islands) and the Chinese coast. Spain claimed possession of the Spice Islands after Ferdinand Magellan's voyage to Asia in 1519, but Portugal eventually bought them (1529). In 1514 the first Portuguese visited the Canton River, gradually took control of Chinese ports and drove the Arabs from the South Pacific. Pepper, cinnamon, ginger and cloves used to flavour salt meat in Europe had been traded by the Arabs who withheld supplies to raise prices. Prices fell dramatically as Portugal brought increasing quantities to Europe.

1550s
PORTUGAL'S DECLINE
By the mid-1500s the empire was in decline. Portugal's population was too small to effectively colonise, and power rested upon a global trade network. Isolated trading posts symbolised Portugal's detachment from local affairs. Fighting disrupted trade with the Gold Coast tribes, after Portugal used rocks from a sacred hill to build Elmina Fort. Portuguese influence weakened among remaining traders who demanded guns, metal and alcohol instead of the novelty goods once offered. In 1580 Portugal was united with Spain. Her merchants were taxed to sustain Spain's European territories, to the detriment of Portugal's empire. The Dutch seized Ceylon and Malacca, and Goa's trade vanished. These weaknesses left Portugal's trade monopoly and territories vulnerable to the challenges it faced from European rivals.

p. 155 ◀ **Distant Voices** ▶ p. 159

As I was going through the forest I heard loud yells on either side of me, such as savages are accustomed to utter, and immediately a company of savages came running towards me.... Then I cried out: 'Now may God preserve my soul'.

Hans Staden, an artilleryman for the Portuguese, describing his capture by the Tupinamba Indians in Brazil (1552)

Spain in the New World
1492–1550

BY THE LATE 1400s, Spain had changed from a land of conflicting Christian and Muslim kingdoms into a single country united by the marriage of Queen Isabella to King Ferdinand in 1469. Their successful military conquests and spiritual crusade against the Moors convinced many in Spain that similar triumphs could be achieved overseas. The search for a route to Asia eventually led to Spain's discovery of a New World which became their overseas empire. The voyages of Christopher Columbus discovered the westward passage from Europe to the Americas. Columbus had spent eight years searching for a sponsor for his voyage to find the westward passage to Asia, and had calculated that Japan was only 2,400 nautical miles from the Canary Islands – in reality a distance of 10,000 nautical miles.

p. 157 ◀ **Triumphs & Tragedies** ▶ p. 162

1492
SAILING TO THE NEW WORLD

Columbus's first expedition embarked in September 1492, with three ships carrying 100 men. In October they first landed on Watling Island and then proceeded to sail around the Bahamas, Cuba and Hispaniola to find Asia, unaware of the significance of the discovery. Columbus was convinced these were Asiatic islands leading to China. Relations with the indigenous peoples (mistakenly called Indians) deteriorated after the Spanish continually demanded provisions, and thefts occurred. His second voyage carried 1,200 people, tools, seeds and animals to begin colonising the largest and most accessible Caribbean islands. Columbus's 1498 voyage found mainland Venezuela and the 1502 voyage found central America. Columbus lost support as the elusive route to the East – and the anticipated riches – failed to materialise. Columbus died in 1506, convinced that the discovery of mainland Asia was imminent.

○ ▶ p.160

1493
DIVIDING THE WORLD

In 1493 Pope Alexander VI had used his spiritual authority to divide the world from North to South Poles between Portugal and Spain, in an attempt to distribute the new colonies and to avoid conflict. Spain received the western hemisphere, and Portugal the eastern hemisphere but disputes over the precise boundary line soon arose. After the Reformation, Protestant rulers would come to challenge the spiritual powers of Rome and begin competing for overseas empires. Although Spain continued to spend vast amounts controlling its colonies and defending its empire, it became weaker internally and consequently vulnerable to challenges from the rising European powers. Spain's control over its overseas possessions weakened as the problems of communication and local efforts to assume greater autonomy across her vast empire grew.

✳ ▶ p. 166

1500s
LATIN AMERICA

Colonists had a devastating impact upon the size, pattern of life and structures of indigenous societies. Disruptions to food production, 'Old World' diseases like smallpox, slavery and war led to South America's indigenous population falling from 57 million in 1519 to four million in 1607. Over 16,000 tonnes of silver and 1,800 tonnes of gold poured into Spain from the Americas in the 150 years after the conquest of Mexico. Despite this wealth the Spanish economy eventually faltered as the influx of riches created a soaring rate of inflation. Agriculture and industry were neglected as Spain became dependent on purchasing imports with her New World riches. Vast amounts of money were spent by the Crown on ambitious schemes and military operations.

✳ ▶ p. 162

1503
SPAIN'S EMPIRE

The Spanish crown exercised tight control over the empire and its trade. All conquistadors gave a proportion of their profits to the royal treasury and Crown representatives often followed their expeditions. All land was owned by the Crown but the Encomienda system granted colonists control over particular areas (and all its indigenous inhabitants). In return the colonists helped the Crown defend the empire and support missionary work within it. The Crown also appointed colonial viceroys and legislators but was still the ultimate decision-maker. From 1503 a 'house of trade' in Seville, Spain, oversaw colonial trade and travel. All colonial exports were brought to Spain by royal 'treasure fleets' and taxes were imposed on imports.

1519
DISCOVERING A NEW CONTINENT

After failing to find sufficient riches in the Caribbean, explorers began to search the interiors of the Americas in the hope of greater reward. These were named after the Italian Amerigo Vespucci, who had travelled to the New World between 1497 and 1504. Conquistadors – military adventurers – launched privately funded expeditions to these areas and settlements were established from 1509. Vasco Nuñez de Balbosa's 1519 journey across the Isthmus of Panama, between North and South America, to the Pacific Ocean was one of the most significant expeditions. Until then, Europeans did not know that this 'Great South Sea' existed and that Asia must be beyond this new continent.

 CONFLICT    ENCOUNTERS   ❖ FACILITIES   ♣ CONQUEST

Amazon, the expedition travelled almost 5,000 km (3,000 miles) down the Amazon to the Atlantic. De Orellana named the Amazon after the legendary Greek female fighters, as he had encountered female warriors during the expedition. Indigenous cultures were often destroyed by the introduction of the language, architecture, customs and religion of Spain. Colonists married indigenous nobility, who liaised between the Spanish and local population.

▲ *Christopher Columbus greets the natives as he lands in the New World.*

▼ *Pope Alexander VI, who divided the world from North to South Poles between the great powers of Spain and Portugal.*

1519
SAILING ROUND THE WORLD

The New World became a desirable destination rather than an obstacle to Asia, as tales of immense riches spread. Spanish explorations reached the east and west coasts of North America down to Argentina in South America. In 1519 Ferdinand Magellan left Spain, explored the east coast of South America, and finally sailed around the southern tip of the continent. On the hazardous voyage through fierce winds and a narrow channel, one ship deserted and another sank. They finally reached the Philippines, where Magellan was killed by the indigenous peoples. The ships continued to India and Africa thereby making the first circumnavigation of the globe, to prove that the world's oceans were linked. Only 18 of the 250 explorers survived the voyage.

✦ ▶ p. 175

1519
THE CONQUISTADORS

In 1519 Hernán Cortés followed a mountainous route to the vast capital of the sophisticated and wealthy Aztec civilisation.

Spanish troops with Indian allies later stormed the Aztec capital of Tenochtitlán (now Mexico City) and seized control of the empire after Montezuma was killed during an uprising in 1521. The second great empire to collapse was the Inca civilisation, after Francisco Pizarro became governor of present-day Peru in 1531. Pizarro rejected the friendship offered by the courtiers of the Inca king, Atahualpa, and massacred them. The Incas, deprived of leadership and terrified by Pizarro's cannon and horses, capitulated to a numerically inferior force in 1534. Conquests also occurred in Guatemala (1523–42), New Granada, present-day Columbia and Ecuador, (1536–39) and Chile (1540–48).

1540
EXPLORING THE AMAZON

Conquistadors like Gonzalo Pizarro and Francisco de Orellana continued overland expeditions in South America. They finally crossed the continent during an expedition to find the legendary golden kingdom of El Dorado. After being carried by a current down the Napo River, a branch of the

p. 157 ◀ **Distant Voices** ▶ p. 161

Of anything they have, if you ask them for it they never say no.... I forbade that they should be given things so worthless as pieces of broken crockery ... though when they were able to get them, they thought they had the best jewel in the world.... They believe very firmly that I, with these ships and people, came from the sky.

Christopher Columbus's report about the Indians to King Ferdinand and Queen Isabella.

The Spice Island
1565–1640

GOLD AND SPICES were responsible for both the Spanish and Portuguese voyages of discovery in the fifteenth century. The Italian cities of Venice and Genoa still dominated the traffic in spices through the Mediterranean ports. For about 100 years, the Portuguese joined with traditional participants in the trade between Europe, the Islamic World and the Far East. The only potential European rival to the Portuguese in south-east Asia for most of the sixteenth century were the Spanish. However, as the sixteenth century drew to a close, there were new entrants to the spice trade, as Dutch and English rivals sought to gain a share of this lucrative commerce.

○ ▶ p. 166 **1565**
THE IBERIAN EMPIRE IN THE FAR EAST

Portugal's strategic network of naval bases and trading posts along the coasts of Africa and the Indian Ocean was not strong enough to keep out rivals, and that had never been its intention. Several agreements negotiated by the two Iberian states denied most of the region to Spain, in return for the Portuguese exclusion from the Americas. In 1565 an expedition from Mexico commanded by Miguel Lopez de Legaspi founded a Spanish settlement at Cebu in the Philippines, but this colony was linked to Spain via Mexico, and so avoided the Portuguese routes across the Indian Ocean. And in 1580, the Spanish king Philip II inherited the Portuguese crown, so that the two empires were united under one ruler.

★ ▶ p. 161 **1577**
ENGLISH PIRACY

English traders wanted to participate in the valuable commerce with the Spanish colonies in the New World. But the Spanish government sought to maintain a monopoly, so that any exchange would take place in Spain. As a result, an undeclared maritime war broke out between England and Spain in 1568. Initially this was confined to the Atlantic, but in 1576 one English captain, Sir Francis Drake, began planning a voyage to the Pacific. He left Plymouth in 1577, sailed around South America, pillaging

Spanish ports along the coast, and reached the Spice Islands in November 1579. He took on a cargo of cloves and continued eastwards, returning to Plymouth in September 1580. Drake's profitable voyage produced several imitators.

▼ *Sir Francis Drake practised piracy during his journey to the New World, causing friction between England and Spain.*

▲ *Spices were a valuable trading commodity in the sixteenth and seventeenth centuries.*

1592
JAMES LANCASTER

The knowledge that Drake brought back to England would probably have been exploited more energetically were it not for the demands of a war with Spain. The defeat of the Spanish Armada in 1588 required virtually every seagoing warship English ports could muster. A sustained assault by the English on the Portuguese spice trade was delayed until 1592, when James Lancaster reached Penang, in the Malay peninsula. From here he sailed into the Strait of Malacca and attacked every Portuguese ship he came across, before sailing for home. Unfortunately for Lancaster, part of his crew mutinied in Bermuda, and made off with his ship. Lancaster's voyage itself was a failure, but the knowledge he gained contributed to the foundation of the East India Company in 1600.

❁ ▶ p. 165 **1595**
THE ARRIVAL OF THE DUTCH

In 1595, Cornelius Houtman took a fleet of four ships from the Netherlands to Java. A group of Dutch investors supported this voyage, with the aim of establishing a permanent Dutch base in the Spice Islands. Houtman succeeded in sailing directly

★ CONFLICT   ⬒ ENCOUNTERS   ❖ FACILITIES   ♣ CONQUEST

across the Indian Ocean, whereas the Portuguese had traditionally followed the coast. In spite of hostility from Portuguese merchants and Javanese rulers, Houtman managed to secure a trading treaty; so, in 1598, the Dutch sent out no fewer than four fleets to the East Indies. At Bantam, on the isle of Java, the Dutch established a permanent base. In 1602 a Dutch East India Company was formed.

1602
BEGINNINGS OF CONFLICT

The English East India Company sought profits in south-east Asia and in 1602 the company established a base at Bantam. The Dutch were already located here, but they were unwilling to share in the wealth of the spice trade. Conflict sprang up between the traders, and the English traders left in Bantam were prevented – sometimes by violence – by the Dutch, Portuguese and even the Javanese, from engaging in commerce. The Portuguese had a fort at Amboina, one of the main ports in the Spice Islands, but the Dutch seized it immediately after the English had reached a treaty with its governor in 1606, rendering the deal void.

1607
AFRICA AND INDIA

Part of the commercial and naval struggle for the control of the Spice Island trade took place outside south-east Asia. The Dutch blockaded Goa and Macassar, both sites of important Portuguese bases. The English helped the Persians to seize Ormuz in 1623. In 1652, the Dutch founded a base at Cape Town, in southern Africa. These events shifted trade between east Asia and western Europe from the traditional Middle Eastern ports to the Dutch-controlled route around Africa. The English, by contrast, found less competition in India. In 1607 a ship of the East India Company visited the port of Surat, and contact was made with the Mogul Empire. In 1612 a permanent trading post was founded there, marking the starting point of the British Raj.

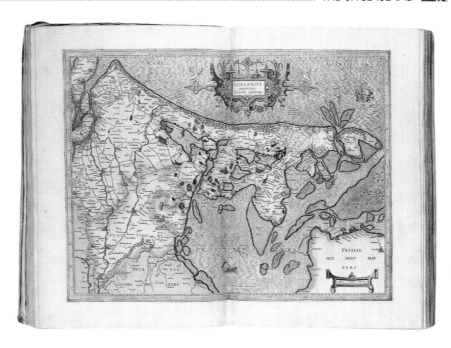

▲ *A sixteenth-century map of the Netherlands; the Dutch expanded their territories in the Indian Ocean.*

1613
JAPAN

The islands of Japan attracted from the European countries of Portugal, England and the Netherlands. In 1613, a ship of the English East India Company, commanded by John Saris, reached Japan and Saris met William Adams who had been shipwrecked there over 10 years before. Adams was a respected figure in Japanese society and he helped the East India Company obtain a treaty to trade with Japanese merchants. Portuguese traders and missionaries had visited Japan since 1543. However, the influences that these contacts were having on Japanese society threatened its uniformity. In 1640, the Japanese expelled all foreigners except a small colony of Dutch traders based at Nagasaki.

★ ▶ p. 164 **1619**
THE DUTCH STRIKE

The Dutch East India Company had started its life committed to trading alone, avoiding the commitments that a proper empire would require. However, after a few years it became apparent to the Board of Directors that a monopoly of trade would ensure higher profits than free competition. In 1619, the Dutch sent Jan Pietszoon Coen to the East Indies. Coen had very clear ideas of

what he wanted to do. First, he founded the Dutch post at Batavia (modern Jakarta) to serve as a centre for all inter-Asian trade. Then, he forced all rival traders out of the islands of south-east Asia. The attacks on the English culminated, in 1623, with a massacre at their main post at Amboina.

p. 159 ◀ **Distant Voices** ▶ p. 163

Whenever the Portuguese go to a foreign land, they mean to stay there for the rest of their days, never wishing to return to Portugal. But when a Dutchman comes to India he says to himself: 'When my six years are up it's back to Holland!' For that reason he never bothers to build very much, whether in the country or the towns. Indeed, when the Dutch capture a fortress or town they usually cut off the landward-facing half of the place, while fortifying the seaward half very strongly, so that they may hold it with few men.

A German mercenary, describing Portuguese and Dutch attitudes in East Asia

Islamic Empires
1500–1757

WHILE EUROPEAN STATES sought trading posts and colonies in the Americas and East Asia during the fifteenth and sixteenth centuries, they sought to bypass a Muslim world that had reached its greatest extent. For Islam, it was a golden age; but the seeds of its decline during the eighteenth and nineteenth centuries were sown by its very success. The Muslim world had little need to trade or exchange knowledge with their neighbours; and its success was due in part to the centralised administration in the hands of a few large empires. Success bred complacency, and technological dynamism in the European world was eroding the Muslim supremacy.

⊕ ▶ p. 169

1501
SAFAVID PERSIA

In 1501 the Safavid clan had brought together many of the Turkic tribes of western and northern Persia and it even threatened to expand westwards into Turkey. A series of defeats in wars with the Ottoman Turks, however, culminating in the final Ottoman victory in 1514, confined the Safavids to the Iranian plateau. The Safavid dynasty encouraged contacts with Europe and Europeans themselves were delighted to engage in diplomatic and commercial relations with a potential enemy of the dangerous Ottoman Empire. The height of Safavid rule came during the reign of Shah Abbas I (1587–1629); Abbas did much to encourage the manufacture and export of silks. But after his death the Safavid Empire went into decline, and in 1722 the dynasty was overthrown by Afghan invaders.

1504
MOGUL INDIA

In 1504 a central Asian tribal leader named Babar took control of Afghanistan. In 1523, he led an army across the Hindu Kush and into India. In 1526, he defeated the army of Lodi, the sultanate of Delhi at Panipat, and established the Mogul dynasty in Delhi. Initially, Mogul rule proved unstable, and another Afghan invasion briefly supplanted them in 1540. But 16 years later the Mogul heir, Akbar, returned from exile in Iran to

rally his followers and re-establish Mogul rule. This empire constantly expanded to the south and east, until it reached its greatest extent in the reign of Aurangzeb (d. 1707). It created a cosmopolitan culture by drawing on both Iran and India for inspiration and skilled artists and technicians.

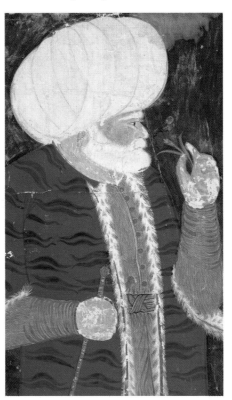

▼ *The Ottoman emperor Suleiman the Magnificent, who led an attempt to capture Vienna in 1529.*

✳ ▶ p. 168

1514
OTTOMAN TURKEY

The greatest Muslim power of the early modern world was the Ottoman dynasty. It emerged from a minor sultanate in western Turkey, which took the lead in wars against the Byzantine Empire and Europe. In 1453 Constantinople fell to the Ottomans, and in 1514 their empire embraced most of Turkey, the Black Sea coast and the southern Balkans. The defeat of Safavid Persia in that year placed the Ottomans in conflict with the 200-year-old Mamluk rulers of Egypt and Syria. In 1516 the Ottomans invaded the Mamluk Empire, and in January 1517 entered Cairo. They now replaced the Mamluks as the dominant military and political power in the Islamic world.

❖ ▶ p. 173

1517
PIRI REIS

On the occasion of the Ottoman conquest of the Mamluks, a Turkish naval officer named Piri Reis presented a huge map of the world to the sultan, Selim. Parts of this map survive, and give some indication of the extent of Muslim scholarship about the rest of the world. It

p. 158 ◀ **Triumphs & Tragedies** ▶ p. 164

1520
THE OTTOMAN WAR AGAINST EUROPE

An energetic young sultan became Ottoman emperor in 1520. Suleiman, who was called 'the Magnificent', extended Ottoman power deep into Europe and across the Mediterranean. His victories over Hungary in 1526 led to a failed attempt to capture Vienna in 1529. In 1538, an Ottoman expedition even threatened the Portuguese trading post of Diu in India. Suleiman's empire, however, had reached its limits. The Habsburg dynasty in Spain managed to stall the Ottoman offensive in the Mediterranean during the 1540s. The failure of the siege of Malta in 1565, and the defeat of the Turkish fleet at Lepanto in 1571, six years after Suleiman's death, ended the immediate Turkish menace towards Europe.

✦ CONFLICT   ᛋ ENCOUNTERS   ❖ FACILITIES   ♣ CONQUEST

included the coasts of India and China, and parts of the Americas. Reis made use of material from Arab, Portuguese and Spanish sources, and may have even used a map drawn by Christopher Columbus. He completed a second map in 1529, which shows the coasts of north and south America. He also compiled a guide to seafaring in the Mediterranean and Persian Gulf, which included information from Portuguese sources.

1610
THE MUSLIM WORLD AND ITS NEIGHBOURS

To Islam, the world has always been divided into two camps: the House of Islam, representing the lands ruled by the faithful, and the House of War, which includes everybody else. While Muslim states tended not to be too interested in going out to the rest of the world, they did welcome visitors who brought useful technology, especially if they chose to accept Islam. A combination of events in about 1610 led to a substantial number of English and Dutch pirates settling in the lands of the Barbary Corsairs of north Africa. These immigrants provided navigational and shipbuilding information that helped transform the Corsairs into the terror of the seas. Jewish physicians who had studied in the West were also much sought after at this time.

1683
THE TURKISH RETREAT

In 1683, the Turks made a second attempt to capture Vienna. This also failed, but this time the Habsburg Empire was able to recover substantial areas conquered by the Turks 150 years before. Even at the time, the peace treaty signed in 1699 was recognised as a turning point in relations between the Turks and Europe. The eighteenth century was an era of continuing retreat by the Turks under Russian and Habsburg pressure until, in 1798, the fringes of their empire became, like India, the battleground for outside powers. The French invasion of Egypt in that year, led by Napoleon, was an attempt to threaten the British position in India.

▲ *Naval battle involving the Barbary galleys.*

1757
THE END OF ISLAMIC INDIA

The Marathas were a new Hindu power, which arose in southern India at the end of the seventeenth century, and was capable withstand the advance of the Mogul armies. The strength of the Marathas combined with internal unrest in the Mogul Empire to overthrow the effective power of the sultan in Delhi. He became effectively a figurehead ruler, and India was once more

▼ *The defeat of the Turks outside Vienna, an event that marked the decline of Ottoman power.*

divided into warring states. These included the European traders, who brought the conflicts from home to India. In 1757, the army of the East India Company, led by Robert Clive, defeated the army of the Nawab of Bengal at Plassey. The effect of this victory was to make England the strongest political power in India.

p. 161 ◀ **Distant Voices** ▶ p. 165

[The Hungarians] are clean in their ways and in their eating, and honour their guests. They do not torture their prisoners as the Austrians do. They practice sword play like the Ottomans. In short, though both of them are unbelievers without faith, the Hungarians are more honourable and cleaner infidels. They do not wash their faces every morning with their urine as the Austrians do, but wash their faces every morning with water as the Ottomans do.

A Turkish traveller, Evliya Celebi, describes two neighbours of the Ottoman Empire, from *The Muslim Discovery of Europe*, by Bernard Lewis

Russia Expands
1480–1796

RUSSIA WAS THE SLOWEST part of Europe to develop. In part, this was because of its distance from the advanced Mediterranean and Middle Eastern civilisations. It was also slow to develop a strong, independent state because of the sheer size of the region. Finally, the successive invasions by crusading German knights, Mongols and Lithuanians during the twelfth and thirteenth centuries denied the loosely knit regime of principalities that had been founded the opportunity to establish a stable system of government. The Russian lands remained under the control of Mongol hordes until the fifteenth century. Internal political divisions among their Mongol overlords eventually allowed the Russians to cease paying regular tribute, and Russia emerged in the second half of the fifteenth century as an important power in eastern Europe.

1480
MUSCOVY EMERGES

In 1480, Moscow defeated an attempt made by the heirs of the Mongols, the Tatar khan of the Great Horde, to reassert the right to tribute. Moscow had long been the most important principality in Russia, in support of the rights of the Russian Orthodox Church and in dealings with the Tatars. Under Ivan III, the first of its rulers to call himself tsar, the territorial expansion of Muscovy moved rapidly. The great trading city of Novgorod, with its vast lands to the north, was annexed in 1478. Other states to

▼ *The Russian conqueror Ivan the Terrible, with his son.*

the north-west of Muscovy were also added. By the end of the reign of Vasilii III in 1533, Muscovy was sufficiently powerful to be treated as an equal by the Habsburg dynasty.

1552
MUSCOVY TURNS EAST

The first major step eastwards by Muscovy occurred in 1552, when Tsar Ivan the Terrible conquered the khanate of Kazan. This event brought the borders of the Muscovite principality to the Urals – the traditional boundary between Europe and Siberia. The tsar granted huge tracts of this new conquest to a leading Muscovite merchant family called the Stroganovs. They came into conflict with the neighbouring khanate of Sibir and, in return for help from the tsar, handed over their estates to him. Fighting in the region continued for several years, but by constructing a chain of forts along the rivers, Russia asserted its control.

★ ▶ p. 169
1558
WARS IN THE WEST

Ivan the Terrible turned his army west in 1558 and invaded the state of Livonia. This was the beginning of a long series of wars with the powers of the region that gradually extended the border of Muscovy westwards. The struggle was with the Baltic powers of Sweden and the united kingdom of Poland-

Lithuania. At the time of Ivan's death in 1584, however, there was little to show for these wars. The most important gain was the port of Narva on the Baltic, but this was lost to Sweden in 1617, after a chaotic period known as the 'Time of Troubles' that saw a Polish army occupy Moscow itself.

1632
THE WAY TO THE PACIFIC

Russian explorers learned of a comparatively advanced Siberian tribe, the Yakuts, in about 1620. The high-quality furs the Yakuts brought to Russian trading posts stimulated the greed of the traders. In 1632, Pyotr Beketov took an armed force to the Lena and conquered the Yakuts. He built a fort on the site of modern-day Yakutsk, and then carried on southwards to the country of another Siberian tribe, the Tungus, and conquered them too. A post in the land of the Tungus, at Butalsk, was the base for a journey eastwards in 1639 by a party of 20 men led by Ivan Moskvitin. This little band followed the Ulya River downstream to its mouth, where it emptied into the Sea of Okhotsk. These were the first Russians to reach the Pacific coast overland.

p. 162 ◀ **Triumphs & Tragedies** ▶ p. 170
1728
BERING'S VOYAGES

In 1724 Tsar Peter the Great hired a Danish navigator, Vitus Bering, to lead an expedition from the Pacific coast to sail west in search of a possible route along the north coast of Russia and Siberia to the Far East. In 1728, Bering put to sea and sailed north into the strait that today bears his name. They found that just north of there the coast of Asia turned westwards, and concluded that a sea separated Asia and North America. The Great Northern Expedition, which took place between 1736 and 1743, made extensive explorations along the northern coast, both from the White Sea and the Pacific. Bering's role took him across the Bering strait to the Alaskan coast, but he died of scurvy in the course of trying to return to Siberia.

★ CONFLICT   𝗦 ENCOUNTERS   ❖ FACILITIES   ⚔ CONQUEST

Turks' expense. Russia also participated with the Habsburgs and Prussia in three partitions of Poland, which extinguished that once powerful eastern European state.

▲ *Peter the Great inspects the shipyards before embarking on his wars of expansion.*

p. 163 ◀ **Distant Voices** ▶ p. 167

The land was here very much elevated; the mountains, observed extending inland, were so lofty that we could see them quite plainly at sea at a distance of sixteen Dutch miles. I cannot recall having seen higher mountains anywhere in Siberia and Kamchatka. The coast was everywhere much indented and therefore provided with numerous bays and inlets close to the mainland.

Vitus Bering's description of Alaska

 ▶ p. 177   **1643**

TO THE CHINESE BORDER

The expedition to the Ulya River uncovered news of large silver deposits along another river to the south. In 1643, Vasiliy Poyarkov travelled to the Amur to find out the truth of it, but behaved so badly towards the local tribe that another expedition led by Yerofey Khabarov in 1649 met with a hostile reception. Khabarov returned in 1651 ready for war. The Amur tribes paid tribute to the Chinese emperor, but that did not deter the Russians. A fort was built at the confluence of the Amur and Sungari rivers. Khabarov and his Cossacks defeated a Chinese assault in April 1652. An uneasy peace between China and Russia in the Amur country continued until the Russians agreed to withdraw in a treaty between the two empires in 1689.

1695

PETER THE GREAT'S WARS OF EXPANSION

In 1682, the 10-year-old Romanov heir Peter became tsar. In 1695 he embarked on a campaign of expansion that resulted in wars with the Turks and Sweden. Although initially Peter experienced more defeats than victories, by the end of his reign – in 1725 – the Russian empire had regained the lands around Narva that they had previously held during the reign of Ivan the Terrible, and also Estonia and Livonia. This had enabled the construction of a new city, christened St Petersburg. Peter's campaigns had also led to the acquisition of land around the Caspian Sea, including the strategic city of Baku. However, his two wars against the Turks produced no lasting gains.

1735

THE TURKS AND POLAND CRUSHED

Successive Russian rulers, from the Empress Anna to the Empress Catherine the Great, initiated wars against the Turks and took part in wider European conflicts throughout the eighteenth century. The first war against the Turks, launched in 1735, ended in a humiliating political settlement in 1739, when the tremendous gains the Russians had made were given up when their Habsburg allies signed a peace treaty. But during the reign of Catherine the Great (1762–96) extensive gains were made at the

▼ *The empress Catherine the Great of Russia.*

To the Ends of the Earth
1769–1900

I N THE FIFTEENTH CENTURY European geographers became convinced that there must be a large unknown land in the southern hemisphere – Terra Australis Incognita – to balance the 'weight' of land north of the equator. On several expeditions the Spanish came close to finding Australia but nobody knew if it really existed. Finally in 1605 Dutchman Willem Janszoon made the first known European landing of Australia on the Gulf of Carpentaria, later naming the land New Holland (1606). William Dampier (1652–1715) became the first Englishman to visit Australia on a buccaneering voyage (1679–91) and led an official expedition to observe the wildlife and indigenous Aborigines (1699–1701).

▲ *An inspection of convicts in the Australian penal colony of New South Wales.*

▲ *Captain James Cook, who led expeditions into uncharted areas of the Pacific from 1769.*

1769
JAMES COOK

There remained many unresolved questions about the Pacific, and the Englishman James Cook (1728–79) helped answer many of these through his forays into the unknown seas in these parts. He plotted many unexplored areas in this part of the world from 1769. Cook produced a chart of New Zealand and, after landing in Botany Bay, he claimed the Australian south-east coast for Britain, calling it New South Wales (1769). Cook also made an exploration of the Great Barrier Reef and proved that New Guinea was not connected to Australia. He made another voyage to New Zealand between 1772 and 1775, before being killed in Hawaii in 1779.

◯ ▶ p. 176 ## 1788
THE PENAL COLONY

Although Spanish and French missionaries, traders and whalers increasingly colonised the Pacific, Australasia was left to Britain, who decided to use New South Wales as a penal colony. Eleven ships carrying 700 convicts, 36 women and guards, plus provisions for two years, arrived in Botany Bay in 1788 and settled around Sydney Cove. Few people travelled beyond the Great Dividing Range which stretched for 4,800 km (7,000 miles) up the east coast. The British had no powerful neighbours to threaten the colony, but faced the problem of economic viability and a population composed largely of criminals. In 1801, however, Napoleon Bonaparte (1769–1821) sent Thomas-Nicholas Baudin to the Australian coast. In response Britain sent Matthew Flinders to survey the entire coastline of the country – which he called Australia.

1794
SHEEP AND SETTLEMENT

By 1800, there were 5,000 convicts around Sydney and the introduction of Merino sheep from South Africa in 1794 had given the colony an export product to attract free settlers. Coastal settlements increasingly sprang up, including Perth (1829), Melbourne (1835) and Adelaide (1836). By the 1830s there were 100,000 settlers. A regular steamship service between Sydney and Britain from 1856 increased the population to one million by the 1860s, by which time convict transportation had ceased. The discovery of gold in Victoria in 1851 led to an influx of settlers, but wool remained the main export commodity. Australia's colonies became self-governing in 1850 and British troops left in 1870.

✳ ▶ p. 170 ## 1810
NEW ZEALAND AND THE FIRST EUROPEAN ARRIVALS

The first European settlers in New Zealand were whalers, escaped convicts from Australia and traders who sold guns to the Maoris and infected them with diseases. Establishing a settlement in New Zealand was problematic as settlers lacked any

✳ CONFLICT   ⌐ ENCOUNTERS   ❖ FACILITIES   ♣ CONQUEST

▲ *Robert Burke and William Wills on their journey across Australia.*

cohesion, economic foundation or organisational structure for a viable colony. The British were reluctant to take responsibility for the islands or to challenge the fierce Maoris. In Britain, however, Gibbon Wakefield (1796–1862) formed the New Zealand Association to support colonisation, but it was not until 1810 that fears of French claims led to a formal declaration of sovereignty. Although a treaty was signed with 45 Maori chiefs, colonisation was obstructed by fierce rebellions (1860–71) as land disputes between Maoris and colonists sparked violence.

1828
EXPLORING AUSTRALIA'S INTERIOR
British explorer Charles Sturt's charting of the great river basins of the Darling (1828), Murumbidgee and Murray Rivers (1829) led to the development of the cities of Victoria and Adelaide. This, in turn, led to the founding of a new colony, South Australia (1834), which Britain populated by selling land to settlers for 60 pence an acre. British immigrant Edward Eyre set out on a trek from Adelaide to Perth in 1841, hoping to find a route for driving livestock. On the journey his companion was killed by two of the Aborigine guides, who fled with the supplies. The remaining Aborigine helped Eyre complete this hazardous trek. Colonisation led to the Aboriginal culture,

land rights and sacred places being destroyed by the British. European diseases and 'pacification by force' until the 1880s devastated the indigenous population.

⟳ ▶ p. 175 ### 1840s
STURT, LEICHHARDT AND MITCHELL
In 1844, Charles Sturt went in search of an inland sea, on a journey to the centre of Australia; instead of finding his sea, though, he found the Simpson Desert. In temperatures reaching 55°C Sturt's team became trapped at Cooper's Creek during a terrible drought, and were eventually forced to abandon the expedition. Later, German explorer Ludwig Leichardt managed to cross north-east Australia, from Brisbane to the Gulf of Carpentaria (1844–45), but he subsequently disappeared with no trace while making an east–west trek across Australia in 1848. Another explorer, Sir Thomas Mitchell, led an expedition in 1845–46 across the Great Dividing Range to find the Baroo River.

1860
CROSSING AUSTRALIA
The first crossing of Australia (1860–61) was completed by Irishman Robert Burke and ex-miner William Wills riding on camels – the first use of the animals in the country. Both unfortunately perished on the return journey. British surveyor John MacDonnell Stuart completed the first south–north crossing (1860–62) on his

third attempt after overcoming water shortages, Aborigine hostility and oppressive heat. During the 1860 trek, Stuart found and named the MacDonnell Ranges and came within 240 km (150 miles) of the centre of Australia. Such crossings enabled the government to begin linking Australia by telegraph and railway. By 1900, explorers had reached most of the 'outback', but the demanding terrain and temperatures they experienced confirmed the belief that much of the interior was unsuitable for settlement.

1875
SETTLEMENT AND ECONOMIC DEVELOPMENT
Sheep farming rapidly grew to become the main source of income for the colony. Europeans, attracted by the temperate climate and abundant pasture, established farms across the South Island. Although settlement was less than Australia, some 300,000 people and over 10 million sheep inhabited the South Island by 1875. The introduction of refrigeration ships (1882) and the suppression of the Maoris, enabled the North Island to develop a trade in frozen lamb and dairy produce. From 1901 settlement on the North Island exceeded that of the South Island. As well as wool, meat and dairy produce the South Island also mined gold after it was discovered in 1861. New Zealand was granted self-government in 1852 and finally became a British dominion in 1902.

p. 165 ◀ **Distant Voices** ▶ p. 169

New Holland is a very large tract of land. It is not yet determined whether it is an island or a main continent, but I am certain that it joins neither to Asia, Africa, nor America. This part of it that we see is all low, even land, with sandy banks against the sea.

William Dampier's description of Australia, from *A New Voyage Round the World* (January 1688)

The Slave Trade
1549–1852

SLAVERY IN AFRICA is as old as history. The ancient Egyptians certainly used slaves, and the word they used to describe them could be translated as 'talking tool' – quite effectively describing how this society perceived them. The Muslim world also made extensive use of African slaves, importing them in considerable numbers across the Sahara. The novelty that the Europeans brought to Africa's trade in slaves, however, was in the shipment of them not just to the neighbouring world of the Mediterranean, but across the Atlantic to the Americas. This forced emigration brought millions of Africans to a new continent and created a new cultural synthesis as African slaves and their descendants adapted their culture to that of their owners.

1549
SLAVERY IN THE NEW WORLD

The Portuguese were the first Europeans to exploit Africa for its slave labour. They had been the first European nation to establish permanent bases on the Atlantic coast of Africa, during the fifteenth century, and these served as collection points for slaves who were then carried to other parts of the empire. In 1549, the Portuguese decided to exploit their Brazilian colony by developing a sugar industry there. Brazil, however, was comparatively underpopulated and the native Americans who lived there were not farmers, so Africans were brought from Guinea and Angola to work the land. Disease and ill-treatment also caused Spanish America to experience labour shortages as the native Americans died in huge numbers. The Portuguese were more than happy to supply slaves in return for Spanish silver.

▼ *Natives of Haiti revolt against French ill-treatment.*

🔲 ▶ p. 172

1562
THE CARIBBEAN AND THE SLAVE TRADE

In 1562, three ships arrived off the coast of Sierra Leone and captured 300 Africans, who were to be taken as slaves to Spanish America. One of the financial backers was the English Queen Elizabeth. This was the first instance of British involvement in the slave trade and it took about 100 years to develop into any size. The settlers of Jamestown, in Virginia, brought slaves to north America in 1619, to grow tobacco, but their numbers were small for several generations. However, in 1625 England acquired Barbados and in 1655 Jamaica, from the Spanish. Planters began to settle there to grow sugar to meet the constantly increasing demand in Europe. The profitability of these operations was immense.

✳ ▶ p. 171

1654
SLAVERY AND EMPIRE

Collection and dispersal points of slaves became important targets in wars. Dutch forces seized posts or constructed new ones in Brazil, and the need to supply slaves to these territories caused the seizure, in 1654, of one of the oldest Portuguese bases in Africa – Elmina near the mouth of the Volta River. Other European states built their own posts on the coast nearby, including the Swedes, the Danes and the Prussians countries almost entirely without American possessions. The islands of the Caribbean were handed round European states like real estate in a modern city. The Dutch captured Curaçao from the Spanish in 1634. The French settled Guadeloupe and Martinique and in 1697 they forced Spain to grant them half of the island of Hispaniola, which eventually became Haiti.

1680s
BRITISH NORTH AMERICA

The colonies of Virginia and Maryland began to attract African labour from 1680 onwards, but many of these were imported via plantations in the West Indies. It was only after the beginning of the eighteenth century that slaves began to arrive directly from Africa to North America in large

▲ *Conflict arose between British and French colonists in North America in the 1740s.*

colonies scattered along the coast of Africa and in the Caribbean, the British were able to seize over 1,500 ships engaged in the traffic. In 1838, slavery was abolished in the British Empire. By 1867, the trade had virtually ceased. But, paradoxically, in the process the British expanded their colonies in Africa, in order to persecute slavers more effectively. Freetown, in Sierra Leone, for example, was founded as a home for slaves released from captured ships.

numbers. In the first 40 years of the century, over 50,000 slaves were brought to Chesapeake Bay, some 90 per cent of them from Africa. The British settlement in the Carolinas, begun in 1663, failed in its attempt to grow tobacco and indigo, but the planned slave labour system soon established itself on rice plantations. This was a wholly African industry, since the rice came from Madagascar, and the growing techniques from West Africa.

 ▶ p. 175 **1741**
THE WAR FOR NORTH AMERICA
The growing wealth of the British colonies along the Atlantic coast of North America – in part based on the profits from slavery – attracted more and more settlers. These newcomers were desperate for land, and this resulted in a series of wars with French colonies in the St Lawrence river valley and around the Great Lakes. Although these coincided with the wars in Europe, they were fought independently. Fighting broke out in 1741, was halted briefly in 1748, and resumed again in 1754. At the end of the conflict in North America, in 1760, the British had pushed the French out of their main colony on the mainland, Québec.

1787
MORAL REVULSION
In 1787, a group of English Quakers organised what was initially a very small community of people to work towards the abolition of the slave trade in Britain.

Although this was a tough battle, it did not last very long. One of the most effective public campaigners was a member of Britain's House of Commons, William Wilberforce (1759–1833). In 1788, he organised a committee to study the slave trade; this revealed many horrifying statistics about the confined spaces and appalling conditions on the ships in which the slaves were transported across the Atlantic. As a result, in 1807, the slave trade was abolished in Britain.

▲ *The philanthropist and reformer William Wilberforce, who led the opposition to the slave trade in Britain.*

⊕ ▶ p. 178 **1800s**
WAR ON THE SLAVE TRADE
For the next 60 years, Britain, largely alone, waged a naval war against the Atlantic slave trade. Using the vast resources of the Royal Navy – then by far the largest fleet in the world – and the chain of bases in the

1805
SLAVERY AND STATE BUILDING
In one place, the abolition of slavery was to have a lasting impact on the course of imperialism in Africa. The Dutch settlers – known as Boers in the Cape of Good Hope – were conquered by a British expedition in 1805, in the course of the Napoleonic Wars (1797–1815). The growing anti-slavery agitation during the 1820s and 1830s alarmed the Boers, for whom slavery was a natural part of God's law. In 1836 a substantial number of them fled the Cape for the high southern African plateau known as the *veldt*. Here they established their own states, the Transvaal Republic and the Orange Free State, where slavery remained permitted until the British forced its abolition in 1852.

p. 167 ◀ **Distant Voices** ▶ p. 171

On a signal given (as the beat of a drum) the buyers rushed at once into the yard where the slaves are confined, and make choice of that parcel they like best. The noise and the clamour with which this is attended and the eagerness visible in the countenances of the buyers serve not a little to increase the apprehensiveness of the terrified Africans.... In this manner, without scruple, are relations and friends separated, most of them never to see each other again.

Olaudah Equiano, describing a slave market on Barbados

The First Decolonisations
1763–1836

p. 164 ◀ **Triumphs & Tragedies** ▶ p. 178

BY THE END of the Seven Years' War (1756–63), the leading western European states controlled the Americas. Britain, the most successful of the nations in the war, had the Atlantic Coast and all of Canada; Spain had much of central and south America and the interior and Pacific Coast of North America; France and the Netherlands held islands in the Caribbean; Portugal controlled Brazil. But these colonies of settlers began to develop economic and political traditions of their own, which soon came into conflict with the authorities in the capitals of their European owners. The movements towards independence and the resulting wars were the first decolonisations in world history.

▲ *Bostonians, disguised as Indians, throw tea overboard in Boston Port in a rebellion against British trade restrictions.*

1774
THE AMERICAN REVOLUTION

A Continental Congress of delegates from the American colonies met in Philadelphia in September 1774. The different colonies themselves began to create their own assemblies. Massachusetts saw one of the most effective ones, and it was here that the British chose to confront the problem. An attempt to seize a store of arms at Concord on 19 April 1775, led to armed warfare. A large colonial army laid siege to Boston, and the Continental Congress appointed a commander – General George Washington (1732–99). Boston was evacuated, but a full-scale war broke out. On 4 July 1776, the Continental Congress declared independence as the United States of America and in February 1778, this was recognised by France.

1778
DEFINING THE BOUNDARIES

French aid to the United States, starting from 1778, tipped the balance of the war in favour of the Americans. In 1781, a large British army trapped at Yorktown in Virginia, surrendered. Fighting an alliance of France, Spain and the United States was beyond British resources. In 1783, a treaty ended the war; but enforcing this independence was not easy. Britain saw no reason to give up valuable fur trading posts around the Great Lakes, while Spain hoped to gain territorial advantages in the lands north of Florida and east of Louisiana. It took a major war with the native Americans of the Midwest and the aggressive deployment of soldiers in the South to secure the 1783 borders. By 1796, the borders of the United States had finally been firmly fixed along the Great Lakes and the Mississippi river.

✱ ▶ p. 176

1763
TAX AND SPEND

The Seven Years' War left Britain with considerable debts, part of which had been the cost of defending the American colonies against French attacks. To the American colonies, it was a violation of their rights as 'freeborn Englishmen'. The crisis became worse after the 'Townshend Duties' of 1767, which were part of a comprehensive package that would restrict the ability of colonial assemblies to influence administrative officials. In 1773, a new crisis began over taxed – but cheap – tea. The colonists rejected the principle of paying any tax and a large shipment of tea was destroyed in Boston harbour – a protest action that became known as the Boston Tea Party. After this episode, the British government was determined to recover the lost revenue, by force if necessary.

▼ *Thomas Jefferson, signing the American Declaration of Independence.*

1791
THE WHITE NIGHTMARE

While the Americans established the right of the governed to approve the actions of the government in 1776, the French

✦ CONFLICT   ⬚ ENCOUNTERS   ❖ FACILITIES   ♣ CONQUEST

Revolution of 1789 established the principle of fundamental human equality. These two strands were tied together in the next major decolonisation, of French-controlled Haiti. In 1791, a huge slave revolt broke out and in 1793 it acquired a poweful leader in the shape of Toussaint L'Ouverture (1743–1803), a former slave turned military genius. After 13 years of largely guerrilla warfare, Napoleonic France finally conceded independence in 1804. For three generations afterwards, slaveholders in the American South and the Caribbean feared the rise of a new L'Ouverture.

1799–1803
THE SECRETS OF SOUTH AMERICA
In 1799, the Spanish monarchy gave approval for a German scientist named Alexander von Humboldt (1769–1859) to conduct a thorough exploration of parts of South America. They were hoping to discover valuable mineral deposits. Humboldt made two expeditions, one along the Orinoco river in Venezuela in 1799–1800 and one along the Andes in 1801–03. His studies added considerable botanical knowledge and also mapped the blank spots in northern South America. Perhaps the most important discovery made by Humboldt was of the value of guano as a fertiliser, which would attract investors from Europe in the nineteenth century to the Pacific coast.

▼ *The Venezuelan general Simon Bolívar.*

✳ ▶ p. 178

1803
EMPIRE BEYOND THE MISSISSIPPI
Many Americans hoped either to annex or found an independent state in the sparsely populated borderlands between Spanish America and the United States. However, a way to get the huge region known as Louisiana, took shape in 1800, when Spain agreed to cede it to France. President Thomas Jefferson (1743–1826) sent diplomats to see if the United States could buy it. Napoleon, France's ruler, agreed, and in 1803 the whole western drainage of the Mississippi River Valley became the property of the US. Jefferson sent two important expeditions to explore this relatively unknown region: that of Meriwether Lewis (1774–1809) and William Clark (1770–1838) followed a northern trajectory in search of a water route to the Pacific; Zebulon Pike (1779–1813) crossed the southern half of the region, reaching Pike's Peak in the Rocky Mountains.

1808
A REVOLUTION OF TRADITION?
In 1808, Napoleon deposed the king of Spain. The inhabitants of Spanish America rejected this change of regime out of hand and, starting in Mexico in 1808, founded their own local councils to rule until the restoration of the king. A confused situation of claims and counter-claims to authority persisted until 1811, when a council in Caracas declared its independence on the proposal of Francisco de Miranda (1750–1816). The struggle of the

Spanish colonies for independence was dominated by the personality of Simon Bolívar (1783–1830), who was both its leading political theorist and most important general. By 1824, the independence struggle had been won on the battlefield, but political change did not extend to social reform.

1818
AN AMERICAN IMPERIALISM
Spanish America was too vast for a single authority. Even an attempt to combine modern Venezuela, Colombia, Panama and Ecuador ended in failure in 1830. For the United States, however, the situation was an opportunity to expand. In 1818, the US forced Spain to sell Florida, under the threat of attack. From 1821, American settlers began moving into Texas, the northernmost part of Mexico; and in 1823, the United States issued what is known as the Monroe Doctrine, instructing European states to keep out of politics in the Americas. But that did not ban American intervention – in 1836, when Texas declared its independence, the United States supported the rebels, in the hope that eventually the territory could be annexed.

---

p. 169 ◀ **Distant Voices** ▶ p. 173

This little fleet altho' not quite so respectable as those of Columbus or Capt. Cook were still viewed by us with as much pleasure as those deservedly famed adventurers ever beheld theirs; and I dare say with quite as much anxiety for their safety and preservation. We were now about to penetrate a country at least two thousand miles in width, on which the foot of civilised man had never trodde; the good or evil it had in store for us was for experiment yet to determine, and these little vessels contained every article by which we were to expect to subsist or defend ourselves.

Meriwether Lewis describes his departure from Fort Mandan

Gunboat Diplomacy
1790–1900

EUROPEAN TECHNOLOGICAL advances during the eighteenth century, especially in the realm of military technology, made it the dominant continent on the planet. Steam power enabled their ships to travel against contrary winds; superior metallurgical techniques enabled Europeans to construct better firearms and more powerful artillery; mass-production techniques enabled them to produce more weapons at a faster rate, and the machinery developed pointed the way to rifling, increasing the accuracy of firearms, and the rapid-fire technology of the machine gun. During the nineteenth century, European colonial adventures increasingly turned to conquest instead of trade, and wars frequently broke out between native states and aboriginal peoples instead of European rivals.

1790
INDIA AND ITS NEIGHBOURS

The British East India Company gradually increased its control over India in a series of wars beginning in 1790. By the end of 1849 there were no independent Indian states left. At the same time, the British had sought to secure the borders of India by interventions in neighbouring regions such as Iran, Afghanistan, Nepal and Burma. Only in Afghanistan did this intervention fail. In 1857, a last attempt to challenge British rule was made when a revolt by Indian soldiers serving under British command, combined with an attempt to recover independence by rulers such as the Rhani of Jhansi and the Mogul emperor. After a fierce struggle in the Ganges Valley, the British emerged victorious.

1793
CHINA IN CHAOS

China's rulers rejected an attempt by Britain to widen the scope for traders in the East Asian Empire in 1793. Trade took place on a controlled basis only, in a few ports. But the most popular import was an addictive drug – opium. The social havoc this wreaked led the Chinese to attempt blocking the supply, causing the First Opium War (1839–42). At the end of this conflict, Britain had acquired Hong Kong

and freer trade had been agreed. China now tipped into chaos: in 1850, a dangerous revolt that threatened the ruling Manchu dynasty broke out in the south of the country. The Tai-ping rebellion eventually took control of central China for many years, until it was suppressed with European help in 1864.

▼ *The British and Chinese meet after the end of the Opium Wars that were waged throughout the early 1940s.*

▶ p. 174

1798
FRANCE AND EGYPT

During the wars between revolutionary France and the rest of Europe, the French government decided to threaten Britain's link with India by invading Egypt. In July 1798, the attacking force arrived off the Egyptian coast. The French conquered Egypt, but abandoned these gains following the defeat of their fleet and army by the British. In 1802, the French army left and after several years of instability, Muhammad Ali came to power in 1809, nominally as the viceroy of the Turkish sultan. Muhammad Ali wanted to be an independent ruler, and pursued this aim single-mindedly, frequently with French support. At the time of his death in 1849, Egypt controlled the Nile Valley as far as Khartoum and both sides of the Red Sea coast.

1801
THE BARBARY CORSAIRS

The Muslim countries of western North Africa had always derived part of their income from what to European eyes was piracy but to Islamic ones was the duty of fighting the infidel. In 1801, the ruler of Tripoli declared war on the United States. This opened a series of minor military

✦ CONFLICT   ⌐ ENCOUNTERS   ❖ FACILITIES   ♣ CONQUEST

▲ *The French invasion of Algiers in 1830, which led to an extended French empire in North Africa.*

engagements between the North African states and European and American powers, that culminated in 1830 with a full-scale French invasion of Algiers. The French combined military might with a policy of settling French colonists in pacified regions. By 1847, the whole of the coastal strip and the fertile land between the Mediterranean Sea and the Sahara Desert had fallen under French control.

❖ ▶ p. 180   **1831–35**
SCIENCE AND IMPERIALISM

The growing value of overseas trade caused governments to demand ever more accurate information about destinations in the far corners of the world. One British voyage to survey the South Atlantic and Pacific coasts of South America carried a naturalist named Charles Darwin (1809–82). His studies of South American plant and animal life during the 1831–35 voyage of HMS *Beagle* contributed to his theory of evolution. Darwin's researches encouraged the exploration of the Amazon Basin between 1848 and 1861 by the naturalists Alfred Wallace (1823–1913), Henry Bates (1825–92) and Richard Spruce (1817–93). The information acquired by scientific expeditions such as these was of great use to investors seeking new natural resources to exploit, and contributed to the development of a colonial economic relationship between South America and Europe.

1845
AMERICAN ADVENTURES

Because the border between Texas and Mexico had never been defined, conflicting claims led to war between the United States and Mexico (1846–48), which resulted in the United States acquiring California and the lands in between as well. In 1845, the United States government finally agreed to

annex the area. This event, together with some armed expeditions by private American citizens to central America, created some ill-will between Latin America and the United States. While the American Civil War raged (1861–65), France and Spain sought to establish control over Mexico and the Dominican Republic respectively. These failed – in Mexico because the armed resistance of the people triumphed in 1867, and in the Dominican Republic because of the expense.

1846
THE SUEZ CANAL

In 1846, a group of Austrian, French and British investors agreed that the time had come to cut a canal between the Mediterranean and the Red Sea, thereby providing a shorter sea route between Europe and the Far East. Muhammad Ali was uninterested in this project, but his successors were more enthusiastic. In 1858, a stock issue raised the money, work began in 1859, and the canal opened 10 years later. The canal was vital to Britain – and Britain now chose to interfere in Egypt's internal politics. In 1881, a group of Egyptian army officers seized control of the country, and the threat to control of the canal caused the British to occupy Egypt in 1882.

1853
JAPAN AND CHINA RESIST

In 1853, a squadron of American warships arrived in Tokyo Harbour. They forced the Japanese government to sign a treaty opening Japanese ports to trade. The leaders of Japan made a determined effort to catch up with the European powers. In 1894, Japan fomented a war with China and emerged victorious in 1895. As part of the peace settlement, Japan acquired Korea, thus becoming one of the powers exploiting

China. In 1899, a resistance movement popularly known as the 'Boxers' began a rebellion in China that resulted, in 1900, in a siege of the foreign diplomats' compound at Peking. An international army, including a Japanese contingent, crushed the rising, ending Imperial China's last hope of regaining control over its borders.

▲ *The Chinese Boxer rebellion of 1900, which was crushed by an international army.*

p. 171 ◀ **Distant Voices** ▶ p. 175

The Company professed to treat the chief of Bharatpur as a son, and then took his Territory; the chief of Lahore was carried off to London, and it has not fallen to his lot to return; the Nawab Shamsuddin Khan on one side they hanged, and on the other side they took off their hats and salaamed to him; the Peshwa they expelled from Poona, and imprisoned for life in Bithur; their breach of faith with Sultan Tippu, is well known; the Raja of Banaras they imprisoned in Agra. Under pretence of administering the country of the chief of Gwalior, they introduced English customs; they have left no name or traces of the chiefs of Bihar, Orissa, and Bengal; they gave the nawab of Farukhabad a small monthly allowance, and took his territory.

The Begum of Oudh, listing the grievances of India

The Scramble for Africa
1788–1902

THE MOTIVES BEHIND the first explorations into the African interior were threefold. Firstly, there was a scientific and geographical interest in revealing the mysteries of this generally unmapped and unrecorded area of the globe. European colonists had largely remained around coastal areas and rarely penetrated inland, leaving whole areas uncharted. Organisations like the Association for Promoting the Discovery of the Interior Parts of Africa (founded 1788) arose to encourage the systematic investigation of the continent. Secondly, Protestant evangelical Christianity motivated missionaries to embark on expeditions to preach and convert. Finally, the anti-slavery movement supported humanitarian missions to penetrate regions where slavery persisted.

1795
EXPLORING THE AFRICAN INTERIOR
At the end of the eighteenth century, expeditions into the African interior began which led to the colonisation of almost the entire continent by the end of the nineteenth century. One of the first great explorers was the British doctor Mungo Park (1771–1806) who led two expeditions to search for the source of the Niger River (1795–96 and 1804–06). In the early nineteenth century, French and German explorers trekked across the hostile Muslim areas of North Africa. In 1824 British explorer Alexander Laing (1793–1826) became the first known European to cross the Sahara from north to south. Frenchman René Caillié (1799–1838) then crossed the Sahara disguised as an Egyptian to visit the once-great commercial centre of Timbuktu (1827–28).

1800s
MEDICINE, MACHINE GUNS AND MOBILITY
A critical element of the exploration and conquest of Africa was a series of inventions and innovations during the period. Firstly, medical advances helped Europeans triumph over diseases. The French development of quinine (1827) helped protect against malaria and dramatically reduced death-rates. Military developments in firepower enabled numerically inferior imperial forces to inflict decisive defeats upon indigenous opposition. Camouflage, mounted infantry, improved fieldcraft and native troops all helped the imperial forces adjust to the challenges of colonial warfare.

Steamships, small enough to navigate inland waterways, enabled explorers to open up great rivers such as the Niger, Zambezi, Nile and Congo. Gunboats, fitted with armour plating and cannon, were able to help capture and patrol territories. Railways, roads and telegraphy also helped relieve the logistical challenges of natural obstacles and vast distances.

1800s
COLONIAL ADMINISTRATION
Colonial control took various forms within Africa. Initially, governments had often left the task of developing trade and settlements to chartered companies such as the Royal Niger Company. As colonisation developed during the 1800s, governments began assuming greater direct control of administrative and defence responsibilities for overseas possessions. France pursued this centralised form of control and encouraged 'assimilation', whereby French culture and language was 'exported' to

THE SCRAMBLE FOR AFRICA 1880–1914

Great Britain
France
Belgium
Germany
Spain
Portugal
Italy

Following their rise in wealth from the fruits of their newly industrialised economies, many European countries turned their attention to expansion. They were motivated by the desire to secure new sources of raw materials and trade and by the dictates of military strategy. They mistakenly saw Africa as an empty continent ripe for exploitation and divided it up accordingly.

✦ CONFLICT   ⌐ ENCOUNTERS   ❖ FACILITIES   ✦ CONQUEST

colonial populations. By contrast, Britain often pursued devolution or indirect control. This normally involved granting various degrees of autonomy to local authorities, often traditional rulers of a given locality. Customary laws and practices would often continue but would be overseen by British officials.

▲ *The Berlin Conference, at which Africa came under European imperial power.*

♣ ▶ p. 177   **1815**
THE AGE OF IMPERIALISM
Imperial expansion was continuous after 1815, as nations sought the prestige of overseas conquest. In Africa this became a 'scramble' as new colonial powers (such as Germany and Italy) increased the momentum to secure territories before their rivals. Peace was maintained between the colonists through the Berlin Conference (1884–85), which helped divide Africa into 'spheres of influence'. Great Britain made the greatest gains, including Egypt (1882), Nigeria (1884), British Somaliland (1884), Southern Rhodesia (1890), Northern Rhodesia (1891) and Sudan (1898). France also made significant gains, mainly in north and west Africa, including French Congo (1875–92), French West Africa (1786–98) and Madagascar (1895–96). During the 'scramble' Germany quickly built up an African and Pacific empire, covering one million square miles and Italy seized Tripoli (1861), Eritrea (1889), Somaliland (1893) and Libya (1912).

1830–64
TRACING THE NIGER AND ZAMBEZI
In 1830 British explorers Richard (1804–34) and John Lander (1807–39) discovered the mouth of the Niger River, which eventually became the passage into the African interior, making the once great Saharan crossroads largely obsolete. From 1849 the British missionary David Livingstone (1813–73) helped map much of southern and central Africa and became the first known European to cross the continent from the west to east coast (1854–56). From 1858–64 he led the Great Zambezi Expedition. He considered the river as 'God's Highway' that would open the interior to Christianity and trade. On his last journey to explore the river systems of central Africa (1866–73), he became stranded by Lake Tanganyika but was rescued in 1873 by American journalist Henry Morton Stanley (1841–1904).

☽ ▶ p. 183   **1858–77**
THE SOURCE OF THE NILE
British explorers Richard Burton (1821–90) and John Speke (1827–64) were the first Europeans to reach Lake Tanganyika (1857) and Speke then went to Lake Victoria, the source of the White Nile (1858). Speke led a further expedition back to the source of the Nile in 1860–63 and became the first known European to visit Uganda. From 1861 to 1864 British explorer Samuel Baker (1821–93) and his wife, Florence, travelled to Lake Albert Nyanza, a feeder of the White Nile. From 1873–75 British explorer Verney Lovett Cameron (1844–94) surveyed Lake Tanganyika and made the first European east–west crossing of Africa. In 1874 Stanley explored Lakes Victoria and Tanganyika to confirm Speke's findings. He then travelled right down the Congo to the Atlantic Ocean (1874–77).

1890s
LATER EXPLORATIONS
In 1879 Stanley returned to the Congo to help develop a colony, Congo Free State, under the personal control of Belgium's king, Leopold (1835–1909). In 1889 two

Germans, Hans Meyer and Ludwig Purtscheller, became the first Europeans to climb Mount Kilimanjaro. One of the final expeditions in the 1800s was made by Mary Kingsley (1862–1900), a British amateur anthropologist and naturalist who travelled to West Africa to explore Angola and the Congo River (1893). While exploring in 1894 she encountered the Fang cannibal tribe and travelled in a native canoe up the Ogooué River and ended her expedition by climbing Mount Cameroon (possibly being the first woman to accomplish this). By the First World War the continent was under almost complete colonial control by France, Britain, Germany, Belgium, Spain, Portugal and Italy.

★ ▶ p. 179   **1899**
THE BOER CHALLENGE TO THE BRITISH EMPIRE
The greatest challenge to British power at this time arose in South Africa, in the form of the Boers (Dutch settlers). Two Boer republics had become enclosed by British territories and conflict between the settlers began to arise. Increasing friction between the Boers and British escalated into war after Cecil Rhodes (1853–1902), prime minister of Cape Colony from 1890–96, attempted to seize the diamond and gold areas of the Boer republics. Throughout the Boer War (1899–1902), the British suffered serious defeats at the hands of the Boers, until many of the Boer communities were placed in concentration camps. Their property was destroyed, denying the soldiers vital supplies, thus turning the fortunes of the war.

p. 173 ◀ **Distant Voices** ▶ p. 177

You cannot make omlettes without breaking eggs. You cannot exercise control over barbarous countries without (occasionally) coming into conflict with their savage rulers and having to shed some blood.

Joseph Chamberlain's view on colonial conquest from *Foreign and Colonial Speeches* (1897)

The Evil Empires
1931–45

THE FASCIST AND MILITARIST regimes that emerged in Germany, Italy and Japan after the First World War created imperialist ambitions that plunged the world into war once again. Fascism emerged from the discontent created by the 1919 Versailles Treaty, the subsequent political instability and economic depression. German fascism (Nazism) fused nationalism with racism to form powerful imperial ambitions. Nazi leader Adolf Hitler (1889–1945) articulated a dream of a German Empire that arose from destroying racial and ideological enemies. Aryan territories around Germany would be united; European domination would then be achieved by creating colonial states or subject lands of less important Aryans or 'inferior' peoples. Italy's fascists, led by Benito Mussolini (1883–1945), articulated a similar imperial ambition and belligerence, but their racism did not dominate their political agenda.

▲ *Norwegian fascist Vidkun Quisling, a Nazi collaborator prior to the Second World War.*

▲ *Officials proclaim the New State of Manchuria.*

1931
THE GREATER EAST ASIA CO-PROSPERITY SPHERE

Japan's invasions were initially perceived as liberating nations from European colonists. Semi-independent governments were appointed, except in the 'inferior' south-east Asia region. Often Japan failed to mobilise occupied areas and faced disorder and hostility instead of co-operation. Local nationalists were often given responsibilities but they used this collaboration to bolster their movements. Japanese barbarity was commonplace with forced labour, massacres and human rights violations. This was first displayed during the Manchuria invasion (1931) and the invasion of China (1937), where 250,000 people died in Nanking alone. China responded by bitterly resisting Japan and 15 million Chinese died from the fighting and appalling conditions.

◉ 1933
THE 'NEW ORDER'

Germany's territorial acquisitions after Hitler took power (1933) began by regaining the Saar from France (1935), then the Rhineland (1936) and Austria (1938). Britain and France declared war after the occupation of Czechoslovakia and Poland in 1939. By 1942, Germany's empire stretched from the Atlantic to the Urals and was bolstered by the support of Italy, Slovakia, Hungary, Bulgaria and Romania. Without sufficient personnel to control the empire, the Nazis depended upon local collaboration. Local fascists, such as Vidkun Quisling in Norway (1887–1945), welcomed the occupiers, but often their ambitions for governing their own nations clashed with Nazi policies. The German occupiers secured public co-operation by threats and punishments – both individual and collective.

1935
THE 'NEW ROME'

Italy's empire, forged by the infamous Benito Mussolini, was a small and short-lived creation. It began with the invasion of Ethiopia in 1935, followed by Albania in 1939 and British Somaliland in 1940. Sections of France, Yugoslavia and Greece also came under its control. Italy, however, lacked the capability and the commitment to retain her conquests. Britain repulsed her attack on Egypt (1940–41) then recaptured East Africa (1941). Public support for fascist imperialism – and the war – was short-lived. Before Mussolini fell from power in 1943 the empire was already strained by deteriorating relations with Germany in the occupied regions they shared, especially over the treatment of Jews.

✳ ▶ p. 181 1936
MILITARISM IN JAPAN

Japan had seen the rise of militaristic and imperialistic movements since 1918. Since Japan's emergence from isolation in the nineteenth century to become modern and industrialised, the nation had developed into a leading military and economic force

 ✦ CONFLICT   🖺 ENCOUNTERS   ❖ FACILITIES   ♠ CONQUEST

within Asia. It had already gained territory from China (1894–95) and Russia (1899–1902) through military conquests. After the First World War it gained former German islands and Chinese outposts. Overseas expansions became a key policy in the inter-war period, with Japan invading Manchuria (1931). After the military took power (1936) they began attacking China (1937). Japan's aim was for a 'Greater East Asia Co-prosperity Sphere', in theory a mutually beneficial trading network; in reality a framework to secure raw materials for Japan and markets for her exports.

1939
THE NAZIS PLUNDER EUROPE

Germany had anticipated a rapid victory, and economic planning focused upon restructuring her empire for the post-war era. The prolonged war, however, presented Germany with pressing needs. Economic squads swarmed into conquered lands to seize raw materials, gold and machinery. Germany assumed control of fuel, materials, currency and prices. Occupation costs were imposed on countries with France paying 10.9 per cent of her national income in 1940 and 36.6 per cent by 1943. German labour shortages were relieved by prisoners-of-war, and 'voluntary' or forced foreign workers were compelled to work in Germany. By 1944, some two million prisoners-of-war and 7.5 million adults and children from across German-occupied Europe were working in Germany.

1939
THE ECONOMY OF THE THIRD REICH

As the needs of Germany's war machine grew, their methods to satisfy it became harsher. Forced labourers suffered intolerable conditions, and many died. Despite this plundering of the human and economic resources of the Nazi Empire, Germany did not achieve any centralisation or real efficiency, although this became critical as Allied attacks increasingly hampered economic activity. By 1944, French industrial output was falling dramatically and agricultural production

reached only 25 per cent of its 1939 output. The economic and administrative control of occupied areas was seriously undermined by 'authoritarian anarchy' arising from bureaucratic weaknesses. Although power was centralised in Berlin it was fragmented into numerous rival agencies.

1939
OCCUPIED POPULATIONS

The effects upon occupied populations were traumatic. Intellectual freedoms were constrained by Nazi doctrine, cultural and religious expression was replaced by the Nazi identity, politics was repressed by propaganda, information was censored and freedom of movement limited. Economic dislocation impoverished populations and food production was directed to Germany. As conditions deteriorated and transport systems faltered, the rationing of populations reached critical levels. One of the most terrifying manifestations of the New Order was the Nazi attempt to achieve racial supremacy. The Nazis aimed to create a demographic transformation in Europe by gathering the German race together. This involved enslaving the Slavs and destroying the Jews. Unlike the barbarism of former conquerors, Nazi violence was not random but systematic and millions were killed with bureaucratic efficiency and cruelty.

1945
1945 AND BEYOND

The evil empires of Germany and Italy had finally collapsed by 1945, at the end of the Second World War. Despite being relatively short-lived, a total of 60 million people had died during their period of power. The human and material cost of these regimes was unprecedented and they opened the eyes of the world to the dangers of such political cults. Their rise, domination and collapse had far-reaching repercussions for the shape of the post-war world, the pre-war colonial powers and the ascendancy of new power blocs. In this short period, the world view of persecution, basic human rights and warfare itself had changed forever.

p. 175 ◀ **Distant Voices** ▶ p. 179

Should we succeed in establishing this Nordic race again from and around Germany ... then the world will belong to us. Should Bolshevism win, it will signify the extermination of the Nordic race.

A view of the Third Reich, by Heinrich Himmler, SS and Gestapo chief

▼ *German prisoners after the Battle of Stalingrad in 1943.*

Cracks and Collapse
1885–1965

THE EUROPEAN COLONIAL EMPIRES remained almost unchanged from the nineteenth century until the Second World War. The only major change involved the German and Turkish colonies which were redistributed as mandates (trusteeships) to the Allies by the League of Nations (1919). By 1965, however, the European empires possessed fewer colonies than they had held four centuries earlier. Although the decolonisation mainly occurred after 1945, its origins lay in the rise of nationalist sentiments from the nineteenth century on. Nationalism – the belief in the union of people who share a common culture, language and belief into one nation state – was the major impulse behind independence movements.

1885
THE FIRST STIRRINGS OF NATIONALISM

Violent resistance to colonial rule had been commonplace for centuries, but the first systematic political challenge arose with the Indian National Congress (est. 1885). This aimed to further the powers of Indians who were already entering local government and the civil service. Similar movements later emerged elsewhere, such as the National Congress of British West Africa (est. 1918) and the South African Native National Congress (est. 1912). Despite these movements, only Britain offered any measure of self-government to its colonies by making Canada, New Zealand, Australia and South Africa into independent 'dominions'. Such freedoms were, however, restricted to colonies where white settlers were a large or dominant section of the population.

1919
INTER-WAR UNREST

During the First World War the imperial empires retained the co-operation of their colonial subjects, but the inter-war period exposed the fragility of their imperial control. Efforts to satisfy Arab aspirations in the Middle East led to Britain establishing the kingdoms of Iraq (declared independent in 1932) and Transjordan. Similar promises made to the Jews for a 'National Home' in Palestine created more complications and violence. The Indian independence movement proved a serious threat to British rule, with growing demands for Indian representation in central government. The 1919 Amritsar massacre of 400 Indians hardened nationalist campaigners, and emergency powers were subsequently introduced to repress protests amid growing violence.

1939–45
COLLAPSING EMPIRES

The Second World War saw the first steps towards the collapse of colonial rule, as European powers became embroiled in a global conflict that exposed deep cracks in the foundations of imperialism. The omnipotence of colonial powers was shattered by the conquests of their homelands or colonies, especially as a result of

p. 170 ◀ **Triumphs & Tragedies** ▶ p. 182
1931
GANDHI AND THE INDIAN STRUGGLE

The 1935 Government of India Act granted limited self-government and pledged to progressively transfer power. Such vague promises failed to satisfy the Indian National Congress. Nationalist leader Mahatma Gandhi (1869–1948) led a campaign of *satygraha*: passive civil disobedience and the boycotting of European goods. In 1931 the British imprisoned Gandhi, but failed to suppress the momentum for change. In the immediate post-war period, war-weary imperial powers were often unable fully to restore colonial control. Civil unrest in India and a naval mutiny (1946) forced Britain to accelerate moves towards independence. In elections Indian Muslims in the north voted overwhelmingly for the Muslim League which demanded a separate state. In August 1947, the country was partitioned into independent India (mainly Hindu) and Pakistan (mainly Muslim).

▼ *The Amritsar Massacre, in which 400 Indians were killed and a further 1,200 injured.*

✦ CONFLICT   ⌂ ENCOUNTERS   ❖ FACILITIES   ♣ CONQUEST

communist North Vietnam. After French capitulation at Dien Bien Phu in 1954, Indochina was divided into Laos, Cambodia, North Vietnam and South Vietnam. The subsequent civil war between North and South Vietnam led to the region becoming a Cold War battleground after US intervention.

1948
THE MIDDLE EAST AND COLONIAL LEGACIES

In the Middle East, France had quickly left Syria and Lebanon (1946), while Britain granted independence to Jordan the same year. With Arab-Jewish hostilites escalating, Britain agreed with the United Nations a plan of partition for Palestine. By May 1948 the British had withdrawn, leaving a newly declared Jewish-Israeli state at war with her Arab neighbours. Some of the old European empires still retain control over small areas, while imperial links are retained in organisations such as the British Commonwealth. In 1982 Britain fought and won a war with Argentina over possession of the Falkland Islands colony in the South Atlantic. Britain returned her last important colonial possession, Hong Kong, to China in 1997.

1956
BRITISH POWER IN FLUX

With little colonial reform in Africa, independence campaigns arose. The first major incident to expose imperial vulnerability was the Kenyan Mau-Mau guerrilla war (1952–56). Nations like Britain became increasingly aware that decolonisation would not disrupt overseas economic interests, but would relieve them of imperial defence and administration. The 1956 Suez Crisis in which France and Britain had to make a humiliating withdrawal from Egypt under US pressure undermined the credibility of the colonial powers and revealed their declining global status. A major review of Britain's imperial position resulted in Ghana becoming the first independent 'black' nation in Africa (1957). By 1964 British prime minister Harold Macmillan (1894–1986) spoke of a 'wind of change', as decolonisation spread through Africa and the Caribbean.

▲ *The French and British were forced to withdraw from the Suez Canal Zone in 1956 after US intervention.*

1956
FIGHTING AND FREEDOM IN AFRICA

In 1956 France left Morocco and Tunisia, but Algerian independence was opposed by the one million Algerians of French descent (*colons*) who rejected the idea of an Arab Muslim state. In 1954 a nationalist Arab rebellion sparked a bitter civil conflict. To halt any withdrawal French army officers sympathetic to the *colons* revolted (1958) and new Premier, Charles de Gaulle (1890–1970), was appointed. De Gaulle withdrew from the colonies of Guinea (1958), Cameroon, Congo, Gabon, Chad and the Central African Republic (1960). Algeria finally gained independence in 1962. The ruling white minority in southern Rhodesia issued declared independence in 1965 and excluded blacks from power. White-dominated South Africa adopted a racist apartheid policy in 1948 and, amid opposition from the British Commonwealth, became a republic (1948).

p. 177 ◀ **Distant Voices** ▶ p. 181

I want freedom immediately, this very night, before dawn if it can be had. Freedom cannot wait for communal unity…. Nothing however should be done secretly. This is an open rebellion….

Gandhi's response to British promises for independence (August 1942)

▲ *Mahatma Gandhi, leader of the Indian Nationalist movement.*

Japanese conquests in Asia. Bargaining for support, Britain offered India post-war independence in return for help during the war. The Indian National Congress demanded this immediately and in an about-face an Indian National Army even fought with the Japanese against Britain. Resistance groups who campaigned against occupation planned to fight both the Axis powers and the imperialists.

1948
FIGHTING WITHDRAWALS

Britain accomplished peaceful withdrawals from Ceylon and Burma (1948), but clung to Singapore and Hong Kong, resisted Indonesian efforts to seize Sarawak and Brunei, and fought a prolonged war against communist Malayan guerrillas from 1948 – but finally granted the country independence in 1957. In 1945, nationalists and communists assumed control in Indochina. France attempted to exert control over the southern nationalists and battled against

The Cold War
1946–98

THE DEFEAT OF GERMANY and Japan in the Second World War (1939–45) changed the structure of imperial power in the world. Now two great powers – the United States and the Soviet Union – challenged each another for global domination and the other states had to choose which side to be on. Some did not want any part in this conflict, but were forced into choosing sides by the two main rivals on the principle that 'those not with us are against us'. The experience of the Second World War had underlined the importance of propaganda as a means of swaying popular opinion and as a result feats of exploration and scientific achievement became as much weapons of ideological war.

▲ *Cartoon depicting Soviet dictator Joseph Stalin.*

1946
THE DIVISION OF EUROPE

The Soviet leader, Joseph Stalin (1879–1953) feared American military power, especially the American monopoly of atomic weapons. When Winston Churchill (1874–1965) gave his notorious 'Iron Curtain' speech in February 1946, the suspicious Stalin denounced it as 'a dangerous act'. In 1947–48 the Communists seized power in eastern Europe, under the domination of the Soviet Union. At the same time the Soviets gave considerable financial support to the Communist parties of France and Italy. In that year, the United States launched the Marshall Plan, giving financial aid to the governments of western Europe. This aid – and other assistance to pro-capitalist parties – helped defeat the communists in elections in 1948.

❖ ▶ p. 183   **1946**
EXPLORATION AND THE COLD WAR

In 1946, Admiral Richard Byrd (1888–1957) returned to Antarctica to lead the largest expedition ever mounted to that inhospitable continent. Operation Highjump involved a fleet of 13 ships and 4,700 men. Highjump charted a large extent of the coastline of the ice pack covering the pole. Expeditions such as these were considered highly prestigious in the ideological war between the United States and the Soviet Union. The scientists involved, however, preferred activities such as the International Geophysical Year (1957–58). Some 12 nations participated in this, involved in projects such as the causes of earthquakes, oceanography, the study of the weather and the crossing of the Antarctic.

1948
GLOBAL COLD WAR

The beginning of the Cold War is normally associated with the Berlin Blockade of 1948. At the beginning of 1949, the Communists triumphed in a civil war in China, while in August, the Soviet Union detonated an atomic bomb. Suddenly, the Communist bloc had been transformed into a genuine global rival to the United States. In 1950, the Communists of North Korea invaded the American-backed South Korea. The United Nations, founded to end such conflicts, intervened when the Soviet Union boycotted a crucial Security Council meeting, and so was not able to use its veto against an American proposal to name North Korea as the aggressor. Hundreds of thousands of American and allied troops now invaded Korea under the flag of the United Nations – the war lasted until 1953.

▼ *Russian troops blockade Berlin at the beginning of the Cold War.*

1954
THE DOMINO ERA

Communists were frequently involved in the highest councils of independence movements, which therefore became suspect in the eyes of the United States. The worst offenders, from this perspective, were the Indochinese Communist, led by Ho Chi Minh (1890–1969). When the French finally agreed to the independence of Indochina, the United States supported an anti-Communist regime in its own state in the south. The war continued because political leaders in the United States had adopted a strategy of containment. Friendly governments were established in states bordering the Communist bloc, and linked by means of military alliances such as the Baghdad Pact of 1955 between Turkey, Iraq, Iran and Pakistan. The strategy was publicised under the less aggressive name of the 'Domino theory'.

▲ *The president of North Vienam, Ho Chi Minh, with the Yugoslav president Marshal Tito.*

1957
THE HIGH WATERMARK OF COMMUNISM

In October 1957, the Soviet Union's considerable investment of resources into rocket technology paid off with the launch of an unmanned satellite called *Sputnik* into space. Politicians and military leaders in the United States were alarmed. The United States had, in 1955, openly declared its intention of launching a space satellite in 1958 as part of International Geophysical Year. The Soviets had kept quiet, and beaten the United States to it. The advantage that the Soviets had in rocket technology enabled them to repeat the feat of beating the United States in what had been christened 'the Space Race'. In 1959, a Cuban civil war ended with the victory of Fidel Castro (b. 1927), a man who openly welcomed the support of Cuba's Communists for his regime.

1960s
THE NEW EMPIRES

The power of atomic and nuclear weapons was such that the risk of global destruction deterred a direct war between the superpowers. Instead they fought by proxy, lending aid to factions in a civil war in Africa in the aftermath of decolonisation, such as in Congo (1960–65) or Angola (1974–75), or to different sides in conflicts in the Middle East. Of all the former colonies, only India was able to keep itself out of the superpower conflict, skilfully holding itself loyal to the non-aligned movement that Jawaharlal Nehru (1889–1965) had helped to found. A new colonial system had emerged, in which any attempt to follow independent policies would result in military intervention, such as in Czechoslovakia (1968) and Chile (1973).

1975
THE END OF THE COLD WAR

So much of the Soviet Union's resources were devoted to military expenditure that it was distorting economic development. After the victory of North Vietnam in 1975, the United States began to reject Soviet overtures to reduce tension between the superpowers. In 1979, when an internal political dispute threatened the stability of a Soviet-sponsored regime in Afghanistan, the Red Army invaded. This intervention allowed the United States to sponsor a guerrilla movement of Islamic militants. By 1985, when Mikhail Gorbachev (b. 1931) emerged as party leader, it signalled an end to old policies. Once the threat of military intervention was lifted, the Communist bloc fell apart. Non-Communists formed a government in Poland in 1989, and in 1991 the Soviet Union itself disintegrated.

1990s
THE EMPIRE OF MONEY?

During the 1990s, the old-style imperialism of military conquest and occupation vanished. Computer technology created such an integrated global economy that it became possible to order something from Japan via the Internet and have it arrive in Europe by air mail within a couple of days. Exploration in search of resources to exploit has now been superseded by space satellites that can help create resource maps of the whole world. Imperial power today resides in the flow of money that can, in a matter of hours, devastate a major economy – as happened in Britain in 1992, in Mexico in 1994–95, and in Russia in 1998.

p. 179 ◀ **Distant Voices** ▶ p. 183

Nothing short of doom awaited the loser, now that battle had begun. When the Soviets shot a Sputnik called Mechta into a heliocentric orbit, the House Select Committee on Astronautics, headed by House Speaker John McCormack, said that the United States faced the prospect of 'national extinction' if it did not catch up with the Soviet space program. 'It cannot be over-emphasised that the survival of the free world – indeed, all the world – is caught up in the stakes.'

A journalist describes the impact of Sputnik on the United States, from *The Right Stuff*, by Tom Wolfe

The Furthest Frontiers
1600–2000

THE POLAR REGIONS are the coldest and most desolate areas on Earth. The first peoples to explore these regions were the Inuit's ancestors, who crossed the Bering Strait into the Canadian Arctic from 15,000 BC. Beginning in the 1400s, the English and Dutch attempted to find a northern passage to Asia as a shorter route to eastern markets. Englishman John Cabot reached Newfoundland in 1497 while attempting to sail to China via the north Atlantic. In the 1500s, the English and Dutch attempted to reach Asia along the north Russian coast. During the eighteenth century, seal hunters and whalers made valuable discoveries while working in Arctic waters. Voyages were also made by Russia, but it was a Swede, Adolf Nordenskjöld, who finally found a north-eastern passage to Asia in 1878.

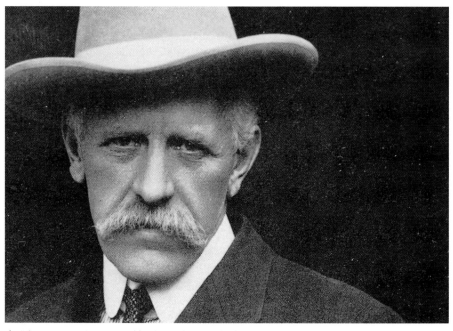

▲ *The Norwegian scientist and polar explorer Fridtjof Nansen.*

1600s
THE ORIGINS OF SPACE EXPLORATION

The physical exploration of space is one that is confined to the late twentieth century. Its roots, however, are much older, and the first explorations of the universe began with astronomy. From the 1600s telescopes were used to observe the night sky. A refractory telescope (using glass lenses to gather and focus light to provide clear images) was built in 1608 and a reflecting telescope (using mirrors to reflect light) appeared in 1668. These primitive machines enabled astronomers to take the first steps towards exploration that went beyond the confines of earth. Later telescopes have gathered radio waves from distant stars and telescopes mounted on satellites now make observations unobstructed by dust, moisture and air currents. These can also detect star or galaxy rays using ultraviolet, infrared and x-rays.

1872
OCEANIC EXPLORATION

Although 70 per cent of the globe consists of oceans, the exploration of them was largely overlooked until oceanography developed in the nineteenth century. This young science has helped penetrate the ocean depths to increase our understanding of the forces that constantly change our planet and phenomena such as earthquakes. The first major exploration was made by scientist aboard HMS *Challenger* (1872–76) which sailed 70,000 km (112,650 miles) through the Atlantic, Indian and Pacific Oceans, collecting 4,417 species of fish and aquatic plant life. From the 1920s, echo-sounders were used to measure ocean depths. Sonar technology now enables up to 60 km (37.3 miles) of ocean floor to be scanned at once.

1909
REACHING THE NORTH POLE

Norwegian scientist Fridtjof Nansen (1861–1930) was a principal polar explorer who completed the first expedition to the Greenland ice cap (1888–89). He then designed a ship capable of withstanding the

p. 178 ◀ **Triumphs & Tragedies** ▶ p. 191

1911
REACHING THE SOUTH POLE

Antarctica was the last continent to be explored. In 1908 Ernest Shackleton's (1874–1922) British expedition set out on a 1,300 km (800-mile) trek to the South Pole, but food shortages forced them to turn back 160 km (100 miles) from their objective. The 'race' to the South Pole began in 1910 between a Norwegian team led by Roald Amundsen and a British one led by Robert Scott (1868–1912). Using Inuit survival skills, dog sledges and fur clothing, the Norwegians advanced faster than the mixture of horses, dogs and motor-sledges used by Scott. Amundsen took seven weeks to reach the pole in December 1911. Scott's team arrived in January 1912 but the entire team perished on the return journey.

★ CONFLICT   🌀 ENCOUNTERS   ❖ FACILITIES   ⚓ CONQUEST

pressure exerted by ice and embarked on an expedition across the Arctic basin in 1893, by drifting with the ice instead of ramming it. After realising the ship was not drifting towards the North Pole he set off with a companion to reach it on specially designed sledges, but was forced to turn back 370 km (230 miles) from their objective. In 1909 American Robert Peary (1856–1920) claimed to have reached the North Pole with Eskimos on sledges. The Japanese adventurer Naomi Uemura made the first solo trek to the North Pole in 1978.

1929
ANTARCTIC EXPLORATION

Ernest Shackleton led a voyage across the continent (1915–17) after drifting in ice for nine months. The crew were forced

▼ *Antarctic explorer Ernest Shackleton.*

into lifeboats after the ship began to be crushed by ice. A small party finally reached their base camp on foot, and all were eventually saved. In 1929 Richard Byrd flew over the South Pole, Amundsen became the first man to reach both poles after flying over the North Pole in 1926, and American Lincoln Ellsworth (1880–1951) made the first flight across Antarctica in 1935. Many nations have laid claims to Antarctica, but conflict has been averted by international treaties which encourage conservation and co-operation in research. The potential to extract minerals from Antarctica may still generate rivalry over the continent.

❖
1930–60
SUBMERSIBLE AND DIVING
TECHNOLOGY

In 1930 the Swiss inventor William Beebe designed a spherical diving machine capable of withstanding water pressure at deep levels and in 1948 Swiss scientist Auguste Piccard (1884–1962) designed a submersible that could dive and surface without assistance from a ship. In 1960 a submersible made a record-breaking descent 11 km (6.8 miles) into the Mariana's Trench in the Pacific Ocean, the world's deepest recorded place. In 1943 Frenchmen Jacques Cousteau and Emile Gaynon designed the first aqualung: cylinders containing compressed air fed to divers through a mouthpiece. This invention opened a new era in exploration as divers could now descend to 60 metres (200 ft) without being constrained by heavy suits or air cables.

1960s
THE SPACE AGE

Entering space required a rocket capable of breaking through Earth's gravity. This was first achieved by American Robert Goddard's (1882–1945) liquid-fuel rocket (1926). In 1957 the first satellite was launched by the USSR. The first manned spaceflight carried Russian Yuri Gagarin (1934–68) in 1961. John Glenn became the first American to orbit Earth in 1962. Russian Valentina Tereshkova (b. 1937) became the first

woman astronaut (1963) and Russian Alexei Leonov made the first space walk (1965). Space exploration became entangled with superpower rivalry and it became a showpiece for displaying technical superiority with obvious military implications. One of the greatest missions was the 'race' to the Moon. In July 1969 the United States won when Neil Armstrong (b. 1930), Edwin (Buzz) Aldrin (b. 1930) and Michael Collins (b. 1930) landed on lunar soil. The first space station was launched by the USSR in 1974.

2000
EXPLORING AND COLONISING:
THE WAY AHEAD

Human space travel still involves considerable obstacles. Prolonged weightlessness causes physical problems. Protective clothing must be worn at all times outside the aircraft because of extreme temperatures and radioactivity. Space debris from previous explorations is now posing a threat as a collision with fast-moving fragments can damage craft and cause depressurisation. Space probes capable of breaking free of gravity are a major part of exploration. They have the ability to send back pictures and signals from distant destinations that would be too hazardous and costly for manned flights. US *Voyager 1* and *2*, launched in 1977, have made some spectacular discoveries during flights to Jupiter, Saturn Uranus and Neptune.

p. 181 ◀ **Distant Voices** ▶ p 187

At three in the afternoon a simultaneous 'Halt!' rang out from the drivers. They had carefully examined their sledge-meters, and they all showed the full distance – our Pole by reckoning. The goal was reached, the journey ended. I cannot say – though I know it would sound much more effective – that the object of my life was attained.

Roald Amundsen's description of reaching the South Pole, from *The South Pole*

Trade and Industry

CULTURAL HISTORIANS argue that it is the capability of human beings to transcend everyday matters that distinguishes them from other species. Military historians note, sorrowfully, that humans are the only animals that engage in violence over matters of abstract principle, such as religion, or for entertainment. It is true, however, that neither the aesthetic nor the sadistic impulse finds outlet among people who lack the ordinary necessities of life – food, shelter and clothing. Humans are not ideally adapted to living on Earth. It is doubtful whether they are even suited to upright locomotion, let alone to combating the intense cold of the polar regions or escaping from predators. To survive, people have had to use their intelligence to compensate for their physical inadequacies. They have had to learn how to manage and exploit their environment without destroying it. They have had to experiment and improvise; to communicate with others in order to share and test ideas; to co-operate and to specialise. The story of trade, industry and agriculture is more than a story of survival: it is a drama of trust and rivalry, of brilliance and diligence, of success and failure. There is no better expression of humanity than the ability to make and share.

KEY THEMES

- 🖳 INVENTIONS
- 🏛 CONSTRUCTION
- $ MONEY
- ⚙ EXPORTS
- ⇔ MIGRATION
- ✕ LABOUR
- ✷ ENERGY
- ⚑ LAND
- ◆ ECONOMY
- 🌿 AGRICULTURE

KEY EVENTS

❶ 3000 BC
RICE CULTIVATION

In the river valleys of southern Asia, the monsoon is a dominant annual feature. Rice became the staple of monsoon cultivation in the third millennium BC. Rice cultivation needs more labour and skill than field crops, but the yield from paddy fields can be very high, thus very dense populations developed in these regions.

❷ 600 BC
METALLIC MONEY

The first coins of the modern type – round and flat, with a value and images or inscriptions marked on the surface – appeared in Lydia (now Turkey), c. 600 BC. They were made from copper and silver. From then on, commodities, land, taxes and services could be valued in terms of money.

❸ 100 BC
THE SILK ROUTE

The Silk Route was a series of land trading routes, altogether more than 6,000 km (3,750 miles) long, that connected the eastern Mediterranean with East Asia. It first opened about 100 BC and was revived under the Mongol Empire in the thirteenth century. Chinese silk, metals, glass and coins were carried along the route.

❹ 1400–1600
EUROPEAN NAVIGATORS

The European navigators of the fifteenth and sixteenth centuries sailed, usually at the command of their rulers, in search of gain. Fortunes were to be made from trade – in ivory, gold, porcelain, tea and spices. Not until the seventeenth century did explorers begin to seek knowledge rather than profit.

❺ 1600 AND 1602
THE DUTCH AND ENGLISH EAST INDIA COMPANIES

The establishment of the Dutch (1600) and English (1602) East India companies gave great power and organisational strength to their respective nations. The most lucrative European ventures were in the smaller islands of the Caribbean, where plantations – worked by imported African slaves – yielded sugar, a commodity much in demand at home.

❻ 1700s
COAL AND IRON

Abraham Darby (1678–1717) developed the use of coal (in the form of coke) for blast furnaces to increase output. This turned Europe and then North America into the workhouse of the world for the next two centuries. At Coalbrookdale, where Darby acquired premises, one of the world's first cast-iron bridges was built in 1799.

❼ 1929
THE GREAT DEPRESSION

The Great Depression was a worldwide economic slump that began in 1929 with the Wall Street Crash. the Crash was caused by excessive investment in the domestic US market that pushed prices up to unsustainable levels. The Crash caused large-scale bankruptcies and unemployment rose by nearly two million.

❽ 1947
GATT

The General Agreement on Tariffs and Trades (GATT) was signed in Geneva in 1947 by representatives of 23 non-Communist nations. It was dedicated to the expansion of multi-lateral trade and settlement of trade disputes.

TIMELINE

	9000 BC	Neolithic farming
	8500 BC	Transition from hunting to farming
	5500 BC	Civilisations grow up along the Nile
	4000 BC	First toolmakers
1	• •**3000 BC**	Early agriculture and industry
	2590 BC	Ancient Egyptian pyramid construction
	1700 BC	First road construction
2	• • • **600 BC**	First metallic money used
3	• • •**100 BC**	Silk Route opened
	AD 300	Maya develop irrigation
	1086	Watermills used to drive machinery
	1300	Firearm technology developed
4	• • • • •**1500**	Mercantilism forms basis of economies
	1600	Ottoman Empire exploits harbours for taxes
5	• • • • • •**1600**	Dutch East India Company established
	1609	First banks open in Amsterdam
	1650	Sugar plantations grow
	1670	Hudson Bay company established
	1694	National debt enables public borrowing in emergencies
	1702	First factory built in Derby, England
6	• • • • • • • • •**1709**	Coke and furnaces make iron construction possible
	1720	South Sea bubble
	1750	Potatoes become Europe's main crop
	1769	Cotton industry takes off
	1783	First public demonstration of the hot air balloon
	1803	First railway opens in South Carolina
	1824	Trade Unions established
	1826	George Stephenson builds railways and locomotives
	1848	Karl Marx develops communist theories
	1850	Mass production of weapons
	1854	Japan's ports opened to world trade
	1855	Blast furnace invented
	1879	First department store opens in Chicago
	1895	Rubber industry develops
	1903	Ford Motor industry established
7	• • • • • • • • • • • **1929**	Great Depression
	1933	Franklin Roosevelt inaugurates the 'New Deal'
8	• • • • • • • • • • • • • •**1947**	GATT signed in Geneva
	1950	Machines replace nearly all personnel on western farms
	1959	Petroleum industry develops in the Persian Gulf
	1960	Computer industry takes off
	1965	Interdependence increases among national economies
	1980	Computers and robots used in industry and in the home
	1990	Rise of the tourist industry
	1994	Crisis in the global economy
	1998	Industrial strength versus agricultural vulnerability

Beginnings
1.5 MILLION–3000 BC

FROM THE TIME *Homo erectus* evolved, about 1.5 million years ago, human beings began to explore and exploit their environment. Necessity is the mother of invention and human beings have always had a greater need than any other animal to invent in order to provide themselves with food, shelter and clothing. They used their intelligence to develop ways of compensating for their physical weaknesses, such as the lack of a prehensile tail or of warmth-giving body hair. They began to learn from luck, experiment or error and to minimise hardship and capitalise on natural advantages such as the terrain or the climate. Working towards common goals, they pooled their skills and learning. Co-operation was the basis of communities.

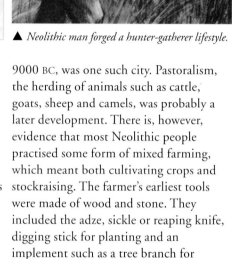

▲ *Neolithic man forged a hunter-gatherer lifestyle.*

1.5 MILLION–5500 BC
THE EARLIEST INVENTIONS

Some of the major developments in agriculture and industry up to 5500 BC include: c. 1.5 million BC, *Homo erectus* began to make better tools than *Homo habilis* – used fire for warmth and protection from animals; 10,000 BC, hunting weapons developed at the end of the Ice Age; 9000 bc,wild cereals harvested with flint sickles in Palestine; 8000 BC, farming and settled villages in eastern Anatolia, some cattle and sheep domesticated, and wheat, barley and pulses grown in Jericho; 7000 BC, metal-working in Anatolia, walled settlement at

Jericho; 6750 BC, pigs domesticated in Iran; 6000 BC, cattle raised in Anatolia; early trade in obsidian and flint; 5500 BC, irrigation practised in Mesopotamia.

9000 BC
NEOLITHIC FARMING

Neolithic farmers lived in simple dwellings such as small houses of sunbaked mud bricks, reed or wood, or even in caves. Where they built dwellings, these were often grouped into villages, which in time grew into cities that survived and flourished on the basis of the production of surplus crops. Jericho, founded around

9000 BC, was one such city. Pastoralism, the herding of animals such as cattle, goats, sheep and camels, was probably a later development. There is, however, evidence that most Neolithic people practised some form of mixed farming, which meant both cultivating crops and stockraising. The farmer's earliest tools were made of wood and stone. They included the adze, sickle or reaping knife, digging stick for planting and an implement such as a tree branch for turning the soil preparatory to planting.

8500 BC
TRANSITION FROM HUNTING TO FARMING

No one knows exactly when hunting and gathering gave way to farming and pastoralism. One of the first known instances happened in the Middle East, *c.* 8500–7000 BC, when people began to cultivate plants and domesticate animals. The next step in human history was the development of civilised – that is, skilled and complex – communities. This took place in the valleys of the Tigris-Euphrates and the Nile rivers *c.* 3500–3000 BC and soon afterwards in the Indus Valley. The conditions required for this evolution were at first geographical. If rich crops were to be harvested year after year from the same fields – permitting people to continue living

▼ *The retreating Ice Age allowed humans to move across land bridges and establish new civilisations.*

💻 INVENTIONS 🏛 CONSTRUCTION $ MONEY ✳ EXPORTS ⇔ MIGRATION

in the same place – the land had to be irrigated. Only where irrigation was needed was co-operation between people required, for digging and dyking. This set-up yielded a surplus of agricultural produce, which allowed some individuals to specialise, in or outside agriculture. It also created the first habits of social organisation.

5500 BC
EGYPT – A GREAT RIVER-BASED CIVILISATION

The first civilisations grew up in the great river valleys – the Nile, the Tigris-Euphrates, the Indus and the Huang He (Yellow River) – where floods guaranteed the growth of crops. In Egypt, where farming is recorded as early as 5500 BC, there was hardly any rain, so canals were dug to bring water from the Nile to their fields. Every July the river rose and covered the fields with water. In November it sank, leaving behind a layer of rich black mud. The Egyptians used a scoop on a pole, called a shaduf, to pour water from the canals on to the fields. They used a light wooden plough, which turned only the topsoil. From about 1600 BC, wheeled vehicles transported farm produce.

5000–1000 BC
INDUSTRIAL DEVELOPMENTS

Some major dates in the development of agriculture and industry between 5000–1000 BC include: 5000 BC, wet rice farming started by village farm communities in China, shaduf used in Egypt for irrigation; 5000–2000 BC, farming spread south in Africa; 4500 BC, earliest plough used, Mesopotamia, first real metalwork; 3500 BC, copper tools in Thailand, corn farmed widely in America; 3100 BC, bronze used in Egypt and Sumer; 3000 BC, farming spread to UK and Denmark from Greece, agriculture in Mexico; 2700 BC, horse domesticated, probably by Ukrainian nomads; 2500 BC, metalworking reached Indus Valley; 1400 BC, start of iron age in western Asia; 1200 BC, horses and chariots used on Saharan trade routes; 1000 BC, iron tools used in Ganges Valley.

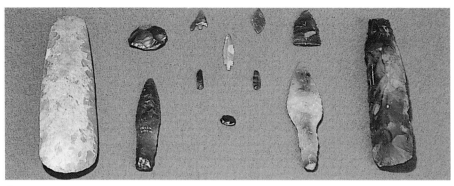

▲ *Early flint and stone tools, including axe and arrow heads.*

▶ p. 197 ## 4000 BC
THE FIRST TOOLMAKERS

Some of the first people to make implements were the flint- and axe-makers of the Neolithic Period (or New Stone Age, *c.* 4000–1000 BC). Flint is a hard stone found in chalk in layers. It can be broken, or 'knapped', into sharp-edged flakes, which make good cutting tools. An example of a flint mine is Grimes Graves in Norfolk, UK. Here people used antlers as picks to chip out the flint. In the mine shafts they worked by the light of candles made with grease and a wick. When the flint was brought to the surface it was broken up and shaped into axe-heads, arrowheads, knives and scrapers. Around 3500 BC flint was used for barter against animal skins, pottery and food.

4000 BC
THE INUIT OR ESKIMOS

The ancestors of today's Eskimos (or Inuit) moved into Arctic North America from Asia about 4000 BC. From Alaska they spread eastwards, reaching Greenland about 2500 BC. They were all nomadic hunters and fishermen. For hunting seal, walrus and caribou, they used *kayaks*, light canoes made of wooden frames with a skin covering, and larger open boats called *umiaks* and sledges. Hunting implements included harpoons, bows and arrows and spears. The Inuit invented other ingenious tools such as the bow drill, which was used to make holes in walrus tusk or other hard materials. The main caribou hunting season was late summer, when the animals were well fed and capable of providing plenty of meat to store for the winter.

3500 BC
THE EARLIEST AGRICULTURE AND INDUSTRY

At the very beginning of Sumerian (modern Iraq) civilisation, *c.* 3500–3000 BC, the earliest forms of industry appeared. The weaving and dyeing of woollen textiles, for example, now emerged, later to provide the cities of the region with a major export commodity. People also learnt for the first time how to measure with the unerring precision needed for construction, especially of canals and dykes. Even more crucial was the measurement of time, because of its critical importance in crop-planting. Priests may have been the custodians of calendars and it was to them that farmers turned for guidance in the organisation of irrigation works and other agricultural tasks. By about 3000 BC, all the readily irrigable land in Sumer had been brought under cultivation and at least a dozen cities, each numbering several thousand inhabitants, dotted the landscape.

p. 183 ◀ **Distant Voices** ▶ p. 189

The farmer wears the same clothes all the time. His fingers are always busy, his arms are dried up by the wind. He rests, when he is able, in the mud. If he is ill, his bed is the bare earth in the middle of his beasts. He scarcely gets home at night before he has to start off again.

The life of a peasant farmer in Egypt, described in an Ancient Egyptian school text

Developments
3000–1000 BC

WELL BEFORE THE BIRTH of Christ, humans had established the most sophisticated and complex societies. Survival was no longer the only purpose of activity. People now began to make not only tools and implements but also artefacts and art objects. They built structures that were not merely intended to protect them from the elements but that would also represent their nature, their beliefs and their aesthetic senses and that would go on standing long after they themselves had died. Most importantly, they created links between themselves and other communities. Specialisation, trade, communications and exchange now became the distinguishing features of humanity. Things were made and ideas were conceived and indulged that were new, original and often inessential, except insofar as they strengthened the interdependence of all human beings.

▶ p. 194

3000 BC
RICE CULTIVATION

In the big river valleys of southern and south-east Asia, notably between Bengal and China, the monsoon was the dominant feature of life: for half the year it rained almost daily, while for the rest of the year there was drought. Rice became the staple of monsoon cultivation in the third millennium BC. Rice-growing differs from grain agriculture in three important ways: rice plants are transplanted from special seed flats, that is, from offshoots; animal power is not essential in the work of cultivation; and rice fields, or paddies, have to be kept under a shallow sheet of water for several months while the rice plants mature. Rice cultivation thus needs a lot more labour and skill than field crops. The yield from paddy fields, however, can be very high. Thus very dense peasant populations developed in the monsoon regions.

3000 BC
SUMER

Lacking stone, the Sumerians of southern Mesopotamia (now Iraq) first built with reeds plastered in mud. Later they constructed huge buildings of sun-dried bricks: the greatest was the Ziggurat of Ur. The earliest surviving potter's wheel, found at Ur, was the first known use made of rotary motion. By 3000 BC the wheel was being used for transport. Another Sumerian invention was glass; and in the third millennium BC, craftsmen were casting in bronze. Since there was no metal in the region, flint and obsidian must have been imported. Networks of trade

▼ *Terraced rice fields in Indonesia.*

existed with the Persian Gulf and, by 2000 BC, with the Indus Valley. The basis of society remained cultivation – of barley, wheat, millet and sesame.

2800 BC
FIRST ARTEFACTS

The first known artefacts were made in the Stone Age. These were arrowheads and axe-heads made by chipping and flaking certain types of stone (such as flint) to produce sharp points and edges. During the Bronze Age, people discovered that metals could be extracted from rock if they heated it. During the subsequent Iron Age, people discovered how to produce and work with iron by heating ore-yielding rocks in furnaces at very high temperatures. The first known man-made iron object, a wrought-iron dagger from Mesopotamia dates from about 2800 BC. The modern tradition of ironwork can be traced back to techniques mastered by the Hittites in Anatolia (now Turkey) *c.* 1500 BC. Between *c.* 1200 and 1000 BC the knowledge of iron metallurgy and the manufacture of iron objects increased and spread widely.

▲ *Reconstruction of an Iron Age village, showing primitive dwellings.*

🏛 ▶ p. 189　**2590 BC**
TRIUMPHS OF THE ANCIENT EGYPTIANS

Between 2630 and 1640 BC the pharaohs, or kings, of Egypt had gigantic stone pyramids made to serve as their tombs. The largest remaining pyramid, at Giza (*c.* 2590 BC), took 84,000 workers 20 years to build. Although the enormous blocks of stone used in construction were placed and measured with amazing accuracy, the simplest tools were used: levers, pulleys, rollers – and human muscle. Pictures and models found in the tombs show what Egyptian life was like. One picture (*c.* 5000 BC) shows a simple boat of bundles of reeds bound together and covered with pitch. Later rowing or sailing ships were used for trading in the Mediterranean region. The Egyptians developed an accurate calendar of 365 days; to measure time, they used sundials and water clocks.

▲ *The massive pyramids in Egypt are a testimony to early invention and engineering.*

◆ ▶ p. 193　**2500 BC**
TRADING IN MESOPOTAMIA

A system of trading, based on market prices and rules for buying and selling, existed in ancient Mesopotamia, *c.* 2500–1700 BC. This is one of the earliest-known systems of its kind in the history of civilisation. To begin with, prices were calculated in barley. Later, silver bars served the same purpose when larger amounts were concerned. Common people rarely did any trading in this way, however, and when they did they usually bartered goods, and therefore never had to use a common standard. Most people remained poor peasants who worked in the fields and paid tax and rent to the king's officials and to wealthy landlords.

1800 BC
LESSONS FROM THE DECLINE OF SUMER

Until about 2400 BC, Sumerian farmers expanded into new land whenever old farmland became degraded or harvests began to diminish. But now they reached the limit of agricultural expansion and their farmland was gradually accumulating salt, the by-product of evaporating irrigation water. The salt poisoned the soil and harvests began to decline until eventually many plots were entirely barren. Over about three centuries, the salts drove crop yields down more than 40 per cent. Production was thus damaged, at a time when the population was growing. Food reserves shrank and with them the prosperity of the society. By 1800 BC Sumerian agriculture had collapsed, dragging down with it a once-glorious civilisation. This episode should provide a lesson to modern policymakers, whose attitude to cropland loss and degradation is often cavalier.

🏛 ▶ p. 192　**1700 BC**
EARLIEST ROADBUILDING

The Assyrians and Persians (*c.* 1700–500 BC) controlled great political and military empires, their success largely attributable to economic and technological advances. For one thing, systematic roadbuilding permitted goods to be concentrated in sufficient supply to keep large numbers of men in the field under arms all year round. Wheeled vehicles using these roads could not only provision the troops, but also keep them moving quickly, cheaply and over long distances. Traders received legal protection and merchants were exempt from military service. Key cities inhabited by merchants and artisans paid a money tribute in return for extensive rights of self-government. The imperial government and field armies both policed the roads to allow passengers unhampered, safe passage. Thus inter-regional traders and the armies entered into an alliance of mutual support.

1000 BC
TRADING LINKS ACROSS NORTH AMERICA

By about 1000 BC communities were established in the eastern woodlands of North America (now the eastern region). Two principal groups were the Adena people of the Ohio Valley (from about 700 BC) and the Hopewell people of the Mississippi basin (from about 100 BC). These people were gatherers, but also grew crops and set up trading links right across North America. They obtained stone from various areas, to make tools, weapons and pipes; copper and silver from the Great Lakes area, for jewellery and musical instruments; mica from the Appalachian mountains for models, badges and decorations; obsidian, a glass-like stone from the Rocky Mountains for knives and spearheads; pottery from south of the Appalachians; and shells and alligator teeth, from the Gulf of Mexico for necklaces.

---

p. 187 ◀ **Distant Voices** ▶ p. 191

In large cities – inasmuch as many people have demands to make upon each branch of industry, one trade alone, and very often less than a whole trade, is enough to support a man: one man, for instance, makes shoes for men, and another for women; and there are places even where one man earns a living by only stitching shoes, another by cutting them out, another by sewing the uppers together, while there is another who performs none of these operations but only assembles the parts.

Cyropaedia, by Xenophon (*c.* 431)

Travel and Exchange
2000 BC–AD 0

NOW THAT WHEELED vehicles existed, crafts such as shipbuilding and roadbuilding had been mastered and the use of animals such as horses for riding and for traction was fully understood, there were few barriers to travel. People did so first and foremost to trade both in necessities and in luxuries. Exchange and barter were the most common modes of trade, but by this time the concept of money was also accepted and the first coins were making their appearance. Travel was also necessary in order to pursue military objectives and in defence of territory. Sometimes, too, a change of climate or geographical circumstances might necessitate migration, such as happened in Africa. People were no longer bound to the place in which they had been born.

$ ▶ p. 198
2000 BC
METALLIC MONEY

The world's first metallic money appeared around 2000 BC. Before that time, cattle had been used for currency, and indeed in some parts of the world they still are. The word 'pecuniary' comes from the Latin word for 'cattle', *pecus*. The first money was made of bronze ingots shaped to resemble cattle. Unlike later coins, which had a fixed value, the value of these coins was determined by weight. Around 800 BC, bean-shaped ingots were introduced. The first coins of the modern type – round and flat, with a value and images or inscriptions marked on the surface – appeared in Lydia (Asia Minor, now Turkey), *c.* 600 BC. They were made in copper and silver. From then on, commodities, land, taxes and services could be valued in terms of money.

▲ *The first metallic money began to appear around 2000 BC.*

1400 BC
ANCIENT CHINESE DYNASTIES

Excavations at Anyang, China – one of the capitals of the Shang dynasty (1400–1100 BC) – revealed a warlike, aristocratic society, which supported a small number of skilled artists who produced highly refined objects for their noble masters. Most of the population were agricultural labourers. The Shang's successors, the Zhou (*c.* 1028–256 BC), believed that the Son of Heaven, or emperor, was granted rule over Earth as long as he behaved piously. Rulership involved the exercise of magical powers. The monarch was, for example, expected to bring rain when it was needed, by performing appropriate rites. A good emperor brought not only peace but also good harvests. In the later Zhou period, rule was dispersed among princes and nobles. To survive, the rulers had to collect larger amounts of taxes and mobilise reliable armies.

❁ ▶ p. 196
800 BC
THE PHOENICIANS

The Hebrew word for the Phoenicians, *kena'ani*, had the secondary meaning of 'merchant' – an apt term to describe these people, who were well known as sea-traders and colonisers and had already established settlements around the Mediterranean (modern Lebanon) by the second millennium BC. Phoenician exports included cedar and pine wood, fine linen, cloths dyed with the famous Tyrian purple (made from the *Murex* snail), embroideries, wine, metalwork, glass, glazed faience pottery, salt and dried fish. The Phoenicians also conducted an import transit trade. The most successful Phoenician colony was Carthage, North Africa, established not long before 800 BC. Phoenicians even exchanged goods with the people of distant Cornwall.

⇔ ▶ p. 193
500 BC
GREEK TRADE

As population grew in ancient Greece (before 500 BC), emigration overseas offered a solution to pressure on living space. Emigrants formed self-governing colonies, which acted as middlemen in the trade between the 'barbarians' of outlying areas and the old cities of the mainland. Trade was particularly boosted when some Greek cities began to specialise in producing wine and olive oil, which could be exchanged for grain, timber and other raw materials and luxuries such as alabaster from Egypt. This trade was fundamentally important in all later Greek and Roman history. It allowed the growth of large cities in the olive- and wine-growing coastlands and it made farmers into vital participants in the towns, indeed into ideal citizens. Greece and Crete also exported pottery and metalwork; while the Romans exchanged wool for spices, gold, grain and silk.

100 BC
SEA ROUTES TO THE EAST

At almost the same time as the Silk Route developed (around 100 BC), shortly before the birth of Christ, Greek-speaking sailors operating from the Red Sea learnt how the regular monsoon winds of the Indian Ocean travelled from the straits of Aden to southern India. Similarly, the sea captains could make voyages across the Bay of Bengal, from the east coast of India to Malaya. From there it was only a short hop across the neck of Malaya (the Isthmus of Kra) to south-eastern Asia, where Chinese vessels were plying the coasts. Thus an almost unbroken sea route linked Rome with China. By this means not only goods but also information and ideas spread throughout Asia.

💻 INVENTIONS   🏛 CONSTRUCTION $ MONEY   ❁ EXPORTS   ⇔ MIGRATION

p. 182◀ **Triumphs & Tragedies** ▶p. 194

100 BC
THE HORSE IN CENTRAL ASIA

An important development in the technique of mounted warfare permitted the widespread stabilisation of civilised governments in central Asia. This was the discovery, by the Parthians, around 100 BC, that horses fed on specially grown alfalfa grew larger, stronger and more beautiful than the shaggy steppe ponies that were known previously. Such horses could carry a much heavier load of armour. If agricultural communities could keep these horses, feeding them on hay and grain where there was no irrigation for the growing of alfalfa, they could defend themselves readily against nomadic raiders. This in turn meant that there was protection for an organised trade route along a well-run, policed – and heavily taxed – caravan route.

▼ *Sea traders from Ancient Crete.*

AD 0
THE SPREAD OF AFRICAN PEOPLES, AGRICULTURE AND LANGUAGE

Around the time of the Christian era, Indonesian root crops and iron tools found their way into Africa, starting somewhere near the Bight of Benin. Suddenly the local people, Bantu-speakers, were able to penetrate the rainforest (in present-day Congo) as slash-and-burn farmers. Later some Bantu-speaking tribes pushed further inland, to the grasslands east of the rainforest. They acquired cattle and then dispersed north and south through the grassy highlands of eastern and southern Africa. The Bantu peoples characteristically had a genetic mutation that gave them some tolerance of malaria. Advancing further east still, they came to the east coast of the continent. A trade language, Swahili, developed from a mingling of Bantu and the language of north African trade, culture and civilisation, Arabic.

▲ *The Sahara Desert, the world's largest desert.*

AD 0
OBSTACLES TO AFRICAN DEVELOPMENT

Although Africa supported coastal trading enterprises and some great kingdoms inland, the continent was slow to develop economically because of three geographical handicaps. One was the climate and terrain: much of the continent was desert or semi-desert and large areas supported rainforests, which typically grow on poor soils and are difficult to clear. Only the highlands of the east and the coastal areas of the south have favourable agricultural land. The second factor was the prevalence of insect-borne diseases, mostly malaria, sleeping sickness and yellow fever, all of which cause considerable weakness in their victims. A third disadvantage was the difficulty of transport and communications over land that was largely high above sea-level. The fact that African peoples spoke hundreds of different languages reinforced the difficulties of communication.

p. 189◀ **Distant Voices** ▶p 193

They transport the wine by boat on the navigable rivers, and by wagon through the plains and receive in return for it an incredibly large price; for one amphora of wine they receive in return a slave, a servant in exchange for a drink.

Bibliotheca Historica, by Greek historian Diodorus

Winners and Losers
AD 0–1000

I N THE EARLY CENTURIES of the first millennium, great civilisations flourished, generally thanks to extensive trade, burgeoning enterprise, overarching territorial ambitions, constant military readiness and a faculty for tolerating, even promoting, social inequities. In Greece and Rome, the agricultural labourers were often slaves. In China, imperial rulers exploited the peasantry. The Vikings were unscrupulous plunderers. State monopolies, taxation and privilege were characteristic of the age. Although the rulers of the great powers carried out significant works such as irrigation and sewage systems for the benefit of the populace, they also presided over increasingly fractured societies, in which the gaps between rich and poor grew ever wider.

✕ ▶ p. 199

AD 0–100
SERFS AND SLAVES IN ANCIENT ROME AND GREECE

In the early years of the Roman Empire, large estates supplying grain to cities were owned by absentee landowners and worked by slaves supervised by hired overseers. The slaves were generally war captives. As their supply diminished, tenants replaced them. Slaves and dependent tenants worked to a fixed schedule and the estate owner claimed a predetermined share of the produce. The *coloni*, tenant farmers, were precursors of the serfs of medieval times. So were the helots in the ancient Greek city state of Sparta. Helots were entirely the property of the state and were required to work as agricultural labourers or domestic servants for individual Spartans, providing a fixed amount of produce for their masters and taking only surpluses for themselves. By the fourth century, serfdom was well established in the Roman Empire and former tenants were attached to the land.

AD 23
TRIUMPH OF THE RED EYEBROWS
Under Emperor Wudi (141–87 BC) the Han dynasty (206 BC–AD 220) expanded south of the Yangzi River, absorbing land as far afield as the borders of modern China. To recoup the costs of their campaigns, the rulers imposed tax increases and state monopolies

over key production items such as iron and salt, and the currency became debased. The population soon outgrew the supply of land. In the first century AD, great provincial families were exempt from taxes while the peasants had to pay more. The reforming ruler Wang Man nationalised the tax-exempt estates, redistributed them among the peasantry, expanded state monopolies and abolished slavery. Maintenance of the water systems was neglected, however. In a peasant uprising led by the 'Red Eyebrows', in AD 23 Wang Man was killed.

🏛 ▶ p. 209 AD 100s
THE ROMANS AS BUILDERS AND MERCHANTS

The ancient Romans invented concrete and were famous for their practical structures, such as sewers, aqueducts (raised channels for bringing water to cities), harbours, bridges and canals. They also built superb roads, brilliantly engineered across marshes, carved along the sides of mountains or tunnelled through hills. They preferred to build the roads straight rather than allowing them to circumvent obstacles. With concrete, the Romans erected the first apartment blocks, called *insulae* 'islands'. Trajan's market in Rome, built during the second century AD, housed about 150 businesses and shops and was thus the world's first shopping centre. Among the trades pursued in the shops were tanning, carpentry and ironmongery. Everyday objects such as keys, household lamps and coins were all hand-crafted.

AD 300–900
THE SUCCESS OF THE MAYA
The Maya arrived in the Yucatán peninsula, Mexico, from central America about 1500 BC. The early Maya were slash-and-burn farmers, working plots called *milpa*. At the height of its greatness, *c.* AD 300–900, the

▼ *The Maya constructed massive, pyramid-style temples and palaces.*

Mayan Empire included more than 40 cities. Many of these had stone pyramids, plazas, temples and palaces, together with an enormous stairway and an observatory from which astronomers and mathematicians could take sightings and measurements. Mayan irrigation and terracing methods were advanced. Their principal food crop was maize. They also grew cotton and had highly perfected techniques of spinning, dyeing and weaving cotton. The Maya domesticated the dog and the turkey but had no 'beasts of burden'. They were the only ancient American people to develop an accurate calendar.

▼ *Rice paddies.*

AD 618–907
CHINA IN THE MIDDLE AGES

The T'ang dynasty (AD 618–907) marked the beginnings of significant economic development. Rice paddies were extended to yield enough rice to maintain an expanded urban population of craftsmen, landlords and officials. Trade was often in foreign hands, especially those of Uighurs and Arabs. According to Confucian doctrine, merchants were social parasites. Nevertheless, external and internal trade grew. The land-owning gentry remained the dominant class, served by others, leaving them free to pursue such gentlemanly activities as painting and poetry. In the eleventh and twelfth centuries China built up a massive iron industry using coal for fuel. Regional specialisation permitted the expansion of trade, and seagoing ships developed overseas commerce on an unprecedented scale. But trade was not entirely respectable, and once a merchant

Figures from the Asante kingdom in Africa.

had made his fortune he generally bought land and took up a more civilised occupation. Tradition and state control triumphed, preventing a thoroughgoing industrial and social revolution.

◆ ▶ p. 198 **AD 750**
THE KINGDOM OF GHANA

The kingdom of Ghana was the first of several west African empires that grew rich on trade. The kingdom, founded around AD 750, was favourably positioned on river plains, and its alluvial gold was carried north on the trans-Saharan routes in exchange for salt, textiles, weaponry, copper goods and horses. Imports came from as far afield as Egypt, Germany and Italy. The Ghanaian state included slaves among its exports, and charged taxes at relay stations along the trade routes. West Africa was a key source of gold until the metal was discovered in the Americas in the fifteenth century. The kingdom reached the height of its prosperity about the tenth century, when it extended from Timbuktu (now in Mali) to the Atlantic Ocean, and its capital had a population of 30,000.

⇔ ▶ p. 195 **AD 885**
THE FURY OF THE NORSEMEN

Until recent times, the prayer book used by the Church of England included the line, 'From the fury of the Northmen, Good Lord, deliver us'. The Northmen were the Vikings or Norsemen from Scandinavia. The Vikings began raiding southwards, particularly into Ireland, Britain and France, in the ninth century. They were brutal and primitive, but they were more than plunderers; they were

also eager to trade. When the Norsemen attacked Paris in AD 885, with a force of 40,000 men and 700 vessels, the Parisians held out for 10 months. Food became scarce and to avoid starvation the Parisians ate roots, acorns, dogs, cats and rats. In the east, Swedish Vikings penetrated as far as the interior of Russia, where they founded settlements and began trading with the Slavs.

1000
THE 'DARK AGES' IN EUROPE

Around the year 1000, German cultivators invented a new type of heavy mouldboard plough, capable of draining wet, low-lying lands and strong enough to work the heavy clay soils that covered much of northern Europe, where the light scratch ploughs known in the Mediterranean and the Middle East proved inadequate. Most of the villages of western Europe were under the control of landlords, who were of origin professional fighting men, equipped with a horse, a lance and armour. Other developments were the construction of windmills and watermills (not new inventions but of much improved design) and the horse collar and horseshoes, which allowed horses to be used as work animals instead of oxen. Trading settlements also grew up at this time. In all these senses, the 'Dark Ages' in Europe were in fact very productive times.

p. 191 ◀ **Distant Voices** ▶ p. 195

The world has grown old and lost its former vigour.... Winter no longer gives rain enough to swell the seed, nor summer sun enough to ripen the harvest ... the mountains are gutted and give less marble, the mines are exhausted and give less silver and gold ... the fields lack farms, the seas sailors, the encampments soldiers ... there is no longer any justice in judgements, competence in trades, discipline in daily life.

Cyprian, Bishop of Carthage (mid-third century AD)

The Turn of the Millennium
1000–1345

THE TURN OF THE SECOND MILLENNIUM was a period of glorious creativity in some regions of the world, notably southern Africa and South America, and of stolid stability in others, especially Europe. While the great city of Zimbabwe was rising to prosperity, on the back of finds of gold, iron and copper, the feudal system in Europe lingered on and in North America the Native Americans were still living directly off the land. New technology came primarily from China. In England, perhaps the most significant event of the era was the great survey of lands and agriculture commissioned by William the Conqueror and recorded in the *Domesday Book*, which has been preserved as a great historical treasure.

▲ *Watermills were used to drive the wheels of industry as early as the eleventh century.*

1000s
ZIMBABWE

At some time between 700 and 1400, large mining operations were carried out at several sites in what is now Zimbabwe. The rock-built city of Great Zimbabwe, built in the mid-fourteenth century (now in ruins), testifies to the scale of this enterprise. Prehistoric farmers were the first to occupy the site, but the state began to develop around the eleventh century, and at its peak extended from Botswana to the coast of Mozambique. It was the centre of a powerful empire, which traded as far afield as China. Zimbabwe produced cotton cloth and smelted and manufactured gold, iron and copper. At its peak the city numbered 10,000 inhabitants. The ruins consist of a tall tower and a dry stone wall.

✺ ▶ p. 204
1086
WATERMILLS

Long before windmills were built in Britain, watermills were used to drive machinery. At the time of the Domesday survey in 1086 there were more than 5,600 watermills. At first they were used for grinding corn, but later waterwheels drove various kinds of machinery. They could move a hammer up and down to scour and tighten the weave in cloth to make it thicker: this process was called 'fulling' the cloth. Hammers were also used in early iron foundries to shape the iron and to grind dyes. There were three types of wheel – undershot, overshot and breast. They differed in the point at which water struck them – from underneath, on top or halfway up.

p. 191 ◀ **Triumphs & Tragedies** ▶ p. 203

1086
DOMESDAY AND AFTER

After William the Conqueror became king of England, he ordered the compilation of the famous *Domesday Book*, a survey of his entire kingdom and all its resources, which became an invaluable social record. William's son Henry I, a vigorous and efficient ruler, organised a secretarial department called the Chancery and a treasury department known as the Exchequer. The latter got its name from the custom of laying out tax payments on a long cloth marked out in squares, or chequers. Each square indicated a certain amount of money. Special markers were placed on them to show how much money had been received and how much was still owing; thus even an illiterate tax collector could see how much money he had yet to collect.

1100s
MECHANISATION IN THE MIDDLE AGES

There were three great mechanically minded centres in the medieval world: China, the Islamic countries and Europe. Two great inventions – mechanical clocks and gunpowder – were transferred along regular trade routes from China and the Islamic countries to Europe in the twelfth century. Europe could readily take advantage of new technology because it was rapidly developing a skilled workforce that could make the equipment it needed. Techno-logical developments arose in stable societies, such as China, and elsewhere where need dictated. Thus, a type of plough was invented in China, where the soils were hard and could not easily be worked by hand. The size of the workforce made a difference. In densely populated countries, such as India, it made more sense to use hand labour than to spend time and money on 'labour-saving' devices.

🔥 ▶ p. 196
1100
THE FEUDAL MANOR SYSTEM

The feudal period in Europe began soon after the fall of the Roman Empire and reached its

 INVENTIONS   🏛 CONSTRUCTION $ MONEY   ✸ EXPORTS   ⇔ MIGRATION

height around 1100. The feudal (from 'fief', an inherited estate) was a self-contained community, often comprising the home of the fief holder (sometimes called 'lord'), a parish church and one or more villages. The manor occupied 350–800 ha (900–2,000 acres) of arable land and owned other land as well. A large manor might have a mill for grinding grain, an oven for baking bread, a wine- or oil-press, fishponds, orchards and gardens. Food, linen and woollen textiles and garments and leather were produced. The arable land was cultivated under a three-field system: one field was sown in autumn, another in spring and the third left fallow. A four-year cycle of rotation of fallow land had come in to use by the eighth century, involving three periods of ploughing in the year.

⇔ ▶ p. 206

1100
NATIVE AMERICANS

The Native Americans came from Asia about 20,000 years ago. They settled in different areas and developed different lifestyles. The Anasazi of the south-west built villages called pueblos consisting of several houses joined together. They grew crops until about 1100 when the climate became too dry. The Sioux followed buffalo herds as they migrated across the plains. The Mohawk (of the north-east) hunted deer, bear and caribou for meat and skins. They also trapped rabbits and beaver. The women cultivated the fields with hoes and digging sticks, planted seeds and tended crops. The most important of

these were the 'three sisters': maize, beans and squash. Mohawk villages consisted of perhaps 50 long-houses each up to 45 m (150 ft) long and housing 20 families.

1300s
FIREARM TECHNOLOGY

The Chinese were the first people to make firearms, including cannon. This technology travelled to Europe in the fourteenth century, giving the users a great advantage over opponents armed only with swords. The barrels of early guns were made of iron strips fastened with iron hoops, or of cast brass and bronze. Later, bell-making foundries learnt how to cast cannon barrels and later still musket and handgun barrels from iron. The new technology had an impact on architecture and ship design. Forts were built in a star shape, which would help to deflect cannonballs, and with their own emplacements for cannon. The acme of shipbuilding in this era was the galleon, which had guns on both flanks showing through gunports.

1345
THE AZTECS AND THE INCAS

The Aztecs founded their city of Tenochtitlán on swampy islands in Lake Texcoco (Mexico) in 1345. Canoes plied the lake and canals. Produce grown on the 'floating gardens', or *chinampas*, were taken to market. Food and clothing, pottery utensils, tobacco pipes and cigarettes were sold, along with luxury items

▼ *The Native Americans hunted the buffalo for food, shelter and clothing.*

▲ *The magnificent front gate and wall of the Aztec capital Tenochtitlán.*

– gold, silver, jade and feathers. Slaves, displayed in wooden cages, were also for sale. The Aztecs used fixed units of value, such as jade necklaces, for barter. The Incas of South America were the other most important contemporary American civilisation. Most Inca commoners worked under a communal system in which they had to farm fields designated for the gods and the emperor, as well as their own. Inca cities had efficient drainage and water-supply systems.

p. 193 ◀ **Distant Voices** ▶ p. 197

William sent agents to every shire in England to find out 'the name of each manor, who held it in the time of King Edward, who holds it now; the number of hides; the number of plows on the demesne, the number of those of the men; the number of villeins; the number of cotters; the number of serfs; the number of freemen; the number of sokemen; the amount of forest; the amount of meadow; the number of pastures; the number of mills; the number of fishponds; how much it has increased or diminished; how much it was all worth then; and how much now; how much each freeman and sokeman held and holds there.

William the Conqueror's great undertaking, the *Domesday Book*

Kings, Emperors and Voyages
1200–1500

FROM ABOUT THE THIRTEENTH CENTURY, commercial interests became paramount in the minds of kings, emperors, sultans and overlords. Conquests and alliances had expanded the territories over which they held sway. To support a standing army, land was needed and, to work it, a plentiful supply of human power. States grew rich on trade, carried by land, for example on the famous Silk Route, or, increasingly, by sea. The Age of Discovery began when rulers – spurred on by greed, ambition or sometimes curiosity – sent out navigators to explore new lands for settlement, forge trading links and discover new routes. Inventions, such as astronomical instruments for taking geographical readings, made possible the great voyages undertaken by, especially, the Portuguese, Spanish and Italians.

▶ p. 205
1200s
REVIVAL OF THE SILK ROUTE

The Silk Route was a series of land routes, altogether more than 6,000 km (3,750 miles) long, that connected the eastern Mediterranean with East Asia. It first opened about 100 BC when Emperor Wudi of the Han dynasty subdued large areas of central Asia by conquest and alliance. Various routes ran from the Chinese capital Chang'an (now Xi'an, Shaanxi province) across northern China to the Mediterranean ports of Antioch and Alexandria. The Silk Route fell into disuse with the rise of militarised and belligerent Islamic states and the fragmentation of the Roman Empire but was revived under the Mongol Empire in the thirteenth century when Marco Polo travelled the route to China, taking three years. Shipments of Chinese silk travelled westwards along the Silk Route, while metals, glass and coins went in the reverse direction.

1200s
MONGOLS AND OTTOMANS

The Turkish advance into Europe and India, starting about AD 900, was temporarily halted in the thirteenth century by a Mongol whirlwind. Genghis Khan created a huge military alliance between the peoples of the Asian steppes and then raided in every direction. Mongol dominance lasted only about 150 years, before the Turks mounted a new offensive. From this arose the Ottoman Empire, headed by a sultan. The sultan required not only a standing army, the famous janissary corps, but also several thousand slaves. At first most of these were war captives; additional numbers were purchased from commercial slave dealers or obtained by conscription. One legacy of Mongol rule in the north (1240–1480) was the subcontracting of tax collection, first to corporations of central Asian merchants and then to Russian princes, who created an enduring bureaucracy of tax gatherers.

▼ *The Mongol warlords were a powerful and much-feared force in the 1200s.*

▶ p. 210
1400s
THE NATIVE PEOPLES OF CENTRAL AND SOUTH AMERICA

From a centre in the high Andes, the Incas developed a strictly centralised empire, which expanded to its greatest extent in the fifteenth century. The empire was linked together by a network of roads, of which the two main ones, running along the coast and inland, were each 3,600 km (2,250 miles) long. Potatoes and maize were the chief crops and the llama was an important resource. Practically every man was a farmer, producing his own food and clothing, which was made of llama wool and cotton. A relay service carried messages in the form of *quipu*, knotted cords, at a rate of 240 km (150 miles) per day. Inca communications networks greatly facilitated their conquest by the Spanish.

1400–1600
EUROPEAN NAVIGATORS

The European navigators of the fifteenth and sixteenth centuries sailed, usually at the command of their rulers, in search of gain. Fortunes were to be made from trade – in ivory from Africa, gold from Brazil, porcelain from China and tea and spices from India and Ceylon (spices were particularly sought after because they hid the taste of rotting food before the days of refrigeration). Among the early explorers were Amerigo Vespucci, an Italian who sailed to the Caribbean and South America; Vasco da Gama (Portuguese), who pioneered the eastern sea route to India; Christopher Columbus (Italian), who made four voyages to the Caribbean; and Ferdinand Magellan (Portuguese), who led the first expedition round the world.

1400–1700
THE KINGDOM OF BENIN

The kingdom of Benin flourished between 1400 and 1700 in the area of modern Nigeria. The Oba, or king, performed ceremonies to ensure the rains and the harvests. The most important festival was the *agwe*, the feast of new yams, which took place at harvest time, in November. A

💻 INVENTIONS   🏛 CONSTRUCTION $ MONEY   ✳ EXPORTS   ⇔ MIGRATION

number of slaves and animals were sacrificed and singing, dancing and 'magic' acts would form part of the festivities. Twice a year the villages had to send a tax to the Oba, consisting of yams, palm oil, pepper and kola nuts. The Oba alone was allowed to trade with the foreigners, who began to visit Benin in the 1840s. Benin sold kola nuts to north Africans and palm oil (for soap), ivory, pepper and slaves to the Europeans.

1405–33
THE VOYAGES OF CHENG HO

Soon after 1400, the Chinese emperor selected a court eunuch named Cheng Ho to be commander in chief of missions to the western oceans to consolidate Chinese supremacy in trade and the arts of seafaring. In the course of his seven voyages (1405–33) – on the first he commanded 62 ships and 27,800 men – Cheng visited Malacca, Ceylon, Calicut, Sumatra, India, Hormuz on the Persian Gulf and the east coast of Africa. In 1424, the new Ming emperor

▼ *At the beginning of the fifteenth century, the Chinese underwent a brief period of exploration and adventure.*

forbade the building of seagoing vessels and suspended naval expeditions abroad. It was believed that imperial resources should not be squandered in distant enterprises but mustered in defence against nomads. In the wake of Cheng's voyages Chinese emigration increased, resulting in Chinese colonisation, notably in south-east Asia, and the accompanying tributary trade, which lasted until the nineteenth century.

1430s
JAPANESE SEAPOWER

After about 1300, Chinese improvements in naval architecture penetrated Japanese society: the compass, adjustable centreboards, keels, cloth sails and generally larger, more serviceable ships. Sea voyaging was now practicable along the Japanese coasts, across to China and south-east Asia and to the nearer Pacific islands. Fishing soon developed into an important industry; and when the Chinese withdrew from the seas in the 1430s Japan rapidly became the foremost naval nation in the region. Samurai (warriors) who had too little or no land took up piracy and quickly became the scourge of the China coast. They brought back rich booty to their home ports, where the interchange between merchants and warriors became intense and important and gave rise to a warlike, self-reliant middle class.

🖥 ▶ p. 205 ## 1488–99
PORTUGUESE NAVAL ARTS AND INVENTIONS

In 1488 Bartolomew Diaz discovered the Cape of Good Hope. Nine years later Vasco da Gama, another Portuguese sea captain, rounded the Cape and in 1499 he completed the first round trip to India. Both had the blessing of Prince Henry of Portugal (d. 1460), nicknamed 'the Navigator', who prepared the way for the great voyages that opened up the entire habitable world to Europeans. Henry's motive was to circumvent and eventually overwhelm the realm of Islam. Henry commissioned astronomers and mathematicians to compile accurate tables of the sun's declination at known latitudes, to help navigators

▲ *Samurai traditions continued in Japan into the twentieth century.*

determine their position. Thanks to these, da Gama spent 97 days out of sight of land, yet steered accurately to the Cape. The Portuguese also took the lead in shipbuilding, constructing stronger vessels with stouter hulls, more masts and several sails.

p. 195 ◀ **Distant Voices** ▶ p. 199

When news were brought that Don Christoph Colonus Genoese [Christopher Columbus] had discovered the coasts of India … insomuch that all men with great admiration affirmed it to be a thing more divine than human, to sail by the West to the East where spices grow, by a way that was never known before, by this fame and report there increased in my heart a great flame of desire to attempt some notable thing….

Sebastian Cabot (1474–1557), Italian-born seaman and explorer, in conversation with Galeacius Butrigarius, papal legate in Spain; as reported by Hakluyt, *Voyages III*

European Expansion
1500–1694

FROM THE EARLY SIXTEENTH CENTURY the Europeans became world superpowers. Their discoveries had taken them all over the world, where they had established trading companies and laid claim to territory. They exported many things: finished goods, notions of law and governance, enterprise and inventiveness, and diseases. Among their imports were foodstuffs, tobacco, coffee and tea, manufactured goods such as cloth, gold and silver, and profits. Although European influence did not predominate everywhere in the world, for example in Africa, it was only a matter of time before European requirements made inroads into other civilisations. Trade, commerce and finance began to be subjected to principles and controls superimposed from above.

1500s
CONSEQUENCES OF EUROPEAN DISCOVERIES

European naval supremacy had three major consequences. The flow of massive quantities of silver and gold from the Americas made prices rise – fourfold in Spain – adversely affecting buyers on fixed incomes while profiting sellers. A second consequence was the spread of American food crops such as maize, the sweet potato and the potato. New food crops increased local food supplies and swelled the population, not least in west Africa, the source of the millions of slaves who were taken to America in the seventeenth and

eighteenth centuries. The third major impact was the spread of disease. In the Spanish New World the population in 1500 was about 50 million; by about 1650 it had shrunk to only four million – despite Spanish immigration.

◆ ▶ p. 201 ### 1500s
MERCANTILISM

With the establishment of empires and colonies by European countries after about 1500, trade became an arm of governmental policy. Each empire tried to acquire as much wealth as possible for as little outlay as possible. This form of international trade, known as mercantilism, embodied the belief

▲ *Tobacco became a valuable trading commodity after the opening up of the New World.*

that foreign exports are preferable to both internal trade and imports, that the wealth of a nation depends on its stock of gold and silver and that governmental interference in the national economy towards such ends is justified, even desirable. The earliest mercantilist efforts were directed towards eliminating internal trade barriers, which had been in place since the Middle Ages. Governments helped industries to grow because they were a promising source of taxation. Colonies were inevitably exploited as sources of raw materials and prevented from trading with other nations.

$ ▶ p. 213 ### 1500s
PAPER MONEY

Paper was first introduced as money in China, probably as early as the seventh century. Being rare, paper was precious. Paper money was widely used during the Ming dynasty, 1368–1644, but it was not until the sixteenth century that Europeans discovered the value of paper money. A

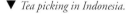

▼ *Tea picking in Indonesia.*

merchant would store his money with a goldsmith, against a receipt promising to pay back the money when it was needed. The merchant could use the receipt to buy goods from another trader, who would then use it to reclaim the money from the goldsmith. In due course, the receipts were used instead of coins. Goldsmiths soon formed organisations called banks to issue notes worth fixed amounts of gold or silver. The first European bank to print its own paper money was the Stockholm Bank, Sweden, in 1661.

✕ ▶ p. 200

1600s
THE DUTCH IN INDONESIA

The Dutch colonists achieved control in the spice islands of south-east Asia early on by a policy of military conquest. Thereafter, they forced local notables to deliver agricultural produce in specified amounts, to be sold on the world market. These local dignitaries thus became, in effect, plantation overseers, while the actual agricultural workers became little more than serfs. The Dutch systematically introduced new crops: the Javanese, for example, were forced to grow coffee from Arabia, tea from China and sugarcane from India. It was a successful strategy, and one which ensured good returns for the Dutch. This was the range of produce that would yield the greatest profits for the colonists.

1600s
CARRYING TRADE

The great European trading companies had to pay for the goods of Asian origin that they brought back to Europe by shipping quantities of gold and silver in exchange. To reduce the outflow of silver, the companies were under constant pressure to export more goods to India. European manufactures such as woollen cloth were, however, inappropriate for the Indian climate. The Dutch and English merchants thus had to try to develop profitable carrying trade between Asian ports. This they successfully did. The English, for example, organised cloth manufacture in western India by advancing money to

spinners and weavers, specifying the cloth they wanted and regulating the amount of such cloth, called 'calico', that reached the market. Along the African and Asian coasts, the cloths were sold or exchanged for goods of similar commercial value.

1600s
THE KINGDOM OF DAHOMEY

The kingdom of Dahomey dominated the region of what is now the southern part of Benin, west Africa, from the early seventeenth to the nineteenth centuries. It grew rich by selling slaves to Europeans in exchange for weapons. The kingdom was an absolute monarchy of a form unique in Africa, with a society rigidly stratified into royalty, commoners and slaves. From about 1680 a regular census of population was taken as a basis for conscription, and in the early eighteenth century an army of female soldiers and bodyguards was formed. Dahomey was organised for war, both in order to expand and to take captives: those who were not sold into slavery were kept to work on the plantations that supplied food for the army and court.

1600 AND 1602
THE DUTCH AND ENGLISH EAST INDIA COMPANIES

The establishment of the Dutch (1600) and English (1602) East India companies gave great power and organisational strength to their respective nations. The Dutch dominated in East Asia. By the 1640s they had driven the Portuguese from Malacca and Ceylon and established themselves in Java, becoming masters of the spice trade. In the Americas the English colonies in Virginia (1607) and Massachusetts (1620) soon overtook the Dutch colony in New York (1626). The French began to colonise Canada, starting at Quebec (1608). The most lucrative European ventures were in the smaller islands of the Caribbean, where plantations – worked by imported African slaves – yielded sugar, a commodity much in demand at home. English, French and Dutch entrepreneurs had, by the 1640s, taken the bulk of this trade away from the Portuguese and the Spanish.

▲ *The opening of the Bank of England in 1694.*

1609
BANKS

The first bank opened in Amsterdam, the Netherlands, in 1609. By the mid-seventeenth century banks were commonplace in Europe. In Japan feudal clans ran banks which issued their own paper money. As paper money became more widely used, the gold it represented generally stayed in storage. Goldsmiths here saw an opportunity: they could lend a little of the actual gold out and make money by charging the borrower for it. Many of the early banks failed because they lent too much gold. If many savers came to collect at the same time there was not enough to go round. To prevent this, most governments now regulate the amount a bank can lend. The world's first central bank, the Bank of England, was established in 1694.

---

p. 197 ◀ **Distant Voices** ▶ p. 201

For where money is the standard of everything, many vain, superfluous trades are bound to be carried on simply to satisfy luxury and licentiousness.

From *Utopia*, by Sir Thomas More (1516)

The Age of Invention
1600–1700

A REMARKABLE NUMBER of scientific inventions appeared in the seventeenth century. From these sprang major developments in trade, industry and agriculture, as in other fields. New economic and monetary systems and procedures were also devised. These advances did not filter through to all levels of society, even in Europe where many of them originated. The European colonies were not unmitigated sources of joy and prosperity, partly because of rivalry between nations. Elsewhere, corrupt practices, greed and hostility stood in the way of uniform progress. Yet the age laid the foundations of the Industrial Revolution and the subsequent agricultural revolution, economic advancement and general improvements in people's living conditions.

1600s
THE OTTOMAN EMPIRE

Between 1500 and 1700 Muslim power advanced in many regions. In Europe it gained ground at the expense of Christianity. In Africa and south-east Asia the local population accepted Islam along with new kinds of trade, market relations and economic activity. By 1600, Muslim traders dominated the eastern Mediterranean and the Indian Ocean after bringing the Portuguese and the Spanish to heel. The Portuguese even admitted Muslim vessels to their ports because they needed the revenue from harbour tolls. By 1700, commercial agriculture was making rapid advances in the Ottoman Empire and peasants in the coastal lands of the Black Sea and the northern Aegean were eating maize originally brought from America. Manufacturing did not, however, advance, mostly because bribes and taxes mopped up any spare capital. Ottoman exports remained almost exclusively agricultural.

1600s
THE INVENTION REVOLUTION OF THE SEVENTEENTH CENTURY

A scientific revolution took place in the 1600s. During this period there was an influx of inventions that were created to help in trade and industry: many items had industrial, agricultural or commercial uses.

▲ *Hans Lippershay, the Dutch inventor of the telescope.*

Among these were the telescope (1608, Hans Lippershey, Dutch); the steam turbine (1629, Giovanni Branca, Italian); the adding machine (1642, Blaise Pascal, French); the barometer (1643, Evangelista Torricelli, Italian); the air pump (1650, Otto von Guericke, German); the reflecting telescope (1668, Isaac Newton, English); the calculating machine (1671, Gottfried Wilhelm Leibniz, German); and the steam pump (1698, Thomas Savery, English). These inventors were the pioneers of modern science and invention, their machines proving the essential step in industrial progress.

1600s
EUROPE IN THE SEVENTEENTH CENTURY

At the beginning of the 1600s about 90 per cent of Europeans lived from the land. Windmills and watermills, animals and humans were the only sources of power, and people depended on the success of the harvest. Products had been brought from the New World and other lands newly visited by European voyagers (but peasants could not afford to buy them). These included maize, tomatoes, potatoes and French beans from America, peaches and apricots from Asia, spices such as mace, cloves, pepper and cinnamon from south-east Asia, and tobacco, also from America, first used in France in the 1860s by Jean Nicot. Between 1600 and 1720 the climate in Europe was unusually severe: during the 'Little Ice Age' crops failed regularly.

✕ ▶ p. 202 ## 1650s
SUGAR PLANTATIONS

The impetus for the slave trade came from the fashion in the 1650s for drinking tea, coffee (first introduced to Europe in 1516) and chocolate. People liked to stir in some sugar to disguise the natural bitterness. The sudden demand led to phenomenal growth in sugar plantations in the West Indies, the ideal place to grow sugarcane — and slaves seemed the ideal means of providing the labour. During the sixteenth century, about 1,000 slaves were imported from the west coast of Africa into the West Indies. Within the next 100 years, another 800,000 were imported. The sugar barons of the eighteenth century were a powerful elite. British slave merchants accounted for 40 per cent of Europe's trade in slaves and made an estimated overall profit of £12 million out of trading more than 2.5 million Africans.

1654
COLONIAL STRUGGLES

Between 1654 and 1664 the Dutch lost Brazil to local insurgents more or less loyal to Portugal and then New Amsterdam to the British, who renamed it New York. In 1763, the French surrendered Canada to the

British after a bitter conflict. American colonists' objections to being taxed by the British government eventually erupted into war (1775–83), the French siding against the British (1778–83) and contributing to their defeat. Russian fur traders established small settlements in the newly discovered Aleutian Islands and on the Alaskan mainland. This spurred the British Hudson's Bay Company to explore and lay claim to all of Canada west as far as the Rocky Mountains by 1789. The Spaniards reacted to Russian colonisation by pushing further up the coast, establishing missions at San Francisco (1775) and Nootka (1789).

▲ *The Bank of England was established by Parliament in 1694.*

1670
THE HUDSON'S BAY COMPANY

The Hudson's Bay Company was founded in 1670, when Charles II of England granted a charter to his cousin, Prince Rupert. The company enjoyed a highly profitable monopoly over trade in furs throughout the Hudson's Bay basin. It also

▼ *Slaves were first used on sugar plantations in the West Indies.*

had the power to establish laws and fix penalties, erect forts, maintain warships and make peace or war with the natives. Conflicts with the French over the fur trade were finally resolved when the British conquered Canada in 1763. In 1821 the company amalgamated with its great rival, the North-West Fur Company, formed in 1759. The Hudson's Bay Company lost its monopoly in 1859 but remained the most important Canadian fur company.

◆ ► p. 204 **1694**
THE NATIONAL DEBT

The rapid rise of England's power was facilitated by the invention of a new instrument of credit: the national debt. This allowed public borrowing for emergencies on very advantageous terms. The central idea was that Parliament should be responsible for repayment. Previously, governmental borrowing had been in the king's name and debts were regarded as his personal obligations. In 1694, Parliament established the Bank of England, one of whose principal functions was to lend money to the government on the understanding that Parliament would guarantee repayment and raise the funds thereto by levying taxes. This meant that costs could be spread over several years. Moreover, as repayment became a near certainty, interest rates fell and the English government was able to borrow from foreigners as well as from its own subjects. Foreign governments were not so well placed.

1700
TARIFFS

A tariff is a schedule of customs duties, sometimes called imposts, generally imposed by a government on imports, but sometimes also on exports. Tariffs were originally levied to raise revenue. In the sixteenth and seventeenth centuries, when national economies and nation states were coming into being, they were imposed mainly as instruments of government economic policy. The purpose might be to protect domestic industries against foreign competition. It was common for a government to levy high, discriminatory tariffs as a means of displaying hostility towards another country. Equally, friendly nations might be accorded preferential treatment. Almost every peace treaty concluded between warring powers in Europe after 1700 contained a most-favoured-nation clause, compelling the two sides to extend to each other tariff treatment as favourable as that accorded to any other nation.

p. 199◄ **Distant Voices** ►p. 203

Whoso commands the sea commands the trade of the world; whoso commands the trade of the world commands the riches of the world.

Sir Walter Raleigh (1608)

Slaves and Runaways
1630–1865

THE SLAVE TRADE began in 1630 and ended in the 1860s. During this terrible period, millions of Africans were captured and exported to sugar and other plantations, particularly in the Americas. This abominable trade caused the deaths of countless people in transit or, later on, while in employment. At the same time, it ensured the prosperity of the slave masters – mainly British, French, Portuguese and Dutch – and the success of their commercial enterprises. Campaigners against slavery came from both within and without the ranks of slaves until eventually the trade, and then the use of slaves, were abolished. In Russia a similar regime permitted what was essentially a system of slavery, in which labourers were required to remain at their posts on pain of death.

✕ ▶ p. 207

1630
THE BEGINNINGS
OF THE SLAVE TRADE

An Englishman, John Hawkins, piloted the first slave ship to Spanish waters in 1562–63. Negro slavery and agricultural plantations began to become important only after about 1630, however, when sugar plantations became firmly established. The entrepreneurs of the slave economy in America were, in the end, mainly Portuguese, English, French and Dutch. Their impact on the native inhabitants was huge. The colonists brought disease, their own religions, culture and styles of life that penetrated initially from the mainly coastal settlements right across the continent. The horse, for example, a Spanish import into America, became the basis of a nomadic lifestyle in which buffalo were hunted. This so-called Plains Indian culture spread across the North American prairies in the seventeenth century.

▶ p. 206

1649
RUSSIAN RUNAWAYS

In Russia in the mid-seventeenth century, the idea of being tied to the land took on an almost literal meaning. The tsar had insufficient money to pay salaries to his officials and to army personnel; instead, he rewarded them with grants of land. Of course, land without peasants to work it was

▲ *Sir John Hawkins, captain of the first slave ship into Spanish territory.*

valueless. To prevent peasants from running away, the tsar had laws passed authorising landholders to chase and capture runaways. A law of 1649 required each man to remain at his post, in the place and walk of life in which he had been born. The practice never quite matched the theory: runaways often escaped from Russian society altogether and settled elsewhere in Asia or Europe. Exceptionally, one might rise to a top official post.

1700s
A TRIANGULAR TRADE

The slave trade was triangular. Ships left British ports carrying cargoes of textiles, weapons, beads, tobacco and other commodities. Arriving at the west coast of Africa, the ships' captains bartered these cargoes for slaves – who had previously been kidnapped by African slave traders. From there, overloaded with slaves, ships sailed to the West Indies and America. On board ship the slaves were packed into the hold, barely able to move. Many died during the voyage and were thrown overboard. Those who survived were traded for sugar, spices, rum and tobacco, which were carried back to be sold in Britain. The slaves were frequently tortured, using branding irons, neck collars, leg shackles and thumbscrews.

1700s
SERFDOM

Serfdom in Russia was a system in which the peasants were theoretically free tenants but were in fact the servants of the landowners, who exploited them mercilessly, demanding ever-larger shares of the crops. By the late seventeenth century, serfs were usually heavily in debt to their masters and were virtually chattel slaves. The system persisted until the mid-nineteenth century in Russia and other parts of eastern Europe. Tsar Alexander II (r. 1855–81) abolished serfdom throughout Russia in 1861. In western Europe, feudalism and serfdom had almost disappeared by the eighteenth century and the French Revolution of 1789 put the final nail in their coffins. Former serfs had by then attained a degree of economic independence and even become small landowners in their own right.

1787
CAMPAIGNERS AGAINST SLAVERY

Notable campaigners against slavery included Granville Sharp (1735–1813), who organised a society to fight slavery in 1787; Thomas Clarkson (1760–1846), who gathered evidence on the slave trade which he published in books and

 INVENTIONS  CONSTRUCTION $ MONEY   EXPORTS   MIGRATION

THE SLAVE TRADE ACROSS THE ATLANTIC, 1500–1865

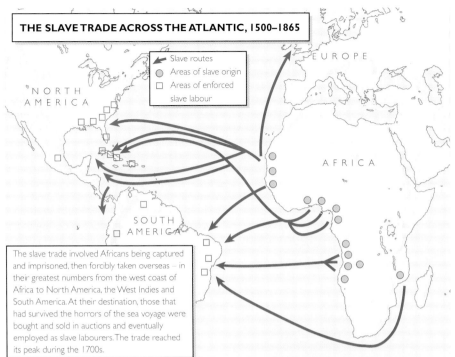

Slave routes
● Areas of slave origin
□ Areas of enforced slave labour

The slave trade involved Africans being captured and imprisoned, then forcibly taken overseas – in their greatest numbers from the west coast of Africa to North America, the West Indies and South America. At their destination, those that had survived the horrors of the sea voyage were bought and sold in auctions and eventually employed as slave labourers. The trade reached its peak during the 1700s.

▲ *Leading English abolitionist Granville Sharp.*

p. 194 ◀ **Triumphs & Tragedies** ▶ p. 207

1850
HELPING SLAVES TO FREEDOM

'One of the best and bravest persons on this continent – General Tubman' was the way a white abolitionist described Harriet Tubman (1820–1913), a former slave who had escaped along a secret route of hiding places known as the 'underground railroad' in America. She then resolved to help others and returned countless times to the South, becoming the most famous 'conductor' on the 'railroad'. With a reward of $40,000 on her head for her capture, Harriet always carried a gun and warned the fleeing slaves, 'you'll be free or die'. Between 1850 and 1861 she rescued more than 300 slaves. During the Civil War (1861–65), she served as a nurse, laundress and spy for the Union (Northern) army. The war took the lives of 620,000 American soldiers, but brought slavery to an end.

pamphlets; the Anti-Slavery Society (founded 1823), which led the campaign to stop the slave trade, but continues to work towards abolishing types of slavery that still exist; Sojourner Truth (1797–1883), a runaway slave who spent more than 40 years preaching against slavery; Nat Turner (1800–31), who organised a rebellion by over 60 slaves, but was captured and hanged; and Frederick Douglass (1817–95), the most important leader of Black Americans after the Civil War.

1807
STEPS TOWARDS ABOLITION

William Wilberforce (1759–1833), a member of Parliament at the age of only 21, soon began working closely with William Pitt, the prime minister, to campaign against the slave trade. Together with friends, nicknamed 'the Saints', he gathered accounts of the horrors perpetrated on British slave ships. Meanwhile, some MPs, having become rich as a result of slavery, continued to vote to perpetuate it. However, Wilberforce gradually won support and by 1807 had managed to stop British ships from trading in slaves. He continued to

campaign, with the Anti-Slavery Society he had set up (1823), to abolish slavery altogether. Just three days before he died, he heard the news of the vote in Parliament, and wrote, 'Thank God, that I should have lived to witness a day in which England is willing to give twenty million pounds for the Abolition of Slavery.'

1833
AFTER SLAVERY

After 1833, the British government stationed a naval squadron in west African waters, with instructions to intercept slavers. Whenever a slave ship was captured, the slaves on board were brought to the British naval base at Sierra Leone and there set free. In East Africa, Arabs carried on the slave trade, which continued to expand until the 1860s, before British diplomatic and naval pressure eventually crushed it altogether (1897). As the slave trade shrank, trade in European machine-made cloth and other products against African raw materials increased. So did the export of European firearms to Africa, enabling hunters to slaughter elephants for the growing ivory trade, not to mention already dangerous regimes.

p. 201 ◀ **Distant Voices** ▶ p. 205

How can you carry on the slave trade moderately? How can a country be pillaged and destroyed in moderation? We cannot modify injustice. The question is to what period we shall prolong it.... My honourable friends, I believe this traffic in slaves to be impolitic; I know it to be inhuman; I am certain it is unjust.... We cannot wait for other nations to act with us. Ours is the largest share of the slave trade, and ours is the deepest guilt. We cannot wait until a thousand favourable circumstances unite together.

Charles Fox, British foreign secretary, in a speech to the House of Commons (1793)

Into the Industrial Revolution
1702–1830

THE INDUSTRIAL REVOLUTION began as a whisper of change in the early seventeenth century and within 100 years had risen to a roar. The first factories and first industries saw the light of day in the early years of the eighteenth century. Industrialisation had an enormous impact on patterns of labour, living conditions, commerce and social structures. Money became more than a means of simple transaction – it was a conduit for control, bargaining, investment and speculation. The pursuit of wealth led sometimes to disappointment and even ruin. The United States of America doubled in size with the Louisiana Purchase of 1803, a cash purchase of land, opening up that great nation to settlement and development.

✱ ▶ p. 206
1702
FIRST FACTORIES
The world's first factory was built in the countryside near Derby, England, in 1702. It produced silk, using a machine to unreel the silk from cocoons. At that time a factory was powered by water, so it had to be near a fast-flowing stream. This usually meant a cramped site in a steep-sided valley. Moreover, the water could drive only a few machines. The steam engine changed all this. The steam boiler was fuelled with coal. The priority now was to be near or within transporting distance (by canal barge, for example) of a mine. Coal yielded more energy per unit than any other known fuel. Factories could now expand. Iron and steel factories continued to be sited near coal and iron fields, whence they got their raw materials, but with the advent of steam trains, other factories began to move away, frequently to 'green-field' sites.

▲ *The cast-iron bridge at Coalbrookdale on the River Severn.*

1709
COAL AND IRON
Abraham Darby (1678–1717) independently developed the use of coal (in the form of coke) for blast furnaces to increase their output. This turned Europe and then North America into the workhouse of the world for the next two centuries. Darby, who had used coke in smelting copper, founded the Bristol Iron Company in 1708. He acquired premises at Coalbrookdale, on the River Severn, near supplies of low-sulphur coal. In 1709 he made marketable iron in a coke-fired furnace; soon he was able to demonstrate the superior cheapness and efficiency of coke by building much larger furnaces than were possible with charcoal as a fuel. The quality of the iron

permitted the manufacture of thin castings, which were as good as brass for making such items as pots and other hollow wares. It was at Coalbrookdale that one of the world's first cast-iron bridges was built in 1799.

◆ ▶ p. 211
1720
THE SOUTH SEA BUBBLE
The first runaway credit boom has become known as the South Sea Bubble. The 'bubble', or hoax, centred on the fortunes of the South Sea Company, founded in 1711 on trade – mainly in slaves – with Spanish America. A boom in South Sea stock occurred in 1720 as a result of the Company's proposal, accepted by the British Parliament, to take over the national debt. Shares rose dramatically in value but within months the market collapsed. Many investors had been persuaded to make unwise investments and were ruined when the 'bubble' burst. A House of Commons inquiry revealed that at least three ministers had accepted bribes and speculated. The South Sea Bubble so discredited joint-stock companies that they were made illegal in all leading countries, and remained so until the nineteenth century.

1750s
CHANGE IN EUROPE
In western Europe, the most important change in agriculture in the mid-eighteenth century was the spread of potato cultivation. In the environment of, for example, Germany, the calorie content of a potato crop was about four times that of a grain crop. In the Balkans and Hungary, maize played a similar role in enlarging food-production capacity. In communications, France led the way in developing all-weather roads and a system of canals that connected with natural waterways. In manufacturing, England took the lead, offering plenty of scope for private enterprise and hands-on inventiveness. New crafts were also created by imitation of the products of other countries. By trial and error, Europeans learnt how to replicate Chinese porcelain.

▦ INVENTIONS   🏛 CONSTRUCTION $ MONEY   ✺ EXPORTS   ⇔ MIGRATION

1769
THE COTTON INDUSTRY

Richard Arkwright (1732–92), an inventor and businessman, invented the spinning-frame, a machine that could produce strong cotton thread in 1769. Arkwright was the first person to use one of James Watt's steam engines to drive machines, for spinning and weaving, in a cotton mill. These machines could spin not just one thread, as on a hand-powered spinning wheel, but hundreds of threads. Manchester in England became the centre of the cotton industry and was sometimes known as 'Cottonopolis'. It grew rapidly during the Industrial Revolution, but the people who worked in the factories lived for the most part in unhealthy, filthy, overcrowded slums without running water, on unpaved streets lacking drains or main sewers.

▶ p. 208

▼ Richard Arkwright's spinning machine, which revolutionised the weaving industry.

1773
TAX REBELLIONS

The Boston Tea Party is the name given to the protest in 1773 by North American colonists against taxation by Britain. The colonists objected to paying taxes on items such as tea, which the British Parliament had imposed without their consent. A small band of rebels dressed up as Mohawk Indians, boarded three ships in Boston harbour and dumped a cargo of tea into the water. The British retaliated with a series of laws to punish the offenders. These were known as the 'Intolerable Acts' and they included a law closing the port of Boston until the money to compensate for the lost tea was paid to the British East India Company.

1776
FREE-TRADE THEORY

The first free-trade theorists were a group of eighteenth-century followers of the economist François Quesnay, known as the physiocrats. They maintained that the free movement of goods accords with the principles of natural liberty; government intervention is justified only to the extent necessary to ensure free markets. This is because a nation's well-being is best secured if individuals are allowed complete freedom to pursue their economic interests. The national advantage represents the sum total of individual advantage. The free-trade system, which prevailed during the nineteenth century, received its most eloquent expression in *The Wealth of Nations* (1776), by the Scottish economist Adam Smith. The policy stood in opposition to mercantilism, which put a high value on national self-sufficiency, guaranteed, if necessary, by high protective tariffs.

▲ America began to open up in the 1800s, and the first railroad was opened in 1830.

▶ p. 209

1803
THE OPENING UP OF AMERICA

In 1803, the United States bought the lands west of the Mississippi River from France for $11,250,000. The Louisiana Purchase doubled the country's size. Thousands of people now began to move westwards to settle in and cultivate the new territories. The new settlers drove out the Native Americans who lived on the plains. The move west picked up speed after the American Civil War in the 1860s. The first American railway was opened in South Carolina in 1830. By 1880, America's rail network was bigger than that of Europe. Rail transport made the development of America possible despite the great distances between places. Goods could be sent cheaply and easily to market in exchange for factory-made equipment for farm use.

p. 203 ◀ **Distant Voices** ▶ p. 207

What goods could bear the expence of land-carriage between London and Calcutta? Or if there were any so precious as to be able to support this expence, with what safety could they be transported through the territories of so many barbarous nations? Those two cities, however, at present carry on a very considerable commerce with each other, and by mutually affording a market, give a good deal of encouragement to each other's industry….

Adam Smith, Scots economist, *The Wealth of Nations* (1776)

Improvers and Movers
1782–1824

A S THE EIGHTEENTH CENTURY wore on, the pace of invention accelerated in many areas: in farming, in civil engineering and in the organisation of the workforce. The invention of an efficient steam engine, capable of driving many kinds of machinery, was almost a revolution in itself. Thomas Telford's road- and bridge-building methods translated effortlessly to sites around the world. As industries developed and expanded, living and working conditions for the employees were sorely neglected. The establishment of a new colony in Australia provided an outlet for the disposal of undesirables, many of whom doubtless welcomed their banishment as a blessed relief and an opportunity for self-sufficiency and individual enterprise.

✹ ▶ p. 214

1782
STEAM

James Watt (1736–1819) was the most important engineer of the Industrial Revolution. While working at the University of Glasgow, he was asked to repair a working model of a steam engine used for pumping water that had been invented by Thomas Newcomen in 1705. Using only a quarter of the coal needed by earlier engines, these were cheaper to run and more powerful. In partnership with

▼ *James Watt's steam-driven engine, based on a model invented by Thomas Newcomen.*

Matthew Boulton in Birmingham, Watt built steam engines that could drive all kinds of machinery, for example to lift coal to the surface in mines. In Watt's first steam engine, a coal fire heated water to make steam. In 1782 he built the first rotary steam engine, with cogs and wheels, so that the engine could turn wheels and drive machinery. The watt, the unit of electrical power, is named after James Watt.

1783
FIRST BALLOONS

Joseph (1740–1810) and his brother Jacques (1745–99) Montgolfier were the sons of a wealthy French paper manufacturer. After several early experiments, Joseph began to think about an 'air machine', which would be filled with a gas that was lighter than air. Hydrogen was already known but, being highly flammable, was dangerous. The Montgolfiers found that air, when heated, becomes lighter and rises. Their first public demonstration of a hot-air balloon was given in 1783, at the invitation of the king and queen, Louis XVI and Marie Antoinette. As the king believed that air travel was too dangerous for people, the balloon carried as passengers a cockerel, a duck and a sheep. Further experiments with people-carrying aircraft were interrupted by the French Revolution.

⇔ ▶ p. 210

1788
SETTLEMENT IN AUSTRALIA

Hardly had Captain James Cook confirmed the existence of the Australian continent than the British established a convict colony there. A group of prisoners and their guards arrived in Sydney, New South Wales, in 1788. In 1803, another penal colony was established inTasmania. Australia had previously been settled by Aborigines; like the Native Americans, these people were dispossessed, hunted, misused and sometimes murdered. By the 1870s there were no Aborigines at all left in Tasmania. From the 1820s, free settlers began to emigrate from Britain to Australia. They generally reared sheep on the rich pasture near the coasts and created a profitable wool industry. Convict shipment ceased in the 1860s.

1793
THE COTTON GIN

Two notable agricultural inventions of the eighteenth century were the cotton gin and the seed drill. The seed drill was developed by the English agriculturalist Jethro Tull (1674–1741) and was a machine that cut a furrow in the soil and then dropped the seed through a tube. It sowed seed in rows, permitting cultivation between the rows and thus reducing the need for weeding. The seed drill featured a rotary mechanism on which all subsequent sowing implements were based. The cotton gin, created in 1793 by the American inventor Eli Whitney (1765–1825), cleaned the cotton by separating the seeds from the fibres of the short-staple cotton plant (work hitherto done by hand). The efficient design remains in use today almost unchanged.

▶ p. 214

1800
FARMING 'IMPROVERS'

Before the nineteenth century in England farming had been a lowly trade, fit only for peasants. By 1800, even the king, George III, had a farm on his estates at Windsor and was nicknamed 'Farmer George'. The change occurred partly because of enclosure. Under the enclosure system, open fields made up of narrow strips were replaced by farms with

▲ *Jethro Tull's seed drill, with its innovative rotary mechanism, which formed the basis for a new generation of farming machinery.*

compact fields. Land that had been farmed communally, even the village common, now belonged to individuals. The gentlemen farmers, known as 'improvers', experimented with new techniques such as crop rotation and soil improvement. Charles, Viscount 'Turnip' Townsend (1674–1738), added turnips and clover (for cattle feed) to the crops. Robert Bakewell (1723–95) cross-bred sheep to create the New Leicester, an animal that put on fat quickly.

1800
HOMES FOR WORKERS

During the Industrial Revolution most poor children in Britain did not attend school, but instead worked for up to 17 hours a day in dangerous and unhealthy factories, for tiny wages. They were often most brutally treated, with whippings and kickings. Robert Owen (1771–1858), manager of a spinning mill at New Lanark, Scotland, resolved to show that he could treat his workers well and still run the business profitably. He built homes for them, set up a cheap shop, reduced their working hours and started the first infants' school in Britain. Of his New Lanark 'experiment' (1800), he said: 'It does not appear to me necessary for children to be employed under ten years of age in any regular work. I instruct them and give them exercise.' His attempt to establish a kind of commune in the USA, called New Harmony, foundered in quarrels, but the ideas lived on.

p. 203 ◀ **Triumphs & Tragedies** ▶ p. 213

1802
ROADS AND BRIDGES

Thomas Telford (1757–1834), nicknamed 'the Colossus of roads', was one of the most important civil engineers of the Industrial Revolution. From 1793 he built canals, including the Ellesmere Canal, to carry raw materials and finished goods from Wales to the River Mersey. In 1802, he was made responsible for building and repairing a network of roads in the Scottish Highlands. He invented a new solid gravel road surface, which could take wheeled vehicles and withstand harsh weather. The 1,400 km (875 miles) of new roads and 11 bridges he built changed the whole way of life in the Highlands. Telford's supreme achievement was the building of a road from London to Holyhead, north Wales, which took 15 years. He used explosives to blast away rock to make new passes. Of the several bridges along the route, the Menai Straits suspension bridge is the most famous.

✕ ▶ p. 215

1824
TRADE UNIONS

Trade unions are organisations of employed workers, formed mainly for the purpose of collective bargaining. Journeymen's guilds existed in the Middle Ages (journeymen being workers hired on a daily basis), but modern trade unionism was a product of the Industrial Revolution. In 1799 the

Combination Law made all unions illegal and they had to function largely as secret societies until 1824, when the law was repealed and unions became legal for negotiating wages and hours of labour. The movement grew steadily in numbers and influence. The Trade Union Act of 1913 allowed a trade union to pursue any lawful purpose. The London dock strike of 1889 was the first instance of the organisation of unskilled labour by trade unions.

p. 205 ◀ **Distant Voices** ▶ p. 209

The effect of trade and commerce with respect to most civilised states is to send out of their countries what the poor, that is, the great mass of mankind, have occasion for, and to bring back, in return, what is consumed almost wholly by a small part of those nations, viz. the rich. Hence it appears that the greater part of manufactures, trade and commerce is highly injurious to the poor as being the chief means of depriving them of the necessaries of life.

The Effects of Civilization on the People in European States, by Charles Hall, English physician and socialist (1805)

▼ *The Clifton Suspension Bridge over the Severn Valley; this was an engineering technique that developed during the Industrial Revolution.*

Dawn of the Modern Age
1826–65

THE EARLY TO MID-NINETEENTH CENTURY was a time of developments that had huge and enduring repercussions. The invention of locomotives and of photography in a sense represented the beginning of the modern age. Equally significant was Japan's emergence into the daylight of international trade and competition after two centuries of seclusion. Mass production transformed industry, turning workers into machine minders rather than craftsmen, but at the same time permitting unheard-of levels of output to cater for the nascent consumer society. The 'get-rich-quick' notion dates perhaps most essentially from this time too. European willingness to make an unscrupulous profit resulted in the Opium Wars in China. In the United States and Australia, thousands of people panned for gold and succeeded only in burying their dreams.

▶ p. 220

1826
FIRST LOCOMOTIVES
George Stephenson (1781–1848) built the world's first successful railways and the locomotives that operated the trains. While working at a coal mine, Stephenson began to think about ways of moving large amounts of coal more efficiently than by horse-drawn wagon. Experimenting with the design (called 'Catch Me Who Can') of Richard Trevithick, he built effective locomotives capable of pulling trains. He was asked to build a railway line to carry coal. The Stockton–Darlington line, northern England, took three years to build. When it opened, Stephenson himself drove the world's first passenger train, pulled by his locomotive, *Locomotion*. Stephenson and his son, Robert, also built the Liverpool–Manchester railway line (1826–30). His locomotive *Rocket*, built for the purpose, reached the the -amazing speed (over a short stretch) of nearly 60 kph (38 mph).

1839
BEGINNINGS OF PHOTOGRAPHY
Louis Daguerre (1787–1851) showed the world the possibilities of photography. Together with Joseph Niepce (1765–1833), who had taken the world's first-ever photograph, he experimented with ways of preserving an image on a metal plate. After

Niepce died, Daguerre continued working on this project, and in 1839 discovered that a plate coated with silver iodide would produce a satisfactory image, which he called a Daguerreotype. Within a decade, thousands of photographic studios had sprung up around the world. Although the public welcomed photography with enormous enthusiasm, a contemporary French artist sadly observed, 'From today, painting is dead'. The Daguerreotype process permitted only one print to be made of each image; William Fox Talbot (1800–77) discovered a means of making any number of prints from the same negative.

1839
OPIUM WARS
In the 1830s, many Chinese had begun to smoke opium and the British and other Europeans were happy to supply the drug, which was produced mainly in India. When Chinese officials forbade its import, European traders got round this by smuggling and bribery. In 1839, the Chinese sent a commissioner to Canton to clamp down on the illegal importing of opium. When the Chinese destroyed a large cargo of the drug, war broke out. The British landed troops and took the city of Shanghai. By the Treaty of Nanking (1842), four ports in addition to Canton were opened to European trade and Hong Kong was ceded to the British. Fighting resumed in 1856 and, in 1860, Anglo-French force seized Peking. Other Western nations received privileges and even went one better, gaining exemption from Chinese law for their nationals living on Chinese territory.

1848
GOLD RUSHES
James Marshall was building a mill on the banks of the Sacramento River, California, in 1848, when a sudden gleam caught his eye. It was gold. Within a year thousands of people, gripped by gold fever, were rushing to California – even from Europe – in the hope of making their fortunes. The same thing happened after gold was discovered in the Australian outback in 1851. Most of the prospectors were unlucky. Eventually the demand for coins outstripped the amount of gold being produced in the world. Minted coins were given a symbolic value unrelated to the amount of metal they

▼ *British and Chinese forces during the Opium Wars.*

💻 INVENTIONS   🏛 CONSTRUCTION $ MONEY   ⚙ EXPORTS   ⇔ MIGRATION

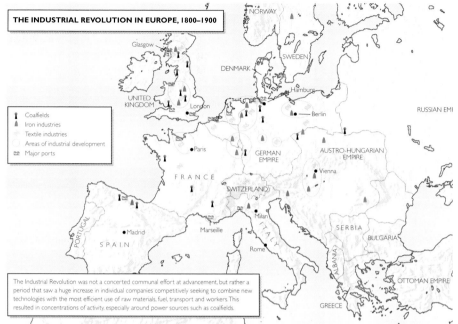

THE INDUSTRIAL REVOLUTION IN EUROPE, 1800–1900

Legend:
- Coalfields
- Iron industries
- Textile industries
- Areas of industrial development
- Major ports

The Industrial Revolution was not a concerted communal effort at advancement, but rather a period that saw a huge increase in individual companies competitively seeking to combine new technologies with the most efficient use of raw materials, fuel, transport and workers. This resulted in concentrations of activity, especially around power sources such as coalfields.

Bay and requested the right to use Japanese ports for trade and as coaling stations for ships plying between Shanghai and San Francisco. The Japanese hesitated and then gave in (treaty of 1854). From then on the Japanese deliberately revolutionised themselves, reckoning that the only way to stave off a Western takeover was to master the skills and knowledge that had made the West so powerful.

▶ p. 215   **1860s**
MASS PRODUCTION

The American Civil War (1861–65) created a demand from the government for guns with interchangeable parts, which could be repaired quickly on the battlefield, as well as being assembled more rapidly and cheaply in the first place. Whereas hitherto all parts had been made in workshops, now they were made in engineering factories. All the parts were standardised. Finishing was no longer done by hand but instead by machine tools. Once these systems were in place, mass production became possible. The skilled craftsman was replaced by the unskilled or semi-skilled worker whose job was to 'mind' a machine or be responsible for one small, specialised operation. This was the basis for the production line, which Henry Ford developed in the USA in the 1920s for motor car manufacture.

contained. Nowadays most gold is stored, nearly half of it at Fort Knox Gold Depository, USA. Only exceptionally is the precious metal used for coins.

1850s
AFRICA AFTER THE INDUSTRIAL REVOLUTION

The Industrial Revolution had consequences in Africa, in terms of spreading trade and communications. Steamboats were introduced to the continent and, as long as they had no rapids to negotiate, they could move up and down a river freely. Railways, circumventing falls and other obstacles, connected with the boats. In the Congo (now the Democratic Republic of Congo), this meant that Belgians could exploit rich copper mines deep in the interior of the country. Where there were no navigable waterways, the railways provided a cheap alternative means of transport. British colonists were thus able to gain easy access to gold and diamond mines in southern Africa and to coffee plantations in Kenya.

1850s
THE INDUSTRIAL REVOLUTION IN EUROPE

In Europe machine shops developed in

Liège, Belgium, after 1807, and soon afterwards in France. Germany took the lead in the 1850s in the new technologies of chemicals and steel. The firm of Krupp, founded in 1811 in the Ruhr region, produced armaments as well as steel wheels for rolling stock on the expanding German railway system. Before the First World War, Krupp pursued a benevolent social policy towards its workers. A major contribution to the steel industry was the invention of the blast furnace for refining ore. This furnace operated on the principle that a blast of air forced through a mixture of solid fuel and ore burns away impurities and converts them to slag, which is insoluble and can be skimmed off.

▶ p. 210   **1854**
THE END OF JAPAN'S SECLUSION

Japan's rulers isolated the country from 1638 on, allowing only a few Chinese and Dutch to reside in the port of Nagasaki and to trade out of Japanese waters. This seclusion could not, however, last forever. Western powers tried to gain admittance and in the end Japanese shore defences clearly could not stop well-armed warships. In 1853, the USA sent four warships to Japan under the command of Commodore Matthew Perry. They anchored in Tokyo

p. 207 ◀ **Distant Voices** ▶ p. 211

We said to the Chinese, 'You have behaved very ill; we have had to teach you better manners; it has cost us something to do it, but we will send our bill in, and you must pay our charges.' That was done, and they have certainly profited by the lesson. They have become free traders too.

Henry Palmerston, English politician, foreign secretary and prime minister; on the Opium Wars, in his election speech at Tiverton, Devon (1847)

Consolidation and Regrouping
1800–95

THE LATE NINETEENTH CENTURY was characteristically an age of consolidation and regrouping, of reacting to, modifying and building on what had gone before, notably during the colonial age and the Industrial Revolution. Africa, for so long treated as a source of labour, its people trampled on and its civilisation scorned by Europeans as non-existent or worthless, now became the scene of an undignified and damaging scramble for acquisition by these same foreign powers. The plantation culture evolved and changed locations. In Europe and North America, modern communications and new means of buying and selling were portents of things to come that would dominate the twentieth century. Marxism, too, was a theory and a movement that arose out of the Industrial Revolution and the social conditions it engendered.

▶ p. 215

1800s
PLANTATION-CROP AGRICULTURE

Plantation-crop agriculture is an intensely commercialised form of agriculture. It originated in the humid tropics and was initially any European planting of export-oriented cash crops under a single management in the areas that had been 'discovered' by the European explorers. The first plantations appeared on the islands in the Gulf of Guinea, but it was the Portuguese sugar plantations in north-eastern Brazil that set the pattern for the new type of crop-growing. A later wave of colonisation in the late nineteenth century revived the system, this time in Asia. Once slavery had been abolished, former slave owners established plantations in India and Sri Lanka. First sugar and then indigo, cotton and tobacco were cultivated in the plantations.

▶ p. 223

1830
THE SCRAMBLE FOR AFRICA

France, whose first major African territory was acquired with the conquest of Algeria in 1830, dreamed of 'civilising' Africa, while building a vast empire across the top of the continent. Britain championed a scheme for a 'Cape to Cairo' railway. British motivation was mixed: trade, territorial power, missionary zeal to Christianise the continent and the wish to populate much of the world with British settlers so as to guarantee the future of the Anglo-Saxon race. The Germans arrived late on the scene (1884) but thereafter expanded rapidly. The Italians tried but failed to take Ethiopia in 1896. The Belgians and Portuguese also staked claims, essentially to African resources. Clashes inevitably occurred between the European imperialists, and indeed contributed to the international tensions that precipitated the First World War.

1837
MODERN COMMUNICATIONS

In linking together the newly industrialised nations in the nineteenth century, communications were as important as transport. Modern mail systems developed from the public penny post, established in Great Britain in 1840. Mail systems became integrated into a global system with the

▼ *A ship laying underwater cables.*

International Postal Agreement of 1875. The electric telegraph, invented in 1837, spread quickly throughout the Western world, its adoption facilitated by the relative cheapness of installing the necessary wires. The first trans-Atlantic cable was laid in 1866. Wireless telegraphy, now called radio, also became a very important means of long-distance communication after Guglielmo Marconi first practically demonstrated it in 1895. Mass-circulation newspapers, fed on news generated by post, telegraph and radio, came into being in the 1850s.

1848
THE COMMUNIST MANIFESTO

The early stages of the Industrial Revolution created social problems. Factory hands crowded into new industrial towns and older cities grew rapidly. From this, Karl Marx (1818–83) deduced that the proletariat (the working masses) were likely to grow even poorer while industrialists grew rich. According to his theory (*The Communist Manifesto*, 1848), this could be resolved only by an uprising of the workers. However, in many places, improvements to public life, welfare and health began to catch up with industrial development: police forces, sewage systems, hospitals, state schools and trade unions all improved the lot of the ordinary person. The reason why Marxism fell on fertile ground in Russia was that the bureaucracy under the tsars was slow to effect such changes.

1870
SEA TRANSPORT

Robert Fulton built the first successful steamboat in 1807. For a long time the steamboats' wasteful use of coal made them unable to compete with sailing vessels on long runs. Better boilers and larger steel hulls, introduced after 1870, allowed steamships to be put to regular use for carrying cargo across the oceans. One result was that grain grown in North America, Argentina and Australia poured into Europe. The opening of the Suez Canal in 1869 and of the Panama Canal in 1914 entirely altered communication routes between different parts of the world. Once wooden ships had been supplanted by those of iron and steel in the second half of the nineteenth century, Britain became the world's leading shipbuilding nation.

◆ ▶ p. 213 **1879**
THE MARKETING REVOLUTION

Marshall Field opened the world's first 'modern' department store in Chicago in 1879. The first F. W. Woolworth Company store, a chain (multiple) store, dates from the same year. The mail-order house made its appearance similarly in the last quarter of the nineteenth century. All three types of enterprise developed enormously, encouraged by increasing urbanisation and efficient transport systems. Even centrally planned economies boasted department stores: Gum, in Moscow, was particularly famous. Self-service supermarkets originated during the Depression. So successful were they that in some areas there were too many of them and they were too large for the area they wanted to serve. They reacted by broadening the range of the goods they handled and many became miniature department stores, offering one-stop shopping.

1884
SOUTH AFRICAN GOLD

South Africa possesses the deepest gold-mines in the world, mining taking place up to a depth of 3,580 m (nearly 11,750 ft). The Rand field, extending roughly east-west through Johannesburg for a distance of more than 80 km (50 miles), was the first to be discovered, in 1884. Production costs are low on the Rand, thanks to its remarkable bedded deposits of very finely divided gold in reefs, or 'blankets', which are continuous over considerable areas. Low-cost labour and coal were also factors in the development of this area. South Africa has dominated gold-mining since the beginning of the twentieth century and is the world's largest producer.

1895
RUBBER

Rubber seeds were brought from Brazil in 1876, but the founder of the natural-rubber industry was H. N. Ridley of the Singapore Botanic Gardens. Ridley's tapping experiments showed that cultivated trees could produce latex continuously without themselves being killed or seriously injured. The first commercial plantings of rubber in

Malaya occurred in 1895 and development was rapid in the European-controlled territories of south-east Asia. Here the temperature and humidity were high all year round and there was a large, cheap and skilled labour force. The rapid growth of the motor-vehicle industry after 1905 greatly stimulated natural-rubber production. The Japanese occupation of south-east Asia in the Second World War, however, blocked much of the world's natural-rubber supply and boosted the development of a massive synthetic-rubber industry, particularly in the USA.

▲ *Tapping rubber trees in Indonesia.*

p. 209 ◀ **Distant Voices** ▶ p. 213

Capitalist production develops technology solely by sapping the original sources of all wealth – the soil and the labourer.

Karl Marx, German-born political theorist, *Das Kapital, I* (1867)

▼ *Gold mining in the Transvaal in South Africa; gold was first discovered here in 1884.*

From High Hopes to Depression
1903–30

WHEREAS THE FRUITS of creative minds had, throughout history, managed to penetrate barriers of ignorance and apathy, it was the First World War that brought official recognition and encouragement to inventors. Motor vehicles and aircraft came into widespread use at the beginning of this most innovative of centuries. While the war created industrial demand, its aftermath in the West (though not in Japan, where industrialisation was being pursued successfully) proved disastrous. The devastation and demoralisation of war were breeding grounds for such political movements as fascism, which seemed to promise security and affluence. World markets and financial institutions, still fairly rudimentary, failed to meet the demands put on them, leading to the Wall Street Crash, the Great Depression and consequent poverty and misery on an enormous scale.

1903
THE MOTOR-VEHICLE INDUSTRY

The motor-vehicle industry is the world's largest industry, employing about one-tenth of all manufacturing workers. Vehicle manufacture began in France, in about 1890, at first in small workshops producing one car at a time. About 10 years later vehicle factories appeared in the USA. In the early days the European makers built all the necessary parts themselves whereas the Americans assembled parts they bought in from other firms. Henry Ford founded the Ford Motor Company in 1903 and five years later invented the famous Model T Ford, which was made on an assembly line using standard, mass-produced parts. In 1908 William Durant founded the General Motors Corporation, like Ford, in Detroit.

1914
THE INVENTION OF INVENTION

The process of invention underwent an important change from 1914 onwards. Before then most inventions had been made by individuals working to their own brief and from their own passion or inspiration. The inventors often had heart-wrenching difficulty in persuading others of the value of their work, let alone in getting the invention put into production. The First World War changed this. From then on, manufacturers and managers analysed where there were bottlenecks or inefficiencies, identified what kind of machine, weapon or process was needed and then commissioned experts to come up with ideas that met the specifications. Invention was thus deliberate rather than accidental, and controlled by technological advance. The rate of invention accelerated enormously and the link between theory and practice became infinitely more direct.

▼ *The famous Ford Model T, the first mass-produced car.*

1914
THE WAR EFFORT

To create and supply the armies of the First World War required overwhelming effort, enterprise and change. Supplies of raw materials had to be found for the manufacture of shells and guns. Labour was needed in armaments plants and other essential industries. Millions of men had to be trained and equipped before they went into the field and were then fed and supplied. The war effort was so great that soon there were shortages of supplies for civilians. People in many parts of Europe had to make do with too little clothing and food and in some areas non-essential products had disappeared altogether. Many new armaments and weapons, such as tanks and poison gas, were used for the first time in this war.

1918
JAPANESE INDUSTRIAL
ETHOS AND DEVELOPMENT

After the First World War, when Japan was keen to industrialise in order to become militarily strong, cheap labour, efficient new machinery and active government participation brought striking success. Japanese samurai traditions persisted, with minor adaptations. Profit was never an end in itself, but was secondary to honour and prestige. The old warrior virtues of courage,

▲ *Samurai traditions continued in Japan well into the twentieth century.*

endurance and loyalty translated smoothly into managerial skills. The relationships between samurai and peasant also carried over into the workplace: managers commanded, workers obeyed and, in return for absolute loyalty, were looked after for life. Similarly, the practice of 'putting out' – hiring outworkers and purchasing their finished products at decent prices – was a system of benevolent patronage. The economic miracle in Japan was not therefore the product of modern, democratic ideas.

1922
EUROPEAN INTER-WAR RECONSTRUCTION

In the inter-war years, life for most Europeans was a sad and difficult business. However great was the relief brought about by the ending of hostilities, there was no going back to the relatively uncomplicated pre-war life. In Britain, the coalfields and some other sectors of industry suffered and there was widespread unemployment. Parts of France were physically devastated and massive public expenditure was needed to restore the land and people's lives to any semblance of normality. In Italy, pervasive dissatisfaction led to political agitation which, in 1922, brought a fascist regime to power. The Fascists exalted military virtues and were prepared to throw national resources into wholesale national reconstruction, even at the expense of group and individual interests. In Germany, economic activity turned sharply upwards in the late 1920s, helped by loans from the USA.

◆ ▶ p. 223
1922
INFLATION

Inflation is the rate of increase in prices. Inflation reduces the value of people's savings and makes the whole economy less efficient. To keep inflation under control, governments now work with trade unions and businesses to limit wage and price rises. Extremely high inflation, normally interpreted as more than 1,000 per cent a year, is called hyperinflation. This happened in Germany in 1922–23. Workers had to be paid twice a day! In Europe in the sixteenth century, prices rose about 400 per cent after silver discovered in Peru brought an abundance of bullion to Europe. Recently, inflation has hit developing countries badly, partly because of the dramatic oil-price increases of 1973–74 and poor harvests worldwide.

p. 207◀ **Triumphs & Tragedies** ▶p. 218
1929
THE GREAT DEPRESSION

The Great Depression was a worldwide economic slump that began in 1929 with the Wall Street Crash. The Crash was caused by excessive investment in the domestic US market that pushed prices up to unsustainable levels, whereupon shareholders switched to selling and prices plummeted. On 'Black Tuesday', 29 October, alone, 16 million shares were traded and $10 billion wiped off share values. The Crash caused large-scale bankruptcies and unemployment rose by nearly two million within six months. Elsewhere in the world too, banks, unable to pay depositors, were forced to close. A shortage of cash meant that less money was available for investment in industry or in farm products. In the USA, drought and dust storms devastated parts of the Midwest and south-west, causing the so-called Dust Bowl.

$ ▶ p. 219   ## 1930s
DECLINE OF THE GOLD STANDARD

The gold standard is a system under which money may be converted, on demand, into gold. It was widely adopted in the second

half of the nineteenth century, principally to make international transactions easier to settle and to stabilise foreign-exchange rates and domestic money supply. Great Britain was the first country to go on the gold standard (1816) followed by the USA (1873). Most countries abandoned it again in the 1930s in the wake of the Great Depression. This was because they believed that their exports would be boosted if they devalued their currencies in terms of foreign exchange. Once this practice had become widespread, however, no country was left with any competitive advantage.

p. 211◀ **Distant Voices** ▶p. 215

The long run is a misleading guide to current affairs. In the long run, we are all dead. Economists set themselves too easy, too useless a task if in tempestuous seasons they can only tell us that when the storm is long past the ocean is flat again.

From *A Tract on Monetary Reform*, by John Maynard Keynes, English economist (1923)

▼ *Panic on the streets after the Wall Street Crash, which sent millions of investors bankrupt.*

The Second World War
1928–45

RESPONSES TO THE disasters and difficulties of the inter-war years continued in the period leading up to the Second World War. In the Soviet Union, Stalin reacted to the need for rapid industrialisation with a programme of collectivisation. In the United States, President Roosevelt inaugurated the New Deal to ease the afflictions imposed by the Depression. In Germany, the Nazis rose to power on the backs of millions of unemployed. Yet positive developments came out of the war, namely the first tentative international agreements on funding, trade, monetary systems and aid, and individual countries' efforts to stimulate production while at the same time restoring damaged infrastructures and national morale. Organic farming, a highly significant movement for the late twentieth century and beyond, originated during this time.

▲ *US president Franklin D. Roosevelt introduced the New Deal in an attempt to relieve the Depression of the 1930s.*

▶ p. 217 **1928**
THE STALINISATION OF RUSSIA

The New Economic Policy (NEP) introduced in Russia in 1921 represented a compromise over the purity of communism: it permitted peasants and small traders to buy and sell freely. The economy thus became partly market-driven and partly directed by state officials without regard to supply and demand. Lack of supplies to the cities thwarted the government's planned industrial development. In 1928 Stalin, the new Russian leader, abandoned the NEP and adopted a policy of collectivisation. Peasants were forced to pool their land and animals to equip collective farms, and each of these had to deliver part of its harvest to the state. Stalin rode roughshod over resistance to collectivisation and continued to requisition grain even if the populace were starving, as happened in 1932–33. The collectivisation programme did, however, permit Russia to industrialise rapidly.

1930
THE NAZIS

The National Socialist German Workers' Party (Nazis), led by Adolf Hitler (1889–1945), achieved national importance in 1930, when big industrialists began to support it. Hitler wanted to make Germany great again by rebuilding the armed forces and putting

people and machines back to work. Hitler became head of the now one-party state in 1933. In 1941, having already annexed or overrun much of Europe, Germany attacked the Soviet Union. The Russians were surprised, but the severity of the winter – in which German supplies ran down, machines failed and men died – repulsed the invaders. Hitler's greatest 'success' consisted of diverting the attention of the German people from the problems of mass unemployment and hyperinflation by channelling their efforts into mobilisation for war.

▼ *Adolf Hitler became leader of the National Socialist German Workers' Party in 1933 and began his plans for an 'Aryan Race'.*

▶ p. 217 **1933**
THE NEW DEAL

In 1933 the US president, Franklin D. Roosevelt, inaugurated a 'New Deal' in response to the depression that afflicted the country. Immediate measures included the provision of employment on public works, government loans to farmers at low rates of interest and restriction of agricultural output to raise prices. Other reforms included old-age and unemployment insurance, measures to prevent forced ('sweated') and child labour, protection of employees' rights to organise protest action against unfair employment practices, and assistance with slum clearance. The New Deal reduced unemployment from 17 million to eight million. Interestingly, the Supreme Court in 1935–36 declared many of the provisions of the New Deal unconstitutional. A major New Deal project was the Tennessee Valley scheme, which harnessed the Tennessee River, providing cheap electricity and protection from floods.

💻 INVENTIONS   🏛 CONSTRUCTION $ MONEY   ✳ EXPORTS   ⇔ MIGRATION

✂ ▶ p. 220

1939
SCHINDLER'S AND OTHER LISTS

During the Second World War, many Nazi concentration camps served as reservoirs of forced labour. Inmates were worked to death in industries such as the I. G. Farben chemicals works and the V-2 rocket factories. From 1939 Oskar Schindler (1908–74) ran an enamelware factory in Crakow, which became a haven for the predominantly Jewish workforce. When the Crakow ghetto was destroyed in 1943, he constructed his own for his workers; later (1944), in the face of the Russian advance, he succeeded – by bluff and bribery – in moving factory and workers to Czechoslovakia. Schindler's factory, supposedly producing munitions for the war effort, in fact made almost nothing usable. Instead, Schindler bought goods cheaply on the black market, sold them to the Nazis and maintained his staff with the profits.

1943
A REVOLUTION IN ARMAMENTS

The Second World War brought a revolution in armaments: aircraft able to fly faster and higher, more powerful tanks and aircraft carriers able to deploy great aerial strike-power. Submarines became faster, more manoeuvrable and with improved armament. They varied in size from ocean-going craft to the coastal type of the 'U' class and the experimental midget, 12 m (40 ft) long, which successfully attacked the battleship Tirpitz in Norway in 1943. The Germans built the V2 rocket, an auto-matically fired weapon, consisting of an aluminium tube tapering to a warhead point. It carried a tonne of explosives. The V2 attained a speed of 4,880 kph (3,000 mph) by gyroscopic control. The first bombs used in war were dropped on Japan in August 1945.

🌿 ▶ p. 217

1944
ORGANIC FARMING

The organic farming movement, known also as biological, regenerative or sustainable farming, was started by Lady Eve Balfour. Not only a talented jazz trombonist and pilot, Lady Balfour was an assiduous agricultural researcher and, in 1944, published *The Living Soil*. Two years later the Soil Association was formed. Organic farming as much as possible excluded the use of synthetically produced fertilisers, pesticides, feed additives and growth regulators. Preferred farming methods therefore included crop rotation, the use of green and animal manures and biological pest and weed control. Organic farming methods are sometimes the only option in underdeveloped and developing areas. In developed countries organic farming is gaining ground, often as a reaction against intensive or factory farming or scares about food safety.

1944
BRETTON WOODS, THE IMF AND THE IBRD

The Bretton Woods Conference was convened in July 1944 to plan currency stabilisation and credit in the post-war era. Representatives of 44 nations took part. Out of Bretton Woods was created the International Monetary Fund (IMF) to support economic development, promote international monetary co-operation, flatten out exchange-rate fluctuations, facilitate international trade and payments and provide short-term credit. The International Bank for Reconstruction and Development (IBRD, the World Bank) was also set up at Bretton Woods to provide loan capital for specific projects in member nations. It has proved particularly valuable in financing

▼ *Scientific advances in agriculture have had a profound effect worldwide.*

projects in health, education and other non-profitmaking areas. The Conference also proposed an informal system for maintaining stable exchange rates between currencies. This worked well until 1973, when the sharp oil price rises in effect ended the agreement.

1945
LIVESTOCK

Most of the world's cattle serve multiple purposes. They provide milk, meat and other products and occasionally draft power. Combinations of physical and economic factors may encourage concentration on either milk or meat production. After the Second World War, governments in most highly developed countries sought to encourage beef production. As with all livestock, productivity varies enormously from region to region. Some animals are intensively reared, with artificial insemination accelerating their rate of reproduction, and advanced feeding and waste-reduction methods. Equally, an enormous livestock population exists in India, where there are 25 million cattle contributing less to the economy than a very much smaller number of highly productive animals. The world's most productive cattle are heavily concentrated in the humid temperate mid-latitudes of the northern hemisphere.

---

p. 213 ◀ **Distant Voices** ▶ p. 217

The air must be the highway of the future for all who would live greatly – whether individuals or communities – those who are laggards in the race must prepare to resign their dreams of Empire or Commonwealth or anything that spells hegemony.... Our leadership of the world has rested upon our infinity of world-contacts, on our primacy in travel and commerce, on our elder brotherly responsiveness to all cosmopolitan problems in their emergence.

The Observer (24 May 1934)

The Post-war Dividend
1945–70s

POST-WAR RECONSTRUCTION became the object of colossal international effort, in the form of aid programmes and trade agreements. Technological advances that had appeared during the war now made the transition to peacetime use – in agriculture, in industry, in marketing and in commerce – which accordingly developed rapidly. New schemes of living and working, such as the Israeli kibbutz, came into existence. The petroleum industry, already a century old by 1959, began to become a world force, capable of exerting as much influence as any international institution or great power. The division of the world into political blocs gave rise not to co-operation but to rivalry, sometimes on a grand scale, as in the nuclear and arms races.

▲ *The development of the H-bomb was perhaps the most significant technological invention to arise from the Second World War.*

1945
TECHNOLOGICAL ADVANCE

The most spectacular technological developments in the post-war decades were in the military field, but a greater number occurred in other areas. Chemical fertilisers, insecticides, herbicides, scientifically designed animal feeds, seed selection and animal breeding changed the face of agriculture beyond all recognition. New drugs were developed, which went into production on an unprecedented scale. Television found its way into millions of homes, especially, to begin with, in Europe and North America. Although these advances brought obvious advantages, they also tended to widen the gap between rich and poor nations. The former had the physical resources and skilled manpower to pursue research; the latter often suffered a 'brain drain'. Scientists and innovators also attained a not wholly enviable status as 'ivory-tower' boffins, remote from the rest of society.

1945
POST-WAR CHANGES IN INDUSTRY

In the first two decades after the Second World War, new industries emerged, based on new technology, such as television and the earliest computers. Production was small at first, with little automation. Customers bought 'essentials' from a market

limited in scope and size. Price was not their first consideration. Customers did expect to replace goods after quite a short time. The result overall was a growth in employment and prosperity. After about 1965, manufacturers concentrated on producing on a larger scale and by more efficient processes. The number of jobs thus declined, even though the market continued to grow. From about 1970 customers were mainly replacing old items rather than buying completely new goods. They expected more efficiency, speed or style, more variety of choice and good value for money. Manufacturing had to become more adaptable. Demand was renewed for skilled workers, rather than the 'machine-minders' from the days of mass production.

1947
GATT

The General Agreement on Tariffs and Trade (GATT) was signed in Geneva in 1947 by representatives of 23 non-communist nations. By 1988 there were 96 members. GATT created an international forum dedicated to the expansion of multi-lateral trade and the settlement of trade disputes. Members agreed to treat all other members equally – the most-favoured-nation policy. In theory this represented a desire to abolish all non-tariff barriers to trade. The eighth round of trade negotiations, the Uruguay Round, continued from 1986 to 1996, and the final agreements resulted in the creation of the World Trade Organisation (WTO), superseding GATT. The WTO incorporates the original principles of GATT, but extends them to include trade in services, intellectual property rights and investment, and, since February 1997, the liberalisation of the telecommunications trade.

1947
POST-WAR RECONSTRUCTION PLANS

In 1947, General George Marshall, the US secretary of state, announced the European Recovery Programme, to help European reconstruction after the war. Known as the

⌨ INVENTIONS 🏛 CONSTRUCTION $ MONEY ⚙ EXPORTS ⇔ MIGRATION

Marshall Plan (1948–53), it was drawn up under the leadership of the USA, Britain and France, and Congress made American funds available, gladly supporting the principle of giving aid to anti-communist governments. Fourteen European nations accepted the aid, including Britain itself. Proposed aid for Britain and its dependencies in the first year consisted of goods to the value of £331 million. Russia and the Russian-dominated countries of eastern Europe refused the offer, instead bringing into force economic plans of their own. Economic development took place in eastern Europe but, without the international co-operation and trade that occurred in western Europe, the region lagged behind.

▶ p. 220

1948
KIBBUTZIM

Under communal tenure, individuals have no rights to ownership of land, which is held collectively. One of the most successful experiments in communal tenure is the Israeli kibbutz (plural, kibbutzim). The first kibbutz was founded beside the River Jordan in 1909. Many more were established after Israeli independence in 1948 – especially along the frontiers of the new nation – and were essential in its defence. Typically they were situated on desert or land of low productivity, which the residents irrigated and farmed. Most, but not all, kibbutzim are based on agriculture, cultivating such crops as cotton, sugarbeet, cereals or, famously, citrus fruits. The essence of a kibbutz is the principle of social equality. People contribute according to their ability and receive according to their needs. Children are reared communally.

1949–70s
THE NUCLEAR AND SPACE RACE

In 1945 only the USA possessed atomic bombs. By 1949 Soviet scientists, working partly on information collected by spies, were able to duplicate the technology and detonated their first atomic bomb. The US government then started work on the H-bomb, a more powerful type of nuclear

warhead, in which energy is derived from hydrogen fusion. The Russians were only a few months behind; both nations exploded their first hydrogen warheads in 1953–54. The next goal was to develop rockets capable of delivering nuclear warheads, which both countries had achieved by the early 1960s. Into the 1970s the armaments race demanded a very considerable part of national resources. A remarkable by-product was the exploration of space. Since rockets could carry warheads they could also launch artificial earth satellites.

1950s
MODERN WESTERN FARMING

On modern Western farms, machines now perform most tasks that were formerly done by hand or with the help of oxen or horses. Tractors can pull or push equipment such as one or more ploughs, a harrow or a seed drill. Combine harvesters can reap, thresh (beat grain to separate it from the husk) and winnow (separate grains from straw and chaff by fanning them). Intensively raised livestock are kept (especially pigs and chickens) in large buildings under controlled conditions of feeding and temperature. Many modern farmers also use fertilisers to improve crop growth and herbicides and pesticides to kill off weeds and insects. Healthy animals are vaccinated against illnesses and sick animals treated with antibiotics.

▶ p. 218

1959
THE PETROLEUM INDUSTRY

The petroleum industry celebrated its first centenary in 1959, when world output attained around one billion tonnes for the first time. The industry began with Drake's well at Titusville, Pennsylvania, USA. The USA was the world's leading producer almost unbrokenly until the 1960s. Its feverish attempts to search for oil had included the digging of more than a million wells. Of the top 10 producers in 1989, the first four, measured in terms of years of reserves, were in the Persian Gulf area. Oil offers tremendous advantages over most other forms of energy: it is a liquid and thus

▲ *Drake's Well in Titusville, Pennsylvania, where oil was first discovered in 1859.*

easier to handle than, for example, coal; it has a higher calorific value than coal, weight for weight; and it can be refined for different purposes.

p. 215 ◀ **Distant Voices** ▶ p. 219

Perfections of means and confusion of goals seem – in my opinion – to characterize our age.

From *Out of my Later Years*, by Albert Einstein, German-born theoretical physicist (1950)

Divergence and Opportunity
1960–79

FROM 1960 TO 1980 divergences between the developing and the developed world began to grow. The latter strode ahead with expansion in construction, industry, mining and trade. The former sometimes got sucked into a vicious circle, where the priorities of security and military preparation took already scarce resources and funds away from struggling economies, thus exacerbating poverty and social disintegration. The news was not all bad, however. In agriculture, high-yielding varieties of grains and other improvements heralded the Green Revolution. Computers, albeit descendants of the first machines of the 1940s, now came into widespread use, soon to create opportunities in almost every country in the world for communication, education, business and trade.

▲ *A hydroelectric dam in Scotland; hydroelectric energy is a perpetual resource, but is difficult to harness.*

✳ ▶ p. 221
1960s
ENERGY PRODUCTION

In the hundred years after 1860, when statistics of energy production first became available, world energy production increased about 30 times. Most of that increase occurred in the few countries that had a high level of economic development. Energy supplies may be regarded as either primary or secondary. Primary energy consists of new increments of energy, whereas secondary energy is primary energy that has been transformed, that is, rendered into a more convenient and usable form. Primary energy resources are of either the perpetual or the accumulated type. The former come from solar radiation and accordingly exist in enormous quantities, but they are difficult and expensive to harness because the energy is dissipated almost as fast as the earth receives it. Hydroelectric, tidal and solar energy are examples. Accumulated resources consist of the fossil fuels such as coal and oil.

1960s
THE GREEN REVOLUTION

The Green Revolution is the term used since about the 1960s to describe the effort to increase and diversify crop yields in developing countries. The American agricultural scientist Norman E. Borlaug is often considered the founder of the Green Revolution. Many countries have taken steps to implement Borlaug's programme for achieving agricultural efficiency. The programme stresses the need to abandon local, traditional strains of plants and breeds of animals in favour of new strains and breeds; conduct research to enable new procedures to be adapted to local conditions; obtain long-term support from local government to apply and extend knowledge; and achieve changes in the infrastructure in order to stabilise the numbers of people in a society and to enhance the quality of their lives.

p. 213 ◀ **Triumphs & Tragedies** ▶ p. 221
1960s
THE RISE OF THE COMPUTER INDUSTRY

The computer industry did not exist until the 1940s and its products were not widely used until the 1960s. This industry is now one of the fastest growing. The largest companies making machines include IBM (which has set the standard, especially for home computers), Hewlett Packard, Apple and Acorn. Other companies make the components used to build computers. Computer hardware is sometimes now made in developing countries where the labour is inexpensive. Components such as silicon chips are still made in industrial countries such as the USA and Japan. The software-operating systems that computers use are written by computer programmers. The largest software company is the Microsoft Corporation, which has a virtual monopoly on computer-operating systems worldwide. Computers continue to become faster and more efficient, with larger memories and more power.

💻 INVENTIONS   🏛 CONSTRUCTION $ MONEY   ⚙ EXPORTS   ⇔ MIGRATION

1963
THE RUSSIAN DROUGHT

In 1963, a disastrous drought in the USSR caused a decline of about 25 per cent in the country's wheat production. The government consequently needed large wheat stocks immediately. It purchased huge stocks from Canada and Australia, to the point where those countries' stocks were reduced almost to nothing. Then, in October 1963, the president of the USA, John Kennedy, authorised the first sales of surplus wheat to the USSR. An order for one million tonnes of wheat, worth nearly $80 million, was placed by Russia with the Continental Grain Co., representing the largest individual sale in the history of the world wheat trade. By March 1964, Russia had contracted for the supply of more than 10 million tons of Western wheat, and had become by far the world's largest importer of the foodstuff.

1965
MODERNISATION WITH MILITARISATIONS

As countries modernised after the Second World War, militarisation became an easy option for many. The military chain of command is an obvious model for government. The mobilisation of resources in the service of government may encourage a sense of national unity in the face of external or internal threats. African, Asian and Latin American governments neglected their social and cultural development by putting disproportionate resources into the purchase of armaments. Sometimes these countries became over-dependent on a single foreign supplier. In 1965, Indian and Pakistani tank forces fought each other for a few days but had no option but to stop when Great Britain, which had equipped both armies, refused to supply either side with the spare parts needed to keep the tanks operational.

1965
THE RISE OF INTERNATIONAL TRADE

International trade has grown enormously as a proportion of total economic activity in the twentieth century. This is due to increasing interdependence among national economies. Protectionist interests within regional trading communities, such as Mercosur (Latin America), may cause them to restrict trade with countries outside their own circle, but equally the regional groupings can serve as first steps towards reaching broader trade agreements. World trade increased five-fold between 1965 and 1976 and then almost doubled again by 1985. Worldwide the trend continued strongly throughout the 1980s and the 1990s, with fluctuations caused by recession in Europe and Japan. In 1995, the total value of exports and imports throughout the world was estimated at US$5 trillion. Trade growth was particularly marked in the oil-exporting developing countries between 1976 and 1982.

1975
MINERALS

In order to use minerals for industrial production, rocks containing the mineral, in the form of ore, must be extracted and processed. Metallic minerals are sometimes combined to form alloys, for example, steel. The extraction and processing of minerals is expensive, energy intensive and requires advanced technology. Many developing companies have rich mineral deposits but lack the capacity to exploit them. Help is often provided in the form of finance and technical expertise from a multi-national corporation. The EU imports 70 per cent of the minerals it needs, including more than 95 per cent of its copper, chromium and manganese. In 1975, to secure its supply, the EU (European Community) signed an agreement, the Lomé Convention, with 45 developing countries to guarantee prices and amounts of important minerals.

$ ▶ p. 224

1979
EMS AND EMU

The European Monetary System (EMS) aimed to aid financial co-operation and to establish monetary stability within the European Union (EU). It came into force in 1979 as a means of correcting the fluctuations in exchange rates that followed the 1974 oil crisis. The central component of the EMS was the exchange rate mechanism (ERM), a voluntary system of partly fixed exchange rates, based on the European currency unit (ECU, the standard monetary unit, the level of which was set according to a basket of currencies of member states). Participating currencies under the ERM were allowed to fluctuate in relation to each other and to the ECU within a fixed band only. The ERM was a stepping stone to European monetary union (EMU), which began on 1 January 1999. Proponents of EMU claimed that a fixed exchange rate would act as an anchor against inflation. Opponents feared loss of national autonomy over monetary and exchange-rate policy.

▼ *The Euro, the new single currency, phased in at the end of the twentieth century.*

p. 217 ◀ **Distant Voices** ▶ p. 221

The real accomplishment of modern science and technology consists in taking ordinary men, informing them narrowly and deeply and then, through appropriate organisation, arranging to have their knowledge combined with that of other specialised but equally ordinary men. This dispenses with the need for genius. The resulting performance, though less inspiring, is far more predictable.

From *The New Industrial State*, by John Kenneth Galbraith, Canadian-born economist and diplomat (1967)

An Interconnected World
1980–90

AFTER COMPUTERS came Computer Integrated Manufacturing – and after that came robots. Such devices, in the hands of capable managers, made manufacturing cheaper. Jumps in oil prices, predominantly in the hands of Gulf states, made manufacturing more expensive. While farming was, on the whole, becoming more productive for a wider range of consumable goods, food scares were causing buyers to doubt the wisdom of consuming such produce. The collapse of communism, its centrally planned economies and its overloaded bureaucracies, pointed up the disparities between different types of economic system. Tourism, a mixed blessing for host countries, is another example of the push-pull interconnectedness of the modern world. In the 1980s, environmental issues came to the fore, with the recognition that, in one world – as the whaling question demonstrates – the action of one nation impinges on all others.

▲ *Robots first began to replace human labour in factories during the 1980s, and have changed the face of manufacturing.*

1980s
ROBOTS

Not only has the computer changed people's personal and business lives, it has also changed manufacturing. In many factories, robots can perform simple tasks faster and more accurately than people. When computers are used to design, make and assemble product parts, this is called

Computer Integrated Manufacturing (CIM). Computers may control robots, which can be adapted to do new tasks very quickly, simply by changing the computer program, whereas people need to be retrained for new tasks. The use of robots makes smaller factories possible: robots take up less space and are flexible. A robot can make a small number of one product and then switch to making a different one. Factories can thus produce the wider range of low-cost products that customers now want.

1980s
FARM SIZES AND WORKFORCE

Almost half the world's workforce is employed in agriculture. The proportion varies widely from region to region. In Africa the figure is nearer to two-thirds, whereas in the UK it is a mere one per cent. Farm size also varies, largely according to purpose. Tea, rubber and cocoa are grown on single-crop plantations, wheat on farms of thousands of hectares. Livestock farms, such as Australian sheep stations, must be large to allow thousands of animals to graze them. Another form of land-extensive agriculture is nomadic herding. In the developing countries of Africa and Asia, subsistence farming – in which the owners grow enough food to feed themselves

and their families – is still frequently found. In the late 1980s, the average Canadian farm (perhaps producing wheat) occupied about 230 ha (570 acres), while the average single smallholding in Indonesia was less than 1.2 ha (3 acres).

1980s
GOVERNMENT SERVICE

In economies at all stages of development, the state has historically usually been by far the largest employer. Some developing countries in the early days of the independence developed a disproportionately large civil service. This was because employment by the state was sometimes regarded as a reward to individuals for having helped the nation to achieve self-determination or prosperity. Often there was little for the new bureaucrats to do, however. The quintessential state bureaucracy, that of imperial China, was particularly rife with favouritism and bribery. When the planned economies, especially in the then Soviet Union and

▼ *The government of China was rife with bribery and corruption.*

 INVENTIONS   🏛 CONSTRUCTION $ MONEY   ✷ EXPORTS   ⇔ MIGRATION

eastern Europe, collapsed in the late 1980s, they took with them their inflated bureaucracies. In capitalist states, too, the need was recognised for a reduction in government's role in the economy.

1980s
WHALING
The Norwegians pioneered the modern whaling industry. They were the first to concentrate on the Antarctic waters and to use floating-factory ships. Japan and the Soviet Union entered the whaling industry after the end of the Second World War. For them, whaling had great advantages, as they lacked large domestic supplies of vegetable oils and were reluctant to use foreign exchange to buy them. The International Whaling Commission, formed in 1946 to regulate whaling, at first set quotas that were too low to protect endangered species. By the late 1980s almost all of the 24 member nations had given up whaling. Currently, Japan formally does not do commercial whaling but hunts whales for 'scientific' purposes. After suspending commercial whaling in 1988, Norway resumed the activity in 1992.

1988
FOOD SCARES
Since about the 1980s, people have been subjected to several 'food scares'. A dangerous form of food poisoning, *salmonella enteriditis*, which was present in eggs, came to public attention in 1988. It was blamed on the practice of recycling chicken carcasses as chicken food. In March 1996 the European Commission placed a ban on exports of British beef and its by-products after it was revealed that a small proportion of animals were infected with a fatal illness called *bovine spongiform encephalopathy* (BSE), which proved to be transmissible to humans as Creutzfeldt-Jakob Disease (CJD). A slaughter programme, costing £1 billion, destroyed nearly a million animals by the end of 1996. Also in the 1990s, a strain of the bacterium *E. coli*, which had contaminated cooked meat, killed several people in the UK.

▲ *Tourist accommodation in the Gambia.*

p. 218 ◄ **Triumphs & Tragedies** ► p. 225
1990
GERMAN REUNIFICATION
On 2 October 1990, the reunification of Germany took place. East Germany, a centrally planned economy, was reunified with West Germany, one of the world's most highly developed and successful economies. In 1988 output per wage earner and wages in East Germany were about half those of West Germany. East German factories consumed almost twice as much energy as West German factories to produce goods of the same value. State control in East Germany had perpetuated inefficiency: people's continuing employment did not depend on their skill or willingness to upgrade. In the free market arena of reunified Germany, many from the east found it difficult to obtain work. Within a year or two, Germany's unemployment rate had soared to three million.

1990
TOURISM
Tourism has become a gigantic business in the last 30 years or so. As people become more affluent, they spend more on holidays. Many developing countries are promoting themselves as tourist destinations in order to earn foreign currency, which they can use to pay for the imports they need. The Gambia, in West Africa, is one country in which tourism has become a major sector of the economy. In 1965 it received just 20 visitors. In 1990 there were 114,000. The gains and losses in the tourism industry can be quite complex. The profits from hotels and other tourist services may go to foreign owners, although taxes paid to the host

government represent a gain. Some of the goods and necessities provided for tourists, such as food and drink, may be imported, at the expense of support for local agriculture and manufacture. On the other hand, the business provides jobs for local people.

✳ 1990
OIL PRICES
From the 1960s the United States and most other non-communist countries were increasingly dependent on oil from the Persian Gulf region. In 1973–74, the Organisation of Petroleum Exporting Countries (OPEC), many of them Arab states, acting in concert, abruptly quadrupled the price of oil. Some countries are particularly vulnerable to any fall in the oil price; in Saudi Arabia, for example, oil and refined petroleum account for about 90 per cent of exports. A further doubling of the oil price in 1979 drove up inflation in several developed countries. Oil is vital to both producer and consumer countries and often engenders conflict. In 1990 Iraq invaded oil-rich Kuwait causing oil prices to leap. An American-led alliance drove the Iraqi forces out but only after they had set fire to most of Kuwait's oil wells.

p. 219 ◄ **Distant Voices** ► p. 223

Recession is when your neighbour loses his job. Depression is when you lose yours.

Ronald Reagan, US president, in his election campaign speech, Jersey City (September 1980)

The Global Economy
1990–99

IN THE 1990S it became clear as never before that the world's economy was essentially a single entity consisting of different parts. No longer was it simply true that if America sneezed, the world would catch cold: snuffles anywhere could just as well bring the United States down with a life-threatening illness. Important issues and concepts were discussed in the 1990s: how do people make a living?; who works where?; who lives where?; what do they own?; to what do they aspire?; what impact does their activity have on the environment?; how do their needs and aspirations impinge on those of others?; and can the planet support the world's population?

1990s
THE ENVIRONMENT
Many of the processes used during the early days of industrialisation were not only primitive and inefficient, but also wasteful of materials and responsible for enormous amounts of pollution. Industries churned out smoke and noxious gases into the air, poured effluent into rivers and the sea, dumped waste and used up non-renewable raw materials and energy such as coal and oil. Few people knew what damage human activity could inflict on the environment in the long term. In the late twentieth century, people began to meet the environmental challenge. Industry found ways of being far less wasteful of raw materials and to contribute far less to pollution. Governments helped with legislation, such as to require factories to use smokeless fuels. Environmental organisations probably did more, promoting awareness and action and conducting research and investigations to substantiate their campaigns.

1990s
FIRST, SECOND AND THIRD WORLDS
Where did the three worlds go? Until the 1990s, economists and politicians commonly referred to the Third World; by this they meant the less developed countries. The terms First World and Second World were used less often. They referred respectively to the advanced industrialised countries; and to the countries of the then communist bloc. When communism collapsed, the Second World as a political concept vanished with it. It is now customary to talk of the 'developing world' instead of the Third World: countries where most people still depend on farming for a living, wages are low and advanced technology is lacking. The UN classifies roughly two-thirds of all independent states in this category. The term 'newly industrialised countries' describes particularly some in East Asia, including Malaysia, Singapore, Korea and Taiwan.

1990s
INDUSTRY VS MANUFACTURING
The word 'industry' is often used interchangeably with 'manufacturing'. Manufacturing is the making of goods by taking raw materials and applying skills and machines to them. Until the mid-twentieth century, more people worked in manufacturing than in any other form of employment. Now, with the advent of automation and more advanced machinery, including computer-assisted processes, no more than 30 per cent of people work in manufacturing. 'Industry' in its widest sense includes manufacturing and the provision of services, mining, extraction and semi-processing and trade. A distinction may be made between heavy and light industry. Heavy industry includes such basic industries as coal-mining, shipbuilding and steel-making, requiring heavy equipment. Light industry refers to the processing in smaller factories of such goods as electronics components and glass.

1990s
MOTOR-VEHICLE OWNERSHIP
Demand for motor vehicles grew enormously as soon as mass production began, first in the USA, then – after the Second World War – in Europe and Japan, where the trend was towards smaller, more reliable and more fuel-efficient cars. Competition in this area meant that the USA gradually lost its lead as the world's greatest car-making country. The Japanese

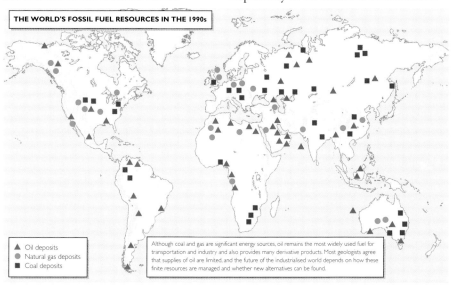

THE WORLD'S FOSSIL FUEL RESOURCES IN THE 1990s

▲ Oil deposits
● Natural gas deposits
■ Coal deposits

Although coal and gas are significant energy sources, oil remains the most widely used fuel for transportation and industry and also provides many derivative products. Most geologists agree that supplies of oil are limited, and the future of the industrialised world depends on how these finite resources are managed and whether new alternatives can be found.

 INVENTIONS   🏛 CONSTRUCTION $ MONEY   ✳ EXPORTS   ⇔ MIGRATION

now produce most of the cars in the world. Although there is no doubt that vehicles damage the environment, principally by emitting exhaust gases, everyone still seems to want a car. Lebanon has (late 1990s) one of the greatest densities of car ownership, with more than one car for every person in the country. By contrast, in China there is only one car for every 2,000 people or so.

◆ **1990s**
SUPPLY AND DEMAND
The price of a commodity tends to depend on supply, that is, the amount available for sale, and demand, the amount that consumers want to buy. The higher the price of a commodity, the more of it suppliers will want to sell. Supply therefore generally increases as the price increases. On the other hand, rising prices discourage buyers. In a free market, a balance is usually achieved between supply and demand by pitching prices at the right level. Governments are responsible for printing money. It might be supposed that if they simply print more, everyone will be richer. In fact, if the money supply increases, people are keener to buy more goods and services. The higher demand leads to higher prices (inflation).

▼ *A modern shipyard, a declining industry in Great Britain.*

⇔ **1990s**
ENVIRONMENTAL CAUSES OF MIGRATION
In the early 1960s there were an estimated one million international refugees or migrants. By 1995 the number had soared to 27.4 million. There are at least as many people again displaced within their own countries. The causes are often related to the environment. Desertification has forced one-sixth of the populations of Mali and Burkina Faso out of their homelands. Inequitable patterns of land distribution in El Salvador caused many peasants to move to neighbouring Honduras. In Ethiopia, the highland farming areas have become largely depopulated because of massive deforestation and soil erosion, along with population growth, unjust systems of land tenure and inefficient agricultural practices. Industrial development – the building of dams, roads and other projects – also displaced around 90 million people between 1985 and 1995.

1990s
IRRIGATION PROBLEMS
In 1900, there were 40 million ha of irrigated land in the world. Growth occurred throughout the twentieth century, notably from 1950 to 1993, bringing the total ultimately to 248 million ha.

However, a key point was reached in 1979, when the expansion in irrigated area began to fall behind population growth. The trend has continued since. Two-thirds of the world's irrigated area is in Asia. During the 1990s, the depletion of aquifers and the diversion of irrigation water to cities were the main causes of the reduction of irrigated aresa. In India water tables are falling in several states, including the Punjab – the country's 'breadbasket'. Where the water table falls, deeper wells are dug – if money is available; if not, irrigated agriculture has to be abandoned.

1992
RIO AND AFTER
One of the signal accomplishments of the UN Conference on Environment and Development in Rio de Janeiro in 1992 (the Earth Summit) was the official linking of environment and development issues. Yet, while the world's population grew by about 450 million in the subsequent five years, biological wealth and diversity diminished; and an estimated 1.3 billion people were too poor to meet their basic needs for food and shelter. The broad goals of the Summit were laid down in Agenda 21, which recognised that 'an environmental policy that focuses mainly on the conservation and protection of resources without consideration of the livelihoods of those who depend on the resources is unlikely to succeed'. By 1996, 117 governments had formed commissions to develop national sustainable development strategies.

p. 221 ◀ **Distant Voices** ▶ p. 225

What is now at stake is nothing less than the viability of the world financial and trade order put in place over the last 20 years. At the centre of the financial system is the dollar, whose intrinsic supremacy the Americans have further exploited by insisting that economic development should be as laissez-faire as possible.

The Observer (6 September 1998)

Is There Room at the Inn?
1990–2000

BUSINESSMEN IN SOME Western countries complain of the difficulty of exporting because of the strength of their currencies. Excessive competition in financial services is causing redundancies. Microchip manufacture has suffered a collapse in demand because of oversupply. The meltdown in the Asian economies (1997–98) made commentators wonder whether world financial systems may not be on the verge of disintegration. Even assuming stable banks and financial institutions, the combination of over-population and under-performing economies gives reason enough for anxiety. Hunger now affects nearly 20 per cent of the world's population. And for those who are now affluent, the indications suggest a future drop in standard of living. Whether wisdom and expertise will be deployed to meet the economic and environmental challenges, only time will tell.

$
1990s
EXCHANGE RATES

The exchange rate is the amount of one country's currency that can be bought with another country's currency. International trade depends heavily on exchange rates. If the currency's value falls, exports from that country will cost buyers less. This will increase demand from buyers, thus favouring exporters. The low value of the currency, however, also makes imports more expensive. In the late 1990s, British exporters complained that the 'strong' pound was damaging their trade by making exports too costly. Fluctuating exchange rates are not good: they make it difficult for businesses to plan ahead. Countries may therefore decide to link their exchange rate to a major currency or to fix variations in exchange rates within agreed bands: the European Exchange Rate Mechanism is one such system.

1990s
HUNGER

Of the 5,500 million people in the world, more than 1,000 million are chronically hungry. Every year between 13 million and 18 million people die of hunger or hunger-related illnesses. Many people suffer from chronic undernutrition, because they regularly and over a long period consume too few calories and other nutrients. Malnutrition occurs when there is a major shortage of a specific nutrient, such as vitamin A (deficiency can cause blindness). Intestinal parasites can hinder proper absorption of nutrients. Seasonal hunger occurs when stores of goods run out before the new harvest can replenish them. Famine, a severe and widespread food shortage, is usually caused by crop failure or damage, but the reasons may be more complex, involving prices, conflict or other problems of access.

1990s
THE POLITICS OF SCARCITY

Surplus was the key feature of the world food economy in the 50 years after the Second World War. Now scarcity is dominant. The economies of Asia, from Pakistan east to Japan, grew dramatically in the 1990s. China's economy grew by two-thirds between 1990 and 1995. Never before have so many people become affluent and therefore moved up the food chain so fast. With demand burgeoning, Japan, South Korea and Taiwan import more than 70 per cent of the grain they consume. Asia is becoming strong industrially but agriculturally vulnerable – particularly as it depends for nearly half its grain imports on the USA, where harvests vary widely from year to year. Intense heatwaves (e.g. in 1988) also shrink grain harvests.

▼ Black Wednesday, the stock market crash that caused a global crisis in 1998.

⌨ INVENTIONS   🏛 CONSTRUCTION $ MONEY   ❋ EXPORTS   ⇔ MIGRATION

1990s
THE WORLD'S POPULATION-CARRYING CAPACITY

Recent trends underline the urgency of improving Earth's population-carrying capacity. There is now little prospect for substantially expanding cropland area, so the key determinant will be land productivity (although the level of consumption also counts). From 1950 to 1990 land productivity grew enormously: grain yield rose from 1.06 tons/ha in 1950 to 2.54 tons/ha in 1990. After 1990, however, the increase slowed down, to less than one-third of the annual growth rate in population over the same period (to 1996). In Japan rice yield per ha did not increase at all after 1984 and in Russia the annual rise, which had been remarkable from 1950 to 1977, slowed dramatically. About 88 million people are added to the world's population each year.

p. 221 ◀ **Triumphs & Tragedies** ▶ p. 232

1990s
CRISIS IN THE GLOBAL ECONOMY

In the late 1990s, an economic crisis occurred in south-east Asia and gradually spread across the world. In July and August 1998 alone, four trillion dollars were wiped off the value of shares worldwide. Commodity prices, including oil and grain prices, collapsed to their lowest level in real terms since the 1930s. The Asian 'miracle' came to grief as a result of massive speculation against fixed currencies. Singapore, for example, had pegged its dollar to the US since the early 1970s and had succeeded in attracting huge flows of inward investment. China's devaluation of its currency in 1994 was the last straw. Just as the other Asian economies were moving into a boom, their fixed link to the dollar was making exports uncompetitive. Inflation rose. One by one the countries were forced off the dollar peg, currencies plunged and stockmarkets crashed. Leading economists suggested exchange controls as the least damaging way out of the crisis.

2000
HUMAN SECURITY

Human security, unlike traditional military security, is about strengthening the social, economic and environmental fabric of societies. World environmental governance is increasingly important, as are debt relief and compacts to reduce poverty, unemployment and social breakdown. A key measure would be the redistribution of land accompanied by guaranteed secure land tenure and improved rural credit and extension (advice). This would create market demand, which in turn helps to stimulate industries that can provide employment outside agriculture. Once this happens, people experience a higher level of social and economic security, which is a crucial factor in limiting population growth. Demilitarisation is another worthwhile means of promoting human security. Such measures cost money, but the choice is between paying now and paying much more later.

2000
FEED GRAIN FOR PEOPLE?

National governments need to assess the merit of using cropland to produce non-essential crops. The five million ha of cropland used for tobacco, for example, could produce 15 million tonnes of grain, enough to feed the 'new' population of the world for nearly seven months. In the US, 10 million tonnes of grain is used to produce ethanol as an automobile fuel. Little grain remains in storage; nor is there any significant idled cropland. The only remaining reserve that can be tapped in a food emergency is the grain harvest that is currently fed to livestock, poultry and fish. There would be a high price to pay. It would therefore be sensible to ration or tax the consumption of livestock products.

▲ *Harvesting the rice in Japan.*

2025
THE FUTURE OF CROPLAND

In 2025 the world's population is likely to be 7.9 billion, and 90 per cent of births then will occur in developing countries. These were 96 per cent self-sufficient in grain in 1969–71 but only 88 per cent so in 1993–95. For thousands of years farmland was treated as an expendable commodity, but food reserves eventually declined along with loss of land. Now the only available means of increasing grain production is to raise crop yields. The gap between food needs and food availability may be narrowed by market forces. Markets do allocate scarce resources, but generally only in the shorter term, and they under-represent the millions of poor but chronically hungry people in the world. Governments must therefore take steps to care for soils and preserve cropland.

p. 223 ◀ **Distant Voices** ▶ p. 229

It is time for lenders to cancel the bulk of the debts owed by [the most severely indebted low-income] governments – some $200 billion – in exchange for a human security conditionality: commitments by the debtors to reduce their military expenditures and armed forces, and to invest resources that otherwise would have gone into debt servicing in areas of social and environmental need.

Michael Renner, 'Transforming Security', in *State of the World 1997*

Science and Technology

KEY THEMES

✳ FOOD

✈ TRANSPORTATION

✉ COMMUNICATION

🏛 HABITATION

⚜ WARFARE

🏙 ARCHITECTURE

✠ MEDICAL SCIENCE

🌿 AGRICULTURE

✪ RESOURCING

📖 KNOWLEDGE

HUMANKIND'S ABILITY to adapt to changing environments, to continually build on the successes and learn from the failures of his forbears, has seen them progress from a primitive people, aware only of their own immediate society and surroundings, to a species that has dominated Earth – and uncovered many of the mysteries beyond it, creating inventions that at first simply allowed them to survive, then gradually went on to enhance their quality of life. In many areas, the twentieth century has seen the greatest scientific growth – in medicine, transport and communications – but the stepping stones to this century's success should not be overlooked. Frequently such success is the result of years of patient experimentation and self-belief. Of course, not all technological advance has proved profitable, or even humane, but much of it has proved so successful that it has become an integral part of the world in which we live today. The world continues to create new challenges, and it seems the very nature of human progress has generated new problems – to the point where our very planet seems under threat; many mysteries also remain: the understanding of the human mind, the curing of many diseases, the exploration of life beyond our own world, and our own universe. As science and technology continue to progress in leaps and bounds, who knows what the next millennium will uncover?

KEY EVENTS

❶ 2700 BC
THE WHEEL AND AXLE

Pressures of trade, industry and warfare provided the necessity which mothered the invention of the wheel and axle in around 2700 BC. Various wheeled vehicles, such as carts, wagons and chariots, pulled by oxen or horses, were adopted rapidly, such was the advantage of using them.

❷ 1000s
GUNPOWDER

Sometime early in the eleventh century the Chinese chanced on the formula for gunpowder. Its potential as a propellant was only fully realised when it got into the hands of warring Europeans looking for an edge over their enemies. It gained its familiar name when it was used in the first cannons.

❸ 1450s
MOVEABLE TYPE PRINTING

The inventive genius of German goldsmith Johann Gutenberg brought printing of age. During the late 1450s he devised a system for using individual type characters, cast in moulds from an alloy of lead, tin and antimony, which were interchangeable within a frame. It was quick and easy to assemble whole pages of type which could all be used time and time again for other jobs.

❹ 1685
ISAAC NEWTON

Isaac Newton laid down the foundation for the discipline of modern physics. He discovered that white light is in fact made up of a spectrum of coloured light and that light seemed to behave as both waves and particles. He also described three laws of motion and defined the nature of weight, mass, force, acceleration and inertia. His most famous work was done on gravity.

❺ 1876
TELEPHONE

In 1876, Alexander Graham Bell made an assemblage of components devised in part by other electrical scientists which he had improved upon for practical application. He had invented the telephone by doing so, and was able to transmit the first ever spoken message via an electrical wire. Important in their own right, were the microphone and loudspeaker he had developed.

❻ 1926
TELEVISION

Ever since the first public transmission of television images in 1926 the television has progressively become the single most important medium for conveying information to the populations of the world. It has become an accepted part of the culture in societies ranging from the most advanced to the those of the 'third-world', such is its magical attraction by providing information for the eye and ear.

❼ 1945
NUCLEAR TECHNOLOGY

There is perhaps no greater symbol of technological development in the twentieth century than the nuclear bomb. It was used to halt the world's greatest war in one fell swoop, yet it was originally conceived as a source of power for the modern age. Indeed, nuclear power stations are now fairly commonplace in the world, despite the inherent risks associated with their production of radiation.

❽ 1953
DNA UNRAVELLED

In 1953 the structure of DNA (deoxyribonucleic acid) was revealed to the world by Watson and Crick. At last, the working mechanism for Darwin and Wallace's evolutionary process was clear. The double helix design held coded information for all living things; it could 'unzip' to duplicate itself and combinations of code, together with mutations in the form of errors, provided the variety necessary for selection of favourable traits to occur.

TIMELINE

Prehistory   First stone tools used
Prehistory   Man learns to manipulate fire
Prehistory   Horticulture and domestication expand
1 • • • **2700** BC   Wheel and axle invented
1000 BC   Permanent housing established; evolution of the plough
1000 BC   Cuneiform used to communicate in Sumeria
1000 BC   Mathematic principles applied to construction and building
1000 BC   Use of clay for bricks and tiles
1000 BC   Weaving and spinning developed
AD **100s**   Galen develops theory of 'Humours'
AD **100**   Invention of the astrolabe
2 • • • • • • **1000s**   Invention of gunpowder
1088   Water clocks invented
1100   Blast furnace invented
1364   Development of firearms
3 • • • • • • • • **1450s**   Gutenburg invents movable type printing
1500s   Paracelsus and Vesalius prove external agents cause disease
1551   Invention of Gunters Chain revolutionises measurement
1580   Mercator introduces latitude and longitude to cartography
1600   Kepler's laws of planetary motion
1608   Invention of the pendulum clock and the telescope
1609   Invention of the microscope; discovery of blood circulation
1614   John Napier publishes his logarithmic tables
4 • • • • • • • • • • **1685**   Isaac Newton's theories
1705   Halley predicts his comet's return
1769   James Watt's begins to develop steam engines
1796   Inoculation and vaccination first used
1800   Mass production techniques for steels, ceramics and textiles
1820   Michael Faraday produces first electric motor
1826   Photography and cinematography developed
1853   Internal combusion engines
1859   First oil rig established at Oil Creek, Pennsylvania
1867   Anaesthetics and antiseptics developed
5 • • • • • • • • • • • • • • **1876**   Alexander Graham Bell invents the telephone
1877   Phonograph and gramophone records invented
1895   Marconi discovers radio waves
1908   Model T Ford produced
1913   Conveyor belts used on production lines
6 • • • • • • • • • • • • • • • • • • **1926**   John Logie Baird demonstrates monochromatic television
1934   Nuclear technology develops
1935   Radar and sonar developed
1936   Circuit boards and microprocessors invented
1938   Photocopiers and faxes invented
7 • **1945**   Rise of nuclear technology
8 • **1953**   DNA unravelled
1980   Virtual reality
1984   E-mail and the internet come in to use

Beginnings of Technology
PREHISTORY

AT A POINT over three and a half million years ago, hominids began using pieces of stone as tools and weapons. By breaking stones to make simple choppers, our ancestors invented the first technology. The early Palaeolithic, or Stone Age, began with the *Australopithecines*, followed by the first member of our genus, *Homo habilis*. As the Homo line carried on evolving, humans became more intelligent and their application of basic technologies in utilising stone and organic materials became more sophisticated. After *Homo habilis* came *Homo erectus*, the forerunner to various forms of human from different parts of the Old World. Eventually *Homo sapiens* appeared as the sole member of our lineage around 30,000 years ago, fully equipped mentally and physically for using technology as a means for survival in many kinds of environment over the planet.

▲ *One of the earliest technologies: a flint arrowhead.*

PREHISTORY
THE CUTTING EDGE OF TECHNOLOGY

The first deliberately shaped stone tools were crude choppers, used for basic predetermined activities such as bludgeoning, butchering and digging. Gradually stone tools became more refined as techniques for making them improved and more specific uses for different designs emerged. Human hands also evolved to feature a fully opposable thumb allowing for a precision grip as well as the power grip. Four essential manufacturing processes: direct and indirect percussion, pressure flaking and abrasion, led to a whole array of stone artefacts being made with a wide variety of applications. They included

handaxes, spear and arrowheads, bone and hide scrapers, shaping burins, and a selection of points and blades for holding in the hand or fixing into handles.

PREHISTORY
ORGANIC TOOLS AND WEAPONS

Bits of wood and bone were probably used as simple tools before stone, so as technology developed organic materials became an important part of the material culture alongside stone materials. Animals and plants supplied many different materials for technology, as well as foods. Organic materials tend to decay and disintegrate far more readily and rapidly than stone however, so there have been far fewer specimens found in comparison with stone artefacts. Animal materials included; bone, horn, antler, ivory, hide, fur, hair, sinew and gut. Plant materials included; wood, bark and fibres. Together with stone and mineral materials, they completed a list of resources which enabled humans to make a kit of all the tools, weapons and other artefacts they needed to survive.

✳ ▶ p. 233　## PREHISTORY
OUT OF THE FLAMES

Naturally occurring fire probably introduced humans to its benefits as a tool and weapon, so humans devised ways for creating fire at

will and developed methods for controlling its use. Two processes were discovered for getting a fire going: striking stone against iron pyrites readily produced sparks; and spinning the end of a straight stick very rapidly in a recess in another piece of wood resulted, with a little skill, in a friction glow. Cooking food served two important purposes: it killed dangerous pathogens in meat; and broke down the chemicals in otherwise indigestible or even inedible foods. Controlled use of fire had the obvious benefit of supplying warmth and deterring predators, as well as helping with hunting and being a very useful tool for working and treating stone and organic materials.

PREHISTORY
SHELTER FROM THE ELEMENTS

Early technology was employed in the design and construction of many kinds of shelter as humans wandered into less congenial parts of the world. Living a hunter-gatherer existence was a nomadic lifestyle, so shelters needed to be only temporary. They had to be easy to erect using the resources available and light enough to transport to a new location if they weren't simply left behind. Bivouacs and tents were the simplest form of shelter, using animals skins or other suitable materials to cover a basic frame made from wood. Caves were used wherever they were available and some were hewn from the rock by early humans using stone tools. The design of shelters depended primarily on the materials close at hand in different environments, and the conditions that the environment imposed on the people living there.

▼ *Prehistoric family of hunter-gatherers.*

PREHISTORY
HORTICULTURE AND
DOMESTICATION

Technology evolved in human hands to make survival easier in a hostile and competitive world. Eventually people became more inclined to stay in one place, rather than wander about. This meant having to employ technology to sustain necessary resources and as a result, hunting and gathering declined as early farming took a hold. The domestication and rearing of livestock meant being able to convert useless plant materials into valuable animal products and it provided for periods of the year when hunting could not be relied upon. Similarly, plants were cultivated in groups and given special treatment to encourage better yields of fruit or seed and so on. Furthermore, animals provided fertiliser for the plants, which in turn provided fodder for the animals. Horticulture and animal husbandry thus became inseparable partners in the farming process.

▼ *The cave paintings at Altamira are some of the finest examples of prehistoric communication.*

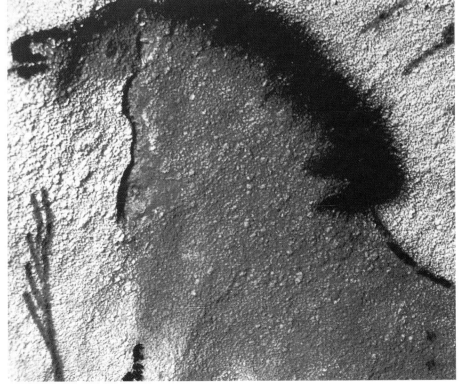

✈ ▶ p. 230 ## PREHISTORY
TRANSPORT OVER LAND
AND WATER

The ability to carry things while walking is one of the defining characteristics of the human species. As technology progressed however, the next logical step was to devise ways for moving things around with less effort and inconvenience, especially as the problem of having to traverse various types of terrain arose with wandering migrations. Panniers and bags helped with carrying relatively small things and simple sledges were developed for dragging larger items around, considerably helped by the eventual use of domesticated animals for supplying traction power. Rafts and dugout logs were the first water transport, eventually leading to the manufacture of skin and frame canoes and dinghies.

✉ ▶ p. 232 ## PREHISTORY
LINE, FORM AND COLOUR

An integral mechanism for technological progress is the communication of ideas and knowledge. Early forms of information and communication technology included drawings, paintings, and etchings onto surfaces and the carving and sculpting of three dimensional artefacts. All kinds of animal, plant and mineral materials were used for expressing and recording human thoughts, as well as the use of language and demonstration. Without communicating previous discoveries and inventions, new generations of people would not have been in a position to generate new developments, because they would have had to start again from scratch. Teaching and learning were disciplines vital for the flow of technological and scientific knowledge from one generation to the next and the tradition has been adhered to ever since.

PREHISTORY
CLOTHING THE NAKED BODY

During the Stone Age people began to migrate to various parts of the world and had to cope with terrain and climates which were not always congenial. For this reason, it became necessary to invent clothing. Ever resourceful, people used the materials available to them in different habitats for making the clothing appropriate to their particular requirements. Since the principal materials for constructing their clothes came in the form of skins from animals which lived in the locality, they found that the warmth and protection supplied by their clothing matched the conditions very well. They were, in effect, utilising the evolutionary adaptations in prey species, to their own ends.

p. 225 ◀ **Distant Voices** ▶ p. 231

Man is a creature adapted for life under circumstances which are very narrowly limited. A few degrees of temperature more or less, a slight variation in the composition of air, the precise suitability of food, make all the difference between health and sickness, between life and death.

Sir Robert S. Ball, *The Story of the Heavens* (1885)

Bronze Replaces Stone
2700–1800 BC

A T FIRST, NATURALLY OCCURRING copper nuggets were hammered into small tools and trinkets. Then it was discovered how to smelt copper ore with charcoal to produce molten metal which could be cast into larger shapes, but although copper was also less brittle than stone, it was not very hard wearing, so stone remained popular. Then came the seminal breakthrough which would begin the metallurgical revolution. It was realised that by mixing molten copper with molten tin, another soft metal, an alloy could be made which was harder than both. Bronze had arrived and it prompted dramatic changes in technology. It replaced stone in many respects and new uses were found for it because it possessed characteristics not previously found in a single material, so the way was opened for more rapid progress.

▲ *Stone relief carving showing the wheel of a chariot.*

✈ ▶ p. 239 **2700 BC**
THE WHEEL AND AXLE

As humans began building settlements and early civilisations started to appear, aided by Bronze Age technology, there came an increased need for an efficient way to transport bulky goods from one place to another. Pressures of trade, industry and warfare provided the necessity which mothered the invention of the wheel and axle in around 2700 BC. Various wheeled vehicles, such as carts, wagons and chariots, pulled by oxen or horses, were adopted rapidly, such was the advantage of using them. The wheel and axle proved to be of vital importance because they effectively opened the door for more effective communications between human populations and provided a far more efficient means for transporting people, equipment and goods; the net result was an infrastructure within and between early civilisations.

☗ ▶ p. 235 **2500 BC**
PERMANENT HOUSING

The advent of sedentary lifestyles meant that by the mid-third millennium BC people started to design and build permanent buildings as a framework for early civilisation. The first settlements comprised simple structures made with wattle and daub walls and a timber frame and roof. Materials and techniques for building advanced rapidly however, and more durable materials began to be used, such as stone, slate, fired clay bricks and roof tiles. The dynamics of the new materials required more precise building techniques; these led to features which were modern concepts at the time. Straight walls with right-angled corners were first seen in this period. They allowed for more economical use of regulated building components as well as making a better use of available space.

⚔ ▶ p. 234 **2300 BC**
TOOLS AND WEAPONS IN BRONZE

Bronze had several distinct advantages in its favour over stone, which made it a far superior material. To start with, a material which could be heated into a liquid and then poured into moulds to cast specific shapes was very useful. Added to this, it could be worked by hammering, cutting and bending into complex shapes and joined together with pins or rivets. Unlike stone it was also very tough and resistant to extremes of temperature, but most importantly it could be easily resharpened to an edge thinner and sharper than stone, without losing much material. Many tools, weapons and artefacts with uses in different areas of human activity appeared in bronze, because it was so versatile, for example domestic, farming, warfare, building and fabrication uses.

✿ ▶ p. 231 **2000 BC**
THE PLOUGH AND SICKLE

Basic forms of farming implement made from stone and organic materials were already in use as bronze was introduced. Digging sticks, stone adzes and axes, the scratch plough and stone blade scythes and sickles had all been developed. Bronze, though, marked a significant improvement in the quality, effectiveness and efficiency of such tools. This was crucially important at the time because higher and more reliable yields from crops were required to feed the growing populations contained within settlements, many of whom now devoted their efforts to new specialised careers, not involved with farming. Bronze blades were tougher, longer and thinner than stone and only took a few moments to resharpen.

▼ *Basic farming machinery, such as the plough and sickle, was being used as early as 2000 BC.*

▲ *Stone relief depicting a carpenter working with primitive tools.*

stone included two or more radiating beams. The oxen or horses were attached to the ends of the beams and trained to walk round in circles. The seed was now fed into the centre of the upper stone and flour spilled from the join between the two. A similar devise called a capstan, operated by humans or animals, was used for moving heavy objects by winding a rope.

✪ ▶ p. 234 **1800 BC**
WEAVING AND KNOTS
The basic principle of interlacing and tying materials together to make new materials and objects with multidirectional strength, provided humans with a technology for many new applications during the Bronze Age. Weaving materials such as strips of wood, canes or rushes, resulted in a plethora of artefacts, including baskets, building and fencing panels and furniture. Weaving twines or threads, spun from animal or plant fibres provided people with various types of cloth. Textiles in turn, were put to all kinds of uses; clothing, sails, sacks, bed linen and so on. Knotting materials instead of weaving them, resulted in netting which saw the beginning of fishing as an industry, now fully capable of supplying the burgeoning civilisations around the Mediterranean.

2000 BC
SAILS, PLANKS AND OARS
Boat building developed rapidly with the introduction of bronze technology, primarily because metal tools allowed for the skilled shaping and joining of planks and timbers required to construct a water-tight vessel. The concept of water displacement had been realised with the first skin and frame canoes, so now boats grew in size to become small ships. The principle of attaching planks to a timber frame provided the blueprint for a wide variety of shapes and sizes of boat. Mortise and tenon joints with locking wedges and dowels provided the structural stability and lapped planks sealed with bitumen provided a strong water resistant hull. The methods for propelling the boat at this time were primarily oars and a square sail if there happened to be a favourable wind.

🌿 ▶ p. 238 **2000 BC**
HYDRAULIC FARMING
The Ancient Egyptians developed a system of hydraulic farming around the rise and fall of the Nile river. They planted seed just before the rains, so that the crops had a good start with plenty of water. The river would swell following the rains and irrigation channels were used to supply the crops with water from the river over the vital growing period. However, the waters of the Nile would get progressively lower, so it became necessary to contain as much water as possible and raise it up to the irrigation channels. This was achieved by using devices called *shadufs*, long pivoted poles with a bucket at one end and a counterweight at the other. The water was lifted with *shadufs* up a series of stepped tanks until it was elevated high enough to reach the irrigation system.

2000 BC
TREADMILLS AND CAPSTANS
Milling cereals was a time-consuming and labour intensive activity, so it made sense to get animals to do the work instead. This was achieved by applying the principle of the wheel and axle to another machine, the treadmill. Two circular millstones were aligned with a vertical axle, and the upper

Burgeoning Civilisations
4000–1000 BC

AS TECHNOLOGICAL DEVELOPMENTS moved into metallurgy, people began to establish lifestyles which reflected their increased knowledge and the potential in its application. Inhabitants of cities tended to adopt certain roles as part of the civilised community rather than pitching in with all activities as used to be the case. Specialising in specific jobs had a two-way effect on society: people lost their general understanding of the technologies involved in different industries through a lack of contact and first-hand experience, yet they gained an intimate knowledge of their own. Members of a society therefore became mutually dependent on one another to supply all that they needed for a good quality of life and found themselves able to push forward and improve the technological area with which they had become so familiar.

▲ *The methods of quarrying and transporting the huge sandstone blocks used in the Egyptian pyramids, are a testimony to ancient engineering techniques.*

 ▶ p. 244 **4000 BC**
WRITING AND SYMBOLS
Leading into the Bronze Age, people had developed ways to record and communicate information using pictures. Eventually the pictures became more stylised and standardised as they evolved into symbols which could be quickly drawn out as a code of meaning, or writing. As early as 4000 BC the process of simplification had reached a stage known as cuneiform writing. It was a system formed of combinations of wedge shaped strokes to make the characters, which were often impressed into clay tablets. Cuneiform remained in use, in many cultural forms, until cursive writing took its place in about the fifth century BC. The Egyptians adopted a form of writing with pictorial symbols, called hieroglyphics, with which they decorated the surfaces of monuments and tombs.

3000 BC
POTTERY AND BRICKS
By the beginning of the Bronze Age, clay bricks and tiles were being used, and pottery had been invented by using the coil and slab method, which involved assembling objects with clay components which were then smoothed to complete a single artefact. In approximately 3000 BC, the potters wheel was invented. At first it was hand rotated but it developed to include a weighted flywheel which enabled potters to draw the clay into shape from one piece, as it span round. Eventually the foot-operated kick-wheel was added, leaving both the potter's hands free and the way was opened for the mass production of pottery and ceramics as demanded by civilisation.

▶ p. 236 **2500 BC**
TOMBS AND TEMPLES
A powerful influence on the successful running of complex civilisations was the sense of cohesion through religious belief. Believing that gods were ultimately in control of them and their environment, and that their leaders were themselves personifications of gods, it was reasoned that as much time and effort as possible should be devoted to keeping them happy. They therefore applied state-of-the-art technology in the designing and building of temples, tombs and other monuments. As the projects became ever more ambitious, so technology was required in order to optimise the resources available. Religion was a major player therefore, in the promotion of innovative ideas during this period, because there was nothing quite like the fear of divine retribution for encouraging people to think creatively.

p. 225 ◀ **Triumphs & Tragedies** ▶ p. 237
2500 BC
PYRAMIDS AND MONUMENTS
The Bronze Age saw many civilisations rise and fall; all of them left behind some legacy of their enterprises in the form of architectural ruins or at least evidence of a monumental achievement during their heyday. The most noted are the Egyptian pyramids which were accurately designed and constructed as tombs for revered kings. High levels of technical expertise went into their making, including precise surveying and preparation of the foundations and strict adherence to geometric constraints as they were slowly assembled block by block. The pyramid was the most stable way to build upwards, before the introduction of pillars or columns and lintels allowed for more lightweight and elaborate use of stone.

✠ ▶ p. 237 **2500 BC**
HEALERS AND EMBALMERS
The Bronze Age witnessed developments in technology related to medical procedures, although implements and techniques were primarily used in the treatment of cadavers as opposed to patients, in accordance with spiritual beliefs. Various knives and other tools were used for minor surgery ranging from lancing abscesses and stitching wounds to extracting rotten teeth and trepanning the skull. Consequently, surgical expertise

▼ *The Egyptians developed a method of preserving dead bodies, known as mummification.*

became the reserve of the undertaker, particularly in Egypt, where a veritable industry centred around the preparation of the dead. Embalming involved the discreet use of implements for the removal of the internal organs, including the brain, which were placed in special jars. The remaining corpse was then treated with ointments, oils and other chemical agents to preserve it, before being swaddled in bandage.

1000 BC
COUNTING THE COST
As soon as people became aware of the value of possessions, it became necessary to make calculations of worth. Number, weight, volume, area, time, and so on, all became measures for making these calculations. Performing such calculations required the creation of written numerals to avoid complex mental arithmetic. Money came into being because trading by barter alone did not always result in a satisfactory exchange of goods. It took many forms initially, as a variety of materials were experimented with. Since money was in essence, a representation of effort, and in turn value, it needed to be made from a material which was itself rare, desirable and difficult to acquire. Metals were the obvious answer, as they had a cross-cultural intrinsic value which could be relied upon in any trading situation.

1000 BC
NATURAL MATHEMATICS
As mathematics began to play a part in assisting with the design and erection of buildings during the Bronze Age, basic principles applied to the engineering of these projects are seen to have been borrowed from nature. Geometric shapes such as circles, oblongs, squares and triangles took prominence along with straight lines and symmetry, all of which are natural phenomena. Human designs adopted such principles because they were discovered to be the optimum way to shape things in the context of maximum strength with economical use of materials. Other natural phenomena – the

perfect horizontal of still water and the perfect vertical of a weighted line, were essential devices in making sure that very heavy buildings stood exactly upright and on level foundations.

✸ ▶ p. 247 **1000 BC**
SELECTING THE BEST
Just as humans effected evolutionary changes in farming technology during the Bronze Age, they also promoted alterations to the crops and animals they farmed. The reason why farmed species changed in appearance from their wild relatives, was because they were subjected to a process called improvement by artificial selection. The genetic survival mechanism in life forms which provides variety for natural selection was being exploited by early farmers, who were simply choosing the best specimens to provide the subsequent generations and modifying the species over time as a result. Similarly, these new farm species would themselves eventually be artificially evolved into different breeds, displaying desirable characteristics appropriate for the environments in which they were being raised and the intended uses of the resources they supplied.

p. 231 ◀ **Distant Voices** ▶ p. 235

I fashioned they great statue resting in its midst; 'Amon-Endowed-with-Eternity' was its august name; it was adorned with real costly stone like the horizon. When it appeared there was rejoicing to see it. I made for it table-vessels, of fine gold; others of silver and copper, without number. I multiplied the divine offerings presented before thee, of bread, wine, beer, and fat geese; numerous oxen, bullocks, calves, cows, white oryxes and gazelles offered in his slaughter yard.

Pharaoh Rameses III, translated from hieroglyphics on the temple of Medinet Habu

Iron Replaces Bronze
1400–500 BC

BRONZE HAD BEEN a very popular and versatile material, and in use for several millennia by the time iron began to be worked into tools and weapons. Iron was a difficult metal to produce at first, despite its superior qualities, so bronze persisted for a long period of overlap in many places. Iron cannot be hammered cold like bronze, but instead must be heated and forged while glowing hot and relatively soft. A new industrial technique had to be built around iron production before it was seen as a practicable metal to use instead of bronze, but it would still take moret han 2,000 years before Europeans were able to use iron in its molten form for casting.

▶ p. 239 **1400 BC**
SMELTING IRON

The earliest method for producing iron was developed by the Hittites from about 1400 BC. They found that crushed iron ore, heated with charcoal, would convert into a spongy form of iron containing pockets of impurities which had then to be beaten out of the metal while soft to attain a piece of metal of workable consistency. The charcoal was removing the oxygen from the iron oxide to leave the metal behind, but other unwanted minerals, known as slag, were held in the metal which formed a honeycomb around them. Without being able to separate the metal from the slag by melting it into a fluid form, being unable to produce a high enough temperature, they had no choice but to pummel the metal so that bits of slag fell out and the metal gradually welded itself into a solid piece.

1000 BC
FROM IRON TO STEEL

Iron smelting furnaces gradually improved and were far more effective at achieving and maintaining higher temperatures. This made it easier to produce and forge wrought iron in the quantities increasingly demanded by the civilisations of the period. Experiments also led to the invention of a harder form of iron known as cementation steel which was made by repeatedly folding and hammering the heated metal with layers of charcoal. By

around 400 BC, the Chinese had already managed, with the aid of sophisticated bellows, to melt iron into a liquid. By raising the temperature of their furnaces above 1,539°C they were able to cast iron into moulds for the first time. Europe would have to wait for some 1,500 years longer.

1000 BC
THE SUPERIOR METAL

The advantages of using iron over bronze, were emphasised by the people who used them. Iron Age civilisations were war-like, and warfare generated two prime motivating factors for making the most of

▼ *Early flint tools; metals eventually superseded these primitive weapons, first bronze and then iron, in around 1400 BC.*

the new metal: The most obvious one was being ahead in the arms race. Iron-made weapons and equipment proved to be far superior and bronze-based civilisations fell quickly under the grey metal. Another important concern was being able to feed an army and therefore maintain the winning edge, especially when facing another iron-based adversary. Iron farming implements made this possible because they were stronger, sharper and more hard-wearing, so productivity increased to meet requirements. Iron ploughshare knife and scratch points also made tilling the fields far more efficient.

1000 BC
NEW METALLIC APPLICATIONS

Throughout the Bronze Age, people still used flint for the tip of the scratch plough, even though it was brittle, because it needed to stay sharp to be effective. Soft metals blunted too easily. Iron on the other hand, possessed the combined qualities of flint and bronze, being hard wearing, but not brittle. With an iron ploughshare knife as well as scratch tip, the plough was improved very considerably. Iron was also far more suitable, thanks to its dynamic properties, for structural tasks such as brackets, bracings and other components as parts of ships, vehicles or machines which had to cope with high levels of vibration and strong forces. The only down side about using iron was its readiness to turn back into iron oxide by rusting, especially in warm salt water.

▶ p. 238 **800 BC**
OFFENSIVE WARFARE

By 800 BC, iron was employed in the manufacture of many manual weapons, but it proved to be so versatile that engineers began using the metal for strengthening and making other working components of various intriguing inventions, designed to out-do their opponents in war. Apart from the more obvious uses for iron, in the manufacture of blades for swords and daggers, and tips for arrows, bolts and spears, there were parts for mechanical devices such as siege and field artillery engines. Some war engines were elaborate devices which hurled projectiles, such as rocks and bolts, towards enemy ramparts and soldiers alike, at very high velocity. Others were designed to allow soldiers to approach ramparts under siege without injury, so that they could attempt to dig beneath the walls or climb over them.

800 BC
DEFENSIVE WARFARE

As weapons for attack became more formidable during the Iron Age, so defensive technology had to counter the trend. Wrought iron armour, helmets and shields were vitally important in fending off strikes and blows from enemy infantry and artillery, even though they weighed the soldier down. Ramparts had to be better designed and constructed to cope with assaults from war engines such as ballisters, catapults and onagers, which were used to hurl various objects at speed, including burning tar which would set light to anything it hit. Sieges could last for several months if a stalemate situation arose, so the outcome was often decided by the ingenuity of engineers applying their technological know-how to outwit the other side.

▶ p. 249 **500 BC**
A CLEANER WAY TO LIVE

Civilisation meant large numbers of people living in close proximity within the confines of a city's parameters. This led to an inevitable problem with both the supply of clean water and the removal of polluted water, or sewage. Without these basic amenities, hygiene levels would fall rapidly, leading to illness and disease. Before they grew too large, containers were used to transport water and sewage to and from cities, unless they were built immediately around a river, which acted as a conveyor for fresh and dirty water. Gradually aqueducts, drains and sewers were experimented with out of necessity in some established cities with varying degrees of success. Eventually though, new cities were designed and built to incorporate the conduits necessary for the adequate functioning of such amenities.

500 BC
FROM THE KILN

The end of the Bronze Age had seen pottery beginning to incorporate glazes and enamels, as well as mineral pigments. During the Iron Age, ceramics developed at a pace and craftsmen became artisans, so much so that their products became an expression of the achievements of civilisation. Incredibly delicate and finely worked pieces of ceramic ware were made, which required great technological skill in the control of kiln temperatures for the multiple firings necessary to create them. As well as vessels, such as vases, ewers and bowls; ceramic tiles were used for lining baths and washrooms. Beautiful mosaics, comprising myriad tiny coloured tiles, were also very popular for covering the floors in houses and other buildings.

p. 233 ◀ **Distant Voices** ▶ p. 237

Others shall shape bronzes more smoothly so that they seem alive (yes, I believe it), shall mould from marble living faces, shall better plead their cases in court, and shall demonstrate with a pointer, the motions of the heavenly bodies and tell the stars as they rise: you, Roman, make your task to rule nations by your government (these shall be your skills), to impose ordered ways upon a state of peace, to spare those who have submitted and to subdue the arrogant.

From *The Aeneid*, by Roman poet Virgil

▼ *The Romans eventually developed sophisticated under-floor heating systems for their villas, known as hypocausts.*

Civilised Minds at Work

550 BC–AD 200

O F THE MANY CIVILISATIONS which waxed and waned during the Iron Age, the Greek and Roman empires have been marked out for their progressive effect on science and technology. The rise and fall of civilisations were actually beneficial in the context of technological development because they tended to disperse new information amongst new populations and they encouraged innovative thought by placing know-how into the hands of people with new problems to solve. The Greeks had more interest in the academic pursuit of knowledge so that they could understand the workings of the world around them, while the Romans, being warlike, placed more emphasis on the practical application of science and technology, so that they could fulfil their empire-building ambitions.

550 BC
UNIVERSAL CURRENCY

Schist is a flint-like black stone which can be used to indicate the purity of gold when rubbed on its surface, by displaying marks in a range of possible colours. Following this discovery, Croesus, ruler of Lydia, was prompted to introduce the first standardised imperial gold coinage, which was called the stater, in 550 BC. The idea was immediately popular and other civilisations around the Mediterranean followed suit. Coinage had the effect of unifying and defining the parameters of the European civilised world, which had previously comprised fairly disparate populations. People from different cultures were able to place their collective trust in the quality of the metal being minted. This resulted in more flexible trade, which encouraged a flow of ideas and information as well as goods.

▶ p. 240 **500 BC**
GREAT MINDS

The Greeks are accredited with having invented the concept of creating a theory or paradigm and pursuing the evidence required to prove it true or false. This was the basis on which they worked and, combined with an environment which actively encouraged scholarly achievement, the Greek civilisation spawned a number of noted thinkers in the fifth century BC who made breakthroughs now regarded as seminal moments in the progress of science and technology. They include Aristotle, Pythagoras, Plato, Archimedes and Euclid, who between them made some astonishing discoveries in mathematics, geometry and physics, as well as expounding various ideas on the universe, atoms, logic and so on, which were to influence scientific thought for many centuries, even though later technology would eventually prove some of their notions to be incorrect.

▶ p. 249 **500 BC**
ROADS AND BRIDGES

To build and maintain an empire it was essential to be able to maintain communications between different regions and the central government. The Romans went to enormous lengths to construct an infrastructure of roads and bridges which could be relied upon to send troops and supplies to trouble spots as quickly as possible. Roman roads consisted of closely fitting stone slabs set on a foundation of hard core made from sand, gravel and masonry rubble, and lined with stone curbing. The land was surveyed to keep the road as level as possible and to find the straightest route from one location to the next. When it came to spanning rivers and valleys, Roman engineers solved the problem with expertly constructed bridges, viaducts and aqueducts.

▼ *The Romans built a huge network of roads throughout their empire.*

✳ FOOD   ✈ TRANSPORTATION   ✉ COMMUNICATION   ♨ HABITATION   ⚔ WARFARE

p. 232 ◀ **Triumphs & Tragedies** ▶ p. 243

250 BC
MAPPING THE ANCIENT WORLD

Greek geographer and mathematician Eratosthenes (*c.* 276–194 BC) was the first map-maker to apply a mechanism to maps which made them practicable for navigation. He included lines of longitude and latitude so that a grid was created, which meant that different locations were referenced in relation to one another according to real space. It was also possible to determine a position at sea or on land on the map according to the predictable movements of the stars throughout the year. Eratosthenes was even able to make a surprisingly accurate calculation of the world's circumference, at a time when most people thought the world was flat.

200 BC
ARCHES AND CONCRETE

Iron Age civilisations typically developed sophisticated methods for building in stone. Technology allowed for the fashioning of close-fitting stone components which were carefully positioned together to gradually assemble impressive monuments and temples, etc. The Romans excelled at building with stone, aided by two very useful inventions. The most obvious architectural invention was the arch. This simple concept was a major breakthrough, because up until then, the lintel had been used which had very limited uses due to its lack of strength. The arch was a dynamic shape which actually became more stable under compression. The second invention was concrete, using a lime-based cement and rubble, which meant being able to fill cavities with a self-containing material.

▲ *The Greek geographer and mathematician Eratosthenes, who made the first practical maps.*

200 BC
MATHS AND GEOMETRY

While the Greeks were pondering philosophically about science and technology, the Romans were far more concerned with putting theory into practice. Their technology, particularly related to engineering and architecture, benefited greatly from the application of geometrical and mathematical formulae, which optimised the use of materials and processes available to them. Mathematics was important for making accurate calculations of criteria such as angles, areas, quantities, dimensions and proportions. Geometry played an equally vital role in determining appropriate structural shapes for maximising strength against economy of materials, as well as imposing a general aesthetic discipline, including symmetry. Strict mathematical principles also governed the design of engines and machines used by the Romans for warfare and construction, to be sure that they performed their tasks properly and safely.

150 BC
GLASS BLOWING

Until the Iron Age, the uses for glass had been restricted to jewellery, ornaments and providing the vitreous powder for ceramic glazes, and so on. The raw material was easy to produce, by heating a mix of sand, lime and soda, which could be tinted by adding various chemicals, but forming it into useful shapes had been the problem. The simple process of blowing air into molten blobs of glass on the end of pipes provided the way forward for glass technology, because it enabled the manufacture of containers and vessels. Glass technology eventually caught up with previous developments in ceramics, and items of glassware became equally ornate and intricately crafted, involving layers with different colours and exquisite engraving.

✠ ▶ p. 242

AD 100s
GALEN AND MEDICINE

Anatomy and physiology became areas of detailed study for the Greeks, because they had a curiosity about how things work and the components of the body seemed to have clearly defined roles. Of course, this was essentially true when it came to muscles, bones and so on, but they had no appreciation of the scientific complexity with which life actually maintains itself, so they came up with other, less scientific explanations. The most noted physician and anatomist of the era, Galen (*c.* AD 129–200), asserted that there must be mysterious energies called humours which gave and maintained life in the body in the form of natural, vital and animal spirits. His idea dominated European medicine for some 1,500 years, until science eventually proved him wrong.

▲ *Claudius Galen's theories on humours that controlled the body formed the basis of medicine for hundreds of years.*

p. 235 ◀ **Distant Voices** ▶ p. 239

The good of men is the active exercise of his soul's faculties in conforming with excellence or virtue. Moreover, this activity must occupy a complete lifetime; for one swallow does not make a spring, nor does one fine day; and similarly, one day of a brief period of happiness does not make a man supremely blessed and happy. It has been well said that the good is that at which all things aim. Therefore, the good of man must be the end objective of the science of politics.

From *Nicomachean Ethics*, by Aristotle, philosophical scientist (384–322 BC)

Chaos Brings Invention
AD 500–1100s

ALTHOUGH, FOR SOCIOLOGICAL and economic reasons, the Middle Ages have been popularly thought of as a period of slow progress, there were plenty of important developments made relating to science and technology. Due to the relative chaos which reigned over European populations, progress in this region tended to be concerned with a need to find practical solutions for tangible problems, by way of making the struggle for survival that much easier. Elsewhere, notably in China and Arabia, continued philosophical and academic pursuits inevitably led to inventions and discoveries, which in turn, filtered through to Europe, using trade, warfare and invasion as their vehicle. As a result, technological and scientific developments maintained momentum throughout the Middle Ages despite the presence of inhibitory agents.

▶ p. 241 AD 500s
STIRRUP AND LONG-BOW

Warhorses were an important means for gaining an advantage over heavily armed opposing infantrymen. This advantage was quickly lost however, if the cavalryman was dislodged from his horse by losing his balance or being pulled off. The solution was the stirrup. This simple invention made all the difference, giving the rider a secure foothold whilst striking his lance or wielding his sword. The crossbow was a weapon favoured by continental troops because it fired bolts at high velocity and could penetrate chain-mail and armour. The Welsh long-bow had a decisive advantage over the crossbow. A well-trained archer could send eight arrows in the time it took to load and fire just one bolt, and with an equal thrust each time.

▶ p. 241 AD 500s
THE MOULDBOARD PLOUGH AND COLLAR

Although suitable for tilling light soils around the Mediterranean, where it originated, the scratch plough was not effective on the deep-rooted clay soils of northern and eastern Europe. The solution came when the concept of turning the soil, rather than opening it, was realised. The mouldboard plough still had the iron-share knife to cut through the soil, but instead of the scratch point behind, it featured a curved wooden board which sliced beneath the roots and flipped the sod upside down as it moved forward, creating a continuous furrow. The new plough changed the landscape, as forests were cleared to make way for larger fields, but not before the horse collar was introduced, enabling farmers to replace oxen with horses to double the traction power.

AD 500s
LATEEN RIG

Boats prior to the Middle Ages were cumbersome to direct and had to be rowed along unless the wind happened to be blowing in the correct direction. The lateen rig was a triangular sail attached to a pivoted boom. It arrived via the Arabs and revolutionised boat propulsion during the Middle Ages, because it did away with a need for oarsmen. It was now possible to sail into the wind, so boats could sail in any direction by tacking. Lateen sails tended to make a boat list, so it was necessary to introduce another new invention, the sternpost rudder. A single, centrally placed hinged rudder would remain deep in the water and could be controlled with enough leverage to maintain course under the strongest winds.

AD 751
PAPER MAKING

In AD 751, a Chinese team set up a factory for making paper in Samarkand, east of the Caspian sea. From there, the Arabs brought the technology to Spain. By the end of the eleventh century, water-powered paper mills were operating in Italy. It was old linen which supplied the principal raw material,

▼ *The rise of the cavalry in the sixth century led to more advanced methods of warfare.*

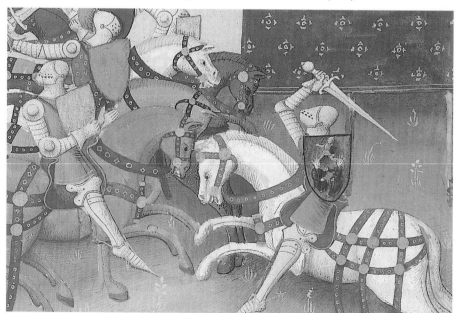

flax fibre, which was soaked and pulped, ready to be lifted in uniform layers with mesh screens made from drawn wires. The drained pulp was then placed between layers of cloth to form a pile, which was then squeezed under a press to remove as much water as possible before hanging each leaf to dry. Paper was far cheaper than alternatives and the net result was an increase in literacy as people became more interested in being able to read.

▲ *The astrolabe, a navigational device first developed by Ptolemy in the second century AD.*

✈ ▶ p. 243 **AD 800s**
NAVIGATION

By the ninth century the Arabs had perfected the astrolabe, a device first conceived by Ptolemy (*c.* AD 100–170), a scientist from Alexandria. It was a device by which the position of the stars could be used to determine a position at sea or on land, by knowing the date, and vice versa. It became the most important instrument for navigation for several hundred years, partly because sailors usually remained within familiar waters and only travelled during a season of congenial weather between May and September. By the late twelfth century the Arabs had knowledge of the lodestone compass, possibly invented in China. Suddenly it was possible to navigate without being able to see the sun or the stars, so confidence in navigating uncharted waters grew.

1000s
WEAVING AND SPINNING

In about the eleventh century two new machines arrived in Europe, which seem to have come via the Arabs from China. They transformed the textile industry in one fell swoop. The horizontal loom featured a mechanism for lifting alternate sets of warp threads and a shuttle for sending the weft thread quickly beneath with each weave. It also featured a device for packing the entire width of the cloth in one action. Using the new loom was far more efficient and therefore more productive than the old vertical technique, so it was just as well that the spinning wheel came along as part of the package, as it meant that yarn could be supplied in adequate quantities to supply the now burgeoning textile industry.

1088
A MEASURE OF TIME

Telling the time had always been an approximation. The sundial and hourglass had obvious limitations and the people who required a timepiece most of all, the Cistercian monks, needed to know the canonical hours at night so that they could rise from their beds and pray. The invention they came up with was the water clock. The mechanical apparatus was fed by a perpetual and regulated supply of water which meant that the clock could run reliably for hours. The water collected slowly in a tank containing a float which rose with the water level and moved a pointer up a vertical dial. In about 1088 the Chinese had invented a water-powered clock with a mechanical escapement and gear mechanism.

⊗ ▶ p. 243 **1100s**
WHAT A BLAST

In the 1100s Europeans at last mastered a technique for producing cast iron, some 1,500 years after the Chinese. The furnace was called a blast furnace in allusion to the blasts of air required to achieve a high enough temperature to melt the iron. Water and sometimes wind power were used to operate the bellows and for crushing up the iron ore to increase its surface area. Blast furnaces gradually grew in capacity

to meet the demand for the new cast iron, but two problems arose as a result. Charcoal began to run short in supply as trees in Europe were increasingly felled, and slag impurities prevented as much as 50 per cent of the iron from being run off for casting.

▲ *Advances in metalworking throughout the Middle Ages provided new and more sophisticated suits of armour.*

p. 237 ◀ **Distant Voices** ▶ p. 241

If a single sparrow should fly swiftly into the hall, and coming in at one door, instantly fly out through another. In that time in which it is indoors it is indeed not touched by the fury of winter, but yet, this smallest of space of calmness being passed almost in a flash, from winter going into winter again, it is lost to your eyes. Somewhat like this appears the life of man; but of what follows or what went before, we are utterly ignorant.

From *Ecclesiastical History of the English People*, by the Venerable Bede (AD 673–736)

Progressing Slowly but Surely
AD 765–1250s

ADVANCES IN SCIENCE and technology still managed to find their way during the uncertainty of the Middle Ages. Amidst the warfare, poverty and illness of the period, simple necessity promoted developments which might make life a little easier to survive. Improved methods for farming and producing goods for trade became vital as populations struggled to subsist in competitive and unstable economies all over Europe. Meanwhile, other nations prospered, primarily because of the trade routes between the Arabian and Asian populations. These regions, imbued with optimism and confidence, tended to nurture innovation in many areas of science and technology as a result of healthy competition and having the time to experiment due to surplus resourcing.

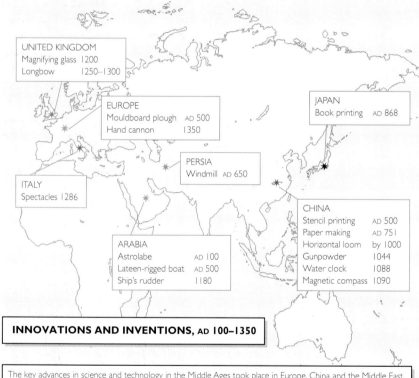

UNITED KINGDOM
Magnifying glass 1200
Longbow 1250–1300

EUROPE
Mouldboard plough AD 500
Hand cannon 1350

JAPAN
Book printing AD 868

ITALY
Spectacles 1286

PERSIA
Windmill AD 650

CHINA
Stencil printing AD 500
Paper making AD 751
Horizontal loom by 1000
Gunpowder 1044
Water clock 1088
Magnetic compass 1090

ARABIA
Astrolabe AD 100
Lateen-rigged boat AD 500
Ship's rudder 1180

INNOVATIONS AND INVENTIONS, AD 100–1350

The key advances in science and technology in the Middle Ages took place in Europe, China and the Middle East. Arab traders were instrumental in the exchange of knowledge between the Islamic world and China, as well as bringing innovations from the East into Europe.

▶ p. 241 **AD 765**
SCIENCE AND ASTRONOMY
When fanatical Christians, and then Muslims, sacked Alexandria at the beginning of the Middle Ages, a vast library of manuscripts was lost, which contained information about every manner of scientific discovery and theory. Incredibly, in AD 765 a Byzantine monastery in Persia was discovered to contain copies of many of the lost works. They were translated from Greek into Arabic in Baghdad and duplicate copies eventually found their way to Muslim-held Spain. By the mid-thirteenth century Spain had become Christian and the manuscripts were translated into Latin. Copies now found their way to all parts of Europe where they were the subject of intense interest, particularly because of the astronomical information which had a directly practical application with navigation.

1000s
MILL POWER
The principle for utilising water or wind power is the same, and both forms of energy were used to drive mills in the Middle Ages. The water or wind was used to turn a drive axle with a wheel or sails. The energy was thus made available in the form of rotary motion, which could in then be used to move machinery in various ways for performing the stages in industrial processes. By fixing cams and trip wheels to the turning axle, a reciprocating or switching motion could be conveyed to parts of machinery for operating devices such as hammers or presses. Similarly, cranks were used to create oscillating movements for pumping bellows and moving saws and knives to and fro.

1000s
MILL APPLICATIONS
Mining, iron smelting and textiles were the industries which benefited greatly from the use of mills as power stations. Mining was often complicated by flooding so the introduction of pumps and bucket conveyors, powered by water mills, made life much easier for miners. Powered capstans were also used to elevate and lower materials and equipment. Mill power was used to crush iron ore and pump the bellows essential for reaching smelting temperature in blast furnaces. Flax fibres were processed and cloth was fulled in water mills. These developments in the applications of mill power were largely responsible for the people of the Middle Ages improving their trade connections and their wealth.

1000s
THE CHINESE INFLUENCE

There are many inventions from the Middle Ages which have been attributed to the Chinese. They found their way to Europe via trade links with the Arabs, who used monsoon winds to traverse the Arabian Sea to India. The inventions of note include, paper, printing, silk, horizontal loom, spinning wheel, lateen sail, sternpost rudder, gunpowder, cast iron and clockwork mechanism. They all played a greater or lesser role in maintaining the momentum of technological progress in Europe where their potential seemed to be realised more acutely through the necessity for Europeans to make ends meet, while the Chinese cultural ethos was more relaxed and collectively oriented.

📖 ▶ p. 257 **1000s**
ROTATION FARMING

The improvements made to farming with the introduction of the mouldboard plough, resulted in surplus production. Nevertheless, people still suffered from malnutrition due to lack of food variety and productivity peaked off as the soils became exhausted of nutrients. The solution was the three-field rotation pattern. Fields were used for two years in succession and then left for a year. The first crop was used as a green fertiliser as well as a food source, and the second was grain, which tended to drain the goodness from the earth, which required being lain fallow for 12 months to recover. Fields were grouped in threes so that each was subject to a different phase in any one year.

👑 ▶ p. 242 **1000s**
GUNPOWDER AND SWORD

Sometime in the early eleventh century the Chinese chanced on the formula for gunpowder. The potential for gunpowder as a propellant was only fully realised when it got into the hands of warring Europeans looking for an edge over their enemies. It gained its familiar name when it was used in the first cannons, which were little more than upturned bells from which large stone

▲ *In the eleventh century, mills began to be used to harness natural energy.*

balls were fired. In the late thirteenth century, Mongols had made repeated attempts to invade Japan. Thanks to a curved sword made from expertly tempered steel, the Japanese won, while the Mongols fumbled with their own inferior weapons.

1098
THE HABIT OF DISCIPLINE

Safe behind the massive walls of their monasteries, the monks of the Middle Ages continued to embrace and take full advantage of new technologies and scientific discoveries. Their literacy, reputation and – most importantly – their neutrality (in a world of warfare), meant that information and ideas were frequently brought to them as a consequence of trade and by people seeking refuge within their walls. The Cistercian order (est. 1098) in particular, did very well from this situation and made enormous progress by establishing very successful iron and textile industries, as well as producing highly prized luxuries such as wines and spirits.

1250s
ARABIC SCIENCE

When Arabic copies of Classical manuscripts were translated into Latin in Spain from the mid-thirteenth century onwards, European scholars were given access to a wealth of information, but it was tempered by elements of superstition or spirituality. Astronomy, medicine and chemistry were accompanied by their alter

egos, astrology, spiritual healing and alchemy, all based on belief systems rather than science, as a way of explaining complex problems which seemed unfathomable by other means. The Arabs, however, put paid to these scientific nonsenses to a certain extent by introducing a logical and reasoned approach to scientific enquiry. A theory was postulated using a paradigm and controlled experiments were performed to look for evidence. If the results failed to confirm a theory, then the case was left open rather than seizing on fantastical notions.

p. 239 ◀ **Distant Voices** ▶ p. 243

Famine extended its ravages to such an extent that one feared that almost the whole human race would disappear. Climatic conditions were so unfavourable that the weather was never suited to sowing, and through the floods there was no way of harvesting. If by chance one could find food for sale, the seller could exact as excessive a price as he liked.... Raging hunger made men devour human flesh. Some persons travelling from one place to another to flee the famine and finding hospitality on the road, had their throats cut in the night and served to nourish those who welcomed them.

Glaber of Cluny, describing conditions in England (1032–34)

The Art of Thinking is Reborn
1364–1592

THERE WAS AN IMPORTANT and fundamental development following the Middle Ages, which helped with the generation of new ideas: correspondence. It became common practice for the prominent scientists and engineers of the era, to send copies of documents about new discoveries, inventions or unsolved problems, to others who may be interested or able to help, wherever in the world they may have lived. As a result, the most significant events in science and technology, speedily became known to the relevant people. This in turn, tended to inspire innovative thought and inquiry; perpetuating a chain of actions and reactions. Being informed of developments elsewhere, became a vital component in making breakthroughs, and it indicated the way forward, where collective effort or teamwork, would become increasingly responsible for providing the impetus behind progress.

▲ *The Swiss physician Paracelsus, the first scientist to refute Galen's theories of humours.*

▶ p. 257

1364
FIREARMS

As cannon became larger and more powerful, gunsmiths were reducing the size of other guns to supply the requirement for firearms. The earliest known firearms are dated 1364. Such weapons were hand-held cannons or arquebuses, which needed two people to operate them, with the heavy barrel supported by a tripod or a pole. Soon, such long arms had been refined to make the weapons more practicable since they could be operated by a single marksman, and light enough to carry in the hand. The musket was favoured for accuracy in the field, while short arms, such as carbines and pistols, were the weapons for close quarters. Firing mechanisms developed from the matchlock to the wheel-lock and flint-lock.

1500s
CANNON AND FORTRESS

Throughout the fifteenth century, cannon barrels developed, to become larger and more powerful. Bronze and brass cannon were dangerous, because they would sometimes explode, having developed fractures with repeated use. Iron was a better option, but casting such large objects was not possible at first, so wrought iron had to be used instead. Wrought iron strips were assembled length-

wise to form the barrel tube and then bound tightly together using contracted hoops, to resist the radial stresses of the blast. By the early sixteenth century, the cast iron cannon had become the state-of-the-art weapon. Such formidable weapons also meant rethinking the design of fortresses. The 'bastion principle' was introduced as a result. Bastion forts had angled walls to eliminate dead ground, so that enemies could always be shot at.

1500s
FINDING THE MARK

Developments with cannon and firearms, with the introduction of gunpowder, were rapid. Soon it became possible to attack from considerable distances. Reaching a distant target could no longer depend on trial and error, so a new science was introduced, called ballistics. Ballistics involved the use of geometry and physics in calculating the required trajectory of a projectile. The calculations were based on a number of key factors, so that the incline and azimuth (vertical and horizontal) angles of the gun barrel were correct. They are: direction, distance, elevation, wind inter-ference and velocity of projectile. A number of devices for making the necessary measure-ments were invented and developed during the sixteenth century.

▶ p. 245.

1500s
PARACELSUS AND VESALIUS

A Swiss physician named Paracelsus (1493–1541) was the first scientist to make a nonsense of Galen's ideas about humours controlling the body and mind. He refuted the theory on the basis that the results of observation and experimentation should override the preconceptions of traditional lore, and that the results of his own studies had suggested scientifically based processes at work. He consequently established the practice of seeking external agents as explanations for disease and infection, making important progress in this area, even introducing laudanum as a painkiller. By 1543 Vesalius, another famous physician of the period, had published his *On the Workings of the Human Body*, which opened the way for microscopic studies in the following centuries.

1500s
MAKING MEASUREMENTS

Edmund Gunter (1580–1626) made detailed mapping possible with the Gunter's

chain; a simple device comprising 22 yardsticks linked together. The chain was used to taking the dimensions of areas of land, which could then be used to calculate larger tracts and areas by triangulation. The theodolite, invented in 1551, was a military ballistics instrument which was used in conjunction with Gunter's chain for measuring the relative elevations of locations. By contrast, Pierre Vernier (*c.* 1580–1637) invented a device for taking very accurate measurements of small objects. In 1621 came the invention of the slide rule, which was used as a standard means for performing mechanically certain arithmetic calculations for several hundred years until the invention of the calculator.

⊛ ▶ p. 250 **1500s**
GLASS AND COAL
Glass for making windows was in increasingly high demand by the end of the sixteenth century in Europe. The enormous growth in the industry had led to a shortage of charcoal because forests had yielded all their timber. At the turn of the seventeenth century, things had become so desperate that alternatives were being sought. Coal was a familiar domestic fuel but too dirty for glass smelting,

▼ *Coal began to be used in glassmaking in the sixteenth century, as an alternative to charcoal.*

until a new underfed furnace was invented which kept the glass free from soot and smuts. This was hailed as such an important event that the use of charcoal for making glass was banned. Soon coal was the driving force behind copper, brass and lead production.

p. 237 ◀ **Triumphs & Tragedies** ▶ p. 244
1581
A REGULATED EXISTENCE
The concept of arriving for and leaving from work at certain times was just one example of the effect clocks had, particularly in towns and cities, where increased efficiency was the underlying motive for introducing clocks. By the middle of the fifteenth century, the steel spring had been introduced for powering clock mechanisms, instead of the weight drive. Smaller clocks could now be made, but springs lose their energy gradually as they unwind, so a device called a *fusee* had to be incorporated. It was a tapered or conical drive wheel which compensated for the loss of energy. In 1581 Galileo Galilei noticed the phenomenon of the pendulum. A hundred years later the pendulum would set a new benchmark in time-keeping accuracy.

✈ ▶ p. 251 **1592**
CARTOGRAPHY
While Mercator was developing ways to portray the lands and oceans of the world onto flat maps, others were directing their attentions toward detailed mapping of more familiar territory. In 1539 Richard Benese, issued a comprehensive volume of instruction on surveying and the use of associated tools and instruments. He had set a precedent which marked the way for modern cartography. In 1592 the first fully surveyed map of England was published by Saxton, showing villages, market towns and rivers. 1592 saw the first surveyed map to include the courses of all principal roads. By the mid-seventeenth century, precise distances were being added to maps, meticulously recorded using foot wheels. The first world atlas of maps became available in France in 1658.

p. 241 ◀ **Distant Voices** ▶ p. 245

It is well to observe the force and virtue and consequence of discoveries, and these are to be seen nowhere more conspicuously than in those three which were unknown to the ancients, and of which the origins, though recent, are obscure and inglorious; namely, printing, gunpowder, and the magnet (Mariners needle). For these three have changed the whole face and state of things throughout the world. Nature cannot be ordered about, except by obeying her.

Comments on Science of the Age, by Francis Bacon (1561–1626)

▼ *An early pendulum-driven clock.*

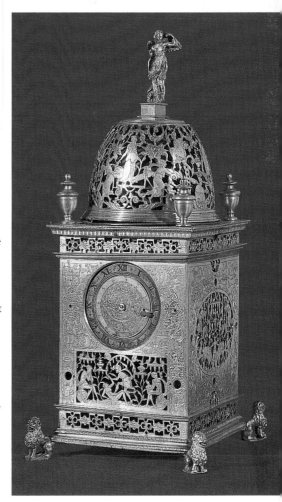

The First Great Names of Science
1450s–1643

THE PERIOD IMMEDIATELY following the Middle Ages saw significant changes in science and technology, because prominent thinkers introduced innovative approaches to scientific enquiry. They were also assisted in their work by the invention of finely crafted instruments, apparatus and gadgets – the paraphernalia that makes the scientist's tool-kit. The overall climate was one for rejoicing in new discoveries which offered a better quality of life, so science was becoming the secular replacement for religion; little wonder that the inquisitions gave scientists a hard time of it all over Europe. However, the invention of printing meant a wide and rapid circulation of scientific information which the religious leaders could do little about, so eventually the great thinkers of the age became venerated.

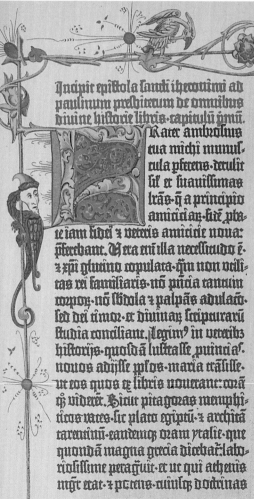

▲ *Page from the first printed Bible by Johann Gutenberg.*

✉ ▶ p. 250   **1450s**
MOVABLE TYPE PRINTING

The inventive genius of German goldsmith Johann Gutenberg (*c.* 1400–68) brought printing of age. During the late 1450s he devised a system for using individual type characters, cast in moulds from an alloy of lead, tin and antimony, which were interchangeable within a frame. It was quick and easy to assemble whole pages of type which could all be used time and time again for other jobs. As a result, printing took off rapidly. Within 30 years most of the western European countries had several printing works and, by the early sixteenth century, most classical manuscripts were made available in print. The first newspaper went on sale in Germany in 1609, where it had all started.

📖 ▶ p. 247   **1543**
COPERNICUS

The reinstatement of scientific enquiry led to an acceleration of progress, as it became the driving force in world culture. As a result, theories began to surface which contradicted popular opinion. Nicolas Copernicus (1473–1543), a Polish astronomer, was the first to suggest that Earth was not the centre of the universe. His observations showed Earth to be rotating around the sun, which he mistakenly took to be the centre of the

universe. Nonetheless, the solar system hypothesis had been born. Christian beliefs were dominant at this time, so any idea which refuted the notion that the universe was centred around humanity, was not well received. Copernicus' major treatise – *The Revolutions of the Celestial Spheres* – was not published until the year of his death.

p. 243 ◀ **Triumphs & Tragedies** ▶ p. 251
1564–1642
GALILEO GALILEI

Italian scientist Galileo Galilei was the founder of a new scientific method. By deducing laws to explain the results of observations and experiments, he reinforced Copernican theory and trod new ground of his own. He showed that different-sized objects with the same density would display the same constant acceleration when released to fall simultaneously, and that, allowing for friction, a body moving on a horizontal smooth surface will neither accelerate nor decelerate. These demonstrations angered contemporary orthodox scientists, because they seemed to contradict logical or instinctive preconceptions about physics. He also used the newly invented telescope to observe that the moon was not a perfect sphere, and that the planets revolved around the sun.

▼ *Polish astronomer Nicolas Copernicus began to investigate the possibility that the Earth was not the centre of the universe.*

▲ *The Flemish mapmaker Gerardus Mercator, who developed the cylindrical globe with lines of longitude and latitude.*

1571–1630
JOHANNES KEPLER

Johannes Kepler (1571–1630) was a German mathematician and astronomer who used mathematics to formulate three laws of planetary motion, which are still the basis for our understanding of the solar system. These state that: each planet has an elliptical path, with the sun centred at one of the points of focus; the plain swept out by the radius vector of a planet will always measure an equal area given the same length of time; and the square of a planetary year is proportional to the cube of its average distance from the sun. If certain measurements were known, then Kepler's laws could be used to deduce the missing data, and they also led to the discovery of new planets due to discrepancies in calculations.

1580
MAPPING THE GLOBE

The curvature of Earth's surface presented itself as a practical problem when it came to drawing maps onto flat pieces of paper. A Flemish map maker named Gerardus Mercator (1512–94), hit on the idea of inventing a cylindrical projection to partially solve the problem. Mercator's projection displayed the lines of longitude and latitude (parallels and meridians) as a grid, which became immediately popular because it meant that courses could be plotted in straight lines with a pair of compasses. All map projections distort reality, however they work, and the flaw in Mercator's was that exaggerations in width occurred moving away from he equator north and south, until the poles were stretched to equal the length of the equator itself.

1608
TELESCOPES AND CLOCKS

The telescope was invented in 1608 by Dutchman, Hans Lippershey (c. 1570–1619), as a military reconnaissance device. Galileo had adapted it within a year, and began to radically change the human view of their position in the universe. The fundamental effect that the telescope had was to call orthodox scientific beliefs into doubt and initiate a revolution in thinking. It is held also, that Galileo noticed the phenomenon by which a pendulum takes the same time to complete a swing, whatever the length of the arc. This led another Dutchman, Christian Huygens (1629–95), to develop the pendulum-regulated clock, which in turn enabled scientists to measure time accurately enough to verify Galileo's astronomical theories.

✠ ▶ p. 257 ## 1609
JANSSEN AND HARVEY

The telescope, which might have been called the 'macroscope', spawned an alter ego in the form of the first optical microscope in 1609. The invention of a Dutchman, Zacharias Janssen (1580–1638), the microscope transformed scientific knowledge of the way things are designed and function at a cellular level. Study by magnification initiated various new approaches to biology, chemistry, geology and so on. William Harvey (1578–1657), an English physician, discovered the circulation of blood thanks to the microscope. This led to more dynamic and progressive approaches to medicine, now that blood was understood to be the medium for transporting vital chemicals to parts of the body.

1643
TORRICELLI

It was found that water could only be sucked up a tube for some 10 m (32 ft), after which it would simply go no higher. This meant having to pump the water in stages to the surface. Evangelista Torricelli (1608–47), set to work on this problem in 1643. He reasoned that the air asserted a pressure which increased with depth. He filled a glass test tube with mercury and then inverted it with the open end submerged in a dish of mercury to keep an air seal. He found that the mercury column dropped to a length of about 76 cm (30.5 in) and stopped, with a small space above it, showing that the weight of air, or air pressure, was supporting the column of mercury, and that the space above must be a vacuum.

p. 243 ◀ **Distant Voices** ▶ p. 247

Knowing that it will afford you pleasure to learn that I have brought my undertaking to a successful termination, I have decided upon writing you this letter to acquaint you with all the events which have occurred in my voyage, and the discoveries which have resulted from it. Thirty-three days after my departure from Cadiz, I reached the Indian Ocean, where I discovered many islands, thickly peopled, of which I took possession without resistance, in the name of our most illustrious monarch.

Letter written to Ferdinand and Isabella of Spain by Christopher Columbus (1493)

The Scientific Revolution
1600s–1725

BY THE SEVENTEENTH CENTURY, science and technology were gathering the pace which would lead to the Industrial Revolution. Scientists had been freed of the shackles of fanatical Christianity, so they were allowed to get on with the job in hand, unhindered and actively encouraged by governments eager to secure dominance over other countries by keeping ahead. The work of scientists after the Middle Ages had done much to lay the foundations for continued discovery and invention, and the application of new knowledge was becoming increasingly ingenious. It seemed that any problem could be solved before long, and this gave scientists and engineers alike, the confidence to make bold steps forward, helping each other inadvertently by making new things possible with each stride.

1600s
RENÉ DESCARTES

René Descartes (1596–1650), was a French mathematician, who made significant discoveries in geometry and optics, a science which he effectively initiated and which was carried on by Newton. By way of explaining the structure of the universe, he opted for a solution which employed mathematical physics, called analytical (or co-ordinate) geometry. He invented Cartesian co-ordinates as a means for using algebraic expressions to define and manipulate geometric shapes which he saw as giving the universe its structure. His experiments with light were centred around the ways the paths of light rays can be altered with the use of lenses and mirrors to magnify, focus and divert images, a science called geometric optics.

1614
JOHN NAPIER'S LOGARITHMS

John Napier (1550–1617), was a Scottish mathematician who concerned himself with developing ways to help with calculation. He invented a mechanical calculating device called Napier's bones, in allusion to the noises it made while operating, but his major contribution to mathematics was the invention of logarithms. He published his logarithmic tables in 1614 and they became the standard means for making multiplication and division calculations until the advent of electronic calculators in the twentieth century. Each logarithm was the exponent or index of a number according to a specified base value. The user simply looked up the appropriate logarithm numbers and added them to make a multiplication, or subtracted them to make a division. The resulting number was then checked in the logarithmic tables to find its real value.

1682
STEAM ENTERS THE PICTURE

The first practical application of steam was in Papin's pressure cooker of 1682. He noticed and recorded the physical forces created by steam as it expanded and contracted, which inspired Thomas Savery to build a steam-operated mine pump between 1698 and 1702. By 1712, Thomas Newcomen (1663–1729) had invented the first 'proper' steam engine, featuring a piston and cylinder. James Watt (1736–1819) was repairing a Newcomen engine when he realised that the design could be improved by incorporating a separate condenser. This allowed the working cylinder to remain hot and increased the efficiency of the engine considerably. The Watt steam engine was such an improvement that it went on to power the Industrial Revolution.

1682
HALLEY'S COMET

English astronomer Edmund Halley (1656–1742) was primarily concerned with the movements of astronomical bodies over long periods of time. He compiled a catalogue of all the stars he could see with his telescope and referred to historical

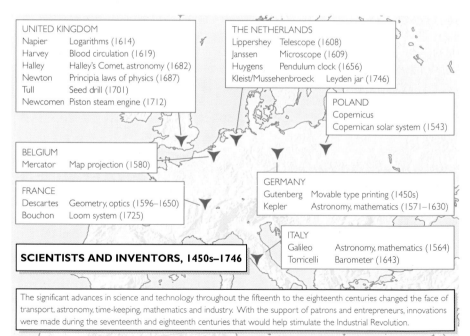

UNITED KINGDOM	
Napier	Logarithms (1614)
Harvey	Blood circulation (1619)
Halley	Halley's Comet, astronomy (1682)
Newton	Principia laws of physics (1687)
Tull	Seed drill (1701)
Newcomen	Piston steam engine (1712)

THE NETHERLANDS	
Lippershey	Telescope (1608)
Janssen	Microscope (1609)
Huygens	Pendulum clock (1656)
Kleist/Mussehenbroeck	Leyden jar (1746)

POLAND	
Copernicus	
	Copernican solar system (1543)

BELGIUM	
Mercator	Map projection (1580)

FRANCE	
Descartes	Geometry, optics (1596–1650)
Bouchon	Loom system (1725)

GERMANY	
Gutenberg	Movable type printing (1450s)
Kepler	Astronomy, mathematics (1571–1630)

ITALY	
Galileo	Astronomy, mathematics (1564)
Torricelli	Barometer (1643)

SCIENTISTS AND INVENTORS, 1450s–1746

The significant advances in science and technology throughout the fifteenth to the eighteenth centuries changed the face of transport, astronomy, time-keeping, mathematics and industry. With the support of patrons and entrepreneurs, innovations were made during the seventeenth and eighteenth centuries that would help stimulate the Industrial Revolution.

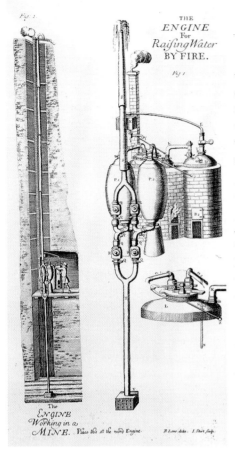

▲ *Thomas Savery's steam-operated mine-pump.*

records to trace the proper motion of stars. He also began work on calculating the astronomical unit, or AU, which is the average distance from Earth to the Sun during its orbit, and the unit by which astronomers measure the distances of other planets. Halley witnessed the comet named after him in 1682, which he correctly identified to be the same comet previously sighted in 1456, 1531 and 1607. He predicted its return in 1785, reasoning that it must follow a parabola; it duly did.

▶ p. 252

1685
NEWTON

Isaac Newton (1642–1727) was an English physicist and mathematician who laid down the foundation for the discipline of modern physics by demonstrating that scientific principles are of universal application. He discovered that white light is in fact made up of a spectrum of coloured light and that light seemed to behave as both waves and particles. He also described three laws of motion and defined the nature of weight, mass, force, acceleration and inertia. His most famous

work was done on gravity, which he expounded in 1685. His law of gravitation fundamentally altered the way scientists understood the universe and was seen to fit well with observations until Einstein came along in the early twentieth century.

▶ p. 255

1701
THE SEED DRILL

Jethro Tull (1674–1741) noticed that sowing seed by hand had various intrinsic problems which could be improved upon by inventing a mechanical device to do the job instead. He developed a seed drill around 1701 which inserted seed in rows beneath the soil as it moved across the field. It had several advantages over hand sowing, so it became popular straightaway. Labour costs were reduced, less seed was lost to birds, the seed was more evenly distributed over the field and planting in rows meant that the crop could be cultivated during the growing season, because it allowed for the access of workers without trampling the plants. With such obvious gains in efficiency and productivity, Tull's seed drill became a familiar sight overnight.

1706
ELECTRICITY ENTERS THE PICTURE

Various experiments were conducted over the early half of the eighteenth century to try to understand the nature of electricity. Francis Hauksbee, invented the Influence Machine in 1706; a glass globe which demonstrated the glow of air molecules by friction and the way electricity would attract various items of metal and threads. In 1745

▼ *Isaac Newton, considered to be the father of modern physics.*

the Leyden jar was developed by Kleist and Musschenbroek as a means for storing electricity , and by 1749 electricity saw its first practical application, firing mines and other explosives. In 1786, Luigi Galvani showed that electricity stimulated movements in frogs' legs by inventing the cathode and anode cycle, which led to fellow Italian, Alessandro Volta, building his Voltaic Pile battery, comprising layers of copper and zinc, in 1796.

1725
THE ORIGINS OF THE JACQUARD LOOM

Before the eighteenth century, weaving patterns into textiles had been a laborious process. A system of strings was used to lift the appropriate weft threads, following instructions in the form of grids on different coloured bits of paper. Automated organs had been made which worked by rotating a drum with pegs protruding from it. The pegs operated the appropriate pipe valves as they passed by. In 1725, Basile Bouchon, the son of an organ-maker realised that the punched paper, used for positioning the drum pegs, could be used in a similar way to operate a loom. His idea was improved upon in 1741 by Jacques de Vauchanson, but it remained unknown until 1800, when Joseph Marie Jacquard improved the mechanism by introducing card sections instead of a paper loop.

p. 245 ◀ **Distant Voices** ▶ p. 249

Whence is it that nature does nothing in vain: and whence arises all that order and beauty which we see in the world?.... Does it not appear from phenomena that there is a Being incorporeal [humans], living, intelligent, omnipresent, who in infinite space, as it were in his Sensory, sees things themselves intimately, and thoroughly perceives them, and comprehends them wholly.

From *Optics*, by Isaac Newton (1704)

A World About to Change
1600s–1787

THE SEVENTEENTH CENTURY onwards saw many people swallowed up into expanding industries. These industries tended to be very labour-intensive however, so large numbers of people were employed to keep everything running. In fact, whole communities started to depend on industry for their livelihood as populations became culturally assimilated. This meant that whole families might end up working for the same company and know no other way of making a living. By the second half of the eighteenth century technology was beginning to automate industrial processes, resulting in social changes. Resistance reared its head, but progress won as machinery run by steam power replaced thousands of people. They in turn, had to be satisfied with unskilled jobs as servants to the machines in industrial environments which were far less than congenial.

1600s
GLASS SHEET

A process was developed in the 1600s which enabled the production of sheet glass for the first time. This meant that large single-pane windows and mirrors could be made and a whole new industry rose up around the process. It involved pouring the required quantity of molten glass onto a casting table, where it was carefully spread and rolled out to an even thickness and allowed to cool slowly, to prevent it cracking. The development of larger, coal-fuelled, furnaces had proved essential for supplying molten glass in sufficient quantities for good-sized sheets. Techniques for making high-quality optical glass were improved in the 1700s allowing for considerable improvement in optical instruments such as the telescope and microscope, which required very precise and accurate lenses.

1600s
TINPLATE

Mild steel proved to be a very useful and versatile material. In sheet form it could be cut and folded to make all kinds of useful objects. It did however, have a drawback: its readiness to oxidise or rust. Rusting would eat away at the metal, weakening it and contaminating anything contained by the steel. In the late 1600s in Germany, a process was developed which would revolutionise the application of mild steel. It was the tinning of steel to make tinplate. The mild steel was rolled into thin sheets and given a thin coating of tin which protected the steel from corrosion. Tinplate would go on to provide the basic material for food canning.

1652
MAGNETISM

Otto von Guericke, (b. 1602), demonstrated how to create a vacuum with his famous horse experiment in 1652, showing that 16 animals could not pull two evacuated brass hemispheres apart until air was let in. He then made a sulphur ball which, when rubbed, would attain magnetic qualities, mysteriously glow in the dark, and make crackling noises. On reading Guericke's work, an American named Benjamin Franklin (1706–90) made a link between the crackling noises and lightning. He then demonstrated that lightning was an electrical force by capturing it down the wet line of a kite into a Leyden jar, and proposed for the first time that electricity flowed because of positive and negative charges.

1670
REFLECTING TELESCOPE

By the time Isaac Newton started his astronomical observations it was very difficult to make telescopes any larger. The design developed by Galileo was a refracting telescope, which required lenses to become bigger and bigger if a greater magnification of the stars was desired. It was Isaac Newton himself who first built the new type of telescope, called the reflector telescope. A concave mirror was used to focus the light collected, instead of a lens. Large mirrors were cheaper and easier to make, and they had the added advantage of being far less heavy and so easier to mount. Newton's first reflector telescope was made in 1670; it led to the construction of some very large instruments which effectively opened up the skies for closer scrutiny.

▼ *Early experiments with magnetism.*

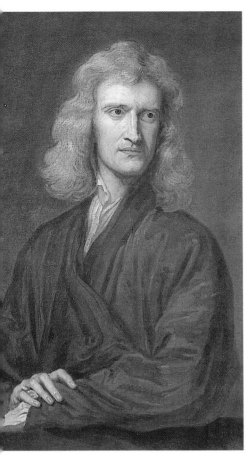

▲ *Isaac Newton – philosopher, mathematician, scientist and astronomer.*

1700s
PORCELAIN

A significant industry of the 1700s, was pottery. Thanks to the established use of coal instead of wood as a fuel, the bottle kilns used for firing the pottery could be made very large. The requirement for the mass-production of quality table- and kitchen-ware was more than matched by demand for bricks and tiles for building and industrial application. Porcelain originated in China many centuries before the eighteenth, but Europeans were now coming to grips with how to produce it. Kaolin, the fine white clay used to make porcelain was supplied to Europe from China until resources were found closer to home. One of the most famous makers of fine porcelain was Josiah Wedgwood (1730–95). His company specialised in making pieces which incorporated white reliefs on a coloured background.

▶ p. 266
1700s
DOMESTIC HYGIENE

Until the 1700s, although homes were supplied with mains water, the pipes were often made from wood. Water and wood made an ideal environment for the growth of germs which would inevitably find their way into the human body. Consequently disease, which was not understood to be caused by micro-organisms at this time, was an intrinsic part of the urban environment. Putting two and two together, the French introduced cast iron water pipes, mains, sewer and drain pipes during the eighteenth century which led to an immediate improvement to community health and prosperity. Other countries soon followed suit, although mild steel became the favoured metal, because it was not brittle like cast iron, which had led to problems with pipes cracking under strain and temperature changes.

1774
PRECISION ENGINEERING

The sextant was an instrument for calculating position by aligning the horizon with a specific star or the sun. When it had a telescope added to it in 1757 its potential for accuracy was improved considerably, but the divisions scribed on the scale (six for each degree) now needed to be marked far

▼ *Josiah Wedgwood, one of the pioneers of the fine porcelain industry.*

more accurately. The solution came in 1774 with the Ramsden dividing engine. It introduced the concept of using a tangent screw or worm gear for making minute adjustments. The worm gear was then incorporated into lathes and other machinery and hailed the beginning of mass production of precision-made components in all areas of industry. The concept of interchangeable parts was also born, because the new machinery would now make things to exactly the same specifications every time.

1787
NICHOLAS LEBLANC

As the West prepared for the Industrial Revolution, the scale of industrial processes began to grow. Just as furnaces were upgrading to produce huge quantities of metal and glass, other vital chemicals needed to be churned out in prodigious amounts. Nicholas Leblanc (1742–1806) introduced an industrial-scale method for producing washing soda or sodium carbonate, called the Leblanc process in 1787. Sulphuric acid and sodium chloride were heated to produce hydrogen chloride and sodium sulphate. The latter was then roasted with limestone and coal to make the sodium carbonate which could be dissolved in water and crystallised. The Leblanc process was a benchmark for chemical processing which influenced many others.

p. 247 ◀ **Distant Voices** ▶ p. 251

I am not yet so lost in lexicography as to forget that words are the daughters of earth, and that things are the sons of heaven. Language is only the instrument of science, and words are but the signs of ideas: I wish, however, that the instruments might be less apt to decay, and that signs might be permanent, like the things which they denote.

From *The Dictionary of the English Language*, by lexicographer Samuel Johnson (1755)

Seeing Into the Future
1700–1895

THE INDUSTRIAL REVOLUTION brought radical changes to science and technology. This was partly due to completely new phenomena such as electricity coming into the picture, but also because there was an enormous acceleration of technological progress. Competitive market forces were principally to blame for this, although it was inevitable also that new technologies would branch out and cause a proliferation of new ideas concerning their potential application. Technology had always followed an exponential path in this respect anyway, and the Industrial Revolution was both the cause and symptom of an explosion in innovative human thought and creativity.

1700s
TEXTILE AUTOMATION

As the Industrial Revolution gathered pace, one of the first large-scale industries to be affected by technological developments was the textiles industry. Many thousands toiled in textile mills where processes had traditionally been very labour-intensive. Then suddenly, engineers started introducing machines for automating processes, thus replacing a need for large workforces. The machines introduced included John Kay's (1704–64) Flying Shuttle in 1733, James Hargreaves's (d. 1778) Spinning Jenny in 1767, Richard Arkwright's (1732–92) Spinning Frame in 1769, Samuel Crompton's (1753–1827) Spinning Mule in 1779 and Edmund Cartwright's (1743–1823) Power Loom in 1785. Added to these, James Watt's steam engine was introduced as a power supply in 1769.

▼ *John Kay's 'Flying Shuttle', invented in 1733.*

✪ ▶ p. 259 **1792**
COAL REFINING AND APPLICATIONS

In 1792, William Murdock (1754–1839) invented an apparatus for processing coal by 'destructive distillation'. By heating coal to very high temperatures without the presence of air, it would break down into component fractions, including gases, liquids and solids, all of which proved to have useful applications during the Industrial Revolution. Coal gas was used for lighting and as a fuel for the first internal combustion engine. Coal tar was used for waterproofing canvas to make tarpaulin. Naphtha was used as a solvent for rubber in the Mackintosh process. Pitch, bitumen and asphalt were used for building road surfaces and other sealing applications, such as in roofing. Coke was the carbon content of the coal bereft of all the other hydrocarbons, and was used as a fuel industrially and domestically.

1820
RUBBER INDUSTRY

By the 1800s, rubber had found limited application but, in 1820, Thomas Hancock invented a machine called the 'pickle', which masticated rubber blocks into a workable material for moulding into shapes. He also experimented with combining rubber with cloth to elasticate it, and welding thin slices of rubber together to make waterproof sheets for hospitals. In partnership with Charles Macintosh (1766–1843) he marketed various versions of a waterproofed coat. The most important use of rubber was for making vulcanised rubber tyres for bicycles and automobiles. Charles Goodyear (1800–60) invented the vulcanising process, by heating rubber with sulphur in 1839. R. W. Thompson invented the first pneumatic tyre in 1845, although John Dunlop (1840–1921) gave pneumatic tyres their place in history in 1888.

✉ ▶ p. 253 **1826**
PHOTOGRAPHY AND CINEMATOGRAPHY

The first photographic image was taken in 1826 by Joseph Niepce (d. 1833) in France. His assistant, Louis Daguerre (1789–1851)

▲ *Louis Daguerre, the father of photography.*

made an improvement known as the Daguerreotype in 1839. The first photographic print-making process using the negative-positive method on paper, was invented in 1835 by William Henry Fox-Talbot, which meant being able to produce duplicate copies. The year 1861 saw the first colour photograph, taken by James Clerk-Maxwell (1831–79), and the invention of the single lens reflex camera, by Thomas Sutton. The first successful attempt at producing a moving photographic image was made by Louis Aimé Augustin Le Prince in New York 1885. The Lumière brothers of France had invented the first practical movie camera and projector by 1895.

✈ ▶ p. 252 **1835**
ASPHALT AND CONCRETE
In the late 1820s, John McAdam (1756–1836) devised a new process for making road surfaces using a mixture of heated bitumen or asphalt and stones, which would set by cooling to provide a smooth durable top layer. The first application was on a road in Vauxhall London, in 1835. His invention was dubbed 'Macadamising' and has remained a ubiquitous form of road surfacing ever since. Portland cement was invented by Joseph Aspdin, of Yorkshire in 1824. It proved to be a very versatile building material indeed. By 1867, steel-reinforced concrete had been patented by Joseph Monier of France. The first reinforced concrete building was erected in America in 1872 and the first concrete road was laid in 1892, also in America.

1859
OIL REFINING AND APPLICATIONS
The first oil rig was established in 1859 at Oil Creek, Pennsylvania by Edwin Drake. Petroleum was destructively distilled to extract the various hydrocarbon fractions comprising it. At first, only the oils were recognised as having any commercial value, but advances in technology during the latter half of the Industrial Revolution, found uses for everything petroleum had to offer. Acetone and ethanol were used as solvents; paraffins and fuel oil were used for oil lamps and heaters; petrol and diesel were used as fuels in internal combustion engines, along with lubricating oils; carbon black was used as a pigment for inks; and petroleum jelly found a medical use. Oil production increased dramatically towards the end of the 1800s as technology became geared around the applications of its chemical constituents.

1860
IRON AND STEEL
Various cast iron structures were being built in the late 1700s, with ever-increasing ambition on the part of engineers. Problems with the brittleness of cast-iron cannon, which had a tendency to fracture and explode, led Henry Bessemer (1813–98) to invent a process for converting pig iron (cast-iron blocks) into steel. The Bessemer process, introduced in 1860, removed excess carbon from the pig iron to produce a metal with slightly more carbon than wrought iron; this was steel. The iron was melted and then had air blown through it, which

▼ *Wilhelm Röntgen, whose experiments with radioactivity led to his discovery of x-rays.*

actually made it hotter, because the oxygen in the air burnt off the carbon held within the iron as carbon dioxide. Steel production increased from 0.5 to 28 million tonnes from 1870 to 1900, such was the demand.

p. 244 ◀ **Triumphs & Tragedies** ▶ p. 254
1895
RADIOACTIVITY AND X-RAYS
While experimenting with a cathode ray tube in 1895, which would later be developed into the television, Wilhelm Röntgen (1845–1923) noticed a new phenomenon. Invisible rays being emitted by the device, which he dubbed X-rays, were causing various chemicals to glow. He then discovered that the rays, although invisible to the eye, would affect a photographic plate. What was more, the X-rays had the ability to travel through some solid materials and not others, which meant that they could be used to see inside the body and look for breaks in bones. Röntgen's discovery made an enormous contribution to medical diagnosis, which had previously relied on a great deal of guesswork and painful manipulation of the patient.

p. 249 ◀ **Distant Voices** ▶ p. 253

I was excited by two motives to offer my assistance, which were love of you and love of a money-getting ingenious project. I presumed that your Engine would require money, very accurate workmanship, and extensive correspondence, to make it turn out to the best advantage; and that the best means of keeping up the reputation, and doing the invention justice, would be to keep the execution part of the hands of the multitude of empirical Engineers, who from ignorance, want of experience and want of necessary convenience, would be very liable to produce bad and inaccurate workmanship.

Letter to James Watt, from Matthew Boulton (1769)

Electricity Comes of Age
1810–1901

AFTER YEARS of experimentation with electricity and magnetism, the two were finally proven to be connected in the early 1800s. This breakthrough was one of the most important events in the history of science and technology. Being able to make and use electricity as a power source changed the lives of humans. Its application in domestic, civil and industrial environments became ubiquitous. Just about all human technological developments from that point involved electricity in one way or another, either in production processes or function and now, modern life would simply grind to a halt if electricity ceased to exist.

▸ p. 257 **1810**
ELECTRIC LIGHTING AND HEATING
The first application of electricity for lighting was in the arc-lamp, invented in 1810 by Humphry Davy (1778–1829). By 1835 the first experiments with incandescent lighting were being carried out by a Scot, James Bowman Lindsay. This involved producing an electrical glow by passing a current through a carbonised cotton thread inside an evacuated glass bulb. In 1878, both Thomas Edison (1847–1931) and Joseph Swan (1828–1914) were independently working on designs for commercially viable electric light bulbs. The first true filament bulb containing an inert gas, was marketed by Edison in 1880. The year 1889 saw the first commercially produced electric heater, designed and built by W. L. Burton and the first electric oven, which was installed in a Hotel in Switzerland.

1820
ELECTRIC MOTOR
In 1820 Hans Christian Oersted (1777–1851) inadvertently proved the connection between magnetism and electricity, by moving a compass needle to align itself with the flow of an electrical current. This led to Michael Faraday (1791–1867) making a prototype dynamo in 1821, by spinning a magnet inside a coil of copper wire, producing an electric current. He then tried a similar experiment to demonstrate that a reverse process would create a rotary motion; the first electric motor. Faraday's prototypes had shown the way to go even though they were not designed to have a functional value. By 1830 an American called Joseph Henry (1797–1878) had built the first electric motor capable of driving machinery.

▼ *Alexander Graham Bell, demonstrating the first telephone.*

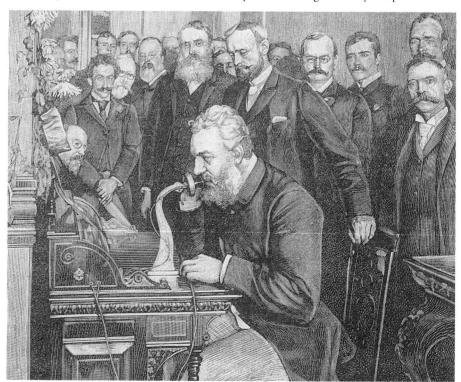

1830s
GENERATORS
As soon as electricity found a practical application it became necessary to produce the electricity required. Faraday's dynamo was the answer. It was an electricity generator in prototype, which simply needed to be improved upon like the electric motor. The dynamo's armature was rotated using another power source, usually steam, to convert the effort into electrical energy, which could be stored in cells or supplied directly to the electrically operated device. It was not until 1880 onwards that electricity was beginning to be supplied domestically. The first power stations for this purpose appeared in England, where the product became popular very quickly as an alternative to gas lighting. Domestic availability of electricity initiated a whole new industry producing electrical appliances for the home.

✈ ▸ p. 254 **1834**
ELECTRIC VEHICLES
Once the electric motor had been made into a working device in 1830, the way was opened for using electricity as a power

supply for moving vehicles. The very first use of an electric motor for supplying traction was in 1834, when American Thomas Davenport moved a vehicle around a short circular track. By 1844, Henry Pinkus had patented the use of the rails themselves for conveying the electrical current to the locomotive, and 1890 saw the first London tube line using Ernst Werner von Siemens's (1816–92) electric locomotives. The first electric car was a motorised carriage from 1839, made by a Robert Davidson, which traversed an indoor surface. The first road-going electric car appeared in 1874. It was a one horsepower, three-wheeler, built by David Salomons.

✉ ▶ p. 258

1835
TELEGRAPH TO TELEPHONE

It was the inventor of the Morse code, Samuel Morse (1791–1872), who built the first electric telegraph in 1835. Electrical pulses were sent along the telegraph wire using his code; at the receiving end, a series of clicks were heard which had to be deciphered by the operator. This was the first modern form of telecommunication. In 1876, Alexander Graham Bell (1847–1922) made an assemblage of components devised in part by other electrical scientists, which he had improved upon for practical application. He had invented the telephone by doing so, and was able to transmit the first ever spoken message via an electrical wire. Important in their own right, were the microphone and loudspeaker he had developed, which found plenty of other applications.

▼ *An early gramophone record player, an idea first demonstrated by Thomas Edison.*

1867
ELECTRIC CELLS AND BATTERIES

For certain applications it was necessary to store electricity for use, as opposed to having it supplied directly from a generator or dynamo. For this reason the electric cell was developed, which later became known as the battery, since the term 'battery' was used to describe a collection of cells. Various forms of electrolytic batteries were invented after the Voltaic Pile was first marketed in 1800. They each had different qualities which meant that they were suitable for a variety of applications. The first dry cell battery was invented in 1867 by Georges Leclanche (1839–82), and Ever Ready began manufacturing them in 1890. They had the advantage of being relatively compact and lightweight, as well as not having to be held upright.

1877
PHONOGRAPH TO RECORD PLAYER

Having invented the telephone, a way for recording audible messages was sought. In 1877, the famous American inventor, Thomas Edison (1847–1931), made the first demonstration of a machine which he called the phonograph. It comprised a tin foil cylinder held on a rotating drum. Sound was converted, via a vibrating needle touching the tinfoil, into a spiralling sound track or line on the surface. When the machine was operated in reverse, a needle would pick up the characteristics of the scribed line and an amplifier transmitted the sound. The gramophone record, a horizontal disc, as opposed to Edison's drum, was invented by Emile Berliner (1851–1929) in 1887. The first gramophone records were made from shellac, a hard resinous substance derived from the lac insect.

1888
RADIO

Both the telegraph and telephone relied on a physical wire link to be able to convey messages. This had obvious limitations, although the first submarine cable was successfully laid across the Atlantic in 1857.

▲ *Guglielmo Marconi, who made the first successful transmission with the use of radio waves.*

In 1888, a German scientist, Heinrich Hertz (1854–94), discovered the existence of radio waves. This led Guglielmo Marconi (1874–1937) to make the first successful transmission using radio waves, which he quickly demonstrated, could be sent without the receiver being visible. In 1901 the first radio transmission all the way across the Atlantic was made, and the domestic 'wireless' was only a few years away. Marconi's invention had an immediate impact on world communications, particularly, early on, with shipping, because the telegraph and telephone could not be used.

p. 251 ◀ **Distant Voices** ▶ p. 255

It was impossible in those days to foresee the eventual results of the attempts I was then making to evolve a method of communicating across space without the use of a material conductor, but even when I had only succeeded in sending and receiving signals across a few yards of space by means of Hertzian waves I had the vision of communicating by this means over unlimited distances.

Guglielmo Marconi (1874–1937), on the invention of radio

Getting Things Moving
1769–1850

MANY OF THE TECHNOLOGIES taken for granted in the modern world have their roots in the nineteenth century. As technology has progressed over the ages, processes have become more complex. This means that new concepts can take a while to develop, a lot of trial and error, and prototyping needs to be carried out. Some products keep on improving as new technologies and materials become available. The Industrial Revolution gave birth to many things which we still use. It can be surprising to learn how early on some inventions first saw the light of day, but if they hadn't appeared as early as they did, things would not have advanced as far as they have done now.

1769
WATT'S ENGINES

Having designed and made his first improved steam engine in 1769, James Watt (1736–1819) went on to introduce various improvements to his engines, to make them suitable for use in different situations. One of his first customers was John Wilkinson, who used the machine for blowing air into his blast furnace. In partnership with Matthew Boulton (1728–1809), Watt added sun and planet gears and centrifugal governors to the engines, making them more reliable and controllable. He also invented a double-acting engine which used steam to drive the piston in either direction along the cylinder alternately. In 1781 he came up with the compound engine, which uses the exhaust steam from one piston to drive another.

✈ ▶ p. 256   1770
STEAM VEHICLES

The first recorded example of a steam engine was a carriage designed for pulling field guns. Nicholas Cugnot designed and constructed it in 1770 in Paris. It was a cumbersome machine; difficult to steer and continually running short of steam. Richard Trevithick (1771–1833) was the first to build a steam-powered locomotive, which he ran on the Penydarren railway in Wales in 1804. By the 1820s, locomotives were becoming a familiar sight and the brittle cast-iron tracks had to be replaced with

wrought iron, as they became heavier and more powerful. The first steam-powered boat was made by Claude d'Abbans and took to the water in 1783. The engine, made by Frèrejean et Cie, rotated a large paddle wheel.

1800s
MASS-PRODUCTION TECHNIQUES

Textiles and ceramics saw huge expansion of their industries in the eighteenth century, bringing a shift of labour force, from working the fields to working in town factories. Henry Maudslay (1771–1831) introduced a new design of lathe in 1800, which revolutionised the production of precision parts. Maudsley went on to develop a production-line for mass producing ships'

blocks. By 1808, he had perfected five machines which needed only 10 unskilled men to operate them; turning out 130,000 blocks a year. American Elisha King Root, began developing mass-production techniques associated with farming. In 1832 he established a factory for producing steel axeheads, and in 1837, John Deere began mass-producing the steel ploughshare.

p. 251 ◀ **Triumphs & Tragedies** ▶ p. 260
1800s
GREAT ENGINEERS

The Industrial Revolution is often remembered for the great achievements of ambitious engineers of the period. Isambard Kingdom Brunel (1806–1859) is probably the most famous of these pioneers. He designed and built a series of iron-hulled steamships between 1837–58, and his bridges include the Clifton Suspension Bridge. Thomas Telford (1757–1834) was a big name in civil engineering. He built the Caledonian canal between 1802–23 and the Menai Road Suspension Bridge between 1819–26. He completed more than 1,200 bridges, churches and harbours. A tunnel-ling engineer called James Henry Greathead (1844–96), invented the Greathead Shield System, which was used for creating the London Underground 'Tube' system during the latter half of the nineteenth century.

▼ *The Clifton Suspension Bridge over the Severn Valley, designed by Isambard Kingdom Brunel.*

1831
TYPEWRITER AND SEWING MACHINE

The first sewing machine was invented in 1790 by Thomas Saint of London, but it was 1831 before the first commercially produced sewing machine appeared, produced by Bartholemy Thimmonier. The first sewing machine to feature an eye-pierced needle, pressing surfaces and double-threaded lock-stitch, was designed and produced by Englishman Elias Howe in 1846. This machine influenced the Isaac Singer (1811–75) design, brought out in 1851, which was the first domestic model. Like the sewing machine, the typewriter had an early start. In 1808, Peligrin Turri of Italy, made a writing machine for a blind friend, which stamped the type characters down onto the paper. The 'qwerty' keyboard was invented by Christopher Latham Sholes in 1872.

▲ *The Hollerith tabulating machine, first used in the US census of 1890.*

1835
CALCULATING MACHINES AND COMPUTERS

Several calculating machines were conceived before the Industrial Revolution. John Napier (1550–1617), Blaise Pascal (1623–62) and Gottfried Von Liebnitz all came up with devices. In the 1720s, a Basile Bouchon devised a machine which worked on the punched card principle of the Jacquard Loom. In 1835, Charles Babbage (1792–1871) conceived and drew plans for his computer named the 'Analytical Engine'. It was never made, but it embodied the principles on which modern digital computers are based. Herman Hollerith, an American, made a tabulating machine which was used to take a census in 1890. It introduced individual punched cards as a means for sending or blocking signals, which could then be counted to calculate the census results.

✳ ▶ p. 264

1841
FOOD PROCESSING AND CANNING

As early as the 1760s, Lazaro Spallanzani (1729–99), an Italian priest, had managed to contain sterilised food in sealed glass jars, by boiling it for an hour or so beforehand. Frenchman, Nicholas Appert, did the same in 1794, but neither of them had understood why it had worked, since knowledge of bacteria was yet to come. By 1812, Donkin and Hall had set up a commercial cannery in England, for supplying the army and navy forces, before making their produce available in shops in 1830. Their cans were made from tinplate, because it was easier to seal and was more durable than glass. The introduction of chlorine salts into the water for the heating process meant that higher temperatures could be achieved. This established an efficient mass production process in 1841.

1850
REFRIGERATION AND FREEZING

The 'compress and release' process was the secret to achieving refrigeration, accomplished in 1850. Alexander Catlin Twining used ether as a coolant and established a commercial refrigeration plant in Cleveland, Ohio, which was able to produce 850 kg (2,000 lb) of ice per day. In 1851, breweries in Germany and Australia had refrigeration systems, using ammonia as a coolant, set up by Von Linde and James Harrison respectively. After 1869, ships were able to transport frozen beef and other perishable produce to distant locations.

A cooling system first demonstrated by John Gorrie (d. 1855) in 1850, but claimed by Ferdinand Carre in 1858, proved to be more reliable on board ships, because it used air as a compression medium for cooling and thus was not prone to leaking.

p. 253 ◀ **Distant Voices** ▶ p. 257

We do not take him for either a rogue or a fool, but an enthusiast, blinded by the light of his own genius, an engineering knight-errant, always on the lookout for magic caves to be penetrated and enchanted rivers to be crossed, never so happy as when engaged 'regardless of cost' in conquering some, to ordinary mortals, impossibility.

Editor of *Railway Times*, on Isambard Kingdom Brunel (1845)

▼ *Italian microscopist and physiologist Spallanzi, investigating the digestive system of a chicken.*

Understanding and Ingenuity
1781–1867

UNDERSTANDING THE WAY things work had a significant effect on peoples' lives by the end of the Industrial Revolution. Scientists had managed to unravel many of the mysteries surrounding the origins of life, the causes of disease and the way that the very fabric of the universe worked. This inevitably led to both beneficial and detrimental changes in equal measure, as humans became instilled with a confidence borne on a wave of progress which told them that anything was possible. Scientific and technological advances were accelerating to a point where something new was being discovered or invented with each passing year, and innovative minds now had the ability to decide on what they wanted to achieve and go about it unhindered.

▲ *The British scientist Edward Jenner, performing the first inoculation against smallpox.*

▲ *Henry Cavendish, who discovered the chemical make-up of water by igniting hydrogen and air.*

1781
ATOMS AND ELEMENTS

Work on gases eventually led to the realisation that materials are either made up of pure elements or they are made from molecules which comprise combinations of elements. Henry Cavendish (1731–1810) discovered hydrogen by experimenting with acids on metals. In 1781, he ignited a mixture of hydrogen and air and was amazed to find that he had created water,

which was thought to be an element. By 1814, a Swedish chemist called Jöns Berzelius (1779–1848) had devised various symbols to represent elements and compounds, and he went on to publish tables indicating atomic and molecular weights of over 2,000 chemicals. The 'Periodic Table', based on atomic mass, was devised by Russian chemist, Dmitri Mendeleyev (1834–1907) in 1869.

✈ ▶ p. 262 **1783**
TAKING TO THE AIR

The year 1783 saw human flight for the first time. The Montgolfier brothers, Jacques and Joseph, designed a hot-air balloon, piloted by Pilatre de Rozier and Marquis d'Arlandes. A month later, the Charles brothers, flew their hydrogen balloon. By 1852, the first powered flying machines appeared. Henri Giffard used a 3-horsepower steam engine to propel a hydrogen filled airship. George Caley (1773–1857) made a variety of model gliders based on birds between 1804 and 1853, when he persuaded John Appleton, his coachman, to make the first manned aeroplane fight across a valley in Yorkshire. Various other aviators experimented with glider flight in the 1890s, including Otto Lillienthal, P. S. Pilcher, L. Hargreave, who flew the first monoplane, and French engineer, Octave Chanute.

1796
INOCULATION AND VACCINATION

In 1796, a British scientist called Edward Jenner (1749–1823) managed to inoculate a boy against smallpox by using cowpox vesicles. Cowpox was a related disease, which caused the boy to develop the antibodies in his system necessary to fight off smallpox. This became known as a non-variolous vaccination, and established the practice of using either dead or related pathogenic organisms for inoculating against serious diseases. Frenchman, Louis Pasteur (1822–95) was the person who actually proved the existence of bacteria and other pathogens, when he demonstrated that heat would halt the fermentation process in alcohol and milk by killing off the yeast micro-organisms. Pasteur developed and successfully used the first rabies vaccine in 1885, in Paris.

1800s
FARMING MACHINERY

The introduction of Tull's seed drill in the early 1700s was the first step in the mechanisation of farming during the Industrial Revolution. A threshing machine was built by Englishman, Thomas Wigful, in 1802 and, by the 1850s, the first combine harvesters, which cut and threshed, were being pulled by horses across Californian wheat fields. John Deere's steel ploughshare was introduced in 1837 and Richard Gatling developed a version using a steam engine for traction. The first multi-purpose steam traction engines saw service in 1857. They were eventually superseded by tractors, the first of which, with a petrol engine, was the 'Burger', built in Chicago from 1889. The tractor changed farming beyond recognition by replacing a need for traction animals and a significant pro-portion of farm labourers to boot.

1807
PERCUSSION IGNITION GUNS

In 1807, Alexander Forsyth (1768–1843) invented percussion ignition for firing projectiles from guns. Johannes Pauly (1766–1820) developed the idea and came up with the first breech loading gun, with centre-fire cartridges, in 1812. By 1835, gun makers Lefaucheux had introduced the pin-fire cartridge and Samuel Colt (1814–62) had invented his first revolver. So much more efficient were percussion-breech loading guns, that both European and American armies adopted them in the 1840s. Richard Gatling (1818–1903) perfected his rapid-fire machine gun in 1862, which was hand cranked and could fire up to 1,200 rounds per minute. This, along with exploding shells, which had been refined since their introduction in 1784 by Henry Shrapnel (1761–1842), changed the face of warfare.

1853
INTERNAL COMBUSTION ENGINES

The very first internal combustion engine was a 3-stroke gas-engine, by Eugenio Barsanti and Felice Matteucci of Florence in

1853. The four-stroke engine appeared in 1876, powered by gas and designed by Nikolaus Otto. The first engine to use petrol was made for propelling a cart by Austrian, Siegfried Marcus in 1870. By 1885 the first practicable petrol engine had been perfected by the teamwork of three engineers. They were Gottlieb Daimler (1834–1900), Karl Benz (1844–1929) and Wilhelm Maybach (1846–1929) who invented the carburettor. The principle of using compression ignition for an internal combustion engine was first explained by Herbert Akroyd (1864–1937) in 1890, and became the first working diesel engine in 1892, thanks to the work of German engineer, Rudolf Diesel (1858–1913).

▶ p. 260 **1859**
EVOLUTION AND INHERITANCE

Charles Darwin (1809–82) worked as a naturalist on board the HMS *Beagle*, between 1831–36. What he saw led to the development of his theory of evolution, but he spent many more years looking for tangible evidence. Alfred Russel Wallace (1823–1913) was 14 years younger than Darwin. He became a professional naturalist, making a living by collecting specimens of plants and animals to send back to Europe from South America and Southeast Asia. By 1858 he had arrived at the same idea of 'evolution by natural selection' as Darwin, and actually sent an outlining essay to Darwin because he was a well-respected naturalist at the time. When Darwin received the essay, he realised he had waited too long and published his famous work *On the Origin of Species* in 1859.

▶ p. 260 **1867**
ANAESTHETICS, ANTISEPTICS AND ANALGESICS

Once scientists began to understand that micro-organisms were responsible for infection and disease, a whole new approach to medicine and surgery was initiated. Joseph Lister (1827–1912) was the first surgeon to introduce an antiseptic, in 1867. He used a spray of carbolic acid (phenol), an extract from coal tar, to kill and inhibit

pathogens. By 1874, Abraham Groves (1847–1935), had introduced the practice of sterilising surgical instruments and wearing rubber gloves. Anaesthesia, although practised for centuries in the form of alcohol, became more of a science at this period. William Morton, an American dentist, coined the word 'anaesthesia' in 1846, when he adopted the use of rectified sulphuric ether. James Simpson introduced chloroform in 1847, and Karl Koller, a German, demonstrated the use of cocaine as a painkiller for the first time in 1884.

▲ *Joseph Lister, the first pioneer of antiseptics and anaesthetics in surgery.*

p. 255 ◀ **Distant Voices** ▶ p. 259

The number of inhabitants is about seven thousand; chiefly engaged in manufactures of linses [linen], worsted stockings woven and knit, and a course sort of woollen cloth called cottons. The carding and the frizzing mills, the rasping and cutting of log-wood by different machines are well worth seeing. The manufacturers employ great quantities of wool.

From *Observation on the Textiles Industry*, by Thomas Pennant (1771)

The Electronic Revolution
1900–55

THE PAST HUNDRED YEARS have seen some remarkable achievements in science and technology. So much so, that the ways people live their lives in 'modern' environments have altered beyond recognition. It is worth remembering though, that many of the things we now take for granted in our man-made habitats were developed around the turn of the twentieth century, or the technologies which have led to them were first being investigated at that time. Generally speaking, technologies became more complex as the twentieth century advanced, but the rate of progress carried on accelerating because of the fundamental mechanism by which newly discovered technologies provide the catalyst and impetus for yet newer developments.

1900s
ELECTRIC APPLIANCES

The introduction of domestic electricity supplies led to an inevitable vogue for electrical 'labour saving' devices for the home. There have been many and various appliances marketed, some of which have become ubiquitous components of the household; others have become obsolete or just didn't take off. The familiar inventions include: iron (1882); kettle (1891); toaster (1893); hair dryer and heater (1899); washing machine (1907); dishwasher (1914); mower (1916); clock (1918); blanket (1927); microwave oven (1947); watch (1957); calculator (1964); and personal organiser (1993). The fact that these devices are so often taken for granted is testament to their usefulness.

1904
VALVES AND TRANSISTORS

A major breakthrough in the development of complex machines run by electricity, came in the shape of the valve tube. It was a sealed glass tube containing a vacuum. Inside the vacuum were a cathode and anode which were able to create a one-way electrical current. This current could be turned on or off with the use of control electrodes, so the valve operated as a switch. The two-diode thermionic valve appeared in 1904 and the three-diode

amplification valve in 1906. Valves were commonly used until the advent of the transistor. The transistor is a semiconductor device with three or more terminals attached to electrode regions. The current between two of the electrodes is controlled by the others. It has the advantages of being smaller and being able to work on much lower voltage.

▼ *John Logie Baird, the man who first demonstrated monochromatic television.*

✉ ▶ p. 264

1926
TELEVISION

The principle which led to the invention of the television was discovered in 1873. It was discovered that selenium, a non-metallic element, was photo-conductive. This meant that electrons fired at it would illuminate the surface and that electrical impulses could therefore by made into images by illuminating dots with varying brightness. It was John Logie Baird who first demonstrated 'black and white' or monochromatic television, in 1926. Only two years later he was able to demonstrate full colour television. In 1908 Campbell Swinton suggested the use of a cathode ray tube as a transmitter and receiver for electrical information. By 1934 the cathode ray tube had been perfected and was adopted as the most suitable device for production televisions.

1930s
SYNTHETICS

Synthetic materials, collectively known as 'plastics', because they can be moulded or formed, have become ubiquitous and frequently used in place of other 'natural' materials. Most are polymeric structures: they have large molecules which are made up of many relatively simple repeated units. Plastics belong in two groups: thermosetting and thermomelting, the latter being recyclable by heating. The first plastics used were celluloid and Bakelite, but by the 1930s polymer plastics began to be developed. They include; polyethylene (polythene), polypropylene, polystyrene, polyester, polyamides (nylon), polyvinylchloride (p.v.c. or vinyl), acrylics, viscose (rayon), epoxies, acetates and polytetraflouroethene (PTFE). Their applications are many and various, for example, moulded components, synthetic fibres, sheeting, resins, adhesives, hardeners, plasticisers, non-stick coatings and so on.

1936
CIRCUIT BOARDS AND MICROPROCESSORS

In 1936 an Austrian named Paul Eisler, living in England, decided that it would be a good idea to incorporate the workings of his home-made radio onto a board. Having invented the circuit board he attempted for some years to sell the idea of printed circuit boards to electronics companies. Necessity in warfare eventually created a need for the rapid reproduction of electronic circuits, which were used to control the proximity fuses for the anti-aircraft shells. After the war the Americans embraced the printed circuit board, which revolutionised a burgeoning electronics industry. By the 1950s America was developing miniature circuit boards using silicon as a semiconductor. These became known as silicon chips, and could comprise many thousands of components all scaled down into a microprocessor.

▲ *Fibre optics were invented in 1955 as a method of carrying coded messages in the form of light pulses; they were first used as telephone cables.*

▲ *Synthetic materials, known as plastics, became popular in the 1930s.*

1945
MICROWAVES

Microwaves are beams of short-wave or high-frequency, electromagnetic radiation or infrared light. Percy LeBaron Spencer invented the first microwave oven in 1945. He discovered the potential of microwaves when they melted a chocolate bar in his pocket. Laser is an acronym for 'Light Amplification by Stimulated Emission of Radiation'. The first laser beam was produced by Theodore Maiman of California in 1960, using a ruby crystal to create a red path of light. Since then, many solids, liquids and gases have been used as laser materials and lasers have found many uses. Communication signalling, cutting, drilling and welding, satellite tracking, weaponry, medical and biological research and surgery have all benefited from laser technology.

1950s
SHAPING MODERN MATERIALS

The introduction of new materials, such as plastics, composites and sheet metals, meant that new ways had to be developed for cutting and shaping them into products. The simplest way to shape a component is to press it into shape: a two-part mould is pushed together under very high pressure, forcing the sheet to take up the desired shape. With plastics, a similar process called vacuum moulding is used to suck the thermo-melting sheet or tube into position. Plastics are often injection-moulded, using very accurate and complex moulding tools which make the desired shape when the plastics is squeezed inside, and then come apart to release the plastic product.

1955
FIBRE OPTICS AND SOLAR PANELS

An optical fibre is a strand of glass with a mirrored cladding, which can convey coded messages sent through it as light pulses. It was first demonstrated in 1955 by Narinder Kapany. The first fibre-optic telephone cables were finally put into service in America in 1977 by the General Telephone Company; one fibre could carry 24 simultaneous calls. By 1988 the first transatlantic cable had been laid; its six fibres could convey 40,000 simultaneous calls. Solar cells are made up of two layers of semiconductor material which create a photo-voltaic current between them when struck by sunlight radiation. The standard materials now used are N and P type silicon. A flow of electrons from P to N and then around a circuit, converts radiation into electricity.

p. 257 ◀ **Distant Voices** ▶ p. 261

The dynamism of discovery permeated not only material life within the scientific civilisation, but also its culture and its art. The scientific revolution was also an economic revolution, inescapable and profound in its human consequences throughout the world.

From *Comments on the Twentieth Century,* by David Thomson (1963)

High Technology is Born
1900–73

THE PROGRESS OF SCIENCE and technology throughout the twentieth century was tempered a great deal by a newly acquired and intimate understanding of the way things work around us. Scientists were able to fathom the depths of atomic, genetic and universal structure, and able to develop laws by which things seem to behave. With this kind of knowledge and advanced equipment to match, the twentieth century became a melting pot for progressive ideas and applications of materials and technologies. The underlying motive for this progress was always to improve the lives of people. Technology began for that very reason, and although some science is pursued out of human curiosity, it usually finds an application which is beneficial.

✠ ▶ p. 267 ### 1900s
MEDICAL SCANNING

Sound waves at frequencies inaudible to humans are used in the ultrasound scanner. The sound waves, emitted by the scanner, penetrate the tissue and bounce back in different ways according to the density and depth of tissue types. The returning waves are interpreted by the scanner in relation to those released and an image is assembled on a screen. The advantage of using sound waves is that they are a non-invasive and safe way of scanning. Use of X-rays has been developed in recent years to result in the CAT (Computerised Axial Tomography) scanner; a machine which uses X-rays to build up a stereoscopic image of the body by building up layer after layer of cross-sectional images with a scintillator.

▼ *Albert Einstein's theories of relativity proved the basis for many scientific discoveries during the twentieth century.*

p. 254 ◀ **Triumphs & Tragedies** ▶ p. 261
1905
EINSTEIN'S THEORIES

Albert Einstein (1879–1955) formulated theories about the nature and structure of the universe which totally transformed human understanding of the way things behave. In 1905 Einstein's *Special Theory of Relativity* was published. In it, he proposed various ideas on the subject of matter, light, space and time, not least that they are all interrelated, hence the name of the theory. He provided complex mathematical formulae to reinforce his ideas and went on to release his *General Theory of Relativity* in 1915 and *Unified Field Theory* in 1953. Einstein's work led to the developments in nuclear fusion and fission, and to Arthur Stanley Eddington (1882–1944) proposing, in 1933, that the universe was expanding from a central point of origin.

1921
THE BEGINNINGS OF MODERN DRUGS

Alexander Fleming (1881–1955) made a significant contribution to medicine by discovering penicillin, which came into use in 1941, in time to save the lives of many war wounded. This was the first of many antibiotics which have been developed since, and have changed the way people look at infection and illness. Another significant breakthrough came in the field of hormones in 1921 when Frederick Banting (1891–1941) and Charles Best (1899–1978) discovered the role of insulin in treating diabetes. Work on hormones has also progressed a long way since that time. Drugs in general, for treating illnesses and for anaesthetics, have seen a science built up around them over the twentieth century, as chemists and physicians have striven to perfect their work, aided by new technologies.

1932
ELECTROSCOPES

In 1932 astronomer Karl Jansky (1905–50) detected the presence of 'radio noise' coming from outer space. This led to the development of radio telescopes, with the realisation that radio waves, instead of light waves, could tell scientists a lot more about the universe. Radio waves have a much lower frequency than those of light, so a radio telescope is in the shape of a large dish, to catch enough information. The first scanning electron microscope (SEM) was developed by Max Knoll and Ernst Ruska between 1928–33. It worked by detecting electrons being bounced off the surface of objects being scanned, creating a visual image on a screen. It can magnify up to 200,000 times.

📖 ▶ p. 263 ### 1934
NUCLEAR TECHNOLOGY

Einstein had shown that matter is lost in the form of heat energy and radiation by nuclear reactions. Nuclear fission is the splitting apart of nuclei by neutrons in a chain reaction. It was first achieved in practice by an Italian

 FOOD    TRANSPORTATION    COMMUNICATION   HABITATION   WARFARE

▲ *Experiments in nuclear technology culminated in the atomic bomb, first tested in 1945; today nuclear energy has myriad different uses.*

scientist, Enrico Fermi, in 1934. Julius Robert Oppenheimer (1904–67) led the team which developed the first fission atomic bomb, tested in New Mexico in 1945. By 1952 a new type of weapon, the Hydrogen bomb had been tested. It was a fusion atomic bomb, which joined the nuclei of hydrogen atoms to make helium atoms and emit lots of heat, thus called a thermonuclear weapon. The first nuclear power station experiments were carries out by Fermi in 1942, and the first working reactor was set up in Russia in 1954.

p. 260 ◀ **Triumphs & Tragedies** ▶ p. 271

1940s
DNA UNRAVELLED

Gregor Mendel (1822–84) performed experiments to demonstrate how particulate inheritance is controlled by dominant and recessive genes. By the 1940s it was realised that genes must be components of DNA (deoxyribonucleic acid). In 1953 James Watson (b. 1928) and Francis Crick (b. 1916) announced their discovery that DNA must be a double helix, with connecting rungs like a twisting ladder. Each rung was a base pair of cytosine-guanine or adenine-thymine, thus forming a double binary code. A different code was thus carried by each gene comprising the DNA strand, and was used to control the production of amino acids in constructing proteins. What was more, the DNA could 'unzip' itself and attract the necessary chemicals to become two identical strands.

1950s
NANOTECHNOLOGY

The invention of the scanning tunnelling microscope (STM) led to a new technology being possible, nanotechnology. Using a process similar to that used in making microchips, the STM is used to etch or

▼ *A strand of DNA, showing a double helix.*

sculpt silicon into minute shapes, which are the components if tiny machines. They are so small that the STM is actually building them using single atoms or molecules. Tiny electric motors have been made which can rotate at several thousand revolutions per second, yet they are less than a tenth of a millimetre in size. The uses for such small machines and devices are potentially very varied. It has been suggested that nano-machines could be injected into the body to perform tasks such as fighting pathogens, delivering drugs or cleaning arteries.

1973
GENETIC MANIPULATION

After it was discovered how DNA and their genes work, scientists set about trying to alter the genes of species to achieve new characteristics. Gene splicing, the insertion of bits of new DNA into an existing DNA strand, was invented in 1973 by American scientists Stanley Cohen and Herbert Boyer. This enabled scientists to produce transgenic species. Transgenic, or genetically engineered, species can thus possess desired characteristics which make them economically more viable through resistance to disease and pests, higher yields and so on; or they may be used to produce valuable chemicals, drugs or hormones for medical use.

p. 259 ◀ **Distant Voices** ▶ p. 263

In effect, we have redefined the task of science to be the discovery of laws that will enable us to predict events up to the limits set by the uncertainty principle. The question remains, however: How or why were the laws and the initial state of the universe chosen?... If we find the answer to that, it would be the ultimate triumph of human reason – for then we would know the mind of God.

From *A Brief History of Time*, by Stephen Hawking (1988)

An Automated Life
1900–61

MACHINES HAVE BECOME an intrinsic part of human life. People use machines for assisting with, or performing, tasks on a daily basis in the modern environment. What were once termed traditional ways of doing things have been superseded by what can be described as a new tradition, because the machines we use are so essential to our existence, in fact, they have made many new ways of doing things possible. The world itself has become a smaller place in the context of our ability to communicate with other people and travel from one place to another. This has given rise to a description of the modern world as a 'global village'.

1900s
TURBINE POWER

The first turbine was invented by Benoit Fourneyron in 1827. It was driven by water and used to power a tinplate rolling mill. The first steam driven turbine, was made by Charles Parsons in 1884, and used for turning an electric dynamo. By the early 1900s, turbines had largely replaced windmill, water-mill and steam-engine power, because they were so much more efficient at converting energy into electricity, although they themselves were powered by water or steam. The steam-powered turbine is now the standard method for turning dynamos in power stations, whether the fuel is coal, oil, gas or nuclear energy. Likewise, hydroelectricity is generated by the force of dammed water pushing the blades of a water turbine.

1903
POWERED FLIGHT

The first manned powered flight came in 1903, when Orville Wright (1871–1948) took to the air in the *Flyer*, built by him and his brother Wilbur (1867–1912), and propelled by a petrol engine. By 1908, Louis Blèriot (1872–1936) had perfected his powered monoplane and established the standard layout for future aeroplanes. The Heinkel He 178, built by Hans von Ohain, was the first plane to use a turbo-jet engine in 1939, superseded by the gas-turbine jet engine, first fitted into the Gloster-Whittle E.28/29 in 1941, and invented by Frank Whittle (1907–96). Modified versions of the Whittle engine went on to become the standard power unit for military and commercial jet planes alike.

✈ 1908
CARS

At first, motor cars were very expensive to own, but by 1908, Henry Ford (1863–1947) had started producing his Model T. It was designed to be affordable by the lay-person and by 1927, 15 million had rolled out of his factories. In 1913, Ford had introduced the first conveyor belt assembly line and truly interchangeable parts, which revolutionised the car industry. After 1918 the motoring era took off; inspired by Ford, other car manufacturers followed suit. Petrol motor lorries and buses appeared in the 1890s but the diesel engine took over in the 1920s and 1930s. The Felix Wankel (1902–88) rotary petrol engine was first used in 1967, but the four-stroke cylinder engine has remained popular.

1913
CONVEYORS

Meat-processing factories in America had introduced conveyor cables for moving carcasses, by the 1890s. Henry Ford (1863–1947) introduced a conveyor to his assembly line for producing the Model T in 1913. After that, conveyors became accepted as part of the route to achieving optimum efficiency in all kinds of industries. Many kinds of conveyor have been developed, for handling unit and bulk materials, according to different process requirements. They include belt, roller, chain, bucket and carousel conveyors. Other conveyors have been invented for carrying people themselves. Escalators, elevators and moving walkways are all conveying machines designed for saving the effort of walking or climbing.

▼ *Louis Blériot made the first cross-Channel flight in his powered monoplane.*

✳ FOOD   ✈ TRANSPORTATION   ✉ COMMUNICATION   ⌂ HABITATION   ⚔ WARFARE

1935
RADAR AND SONAR

Radar, an acronym of Radio Direction and Ranging, was invented in 1935, as a way of locating enemy aircraft, by Robert Watson-Watt (1892–1973). It works by emitting radio waves at regular intervals, which bounce back if an object is within range. A receiver translated the returning radio waves into a visual location dot on a screen. Sonar is an acronym for Sound Navigation and Ranging. It works in a similar way to radar, except that it uses ultrasonic waves, because radio waves will not travel through water. Sonar serves the equivalent purpose to radar, but in a marine environment and was invented by Frenchman, Paul Langevin (1872–1946) in 1914 for detecting German U-Boats.

1957
SATELLITES AND PROBES

Satellites have been orbiting Earth since *Sputnik I* was launched by Russia in 1957. Many satellites are used to observe or scan the Earth for geological information, some are spy satellites, others track the weather, still more are there to make astronomical observations, such as the Hubble telescope, launched in 1990. Communications satellites receive and transmit information from one place to another on the Earth's surface, and are usually in geostationary orbits. The first probe was the Russian, *Luna 3*, which sent back pictures of the dark side of the moon in 1959. A number of probes have been sent on voyages of astronomical discovery since.

▼ *The Hubble telescope, launched in 1990, has provided much previously unknown astronomical information.*

▲ *The launch of the NASA space shuttle* Columbia.

1960s
WATER TRANSPORT

Like locomotives, boats and ships have changed little in essence, over the span of the twentieth century. The introduction of the diesel and petrol engine with the propeller shaft, has led though, to vast ships being constructed. The first supertanker was launched in Japan in 1964. Some tankers and ferries are so large that they have bow-thrusters and stabilisers to help them negotiate their passage through harbours. Submarines and hydroplanes appeared in the early 1900s and the first hydrofoil service began in 1953. Lift is created by the 'wing' which holds the boat hull out of the water and reduces drag. 1962 saw the hovercraft become a part of transport history. It had been invented in 1955 by Christopher Cockerel and developed over the next seven years.

1961
SPACE TRAVEL

The first human in space was Russian cosmonaut Yuri Gagarin (1934–68), who completed a single orbit of Earth aboard *Vostok I* in 1961. In June 1969 Neil Armstrong (b. 1930), accompanied by Edwin 'Buzz' Aldrin (b. 1930) and Michael Collins (b. 1930), were the first to land on the lunar surface in the *Apollo 11* module. The first re-usable space craft was the NASA Space Shuttle *Columbia*, first launched in 1981. The first permanently manned space station was Mir, established by the Russians in 1986. The experiences of cosmonauts and astronauts, having lived for long periods in space stations, have been carefully researched as part of the preparation for planned missions to Mars in the twenty-first century, which will take several months' travel.

p. 261 ◄ **Distant Voices** ► p. 265

It is a natural suggestion that the greater difficulty in elucidating the transcendental laws is due to the fact that we are no longer engaged in recovering from Nature, what we ourselves have put into nature, but are at last confronted with its own intrinsic system of government.

Arthur Eddington (1882–1944), on developments in modern physics

Computer Commuters
1883–1999

THE LAST DECADE of the twentieth century has seen a radical change in the routine by which people in modern environments live their lives. This is almost entirely due to computer technology. The processor is now a ubiquitous feature in the home and workplace, not to mention in many other places, such as shops. They do not literally have minds of their own – yet – but they can think well enough to remove the laborious nature of many tasks. An ability to communicate electronically has also had a significant impact on methods for getting jobs done. It is quite possible to work for people and yet never meet them, perhaps never even know what they look like or sound like.

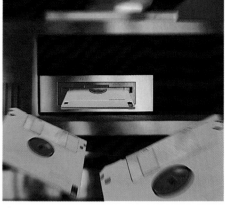

▲ *Computer technologies are constantly changing and improving; the first computers were the size of a room, today they can fit in the palm of the hand.*

1883
VENDING MACHINES

Percival Everitt was the father of vending; he introduced a coin-operated, automatic, postcard vending machine, to Mansion House Underground station, London, in

▼ *Percival Everitt introduced the first vending machine to a London Underground station in 1883.*

1883. By 1887, The Sweetmeat Automatic Delivery Co., launched by Everitt, was dispensing a wide range of goods from vending machines. They included cigarettes, eggs, quinine, biscuits, scent, condensed milk, sugar, and accident insurance! By the early twentieth century, there were coin-operated juke boxes, telephone kiosks, gas meters, ticket machines and so on. Developments in vending machines have branched out in various directions over the years. The first cash dispenser was unveiled in 1967 and there are machines which process as well as dispense products, such as photo-booths and hot-beverage machines, which are controlled by microprocessors.

1938
PHOTOCOPIER AND FAX

Before 1938, techniques for duplicating documents were messy and too slow to be economically viable. Chester Carlson managed to solve this problem by inventing the xerographic copier. It used an electromagnetic plate to attract powder ink to the paper, which was then fixed. The photocopier was born and it was a quick dry process. A small company bought the rights to produce and market the machine, which resulted in the Xerox Corporation. It was also the Xerox corporation who manufactured the first fax machine, in 1966, for office and domestic use via a telephone line. It was called the Magnafax Telecopier.

✉ ▶ p. 265 **1948**
COMPUTER PROCESSORS

The first computer with an electronic memory was built by Tom Kilburn and Fred Williams at Manchester University in 1948. The floppy disc was invented two years later, by Yoshiro Nakamats, for IBM. By 1969, computers had become fully transistorised and featured the micro-processor, invented by American, Edward Hoff. The personal and microcomputer were refined during the 1970s and the first laptop appeared in 1983. By the 1990s, computers had evolved in a few directions according to application, but the two dominant formats or languages were IBM and Apple Macintosh.

1950s
AUDIO-VISUALS

The first video recording and playing equipment was developed over the 1950s and in the Betamax format. In 1976 the VHS format was introduced, which subsequently dominated the market through more effective marketing as well as being a better product. The magnetic tape, used for video, was also adopted for storing audio and computer information. In fact it was first invented in 1929, and became the most ubiquitous medium for recording electronic information until the arrival of the compact disc in 1980, by Phillips. Music CDs, CD-Roms and CD mini-discs have largely taken over now.

1961
ROBOTICS

The first industrial application of a robotic machine came in 1961. General Motors, in America, introduced the Unimation 1900 into their car assembly line. By 1980, General Motors had a 'seeing' robot, which was able to select and separate components by recognition. Most robots are used to complete tasks which they can perform more effectively than humans, usually because the job is boring or laborious, which may lead to problems with concentration. Some robots though, have proved very useful in situations which are too dangerous or simply impossible for humans to function in. Good examples of these are bomb-disposal robots and roving robots used on the surface of other planets. There are also nano-robots being developed and sophisticated robotic prosthetics.

1980s
VIRTUAL REALITY

In 1958, an American scientist, William Higginbotham, invented the first video game. By 1971, a commercially produced model, known as 'Computer Space' was brought out by Nolan Bushnell, and 1983 saw the first home video game system, by Nintendo. Flight simulators were first developed in the 1980s, comprising an artificial cockpit mounted on hydraulically operated legs. The concept of virtual reality was thus born and developments have continued apace. Stereoscopic helmets, data body pads and data gloves have been experimented with in conjunction with hydraulically operated platforms, in attempts to fool the human mind into believing what it sees and feels. Applications for virtual reality, so far include: military and surgical training, architectural design and entertainments.

✉ 1984
E-MAIL AND INTERNET

The technical foundations for the internet and WWW (World Wide Web) were developed as a project, funded by the Advanced Research Project Agency (ARPA), to build an electrically run communications network able to withstand damage by nuclear warfare. Work began in 1984, and with extra funding from the United States' National Science Foundation, was able to link up American universities, via five super computing centres. By the early 1990s the service became cheap enough for domestic use. Sending and receiving e-mail (electronic mail), searching for information on the internet and advertising on web sites became a familiar feature of modern life by the end of the twentieth century.

1990s
PERIPHERAL DEVICES

The computer processor has become a multifunctional 'nerve centre' for information and communication technology, in both the workplace and home. There are various essential accessories, known as peripheral devices, which plug into the processor and enable the effective use of it. Peripherals include: monitors; keyboards; scanners; printers; mice; modems; microphones; videophones; speakers; floppy disc and CD ROM units. Together with the processor, the peripherals make up the ICT (Information and Communication Technology) kit, which can be assembled according to the specific requirements of the individual user. The memory size of the processor can be increased by the insertion of extra silicon chips.

p. 263 ◀ **Distant Voices** ▶ p. 267

History is more or less bunk. It is tradition. We do not want tradition. We want to live in the present and the only history that is worth a tinker's damn is the history we make today. What we call evil is simply ignorance bumping its head in the dark.

Industrialist Henry Ford (1863–1947), responding to trade unionists

▼ *The computer processor became a household item in the last decades of the twentieth century.*

The Variety of Technology
1900–2000

JUST AS THERE are specific scientific and technological features which will be remembered as the most significant developments of the twentieth century, there are lots of other inventions and applications of technology which have made significant changes to the lives of the people living through that era. They may be less ground-breaking in terms of historical progress but they are commonplace in our lives because we have decided that we want them to be available to us on a daily basis. More importantly, they are often components of our working and living environment, which enable us to function more effectively by making our routine easier and more comfortable, usually without us sparing a thought for their significance or importance.

1900s
PNEUMATICS AND HYDRAULICS

Modern uses for pneumatics include: pneumatic tyres, compressor applications, some aerosols, aqua lungs, vacuum forming and vacuum cleaning. Liquids cannot be compressed like gases, but they can be pressurised, so they can be used to exert high pressures in machinery. The first hydraulically operated machine was a press, made by Joseph Bramah (1748–1814) in 1795. The use of a small piston feeding a larger one, results in a gain in power measured against a loss in movement. As well as machinery, other modern applications for hydraulics are seen in vehicle braking systems, jacks and suspension units, which actually use fluid to dampen sudden movements.

1900s
PUMPS

Pumps are used as vital components in all kinds of modern equipment for moving liquids and gases. They fall into two main groups: reciprocating and rotary. Reciprocating pumps use a chamber, which expands and contracts, to produce a pumping action. Some use a piston, which moves up and down a cylinder, drawing the medium in and out using valves. Others use a diaphragm membrane which flexes back and forth. Rotary pumps all involve

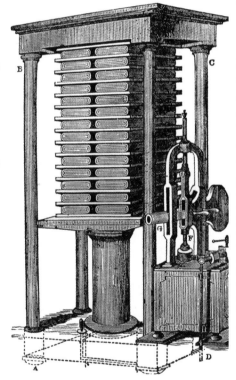

▲ *Joseph Bramah's hydraulically operated press.*

rotating components to create the flow required. Gear pumps are often used to pump oil in engines. Rotary vane pumps are used in petrol stations. Centrifugal pumps are frequently used for water. The peristaltic pump was developed for use in dialysis machines, where the circulating bodily fluids must remain uncontaminated.

▶ p. 267

1900s
GADGETS

There have been many useful gadgets introduced over the twentieth century, which are not technologically significant, but nonetheless are important for our daily routine in the modern environment. They include: safety razor (1901); lipstick (1915); electric razor (1931); aerosol canister (1941); ball point pen (1944); disposable pen (1953); quartz watch (1960); electric toothbrush (1961); tab opening drink can (1962); colour polaroid camera (1963); digital watch (1971); disposable lighter (1973); disposable razor (1974); disposable camera (1986). The use-once-and-throw-away philosophy is indicative of the ethos of modern society, where new is perceived to be good and old bad.

1910
MODERN LIGHTING

Neon lights were first used in 1910 as part of an advertising sign at the Paris Motor Show. The first successful fluorescent strip or tube lighting was made available in 1938, by General Electrics Co., America. Some fluorescent bulbs work by heating sodium vapour or neon gas until the atoms emit a glow of light. Others electrify mercury vapour, which gives off invisible ultra-violet light. This is then converted into visible light when it strikes a phosphor coating on the inside of the glass. Fluorescent light is produced more efficiently than filament light, and the bulbs last longer, because they do not produce destructive levels of heat. Tungsten filament lights are often used when very bright light is required, such as illuminating sports grounds or film sets.

1926
ROCKETS AND MISSILES

The first liquid fuel rocket was fired in 1926, by Robert H. Goddard, in America. A German named Wernher von Braun, developed the principle during the 1930s and made the V2 liquid fuel rocket used by the Nazis, between 1943–45. After the Second World War, he travelled to America, where his work led to the series of Saturn rockets which launched the Apollo missions

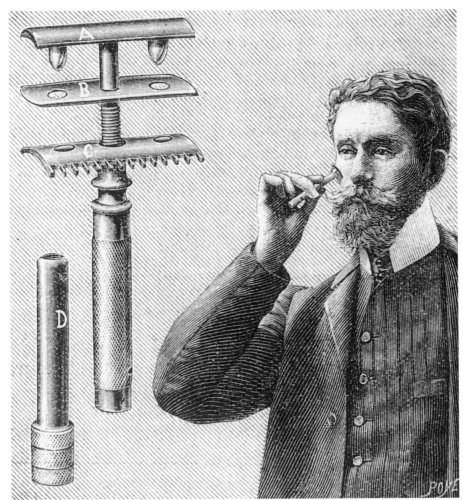

▲ *Illustration showing the first Gillette safety razor, with disposable blade.*

in 1967 and heart surgery has come on in leaps and bounds since then. Progress with prosthesis and osteoplasty have had a huge effect on the welfare of patients. Likewise, brain surgery and techniques for removing cancers have received plenty of attention, especially in the latter part of twentieth century. These have been improved with the aid of very complex computer-controlled machinery, which can support life while surgical procedures are being carried out.

2000
HEATING AND INSULATION

Producing and conserving warmth, have become issues for concern at the end of the twentieth century. Central heating systems which circulate hot water around buildings via radiators, have become a familiar domestic feature, which has meant that people have become more used to living in warm environments and consume more energy as a result. For this reason, the watchword has become 'efficiency', and methods of insulating buildings have become important. Glass wool roofing and wall insulation along with double glazing, have become standard requirements for the modern building. Alternative power sources are also being sought, as sustainable resources will eventually supersede traditional finite sources – the fossil fuels such as coal, oil, gas. Solar-, aero- and hydro-electricity will inevitably take their place.

between 1961–72. Space rockets have since been superseded by Space shuttles, and there are current developments using laser technology as the propellant force. Use of both liquid and solid fuel rockets has carried on evolving in the realm of weaponry. Some very sophisticated missiles with guidance systems have become the state-of-the-art weapons in recent years.

1950s
DIGITAL CODING

The term digital means to be made up of numbers, as digital information is indeed a numerical code. The numbers used are usually binary, which means just two numbers which run in sequences. The numbers 1 and 0 are used, representing 'on and off' in effect. Different sequences comprise each piece of data, which is deciphered using a

microprocessor within the machine using the digital information. Digital has become the prime means for the coding, storage, transmission, processing and reconstructing of information. It was adopted readily by industries concerned with computer, audio and visual information because it offered the advantage of virtually eliminating any degradation or distortion of signals, during transmission, storage, processing and so on.

1958–2000
MODERN SURGERY

There have been significant advances in surgical technology and techniques over the twentieth century. The introduction of the endoscope in 1958, the invention of Basil Hischowitz, has led to developments in keyhole surgery, assisted by lasers. Christian Barnard performed the first heart transplant

p. 265 ◀ **Distant Voices** ▶ p. 271

However, it is my judgement in these things that when you see something that is technically sweet you go ahead and do it and you argue what to do about it only after you have had your technical success. This is the way it was with the atomic bomb. I do not think anybody opposed making it; there were some debates about what to do with it after it was made.

J. Robert Oppenheimer (1904–67), on the development of nuclear technology

Religions, Belief and Thought

WE TAKE FOR GRANTED today the great diversity of human ideas, but the history of thought – of religious, philosophical and political ideas – has been a slow and painful one. Throughout most of history, in most nations, merely expressing a new idea was likely to result in death by torture. The fate of Jesus was typical. Many of the greatest theologians and teachers were denounced in their time as heretics. Even at the height of democracy and freedom of thought in ancient Greece, Socrates was put to death for his teachings, and in more recent times political thinkers such as Jean Jacques Rousseau, Karl Marx and Peter Kropotkin have spent much of their lives in exile. Whenever an oppressor has sought to take control of a country they have imprisoned the intellectuals and burned the libraries. Despite this oppression, or indeed because of it, our modern views on spiritual and political freedom, on reason, justice, democracy and human rights can be traced to these same thinkers.

KEY THEMES

- 📖 SCRIPTURES
- ✝ SAINTS
- ✎ SCHOOLS
- ✳ REVIVERS
- ⦁➤ PHILOSOPHERS
- ▦ THEORIES
- ✴ SCHOLARS
- ✿ PROPHESIES
- ✚ FOUNDERS
- ✺ MYSTICS

KEY EVENTS

1 500 BC
THE SPIRITUAL REVOLT

The fifth century BC was a time of spiritual revolt against the established priesthoods across the world. In India, the Buddha challenged the Brahmins and promoted meditation and monasticism for all castes of society. In China, the founders of Taoism challenged traditional court rituals and Confucian teachings. In Israel, the prophet Isaiah denounced the established powers and called for a spiritual renewal.

2 500 BC
THE BIRTH OF REASON

Greek thought, from around 500 BC onwards, was quite different from anything that had preceded it. For the Greeks, truth did not have to be inherited, because people had within themselves the capacity for reason and for the direct apprehension of truth. Plato and Aristotle, by developing Socrates' method and theory of logical debate, created the foundation for modern philosophy.

3 1150
THE RISE OF THEOLOGY

Western thought has two roots – the Judeo-Christian religion and the Greek philosophy of Plato and Aristotle. It was through the Arabic philosopher Averroës that these two were united and through St Thomas Aquinas that this integrated theory was turned into a Christian theology. The theology of the medieval scholastics was, for many centuries, the only view of the world to be tolerated.

4 1600s
THE BIRTH OF MODERN SCIENCE

Francis Bacon (1561–1626) and René Descartes (1596–1650) are generally seen as the founders of modern science. Bacon stated that science should be about the collection and organisation of observed facts so that general principles could be derived from them. Descartes argued that all matter ultimately consisted of measurable particles and that all we need to do is to measure how these particles behave. All other properties, such as colour and texture are unreal or can be reduced to the basic quantities of size and shape.

5 1748
THE METHODISTS

John Wesley was the founder of the Methodist movement, an offshoot of the Church of England. The name derives from the methodical approach he derived from the Bible for developing personal devotion. Wesley promoted his approach through outdoor sermons across Britain, to which he dedicated 12 years of his life. The movement was reinforced by a profuse production of hymns written by John's brother, Charles.

6 1750
THE POLITICAL RESPONSE

The oppressiveness of factory work led workers to unite to protect themselves and to press for better conditions. Unions gave workers the power to negotiate with their bosses and, at first, these groups were ruthlessly suppressed. The vision of a new society run by, and for, the workers led to the French Revolution and inspired the American Revolution.

7 1800s
THE REDISCOVERY OF NATURE

Analytical science and the Industrial Revolution created a world in which nature was seen as nothing but bits of matter that could be used as raw materials for human profit. The growth of industry led to the destruction of nature and to human suffering. There were many responses to this situation. Wordsworth and the Romantics, Thoreau and the American Transcendentalists, and John Muir advocated spiritual communion with nature and campaigned for simple living and conservation.

8 1900s
THE DISCOVERY OF THE UNCONSCIOUS

The twentieth century saw the rise of psychology – a discipline that has come in for much criticism from philosophers such as Karl Popper, as most of its theories cannot be proven and because the few testable theories have not performed well. The lack of evidence in psychology has also been criticised – Freud reduces all problems to sex, Adler to the will to power and Skinner to past programming – models which contradict one another.

TIMELINE

1900 BC		Abraham and the Promised Land
1500 BC		Hindu *Vedas* written
900 BC		Beginnings of Orphism
850 BC		Homer's *Iliad* and *Odyssey*
700 BC		Classical Hinduism and the *Upanishads*
586 BC		The Pali Scriptures and the Mahayana Tradition
551 BC		Confucius and the Perfect Order of Heaven
530 BC		Pythagoras
①	**500 BC**	Spiritual revolt in the East
②	**500 BC**	Birth of Reason in Ancient Greece
371 BC		Mencius (Meng Tzu)
300 BC		*Tao Te Ching*
179 BC		Tung Chung Shu integrates Confucian thought
7 BC		Birth of Christ
AD 70		Christians flee to Syria, rise of the Evangelists
AD 100		Adoption of Confucianism by the Han dynasty
AD 200s		Plotinus establishes neo-Platonism
AD 500		Rise of Chan and Zen influences
AD 500		T'ien Tai integrates Buddhism into his ideas
AD 570		Birth of the Prophet Muhammad
AD 618		First Taoist monasteries
AD 700		Rise of Tibetan Buddhism
AD 960		Neo-Confucianism becomes state religion of the Sung dynasty
1096		Crusades begin
③	**1150**	Ibn Rushd (Averroës) and the rise of theology
1225		St Thomas Aquinas
1485		Lord Chaitanya and Hare Krishna
1517		Martin Luther's protest against Catholic corruption
1572		St Bartholomew's Day Massacre
④	**1600s**	Era of Bacon and Descartes
⑤	**1748**	John Wesley founds the Methodist Church
⑥	**1776**	Adam Smith publishes *The Wealth of Nations*
1844		Joseph Smith establishes the Mormon Church
1848		Karl Marx writes the *Communist Manifesto* and *Das Kapital*
1856		Sigmund Freud's theories
⑦	**1859**	Theories of Evolution developed by Darwin and Wallace
1869		Gandhi campaigns against Apartheid in India
1883		William Morris creates the Socialist League
⑧	**1900s**	The discovery of the unconcious and rise of psychology
1922		Wittgenstein explores the nature and limits of language
1927		Martin Heidegger develops theories of Existentialism
1943		John-Paul Sartre publishes *Age of Reason*
1949		George Orwell's *1984*
1958		Weber's *The Protestant Work Ethic and the Spirit of Capitalism*
1961		Michael Foucault writes *Madness and Civilisation*
1976		Genetic Determinism outlined by Dawkins in *The Selfish Gene*
1979		James Lovelock and the Gaia Hypothesis
1980		The resurgence of Islam

Hinduism
2000 BC–AD 1485

HINDUISM TEACHES that we are not simply our bodies, but are immortal souls (Atman) and that these are of the same substance as God (Brahman). Souls are reborn in new bodies after each old one dies and, according to the law of Karma, people's thoughts, words and deeds determine the nature of their future lives. One who lives perfectly will not be reborn at all but will be liberated from the material world and reunited with Brahman. Some Hindus believe that all souls are already part of Brahman and that our suffering is only an illusion. These people therefore seek liberation from delusion through study and insight meditation (*jnana* yoga). Other Hindus believe we have really separated from God, but that we will be reunited if we express love of God (*bhakti* yoga) or do good deeds (*karma* yoga).

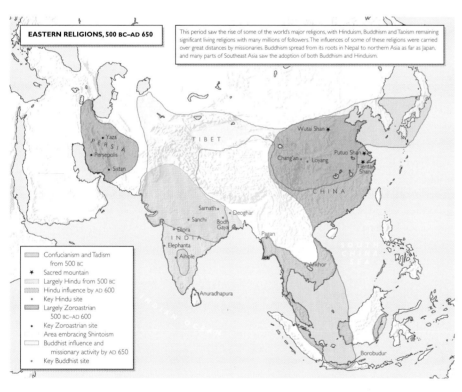

EASTERN RELIGIONS, 500 BC–AD 650

This period saw the rise of some of the world's major religions, with Hinduism, Buddhism and Taoism remaining significant living religions with many millions of followers. The influences of some of these religions were carried over great distances by missionaries. Buddhism spread from its roots in Nepal to northern Asia as far as Japan, and many parts of Southeast Asia saw the adoption of both Buddhism and Hinduism.

Confucianism and Tadism from 500 BC
* Sacred mountain
Largely Hindu from 500 BC
Hindu influence by AD 600
Key Hindu site
Largely Zoroastrian 500 BC–AD 600
Key Zoroastrian site
Area embracing Shintoism
Buddhist influence and missionary activity by AD 650
Key Buddhist site

2000 BC
MOHENJO DARO AND HARAPPA
The word 'Hindu' is the Persian name for the people who lived beyond the Indus River in India and it is in the early civilisations of the Indus Valley that Hinduism, the world's oldest living religion, has its roots. The earliest towns date back further than 3000 BC and the two cities of Mohenjo Daro and Harappa, at their peak around 2000 BC, were the largest in the world. Around 1900 BC, the civilisation began to decline and around 1500 BC the region was overrun by Aryan invaders from the north, who brought with them the Sanskrit language (related to Greek) the caste system, and belief in many nature gods corresponding to the Greek ones. Modern

Hinduism is probably a synthesis of the traditions of these two peoples.

▶ p. 278 **1500 BC**
THE VEDAS AND THE VEDIC AGE
The earliest Hindu scriptures are the four *Vedas* and the earliest of these is the *Rig Veda* ('song of wisdom'). This dates from around 1500–1000 BC and consists of 1,000 hymns that were mainly for the Aryan priests (Brahmins) to use during rituals. The hymns are directed towards nature gods such as Agni, the god of fire and Indra, the sky god, and some of these may have been used by Brahmins before their arrival in India. The *Rig Veda* was followed by the other three *Vedas*, or 'books of wisdom': the *Sama Veda*, *Yajur Veda* and *Atharva Veda* and, around 800 BC, by the *Brahmana* scriptures.

700 BC
THE EMERGENCE OF CLASSICAL HINDUISM
The *Upanishads*, compiled from 700–600 BC from earlier texts dating back to 1200 BC, are the world's earliest books of metaphysical speculation. These consist of interpretations of the *Vedas* (known as vedanta) and they present the idea of Brahman as the Universal Being who unites the Trimuri, or trinity, of Vishnu, Brahma and Shiva (respectively the creator, maintainer and destroyer of life). This doctrine provides an underlying theology that unites the Vaishnavite, the worshipper of Vishnu, the Shaivite, devotee of Shiva, and the followers of other gods in the Hindu pantheon. The two great mythical epics of Hinduism, the *Ramayana* and the *Mahabharata* were written between 500 and 200 BC. The latter contains the *Bhagavad Gita* (500 BC) which has today become the most important and most widely read of the Hindu scriptures.

▶ p. 275 **AD 700s**
SHANKARA AND NON-DUALISM
Shankara, who lived around the eighth century AD, was India's most famous scholar of Vedanta (which means the interpretation of the *Vedas* and *Upanishads*). He was a wandering teacher and may have established

several monasteries for ascetics. His doctrine of *Advaita*, or non-dualism, is expressed in works such as the *Atma Bodha* ('Knowledge of Spirit'). In this teaching nothing exists except God – God is all things and all things are God – and in particular the *Atman* (the soul or true self) is identical with Brahman (God or the universal self). To him the purpose of the spiritual life is to discover God in yourself and to realise that you are nothing but God. *Advaita vedanta* is the belief held by the majority of Hindu scholars today, but is challenged by the followers of Ramanuja.

✿ ▶ p. 273 **1100s**
RAMANUJA

Ramanuja (d. 1157) was a Vedanta scholar and the main critic of the teachings of Shankara. He taught that the Atman (the soul or true self), is distinct from Brahman (God or the universal self), but that it is an expression of Brahman and can re-enter into communion with Brahman. In other words, we come from God and can return to God. Liberation (*moksha*) from delusion (*samsara*) comes through the reconnection (*yoga*) of

p. 261 ◀ **Triumphs & Tragedies** ▶ p. 272
1000–26
MUSLIM INVASIONS

The expansion of Islam to the west around AD 900, had little impact on India for several centuries, until the invasions by Mahmud, a king of Ghazni, a province in Afghanistan. Between 1000 and 1026 he led annual campaigns to capture Indian territories, such as the Punjab, and to destroy and seize the wealth of Hindu temples in the main holy towns of Mathura, Thanesar, Kanauj and Somnath, in the hope that the population would convert to Islam. At Somnath, over 50,000 died in defence of the temple. This and the next two centuries were a 'dark age' for Hinduism, as repeated Islamic invasions from the north-west, by Afghans and Turks, devastated the country. With the loss of the temples and academic centres, philosophy and religious thought declined to be replaced by a vast jumble of superstitions.

Atman and Brahman. This teaching is known as *Visishtadvaita vedanta*, or qualified non-dualism. The philosophy, articulated in his *Commentary on the Vedanta Sutra*, provided a justification for the practice of *bhakti yoga*, or reconnection through devotional worship.

1440
THE BIRTH OF KABIR

Kabir (1440–1518) was born into a weaving family from the Hindu holy city of Benares. His father was a Muslim and his mother is believed to have been a Hindu. He sought to reconcile the mystical forms of Hinduism (in its Vaishnava form) and Islam (in its Sufi form) through worship of Rama/Allah as the one Supreme God. He rejected the polytheism of popular Hinduism and taught that there was one God who had many names. He is known as the 'saint poet' and is remembered both for the many *bhajans* (devotional songs), that he wrote and as a teacher of Guru Nanak (1469–1539), the founder of the Sikh religion. His teachings helped to reduce conflict between Hindus and Muslims.

✚ ▶ p. 272 **1485**
THE BIRTH OF LORD CHAITANYA

Chaitanya was born in Bengal in 1485 and became the founder of a major Vaishnava sect

▼ *The Hindu god Krishna (left), one of the avatars of Vishnu.*

– which is named after him. His teaching was that of passionate devotion, *bhakti*, directed towards Krishna, the latest avatar of Vishnu. His teachings follow on from the tradition of Ramanuja. The practice he taught of devotion and remembrance through continual chanting of the mantra 'Hare Krishna' ('praise Krishna') is today principally associated with the International Society for Krishna Consciousness. The traditional Hindu teaching of non-violence (*ahimsa*) was given great emphasis, particularly in relation to a strictly vegetarian and healthy diet, and in the care of cows, which are sacred to Krishna.

p. 267 ◀ **Distant Voices** ▶ p. 273

He who sees that the Lord of all is ever the same in all that is, immortal in the field of mortality – he sees the truth. And when a man sees that the God in himself is the same God in all that is, he hurts not himself by hurting others: then he goes indeed to the highest Path. He who sees that all work, everywhere, is only the work of nature; and that the Spirit watches this work – he sees the truth. When a man sees that the infinity of various beings is abiding in the ONE, and is an evolution from the ONE, then he becomes one with Brahman.

Bhagavad Gita 13, 27–30

Judaism
1900 BC–AD 1700

THE CENTRAL TEACHING of Judaism is that there is one God, who created the world as a garden. Although the disobedience of the first people led to the destruction of the garden, God maintained a covenant with His chosen people and promised them a fertile land. As the Prophet Isaiah taught, the land would be fruitful for the righteous or turn to desert for the greedy and selfish. The history of Judaism has been a long and tragic one of exile and persecution. Since Abraham spoke of the Promised Land nearly 4,000 years ago, the Jews have lived there in peace for fewer than 1,000 years. Following the Holocaust in the Second World War, many of the 20 million survivors have moved to the new state of Israel.

▲ *King David, the founder of Jerusalem.*

✿ ▶ p. 273 **1900 BC**
ABRAHAM AND THE PROMISED LAND

The great prophet Abraham was born in the ancient city of Ur in Mesopotamia, one of the earliest cities in the world, in around 1900 BC. His original name was Abram. God appeared to him on several occasions, promising him

▼ *Moses surveying the Promised Land, after the flight of the Israelites from Egypt.*

and his people the land of Canaan. According to tradition, when he and his wife, Sarah, were 100, she gave birth to Isaac. Abraham was later called by God to sacrifice Isaac and he was preparing to do so when angels intervened. This story has been interpreted in many ways – as a criticism of the tradition of human sacrifice, as a call to obedience to God and as a precursor to the sacrifice of Jesus. Muslims believe that he built the Kaaba in Mecca for the worship of the One God.

p. 271 ◀ **Triumphs & Tragedies** ▶ p. 273
1250 BC
MOSES AND THE EXODUS FROM EGYPT

Around 1250 BC, after centuries working as oppressed labourers in Egypt, the tribes of Israel, under the leadership of Moses, were authorised to depart. For the next 40 years, as documented in the book of Exodus, Moses led the people through the desert in search of the 'Promised Land', the land of Caanan. During this time, God revealed to Moses the central teachings of Judaism; these included the Ten Commandments, revealed on Mount Sinai and carved into stone tablets by Moses. These were kept in a portable shrine, the Ark of the Covenant, during their wanderings. Moses died within sight of the land, which the tribes eventually occupied.

✚ ▶ p. 291 **995 BC**
KING DAVID BUILDS JERUSALEM

David, Israel's greatest king, was originally a shepherd and musician from Bethlehem and is best known for his allegorical defeat of the Philistine giant Goliath – he probably became the leader of a small Hebrew army that defeated a larger Philistine one. He was elected king of the Hebrews, united the various Jewish tribes and, in 995 BC, captured the small town of Jerusalem, which he rebuilt as his capital. Thereafter it has been known as the City of David. The Ark of the Covenant was later moved to the new city, making it the religious centre of the nation. He was also responsible, according to tradition, for the creation of many of the Psalms – although some appear to have been written at a later date.

967 BC
KING SOLOMON AND THE TEMPLE

David's son, King Solomon, was renowned for his wealth and his wisdom. He ruled from 967 to 928 BC, during which time he brought considerable wealth to the nation through trade with the Phoenicians. Much money was raised through taxes to built a vast temple in Jerusalem to house the Ark of the Covenant – a project that took 14 years and employed the services of thousands of Phoenician craftsmen. The Temple was destroyed and rebuilt on several occasions in the following centuries. It was destroyed in 586 BC by the Babylonian king, Nebuchadnezzar II, who sent 1,500 leaders of the population as slaves to Babylon for 48 years. The final destruction took place under Titus, son of the Roman emperor, Vespasian, in AD 70.

▲ *The expulsion of the Jews from Spain.*

✿ ▶ p. 284   800 BC
THE PROPHECIES OF ISAIAH

The Prophet Isaiah lived at a time of great conflict and danger for Israel, around 800 BC. Faced with the threat of invasion he prophesied that unless the people of Israel had faith and lived honestly, the land would become desert and the nation would be destroyed. God is depicted as the judge of the Israeli nation, punishing sinfulness through drought and plague and rewarding virtue through rain and harvest. Isaiah forecast that the people would revive their faith and that in response the desert would blossom and the gardens of paradise would appear on Earth. There is evidence that the biblical book of Isaiah was written partly by him and partly by one or two later prophets.

p. 272 ◀ **Triumphs & Tragedies** ▶ p. 276

AD 70
DESTRUCTION OF THE TEMPLE AND THE DIASPORA

The final destruction of the Temple by the Romans, took place in AD 70. When the Jews resisted Roman laws, the emperor, Vespasian, sent his son, Titus, to capture the city. The population put up massive resistance and so was severely punished when they were defeated. Following this, the Jewish people were dispersed around the world – an event known as the Diaspora. Many travelled initially to Syria, Egypt and Hellenic territories. In later centuries, both the Christians under Constantine and the Muslims put to death anyone who converted to Judaism, but the strong religious and family traditions enabled the Jews to remain as a distinct people. The remaining wall of the Temple, the Wailing Wall, remains to this day a focus of pilgrimage.

1492
EXPULSION FROM SPAIN

Many of the Jews dispersed from Israel settled throughout Europe, where oppression by Christian governments occurred on a regular basis. Anti-Semitism grew during the Middle Ages and, in many cities, Jews were forced to live in separate enclaves or 'ghettos'. A dramatic example of this occurred in Spain when the Moors (Moroccanili Muslims), who ruled the south (Andalusia), were defeated in 1492. The Moors had promoted religious tolerance and theological dialogue between the faiths. When they were defeated all non-Christians, both Muslims and Jews, were expelled or sentenced to death by the Spanish Inquisition (and much of their money was used to finance Columbus's expedition to America).

✝ ▶ p. 282   1700
THE BA'AL SHEM TOV AND HASIDISM

Rabbi Israel ben Eliezer, the 'Ba'al Shem Tov' or 'master of the good name', was born in the Ukraine in 1700. After living in Spain, he worked as a lime digger in Romania. He became a herbalist and earned the title of 'ba'al shem', and whilst practising this he promoted his religious teachings

through simple stories and parables. His teachings of joy in response to the immanence of God in the world and of the superiority of spiritual emotion over intellectual religious understanding proved highly popular amongst the uneducated Jews of eastern Europe. He meditated in the forests, taught that God was present in nature and was prone to spontaneous singing, dancing and storytelling. The emphasis upon sincere prayer and continual awareness of God's presence differed markedly from the legalistic and oppressive Judaism of his time.

p. 271 ◀ **Distant Voices** ▶ p. 275

For you shall go out with joy, And be led out with peace. The mountains and the hills Shall break forth into singing before you. And the trees of the field shall clap their hands. Instead of the thorn shall come up the cypress tree And instead of the briar shall come up the myrtle tree.

Isaiah 55:12–13 (foretelling the restoration of the harmony of the Garden of Eden, should the people of Israel live in accordance with the Covenant)

Buddhism
586 BC–AD 700s

THE CENTRAL CONCEPT of Buddhism is enlightenment. Through understanding the nature and causes of suffering man can end it and realise perfect consciousness. Like some Hindus – such as Shankara – Buddhists deny the reality of a separate self and believe in a single reality. Erroneous belief in the self is believed to lead to greed, hatred and delusion – these are known as the 'three fires', that cause suffering for all beings. Through meditation man can recognise the error of these desires and become free from them. In the Theravada tradition, the emphasis is on seeking one's own salvation. In the Mahayana tradition, the goal is to help free all beings from suffering.

586 BC
THE LIFE OF SIDDHARTA GAUTAMA (THE BUDDHA)

Siddharta was born into the family of a minor king of the Sakya clan in present-day Nepal in the fifth century BC. Although protected from the sufferings of the world, his curiosity led him to encounter an old man, a sick man, a corpse and an ascetic. Shocked by the suffering he encountered, he became an ascetic, but later realised that self-punishment was a form of delusion. Attaining enlightenment under a bodhi tree in what is now Bodh-Gaya, India, he set out to teach his Middle Way. This involved recognising the Four Noble Truths – that there was suffering, that it had a cause, that it could be overcome and that practice of the Noble Eightfold Path was the means by which to overcome it. This path involved meditation, self-discipline and non-violent living.

269–232 BC
THE REIGN OF KING ASOKA

India's greatest king, Asoka, started his 40-year reign with a military campaign to expand his empire. Shocked by the slaughter, he adopted Buddhism, turning it from a small sect into the state religion. He established laws based on Buddhist principles and these were carved on pillars throughout India. Hospitals and many other public buildings were constructed, sculptures illustrating the life of the Buddha were commissioned and trees were planted. With his encouragement, Buddhism spread to Sri Lanka, where the simple and formal Theravada tradition took root, and also to central Asia, where the emphasis was on the more intellectual Mahayana tradition. Sadly, after his death, this flourishing empire soon fell apart.

▼ *Asoka, king of India, who turned Buddhism into a state religion.*

✎ ▶ p. 277

232 BC
THE THERAVADA TRADITION

Theravada (the 'doctrine of the elders') was the earliest, simplest and most orthodox form of Buddhism. It put great emphasis upon the following of the Noble Eightfold Path and upon each practitioner overcoming their own delusions and 'seeking their own salvation with diligence'. Mahinda, the son of King Asoka, according to tradition, took the teachings of the Buddha to Sri Lanka, where it became the royal religion of the nation. It was there also that the Pali Scriptures were first written down. From there, the scriptures and the tradition of the royal religion were spread to neighbouring countries such as Burma and then Thailand, Laos, Cambodia and Java.

200 BC
THE MAHAYANA TRADITION

Based upon the Buddhist belief that the self is illusory, the Mahayana Tradition – the earliest known scriptures of which date from the second century BC – does not teach that we should each separately seek our own liberation, but instead that we should, upon attaining enlightenment, seek to liberate all beings, as the Buddha had done. Later schools developed the belief that most people could not save themselves and that they should therefore appeal for the help of bodhisattvas – near-Buddhas who had chosen to delay their own entry to nirvana in order to help others achieve enlightenment – through devotional prayer (*puja*) and mantras. In China this practice gave birth to the Chan Hua-Yen and Tendai Buddhist traditions, which all spread to Korea, Japan and Vietnam. In Tibet this formed the basis of the Vajrayana tradition.

AD 500s
CHAN AND ZEN

The Chan school was traditionally brought to China by the sixth-century Indian monk Bodhidharma and was systematised by Hui-neng (the '6th Patriarch') in the T'ang dynasty. The name derives from *Dhyana*, Sanskrit for 'meditation', and the central practice is the direct realisation of reality

📖 SCRIPTURES   ✝ SAINTS   ✎ SCHOOLS   ❋ REVIVERS   �)) PHILOSOPHERS

through meditation. Chan was influenced by the *Diamond Sutra* and also by the teachings of Taoism and the Hua-Yen school. Hui-Neng's Southern School taught that enlightenment was instantaneous whereas Shen Xui's Northern School taught that it was gradual. In Japan Chan was called Zen; this came from the Southern school and took two forms – the Soto Zen, taught by Dogen (1200–53), emphasises *zazen* meditation, whereas the Rinzai Zen taught by Hakuin (1686–1769) used *koans*, unanswerable riddles to force the mind out of the delusory world of words.

▼ *The Buddhist religion was based on the life of Siddharta Gautama Buddha.*

AD 500s
T'IEN TAI

The Chinese scholar, Chih-I (AD 538–597) made major strides in the integration and synthesis of the many different Buddhist ideas entering China. He classified these into eight teachings and developed T'ien Tai (Tendai in Japan) as an attempt to unite these into a single philosophical system. The school is named after the mountain where he founded his main monastery. He felt that each of these eight teachings came from the Buddha and that each was suitable for a different audience. Each person should choose the teaching most suitable for their current situation. He felt, however, that all these teachings were compatible and that they were summed up most concisely in the text of the Lotus Sutra.

AD 700s
HUA-YEN AND PURE LAND

Fa-Tsang (AD 643–712) founded the Hua-Yen school, based upon his interpretation of the Avatamsaka or Hua-Yen Sutra (Flower Ornament Sutra). This stresses the total interdependence of all things. The teaching greatly influenced Chan (Zen) Buddhism. In combination with the T'ien Tai school, it led to the emergence of Pure Land Buddhism in Japan. Pure Land teaches that the faithful, those who chant the mantra 'Namu-Amida-Butsu' ('I take refuge in the name of the Amida Buddha'), will be reborn in the Pure Land of Sukhavati. There are two major Pure Land schools today, the Jodo school of Honen (1133–1212), and the reformist Jodo Shin school of Shinran (1173–1262). A militant form was developed by Nichiren (1222–85), who taught salvation through chanting 'the name of the Lotus Sutra' (Nam-Myoho-Renge-Kyo).

✳ ▶ p. 276 ### AD 700s
VAJRAYANA: TIBETAN BUDDHISM

By tradition, Buddhism was introduced to Tibet in the eighth century by the Indian monk

Padmasambhavain, who founded the Nying-ma tradition and introduced Dzogchen meditation. Atisha (AD 982–1034), another Indian monk, was responsible for the second wave of Buddhism, resulting in the Kadam-pa order. The Tibetan scholar and householder, Marpa, founded the Sakya order. His disciple the poet and ascetic monk, Milarepa (1040–1123), is seen as the founder of the Kagyu order, which was further developed by his disciple, Gampopa (1079–1153). The various schools of Tibetan Buddhism were synthesised and united by Tsongkapa (1357–1418) to create the Gelug-pa tradition, currently headed by the 14th Dalai Lama.

▲ *The ascetic monk Milarepa, founder of the Kagyu order.*

p. 273 ◀ **Distant Voices** ▶ p. 277

[The Middle Path] is simply the Noble Eightfold Path, namely, right view, right thought, right speech, right action, right livelihood, right effort, right mindfulness, right concentration. This is the Middle Path realised by the Tathagata, which gives knowledge, and which leads to calm, to insight, to enlightenment, to Nirvana.

From the First Sermon of the Buddha: 'Setting in Motion the Wheel of Truth' (551 BC)

Confucianism
551 BC–AD 1500s

A T THE CORE of Confucius's teaching, as contained in his *Analects*, is guidance on the cultivation of moral character as the foundation of social order. The ideal man or gentleman, chün tzu, should act in accord with tradition, the requirements of ritual and etiquette and his station in society. In practice, this involved the practice of obedience and respect for ancestors, fathers, rulers, husbands, elder brothers and the practice of benevolent paternalism towards sons, subjects, wives and younger brothers. Underlying these teachings is the belief that through rituals and cultivating the right character, man can help bring about on Earth the Order of Heaven.

▲ *The Chinese philosopher Mencius, a disciple of Confucius.*

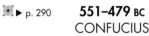 ▶ p. 290
551–479 BC
CONFUCIUS

China's great sage, K'ung Fu-Tze ('Master K'ung') is generally known in the West by his latinised name, 'Confucius'. He came

▼ *Confucius, the founder of Confucianism, whose teachings encouraged social order and harmony.*

from an aristocratic but poor family in the state of Chou and was orphaned at an early age. At this time China was in a state of chaos and had divided into many warring states. Much of Confucius's teachings, which could more accurately be described as moral and political rather than religious, were directed towards restoring the kind of social order that was believed to have existed in ancient times. To Confucius this was a matter of restoring to Earth the perfect Order of Heaven, *T'ien ming*. This could be done through virtuous living and the correct practice of the ancient rituals.

371–289 BC
MENCIUS

'Mencius' is the latinised name of Meng Tzu. He was the best-known disciple of Confucius and his writings are the most important source of Confucian philosophy. He taught that the highest aim of the state was to protect the welfare of the people, that the wise emperor is the one who rules in accord with the Order of Heaven (*T'ien ming*) and that an unjust ruler should be overthrown. He believed that the heart/mind (*hsin*) of man was naturally good and that it should be cultivated to realise its full potential. His teachings – philosophical dialogues and (often entertaining) meditations are found in a book bearing his name, compiled by his followers in the second century AD.

p. 273 ◀ **Triumphs & Tragedies** ▶ p. 281
212 BC
THE BURNING OF BOOKS

The greatest set-back to the development of Confucianism occurred when the emperor, Huang-Ti, founder of the Ts'in dynasty, came to power. Huang-Ti reunited China through military force and built the Great Wall using slave labour. He advocated a philosophy known as Legalism, which denied the existence of morality and stated that the use of strict laws was the only way to maintain social order. In 212 BC he decided to burn all the books in the country – especially those of Confucius and Mencius. This was done to ensure that no record of previous governments survived. Many scholars were put to death and the central writings only just survived. It is ironic that the writings, which advocate a strong centralised state, suffered so badly at the hands of just such a state.

179 BC
TUNG CHUNG-SHU

Tung Chung-Shu played an important role in the integration of Confucian thought with other Chinese ideas. He linked, for example, the Confucian teachings about right relationships (father-son, ruler-subject, and so on) with the Taoist cosmological concept of the complementary nature of opposites (Yin and Yang), to form a philosophical basis for the definition of harmonious and virtuous relationships. Although not a founder of new religious thought in China, the ideas he developed through already established practices, and the combination of new ideas with old, paved the way for further changes in Eastern philosophy and belief.

136 BC
ADOPTION OF CONFUCIANISM BY THE HAN DYNASTY

Whilst many of Confucius's teachings were liberal and humanist, the conservative emphasis on law and order, obedience and tradition made it an attractive and useful philosophy for the generally authoritarian governments of China in early times. In 136 BC, the first emperor of the Han dynasty, Liu Pang, declared Confucianism the formal religion of the country. In 124 BC, Wu-Ti founded a college to encourage the study of Confucianism. Those who studied here were later given positions of authority within the government, and from this time Confucianism became the principal source of education of the ruling classes. Five Confucian texts (the *Five Classics*) were chosen as the central works up which this education was to be founded.

AD 960–1297
HU YUAN AND NEO-CONFUCIANISM IN THE SUNG DYNASTY

After several centuries in which Buddhism was powerful, Confucianism regained its status and became the state religion of the Sung dynasty (AD 960–1297). In its revived form, known in the West as Neo-Confucianism, the teachings are systematised and integrated with other strands of Chinese thought – such as Buddhism and Taoism. Hu Yuan (AD 993–1059) can be seen as the founder of Neo-Confucianism, which then split into two schools inspired respectively by Chu Hsi (1130–1200) and Wang Yang-Ming (1472–1529). From this time, Neo-Confucianism provided the basis of the examination system used to select government

▲ *Monks in modern-day China.*

officials. The emphasis continues to be on ethics but self-cultivation is interpreted as the control of an innately feeble *hsin* (heart/mind). Public observance of Confucian rituals, especially ancestor worship, became obligatory for almost 1,000 years.

✎ ▶ p. 280

1100s
CHU HSI AND THE SCHOOL OF PRINCIPLE

The Neo-Confucian Scholar, Chu Hsi (1130–1200), was the greatest thinker of the School of Principle (Li). This school believed in the Mind of Heaven, or Ultimate Principle, which was reflected in all material things. As a result of this, Chu Hsi taught that careful study of anything could lead back ultimately to the discovery of the Mind of Heaven. The School of Principle therefore encouraged scientific investigation and attempted a deeper understanding of the material world. This was directly contradictory to Buddhist introspection, and belief in abandonment of all things material, the root of unhappiness. This view was challenged by Wang Yang-Ming and others of the School of Mind.

1500s
WANG YANG-MING AND THE SCHOOL OF MIND

Wang Yang-Ming was a leading Neo-Confucian scholar, and the principal thinker in the School of Mind. This school challenged the scientific and material teachings of Chu Hsi and the School of Principle. Instead, Wang Yang-Ming taught

that the human mind was a perfect reflection of the Mind of Heaven, and that we should discover the Mind of Heaven only through study of the workings of our own mind. The School of Mind therefore encouraged self-cultivation and understanding through introspection and meditation during daily activity, and incorporated many Buddhist and Taoist ideas and beliefs, particularly on the practice of meditation. These teachings spread rapidly to Korea and Japan.

p. 275 ◀ **Distant Voices** ▶ p. 279

The Master said, 'What the gentleman seeks, he seeks within himself; what the small man seeks, he seeks in others'. The Master said, 'The Gentleman is conscious of his own superiority without being contentious, and comes together with other gentlemen without forming cliques.' The Master said, 'The gentleman does not recommend a man on account of what he says, neither does he dismiss what is said on account of the speaker'. Tzu-kung asked, 'Is there a single word which can be a guide to conduct throughout one's life?' The Master said, 'It is perhaps the word 'shu' – i.e. do not impose on others what you yourself do not desire'.

The Analects of Confucius, Book XV, 21–24

Taoism
604 BC–AD 742

TAOISM SHARES with Confucianism the belief in Heaven as perfect and as the source of order and harmony on earth. However, whilst Confucius taught how to impose this order, Taoists believe it can only be achieved by allowing it to happen naturally. Taoists believe that order and harmony are natural and that disorder comes about through our attempts to interfere with nature. Right behaviour comes about through living spontaneously and through direct connection with nature. The formal behaviour of Confucians was seen as artificial and resulting in pride and hypocrisy. The highest virtue in Taoism was humility and unselfconsciousness rather than being a gentleman. Human well-being comes from co-operating with nature and human nature and not through trying to control it. The philosopher Rousseau held similar views.

▲ *A meeting between Confucius and the Taoist scholar Lao Tzu, now believed to have been a mythical character.*

400 BC
'THE WAY'

The 'Tao'or 'Dao' means 'the Way', and this idea is central to Taoist thought and practice. The main texts of the faith – the *Tao Te Ching* and the writings of Chuang Tzu – are believed to date from around the fourth century BC, and in these works, the idea of the Way was impossible to describe or define exactly and is seen rather as an all-encompassing idea – the power behind, the path towards and the practices of Taoism. Also central to Taoist philosophy is the balance of the two opposing yet complementary forces of Yin and Yang. The correct harmony and interplay of these two forces is essential in maintaining the well-being of all matters, both human and natural.

350 BC
CHUANG TZU

The earliest Taoist sage who is likely to have existed is Chuang Tzu, whose teachings are to be found in a book of the same name. *Chuang Tzu* articulates the Taoist teaching that one should live in accordance with the Way (*Tao*), the order of nature, and abandon Confucian artificiality, the pursuit of wealth and power and attempts to coerce either people or nature. The world is continually changing and so spontaneity and intuition are our only guides to a sane

life. The person who lives this way will attain virtue (*Te*). The *Chuang Tzu*, which is the most philosophical and coherent of the Taoist scriptures, contains many amusing criticisms of orthodox Confucianism.

▼ *Taoism challenged the social orientation of the teachings of Confucius.*

📖 ▶ p. 282
300 BC
THE TAO TE CHING

The principal book of Taoism, the *Tao Te Ching* (*Book of the Way and its Virtue*) is traditionally ascribed to Lao Tzu ('Old Man'), an older contemporary of Confucius. Scholars now generally agree that he is a mythical character, possibly invented by critics of Confucianism. The teachings in the *Tao Te Ching*, which was

probably compiled from earlier works around 300 BC, challenge the ritual formalism and social orientation of Confucianism and advocate spontaneity, humility, the rejection of worldly success and political power and the pursuit of a mystical communion with nature. They declare that the order of nature and the natural way of life cannot be reduced to written formulae and sets of rules; as the opening sentence reads 'The Tao that can be spoken of is not the eternal Tao'.

AD 50
DECLINE OF TAOIST THOUGHT

From around the middle of the first century AD, there was a marked decline in philosophical and contemplative Taoism. The pursuit of a natural and spontaneous way of life, by allowing oneself to follow freely the currents of the Tao, turned into the pursuit of eternal life – or Hsien. This new form of Taoism saw the rise in use of magic potions and forms of sexual yoga. Contemplation of the ineffable 'order of nature' was gradually replaced by the worship of countless household gods and the practices of divination, alchemy, astrology and magic. Hsien Taoism flourished under the influence of Chan Tao Ling and Chang Lu.

✴ ▶ p. 280
AD 100s
LIEH TZU

Lieh Tzu, one of the most important names in Taoism, may never have existed. He is described as a Taoist immortal who is able to 'ride the wind'. *Lieh Tzu*, the book attributed to him, appears to be an edited compilation of various works. The contents are similar in style to those of the *Chuang Tzu* and may originally have been by the same author(s). They are, however, more confused than the *Chuang Tzu*, suggesting that they were written or compiled later, possibly in the first to second centuries AD. One reason for this view is that the *Lieh Tzu* contains little criticism for Confucianism, but is critical of Hsien Taoism, which taught how to attain immortality through occult practices and which began to emerge from the first century AD. The book advocates instead the traditional contemplative form of Taoism.

AD 100s
CHANG TAO LING AND CHANG LU
Chang Tao Ling (AD 34–156), is traditionally described as a Taoist immortal who could 'ride the wind' and who received his powers and title of 'Heavenly Master' directly from Lao Tzu. He was a magician who established a semi-independent Taoist state in south-west China. His grandson, Chang Lu, was responsible for turning Taoism into a formal religion based upon the pursuit of immortality, or Hsien. The order is commonly known as 'The Way of Five Pecks of Rice' because this was the tax they collected from all citizens. He expanded his grandfather's state and created a hierarchy of priests and annual calendar of ceremonies. This order, known as the 'Orthodox One' sect, is the largest Taoist group existing today, and is still led by the 64th descendant of Chang Tao Ling.

AD 600s
SUPPORTED BY THE T'ANG DYNASTY
Whilst not the natural religion of a government, Taoism received state patronage at a time when Buddhism and Confucianism were being suppressed. Emperor Kao-Tsung (AD 649–683) brought in legislation to ensure that there was a Taoist monastery in every prefecture (county). This ensured the protection of Taoist teachings, but also brought them under state control. The result was that the outward rituals flourished, whilst the underlying philosophy declined. During this time many Taoist temples were built and in AD 742 Chuang Tzu was formally canonised. The Taoist Canon – *Tao-tsang*, the most comprehensive collection of Taoist writings – was compiled at this time.

AD 600
THE TAOIST INFLUENCE ON CH'AN (ZEN) BUDDHISM
During the T'ang dynasty, the Ch'an (Zen) school of Buddhism developed in China, a tradition that grew from the Hua-Yen school and the teachings of the Diamond Sutra, but which incorporated in an almost unaltered form many traditional teachings of Chuang Tzu and philosophical or contemplative Taoism. This form of Buddhism avoided the later Taoist practices, those of the occult Hsien Taoism, and instead concentrated on practices such as the understanding of the rhythm of nature and how to live in harmony with this. Due to innate similarities, these were easily united these with the meditation practices already established as part of the Buddhist philosophy.

> p. 277 ◀ **Distant Voices** ▶ p. 281
>
> *When Chuang Tzu was about to die his disciples began planning a splendid funeral. But he said: 'I shall have Heaven and Earth for my coffin; the sun and moon will be the jade symbols hanging by my side; planets and constellations will shine as jewels all around me, and all beings will be present as mourners at the wake. What more is needed? Everything is amply taken care of.*
>
> *Chuang Tzu*, XXIII, 14

▼ *Taoist monks pictured in ceremonial dress in China.*

Greek Thought
850 BC–AD 270

GREEK THOUGHT, from around 500 BC onwards, was quite different from anything that preceded it. In other civilisations, the purpose of philosophy was to explain the meaning of the traditional scriptures that had been revealed to them and to prove their validity. For the Greeks, truth did not have to be inherited, because people had within themselves the capacity for reason and for the direct apprehension of truth. The nature of the higher world (of mind, number or archetype) could be discerned in the order of the visible world – in music, geometry and the movement of the planets. They were therefore prepared to follow the logic of their arguments, wherever this led, and to reject any traditions that appeared illogical.

850 BC
HOMER, THE GREEK GODS AND THE TROJAN WARS

The *Iliad* and the *Odyssey*, attributed to the blind poet, Homer (*c.* 850 BC), are the earliest and greatest Greek epic poems, and provide a detailed picture of early Greek religion. This could be described as an anthropomorphic polytheism derived from earlier nature gods. The many gods, both male and female, who live on Mount Olympus, are ruled over by Zeus, the powerful thunder god. Other gods include Apollo, the sun god, Demeter, the goddess of harvests and Neptune, god of the sea. All have different human personalities, they can plot against one another and be influenced through prayers and sacrifices. There was no central dogma, theology or revelation, although later philosophies made use of the ancient myths.

▲ *Marble bust of the Greek poet Homer.*

 ▶ p. 283
600 BC
ORPHISM

Orphism was a mystic cult, dating from around the sixth century BC, supposedly based on the teachings of the divine musician and poet Orpheus. Followers and wandering priests participated in the ascetic Orphic rites to purify themselves. They abstained from meat and fish (since animals were seen as fellow beings) and practised meditation. These practices were necessary because it was believed that, although humans contained the pure soul of the god

Dionysius (a son of Zeus), Zeus created their bodies from the ashes of the evil Titans. The soul (as in Hindu belief) would continue to be reincarnated in impure bodies – to remain trapped in the 'circle of generation' or 'mortal coil' – until it was purified and made divine again.

❋ ▶ p. 282
600 BC
PYTHAGORAS

Pythagoras was both a mathematician and a mystic. His Pythagorean Brotherhood was a religious community which studied the spiritual significance of numbers – such as the relationship between musical notes and the lengths of strings, and the relationship between the lengths of the sides of triangles. These were seen as ways of discovering the divine order in the natural world. Many of his beliefs, like those of Orphism, appear, surprisingly, to be Hindu in origin (Greek and Sanskrit are related languages). These include the idea that souls can reincarnate after death in other humans or animals, the practice of vegetarianism for this reason and the practice of strict asceticism to overcome the desires of the body. His beliefs greatly influenced Plato.

▼ *Depiction of the Greek mythological character Bacchus, with satyrs.*

▲ *The Greek philosopher, Plato.*

p. 276 ◀ **Triumphs & Tragedies** ▶ p. 282

399 BC
PLATO AND THE DEATH OF SOCRATES

Plato's teacher, Socrates, was put to death for his teachings in 399 BC. This event is recorded in Plato's *Dialogues*, which are a form of memorial to Socrates and which contain many discussions ascribed to him. He argues that knowledge can only exist if there are eternal things to which knowledge can refer, and as material things change, they must therefore be only expressions of unchanging Forms. He believed in Forms such as the Good, the True and the Beautiful, which all things expressed to greater or lesser degree. In his *Republic* he depicts a State based on his ideals and ruled by philosophers. This was the inspiration for many other visions such as the *Utopia* of Thomas More. His ideas were promoted through his Academy, the first centre of higher learning, and developed by his pupil Aristotle.

▶ p. 285

367 BC
ARISTOTLE

Aristotle studied at Plato's Academy from 367 BC and went on to become a teacher to Alexander the Great. Whilst developing many of Plato's ideas, he rejected the theory of Forms, arguing instead that material things were the primary reality and that any properties that they had, such as colour or taste, were just aspects or properties of that matter. His rigorous use of logic and his rejection of all unnecessary hypotheses resulted in him being seen as the founder of logical theory. He believed in reason as humankind's distinguishing feature, but his thought covered almost every subject from politics to literature, logic to psychology and ethics to science.

341–271 BC
EPICURUS

Epicurus was a materialist; he taught that the gods were immortal physical beings, but that they did not control the world or judge or punish humans. There was no life after death and the good life involved the enjoyment of reasonable pleasure, the cultivation of contentment and freedom from responsibilities and from physical pain. We should 'eat, drink and be merry – for tomorrow we die'. The gods in Olympus, free from pain and responsibility, were seen as providing the ideal model for this lifestyle. Epicurus established a school of philosophy, the Garden, in Athens to study and practise this way of life. He was opposed by the rival Stoic school.

334–262 BC
ZENO OF CITIUM AND STOICISM

Zeno of Citium (334–262 BC) taught that the gods were merely natural forces and that the world was really controlled by mind. He believed that there was no other purpose in life than to exercise reason, and so people should live rationally, in accord with nature and with acceptance of their eventual extinction. Zeno was inspired by Socrates' calmness and courage in the face of his fate. Stoicism at times had the support of most of the educated population of Greece and Rome. Roman Stoics included Epictetus, Seneca and Marcus Aurelius. The school was opposed by the Epicureans, who had similar beliefs about the world but who felt that in response to our mortality we should 'eat, drink and be merry'.

※ ▶ p. 286
AD 200s
PLOTINUS AND NEOPLATONISM

Plotinus (AD 204–270) was probably born in Egypt and in later life lived in Rome. He founded the school of Neoplatonism, a radical restructuring of Plato's teachings. For example, he believed that physical forms derived from archetypal ideas, themselves derived from the Good, the True and the Beautiful. He also expounded the idea of the One – the ultimate and unchanging source of reality, of which the world is a reflection. His teaching formed the basis for the spiritual practice of seeking union with the One by rising above the worlds of form and ideas through meditation. Plotinus's influence on Christianity is illustrated in the opening lines of the Gospel of St John, literally: 'At the origin is the word.'

p. 279 ◀ **Distant Voices** ▶ p. 283

The One is all things and no one of them. The source of all things is not all things but transcends them. All things return to it – seeking nothing, possessing nothing, lacking nothing, the One is perfect and has overflowed and in its exuberance has produced the new: This product has turned again to its begetter and been filled and has become its contemplator.

Plotinus, *2nd Tractate of the Enneads*

Early Christianity

7 BC–AD 547

CHRISTIANITY WAS originally one of several Jewish sects created in response to the formalism of the priestly tradition and the decadence and materialism of city life. These groups sought a more direct spiritual connection with God, with less emphasis on rules and regulations. To them God was not a distant king who only spoke to priests, but a father who cared directly for all his children. Like a father, God would provide for all material needs, so the pursuit of wealth should be abandoned. Jesus's statement that he was the 'Son of God' caused the split with Judaism. To all the main Christian denominations since the Council of Nicaea, Jesus was God born as a man, although the Bible states that the human race are all sons of God. To Jews and Muslims he was a major prophet.

p. 281 ◀ **Triumphs & Tragedies** ▶ p. 287

7 BC
THE LIFE OF CHRIST

Born in Galilee around the year now calculated to be 7 BC, Jesus showed interest in religious matters from an early age. His cousin, John the Baptist, was at that time a radical and ascetic preacher who was highly critical of the Jewish establishment. Jesus underwent the ritual of baptism in the Jordan River, which symbolised the cleansing of the spirit. After a retreat into the wilderness, he became a wandering preacher and attracted a large following. He rejected the pursuit of wealth and the use of violence, proclaiming that these would prevent man from entering the Kingdom of Heaven. His message that we can all, like him, become sons of God, led to his persecution by the priesthood. The traditional teaching of the church is that, after his crucifixion, Jesus rose from the dead.

✟ ▶ p. 286

AD 67
THE DEATH OF ST PAUL THE APOSTLE

St Paul (Saul of Tarsus) was a Jewish tent-maker and originally an opponent of Christianity. His sudden conversion experience on the road to Damascus marked the starting point of his promotion of Jesus's teachings. His many letters to the new churches around the Mediterranean are recorded in the New Testament. He became involved in the controversy over whether Christianity was a form of Judaism – and so only open to Jews – or a faith that was open to all. He concluded that it was open to all and that the teachings of the Torah, such as circumcision, did not apply to Christians of non-Jewish origin. This made him unpopular with the Christians of Jewish origin, who persuaded the Romans to arrest him. He was executed in Rome in AD 67.

📖 ▶ p. 285

AD 70
THE EVANGELISTS

The four Gospels in which the life of Christ is described, consist of three similar, or synoptic, Gospels by Matthew, Mark and Luke, and a later, more theological one, by John. Surprisingly little is known about these four evangelists. The earliest Gospel, that of Mark, was probably written around AD 70, but the author may never have met Jesus. The Gospels of Matthew and Luke were both written in Antioch, Syria, around AD 80 and 90 respectively. Both appear to be derived largely from the Gospel of Mark and from another version, now lost, known to scholars as the 'Q Source'. John clearly lived later and was probably a Greek. It is assumed that Luke also wrote the *Acts of the Apostles* and that John may have written the *Book of Revelation*.

❋ ▶ p. 290

AD 300s
THE DESERT FATHERS

The monastic life and the practice of contemplative prayer originated with the lives of the 'desert fathers', saints and hermits who lived alone and in small communities in the deserts of Syria and North Africa, especially around Alexandria. St Antony of Egypt (AD 251–356), a pupil of St Paul of Thebes, is referred to as the father of Christian monasticism. He created a loose community of hermits, whose lives were based upon work and prayer (*labore et orare*). Other important saints include Athanasius (AD 298–373) and the colourful St Simeon Stylites (AD 390–459) of Syria, who lived for 36 years on top of a tall pillar, to escape from his many followers.

AD 325
CONSTANTINE AND THE COUNCIL OF NICEA

The Roman Emperor Constantine (AD 280–337) adopted Christianity as the state religion and founded Constantinople as its new capital in AD 330. In doing so, he became in effect head of a religion that had previously been a threat to the state. With the power of the state behind it, the Church

▼ *Moses and the burning bush (top) and Moses receiving the Ten Commandments (bottom).*

was able to resolve theological disputes by legal rather than philosophical means. At the Council of Nicaea, called by Constantine in 325, the teachings of the theologian Arius (AD 250–336), who believed that Jesus was not God, were declared heretical and religious orthodoxy was defined. At this time, the Church began to implement punishments for heresy; Constantine ordered that Christians who refused to eat pork should be killed by drinking molten lead.

AD 400s
THE EARLY CHURCH IN ASIA AND AFRICA

Following the destruction of the Jewish Temple in AD 70, the Christians of Jerusalem fled mainly to Syria. Here Nestorius (AD 381–451) created the Syriac, or 'Nestorian' church, which taught (like Arius) that Jesus was not himself God, but was a human made divine by God. After reaching Chaldea (Mesopotamia), Nestorian Christianity spread rapidly to central Asia, China and India. By the third century, a Christian sect, based on the teachings of St Thomas, was active in south India. Meanwhile, the hermits of Egypt gave birth to the Coptic Church, whose teachings soon spread to Ethiopia, where it has been the dominant

faith for 17 centuries. Many of these churches survive to this day.

✎ ▶ p. 303   ### AD 431
THE CELTIC CHURCH

Christianity was brought to Ireland by St Patrick (c. AD 390–460) in AD 431. He had previously lived and studied in monasteries in Gaul and Britain. From Ireland, St Ninian and St Columba brought Celtic Christianity to south-west Scotland. St Columba built the monastery on Iona. From there, it was brought to Northumberland, where the great monastery of Lindisfarne was founded, and where the theologian and historian the Venerable Bede (AD 673–735) studied at the monasteries of Wearmouth and Jarrow. Celtic Christianity derived much from the traditional Celtic culture and this is evident in the importance of the natural world in their theology, in the artwork of their illustrated bibles such as the *Book of Kells* and the *Lindisfarne Gospels* and in the monastic life where monks and nuns lived together.

AD 480–547
ST BENEDICT OF NURSIA

Born in Umbria, Italy, to a noble family, Benedict became the founder of the first major monastic order. Shocked by the decadence of Roman society encountered

during his education, he went to live as a monk in a cave near Rome. His growing number of followers invited him to be their Abbot and eventually he founded 12 monasteries, the final one at Monte Cassino – later to become the focus of European monasticism. Benedict is known mainly for his monastic Rule, which was enlightened and humane for its time. This involved simple but comfortable living, abstinence from meat, regular prayer, the shared ownership of possessions and communal consultation on major issues.

▼ *St Anthony of Egypt, founder of the Desert Fathers.*

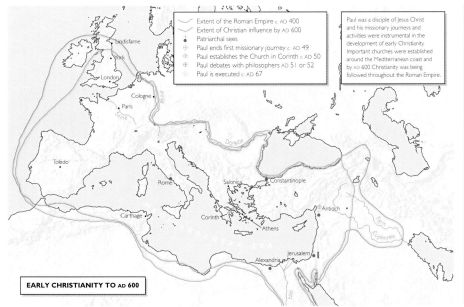

Extent of the Roman Empire c. AD 400
Extent of Christian influence by AD 600
● Patriarchal sees
⊕ Paul ends first missionary journey c. AD 49
⊕ Paul establishes the Church in Corinth c. AD 50
⊕ Paul debates with philosophers AD 51 or 52
⊕ Paul is executed c. AD 67

Paul was a disciple of Jesus Christ and his missionary journeys and activities were instrumental in the development of early Christianity. Important churches were established around the Mediterranean coast and by AD 600 Christianity was being followed throughout the Roman Empire.

EARLY CHRISTIANITY TO AD 600

p. 281 ◀ **Distant Voices** ▶ p. 285

We brought nothing into this world and it is certain we can carry nothing out. And having food and clothing, with these we shall be content. But those who desire to be rich fall into temptation and a snare, and into many foolish and harmful lusts which drown men in destruction and perdition. For the love of money is the root of all evil, for which some have strayed from the faith in their greediness and pierced themselves through with many sorrows.

1 Timothy 6:7–11

Islam
1900 BC–AD 1273

MUSLIMS TAKE PRIDE in the simplicity of their faith. It is based upon the teaching that there is but one God, who created the world, and that His message to humankind, the Qu'ran, was revealed to the prophet Muhammad in AD 610. This message is that the existence of the world and each thing in it is direct evidence of the work of God and that we should therefore remember Him continually. Those who remember God, will receive forgiveness and mercy. Within a few years of the establishment of the Islamic faith, it had spread from Arabia as far as Morocco, Persia and Turkey. Today it has a billion followers.

1900 BC
IBRAHIM (ABRAHAM)

To Muslims Ibrahim, or Abraham, who lived around 1900 BC, is seen as the first prophet of monotheism. To Muslims he is one of a series of prophets, the first of whom was Adam (the first man). The role of each succeeding prophet was to help fulfil the promise made by Allah to Adam in providing guidance to his children on Earth. Other prophets included Nuh (Noah), Musa (Moses) and Isa (Jesus) and ended with Muhammad, the Final Prophet. Abraham attacked the idol worship practised by his father and together with his son Ismail, built the Kaaba in the holy city of Mecca for the worship of the One God.

❦ ▶ p. 299   ### AD 610
THE PROPHET MUHAMMAD

Muhammad, the prophet of Allah, was born in AD 570 in Arabia. As he grew up, he became known as 'the Trustworthy One'. He worked for a wealthy widow, Khadijah, whom he later married. In 610 he received his first revelations from the Angel Gabriel in a cave outside the holy city of Mecca, during a solitary retreat. To Muslims, he was the Final Prophet, the last in the line that included Abraham and Moses, and his message was to have faith in the One True God. His first converts were Khadijah and his cousin, Ali. As

Muhammad's support grew, the opposition he experienced from the polytheists in Mecca, who used the Kaaba for idol worship, also increased.

AD 622
FLIGHT TO MEDINA AND CAPTURE OF MECCA

The hostility Muhammad experienced from the population of Mecca as a result of his teaching the word of Allah, led eventually to his being driven from the city, and he lived for several years in a valley just outside it. Persecution followed him here, though and, in AD 622, in an event later known as the Hegira ('flight'), he fled to Yathrib (later Medina), which had a sympathetic Jewish population. This event is used as the starting point of the Muslim calendar. Over the next eight years he led raids on the camel caravans to Mecca, destroying the Meccan economy and enriching that of Medina. In 630 he captured Mecca and cleared the idols from the Kaaba. Returning to Medina, he died two years later.

AD 632
THE EARLY SUNNI CALIPHATE

The first caliph, or successor to the Prophet as seen by the Sunni sect, was Abu Bakr. He had been a close friend and follower of the Muhammad, and was nominated as the Prophet's successsor on his death, despite suggestions that Muhammad's cousin Ali should become leader (and, indeed, the Prophet's own wish that he should become so). Abu Bakr was succeeded by Umar, who was assassinated in AD 644. The third caliph was Uthman ibn Affan, who compiled the standard Qur'an from the *surahs* (chapters) written down by the Prophet; he was murdered by his own soldiers in 656. These three caliphs, together with Ali, became known as the Rightly Guided Caliphs.

▼ *The Prophet Muhammad was forced to flee from the holy city of Mecca to Medina in AD 622.*

📖 SCRIPTURES   ✝ SAINTS   ✎ SCHOOLS   ❋ REVIVERS   ➡ PHILOSOPHERS

AD 656
ALI IBN ABI TALIB

Ali was a cousin of Muhammad and was adopted by him as a child. He married Muhammad's daughter, Fatima. Together with the Prophet's wife Khadijah, he was the first to realise and accept that Muhammad was indeed Allah's chosen emissary. On the death of the Prophet, Ali was seen by the Shi'ite sect as the rightful successor, and Muhammad himself had expected that his cousin would continue his work. Three caliphs were to come, though, before Ali eventually became the 4th in AD 656. Shi'ites treat him as the 1st Imam. He was murdered in a mosque by opposing Muslims in 661.

●◆ ▶ p. 294 ## 1126
IBN RUSHD (AVERROËS)

Ibn Rushd (1126–98), known in the medieval West as Averroë's, was an Islamic philosopher, best known for his inter-pretation of the works of Aristotle and his reconciliation of these ideas with monotheistic religion. He lived in Muslim Spain, and many Europeans travelled there to study under him. It is through him that western Europe rediscovered the Classical learning of Aristotle that had disappeared from Europe in the Dark Ages, and it is as a result of his interpretation that Aristotle became a major source of inspiration for Thomas Aquinas and for Christian scholastic theology. Such influences laid the foundation for the Renaissance that was later to sweep through Europe.

📖 ▶ p. 300 ## 1165–1240
MUHYIDDIN IBN 'ARABI

Ibn 'Arabi, mystic, philosopher, poet and sage, was given the title Muhyiddin ('the revivifier of religion') by his followers. He was born in Andalusia, Spain, at the height of Islamic culture there, and came in touch with the teachings of all three Western religions. His highly influential *Fusûs al-Hikam*, the 'bezels of wisdom' is a brief summary of his teachings, whilst the *Futûhât al-Makkiyya* is a vast encyclopedia

▲ *The mosque of Ali in Cairo.*

of his ideas. His key doctrine is the Unity of Being, that ultimately there is no self but God and that all things are ultimately one because they are ultimately God. He taught that all religions, whilst having different starting points, led to this insight.

1207–73
RUMI

Mevlana Jalaluddin Rumi was the founder of the Mevlevi Sufi order, a leading mystical brotherhood of Islam. The devotees are often known as 'whirling dervishes' because of their ecstatic spinning dance and chanting of prayers. Rumi was born in Balkh, Afghanistan, to a family of learned theologians. As he grew older he became a student of the wandering dervish, Shamsuddin of Tabriz. Escaping the Mongol invasion, he eventually settled in Konya, Turkey, where he wrote his major metaphysical work, the *Mathnawi*, and many discourses and

poems. The Mathnawi was written poetically, but laid out all the principle ideas and beliefs of the Sufi sect.

p. 283 ◀ **Distant Voices** ▶ p. 287

Your God is one God. There is no god but Him. He is the Compassionate, the Merciful. In the creations of the heavens and the earth; in the alternation of night and day; in the ships that sail the ocean with cargoes beneficial to man; in the water which God sends down from the sky and with which He revives the earth after its death, dispersing over it all manner of beasts; in the disposal of the winds, and in the clouds that are driven between earth and sky: surely in these there are signs for rational men.

The *Qur'an* 2:163–165

Medieval Christianity
1096–1359

BY THE MIDDLE AGES, Christianity had become highly institutionalised and was under the firm rule of the Church hierarchy. The monastic tradition had, however, flourished. The purpose of theology and philosophy at this time was to prove and explain the officially sanctioned teachings of the church. Creative thought was a highly dangerous activity and many philosophers – even some of those subsequently recognised as the most orthodox – were put to death or silenced for heresy. Within the monasteries, however, the actual practice of contemplation and spiritual living was able to flourish where inspired teachers appeared, whilst in the outside world the Church became increasingly involved in political and military activities, culminating in the decidedly un-Christian crusades.

1096
THE CRUSADES

It is one of the ironies of history that more than four centuries of war were dedicated to promoting the teachings of the prophet of

▼ *Christian crusader knights, who launched their first campaign in 1096.*

peace. In all, there were eight crusades to attempt to free the Holy City of Jerusalem from Muslim control, starting in 1096. These all ended either with temporary success after bloody battles, or in complete chaos. The Fourth Crusade never reached Jerusalem and the soldiers, impatient to attack something, plundered the Christian city of Constantinople. The Children's Crusade of 1212 resulted in 20,000 children being sold as slaves in Egypt. The crusades continued after the Christians were driven from the Holy Land in 1291. Thereafter, the crusaders tried to resist the Turkish advance in the Balkans. The Muslims advanced eventually as far as the Danube, conquering Constantinople in 1453.

1098–1179
HILDEGARD OF BINGEN

St Hildegard entered a Benedictine convent at the age of eight and became an anchoress, a solitary contemplative, at an early age. In 1141, she had a vision that God asked her to write down all her thoughts and visions – 'the heavens were opened and a blinding light of exceptional brilliance flowed through my entire brain. And so it kindled my whole heart and breast like a flame, not burning but warming ... and suddenly I understood of

the meaning of expositions of the books ...'. For many years she communicated her visions, distinctive for their ecological and egalitarian content, in the form of many books, paintings and music. She also wrote extensively on herbal medicine and nutrition. In 1150 she moved her convent to Bingen and later created her own convent at Eibingen.

✝ 1181–1226
ST FRANCIS OF ASSISI

St Francis, the founder of the Franciscan Order of friars, has been called the Second Christ, and he did more to re-establish the simple teachings and way of life of Jesus than anyone since St Antony of Egypt. He was born into the family of a wealthy merchant, but following several religious experiences, he abandoned this way of life and gave away all his possessions to become a wandering friar. His reverence for nature, as expressed in his *Canticle to the Sun*, is similar to that found in Celtic Christianity. When large numbers began to follow him, he created a simple Rule for them to follow: this included complete poverty, abstinence from meat and service to the poor. Today his Order is one of the largest in the Catholic and Anglican churches.

✳ ▶ p. 288 1225–74
THOMAS AQUINAS

St Thomas Aquinas was the son of the Count of Aquino and he entered an Italian Dominican monastery at the age of five. At 14, he began his studies at the University of Naples. His principal contribution was his *Summa Theologiae*, in which he argued that the teachings of Aristotle were fully in accord with the traditional teachings of the church. Here he argued that knowledge could be obtained both through reason, as Aristotle had done, and through faith in revelation. Revelation, he said, comes in two forms, the scriptures and the natural world. His approach was to use reason to prove the revealed teachings of the church. His *Summa contra Gentiles* was an attempt to use reason alone to convince the Arabs of Spain and North Africa of the truth of Christianity.

   📖 SCRIPTURES   ✝ SAINTS   ✎ SCHOOLS   ✳ REVIVERS   ➤ PHILOSOPHERS

▲ *Francis of Assisi (left) and Bernard of Clairvaux.*

1260–1327
MEISTER ECKHART

Johannes Eckhart, known as Meister Eckhart (1260–1327), was a German theologian and mystic of the Dominican Order. His German sermons provided guidance in apophatic spiritual practice, whereby the practitioners freed themselves from any concept of God or desire for that concept, so that the real and unnameable God may be free to be born in him. In recent years, the similarities of this approach to Buddhism have aroused great interest. Meister Eckhart's Latin theological works provided a philosophical defence of his teachings. Although he was denounced as a heretic in his lifetime, he has since been recognised as one of the most important Catholic theologians.

1266–1308
DUNS SCOTUS

John Duns Scotus (1266–1308) was a philosopher and scholastic theologian, named after his birthplace, Duns, in Scotland. He joined the Franciscan order and, as a monk, he studied and lectured at Oxford and Paris. He taught, like Thomas Aquinas, that knowledge had two sources, philosophical reason and divine revelation. These teachings were derived from Aristotle and Avicenna, but he rejected their view that mankind could only know the common essences of things, and stated instead that man could directly know the unique nature of each thing. Duns Scotus also argued for the 'proof' for God's existence, and exhorted evidence as the basis for belief.

p. 282 ◀ **Triumphs & Tragedies** ▶ p. 291
1274
EAST AND WEST DIVIDE

The division of the Western Roman Catholic and Eastern Orthodox Churches was a gradual process precipitated by growing differences in cultures and viewpoints that became increasingly obvious throughout the thirteenth century. The real cause was probably the division of the Roman Empire into two halves, centred on the capitals of Rome and Constantinople. This division led to dispute over the status of the pope, the Bishop of Rome. Theologically this division was reinforced by dispute over the 'filioquie clause', a technical theological point that was probably given importance for political reasons. By the time Thomas Aquinas's treatise, Against the Errors of the Greeks, was published in 1274, the division had become irreconcilable.

1296–1359
GREGORY PALAMAS

Gregory Palamas (1296–1359) was a major medieval contributor to the development of Greek Orthodox spirituality. As a monk he lived in the independent monastic state of Mount Athos and, after a Turkish invasion, fled to Thessalonica, where he was eventually made Archbishop. He developed the Hesychasm, a form of contemplative monasticism based upon constant recitation of the Jesus Prayer: 'Lord Jesus Christ have mercy upon me, a sinner'. Gregory taught that, with God's grace, man could discover the Uncreated Light, a direct experience of God's energies. He was also responsible for attempts to achieve theological reconciliation with the Catholics and was one of the best-known Christian mystics of the Middle Ages.

p. 285 ◀ **Distant Voices** ▶ p. 289

This above all else is needful: you must lay claim to nothing! Let go of yourself and let God act with you and in you as he will. This work is his, this word is his, this birth is his, in fact every single thing that you are. For you have abandoned self and have gone out of your soul's powers and activities, and your personal nature. Therefore God must enter into your being and powers, because you have bereft yourself of all possessions and become as a desert.

Meister Eckhart, *German Sermons and Treatises* (1260)

▼ *St Thomas Aquinas.*

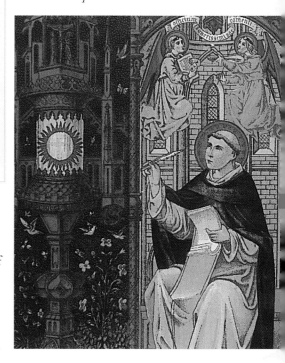

Renaissance Philosophy
1482–1602

B Y THE END OF THE MIDDLE AGES, Western thought was in decline. It was confined to the monasteries and rigidly controlled by the Church. The teachings of the Scholastics were otherworldly and were learned by rote in Latin. Corruption was rife and the popes had more interest in politics than spiritual practice. The liberal intellectual revival that brought learning out of the cloisters was known as the Renaissance. This began in the city of Florence and slowly spread to northern Europe and England. It was sparked by two events – the introduction of printing in 1451 and the arrival of Greek scholars and Classical texts following their expulsion from Constantinople by the Muslims in 1453. Study of Plato and other Classical writers inspired humanist philosophies centred upon man and the world.

❋ ▶ p. 303

1482
MARCILIO FICINO'S *THEOLOGICA PLATONICA*

Marsilio Ficino (1433–99), a Florentine priest, played an important role in reviving the thought of Plato during the Renaissance. He established a Platonic Academy near Florence, where he wrote many commentaries on the works of Plato and Plotinus. He also translated Plato's works from Greek into Latin. His major treatises include the *Theologica Platonica* (1482), in which he explored Plato's religious thought, his theory of the immortality of souls and his views on platonic love. Ficino's particular interest was in integrating the thought of Plotinus and the Neoplatonists with Christianity, but he felt that these teachings existed in all religions. His view of a an ideal life was based on these teachings, and he believed contemplation was the means to reach such higher levels of truth and understanding.

1489
PICO DELLA MIRANDOLA'S *HEPTAPLUS*

Count Giovanni Pico della Mirandola (1463–94) was one of the greatest Renaissance philosophers. He studied at the University of Bologna, after which he became a wandering scholar, visiting universities throughout Italy and France. He later settled in Rome, where he created one of the most extensive libraries of his time. He was inspired by the writings of Plato and especially those of Plotinus and the Neoplatonists. These are explored in his *Oration on the Dignity of Man*, which presents man as a microcosm reflecting the order of the universe. In 1489, he published the *Heptaplus*, in which he gives a mystical explanation of the origins of the cosmos.

1511
DESIDERIUS ERASMUS'S *IN PRAISE OF FOLLY*

Erasmus was the central figure in the development of liberal humanist Christianity in the Renaissance. Born in Rotterdam, he became a priest in 1492. He criticised the corrupt state of monastic life and scholarship, especially the stale dogmatism of the teachings of Aquinas, Ockham and Scotus – all derived from Aristotle. Instead, he advocated a return to the study of original texts such as the original Greek New Testament and the writings of Plato. His views were published in his satirical *In Praise of Folly* in 1511. Unfortunately, his moderate criticisms were attacked as heresy both by the Catholic authorities and by their new opponents, the evangelical Protestants, such as Luther and Calvin.

1513
MACHIAVELLI'S *PRINCE*

Niccoló Machiavelli (1467–1527), was responsible for a revolution in political thought as a result of the publication of his *Il Principe* ('The Prince') in 1513. In common with other Renaissance thinkers, his views are secular; they centre on man and the world and they are inspired by Classical literature. His advice to the Italian city states and their princes was based not upon religious principles, such as the Divine Right of Kings, but simply upon doing whatever worked. This empirical and pragmatic approach can be seen as a precursor to the Scientific Revolution. He looks at past events, such as the lives of Romulus, Theseus and Brutus, as described in Livy's *Histories*, for lessons about the most effective ways for a state to maintain its power.

▼ *The Renaissance Christian humanist Desiderius Erasmus.*

▲ *Niccoló Machiavelli, the secular Renaissance thinker.*

 ▶ p. 293

1518
THOMAS MORE'S *UTOPIA*

Sir Thomas More (1478–1535), Lord Chancellor of England, was the principal figure in the English Renaissance. He was a humanist Christian and, like his contemporary, Erasmus, regarded the happiness and well-being of humanity as the highest Christian ideal. His beliefs and his critique of the political and religious situation of his time are to be found in his *Utopia*, published in 1518. This depicts an imaginary society, inspired partly by Plato's *Republic*, that lives in accord with basic Christian teachings such as the absence of private property, non-violence, the abolition of hunting, religious tolerance, humane penalties for crimes and the rejection of wealth. He was executed for treason against Henry VIII in 1535.

1571
MICHEL DE MONTAIGNE'S *ESSAYS*

Michel de Montaigne (1533–92), was a French aristocrat who, until 1571, worked in the legal and political sectors of society. At this time, he decided to withdraw from this public life and instead he turned to study and writing. The result of his reflections were his *Essays*. These expounded his belief that true knowledge could only be attained by faith and its consequent revelations; the human mind alone, with all its capacity for reason, did not allow this true knowledge. The *Essays* were an exercise in individual ideas and belief, and marked a high point in the Renaissance trend for self-investigation, discovery and understanding.

1584
GIORDANO BRUNO'S *ON THE INFINITE UNIVERSES*

Filippo Bruno was born in northern Italy; he took the name Giordano when he became a Dominican monk. As a monk he studied Aristotle and Thomas Aquinas but in 1576, fearing prosecution for heresy, he fled and then wandered in northern Italy and Switzerland – where he encountered Protestantism. His writings, such as *On the Infinite Universes and World* (1584), attracted the attention of the Inquisition. After imprisonment for eight years, he refused to recant and was burned at the stake by the Church. Although many of his ideas seem strange today, his freedom of thought and his views on the unity of the world had much influence on seventeenth-century philosophy.

1602
CAMPANELLA'S *CITY OF THE SUN*

Tommaso Campanella (1568–1639) was born in southern Italy and became a Dominican monk when he was 14. He rejected the Scholastic and Aristotelean philosophy that he was taught and claimed that all knowledge of the world was obtained directly through the senses. This strictly empirical position contrasts with his later interest in astrology and white magic. Although denounced as a heretic and imprisoned for almost 30 years for holding these views, he spent several of his final years acting as astrological adviser to the pope. His *The City of the Sun* (1602) depicts an imaginary society governed by philosophers, in which the state provides education to all, there is no private property and all things, including wives, are held in common.

p. 287 ◀ **Distant Voices** ▶ p. 291

According to their system, plates and drinking vessels, though beautifully designed, are made of quite cheap stuff like glass or earthenware. But gold and silver are the normal materials, in private houses as well as communal dining-halls, for the humblest items of domestic equipment, such as chamber pots. They also use chains and fetters of gold to immobilise slaves, and anyone who commits a really shameful crime is forced to go about with gold rings on his ears and fingers, a gold necklace round his neck, and a crown of gold on his head. In fact they do everything they can to bring these metals into contempt.

From *Utopia*, by Thomas More (1518)

▼ *Tommaso Campanella.*

Christianity in Reform
1500–1748

THE CORRUPTION AND DECAY of the medieval Catholic Church and monasticism had a number of reactionary consequences: it led to the humanist revival of the Renaissance; to the political breakaway of the Anglican church under Henry VIII in England; and to the more fundamentalist and puritanical response of the Protestants under reformers such as Martin Luther and John Calvin. The dissatisfaction with the state of the church became increasingly widespread throughout Europe, and eventually it forced the Catholic Church to assess its position and take on board many reforms. From around 1550, there was a spiritual and institutional revival across the continent known as the Counter-Reformation.

▼ *Leader of the European Reformation, Martin Luther (far left).*

❀ ▶ p. 301
1500s
COUNTER-REFORMATION AND CATHOLIC MYSTICS

The recovery of the Catholic faith was aided by the emergence of several spiritual thinkers, including three Spanish saints. St Teresa of Avila (1515–82), the Carmelite mystic, is famous for her ecstatic visions; St John of the Cross (1542–91), who was inspired by her, wrote of his own mystic experience of abandoning self in *The Dark Night of the Soul*; and the third, Ignatius Loyola (1491–1556), was a Spanish theologian and military leader. After a serious injury, Ignatius adopted a religious life and studied spiritual practices – as described in his *Spiritual Exercises*. His highly intellectual Jesuit Order, of which he was the general, was organised along military lines with the objective of tracking down Protestant heresy and restoring the true faith.

✳ ▶ p. 298
1517
MARTIN LUTHER

In 1517 the German monk and theologian, Martin Luther (1483–1546), nailed to the door of his local church a long condemnation of the church's practice of selling 'indulgences' – documents that promised the buyer a reduction of time in purgatory. He declared that salvation came through faith and not through such acts. This practice was just one of many examples of the corruption

of the Church at that time. Desiderius Erasmus responded to this situation by promoting humanism, but Luther instead called for a strict adherence to the basic teachings of the Bible, which he translated into German, and a rejection of everything else – monks, ritual, the decoration of churches and the veneration of saints.

1533
JOHN CALVIN

John Calvin, born in France, was inspired by the protestant teachings of Martin Luther. Expelled from France in 1533 he moved to Geneva, where he turned the city into a repressive theocratic dictatorship. Worship, beliefs and morals were imposed by force and opponents were excommunicated or executed. His follower, John Knox, introduced a similar regime into Scotland. Fanaticism during this time took many forms – approximately 100,000 women were tried as witches; music and festivals were banned; and persecution of Jews was widespread. Calvin's teachings, whilst they shared the simplicity of Lutheranism, differed in that he believed in predestination and opposed the ordination of bishops. These differences later became the basis for several wars between the Protestant states of Germany.

1534
HENRY VIII AND THE ANGLICAN CHURCH

The origins of the Anglican Church were not primarily theological or religious, but really resulted from Henry VIII's anger at the pope's refusal to grant him a divorce from his first wife, Catherine of Aragon. Secession from the Catholic Church, which controlled the whole of western Europe, was only possible because of the very low esteem in which it was generally held at the time. Whilst its clergy were Catholic by education and theology, it was supported by the new Protestant movement in northern Europe, and this wide range of theological views remains in the Anglican church to this day. Protestant influence was a significant factor (or excuse) behind Henry's decision to dissolve the monasteries and seize church treasures.

▲ *The massacre of the Huguenots in France.*

▼ *George Fox, founder of the strict puritanical group known as the Quakers.*

peace issues and social justice and for the democratic way in which they run their affairs. An American offshoot, the Shakers, was founded by Mother Ann Lee in 1774.

p. 287 ◀ **Triumphs & Tragedies** ▶ p. 297

1562
WARS OF RELIGION

Reformation in northern Europe and Counter-Reformation in southern Europe split France down the middle. A massacre of the Huguenots (French Protestants) at Vassy in 1562 led to seven civil wars over the next 18 years. These were fuelled by German and British support for the Huguenots and Spanish and Italian support for the Catholics. On 23 August 1572, more than 8,000 Huguenots were killed in the St Bartholomew's Day Massacre in Paris. The shocked response from other European nations forced a truce, but conflict continued to flare up. In 1627 Cardinal Richelieu, on behalf of the French government, led the siege of the Protestant stronghold of La Rochelle, and from 1618 to 1648 Austria and Germany were engulfed in the devastating Thirty Years' War.

1600s
NON-CONFORMISTS

Non-Conformism is a loose category for Christians who did not conform to the practices of the established churches. Their development is complex because preachers often acquired their own beliefs through inspiration from several sources, but by the nineteenth century several distinct denominations had emerged. These included the Presbyterians, Congregationalists, Baptists, Quakers, Unitarians and Methodists. These non-conformist groups were generally opposed to the ordination of Bishops, to links with the state and to the use of ritual and imagery in religious practices. Most denominations were influenced either by John Calvin, who believed in predestination, or by his critic, Jacobus Arminius, who believed in salvation through faith.

1646
GEORGE FOX AND THE QUAKERS

The Society of Friends, or 'Quakers', was founded in England by George Fox (1624–91). Following his own inner experiences in 1646 and 1647, he rejected the formal institutions of the church and emphasised direct awareness of the divine. Quaker meetings involve no liturgy or ritual and are characterised by long periods of silence and contemplation – during which they were once said to 'quake' in awe of God, hence their name. Quakers are renowned for their active concern with

✚ ▶ p. 301 ## 1748
JOHN WESLEY AND THE METHODISTS

John Wesley was the founder of the Methodist movement, an offshoot of the Church of England. The name derives from the methodical approach he derived from the Bible for developing personal devotion. Wesley promoted his approach through outdoor sermons throughout Britain, to which he dedicated 12 years of his life. It was his decision to employ lay preachers in support of his mission, then to ordain them, that led to a split with the Church of England, and in 1748 he created the Methodist church. The movement was reinforced by a profuse production of hymns written by John's brother, Charles. The Methodists proved popular throughout England and soon spread to Wales. It was not long before their influence had extended across the Atlantic to America.

p. 289 ◀ **Distant Voices** ▶ p. 293

I design plain truth for plain people.

From *Sermons for Several Occasions*, by John Wesley

The Impact of Science
1600–1976

THE GREEKS were responsible for the development of philosophical logic, but had little interest in direct observation, and none in experimentation. The rediscovery of Greek philosophy in the Renaissance, combined with experimentation, led to empirical science. Pure science was highly successful in creating a logical model of the world, especially in the areas of physics and astronomy. Its conclusions were disputed more in the areas of biology, such as Darwin's theory of evolution. The application of science to questions concerning ethics (for example utilitarianism), the management of factories (for example Taylorism) and the workings of the human mind (for example behaviourism) have led to accusations that it is being used outside its legitimate sphere.

▲ *Germany's greatest literary figure and philosopher, Johann Wolfgang Goethe.*

1600s
RENÉ DESCARTES, FRANCIS BACON AND REDUCTIONISM

Seventeenth-century philosophers Bacon and Descartes are generally seen as the founders of modern science. Bacon stated that science should be about the collection and organisation of observed facts so that general principles could be derived from them. Before him, the tendency was either to indulge in theoretical speculation or simply to describe the world without explaining it. Descartes argued that all matter ultimately consisted of measurable particles and that all we need to do is to measure how these particles behave. All other properties, such as colour and texture are unreal or can be reduced to the basic quantities of size and shape. In addition to matter, his theory allowed for two other substances: mind and God; however later reductionist materialists, such as B. F. Skinner and Richard Dawkins have dispensed with these.

▼ *The seventeenth-century philosopher René Descartes (far right).*

1700s
GOETHE'S CRITIQUE OF REDUCTIONISM

Johann Wolfgang Goethe (1749–1832), Germany's greatest literary figure, was one of the foremost critics of reductionist science in the eighteenth century. He argued that as the natural world can only be known through subjective and qualitative experience, the process of reducing these experiences to mathematical quantities was not empirical. He felt that scientists were deliberately blinding themselves to the reality of the natural world and replacing it with an abstraction. This allowed them to treat nature as an inanimate object and to exploit it for their own ends. To counter this problem, he attempted to develop a theory of colour that incorporated the direct sensory experience of different colours. It is generally felt that his critique is of more value than the alternatives he developed.

1859
EVOLUTION AND SOCIAL DARWINISM

The Origin of Species by Means of Natural Selection, by English biologist Charles Darwin (1809–82), was published in 1859. Alfred Russel Wallace independently reached similar conclusions about the nature and process of evolution. The idea that species had developed over time, and that humans had developed from apes, shook the intellectual world and Christianity. Other scientists, using his idea

📖 SCRIPTURES   ✝ SAINTS   ✎ SCHOOLS   ✳ REVIVERS   ➥ PHILOSOPHERS

of the 'survival of the fittest', concluded that Europeans had conquered the world because they were more evolved. Social Darwinists believe that life is an endless struggle and that only the most assertive and aggressive people, businesses and nations survive. Peter Kropotkin, in his *Mutual Aid*, countered this argument by pointing out that the ability to co-operate was a form of fitness that encouraged survival.

▣ ▶ p. 295

1861
UTILITARIANISM

Jeremy Bentham's (1748–1832) utilitarian theory of ethics is that an act is good to the degree that it contributes to the greatest happiness of the greatest number. If an act gives one unit of pleasure to three people and causes two units of pain to another person then it is better to do this act than not to do it. This 'scientific' approach to ethics distinguishes it from approaches, such as the Christian one, which are based on justice or on the intentions of the person acting. The name 'utilitarianism' was first used in the eighteenth century by opponents of the movement as a term of abuse, but its position was developed by Bentham's student, John Stuart Mill (1806–73) in his book, *Utilitarianism* (1861).

▲ *Jeremy Bentham, the founder of the utilitarian theory of ethics.*

1900s
SYSTEMS THEORY AND THE
REDISCOVERY OF HOLISM

Study of complex systems, such as computer programmes, ecological systems, human communities and the human body, has led

scientists to realise that it is impossible to try and understand these structures by analysing each of their components. In the absence of this detailed knowledge, it is still possible to predict the behaviour of these systems with statistical models and general principles of systems theory. Complex systems are self-organising and naturally maintain themselves unless severely disrupted. This understanding provides a basis for an approach to medicine centred upon allowing the body to heal itself, an approach to sociology based upon allowing communities to develop naturally, an approach to agriculture based upon allowing nature to maximise its own productivity.

1911
TAYLORISM AND THE
RATIONALISATION OF
MANAGEMENT

Frederick Winslow Taylor (1856–1915) was the originator of 'scientific management', a means of rationalising work in factories and maximising efficiency. After a professional education, he chose to become a machine shop labourer in 1878, and soon progressed to the role of Chief Engineer. He believed that there was 'one best way' of doing each task and his time-motion studies involved analysing, timing and improving every movement and action of production workers. His central work, *The Principles of Scientific Management*, was published in 1911. Critics of Taylorism saw the practice as turning craftsmen into robots and maximising exploitation, while supporters claimed that Taylor had helped to increase the income of manual workers.

1913
THE BEGINNINGS OF
BEHAVIOURISM

Behaviourism is a school of psychology based on empirical science. It originated in about 1913, pioneered by J. B. Watson (1878–1958), and outlined in his book *Behaviourism* (1925). Behaviourists believe that the only valid form of psychology is the study of how animals and humans physically respond to stimuli, rather than

concentrating on introspection. B. F. Skinner states the position in its purest form in his *Beyond Freedom and Dignity* (1971), in which he presents the mind as an automatic machine and rejects the idea of free will. He concludes, controversially, that our minds should be scientifically programmed by psychologists to ensure socially beneficial behaviour.

1976
GENETIC DETERMINISM

In *The Selfish Gene* (1976), Professor Richard Dawkins (b. 1941) argued that the process underlying life and evolution is the survival and replication of the fittest gene. Derived directly from Darwin's theory, Dawkins suggested that plants and animals were merely the machines that genes used to survive. Although accused of reductionism by his opponents, he argued that any basic unit that self-replicated – whether a gene, a process or an idea – was capable of evolution through natural selection. This meant that not only would individual animals evolve, but so would artefacts, cultures and religions, communities and ecosystems. He also argued that 'God' was merely an idea that used a whole range of effective techniques to survive; a potential weakness of this argument is that it could be applied to any idea, including his own.

p. 291 ◀ **Distant Voices** ▶ p. 295

Then I at once saw, that the ever present variability of all living things would furnish the material from which, by the mere weeding out of those less adapted to the actual conditions, the fittest alone would continue the race. There suddenly flashed upon me the idea of the survival of the fittest. The more I thought over it, the more I became convinced that I had at length found the long-sought-for law of nature that solved the problem of the Origin of Species.

Alfred Russel Wallace on *The Origin of Species*

Merchants, Capital and Industry
1200–1973

THE OPENING OF TRADE ROUTES to Asia in the fourteenth to fifteenth centuries brought prosperity to the city states of Italy, and a new merchant class came into being. Technology, which had developed initially in the monasteries, grew rapidly as a result of the rise of science. When the merchant class gained control of manufacturing technology, a completely new economic system – industrial capitalism – was created. The spinners and weavers, who originally worked at home with hired machinery, were forced into factories by the machine owners in order to maximise their productivity; they experienced none of the new wealth and freedom. Although the employers used biblical reasons to defend the new work ethic, it was soon to be challenged by socialists, humanists, anarchists, romantics and ecologists.

▲ *Poor working conditions caused grave concern amongst philanthropists right up until the twentieth century.*

1200–1400
THE RISE OF THE MERCHANT CLASS
The opening of trade routes to the East in the thirteenth and fourteenth centuries brought great wealth to the Italian city states, especially Genoa and Venice. These cities competed aggressively for control of supplies of silk and spices and they were the first nations to have trade as their principal source of income. As a result of this trade a new social class, the merchants, appeared between the aristocracy and the peasants, with a corresponding set of social values. Traditionally, wealth and poverty were seen as accidents of birth or the will of God – and to the monks poverty was seen as a virtue. The merchants instead began to see wealth as a virtue and as God's reward for hard work and intelligence.

1680
LAISSEZ-FAIRE ECONOMICS AND FREE TRADE
Laissez-faire is a French expression meaning 'leave it alone'. It was introduced by Legendre, a French merchant, in 1680. He recommended that the government did not fix or adjust prices or impose complex trade laws and tariffs, as he felt this only obstructed free trade and caused poverty. Instead a more relaxed economic system was encouraged, along with unhindered international trade. Legendre's ideas proved immensely popular both in his native France and abroad. The name *laissez-faire* was later given to a school of French economists who held this view and who stated that 'to govern better, it is necessary to govern less'.

1700s
THE INDUSTRIAL REVOLUTION
The seeds of the Industrial Revolution of the eighteenth and nineteenth centuries. started before the creation of factories, and began in the villages of Lancashire, England, with technological advances in domestic textile production. Hargreaves's Spinning Jenny, for example, enabled spinners to increase their productivity beyond anything they had been able to achieve previously. Because the machines were expensive, though, they had to be hired rather than purchased, and this made spinners dependent upon the machine owners. Capitalists claim that the owners provided employment opportunities for the craftsmen, whilst socialists state that their ownership of the means of production was the start of massive exploitation of factory workers.

1700s
THE CREATION OF THE FACTORY
Skilled spinners and weavers, who worked at home using small hired machines, were forced by the owners to work in factories, so that they could be supervised and be made to work longer hours. Later the machines were enlarged and powered by steam and men were replaced by cheaper women and children. Dr Andrew Ure stated, in his *The Philosophy of Manufactures* (1835), that 'the constant aim and tendency of every improvement in machine to supersede human labour altogether, or to diminish its cost by substituting the industry of women and children for that of men; or that of ordinary labourers for trained artisans'. Had craftsmen retained control of their own labour we might, today, have had advanced domestic industries instead of vast production plants.

●● ▶ p. 298 **1776**
ADAM SMITH: *THE WEALTH OF NATIONS*
Adam Smith (1723–90) was a Scottish economist and philosopher – and the founder of modern economics. His most important publication, *An Inquiry into the*

▲ *Scots philosopher Adam Smith, author of* The Wealth of Nations.

Nature and Causes of the Wealth of Nations (1776), explored the function of the market and explained how free trade, free enterprise and the free division of labour could work for the benefit of all. He described this as the action of a 'hidden hand'. In common with the French *laissez-faire* economists, he advocated free international trade. He also wrote and lectured extensively on social ethics, justice and meaningful work. He is seen today as a politically 'right-wing' thinker who advocated the selfish pursuit of profit. He was also the author of the *Theory of Moral Sentiments* (1752) and donated the majority of his own wealth to charity.

1859
JOHN STUART MILL AND THE LIBERAL RESPONSE

John Stuart Mill, born in London in 1806, had mastered Greek by the age of three and Latin by the age of four. He was a Liberal MP and the most significant founder of

Liberal philosophy. He advocated a free market consisting of workers' co-operatives, and pointed out that true human needs are not effectively valued by the economy. For this reason, he argued that, in the interests of people and the environment, there should be a limit to both economic and population growth. In his *Utilitarianism* (1861), he argued that man should act to bring the greatest good to the greatest number, but in his *On Liberty* (1859), he argued that we should never coerce anyone except in self-defence.

▦ ▶ p. 296 **1905**
THE PROTESTANT ETHIC

The Protestant Ethic and the Spirit of Capitalism (1905), by sociologist Max Weber (1864–1920), has had significant influence on our understanding of capitalist attitudes and values. Weber traces the view that maximising profit is the purpose of life and that leisure is evil to the teachings of John Calvin, notions that were common amongst early industrialists. Calvin taught that profit was God's reward to the obedient and hard-working, and that poverty was a result of sinful laziness. Biblical quotes supporting this view were often written on the walls of workshops. This marked a turning point in generally held work ethics and a demonstrated a major shift from the medieval belief that 'blessed are the poor'.

1973
POST-INDUSTRIALISM AND THE REDEFINITION OF WORK

Sociologist Daniel Bell (b. 1919) argues that the original Protestant work ethic underlying capitalism will collapse as a result of the massive productive capacity of modern technology. This is argued in his books, *The End of Ideology* (1960), *Towards a Post Industrial Society* (1973), *The Coming of Post Industrial Society* (1973) and *The Cultural Contradictions of Capitalism* (1976). Modern capitalism requires consumers in pursuit of leisure and so is moving us towards a world where work is no longer seen as a virtue. Professor Charles Handy points in a similar direction,

predicting the end of the full-time nine-to-five job and forecasting instead that people will increasingly work part-time on a freelance basis.

p. 293 ◀ **Distant Voices** ▶ p. 297

The man whose whole life is spent in performing a few simple operations has no occasion to exert his understanding. He naturally loses, therefore, the habit of such exertion and generally becomes as stupid and ignorant as it is possible for a human creature to become. But in every improved and civilised society this is the state into which the labouring poor, that is the great body of the people, must necessarily fall, unless government takes some pains to prevent it.

Adam Smith, author of *The Wealth of Nations*

▼ *The founder of Liberal philosophy, John Stuart Mill.*

Socialism, Marxism and Revolution

1381–1960s

THE OPPRESSIVENESS of factory work eventually led workers to unite to press for better conditions. Unions gave workers the power to negotiate with their bosses, although at first these groups were ruthlessly suppressed. The origins of revolutionary socialism go much further back than the industrial age, though, to events such as the Peasants' Revolt of 1381, the English Civil War of 1642–49 and the French Revolution, but it came of age in response to the factory system. Karl Marx developed the most comprehensive economic and social thinking behind socialism and communism. Despite his predictions, revolution did not happen in industrial nations, but in feudal countries like Russia and China and in colonies such as Vietnam and Cambodia. In all cases, the imposition of equality involved tyranny and the murder of millions.

▲ *John Ball preaching to the peasants during the revolt of 1381.*

1381
THE ENGLISH PEASANT REVOLT

In 1381, inspired by the radical sermons of a priest, John Ball, and led by Wat Tyler, 30,000 peasants from across southern England marched to London to challenge Richard II to abolish serfdom. John Ball preached 'things cannot go right in England and never will, until goods are held in common and there are no more villeins and gentlefolk, but we are all one and the same. In what way are those whom we call lords greater masters than ourselves? How have they deserved it? Why do they hold us in bondage? If we all spring from a single father and mother, Adam and Eve, how can they claim or prove that they are lords more than us, except by making us produce and grow the wealth which they spend?'. After looting London, the rebels were eventually crushed.

1789
THE FRENCH REVOLUTION

'Liberté, Egalité, et Fraternité' was the rallying cry of the revolutionaries who stormed the Bastille in 1789. This was the start of the Revolution that would eventually overthrow the monarchy. There followed a series of political events that abolished the absolute power of the king and the rich landowners and replaced it with a Republic elected by all the people. The new government adopted the 'Declaration of the Rights of Man and of the Citizen', declaring everyone equal and free and subject to fair taxes. Perversely this was imposed through a regime that became known as the 'Reign of Terror', led by Maximilien Robespierre. The Revolution, despite its violence and tyranny, inspired political radicalism across Europe.

1834
TRADE UNIONS

In 1834, six leaders of the Friendly Society of Agricultural Labourers, who had met in Tolpuddle, Dorset, were arrested for 'administering unlawful oaths'. This action was taken after the six men entered into an agreement not to work for less than 10 shillings a week. The government, fearing such actions would inspire rural unrest, pressured the judge to transport them to Australia, 'not for anything they had done, but as an example to others'; a sentence that was passed, earning the men the title of the Tolpuddle Martyrs. Their punishment resulted in public outrage and eventually their sentence was repealed. Subsequently, the Trade Union movement expanded rapidly.

▲ *Karl Marx, whose communist ideas were to have a significant impact on the shaping of the twentieth century.*

▶ p. 306 ## 1848
KARL MARX AND COMMUNISM

Karl Marx, a middle-class German Jew, studied philosophy at the University of Berlin before editing a radical newspaper. After the failed 1848 revolt in Germany, he fled to England, where he wrote *The Communist Manifesto* and *Das Kapital*. In these, he attempted to provide a scientific foundation for socialism (countering the utopian socialism of Proudhon and Bakunin). Like the English economists, he saw production as based on land, labour and capital, but he pointed out that whoever controlled the mode of production also controlled the economics and politics of the country. Control by landowners causes feudalism, control by investors causes capitalism and control by labourers causes socialism. Public ownership of the means of production was seen as the necessary basis for fair and meaningful work.

1863
THE CO-OPERATIVE MOVEMENT

Co-operatives were businesses that were owned and run by the workers and/or the customers, thereby ensuring fair distribution of profits and suitable working conditions. The first successful retail co-operative was created in Rochdale in 1863. The 'Rochdale Pioneers', as they were known, began a movement that soon involved thousands of branches. By the end of the year, the North of England Co-operative Wholesale Society had brought together 300 retail co-ops, and in within 10 years the Co-operative Wholesale Society had been created to support these enterprises. The expansion of the co-operatives was backed by the Co-operative Party, which later merged with the Labour Party.

1893
THE LABOUR PARTY OF GREAT BRITAIN

The Reform Act of 1884 extended the right to vote to much of the working class in Britain. Traditionally, the working classes had sought representation through the Liberal Party but, with the extended franchise, a new Labour Party was formed by Keir Hardie of the Lanarkshire Miners' Union. With the support of the Trade Unions, and wholeheartedly backed by the miners, Keir Hardie became an MP in 1892 and the Labour Party won 40 seats in 1910. The party advocated a number of social reforms, which included abolishing child labour and introducing an eight-hour day. In 1924 Labour, in alliance with the Liberals, won their first election and Ramsay MacDonald was elected prime minister.

▲ *Mao Zedong, the leader of the Communist Party in China and founder of the People's Republic in 1949.*

p. 291 ◀ **Triumphs & Tragedies** ▶ p. 308

1949
MAO ZEDONG AND COMMUNISM IN CHINA

Mao Zedong (1893–1976), Chinese Communist leader was chairman of the Communist Party of China and the principal founder of the People's Republic of China. Mao helped found the Chinese Communist Party in Shanghai in 1921. In 1927, their then-allies launched a military campaign against the Communists, who retreated to rural areas where they gained the support of the peasants. After Nationalist forces surrounded them in 1934 the Red Army retreated 9,650 km (6,000 miles) to the north-west in the Long March. In 1949 they eventually captured most of China and declared the People's Republic. Chairman Mao promoted rural develop-ment, equality and the pursuit of economic self-reliance in the villages, but his government was extremely authoritarian and up to 100 million dissidents may have died in his labour camps.

1960s
SOCIALISM IN AFRICA AND SOUTH AMERICA

African and South American socialism was distinctive from socialism in other countries, in that it was generated in response to the economic and cultural impact of colonialism. In Tanzania, Julius Nyerere sought to reinstate traditional village socialism with his *Ujama'a* or self-reliance system. Nyerere went on to become president of the Republic of Tanganyika, when it was established in the 1960s. In South America, Paolo Friere, in *Pedagogy of the Oppressed*, called for a grassroots education that would help people to control their own lives and Ivan Illich attacked the disempowering impact of institutions. Liberation Theology is a Christian expression of such ideas.

p. 295 ◀ **Distant Voices** ▶ p. 299

When Adam delved and Eve span who was then a gentleman?

John Ball, revolutionary priest (1381)

Utopian Visions and the Challenge to the State
1762–1973

THE AGRICULTURAL and Industrial Revolutions brought misery and disruption to millions and, as landless peasants poured into the new manufacturing towns, conditions soon became intolerable. Children as young as six worked 18 hours a day in mills and coal mines, and pollution and disease reduced the average lifespan in some towns to around 15 years. Many thinkers, concerned with the situation, sought to develop visions of a better world. Socialism began to flourish amongst the workers, but it seemed to carry with it the danger of tyrannical government and offered no alternative to the factory system. In general, the alternatives proposed involved finding new equivalents to the traditional self-reliant villages that had been lost – self-governing communities free from employers and state control.

●◆ ▶ p. 307 **1762**
JEAN-JACQUES ROUSSEAU'S *EMILE*
Rousseau (1712–78) was renowned as the greatest liberal thinker and advocate of democracy and freedom in the eighteenth century. His writings covered every discipline from education to politics and from theology to science but all were held together by his underlying belief in the innate goodness of human nature and the natural world and the corrupting influence of artificial culture. In his *Emile* (1762) he presented healthy education as a result of innate curiosity about the world and not as a result of coercive lessons. The only healthy governments were those that emerged from a social contract between free and equal citizens. Christian living involved allowing God to act in our lives and in nature and in minimising our ignorant interference with this process.

1792
ROBERT OWEN AND NEW LANARK
Robert Owen (1771–1858), a manager of a spinning factory in Manchester, disillusioned with poor working conditions, became a practical utopian. He sought in 1792 to create a new type of community in the village of New Lanark, where originally children as young as five worked 13 hours a day. He created schools, increased the minimum working age to 10 and decreased the working day to 10 hours and supported trade unions, factory reform, votes for all. Disillusioned with the slow results, he started another community, New Harmony, in the United States, which his son then managed. His ideas were published in *A New View of Society* (1814) and he addressed Parliament on this subject in 1816.

▼ *Eighteenth-century liberal thinker Jean-Jacques Rousseau.*

1883
WILLIAM MORRIS AND THE SOCIALIST LEAGUE
William Morris (1834–96) made his living as a designer, creating naturalistic textiles and wallpapers, which remain as popular now as they were in their day. He was also a visionary poet and writer. In 1883, he created the Socialist League, but he opposed the authoritarianism of state socialism, advocating instead a socialism inspired by the medieval workers' guilds. His poem *The Earthly Paradise* (1868–70) and his novel *News from Nowhere* both depict a visionary and utopian society – a kind of medieval socialist world with minimal government and no material possessions, founded on co-operative work, craftsmanship and small communities. Along with many other groups at the time, such as the Fabians, the Socialist League wanted a move away from the capitalism that had characterised recent years.

✳ ▶ p. 300 **1888**
LEO TOLSTOY'S *KINGDOM OF GOD*
Count Leo Tolstoy (1828–1910), the Russian novelist and anarchist is renowned both for his great works of literature – *War and Peace* and *Anna Karenina* – and for his radical Christian pacifism. In 1888 he gave away all his material possessions to his wife, and instead lived under her roof as a peasant. He also emancipated his serfs. Like Gandhi, Tolstoy looked to the origins of his religious tradition for the basis for a free, non-violent and natural way of life. This is reflected in the simple and direct style of his novels and is argued more explicitly in his political works. These include *The Kingdom of God is Within You* (1893) and *Patriotism and Government* (1900), in which he argued that Christians had a moral duty to refuse military service.

1902
PRINCE PETER KROPOTKIN'S *MUTUAL AID*
Prince Peter Kropotkin was born into a noble Russian family. Following exile from Russia for his anarchist views, he settled in

▲ *Mahatma Gandhi, who headed a campaign for justice in India.*

London. His *Fields, Factories and Workshops* (1899) was a study of how small villages and decentralised communities could produce all their own food and material needs without relying upon landowners, big business, factory owners or the state. *Mutual Aid* (1902), was a refutation of the views of the Social Darwinists, who justified capitalism on the basis that it encouraged the survival of the fittest. As a biologist and anthropologist, he was able to show that evolution often resulted in mutually beneficial co-operation between animals and between peoples in primitive societies. He rejected the comm-unist alternative to capitalism because he felt his research proved that co-operation could arise naturally without being imposed by the state.

1914
MAHATMA GANDHI'S CAMPAIGN FOR FREEDOM

Mohandas Karamchand Gandhi (1869–1948) was born in Bombay and studied law in England then, as a barrister, moved to South Africa. He experienced the apartheid policy when he was thrown out of a first-class railway carriage at Pietermaritzburg in 1893. From then he campaigned for justice using non-violence (*ahimsa*), or what he called *satyagraha* or 'truth force'. On returning to India in 1914, he dedicated himself to obtaining Indian independence from the British Empire through non-violent action. Protests such as the salt march – where 60,000 were arrested for breaking a British ban on making salt –

destroyed the credibility of British rule. With independence, the country underwent partition into Muslim Pakistan and largely Hindu India and over one million died in religious conflict. Hindu extremists, angered at this policy, assassinated him in 1948.

✿ ▶ p. 305   **1932 AND 1949**
BRAVE NEW WORLD AND *1984*

Brave New World (1932) and *1984* (1949) are dystopias, not visions of an ideal world but their opposite. In *1984*, George Orwell illustrated an authoritarian communist world, similar to Stalin's Soviet Union – a world in which everything was controlled by Big Brother and his Thought Police for the benefit of the masses. In *Brave New World*, by contrast, Aldous Huxley described a world in which the arts of the salesman are used by the government; where people were genetically

▼ *Aldous Huxley, author of the dystopian novel* Brave New World.

engineered and psychologically normalised to fit into society; where brainwashing and subliminal advertising were used to keep people consuming and to prevent them thinking. All these were considered the possible future of the consumer society.

1973
SCHUMACHER'S
SMALL IS BEAUTIFUL

E. F. Schumacher's *Small is Beautiful: A Study of Economics as if People Mattered* was published in 1973. In it he challenged the vast institutions that were emerging in both capitalist and communist countries and called for small communities, decentralis-ation and technology on a human scale. Excessive size was, he believed, the cause of unemployment, poor working conditions, inequality and a decline in freedom. In particular he was keen to help poor countries develop without suffering the problems of what he termed 'giantism', and to this end he helped develop 'Intermediate Technologies', machines that could be owned and used on a village scale – an approach that has now been widely adopted.

---

p. 297 ◀ **Distant Voices** ▶ p. 301

For conditions even remotely comparable to those now prevailing we must return to imperial Rome, where the populace was kept in good humour by frequent, gratuitous doses of many kinds of.... But even in Rome there was nothing like the non-stop distraction now provided by newspapers and magazines, by radio, television and the cinema. In Brave New World *non-stop distractions of the most fascinating nature are deliberately used as instruments of policy, for the purpose of preventing people from paying too much attention to the realities of the social and political situation.*

Aldous Huxley, on government use of brainwashing, from *Brave New World Revisited*

Spiritual Revival in the Nineteenth Century
1800–75

RELIGION IN THE nineteenth century was, in many cases, characterised by a move from dogma and sectarianism to universalism, egalitarianism and a more experiential and participatory spirituality. This shift resulted in several new forms of Judaism and the foundation of a number of different schools of thought and belief. New religions such as Baha'i and Theosophy took hold and spread throughout their native countries and beyond. Teachers such as Ramakrishna taught that all religions are one and advocated policies of world peace. Outside the bounds of traditional religion, the English Romantic movement and the American Transcendentalist movement celebrated solitary spiritual communion with the natural world.

▲ *One of the founders of the American Transcendentalist movement, Henry David Thoreau.*

 ▶ p. 306

1800s
THE ROMANTIC MOVEMENT

Romanticism was an artistic and literary movement of the early nineteenth century, which flourished primarily in England and Germany. Romantics rejected the rationality and objectivity of Classical thought and embraced free self-expression, subjectivity, individuality, solitude, spontaneity and communion with nature. Key figures include poets such as Wordsworth, Coleridge, Shelley and Byron and

▼ *English poet, critic and leader of the nineteenth-century Romantic movement, Samuel Taylor Coleridge.*

philosophers such as Schelling. Schelling's transcendental idealism was based upon the view that the ultimate reality is mind, which is present in all things, and that nature is mind in the process of becoming. Nature can, therefore, never be adequately understood by the mechanistic analysis of science but only through the aesthetic and spiritual perception of the mind.

1800s
AMERICAN TRANSCENDENTALISM

Ralph Waldo Emerson (1803–82), with his colleague Henry David Thoreau (1817–62), initiated a philosophical and literary movement, known as American Transcendentalism, which drew upon the teachings of the *Bhagavad Gita* and other Eastern texts to provide a basis for experiencing the divine in the natural world. The basis of their belief was the oneness of life in all its forms. Despite its somewhat exotic origins, the movement's values, such as self-reliance and simple living, fitted well with American society and have inspired many significant events from the first World Parliament of Religions in Chicago to the conservation movement and the creation of national parks. The Transcendentalists were greatly influenced by the Romantic movement in Europe at the time.

1827
JOSEPH SMITH AND THE BOOK OF MORMON

The Church of Jesus Christ of Latter Day Saints – more commonly known as the Mormons – was founded by an American Christian, Joseph Smith (1805–84), following a vision in 1827 in which he was shown the *Book of Mormon*. Although the original was supposedly written in an American Indian language on golden plates buried under his parents' farm, he published a translation in 1830 and declared himself the priest of the new church. The *Book of Mormon* was not intended to replace the Bible, but to supplement it. Smith was killed by opponents in 1844, and eventually Smith's supporters were driven out of several states. They were led by Brigham Young (1805–77) to Utah where they founded a community at Salt Lake City.

1840s
REFORM AND CONSERVATIVE JUDAISM

The 1840s marked the emergence of several distinct movements in Judaism that split from traditional Orthodoxy. These were rooted in recognition by Jews that they were citizens of their host nations and not a nation within a nation. Reform Judaism, which developed amongst immigrants to the United States, was an attempt to adapt Judaism to Western society by distinguishing between the unchangeable and universal teachings of Judaism and those that were merely cultural traditions. Conservative Judaism made a similar distinction but treated far more of the teachings as unchangeable. This approach was opposed by the Zionists, who saw themselves primarily as citizens of the future nation of Israel – a stance that brought them into conflict with the societies in which they lived.

▼ *The founder of the Church of Jesus Christ of the Latter Day Saints, or Mormons, Joseph Smith, with his wife.*

1847
THE MORMON COMMUNITY

After Joseph Smith's death, leadership of the Mormons fell to Brigham Young (1805–77). In 1847, they set off to found a new community for themselves away from the persecution that had previously dogged them; they eventually settled in Salt Lake City in Utah. The Mormon practice of polygamy, amongst others, resulted in continued persecution and violence, however, and many members, also disagreeing with the strict discipline and dictatorial power of their leader, formed splinter sects of the Church. Polygamy was eventually outlawed, and Mormon communities thrive across the United States to this day.

✳ 1860s
SRI RAMAKRISHNA

Ramakrishna was a Hindu mystic from Bengal, and has since become one of the most popular saints of the Hindu faith. As a priest he practised *bhakti*, devotional prayer to the god Kali. He then experimented with prayer, meditation and worship in several of the major religions, including Islam and Christianity, having ecstatic visions as a result of each of these. He is chiefly remembered for teaching that there is one God common to all religions, despite the different names attributed to this God. His life is commemorated in the work of the Ramakrishna Mission, an order of Hindu monks, created by his disciple, Swami Vivekananda (1863–1902).

✚ ▶ p. 304 1863
THE BAHA'IS

Bah'u'll'h (1817–92), who was born in Tehran, was the founder of the Baha'i faith. In 1844 he joined the Babi movement, an Islamic Shi'ite sect led by Hadrat-I A'la, 'the Bab' (1819–50). In 1863, following revelations in a dungeon, he declared that he was the Divine Messenger prophesied by the Bab, the latest in a series including Moses, Zoroaster, Buddha, Christ and

Muhammad. His book, the *Kitab-I-Aqdas*, 'the most holy book', is the principal scripture of the faith, but the scriptures of all the major faiths are used in worship. His teachings bring together mysticism and contemporary concerns such as interreligious harmony, disarmament and world government – concerns that are strongly promoted by the seven million Baha'is throughout the world today.

1875
THEOSOPHY

Theosophy is a populist occult school that mixes a range of Eastern, ancient Egyptian and Neoplatonic ideas. It was promoted by the Russian-born Madame Helena Blavatsky (1831–91), who claimed to receive the teachings telepathically from Tibetan mahatmas, and was a great exponent of the Hindu faith. The Theosophical Society, founded in New York by Blavatsky and O. S. Olcott (1832–1907) in 1875, introduced Eastern ideas, in a rather confused form, to large numbers of Westerners. The basis of its teaching is concerned with divine revelation, and the school promoted investigation into the unexplained and untapped powers of both man and nature.

p. 299 ◀ **Distant Voices** ▶ p. 303

As one and the same material, water, is called by different names by different people, one calling it water, another eau, a third aqua, and another pani, so the one Sat-chit-ananda, the everlasting-intelligent-bliss, is invoked by some as God, by some as Allah, by some as Jehovah, by some as Hari, and by others as Brahman. As one can ascend to the top of a house by means of a ladder or a bamboo or a staircase or a rope, so divers are the ways and means to approach God, and every religion in the world shows one of these ways.

Sri Ramakrishna

Psychology
1890–1971

THE INTRODUCTION of the concept of the unconscious mind has had a major impact upon the way that we treat mental illness and behaviour problems in the twentieth century. Psychology has, however, come in for much criticism from philosophers, such as Karl Popper, because most of its theories cannot be either officially proven or falsified, and because the few theories that can be tested have not performed well. The flexibility of the science has also been criticised, as many different interpretations and understandings can be drawn from it, for example, Sigmund Freud reduced all problems to sex, Alfred Adler to the will to power and B. F. Skinner to past programming – models that contradict one another.

1890s
FRITZ PERLS AND GESTALT THERAPY

Gestalt psychology is a tradition that sees human experience and subjectivity as an indivisible and immediate whole that cannot meaningfully be divided into parts or be analysed in historical terms. Further than this, the whole proves to be greater that the sum of the individual parts. The movement emerged in Germany in the 1890s; Gestalt therapy, the therapy based upon this theory, was developed by Dr Fritz Perls. The emphasis of the therapy is upon providing the patient with practical help to enable them to live in the present, rather than on the provision of lifelong psychoanalysis. The therapy is also experiential rather than intellectual in approach, involving the whole person.

1910
SIGMUND FREUD

Freud (1856–1939) is credited with being the inventor of psychoanalysis. His first major work was *The Interpretation of Dreams*, which he was inspired to write in response to the many dreams that he had following the death of his father. In developing these ideas, he began to concentrate on the concept of the unconscious mind, of which dreams were the most common example, which he analysed in terms of competing forces – the *ego*, the *superego* and the *id*. Behaviour patterns in his patients, such as anxiety, phobias, hysteria and obsessions, were classified as neuroses – the consequences of repressing disturbing thoughts. Through psychoanalysis these repressed emotions would enter the conscious mind.

1912
ALFRED ADLER'S *NEUROTIC CONSTITUTION*

Alfred Adler was a student of Sigmund Freud, and part of his inner circle in Vienna. Despite being a follower of Freud's studies, Adler rejected his exclusive emphasis upon sexuality as humankind's unconscious motivator, and stressed instead the will to power and the inferiority complexes that occurred when this was obstructed. These theories are explored in his major work *The Neurotic Constitution* (1912). Adler also felt that Freud over-emphasised the role of the unconscious to the extent of denying free-will and the role of conscious creativity. Due to the nature of his beliefs, Adler can be seen as an early advocate of a humanist psychology.

1912
CARL GUSTAV JUNG

Another student of Freud, Carl Gustav Jung (1885–1961) likewise rejected Freud's heavy emphasis upon sexuality as the principal driving force of unconscious thought. Jung focused instead upon the spiritual, and drew much inspiration from the study of the practices, beliefs and symbols of differing religions, publishing *Symbols of Transformation* in 1912. He felt that man's unconscious thoughts were not unique to each individual, reflecting personal thoughts and desires, but rose from a collective unconscious and therefore the symbols and thoughts that arose in dreams were timeless and universal archetypes. Jung reached these conclusions after noting similarities between patient's hallucinations or delusions, and finding that these could not always be linked to the patient's personal experiences.

▼ *Sigmund Freud, the founder of psychoanalysis.*

📖 SCRIPTURES   ✝ SAINTS   ✎ SCHOOLS   ❋ REVIVERS   ➥ PHILOSOPHERS

▲ *Carl Gustav Jung, a pioneer of psychoanalysis along with Sigmund Freud.*

1920s
ROBERTO ASSAGIOLI AND PSYCHOSYNTHESIS

Dr Roberto Assagioli was the founder of psychosynthesis. He was another student of Freud, and whilst he valued many of Freud's insights, he felt that they did not reveal anything about the higher aspirations of the human mind. He set to work investigating further the working of the mind, taking his studies a step beyond Freud's theories. Through his research at his Centro di Studi di Psicosintesi in Florence, Assagioli developed the idea that people have multiple personalities, some conscious, some unconscious, and that a central goal of therapy is to integrate these and so make a whole and united mind. This field of psychiatry became known as psychosynthesis.

1950s
ABRAHAM MASLOW

Abraham Maslow and his colleague Carl Rogers were the founders of humanistic psychology, a school that emerged in the USA in the 1950s. Whereas earlier psychology focused on the study of psychological illness and abnormality, Maslow studied the behaviour of people who were mentally healthier than average. For him the aim of therapy was to remove all the inner obstacles to the open-ended process of 'self-actualisation', of achieving one's true potential. He saw human needs as existing in a hierarchy; when lower needs, such as food and shelter are satisfied then higher needs, such as love and acceptance, become the principal motivators. His study of self-actualising people revealed that they were spontaneous, creative, lacked inhibitions, were interested in the world rather than being self-centred.

1960s
R. D. LAING AND ANTI-PSYCHIATRY

R. D. Laing (1927–89) was one of the most radical critics of psychiatric practice of the twentieth century. In his books *The Divided Self* (1960) and *Sanity, Madness and the Family* (1964) he rejected the orthodox view that schizophrenia was simply an illness and saw it instead as a normal response to an impossible social situation. He therefore favoured group therapies and attacked chemical therapies and electric shock treatments. He also viewed madness not as a sign of mental decline but as a phase through which the mind needs to pass whilst healing itself. This led him to see the therapist as a companion on a journey through madness.

❋ ▶ p. 308 **1971**
BEYOND FREEDOM AND DIGNITY

Behaviourists teach that psychology should only study physical behaviour – how a human or animal responds to a stimulus – and should not attempt to speculate about feelings, emotions or the unconscious mind. The movement was established in 1913 by J. B. Watson, but was popularised by B. F. Skinner (1904–90). In Skinner's book *Walden II* (1948), he stated that a better society should be created by programming people to modify their behaviour. Later he addressed further problems in *Verbal Behaviour* (1957), which investigated the existence of language and its conditional development. In his *Beyond Freedom and Dignity* (1971) he denied that humans have free will or responsibility for their behaviour.

p. 301 ◀ **Distant Voices** ▶ p. 305

The man whom we can with justice call 'modern' is solitary. He is so of necessity and at all times, for every step towards a fuller consciousness of the present removes him further from his original 'participation mystique' with the mass of men – from submersion in a common unconscious. Every step forward means an act of tearing himself loose from that all-embracing, pristine unconsciousness which claims the bulk of mankind almost entirely.

Carl Gustav Jung

▼ *R. D. Laing, who strongly opposed the practice of psychiatry in the twentieth century.*

The Rediscovery of Nature
1790–1992

ANALYTICAL SCIENCE and the Industrial Revolution created a world where nature was seen as nothing but bits of matter that could be used as raw materials for human profit. The growth of industry led to the destruction of nature and to human suffering. There were many responses to this situation. The Romantic movement in Europe and the American Transcendentalists advocated spiritual communion with nature and campaigned for simple living and conservation. Campaigning groups such as the Sierra Club, Earth Day and the German Green Party emerged to protest at the destruction. Scientists such as Goethe, Lovelock and von Bertalanffy developed the concepts of holism and systems thinking as an alternative to reductionism.

1790s
WILLIAM WORDSWORTH'S INSPIRATION

William Wordsworth (1770–1859), who lived for most of his life in the Lake District, is England's greatest nature poet. With him, the medieval view of nature as desolate and demonic was overturned; instead it was seen as a source of inspiration and spiritual renewal, a sanctuary where the divine could be encountered. His own experiences of nature during his long walks in the Lake District and the Wye Valley, and during his tour of Europe in 1790, are the source of inspiration of most of his poetry. Like his friend and colleague, Samuel Taylor Coleridge, his political views, at least in his youth, were radical and initially he was an enthusiastic supporter of the French Revolution. His major works include 'The Prelude' (1805) and 'The Recluse' (1814).

1845
HENRY DAVID THOREAU

Between 1845 and 1847, Henry David Thoreau lived alone in the woods at Walden Pond, Massachusetts. 'I went to the woods because I wished to live deliberately, to front only the essential facts of life, and see if I could not learn what it had to teach, and not, when I came to die, discover that I had not lived.' Together with the essayist Ralph Waldo Emerson he was a founder of

▲ *The Romantic poet William Wordsworth.*

American Transcendentalism, a spirituality of nature inspired by Eastern religions. Imprisoned for a night in 1846 for not paying his taxes, which the government was using to finance a war with Mexico and the continuance of slavery, he wrote *On the Duty of Civil Disobedience*. In this – one of the most important political essays in American history – he argued that citizens had a moral duty to break unjust laws.

1892
JOHN MUIR AND THE SIERRA CLUB

John Muir (1838–1914) was the founder of the US National Park system and of the Sierra Club (1892), one of the earliest and largest conservation groups. He was born in Dunbar, Scotland, and moved to America with his farming family in 1849. There he travelled throughout the nation, working as a shepherd and labourer in wilderness areas. His love of the natural world led him to writing, his first work being *Studies in the Sierra* (1874), and these brought him into contact with other writers such as Ralph Waldo Emerson. His book *Our National Parks* (1901) attracted the attention of President Theodore Roosevelt, who visited his log cabin and there developed the Conservation Corps, a national scheme to mobilise conservation activities.

1949
ALDO LEOPOLD: THE ECOSYSTEM

Aldo Leopold (1887–1948) worked as a conservationist for the US Forest Service. His major work – *A Sand County Almanac* (1949) – was published posthumously, and in it he introduced the concept of the ecosystem as an interacting web of living organisms that had its own natural balance. The work stated that in order to manage an ecosystem, it was necessary to 'think like a mountain' and obtain an overview of the whole system. His *Land Ethic* was based on the moral maxim that 'a thing is right when it tends to preserve the integrity, stability and beauty of the biotic community. It is wrong when it tends otherwise'. His beliefs have greatly influenced modern views on ecology.

1970s
THE EMERGENCE OF THE GREEN MOVEMENT

Amongst the first of the new 'Green' parties that arose during the 1970s to tackle increasing environmental problems, was Greenpeace. This was founded in British Columbia in 1971, in opposition to the nuclear testing in the United States. In the US itself, the Green Party was established

📖 SCRIPTURES   ✝ SAINTS   ✎ SCHOOLS   ✳ REVIVERS   ⚭ PHILOSOPHERS

▲ *Carl Gustav Jung, a pioneer of psychoanalysis along with Sigmund Freud.*

1920s
ROBERTO ASSAGIOLI AND PSYCHOSYNTHESIS

Dr Roberto Assagioli was the founder of psychosynthesis. He was another student of Freud, and whilst he valued many of Freud's insights, he felt that they did not reveal anything about the higher aspirations of the human mind. He set to work investigating further the working of the mind, taking his studies a step beyond Freud's theories. Through his research at his Centro di Studi di Psicosintesi in Florence, Assagioli developed the idea that people have multiple personalities, some conscious, some unconscious, and that a central goal of therapy is to integrate these and so make a whole and united mind. This field of psychiatry became known as psychosynthesis.

1950s
ABRAHAM MASLOW

Abraham Maslow and his colleague Carl Rogers were the founders of humanistic psychology, a school that emerged in the USA in the 1950s. Whereas earlier psychology focused on the study of psychological illness and abnormality, Maslow studied the behaviour of people who were mentally healthier than average. For him the aim of therapy was to remove all the inner obstacles to the open-ended process of 'self-actualisation', of achieving one's true potential. He saw human needs as existing in a hierarchy; when lower needs, such as food and shelter are satisfied then higher needs, such as love and acceptance, become the principal motivators. His study of self-actualising people revealed that they were spontaneous, creative, lacked inhibitions, were interested in the world rather than being self-centred.

1960s
R. D. LAING AND ANTI-PSYCHIATRY

R. D. Laing (1927–89) was one of the most radical critics of psychiatric practice of the twentieth century. In his books *The Divided Self* (1960) and *Sanity, Madness and the Family* (1964) he rejected the orthodox view that schizophrenia was simply an illness and saw it instead as a normal response to an impossible social situation. He therefore favoured group therapies and attacked chemical therapies and electric shock treatments. He also viewed madness not as a sign of mental decline but as a phase through which the mind needs to pass whilst healing itself. This led him to see the therapist as a companion on a journey through madness.

※ ▶ p. 308   1971
BEYOND FREEDOM AND DIGNITY

Behaviourists teach that psychology should only study physical behaviour – how a human or animal responds to a stimulus – and should not attempt to speculate about feelings, emotions or the unconscious mind. The movement was established in 1913 by J. B. Watson, but was popularised by B. F. Skinner (1904–90). In Skinner's book *Walden II* (1948), he stated that a better society should be created by programming people to modify their behaviour. Later he addressed further problems in *Verbal Behaviour* (1957), which investigated the existence of language and its conditional development. In his *Beyond Freedom and Dignity* (1971) he denied that humans have free will or responsibility for their behaviour.

p. 301 ◀ **Distant Voices** ▶ p. 305

The man whom we can with justice call 'modern' is solitary. He is so of necessity and at all times, for every step towards a fuller consciousness of the present removes him further from his original 'participation mystique' with the mass of men – from submersion in a common unconscious. Every step forward means an act of tearing himself loose from that all-embracing, pristine unconsciousness which claims the bulk of mankind almost entirely.

Carl Gustav Jung

▼ *R. D. Laing, who strongly opposed the practice of psychiatry in the twentieth century.*

The Rediscovery of Nature
1790–1992

ANALYTICAL SCIENCE and the Industrial Revolution created a world where nature was seen as nothing but bits of matter that could be used as raw materials for human profit. The growth of industry led to the destruction of nature and to human suffering. There were many responses to this situation. The Romantic movement in Europe and the American Transcendentalists advocated spiritual communion with nature and campaigned for simple living and conservation. Campaigning groups such as the Sierra Club, Earth Day and the German Green Party emerged to protest at the destruction. Scientists such as Goethe, Lovelock and von Bertalanffy developed the concepts of holism and systems thinking as an alternative to reductionism.

1790s
WILLIAM WORDSWORTH'S INSPIRATION

William Wordsworth (1770–1859), who lived for most of his life in the Lake District, is England's greatest nature poet. With him, the medieval view of nature as desolate and demonic was overturned; instead it was seen as a source of inspiration and spiritual renewal, a sanctuary where the divine could be encountered. His own experiences of nature during his long walks in the Lake District and the Wye Valley, and during his tour of Europe in 1790, are the source of inspiration of most of his poetry. Like his friend and colleague, Samuel Taylor Coleridge, his political views, at least in his youth, were radical and initially he was an enthusiastic supporter of the French Revolution. His major works include 'The Prelude' (1805) and 'The Recluse' (1814).

▲ *The Romantic poet William Wordsworth.*

1845
HENRY DAVID THOREAU

Between 1845 and 1847, Henry David Thoreau lived alone in the woods at Walden Pond, Massachusetts. 'I went to the woods because I wished to live deliberately, to front only the essential facts of life, and see if I could not learn what it had to teach, and not, when I came to die, discover that I had not lived.' Together with the essayist Ralph Waldo Emerson he was a founder of

American Transcendentalism, a spirituality of nature inspired by Eastern religions. Imprisoned for a night in 1846 for not paying his taxes, which the government was using to finance a war with Mexico and the continuance of slavery, he wrote *On the Duty of Civil Disobedience*. In this – one of the most important political essays in American history – he argued that citizens had a moral duty to break unjust laws.

✚ 1892
JOHN MUIR AND THE SIERRA CLUB

John Muir (1838–1914) was the founder of the US National Park system and of the Sierra Club (1892), one of the earliest and largest conservation groups. He was born in Dunbar, Scotland, and moved to America with his farming family in 1849. There he travelled throughout the nation, working as a shepherd and labourer in wilderness areas. His love of the natural world led him to writing, his first work being *Studies in the Sierra* (1874), and these brought him into contact with other writers such as Ralph Waldo Emerson. His book *Our National Parks* (1901) attracted the attention of President Theodore Roosevelt, who visited his log cabin and there developed the Conservation Corps, a national scheme to mobilise conservation activities.

1949
ALDO LEOPOLD: THE ECOSYSTEM

Aldo Leopold (1887–1948) worked as a conservationist for the US Forest Service. His major work – *A Sand County Almanac* (1949) – was published posthumously, and in it he introduced the concept of the ecosystem as an interacting web of living organisms that had its own natural balance. The work stated that in order to manage an ecosystem, it was necessary to 'think like a mountain' and obtain an overview of the whole system. His *Land Ethic* was based on the moral maxim that 'a thing is right when it tends to preserve the integrity, stability and beauty of the biotic community. It is wrong when it tends otherwise'. His beliefs have greatly influenced modern views on ecology.

1970s
THE EMERGENCE OF THE GREEN MOVEMENT

Amongst the first of the new 'Green' parties that arose during the 1970s to tackle increasing environmental problems, was Greenpeace. This was founded in British Columbia in 1971, in opposition to the nuclear testing in the United States. In the US itself, the Green Party was established

▲ *The first Earth Day was held in April 1970, and drew attention to environmental issues.*

conscious. Although this is a view that is held by many of his supporters, it actually forms no part of Lovelock's theory. His studies of atmospheric chemistry, which led him to discover the hole in the ozone layer and the wide distribution of pesticides, have also provided much evidence for the theory. His work was largely responsible for the greater awareness of the effect man-made products and actions have had on the planet.

✿
1992
SUSTAINABILITY: THE RIO DECLARATION

The Rio Declaration on Environment and Development was signed at the largest-ever meeting of heads of governments, held in Rio de Janeiro, Brazil, in 1992. The Declaration was signed by 169 nations, indicating a worldwide awareness of the necessity to take action on environmental issues. Whilst the agreement was important for this reason, many have pointed out that it is worded so as to avoid committing any individual nation to taking significant action. Questions have also been raised over whether its support for accelerated economic growth can be reconciled with its advocacy of 'sustainability'.

two years later. Environmental politics had its first major impact in Germany in 1987, where the Green Party, *Die Grunen*, obtained several seats in the German government. Growing out of massive demonstrations against nuclear power, this was the most significant shift in the European political scene since the Second World War. Since this time, the influence of 'Green' politics has continued to grow.

1970
EARTH DAY

On the first Earth Day, on 22 April 1970, millions of Americans joined in teach-ins, demonstrations and rallies in major cities across the country, to show support for the protection of the environment, and awareness for the dangers caused by pollution and other environmental issues. The Earth Day received an amount of

corporate opposition, but ended as a great success. The long-term consequences of this event were substantial, leading to important legislation, including the establishment of the Environmental Protection Agency, a 25 per cent reduction in air pollution and the rehabilitation of half of the polluted rivers of the US. The Earth Days, which are held every year, remain major events.

1979
JAMES LOVELOCK AND THE GAIA HYPOTHESIS

The Gaia hypothesis was first outlined by biochemist James Lovelock in his major work, *Gaia* (1979). The hypothesis suggests that the planet Earth, its soil, oceans, atmosphere and biosphere all constitute a self-regulating system that can be thought of as living. He has often been accused by scientists of arguing that the Earth is

p. 303 ◀ **Distant Voices** ▶ p. 307

In the woods a man casts off his years, as a snake his skin, and at what period soever of life is always a child. In the woods is perpetual youth. Within these plantations of God, a decorum and sanctity reign, a perennial festival is dressed, and the guest sees not how he should tire of them in a thousand years. In the woods we return to reason and faith.... Standing on the bare ground, my head bathed in the blithe air and uplifted into infinite space, all mean egotism vanishes. I become a transparent eyeball; I am nothing: I see all; the currents of the universal Being circulate through me; I am part and parcel of God.

Ralph Waldo Emerson

Philosophy in the Twentieth Century
1903–78

THE DISTINCTIVE NATURE of twentieth-century philosophy is the recognition of the limits of proof and knowability. Heidegger and Sartre pointed out that we do not come into the world with a predefined purpose but must create this for ourselves. Popper and Kuhn showed that scientific ideas are not provable but are merely models of reality that may collapse and require replacement at any moment. Foucault showed that 'the normal person' is not an objective reality but an idea that develops over time in response to political and social processes. Einstein concludes that even the 'laws of physics' are not absolute but relative to one another. Underlying all this is a focus upon the limits of language, a recognition that words and names are human inventions and have no direct relation to the physical reality of the world.

▲ *Philosopher Ludwig Wittgenstein.*

1903
BERTRAND RUSSELL'S
PRINCIPLES OF MATHEMATICS

Bertrand Russell, the 3rd Earl Russell (1872–1970), was the founder of British analytic philosophy and a major figure in mathematical logic. His most significant work was his *The Principles of Mathematics* (1903), in which he came to the conclusions that mathematics was an extension of the theories of logic, the subject of which remained beyond the realms of the mind. As well as being a philosopher and historian, he developed a reputation as a pacifist and radical social critic. His analytic philosophy involved reducing philosophical arguments into their constituent parts and linguistically analysing their meaning. In pursuing this path, he has been accused of leading philosophy into a dead end.

1922 AND 1953
LUDWIG WITTGENSTEIN'S
PHILOSOPHIES

Ludwig Wittgenstein (1889–1951) was Professor of Philosophy at Cambridge University between 1939 and 1947. His two very different books, *Tractatus Logico-Philosophicus* (1922) and *Philosophical Investigations* (1953) explore the nature and limits of language and thought. In them, he argued that factual language was nothing but a way of creating pictures of the world, that all logical statements were, by their own definition, true (that is, tautologies) and that language was in itself incapable of communicating aesthetic, ethical or religious insights. He showed, therefore, that thought and language were not about describing objective reality but rather about constructing coherent, meaningful and shared models of the world.

1927
MARTIN HEIDEGGER'S
BEING AND TIME

Martin Heidegger (1889–1976) was responsible for a highly original exploration of the nature of being and of our experience of existence. This was introduced in his *Being and Time* (1927). He asserted that to *be* was not to exist like an object but to choose who one is. He saw subject and object as two concepts derived from the single prior reality of existence – because of this he can be seen as one of the originators of existentialism. To the extent that we allow external events to determine our nature he felt we live inauthentically, to the extent that we create ourselves we live authentically. This concept was developed further by Jean-Paul Sartre.

1934
SIR KARL POPPER'S *LOGIC*

The Viennese philosopher, Karl Popper (1902–94), argued that it is never possible to have certain knowledge. In his *Logic of Scientific Discovery* (1934) he shows that no scientific hypothesis can be proved – it can only be falsified. Indeed if it could never be falsified it would not be a scientific theory. Therefore, every good scientific theory is simply a model that has yet to be disproven. His opposition to the concept of certainty led him, in his *The Open Society and its Enemies* (1945), to criticise authoritarian models of human society and historicism, such as those proposed by Plato and Karl Marx.

▲ *Viennese philosopher Karl Popper.*

1945
JEAN-PAUL SARTRE AND EXISTENTIALISM

'Existence precedes essence' and 'man makes himself'; these phrases encapsulate the atheist existentialism of the French philosopher Jean-Paul Sartre (1905–80). In the absence of a God who created us with a purpose, he pointed out, we arrive in the world with nothing but our own existence. This problem is explored in his *Being and Nothingness* (1943). We have no choice but to decide for ourselves who we are – we must invent our own essence. The self is not an entity but a project, not something that has being but something that is forever becoming. Whoever defines themselves by their current role in life lives in 'bad faith'. It is a philosophy that gives each of us an enormous responsibility but also complete freedom.

1961
MICHEL FOUCAULT

The French philosopher, Michel Foucault (1926–84), sought to understand the origin and nature of institutional controls over how man perceives himself. In his *Madness and Civilisation* (1961) and his *Discipline and Punish* (1975) he explored the origins and development of concepts and normality by looking at the history of punishment and of asylums, of how different social outsiders were repressed in different ways, the social punishment of being different. He came to the conclusion that state concepts of normality are internalised and determine how people see themselves. The 'work of freedom', he decided, was for man to step outside these definitions and to create himself.

1962
THOMAS KUHN

Thomas Kuhn (1922–96), Professor of Philosophy at Massachusetts Institute of Technology, was responsible for a new understanding of how scientific models of the world develop. His major work was *The Structure of Scientific Revolutions* (1962), in which he rejected the view of empiricists that mankind was slowly evolving towards truth, and instead argued that man was simply creating coherent models that map reality, and that these collapse and are replaced whenever experiments reveal insoluble contradictions in the model. He called each of these accepted sets of theories paradigms. He concluded, like Karl Popper, that scientific theories cannot be true, but should be valued in accordance with their usefulness.

1978
JACQUES DERRIDA AND DECONSTRUCTIVISM

Jacques Derrida was born in Algeria in 1930. His thought developed as a response to that of Heidegger, although he was also influenced by Friedrich Nietzsche and Ferdinand de Saussure. He felt that metaphysical philosophy was without meaning, that it had reached the end of its history and that the only true philosophy concerned the nature of being. His greatest work is *Writing and Difference* (1978). The question he asks is: 'what can we say about Being without resorting to any metaphysical assumptions?'. He tries to answer this by deconstructing philosophical statements on this matter and showing their limitations, contradictions and false assumptions.

p. 305 ◀ **Distant Voices** ▶ p. 309

Atheistic existentialism … states that if God does not exist, there is at least one being in whom existence precedes essence, a being who exists before he can be defined by any concept and that this being is man, or, as Heidegger says, human reality. What is meant here by saying that existence precedes essence? It means that, first of all, man exists, turns up, appears on the scene, and, only afterwards, defines himself.

Jean-Paul Sartre

▼ *One of the great leaders of the Existentialist movement, John-Paul Sartre.*

Religion in the Twentieth Century

1893–1980

EUROPEAN COLONIALISM had a profound impact on the civilisations of all the other continents. Flourishing cultures and traditions were suppressed and undermined by the arrival of merchants, governors and missionaries. In Africa, Australia and the Americas tribal religions were banned and the Churches were encouraged to re-educate the populations. In China and Southeast Asia, revolutions inspired by Western ideas led to the abolition of Buddhism, Confucianism and Taoism. With the collapse of Colonialism then the decline of Communism, new versions of old religions are emerging. Tribal societies are rediscovering their cultures and turning to their religious traditions to defend their lifestyle and environment. A politically radical Buddhism is taking form in Southeast Asia. Islam is reviving in a fundamentalist form and liberation theology is uniting socialism and Christianity in Latin America and Africa.

▲ *After the revolution of 1949, Confucianism was abolished in the new Republic of China.*

✳ 1893
SWAMI VIVEKANANDA AND THE REDISCOVERY OF HINDUISM

Swami Vivekananda (1863–1902) was a disciple of Ramakrishna and the most important figure in the recent systematisation of Hindu thought. In developing a philosophy that brought together all the main strands of the Hindu tradition from *advaita* (meditation) to *bhakti* (devotion) he virtually created modern Hinduism. The central teaching is that God is beyond all concepts and images and can be known directly through meditation but that God also takes many forms and so devotional worship is also a true form of religion. As well as providing a means to unite Hinduism, it provided a means to bring harmony between all faiths, and this resulted in worldwide attention when he spoke at the 1893 World Parliament of Religions.

1912
THE DISESTABLISHMENT AND ABOLITION OF CONFUCIANISM

In 1912, the emperor of China was overthrown by the Chinese Republicans led by Sun Yat Sen. Confucianism, which put great emphasis upon loyalty to the emperor, was seen as a threat to the new regime and was disestablished, although it was allowed to continue. After the revolution in 1949, Confucian teachings were condemned by the Communists as élitist and reactionary, and the faith was abolished from the Republic of China. At the same time, all schools and colleges under the control of Western missionaries were seized and nationalised. It is significant that the concept of an authoritarian state run for the welfare of the people has had much influence upon the contemporary government of China.

1941
THE HOLOCAUST AND THE FOUNDATION OF THE STATE OF ISRAEL

Anti-Semitism began to return to France, Germany and Eastern Europe in the late nineteenth century. From 1941, Germany embarked upon the rounding up and systematic murder of all the Jews in Europe and by the end of the war in 1945 no fewer than six million had died. In 1948, Britain, following its victory in the Second World War, decided to offer its Palestinian territory as a homeland for the Jewish refugees in Europe. This return to the 'Promised Land', after 2,000 years of exile has had a profound effect upon the Jewish people. A millenarian sense of hope has helped them to build a modern nation in just a few decades, but it has also encouraged a nationalism that has led to the oppression of the Palestinians and ongoing conflict with their Arab neighbours.

p. 297 ◀ **Triumphs & Tragedies**
1950s
THE DESTRUCTION AND REVIVAL OF BUDDHISM

Communist revolution in China, Vietnam, Laos and Cambodia led to the abolition of Buddhism, the destruction of nearly all the temples and the murder of most monks. In Cambodia only eight monks survived. In Sri Lanka, colonialism virtually destroyed the tradition. A new Buddhism concerned with peace work and community building has emerged. Dr A. T. Ariyaratne's Sarvodaya movement in Sri Lanka involves almost every village, in Cambodia Maha Ghosananda leads massive peace walks across regions sown with land mines, in Vietnam Thich Nhat Hanh, now exiled, founded Tiep Hien, the Order of Interbeing, and in Thailand Sulak Sivaraksa challenges the government's westernisation policy. Buddhism is one of the fastest growing religions in Western nations. Today severe oppression of Buddhism continues in Burma and Tibet.

 SCRIPTURES   ✝ SAINTS   SCHOOLS   ✳ REVIVERS   ➡ PHILOSOPHERS

▲ *The practice of Buddhism was viciously outlawed in Indonesia in the middle of the twentieth century.*

1950s
THE WEST TURNS EAST

The American 'beat' poets of the 1950s, including Allen Ginsberg, Jack Kerouac and Gary Snyder, drew upon Buddhism as a philosophy for rejecting the materialism and 'work ethic' of the Western world. Their example inspired the counter-cultural hippie movement of the 1960s. The Beatles, the greatest pop group of their era, became followers of the Maharishi, and following the trend, thousands of young people travelled to India or began to follow Eastern teachers of many different faiths – Hindu, Buddhist and Sufi. Within 10 years, Eastern practices such as meditation and yoga had become almost

▼ *From the earliest days of exploration, native peoples were forced to accept the religion of the new settlers; this underwent an about-face towards the end of the twentieth century.*

universally available to the public. The general turn towards eastern religions as a more positive and less repressive order has continued into the 1990s.

1960s
THE REVIVAL OF FIRST NATION RELIGIONS

The traditional way of life and the beliefs and practices of the Native Americans, had gradually been eroded by white settlers on their lands since the nineteenth century. Since the 1960s the oppressed and declining society of the Native American Indians has undergone a revival. Increased communication between tribes, supported by a growing number of sympathetic whites, has led to the development of a pan-Indian ecological spirituality. Central texts include the words of Black Elk, whose teachings about the Great Spirit have parallels with Christianity, and the speech of Chief Seattle, who asked, in response to a government bid for their land 'if we do not own the freshness of the air and the sparkle of the water, how can you buy them?'.

1961
CHRISTIANITY IN THE THIRD WORLD

Criticism of colonialism and the brutality of missionaries dates back to the time of Bartólòme de Las Casas (1474–1566), a Spanish Dominican missionary who defended the rights of indigenous peoples in Latin America. Frantz Fanon's (1925–61)

book about colonialism in Algeria, *The Wretched of the Earth* (1961), was one source of the modern Liberation Theology movement. Liberation Theology sees Christ as the friend of the poor, who lived amongst them and died for them. It stresses biblical opposition to the pursuit of wealth and biblical teachings on justice. Archbishop Oscar Romero, who was assassinated by the El Salvador government for speaking out for the poor, is their leading martyr.

1980
THE RESURGENCE OF ISLAM

The Islamic revival that has shaken Iran, Afghanistan, Algeria and most of the Muslim world since 1980 has several aspects that are hard to disentangle. It is both a spiritual revival, although most of the mystic sects have been subjected to harsh oppression, and a militant response to the economic and intellectual dominance of the West. The Islamic Revolution in Iran, led by Ayatollah Khomeini, marked the start of the movement, which inspired the Taliban movement in Afghanistan, the Hezbollah in Palestine and terrorist groups in many other nations. It is probably too early to tell whether the intellectuals, whose main concerns are cultural and spiritual, will gain the upper hand or whether the fundamentalists will instigate increasingly violent attacks on secular societies.

p. 307 ◀ **Distant Voices** ▶

This is the concentration camp and crematorium at Auschwitz. This is where people were turned into numbers. Into this pond were flushed the ashes of four million people. And that was not done by gas. It was done by arrogance. It was done by dogma. It was done by ignorance. When people believe that they have absolute knowledge, with no test in reality, this is how they behave.

Dr Jacob Bronowski, filming *The Ascent of Man* at Auschwitz (1973)

Glossary

Anarchism
Political theory advocating a society that runs without coercive authority from government, religion, education or industry, imposing limits on individuals' freedom.

Anglicanism
Belief in the Christian teachings and doctrine of the Church of England as opposed to that of the Roman Catholic Church.

Anglo-Saxon
Germanic Angle, Saxon or Jute tribes that settled in England from the fifth century, taking advantage of Roman withdrawal to set up individually ruled kingdoms or provinces.

Apartheid
Afrikaans word to describe the former segregation of races in South Africa, based on a belief in white superiority.

Arabs
Term first used in the ninth century BC to describe Semitic people from Arabia, whose descendants settled throughout North Africa and the Middle East.

Avars
Nomadic people from central Asia who defeated the Huns in the sixth century and the Slavs and Bulgars in the seventh century; they were crushed by Emperor Charlemagne c. AD 800.

Boers
Seventeenth-century Dutch, Flemish and Huguenot settlers to South Africa, who waged war with British colonists 1899–1902; their descendants are known as Afrikaners.

Bolshevism
Political ideology rooted in the establishment of a workers' socialist state, leading to the Russian Revolution in 1917.

Bretons
Celtic people, and language, of Brittany in France, who were descended from those who left Britain after the Anglo-Saxon invasions in the fifth century.

Bronze Age
Period dating from around 3000–2000 BC, when people began using metal-making technology based on copper and its alloys.

Buddhism
Eastern religion based on the teachings of the sixth-century Buddha; these are founded in the destruction of mortal desires – and thus unhappiness – which can be attained by following virtuous paths.

Byzantium
Ancient Greek city, the capital of a Mediterranean empire with a distinctive architecture and orthodox religious art.

Carolingian
Term relating to the Frankish royal dynasty which ruled France from the eighth to tenth centuries, during which time it became Europe's most powerful Christian kingdom.

Catholicism
Division of Christianity characterised by worship of the Virgin Mary, repentance and forgiveness, and the power accorded the pope as God's representative on Earth.

Christianity
World religion derived from the teachings of Christ, the son of God, who came to earth, suffered persecution for his teachings and was crucified, before rising from the dead and ascending into Heaven.

Cold War, the
Ideological and political tensions, dating from the end of the Second World War (1945) to the 1990s, between the Soviet Union and the United States; characterised by nuclear threats, arms races, espionage and destabilising governments.

Colonialism
Practise in which one country dominates another for economic gain, imposing its own language and culture to control native peoples.

Communism
Classless economic system of public ownership, where producing goods and food is a communal activity for the general good; made popular in the nineteenth century by theorists such as Karl Marx and Friedrich Engels.

Confederacy
Alliance of self-determining states, such as the states of the American South during the Civil War (1861–65).

Constitutionalism
Belief maintaining that states be defined by a body of fundamental laws on government and the judiciary, concerning individual freedom.

Counter-Reformation
Sixteenth-century movement initiated by the Catholic Church, using the Inquisition and the Jesuit movement, to counter the spread of Protestant factions during the Reformation.

Crusades
Series of wars in the eleventh to thirteenth centuries, ostensibly to recover Palestine, the Holy City, from Muslim control, but generally acknowledged as imperialist in foundation.

Democracy
Political system whereby a country is governed by the people, usually through elected representatives, but sometimes through referendums.

Divine Right of Kings
Christian political belief that a hereditary monarchy is approved by God, and is thus unquestionable; the sovereign is answerable only to God, so rebellion against the monarch was considered blasphemous.

Ecology
Study of organisms, their relationships and environments in eco-systems; but also pertains to conservation of habitat, species and control of pollution.

Empiricism
Philosophical view that bases knowledge of the world on experience gained through the senses, rather than through inherent knowledge.

Enlightenment, the
Seventeenth-century intellectual movement, where rational thought and science came to bear over the irrationality and superstition characteristic of earlier periods.

Environmentalism
Theory based in the belief that environmental influences are the primary factors in determining behaviour or activism which aims to preserve the planet.

Fascism
Authoritarian political movements, particularly powerful in the 1930s–'40s, where democracy and liberalism were abandoned in favour of nationalistic ideology; fascist regimes often fell under the leadership of a dictator.

Feminism
Intellectual and political thinking which argues women's rights to equality in education, law and the workplace.

Feudalism
Social and legal system, whereby peasant farmers worked a lord's land in exchange for small pecuniary rewards, protection and service in battle.

Franks
Germanic people who dominated France and Germany after the Roman era, building a powerful Christian empire up to the ninth century.

Frisians
Germanic people who settled Germany and the Netherlands in prehistoric times by conquering the Celts; the Frisians were eventually overthrown by Charlemagne.

Gaul
Area of Europe during Roman times, covering what is now France and stretching to northern Italy and the Netherlands.

Habsburg Empire
European imperial dynasty dating from the fifteenth to twentieth centuries; the Habsburgs originated in Austria, but incorporated eastern Europe, Spain and the New World.

Hinduism
Dominant religion of India; Hinduism is characterised by a complex system of customs and beliefs including reincarnation and a caste system, as well as numerous gods.

Holy Roman Empire
Denotes from the thirteenth-century lands ruled by successive German kings, which, at its height covered much of central Europe.

Huguenots
French Calvinist Protestants, who were involved in the French wars of religion against Catholics (1562–98); they co-existed for a time, then fled the country as the persecution increased.

Humanitarianism
Line of thought and action in which the interests of mankind override personal or national interests, as in environmental policy and Third-World aid.

Huns
Fierce nomadic Mongol tribes, dating from 2 BC, who invaded China and Europe, dominating the Germanic peoples until the death of Attila in AD 453.

Imperialism
Policy and practice of a state to influence or conquer others in order to expand its wealth, power and influence.

Industrial Revolution
Process by which Britain and other countries were transformed into industrial powers during the eighteenth and nineteenth centuries, by means of technological advance and invention.

Inquisition
Roman Catholic practice operating across Spain, France, Italy and the Holy Roman Empire throughout the thirteenth to nineteenth centuries in an effort to suppress heresy.

Internationalism
Viewing politics or economics in a global way, ideally through the practice of co-operation between nation states.

Iron Age
Period dating from around 1000–500 BC during which barbarian tribes began to use iron rather than bronze; contemporaries of classical Mediterranean and African civilisations.

Islam
Religion founded in the seventh century by the prophet Muhammad, messenger of Allah; Islam emphasises God's omnipotence and inscrutability.

Jesuits
Roman Catholic order founded in the sixteenth century, aiming to protect the Church against the Reformation through missionary work.

Judaism
Religion and cultural tradition of the Jewish people; Judaism follows one God and is based on the Pentateuch.

Liberalism
Thinking which attaches importance to the civil and political rights of individuals, and their freedoms of speech and expression.

Libertarianism
Theory upholding the rights of an individual above all else, seeking to reduce a state's power to safeguard these rights.

Lombards
Germanic people who invaded Italy in the sixth century, settling in what is now Lombardy; conquered by Emperor Charlemagne in AD 774.

Magyars
Ethnically mixed people who settled in Hungary in the ninth century; they eventually raided deep into Italy, France and Northern Europe.

Mameluke Empire
Dominating Egypt and west of the Gulf from 1250–1517, the Mamelukes, descended from freed Turkish slaves, remained Egypt's ruling class until 1811.

Marxism
Economic ideology, framed by nineteenth-century thinker Karl Marx, that feudalism, capitalism and socialism should be replaced by a classless society.

Medieval
Cultures and beliefs of the Middle Ages, dating from the Roman Empire's fifth-century decline to the fifteenth-century Renaissance.

Medici
Powerful Italian dynasty native of Florence, ruling the city 1434–1737, overseeing the flourishing Renaissance period.

Mercantilism
Economic theory, developed in the sixteenth to eighteenth centuries, that a nation's prosperity depended on how much bullion or treasure it held.

Middle Ages
European period from the fall of the Roman Empire to the fifteenth-century Renaissance; marked by feudalism, Catholic dominance and religious art.

Moguls
North Indian dynasty 1526–1858 of great artistic, architectural and commercial achievement; overthrown by the British in the nineteenth century.

Mongols
Nomadic tribes that conquered central Asia and attacked eastern Europe in the thirteenth century, building an empire under Genghis Khan.

Moors
North-west African Muslims of mixed Arab and Berber origin, who dominated southern Spain AD 711–1492 when they were converted to Christianity

Nationalism
Ideological movement to build national identities, reviving interests in native languages, histories and traditions; extreme nationalism is viewed as fascism.

Nazism
German fascist regime of the National Socialist Party, led by Adolf Hitler, who desired an empire for what he called his 'Aryan' race.

Neolithic
Final part of the Stone Age period, marked by the development of agriculture and forest clearance, dating from around 8000–3000 BC.

Normans
Viking 'Northmen' who settled in France, then expanded and took control of what is now Normandy, then conquered England under King William I.

Ottoman Empire
Turkish Muslim empire 1300–1920, stretching to Hungary, southern Russia and north Africa; the empire crumbled after supporting Germany during the First World War.

Pacifism
Belief that war cannot be justified and is immoral; those who refused to fight on such grounds were termed 'conscientious objectors'.

Paleolithic
Stone Age period, divided into lower, middle and upper eras, dating from approximately one million years ago to around 10,000 BC, the start of the Mesolithic Stone Age; paleolithic times saw modern man develop from earlier types.

Prehistoric
Period that covers from the beginning of life on earth, 3.5 billion years ago, to approximately 3500 BC, when humans began to keep records.

Protestantism
Christian religious faith that takes its name from Martin Luther's protest against Roman Catholic corruption in 1529, which precipitated major splits in European Christianity.

Racism
Belief in the superiority of one race over another, often manifesting itself in social and civil discrimination or violence.

Reformation
Sixteenth-century European movement to reform the Catholic Church; used by Henry VIII to separate the Church of England from Rome.

Renaissance
Fourteenth to seventeenth century European intellectual and artistic movement, ending the Middle Ages with its emphasis on science and exploration.

Republicanism
Support for a system where heads of state are not monarchs; only once realised in England under Oliver Cromwell, who was named 'Lord Protector'.

Semites
Peoples of ancient cultures in the Middle East, speakers of Semitic languages and founders of Islam, Judaism and Christianity.

Socialism
Belief in a classless society characterised by equal access to education and employment through state intervention and ownership of major industries and utilities.

Soviet
Countries dominated by communist Russia after 1922, i.e. Estonia, Ukraine, Uzbekistan were termed Soviets within the Union of Soviet Socialist Republics (USSR).

Stone Age
The earliest period of human culture, marked by the use of stone implements and covering Paleolithic, Mesolithic and Neolithic times.

Suffragism
Belief in the extension of suffrage, generally to women and the working classes, traditionally denied the right to vote.

Taoism
Chinese philosophical system dating from the sixth century BC; characterised by a belief in the opposing forces of yin and yang, which balance the universe, and the 'way', which stresses harmonious existence with the environment.

Tartars
Muslim Mongol followers of Genghis Khan; the Tartar state was conquered by Russia in 1552, now the Republic of Tartarstan.

Vikings
Medieval Scandinavian warriors, traders and settlers; Vikings travelled vast distances by sea and river, often pillaging and plundering from foreign lands.

Bibliography

The authors and publishers readily acknowledge the work of a large number of scholars and published works on which they have drawn in the preparation of this book. Artwork and text references have been drawn from a wide variety of sources. Among them are the following books which can provide a good source of further information:

Adams, R. E. W., *Ancient Civilizations of the New World*, Boulder, 1992

Addington, L. H., *The Patterns of War Since the Eighteenth Century*, Indianapolis, 1984

Bakewell, P., *A History of Latin American Empires and Sequels, 1450–1930*, Oxford, 1997

Ball, S. J. *The Cold War: An International History, 1947–1991*, London, 1998

Banks, A., *A Military Atlas of the First World War*, London, 1975

Bechert, H. & Gombrich, R. (Eds), *The World of Buddhism*, London, 1984

Black, C. F., Greengrass, M., Howarth, D. et al, *Cultural Atlas of the Renaissance*, Oxford, 1993

Bohlander, R. E. *World Explorers and Discoverers*, New York, 1992

Boorstin, D. J., *The Discoverers*, London, 1991

Brogan, Hugh, *The Pelican History of the United States of America*, London, 1986

Brogan, Patrick, *World Conflicts*, London, 1985

Bruce, George, *Collins Dictionary of Wars*, London, 1995

Burkholder, M. A. & Johnson, L. L., *Colonial Latin America* (3rd Ed.), New York, 1990

Calvocoressi, Peter, *World Politics Since 1945*, New York, 1991

Cameron, R., *A Concise Economic History of the World: From Paleolithic Times to the Present*, New York, 1997

Carruth, Gorton, *The Encyclopedia of World Facts and Dates*, New York, 1993

Cartledge, P. (Ed.), *The Cambridge Illustrated History of Ancient Greece*, Cambridge, 1998

Cavendish, R. et al, *Journeys of the Great Explorers*, Basingstoke, 1992

Chacoliades, Militiades, *International Economics*, New York and London, 1990

Chant, C., & Goodman, D., *Pre-Industrial Cities and Technology*, London, 1999

Clutterbuck, Richard, *International Crisis and Conflict*, London and Basingstoke, 1993

Collier, S., Skidmore, T. E. & Blakemore, H., (Eds), *The Cambridge Encyclopeadia of Latin America and the Caribbean*, Cambridge, 1985

Cooper, David E., *World Philosophies: An Historical Introduction*, Oxford, 1996

Cunliffe, Barry (Foreword), *The Cassell Atlas of World History*, London, 1997

Davidson, Gienapp, Heyrman et al., *Nation Of Nations: A Concise Narrative of the American Republic*, New York, 1996

Dawson, Lorne L. (ed.), *Cults in Context: Readings in the Study of New Religious Movements*, Toronto, 1996

Day, A. E., *Search for the Northwest Passage*, New York and London, 1986

Eliade, Mircea, *A History of Religious Ideas*, Chicago, 1984

Fagan, B. M., *Peoples of the Earth: An Introduction to World Prehistory*, New York, 1998

Flatlow, Ira, *They All Laughed: From Lightbulbs to Lasers*, New York, 1992

Friend, W. H. C., *The Rise of Christianity*, London, 1984

Gilbert, Martin, *Second World War*, London, 1989

Goodman, M., *The Roman World, 44 BC–AD 180*, London, 1997

Grove, Noel, *National Geographic Society: Atlas of World History*, Washington, 1997

Hall, Michael, *Leaving Home*, London, 1997

Hanbury-Tenison, R. (ed.), *The Oxford Book of Exploration*, Oxford, 1993

Harding, David (Ed.), *Weapons: An International Encyclopedia from 5000 BC to 2000 AD*, London, 1980

Hart, L., *The History of the Second World War*, London, 1970

Herrin, J., *The Formation of Christendom*, Oxford, 1987

Hillier, Bevis, *The Style of the Century*, London, 1983

Hobsbawn, E. J., *Industry and Empire*, London, 1990

Hobsbawn, E. J., *The Age of Extremes, 1919–1991*, London, 1994

Hughes, Robert, *The Shock of the New*, London, 1991

Kenyon, N. D. and C. Nightingale, *Audiovisual Telecommunications*, London, 1992

Kinder, Hermann & Hilgemann, Werner, *The Penguin Atlas of World History, Vols 1 & 2*, London, 1995

La Feber, W. America, *Russia and the Cold War, 1945–1996*, New York, 1997

Ling, Trevor, *A History of Religion East and West*, London, 1977

Litvinoff, M. *Atlas of Earthcare*, London, 1996

Loudon, Irvine, *Western Medicine*, Oxford, 1997

Lundestad, G. *East, West, North, South: Major Developments in International Politics, 1945–1996*, Oslo, 1997

Macfarlane, L. J., *The Theory and Practice of Human Rights*, London, 1985

Maisels, C. K. *The Near East: Archeology in the Cradle of Civilization*, London, 1993

Mallory, J. P., *In Search of the Indo-European: Language, Archeology & Myth*, London, 1989

McEvedy, C. *The Penguin Atlas of the Pacific*, London, 1998

Messadie, Gerald, *Great Modern Inventions*, Edinburgh, 1991

Messenger, Charles, *The Century of Warfare: Worldwide Conflict from 1900 to the Present Day*, London, 1995

Moore, R. I., (Ed.), *The Hamlyn Historical Atlas*, London, 1981

Morison, Samuel Eliot, Commager, H. S., Leuchtenburg, W. E., *A Concise History of the American Republic (2nd edition)*, Oxford, 1983

Myers, N. (Ed.), *The Gaia Atlas of Planet Management*, London, 1985

Nigosian, S. A., *World Faiths (2nd Ed.)*, New York, 1994

Pakenham, T. *The Scramble for Africa, 1876–1912*, London, 1991

Parker, G. (Ed.) *The Times Atlas of World History (4th ed.)*, London, 1996

Porter, A. N., *Atlas of British Overseas Expansion*, London, 1991

Quirke, S. & Spencer, J. *The British Museum Book of Ancient Egypt*, London, 1992

Sabrine, George H. and Thomas L. Thorson, *A History of Political Theory*, Orlando, 1973

Sasson, J. M. (Ed.) *Civilizations of the Ancient Near East (Vol. II)*, New York, 1995

Smallwood, A. D., *The Atlas of African-American History and Politics: From the Slave Trade to Modern Times*, New York, 1998

Solomon, Robert C. and Kathleen M. Higgins, *A Short History of Philosophy*, Oxford, 1996

Spiegel, S. L. & Wehling, F. L., *World Politics in a New Era*, Fort Worth, 1999

Starr, Chester G., *A History of the Ancient World, 3rd Edition*, Oxford, 1983

Taylor, A. J. P., *From the Boer War to the Cold War*, London, 1995

The DK Science Encyclopedia, London, 1998

The New Grolier Multimedia Encyclopedia, USA, 1991

Thomas, H. *The Slave Trade: The History of the Atlantic Slave Trade, 1440-1870*, New York, 1997

Tomlinson, Jim, *Public Policy and the Economy Since 1900*, New York, 1990

Tucker, S. C. *The Great War*, London, 1998

Williamson, E. *The Penguin History of Latin America*, London, 1992

Wilson, A., *Transport*, London, 1995

Woolf, Stewart (ed.), *Nationalism in Europe*, London, 1996

Author Biographies and Picture Credits

JEREMY BLACK
General Editor
Jeremy Black is Professor of History at the University of Exeter. His books include *History of the British Isles, Maps and History, War and the World 1450–2000* and *Why Wars Happen*. He is a member of the councils of the Royal Historical Society and the British Records Association.

PAUL BREWER & ANTHONY SHAW
Exploration and Empires
Paul Brewer has contributed to several historical encyclopedias, as well as a work on the Second World War. Anthony Shaw has written over 50 books; his specialist interests include military history.

MALCOLM CHANDLER
Power and Politics
Malcolm Chandler is a historian and author, who has written widely on all manner of historical subjects, particularly for schools.

GERARD CHESHIRE
Science and Technology
Gerard Cheshire is a specialist science writer, whose recent works have included articles for *BBC Wildlife Magazine* and many part-works.

INGRID CRANFIELD
Trade and Industry
Ingrid Cranfield is an experienced author and editor. Her works include *The Challengers*, a survey of modern British exploration and adventure and she contributes frequently to periodicals, encyclopedias and compilations.

BRENDA RALPH LEWIS
Society and Culture
Brenda Ralph Lewis has been writing on historical subjects for 35 years. She has published 85 history books, and has contributed to many others, as well as to numerous magazines and BBC programmes.

JON SUTHERLAND
War and Peace
Jon Sutherland is an experienced writer, whose specialist interests include military history. He has written over 50 books.

ROBERT VINT
Religions, Belief and Thought
Robert Vint is a lecturer and educationalist at the Religious and Environment Programme; he has contributed widely to books and magazines on all aspects of religion and belief.

Index